THE
WISDOM SEEKERS

GREAT PHILOSOPHERS
OF THE
WESTERN WORLD

*From the Presocratics
to the Renaisssance*

VOLUME I

JAMES L. CHRISTIAN

Professor Emeritus

Santa Ana College

WADSWORTH

THOMSON LEARNING

Australia • Canada • Mexico • Singapore • Spain
United Kingdom • United States

Executive Editor: **David C. Tatom**
Editorial Assistant: **Rachel Pilcher**
Market Strategist: **Adrienne Krysiuk**
Project Editor: **Claudia Gravier**
Print/Media Buyer: **Elaine Curda**
Permissions Editor: **Shirley Webster**
Text Designer: **Vicki Whistler**

Photo Researcher: **Lili Weiner**
Copy Editor: **Kay Kaylor**
Illustrator: **Carol Zuber-Mallison**
Cover Designer: **Vicki Whistler**
Cover Printer: **Von Hoffmann Graphics**
Compositor: **Impressions**
Printer: **Von Hoffmann Graphics**

Printed in the United States of America
1 2 3 4 5 6 7   202   05 04 03 02 01

For more information about our products, contact us at:
Thomson Learning Academic Resource Center
1-800-423-0563

For permission to use material from this text, contact us by:
Phone: 1-800-730-2214
Fax: 1-800-730-2215
Web: http://www.thomsonrights.com

Library of Congress Catalog Card Number: 2001094475

0-03-075137-3

Asia
Thomson Learning
60 Albert Street, #15-01
Albert Complex
Singapore 189969

Australia
Nelson Thomson Learning
102 Dodds Street
South Melbourne, Victoria 3205
Australia

Canada
Nelson Thomson Learning
1120 Birchmount Road
Toronto, Ontario M1K 5G4
Canada

Europe/Middle East/Africa
Thomson Learning
Berkshire House
168-173 High Holborn
London WC1 V7AA
United Kingdom

Latin America
Thomson Learning
Seneca, 53
Colonia Polanco
11560 Mexico D.F.
Mexico

Spain
Paraninfo Thomson Learning
Calle/Magallanes, 25
28015 Madrid, Spain

For Lori,

who said to me each morning after breakfast, "Go and write us a big book."
My everlasting thanks for that support, and for love, intellect, sparkling smiles,
and while still in this world, *eudaimonia.*

To grow into youngness is a blow. To age into sickness is an insult. To die is, if we are not careful, to turn from God's breast, feeling slighted and unloved. The sparrow asks to be seen as it falls. Philosophy must try, as best it can, to turn the sparrows to flights of angels, which, Shakespeare wrote, sing us to our rest.

RAY BRADBURY

INVITATION AND ACKNOWLEDGMENTS

TO THE STUDENT OF PHILOSOPHY

The Greek Cynic Antisthenes once confessed "I needed wisdom, so I went to Socrates." In our Western tradition it is Socrates, more than any other, who has come to stand for wisdom and the search for wisdom. It is true that he once declared, with feeling, "Wisdom! What wisdom? I certainly have no knowledge of such wisdom!" But others kept returning to him because they sensed that what he did have, whatever its name, was rare and very precious.°[1]

This book has been written from the perspective of a pearl diver. In the pages that follow, you will find that some philosophers like to argue, others like to analyze ideas or language, still others want to outline the universe as it exists or should exist; and some few dedicate themselves to saving the world or trying to move the masses.

But a pearl diver seeks a special treasure in the form of a wisdom that comes from careful and honest thinking, well-founded facts, valid inferences, and clear understandings. Along the way he too may enjoy arguing, criticizing, and judging; but in the end what he seeks is a pearl of greater price. Under and behind and through a philosopher's ponderings one can always sense a questing spirit that, after the analyses and dialectics are over and done with, would be happy to settle for a few pearls.

As you read ahead and become acquainted with the lives and thoughts of some of the noblest thinkers ever, you might do well not to forget the simple prayer of Socrates:

Ὦ φίλε Πάν τε καὶ ἄλλοι ὅσοι τῆδε θεοί—Beloved Pan, and all ye other gods who haunt this place, make me beautiful within, and grant that whatever happens outside of me will help my soul to grow. May I always be aware that true wealth lies in wisdom, and may my "gold" be so abundant that only a wise man can lift and carry it away. For me that is prayer enough.[2]

TO THE TEACHER

All textbooks have strengths and weaknesses of course, and we adopt them, don't we, in terms of the first and despite the second? For some decades now teachers of philosophy and the history of philosophy have had not a few excellent textbooks to choose from, and it feels as though, during thirty-five years of teaching philosophy, I have used them all! During that tenure, four observations about the field and the textbooks we use to teach it have appeared increasingly clear to me:

°**Sidenotes** *are used for clarification, comment, and cross-referencing and will be found in adjacent margins throughout the book;* **endnotes** *give sources and can be found at the ends of chapters.*

It is not easy, Socrates, for anyone to sit beside you and not be forced to give an account of himself.
THEODORUS THE CYRENAIC

When Empedocles remarked to [Xenophanes] that it is impossible to find a wise man, "Naturally," he replied, "for it takes a wise man to recognize a wise man."
DIOGENES LAËRTIUS

We are drowning in information, while starving for wisdom. The world henceforth will be run by synthesizers, people able to put together the right information at the right time, think critically about it, and make important choices wisely.
EDWARD O. WILSON

I don't know if the truth can make us free, but I do believe that our unique mentality thrives on this form of soul food, whatever the pain of lost illusions.
STEPHEN JAY GOULD

---

[1] Diogenes Laërtius, *Lives of Eminent Philosophers*, II.78; Plato, *The Apology*, 21b. When a paragraph contains more than one source (as in this case), all sources are referenced together by the number at the end of the paragraph.
[2] Plato, *Phaedrus*, 279

(1) That the "classical" interpretation of Western philosophic thought (the "received tradition") is often biased and arbitrary, so that when one goes back to a philosopher's own writings (when possible) and interprets them in light of more recent scholarship and insight, his concepts re-emerge in a somewhat different light;

(2) That philosophic ideas are commonly couched in esoteric language that makes them unnecessarily difficult and renders many concepts virtually inaccessible to most readers or students of philosophy. Of course there is an obvious cause for this: the philosophers themselves often wrote in a turgid prose that even specialists have difficulty understanding;

(3) That many historical ideas and statements seem to modern eyes absurd—silly, ridiculous, stupid, choose your adjective—until seen in the context of the philosopher's life, at which time, for the first time, they begin to make good sense. The question, "How could he believe that?" is a reasonable question, and very often it gets answered only when we allow the philosopher to speak for himself out of the depths of his own existence;

(4) That dialectical criticism as traditionally practiced is commonly lacking in empathetic insight into the immediate living concerns of the thinker and therefore misses the most important fact of all: what his philosophy meant to him.

These observations may imply only that teachers have different approaches to understanding and teaching the history of philosophy. In any case, the present text attempts to address these concerns.

Lastly, in these volumes the lives of the philosophers have been included along with their thought. The objective sciences can be severed from those who do them, but philosophy cannot. Of course, certain kinds of endeavors—in logic, mathematics, geometry, and physics—once they pass over from philosophy to science, can stand by themselves; but until they make that transition and are appropriately reclassified, they remain intimate representations of the man or woman who created them. For in truth our ideas are expressions of our deepest selves. Philosophy illuminates life, and life illuminates one's philosophy. This does not mean that, if a teacher or student so chooses, a thinker's creations cannot be studied in isolation from the creator; sometimes we must do this because of constraints of time and strength. But to do so will always, to some extent, diminish our understanding and appreciation of the man and/or his thought.

My fondest wish is that more thinkers of the *other* sex had chosen, or been allowed, to do philosophy. What few women philosophers did make contributions to Western thought and are known to us—Hipparchia, Arêtê, and Hypatia are perhaps most prominent—are here included. Someday, hopefully, a sensitive civilization will evolve that realizes what it has lost and set out to create a balance that recognizes its most valuable natural resource.

I do not know how to teach philosophy without becoming a disturber of the peace.

BARUCH SPINOZA

In order to reach the Truth, it is necessary, once in one's life, to put everything in doubt—as far as possible.

RENÉ DESCARTES

ACKNOWLEDGMENT AND APPRECIATION

Without special friends this book would not exist. Most are deceased: Diogenes, Aristotle, Epicurus, Marcus, *et al.*, through time and duration to Bergson, Camus, and Campbell. My deepest debt is to the living. Through eight years of joyous labor the following individuals have, in diverse ways, gifted me with their time, creativity, patience, and supportive silence. I am indebted to:

Peter Angeles, for reminding me (when I most needed it) that intellectual nobility and humanness go hand in hand and that both are very alive and well.

Ted Kneupper, Bob Badra, Terri Burke Venerable, Bert Williams, George Kinnamon, Dean Dowling: you reassure, even from great distances, that there are good men and women in the world for whom one continues to work.

Ray Bradbury, from whom I learned a writer's basic lessons: Don't think (my mind will do that for me), and never listen to carping critics (a writer is his own best critic).

Sarah Villamil, for smoothing over rough times, for balancing your loves, for friendship, for being willing to share her with me.

Robert and Louise McCall, for reminding us that the purpose of life is to see as much beauty as possible, and for being shining examples of how to shelter a creative Muse.

D. J. Atkinson, who, like Ganesha, removes obstacles by cutting the world to size, rendering it a trifle saner, and making it a better place to live.

Ahmad Motlagh: for faring well in the heart of the Absurd, for proving that integrity can survive quite nicely even in the harsh ecosystem we mistakenly call "the real world."

Dr. Fernando Montelongo; Yrama Perez, Monica Hernandez, Claudia Yudice: for creating a healing fellowship where wounded human beings can find solace, and in loving hands, find healing for bodies, hearts, and minds.

Catherine Preece Rhodes, for resurrecting from the archives the astonishing riches of great minds and making them available just when I was ready for them.

Bob Putman, for taking on the task of being, for our time, a reincarnation of the Gadfly himself; it's reassuring to know that Socrates is still present in the Agora, forcing us to take time out from our nonsense and think about what we are doing.

Robert and Anna Maria Smith: for friendship that endures still with fire and light; you have illuminated the way for so many. *Sois sage!*

I am grateful to my family and friends for patience and love: Cathy Christian, Carla Christian, Mark Clairemont, Marcia Christian, Sherrie Martin, Reinar Christian, and Laurie Sue Cooper.

To my wife Lori Villamil-Christian a special word of love for sharing the pain of bad times and the joy of good times, and for walking with me; but most of all for just being who and what you are.

At Thomson: David Tatom gave at least one author the gift of making him feel secure during the publishing process; so from one jittery author, David, thank you. It has been a privilege and the happiest of experiences to work with Claudia Gravier, project editor; Rachel Pilcher, editorial assistant; Vicki Whistler, art director, Holly Lewerenz, production manager; and Shirley Webster and Lili Wiener, photo research.

James Christian
November 2001

CONTENTS

CHAPTER 1

PROLEGOMENA TO THE HISTORY OF PHILOSOPHY

Aristotle defines philosophy as the attempt to escape from "an awesome feeling of ignorance"; Socrates shares his love of ideas; guidelines are suggested for reading the lives and thoughts of Western thinkers; and the philosophers speak for themselves.

SOMETHING OF THE MARVELOUS

In the spring of 345 BC Aristotle and his bride Pythias settled at Mytilênê, the capital city of the northern Aegean island of Lesbos. Surrounded by a small company of congenial friends, they spent two happy years there. In the center of the island lies the big Pyrrha Lagoon, and historians know he spent time observing the tidepool creatures, studying the habits of shellfish and lobsters, and dissecting fishes. Aristotle loved nature, and, although he came to see everything through the eyes of a biologist, he was fascinated by the entire range of natural phenomena. "In all natural things there is something of the marvellous," he wrote. He wondered about the nature of rainbows, explained the misty glow of the Milky Way, pondered the cause of seasons, and tried to account for snow, frost, dew, wind, thunder, and earthquakes. Sometime later he wrote:

> A sense of wonder started men philosophizing, in ancient times as well as today. Their wondering is aroused, first, by trivial matters; but they continue on from there to wonder about less mundane matters such as the changes of the moon, sun, and stars, and the beginnings of the universe. What is the result of this puzzlement? *An awesome feeling of ignorance!* Men began to philosophize, therefore, to escape ignorance. . . .[1]

This passage from Aristotle's *Metaphysics* goes to the heart of the human impulse that drives philosophy. "Men began to philosophize . . . to escape ignorance." We humans begin with the close-in puzzlements that touch the practicality of our daily lives; but, then, with the mounting liberation of our curiosity, we extend our wonderment to the rest of the cosmos and its baffling contents; and as we do so, we become increasingly agitated at the expanding range of our not-knowing. "What is the result of this puzzlement?" Aristotle asks. "An awesome feeling of ignorance!" This is an intolerable feeling, and waking humans will do everything possible to escape from it.

The history of philosophy is the story of the unceasing human struggle to escape this condition of ignorance.

Man cannot live without seeking to describe and explain the universe.
SIR ISAIAH BERLIN

Have you not noticed that opinions divorced from knowledge are ugly things?

SOCRATES

Aristotle of Stagira

*Philosophy asks the simple
question, What is it all about.*
ALFRED NORTH
WHITEHEAD

*For man, the unexamined life is
not worth living.*
SOCRATES

*Parmenides introduced thought to
replace imagination* [phantasias].
TIMON OF PHLIUS

*To live an entire life without
understanding how we think, why
we feel the way we feel, what
directs our actions is to miss what
is most important in life, which is
the quality of experience itself.*
MIHALY
CSIKZENTMIHALYI

*A female student in one of Joseph
Campbell's lecture courses once
asked, "What about the woman?"
"The woman's the mother of the
hero," Campbell replied. "She's
the goal of the hero's achieving;
she's the protectress of the hero; she
is this, she is that. What more do
you want?" The woman said, "I
want to be the hero."*

INVITATION

It is a beautiful story, beautiful because it is the record of the best thoughts we humans can invent when we give in to the urge to know and understand. It is also a frustrating story because the best thinkers were attempting to achieve the impossible—and they knew it. They were trying to understand how the world works, who we are, and what our place is in the scheme of things; and they were seeking better ideas to live by—what we might call wisdom. But at their time and place, with only a rudimentary database of empirical information, their best efforts to understand the world inevitably would fall short of their goal. As for wisdom, none of us is barred from seeking it, but how many of us find it? Still, these thinkers were gifted with inquisitive minds that wouldn't quit, and in the long run their achievements were staggering in depth and breadth. It is in their insights, as well as in their dogged persistence, that they triumphed and bequeathed to us a legacy worthy of our time and attention.

The book you're holding and its companion volume tell the story of Western philosophic thought from about 600 BC to the present. Though written primarily as a textook, it is best thought of as a very personal invitation, to you, to get to know some of the great men and women who have predated us on our planet. It invites you to do this in an empathetic manner by probing as deeply as possible into their lives and thoughts.

This is a story of rebellion, wonderment, and creation. Almost without exception, philosophies are produced by intellectual malcontents, by men and women who dream of achieving perspectives superior to those the world stands ready to offer. If you would like to acquaint yourself with a select few of these people, then open this book at any place, at any time.

CRITICAL PHILOSOPHY

Most of the philosophers biographed here felt they should be doing something—such as arguing, teaching, preaching, or writing—and they engaged in endless bickering over exactly what that doing should be. But if we listen carefully to Aristotle, it appears that philosophy is more a feeling-attitude than a doing. Driven by "an awesome feeling of ignorance," the heart and soul of philosophy is the human impulse to know and understand. Philosophy is the spirit of critical wonderment. Religion and science also arise from this impulse to know, but religion differs from philosophy in that it usually stresses uncritical acceptance of ideas ("on faith") rather than critical discrimination. And science, a pragmatic particularization of the impulse to know, is usually reluctant to indulge in speculative connections and larger questions of meaning; only rarely do scientists professionally attempt to comprehend the Big Picture.

In this book, philosophy is understood as this impulse expressing itself in critical thinking about thinking, whose proximate goal is to get in touch with the truth about reality and ultimate goal is to better see the Big Picture—to understand the world and our place in it.

TOOLS OF INQUIRY

Socrates loved ideas. He worked with ideas, played with ideas, brooded over them, and treated them as valuable tools for getting the work done. It mattered not what the ideas were, where they came from, or who held them. The Sophist educators of his day were advocating a philosophy of ideas Socrates thought insidious; to them, ideas were little more than instruments for winning arguments, and for this the truth was virtually useless. So the Sophists took all sides of a question and made elenctic debate a fine art. But Socrates thought that debating just to play word games, or to stroke one's ego, was absurd when, dedicated to the pursuit of truth, exchanging ideas could become a precious process through which the human soul could become *sophos* and societies could know peace.

So, in his search for clarity and truth, Socrates carried on dialogues in which he explored ideas. In Plato's *Republic* he explores the idea of justice. In the *Lachês* he helps two old soldiers analyze the meaning of valor or courage. In the *Ion* he focuses on artistic inspiration. In the *Euthyphrô* he works with the possible meanings of piety. In the *Hippias Major* he concentrates on beauty, while in the *Lysis* he delves into friendship. In all his conversations (later in life anyway; earlier he tended to be more adversarial) Socrates deferred to the thinking of each individual and led that person at his own pace as they examined the meaning of his ideas. This Socratic love of ideas is prerequisite to doing good philosophy, and it is one of the Greeks' golden legacies.

This attitude toward the function of ideas sharply contrasts with everyday situations when we attack the holder of ideas rather than the ideas themselves. For an extended period following the Athenian era, the majority of thinkers failed miserably to honor this Greek legacy. After about AD 200 it became standard practice for philosophers and theologians to aim their attacks not at the ideas thought but at the thinkers who were judged to be propagandists for "heretical" beliefs. A person who entertained a "wrong" idea was considered depraved and where possible was excommunicated, tortured, and frequently executed.° The employment of ideas as weapons is a tragic legacy of post-Athenian intellectual orthodoxies, and it endures into modern times.

However, those who plant themselves in the Socratic tradition will honor ideas whatever their source. They will listen to these ideas, attempt to understand meanings and implications, and show respect for others' thoughts by taking serious time to think about them and respond to them. Above all, they will refuse to make the holder of different ideas an adversary but will consider that person a coworker in the search for the truth. Of course, honoring ideas doesn't mean allowing them to slip by unexamined. All ideas—especially familiar *archai* (assumed "starting points") which we tend to overlook—must undergo critical scrutiny.

PHILOSOPHIC MOTIFS AND QUESTIONS

You will find certain motifs repeated throughout Western philosophy because they are perceived as both vitally important and peculiarly stubborn. Keep the following motifs in mind as you read, and, as guidelines, ask questions similar to those suggested here about each philosopher's life and thought.

1. Are the philosopher's thoughts truly philosophic? Is his mode of thinking essentially philosophic—or something else? In the following chapters you will encounter a surprising spread of convictions about what defines a true philosopher. Should he be exploring nature, analyzing concepts, or dissecting language? Should he be defending religious beliefs, constructing a metaphysics, or setting out to alleviate the social and economic conditions that bring humans so much misery? Should he be helping people maximize their pleasures and pursue happiness? Or should he be dedicated (as the Cynics believed) to keeping the world off our backs?

Thoroughgoing and rigorous philosophic activity always demonstrates five characteristics: 1. It is an intellectual activity of the rational mind. 2. Its subject is ideas

Let us at least talk about it, you wisest of men, even if it seems bad. Silence is worse; all truths suppressed become poisonous.
FRIEDRICH NIETZSCHE

It is greed to do all the talking and not be willing to listen.
DEMOCRITUS

See pp. 215f., 223ff., 285–290.

What is the first business of one who practices philosophy? To get rid of self-conceit. For it is impossible for anyone to begin to learn that which he thinks he already knows.
EPICTETUS

But I implore you, by my love and hope: do not throw away the hero in your soul! Keep holy your highest hope!
FRIEDRICH NIETZSCHE

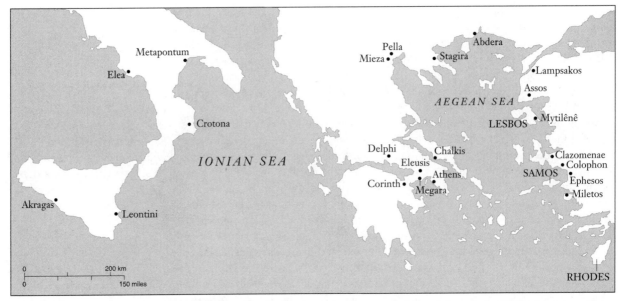

Philosophic thinking first radiated from the Ionian coast during the sixth century BC and spread through the Mediterranean world. During the sixth and fifth centuries major thinkers came from Miletus, Ephesus, Colophon, Samos, Abdera, and from Sicily and Italy in the far west. With the flowering of Greek art, architecture, literature, drama, and philosophy in the fifth century, Athens became the dominant influence in the spheres of intellect and the creative arts. Philosophically, all roads led to Athens.

Snatching the eternal out of the ever-fleeting is one of the great tricks of human existence.

TENNESSEE WILLIAMS

The truth must essentially be regarded as in conflict with this world; the world has never been so good, and will never become so good, that the majority will desire the truth.

SØREN KIERKEGAARD

°*This valuable word is given special definition in philosophy; see lexicon.*

Zeus is no more; the whirlwind reigns instead.

ARISTOPHANES

(ideas about real or experiential objects/events or ideas about other ideas). 3. It is critical in its examination of ideas. 4. It is a sincere search for clarity and truth. 5. It exempts no idea from critical scrutiny. (It also may evidence other qualities—a passion for order, for example, or methodical doubt—but these five are the quintessential ingredients.)

Many of the philosophies dealt with here fail to meet all five criteria. It is appropriate, therefore, to ask each thinker about the rigor of his thinking. If in the end we must evaluate a philosophy on "a scale from one to five," at what point might it cease to be philosophy because it is clearly "something else"? If it is less than rigorous in a philosophic sense, what, then, are the motives behind his thinking and writing? What is he really seeking? What kinds of answers would be required to allay his restlessness and bring quietude to the passions that drove his quest?

2. Does the philosopher recognize the self-centric nature of thinking? Zeno of Elea once said that if something exists, then it has to exist somewhere. It's difficult to argue with him. It turns out that events can occur in only two possible "somewheres": "out there" in the real° world or "in here" in our experiencing. It seems, at first glance, that we shouldn't have much trouble locating the "place" where objects/events occur. Obviously, the hurricane is "out there" and so also are the Moon, the meadowlark singing on the fencepost, and other people, while my headache is "in here" along with my thoughts, memories, anger, love, loneliness, and annoyance with national politics.

Now, it always has been an essential goal of philosophy to think clearly about whatever the philosopher is thinking about, and to do this it is crucial to think about ideas where they are and not where they are not. If we attribute the wrong context to ideas, we are in danger of misinterpreting them. Thus a sharp distinction between the knowing subject, the thinker, and the objects known becomes of the utmost significance in Western philosophic thought. It is obviously important for clear thinking that I think of my headache as occurring in my head and not treat it as though it is perched out there on the fencepost.

Oddly enough, establishing the "geographic location" of the objects of thought often proves to be as difficult as it is necessary. To show why this is so, ask whether the following entities are best thought of as located in the experiencing self or in the real world apart from us experiencers: green, shape, music, saltiness, temperature, evil, perfection, guilt, beauty, wisdom, opposites (e.g., up/down, male/female), essence, infinity, gravity, time, star, death, eternity, nature, evolution, health, inch, season, $2+2=4$, $E=mc^2$, law, nationality, religion.

Moreover, is our philosopher aware of the symbolic nature of thinking? As experiencing selves we exist "in here," while the world we want to know about is "out there." And the only way we can know *about* it is to create thought-symbols to represent what we perceive as "out there." All thinking is representational in just this way. We inherit a great mass of ready-made symbols from our culture and then go on to create symbols of our own. If we choose to work in a specialized field (DNA technology, say, or chemistry), we then adopt and create new symbols to represent the perceived realities in that field. The choice of an appropriate set of symbols is an important first step for apprehending any reality.

To illustrate, physicists will tell you that their defined task is to study motion. To do this they ignore the world of individual things that are the stuff of immediate experience—this lightbulb, this pumpkin, this bluejay (remember that singular objects and fields are all that actually exist)—and focus on the perceived motion of these objects. They then represent that motion with universal abstractions in the form of words, numbers, equations, and formulas. What we think about, therefore, is not reality but the symbols we have created to represent reality, and a careful thinker will make every effort not to confuse the two. °

Is it any wonder that much of our thinking is unclear and confused as we talk about qualities, events, and "things" without precise location and definition? It therefore is important to ask of each philosopher whether he demonstrates an awareness of the subject/object problem and whether he makes an effort to think about his subject matter with some degree of precision. Whatever his perspectives or semantics, is he aware of the egocentric predicament and its epistemological implications? Does he see that a great gulf exists between reality and his experiencing of it? Is he aware of the symbolic nature of thought? Does the philosopher indicate he knows the difference between the symbol and the thing symbolized—or does he confuse the two? Does he distinguish, even in an elementary way, between "primary qualities" and "secondary qualities"? Does he tend to project elements of experience into the realm of the real? In ethical theory (if he has one), does he insist his values are real and therefore should be adopted by anyone who accurately perceives the truth of reality? Does he fail to show any awareness of the knower/known problem? Would acknowledgment of the subject/object distinction tend to invalidate his philosophy? (See pages 199–205; Vol. II.)

3. **Does the philosopher resist the limitations of time and place?** That is, does he attempt to break out of the confinements imposed by the assumptions and values of his own era? To a large extent all of us are trapped in the thought-culture of our age, but we usually do little about it because we are not deeply aware of its existence. Someone has remarked that a fish would be the last creature in the world to recognize water because he is always immersed in it. In this sense we are all fish, but a few—who intuit that water can't be everything—strive to bear witness to the existence of other realities. This time-place awareness is endemic to the philosophic enterprise, and we commonly

I laugh with one face, I weep with the other.
SØREN KIERKEGAARD

°*This distinction between subject and object has now been challenged at the deepest level by twentieth-century physics; see Vol. II, Chap. 18..*

The fool, with all his other faults, has this also: he is always getting ready to live.
EPICURUS

For one swallow does not make a summer, nor does one day; and so too one day, or a short time, does not make a man blessed or happy.
ARISTOTLE

Philosophy is really a form of homesickness.
NOVALIS

find thinkers experiencing a kind of nausea when they realize the depth of their encapsulation and the enormous difficulty of emerging out of it.

Anthropologist Ruth Benedict sees the time-place predicament in this way:

> The life history of the individual is first and foremost an accommodation to the patterns and standards traditionally handed down in his community. From the moment of his birth the customs into which he is born shape his experience and behavior. By the time he can talk, he is the little creature of his culture, and by the time he is grown and able to take part in its activities, its habits are his habits, its beliefs his beliefs, its impossibilities his impossibilities.[2]

This is an excellent description of the predicament that restive intellects of every age have sought to escape, and for not a few it was this longing for transcendence that energized their work. Sundering the bonds of Earth and spreading wings may have been a dream-fantasy, but it was only too clear to them that the limits of the world were unacceptable. They felt they had no choice but to make every effort to unchain themselves and resist enslavement by the *Zeitgeist*.°

°*See lexicon.*

In *The Problems of Philosophy* Bertrand Russell views the life of encapsulated man as "feverish and confined."

Live dangerously. Build your cities on the slopes of Vesuvius.
FRIEDRICH NIETZSCHE

> The private world of instinctive interests is a small one, set in the midst of a great and powerful world which must, sooner or later, lay our private world in ruins. Unless we can so enlarge our interests as to include the whole outer world, we remain like a garrison in a beleaguered fortress, knowing that the enemy prevents escape and that ultimate surrender is inevitable. In such a life there is no peace, but a constant strife between the insistence of desire and the powerlessness of will. In one way or another, if our life is to be great and free, we must escape this prison and this strife.[3]

How much, then, is the philosopher aware of his vulnerability to encapsulation? How large a role does that possibility seem to play in his thinking? How diligently does he seek to avoid it? What tenets do we find in his philosophic doctrine that seem to have been designed (consciously or unconsciously) to break the bonds of time and place?

4. What was the philosopher trying to see? All learning might be described as attempts to expand our seeing capacities. When a geologist looks at the many-layered strata in the walls of the Grand Canyon, he can see what the rest of us cannot possibly see: upheavals of continental masses, the waxing and waning of oceans, the deposition of sediments, and the fossil record of a billion years of life and death. Similarly, a trained astronomer peering at the stars can see literally a different sky from what a boy of age five can see. A professional biologist studying the plant and animal life of a riparian spring sees life-forms and ecological relationships that an untrained eye cannot see. All specialists develop special eyes that allow them to peer deeper into their chosen world and to see what the rest of us are blind to.

In just this way a philosopher also is obsessed with seeing. If by temperament he is a synoptist of the Aristotelian variety, then he wants to see everything! He longs to possess the seeing of the geologist, astronomer, musician, biologist, psychologist, logician, linguist, ethicist, painter, sculptor, and every other specialist. Every mystery, every contradiction, every puzzling phenomenon is an invitation to see, and a view of the Big Picture never ceases to beckon. However, the majority of Western thinkers concentrated on delimited plots of obscurity and labored to see there as much as the constraints of intellect, knowledge, and time would allow.

Ask, therefore, what each of the Western philosophers included in this book was attempting to see. For instance, Democritus was trying to see the invisible components of matter ("atoms") and to understand how they cluster together to create the real objects of perception. Pythagoras was attempting to see and understand the mathematical structure of the cosmos. Plotinus was bent on beholding the secrets of a spiritual universe that lay behind and above the material world. Descartes was attempting to see the nature of mind and body and how they interact. Darwin was trying to see into the mechanisms that produce speciation. Ultimately, despite other preoccupations, each thinker wanted to see an essential something that he believed to be of great importance to his or humanity's vision of truth. What exactly was he trying to see? What factors in his life drove him to concentrate on that area as especially significant? Judged by twenty-first-century hindsight, would we conclude that the philosopher succeeded in seeing what he was attempting to see? Is it possible that his seeing was illusory? What degree of precision (logical coherence or empirical verifiability) did he attain in his seeing? And if his seeing is judged to be illusory, what difference would that really make to him, to us, and to the history of philosophy? (See especially p. 39)

5. What is the philosopher's dominant mode of thinking? Does the philosopher you're studying mostly think about things, look at things, or try to solve problems? In philosophical language, we are asking if his intellect functions primarily in the logical mode, in the empirical mode, or in the life-affirming and problem-solving mode of a pragmatist. Is he best thought of as belonging to the idealist, the empirical-realist, or the pragmatic tradition?

Logicians are most comfortable with abstract concepts and formal connections; their forte is mathematics and logic, and indeed Spinoza and Leibniz modeled their entire philosophies on mathematical and geometric paradigms. Logicians belong to the idealist tradition initiated by Pythagoras, the Eleatics, and Plato; carried forward in the intellectual philosophies of the Gnostics, Neoplatonists, and Scholastics; and brought to flower in the great thought systems of Descartes and Hegel.

Empiricists insist that the job of philosophy is, in Richard Feynman's words, to look at the world and figure out "what in hell's going on out there." They believe that the philosophical impulse to know and understand should push on to a better understanding of "the moon, sun, and stars" and everything else under the heavens. It is probably true that empiricists feel more comfortable with less formal ideas that include a modicum of substantive content. Questions empiricists ask include: Can the mind know the truth of reality? What exactly takes place in an act of perception? When a physicist (e.g., an Einstein or a quantum theorist) says he has captured reality with thought, what has he actually seen? Has he settled (perhaps too soon) for an apprehension of reality without comprehension? Can we still make the classical distinction between primary and secondary qualities? Or is consciousness so deeply involved with reality that the two are inseparable?

Pragmatists argue that philosophy's job is to help struggling humans live each day as well as possible. Socrates taught that philosophy leads to wisdom, which leads to the Good Life. The Greek pragmatists Zeno of Kitium, Epicurus, and the Stoics believed that philosophy is the preeminent instrument for making our lives happy. Over the entrance to Epicurus's Garden was the inscription "Guest, thou shalt be happy here, for here happiness is esteemed the highest good." The American pragmatists argue that ideas attain meaning only when applied to concrete situations. For the most part, pragmatists' questions are aimed at enriching our lives: What can I believe? How can I maintain peace of mind in a hostile world? How can I protect my integrity in a dishonest world? How can I hold onto even a semblance of nobility

The empiricists want only correspondence theories of truth; the idealists, only coherence theories; where both are equally important, and simple elegance or beauty the final crown.

KEN WILBUR

Bertrand Russell once remarked that reading "Pragmatism" is like taking a bath in water that heated up so imperceptibly you didn't know when to scream.

HORACE KALLEN

The only true wisdom lives far from mankind, out in the great loneliness, and can be reached only through suffering. Privation and suffering alone open the mind of a man to all that is hidden to others.
IGJUGARJUK (NORTH CANADIAN CARIBOU ESKIMO SHAMAN)

It is man's especial privilege to love even those who stumble.
MARCUS AURELIUS

°See pp. 131–133.

In the depth of winter, I finally learned that within me there lay an invincible summer.
ALBERT CAMUS

To be surprised, to wonder, is to begin to understand.
JOSÉ ORTEGA Y GASSET

through pain and suffering? How can I live each day with hope and joy knowing that I will soon cease to be?

These three modes of intellect look at the world through different eyes and see different things, and the failure of each to understand the others is a matter of record. Abraham Maslow's proverbial quip applies to all three: "If the only tool you have is a hammer, you tend to treat everything as if it were a nail." Still, all three modes of thought are unqualified success stories in the intellectual history of the West.

It is therefore appropriate to ask these questions of each philosopher: Is his thinking style primarily that of a logician, an observer of things, or a prophetic analyst who works to lay better foundations for understanding the problems of daily life? Does his intellectual mode limit his capacity to see through other eyes? If so, what allowances must we make in order to achieve the fullest appreciation of his labors and insights?

6. Can we discern in the philosopher's life the roots of his philosophy? All philosophy is self-serving. Whatever the more objective reasons we give for philosophizing, we philosophize because we must, and the ideas we create are designed to meet fundamental life needs. It is a commonplace observation that novelists such as Hemingway and Steinbeck always write about themselves. This is certainly true of philosophers. "The great poet dips only from his own reality," Nietzsche said; your ideas must come "out of your own fire." When sufficient records are available, we always find that the leaves and flowers of the tree have roots that run deep into the soil of the past. "What's running the show," Joseph Campbell writes, "is what's coming up from way down 'below.' "

Plato philosophized in order to come to terms with the unbearable tragedies he experienced in his youth.° Epicurus's philosophy of love reaffirmed life and rescued normal human pleasures from the nihilist influence of Plato's otherworldliness. Plotinus's philosophy was created to reassure himself that this world (which he hated) is merely an unreal shadow of a spiritual universe. Augustine's worldview gave meaning to an anguished existence shattered by abuse, rejection, and guilt. Having been ostracized from family, friends, and religious heritage, Spinoza's geometric idealism nourished his soul out of bitterness into love and reassured him that God (drastically redefined) was still there.

The Swiss psychoanalyst Alice Miller provides just one example of the kind of deep illumination made possible by advances in the behavioral sciences during the twentieth century. She writes that Nietzsche's works "reflect the unlived feelings, needs, and tragedy of his childhood." "Most of Nietzsche's writings owe their persuasiveness specifically to his ability to express the experiences he stored up at a very early age." "The truth asserts itself so obviously that it is virtually impossible to deny it: the truth of a mistreated child who was not allowed to cry or defend himself." Nietzsche needed his entire philosophy "to shield himself from knowing and telling what really happened to him."[4]

A long-accepted philosophic dogma has been that biography has no significance for understanding the thoughts of a great thinker; his ideas must be allowed to stand by themselves. This approach can be very productive, and good reasons exist to support it. Facile distortions of a philosopher's thoughts are almost inevitable once personal elements are allowed to enter the picture. In his study of Nietzsche, Walter Kaufmann was justifiably angered by "the fashion of trivializing Nietzsche's ideas psychologically."[5] A philosophic idea, he asserts, develops according to its own inner logic without causal connection to the philosopher's emotional life. Since all of us think of ourselves as amateur psychotherapists, his point is very important: We should make every effort not to dive into waters too deep for our oxygen supply. A second reason for denying the whole person's entry into philosophic criticism is that objective analysis of ideas strictly for their own sake becomes more difficult, especially if we want to argue for their validity. If we are bent on defending the truth of an idea, then linking it to our all-too-human needs and neuroses can make that pursuit seem misconceived.

It is a fine line but very important. On the one hand, it is certainly true that it is easy to dismiss a thinker's ideas once we "understand" them as the arbitrary creations of his "psychological condition." On the other hand, Western philosophy is littered with doctrines from the minds of thinkers who believed with all their hearts that their ideas embodied the truth of things, when, in fact, after critical review those ideas turn out to be expressions of unconscious impulses with no truth value at all for the apprehension of reality. Actually, our philosophies *are* expressions of who we are; we use them to report our deepest selves and most authentic loves, hates, dreams, and fears. "A philosophy," William James said, "is the expression of a man's inner character." Only in mathematics, physics, the geometries, and the logics can ideas stand entirely by themselves. In all other areas our thoughts and our lives are bound together and illuminate one another.

We can ask these questions of each thinker: Does a discernible connection exist between the philosopher's ideas and the known facts of his life? Does that connection shed light on his thinking? Does he demonstrate an awareness of the relationship? Does he make truth claims for ideas that appear to be more the products of deeper currents than attempts to clarify thought? If it is obvious his ideas are the creations of personal need, can we appreciate them despite that fact? or appreciate them even more because that is the case? Or, in this instance, is it best to let his thoughts stand by themselves?

THE PHILOSOPHERS CAN SPEAK FOR THEMSELVES

All the philosophers biographed here were extremists—extremely perceptive, extremely strong willed, extremely original, and extremely individualistic as people and in stating their positions. "If I am not I, who will be?" Thoreau wrote. "From becoming an individual no one, no one at all, is excluded, except he who excludes himself by becoming a crowd," Kierkegaard said; "If I were to desire an inscription on my tombstone, I should desire none other than 'that individual.'" They challenged the orthodoxies of their time, ferreted out hypocrisies, created new ideas, and demanded that everyone be responsible for their thoughts and actions. They are human, of course, "all-too-human" (in Nietzsche's words): The men are chauvinists; they are often blind to the obvious and abandon common sense altogether; they become wrathful over small things; and they often dive deep for pearls and then throw them away. Still, their seeing can inspire, they are master craftspeople in the use of language, and in the final analysis they are probably the best role models the human race has yet produced. Better than anyone, they can tell you what philosophy is all about.

Every thinker puts some portion of an apparently stable world in peril.

JOHN DEWEY

ON PHILOSOPHY AND PHILOSOPHERS

The right way to seize a philosopher, Crates, is by the ears.
(ZENO THE STOIC)

In studying a philosopher, the right attitude is neither reverence nor contempt, but first a kind of hypothetical sympathy, until it is possible to know what it feels like to believe in his theories. . . . When an intelligent man expresses a view

Execute every act of thy life as though it were thy last.
MARCUS AURELIUS

Paul Gauguin. *D´ où venons-nous? Que sommes-nous? Où allons-nous?* 1897 "Where do we come from? What are we? Where are we going?" *With paint and canvas Gauguin asks the ultimate human questions. On the right we see three young women and a baby, symbolizing the sources of life; they ask, Where do we come from? On the left an old woman awaits death in the presence of a white bird representing the afterlife; she asks, Where are we going? In the center a youth, reaching for life, asks What are we? No answers, just questions.*

which seems to us obviously absurd, we should not attempt to prove that it is somehow true, but we should try to understand how it ever came to seem true.
(BERTRAND RUSSELL)

Those who pursue an education but stop short of studying philosophy are like the suitors of Penelope; they found it easier to woo the maidservants than to marry the mistress.
(ARISTIPPOS OF CYRENE)

There are nowadays professors of philosophy, but not philosophers. . . . To be a philosopher is not merely to have subtle thoughts, nor even to found a school, but so to love wisdom as to live according to its dictates, a life of simplicity, independence, magnanimity, and truth. It is to solve some of the problems of life, not only theoretically, but practically.
(HENRY DAVID THOREAU)

The moment a man questions the meaning and value of life, he is sick, since objectively neither has any existence; by asking this question one is merely admitting to a store of unsatisfied libido to which something else must have happened, a kind of fermentation leading to sadness and depression.
(SIGMUND FREUD)

[My philosophy is] a lucid invitation to live and to create, in the very midst of the desert.
(ALBERT CAMUS)

Philosophy is at once the most sublime and the most trivial of human pursuits. It works in the minutest crannies and it opens out onto the widest vistas. . . . No one of us can get along without the far-flashing beams of light it sends over the world's perspectives.
(WILLIAM JAMES)

Philosophy is a battle against the bewitchment of our intelligence by means of language.
(LUDWIG WITTGENSTEIN)

Real intelligence enables us to penetrate to the inside of what we are studying, to reach the very bottom of it, to breathe its spirit, to feel the rhythm of its soul.
(HENRI BERGSON)

A philosophic system is an integrated view of existence. As a human being, you have no choice about the fact that you need a philosophy. Your only choice is whether you define your philosophy by a conscious, rational, disciplined process of thought . . . or let your subconscious accumulate a junk heap of unwarranted conclusions.
(AYN RAND)

Be a philosopher; but amidst all your philosophy, be still a man.
(DAVID HUME)

ON TRUTH AND WISDOM

We must not assume that what convinces us is actually true.
(THE SKEPTICS)

I always had an intense desire to learn to distinguish the true from the false, so as to act clear-sightedly and to walk with assurance in this life.
(RENÉ DESCARTES)

What is truth but to live for an idea? . . . It is a question of discovering a truth which is true for me, of finding the idea for which I am willing to live and die.
(SØREN KIERKEGAARD)

Let us not pretend to deny in our philosophy what we know in our hearts to be true.
(CHARLES S. PEIRCE)

We have to live today by what truth we can get today, and be ready tomorrow to call it falsehood.
(WILLIAM JAMES)

Truth has no special time of its own. Its hour is now—always.
(ALBERT SCHWEITZER)

There are no whole truths; all truths are half-truths. It is trying to treat them as whole truths that plays the devil.
(ALFRED NORTH WHITEHEAD)

I know nothing except the fact that I know nothing.
(SOCRATES)

Where nobody knows anything, there is no point in changing your mind.
(BERTRAND RUSSELL)

Educated men are as much superior to uneducated men as the living are to the dead.
(ARISTOTLE)

We must not spoil the enjoyment of the blessings we have by pining for those we have not.
EPICURUS

Albert Schweitzer and friend at Lambaréné

For nothing is so conducive to greatness of mind as the ability to examine systematically and honestly everything that meets us in life.
(MARCUS AURELIUS)

Nec credi posse aliquid nisi primitus intellectus. *Nothing is to be believed, until it has been understood.*
(PETER ABÉLARD)

I do not know what I may appear to the world; but to myself I seem to have been only like a boy playing on the seashore, and diverting myself in now and then finding a smoother pebble or a prettier shell than ordinary, whilst the great ocean of truth lay all undiscovered before me.

(SIR ISAAC NEWTON)

Give to the intellect, wisdom to comprehend that one thing; to the heart, sincerity to receive this understanding; to the will, purity that wills only one thing.
(SØREN KIERKEGAARD)

ON POLITICS, SOCIETY, AND CULTURE

To know that we know what we know, and to know that we do not know what we do not know—that is true knowledge.
CONFUCIUS

Man is by nature a political animal.
(ARISTOTLE)

I am not an Athenian or a Greek, but a citizen of the world.
(SOCRATES)

As emperor, Rome is my city and my country; but as a human being I belong to the world.
(MARCUS AURELIUS)

Until philosophers are kings, or the kings and princes of this world have the spirit and power of philosophy, and political greatness and wisdom meet in one . . . cities will never have rest from their evils—no, nor the human race.
(PLATO)

The height of injustice is to seem just without being so.
(SOCRATES)

Neglect of an effective birth control policy is a never-failing source of poverty which, in turn, is the parent of revolution and crime.
(ARISTOTLE)

What experience and history teach is this: peoples and governments have never learned anything from history and acted according to what one might have learned from it.
(G. W. F. HEGEL)

The people are absolved from obedience when illegal attempts are made upon their liberties or properties.
(JOHN LOCKE)

If you begin by saying, "Thou shalt not lie," there is no longer any possibility of political action.
(JEAN-PAUL SARTRE)

Politics are for the moment. An equation is for eternity.
(Albert Einstein)

There is no political alchemy by which you can get golden conduct out of leaden instruments.
(Herbert Spencer)

ON MORALS, ETHICS, AND THE GOOD LIFE

Assist a man in lifting a burden, not in laying it down.
(Pythagoras)

Whatever man thou meetest, put to thyself at once this question: What are this man's convictions about good and evil?
(Marcus Aurelius)

People are fools who live without enjoyment in life. Pleasure and absence of pleasure are the criteria of what is profitable and what is not.
(Democritus)

For some, despising pleasure is itself most pleasurable; they derive more pleasure from despising pleasure than from the pleasures themselves.
(Diogenes the Cynic)

Everyone must come out of his Exile in his own way.
Martin Buber

Prize not anything as being to thine interest that shall ever force thee to break thy troth, to surrender thine honor, to hate, suspect, or curse anyone, to play the hypocrite, to lust after anything that needs walls and curtains.
(Marcus Aurelius)

I have discovered that all human evil comes from this, man's being unable to sit still in a room.
(Blaise Pascal)

This sovereignty of the male is a real usurpation, and destroys that nearness of rank, not to say equality, which nature has established between the sexes.
(David Hume)

Two things fill my mind with ever-increasing wonder and awe: the starry heavens above me and the moral law within me.
(Immanuel Kant)

And if a friend wrongs you, then say: "I forgive you what you did to me; but that you have done it to yourself—how could I forgive that."
(Friedrich Nietzsche)

The only obligation which I have a right to assume is to do at any time what I think right.
(Henry David Thoreau)

A man is ethical only when life, as such, is sacred to him, that of plants and animals as that of his fellow men.
(Albert Schweitzer)

Never do anything against conscience even if the state demands it.
(Albert Einstein)

Life is not worth living for the man who has not even one good friend.
(DEMOCRITUS)

Without friends no one would choose to live, though he had all other goods.
(ARISTOTLE)

Friendship is based on equality.
(ARISTOTLE)

As yet woman is not capable of friendship. But tell me, ye men, who of you are capable of friendship?
(FRIEDRICH NIETZSCHE)

ON LIFE, DEATH, AND LIVING

Life is not a problem to be solved but a mystery to be lived.
(JOSEPH CAMPBELL)

No one can be really good without an accurate knowledge of the Nature of the Universe and what makes him human.
(MARCUS AURELIUS)

Above all, have respect for yourself.
(PYTHAGORAS)

Don't forget what happens to the audience at tragedies, will you? Even while they're weeping, they're enjoying themselves.
(SOCRATES)

Words ought to be a little wild for they are the assault of thoughts on the unthinking.
JOHN MAYNARD KEYNES

If you are alone you are completely yourself, but if you are accompanied by a single companion you are only half yourself.
(LEONARDO DA VINCI)

Why then do you live at all, if you do not care to live well?
(DIOGENES THE CYNIC)

When it is time to go . . . we will leave life crying aloud in a glorious triumph-song that we have lived well.
(EPICURUS)

I am saddened that my tongue cannot live up to my heart.
(AUGUSTINE OF THAGASTE)

Madame Curie never heard the birds sing.
(ALBERT EINSTEIN)

Behave not as though thou hadst ten thousand years to live. Thy doom hangs over thee. While thou livest, while thou mayest, become good.
(MARCUS AURELIUS)

The whole life of a philosopher is a preparation for death.
(CICERO)

A free man thinks of nothing less than of death; and his wisdom is a meditation not on death but on life.
(BARUCH SPINOZA)

Wretched, on the threshold of my adult life, I used to pray, "Lord give me chastity and continence: but not yet."
(AUGUSTINE OF THAGASTE)

To live is to be where and with whom one likes.
(JOHN LOCKE)

[Written about 1637 as he was going blind] *These heavens, this earth, which by wonderful observation I had enlarged a thousand times . . . are henceforth dwindled into the narrow space which I myself occupy.*
(GALILEO)

One must separate from anything that forces one to repeat No again and again.
(FRIEDRICH NIETZSCHE)

If a plant cannot live according to its nature, it dies; and so a man.
(HENRY DAVID THOREAU)

There is no sure cure for birth and death save to enjoy the interval.
(GEORGE SANTAYANA)

We have two ears and only one mouth so we can hear more and talk less.
(ZENO THE STOIC)

Desiderium sinus cordis. *It is yearning that makes the heart deep.*
(AUGUSTINE OF THAGASTE)

There's something rather . . . exhilarating about putting yourself on the side of life, instead of on the side of protective ideas.
(JOSEPH CAMPBELL)

We should not pretend to understand the world only by intellect; we apprehend it just as much by feeling.
(CARL JUNG)

Be patient . . . because it wasn't your parents who made the world.
(ARNOLD TOYNBEE)

Immortal God! What a world I see dawning! Why can I not grow young again?
(DESIDERIUS ERASMUS)

ON RELIGION

Fecisti nos ad Te, et inquietum est cor nostrum, donec requiescat in Te. *Thou hast made us for Thee, and our heart is restless till its rests in Thee.*
(SAINT AUGUSTINE)

I have found it necessary to deny knowledge *in order to make room for* faith.
(IMMANUEL KANT)

If oxen [and horses] and lions had hands or could draw with their hands and create works of art like those made by men, then horses would draw pictures of gods like horses, and oxen of gods like oxen, [and lions of gods like lions,] and they would make the bodies [of their gods] in accordance with the form that each species itself possesses.
(XENOPHANES)

A triangle, if it could speak, would in like manner say that God is eminently triangular, and a circle that the divine nature is eminently circular; and thus would every one ascribe his own attributes to God.
(BARUCH SPINOZA)

Truth is one, the sages speak of it by many names.

THE VEDAS

Voltaire (1694–1778), the "laughing philosopher."

If I make it to the top of the mountain, I won't want to be bothered by phone calls.
LORI VILLAMIL

Le coeur a ses raisons que la raison ne connaît point. *The heart has its reasons which reason cannot understand.*
(BLAISE PASCAL)

In religion finite life rises to infinite life.
(G. W. F. HEGEL)

The will of God [is] the sanctuary of ignorance.
(BARUCH SPINOZA)

In truth there was only one Christian, and he died on the cross.
(FRIEDRICH NIETZSCHE)

God is dead. God remains dead. And we have killed him. . . . What was holiest and most powerful of all that the world has yet owned has bled to death under our knives. Who will wipe this blood off us?
(FRIEDRICH NIETZSCHE)

I should only believe in a God that would know how to dance.
(FRIEDRICH NIETZSCHE)

God is a comedian playing to an audience that is afraid to laugh.
(VOLTAIRE)

If you think your belief is based upon reason, you will support it by argument, rather than by persecution, and will abandon it if the argument goes against you. But if your belief is based on faith, you will realize that argument is useless, and will therefore resort to force either in the form of persecution or by stunting the minds of the young.
(BERTRAND RUSSELL)

Generally speaking, the errors in religion are dangerous; those in philosophy only ridiculous.
(DAVID HUME)

ON BEAUTY

Beauty is a gift of God.
(ARISTOTLE)

What do you feel when you see your own inward beauty?
(PLOTINUS)

Only as an aesthetic phenomenon is the world justified.
(FRIEDRICH NIETZSCHE)

Beauty in things exists in the mind which contemplates them.
(DAVID HUME)

The perception of beauty is a moral test.
(HENRY DAVID THOREAU)

I tell you: one must have chaos within one to give birth to a dancing star!
(FRIEDRICH NIETZSCHE)

ENDNOTES

1 Aristotle, *Metaphysics*, I, 2.
2 Ruth Benedict, *Patterns of Culture* (Mentor, 1948), p. 2.
3 Bertrand Russell, *The Problems of Philosophy* (Oxford University Press Galaxy Book, 1959), pp. 157f.
4 Alice Miller, The Untouched Key: *Tracing Childhood Trauma in Creativity and Destructiveness* (Doubleday, 1990), pp. 43ff., 75ff., 80ff., 120ff., 131ff.
5 Walter Kaufmann, *Nietzsche: Philosopher, Psychologist, Antichrist* (The World Publishing Co., Meridian Books, 1956), pp. 30f.

THE PRESOCRATICS

THE DAWNING OF
CRITICAL PHILOSOPHY

PART

1

CHAPTER 2

THE MILESIANS OF ASIA MINOR

Three philosophers from Miletus ask probing questions about matter and motion and thus initiate the Western tradition of critical philosophy as well as (faintly) the science of physics; this can be thought of as the beginning of a new empirical perspective for looking at the world.

THE FIRST PHILOSOPHERS

Philosophizing began in the Western world when a fundamental change occurred in the way we think about the world and our place in it. The records are sketchy, but by all accounts this change began along the Ionian coast of Asia Minor at the opening of the sixth century before Christ, and the name of one man, Thales, is associated with these beginnings. He lived at Miletus, a Greek frontier colony on the southwest coast of what is now Turkey. So great was his fame as an astronomer, mathematician, and philosopher that he was counted as the first of the Seven Sages of ancient Greece, and two centuries later the great Greek philosophers frequently referred to him. Though myth and legend surround his name, it is clear the historical Thales was an innovative thinker who powerfully influenced the shaping of a fresh intellectual spirit.

Thales was followed by a famous pupil, Anaximander, who in turn had a disciple named Anaximenes. All lived in Miletus and are known as "the Milesians" or "the Milesian hylozoists" since all three concluded that, in some mysterious way, matter is alive. (*Hylê* is the Greek word for *matter* and *zoê* for *life*, hence "living matter.")

IN THE HISTORY OF PHILOSOPHY

Thales is remembered (1) as the first critical philosopher/scientist or, better, as an appropriate symbol for the emergence of critical philosophy in the Western world; (2) for predicting the solar eclipse of 585 BC, implying an awareness of order in nature; (3) for suggesting that water is the world's primal stuff; and (4) for concluding that everything must have soul.

Anaximander is credited with the ideas that (1) everything is constructed out of some essential matter *(apeiron)* that is quite other than the substances we observe; (2) motion is created by the interaction of opposites; and (3) all living organisms, including humans, evolved from more primitive life-forms.

Thucydides believed that nothing significant had happened in time before the events which he described, and that nothing significant was likely to happen thereafter.
EDWARD HALLETT CARR

Of all things that are . . . the most beautiful is the universe, for it is God's workmanship.
THALES

As our soul, being air, holds us together, so do breath and air surround the whole universe.
ANAXIMENES

Thales of Miletus (c.640–c.562 BC)

Anaximenes is noted for his theory that everything can be explained through the rarefaction and condensation of air.

The craving for an interpretation of history is so deep-rooted that, unless we have a constructive outlook over the past, we are drawn either to mysticism or to cynicism.

F. POWICKE

MILETUS

Today the ruins of ancient Miletus rise from stagnant waters like a ghost-city conjured by a haunted mind on a bad day. As one approaches from the northwest, the massive remains of the marble city extend out from a low hill on a flat coastal plain. An enormous Roman amphitheater, now crumbling and overgrown with weeds and wildflowers, dominates the hill; at its base acres of broken blocks litter the ground, scattered memories of what was once a thriving metropolis. A footpath around the southern end of the hill leads to sprawling ruins: city streets laid out in neat squares and lined with fluted columns and pedestals, a stadium, public baths, and a temple dedicated to Athena—their faded majesty still reflected in the monumental Hellenistic gateway to the south market. A block farther on one comes upon a vast panorama

When eras are on the decline, all tendencies are subjective; but on the other hand when matters are ripening for a new epoch, all tendencies are objective.

GOETHE

Today Miletus rises ghostlike from marshes on the southwest coast of Turkey, giving a visitor only a faint reminder of the glory the city enjoyed in the sixth century BC with its white marble temples, stadia, gymnasia and industrious populations.

of structures that appear to float on water: municipal buildings, temples, shops, agoras, thermal baths, and gymnasia. The impression is that of a mirage dancing on the surface of the marshes.

Thales knew a quite different city. In 600 BC Miletus was the magnificant harbor city of a seafaring people who traveled the length of the Mediterranean Sea. The central area of the city was situated on a low promontory jutting for a mile into the Latmic Gulf; its gleaming white marble walls and buildings were visible far out to sea. Ionia was the eastern frontier region of Greek culture and influence, and, along with scores of other cities on the Aegean coast, Miletus had been settled by Greeks from the mainland. In turn, Miletus and other bustling Ionian cities sent out their colonies and extended their influence. Miletus alone established some sixty colonies along the northern coast of Ionia and on the shores of the Black Sea—"like frogs around a pond," Plato said. Scores of naval vessels anchored in the harbors of Miletus visited Phoenicia and Egypt in the east and sailed as far as Sicily and Italy in the west.

Miletus occupied less than a square mile. From the harbor gate it was a ten-minute walk to the theater, where Thales could listen to political leaders and common citizens speak on soapbox issues. Another ten-minute stroll took him to the stadium, where he could watch daily athletic contests such as wrestling, footracing, and javelin- and discus-throwing. Five minutes away the city's magistrates conducted business in the main courthouse. A few minutes farther in the center of the city, vendors in the agora displayed copperware from Cyprus; blue glassware and precious stones from Egypt; amphorae and stoneware from Civilia; spices, herbs, and perfumes from Phoenicia and the Orient; wheat and pickled fish from the Black Sea; wool from Italy; and grain, olives, and figs from the Phrygian highlands. North of the agora was the great hall and high altar dedicated to the goddess Artemis, the Huntress. Miletus was a thriving metropolis, full of action, full of struggle, and full of life.

In 600 BC Miletus was a thriving commercial city spread over a promontory extending into the Latmic Gulf; on its eastern flank the famous Lion Gate welcomed ships from other trading cities of the Mediterranean and Black Sea. Miletus became a center for the exchange of ideas, and out of it came new ways of looking at the world, new values, and new assessments of what it means to be human.

History cannot be written unless the historian can achieve some kind of [sympathetic] contact with the mind of those about whom he is writing.
EDWARD HALLETT CARR

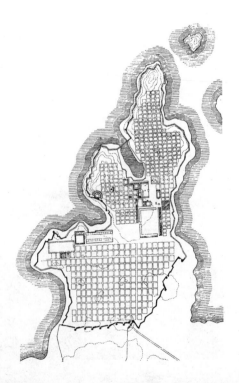

Far-reaching changes were taking place in these cities of the eastern Aegean. Ionia was a cultural meeting place of two frontiers—the East and West. Ideas challenged ideas; clichéd ways of thinking gave way to creative responses. An increasing number of bright intellects could put ideas together in new ways and develop concepts that better described an expanding world.

Historians sometimes depict this historic explosion as first occurring in Athens, and the Athenians did begin to explore democracy on a grand scale, experiencing and exploiting freedom as no one had before. With this freedom a new and joyous creativity emerged. But all this is rightly seen as the culmination of an intellectual ferment that had begun a century earlier in Ionia. As travelers and traders, the Ionians had discovered that if markets were to flourish and businesses to succeed, entrepreneurs must be open to, and tolerant of, new and strange customs and manners, ethical and political attitudes, religious beliefs and practices, and esthetic sensibilities. Such conditions inevitably encourage pragmatism and adaptability, and a softening of old rigidities; they foster new and fertile ways of thinking.

Furthermore, this openness was abetted by an astonishing fact of Greek life: no established religious orthodoxy and no ordained priesthood existed to enforce any kind of doctrinal conformity. The Greeks never developed a separate order of religious leaders as authoritative keepers of secret knowledge and sacred practice and revered for their special status in society. To be sure, a full pantheon of gods and goddesses existed, each with his or her cultic myths, holy places, altars, and festivals. The Greeks practiced a variety of mystery religions, most of them fertility cults celebrating the cycle of the seasons. But no single religious establishment ever became sufficiently strong to empower it into a theocracy; no one in Greek society possessed the authority to impose an orthodox set of dogmatic beliefs on a believing populace.

Thus, because they (1) lived along a great cultural frontier where an exchange of ideas occurred and narrow horizons expanded, (2) were traders and travelers encountering new ideas, and (3) were free of religious conformity, the Greeks on the Ionian coast experienced an unprecedented release from constraints and enjoyed a hitherto unknown degree of personal freedom. These special conditions encouraged creative individualism, and out of it philosophic thought began to develop.

We can be sure Thales and his pupils were not the only ones engaged in this intellectual adventure. Numerous individuals must have felt this freedom and exploited it in their daily lives, but the historical records don't allow us to know of them and pay them our respects. Only the names of a few of the most prominent thinkers have come down to us, and we knowingly use them as symbols of the philosophic venture.

The true mystery of the world is the visible, not the invisible.

OSCAR WILDE

We are forced to fall back on fatalism as an explanation of irrational events, that is to say, of events the rationality of which we do not understand.

LEO TOLSTOY

When you read a work of history, always listen out for the buzzing [of the bees in his bonnet]. If you can detect none, either you are tone deaf or your historian is a dull dog.

EDWARD HALLETT CARR

THALES: THE PRIDE OF MILETUS

THE MAN

Thales lived at Miletus from about 640 BC (the first year of the thirty-fifth Olympiad) to about 562 BC (he died during the fifty-eighth Olympiad). He was a contemporary of Solon, the great Athenian lawgiver, and of the gold-rich King Croesus of Lydia (whose gold didn't prevent his capture by the Persians). By vocation Thales was an engineer. We know that the Persians trained their military engineers at Miletus, and Thales may have been attached to the Persian army as an engineer or instructor.

Most traditions tell us Thales came from a distinguished Milesian family and that his parents were named Examyos and Cleobulina; however, one tradition (from the historian Herodotus) claims he had been exiled from Phoenicia and later naturalized

Of all things that are, the most ancient is God, for he is uncreated. . . .

The greatest is space, for it holds all things.

The swiftest is mind, for it speeds everywhere.

The strongest, necessity, for it masters all.

The wisest, time, for it brings everything to light.

THALES

Let not idle words prejudice thee against those who have shared thy confidence.

THALES

°*Plato uses this story as a metaphor to point out the dangers for "all who pass their lives in philosophy"; see the* Theaetetus, *174A–B.*

All things are full of gods.

THALES

as a Milesian citizen. One account says he was married and had a son named Cybisthus, but also a charming story exists telling us that when his mother first urged him to marry, he replied that the right time had not yet arrived. When she later urged him to marry, he informed her that the right time was long past. Once asked why he had no children of his own, he said it was because he loved children. (Cybisthus may have been his sister's son he had adopted.)

Thales loved solitude, lived quietly, and tried to stay out of public affairs. When he died at age seventy-eight, a statue was erected in his honor bearing this inscription:

> Pride of Miletus and Ionian lands,
> Wisest astronomer, here Thales stands.

Thales was preeminently an astronomer, and two treatises, *On the Solstice* and *On the Equinox*, are attributed to him (along with a book called *Nautical Astronomy*, though his authorship is doubtful). It was said he calculated the size of the Sun and Moon as 1/720th of their respective orbits or a half a degree in diameter.

A story is told that one night while he was walking across a field he looked up at the stars and failed to watch where he was going. He fell into a ditch. The servant woman with him exclaimed, "How can you expect to know about the heavens, Thales, when you can't see what lies at your feet?"°

Diogenes Laërtius, the third-century AD compiler and biographer, undoubtedly conveys something of Thales' sagacity and humor in his *Lives of Eminent Philosophers*:

> [Thales] held there was no difference between life and death. "Why then do you not die?" someone asked him. "Because," said he, "there is no difference."
>
> To the question which is older, day or night, he replied: "Night is the older . . . by one day."
>
> Someone asked him whether a man could hide an evil deed from the gods: "No," he replied, "nor an evil thought."
>
> To the adulterer who inquired if he should deny the charge upon oath, he replied that perjury was no worse than adultery.
>
> Being asked what is difficult, he replied, "To know oneself." "What is easy?" "To give advice to another." "What is the most pleasant?" "Success." . . .
>
> To the question what was the strangest thing he had ever seen, his answer was, "An aged tyrant."
>
> "How can one best bear adversity?" "If he should see his enemies in worse plight."
>
> "How shall we lead the best and most righteous life?" "By refraining from doing what we blame in others."
>
> "What man is happy?" "He who has a healthy body, a resourceful mind, and a docile nature."
>
> He tells us to remember friends, whether present or absent; not to pride ourselves upon outward appearance, but to study to be beautiful in character.
>
> "Shun ill-gotten gains," he says. "Let not idle words prejudice thee against those who have shared thy confidence."
>
> To him belongs the proverb "Know thyself."[1]

Nous is quickest of all, for it runs through everything.

THALES

Another account documents Thales' reputation for practical wisdom. We are told he was mocked for his poverty, his taunters implying that philosophy was quite useless. His response . . . but let Aristotle recount the episode:

According to the story, he knew by his skill in the stars while it was yet winter that there would be a great harvest of olives in the coming year; so, having a little money, he gave deposits for the use of all the olive-presses in Chios and Miletus, which he hired at a low price because no one bid against him. When the harvest-time came, and many were wanted all at once and of a sudden, he let them out at any rate which he pleased, and made a quantity of money. Thus he showed the world that philosophers can easily be rich if they like, but that their ambition is of another sort.[2]

Still another story from the historian Herodotus[3] places Thales with King Croesus as he was attempting to move his army across the Halys River where no bridge existed and at a point too deep to ford. "It is said that Thales, who was then serving with the army, switched the course of the river, causing it to flow behind the army instead of altogether in front of them." It seems Thales went upriver a ways and directed the diggers to cut a channel off from the river. Thus divided into two smaller streams, the river could be easily crossed.

The one event that places Thales at a specific time and place was his prediction of the solar eclipse of 585 BC.[4] With his knowledge of astronomy, and probably by using Babylonian tables of solar and lunar orbits, he predicted the year when the eclipse would take place in western Ionia. It occurred as foretold, and in the heat of battle between the Medes and Persians "the day suddenly turned into night." Awestruck and frightened, both armies were routed by the event.

This "shift from day to night," Herodotus writes, "had been foretold to the Ionians by Thales of Miletus, who set as its limit the year in which it actually occurred." Thales' prediction appears to be the beginning of some kind of concept of natural order. It was the discovery, or the realization, that an event occurs because it follows of necessity specific causation patterns dictated by nature.

Thales spent some time in Egypt studying with the priests, who taught him how to inscribe a right-angled triangle in a circle, knowledge he was so grateful for that he sacrificed an ox in thanksgiving.° He measured the height of pyramids by measuring their shadows after noting the time of day when a man's shadow equalled his height. This is pure abstract geometry at work. He also employed elementary trigonometry to measure the distance of ships at sea, and he wrote a star guide for nagivators.

Thales' knowledge of astronomy was considerable. In addition to predicting the eclipse, he correctly explained the mechanics of solar and lunar eclipses as, respectively, the passing of the Moon between Sun and Earth and the Earth between Sun and Moon. He concluded that the lunar phases indicate that the Moon is lighted by the Sun and is not giving off light from itself; the phases reveal its position relative to the Sun. He also determined the dates of the summer and winter solstices and plotted the Sun's course between them. Thales is credited with dividing the year into four seasons and 365 days.

THE GREEK MIRACLE

Thales asked questions philosophically. He phrased them rationally, and apparently in different ways, in the hope of finding answers that correspond to observed facts. He was not into believing, so he seems to have had no need to honor traditional beliefs. Both religion and philosophy are designed to meet the human need for an understanding of how the world works and what our place is in it, but they differ in how they find answers to these questions. Thales represents an early empirical attempt to find answers based on observation.

When we take up a work of history, our first concern should be not with the facts which it contains but with the historian who wrote it.
EDWARD HALLETT CARR

It would not do for a student to answer every question in history by saying that it was the finger of God. Not until we have gone as far as most in tidying up mundane events and the human drama are we permitted to bring in wider considerations.
FR. M.C. D'ARCY

History is the historian's experience. It is "made" by nobody save the historian: to write history is the only way of making it.
MICHAEL OAKESHOTT

Know thyself.
THALES

°*Pythagoras did the same (see p. 47), which may be a commentary on the high value both placed on mystical knowledge.*

Before Thales, physical events were almost universally explained as the result of supernatural causes. Since people believed all sorts of gods and goddesses, godlets, demigods, demons, ancestral ghosts, and a host of other spirits good and bad inhabited the cosmos, it was reasonable to conclude that all events of human experience occurred because they had been willed. If lightning struck, Zeus had hurled another thunderbolt. When the Sun moved through the heavens, all knew that Apollo was driving it in his fiery chariot. If the Greeks lost the battle of Troy or if Jason's ship slipped safely between the rocks of Scylla and the whirlpool of Charybdis, then the Olympians were again playing their unnerving games.

And so, before the advent of careful thinking, people attributed *natural* events to *supernatural* causes. G. K. Chesterton once remarked that for those holding this pre-critical worldview, the Sun moved across the sky each day only because God got up before the Sun and said to the Sun, "Sun, get up and do it again."

These early Greek thinkers, it seems, were not quite satisfied with all this. They apparently realized that if to every question you ask you have but a single answer—"The gods willed it"—then in fact you know nothing meaningful or useful. Why did crops fail this spring? "Because the gods willed it." Why did the Trojans lose the war? "The gods willed it." Why did my chariot's axle break? "The gods willed it." Why did my daughter die? "The gods willed it." Why did Mount Aetna erupt and bury the city? "The gods willed it." We can repeat such questions forever and not realize that we haven't achieved any significant results other than a modicum of reassurance. To an intellect who has developed even a rudimentary awareness of how we think—to a mind that thinks causally and connects events—it is obvious such answers are facile and unproductive.

The Milesians seem to have sought a different kind of explanation. When they asked about the cause of events, they assumed that the answer might be found in "nature," in the processes of nature, or within matter itself. In seeking causes, they shifted the *location* where they expected to find answers. This shift to an empirical way of looking at the world, however tentative it may have been for the Milesians, is a critical moment in the acquisition of knowledge. It has been called the "Greek Miracle."

Thales, therefore, is important in the Western philosophic tradition. Scientific thinkers first look at the world to find out what is going on. Careful observers don't *begin* with answers. They first observe and gather information and then attempt to account for what they have observed. In the broadest sense, science is nothing more and nothing less than looking carefully at the world to find out what is happening.

On Thales *Thales, too, to judge from what is recorded about him, seems to have held soul to be a motive force, since he said that the magnet has a soul in it because it moves the iron.*

ARISTOTLE

FLOATING DISK

From the beginning of human musings, accounting for the origin and structure of the world has been a frustrating obsession. Ancient cosmologists placed the Earth on the shoulders of Atlas, on the back of an elephant, or on the shell of a giant tortoise. Such conjectures indicate that the problem was overwhelming; without scientific knowledge the question was unanswerable.

Thales concluded that the Earth is (or is like) a disk or drum (a drum is one section of a marble column) floating on an ocean of water. Like a piece of wood rising and falling as waves undulate beneath it, it stays in one place as it floats. This theory explains earthquakes fairly well; the Earth is shaken about like a boat riding the waves.

Aristotle pointed out that Thales' idea fails to answer the question. The Earth may be floating on water, but what is the water floating on? "As if the same problem didn't logically arise for the water supporting the Earth as for the Earth itself!"[5] Aristotle is right, of course. The Earth is riding on the back of an elephant standing on the back of another elephant standing . . . ad infinitum; as the quip has it, it's elephants all the way down. Asking what the water is floating on is a perfectly logical next question.

Thales' explanation may have been intuitive wisdom. Assuming, as nearly all ancients did, that the Earth is flat, then reason insists it must be resting on *something*. If you go down to the shore, what do you find? At Miletus you find water; water surrounds in every direction except up. It was reasonable for Thales to speculate that the world is floating on water. What, then, of Aristotle's criticism? Thales was probably aware of the problem (we don't know this for sure), but given his awareness of the limits of his knowledge and his timely assumptions, he may have seen that no further answer could be found.

WATER

Not only does the world rest on water, it developed from water in the beginning and, in its essence, is still water today. Aristotle wrote that Thales "declared the first principle to be water." The Greek word *hydor* denotes any substance in liquid form. Thales may have had in mind the scenario of a watery chaos out of which all things originally emerged.

It is difficult to decide whether Thales was drawing on prevailing ideas or whether his theory of origins was the product of his own empirical reflections. He must have been acquainted with origin myths from the East. In the Babylonian genesis story, *Enuma elish* ("When from above"), the primeval sweet waters (the male principle) and the primeval salt waters (the female principle) mingle to produce the gods and eventually the world. Similarly, the Hebraic genesis story speaks of *tehom*, an abyss of chaotic waters that predated God's (Elohim's) creation.

On the other hand, this idea may have been an intuition on Thales' part. This is Aristotle's reading of it:

> Probably the idea was suggested to him by the fact that the nutriment of everything contains moisture, and that heat itself is generated out of moisture and is kept alive by it. For of course it is assumed that whatever something is generated out of must be its first-principle. He drew his notion also from the fact that the seeds of everything have a moist nature; and of course the first-principle of moist things is water.[6]

Thales may have come across fossil mollusks in the geologic strata of surrounding mountains and inferred from this that, at some time past, everything was under the sea and that all life emerged from the water. Several later philosophers— among them Thales' pupil Anaximander—were puzzled by the fossil record and made this inference. In any case, Thales believed that things not only originated from water but also still are water in some form. Why water? Perhaps because the world of things comes in three obvious forms—solids, liquids, and gases; and the one familiar substance found in all three forms is water—as ice, liquid water, and gaseous vapor.

MOTION

Thales also was puzzled by motion and change. To even a casual observer the world and its multifarious components are forever in motion; nothing we experience ever stands still. Everything also changes, seemingly on some internal schedule—if not in a minute or hour, then in the span of days or years. Nothing endures, and a "Why?" seems trite and futile. If we think twice about the *cause* of motion, we may feel we are faced with a cosmic paradox.

On the Physicists *Those who
assumed innumerable worlds, e.g.
Anaximander, Leukippos,
Democritus, and, at a later date,
Epicurus, held that they came
into being and passed away*
ad infinitum, *some always
coming into being and others
passing away.*

SIMPLICIUS

°See p. 192.

Thales' answer appears to have been inferred from his experience with magnetic stones. As Aristotle tells us, "Thales conceived of soul as somehow a motive power, since he said that the magnetic stone has soul in it because it sets a piece of iron in motion."[7] ° Magnets, that is, have souls. The Greek word for "soul" is *psychê*, but its connotations were not those of Judeo-Christian tradition—a spirit-person who survives into an afterlife when the body dies. For the Greeks, *psychê* is the animating principle of living things, like an electric current pulsating through the body causing it to move. Thales thus could explain the push and pull that comes from inside a magnet: *Something* resides within the magnet empowering it to set ferrous objects in motion.

You may think Thales is reaching, but have you ever toyed with a pair of bar magnets? Turn them so that the positive poles are together. You can push with all your strength, but the magnets won't touch. Then turn one of them around. They bang together and lock, and it takes considerable effort to pull them apart. Why? Play with them and try to feel Thales' state of mind. Magnets have souls, of course.

From his observation of magnets' behavior Thales could generalize. Magnets, like all else, are made of water, and, like magnets, water must be alive with soul. Motion therefore has its provenance from within living substances.

ANAXIMANDER: THE BOUNDLESS IS THE FIRST PRINCIPLE

Thales' pupil Anaximander is a shadowy figure but is generally thought to have possessed one of the good minds of antiquity. We have no portrait of him and only one fragment of text. For information about him we must rely on the testimony of Aristotle, writing more than two hundred years later, and on even later Greek and Latin writers.

On Anaximander *Among those
who say that the first principle is
one and movable and infinite is
Anaximander of Miletus. . . . He
says that it is neither water nor
any other one of the things called
elements, but the infinite is
something of a different nature,
from which came all the heavens
and the worlds in them.*

SIMPLICIUS

See physis *in lexicon.*

Of his life we know little. His father was Praxides. One report says he had a son. We know he traveled. At Sparta in the Peloponnesus he set up a sundial to count the hours and a *gnomon* (a sort of T-square) to measure the solstices and equinoxes. He wrote a book titled *On Nature* (so did everyone else, it seems; at that time the word "nature" [Greek *physis*, whence "physics" and "physical"°] referred to everything "out there" in nature). He developed a star chart and is credited as the first to draw a map of the known world. He climbed in the mountains of Asia Minor where he found fossils of sea creatures. He seems to have had some practical political ability since the Milesians chose him as the leader of their new colony, Apollonia, in the Black Sea. Miletus was famed for producing engineers, and, like Thales, Anaximander was probably an engineer by profession. He was born in the second year of the forty-second Olympiad (611 BC) and lived to be a little more than sixty-four years old.

FRAGMENT

Whereas nothing Thales wrote has come down to us, a single cryptic fragment from Anaximander has been preserved by the Greek writer Simplicius in his commentary on Aristotle.[8] Cryptic it is!

*All things arise out of the
Boundless. . . .*

ANAXIMANDER

The Unlimited *[apeiron]* is the first-principle *[archê]* of things that are. It is that from which the coming-to-be [of things and qualities] takes place, and it is that into which they return when they perish, by moral necessity, giving satisfaction to one another and making reparation for their injustice, according to the order of time.

Anaximander refers to this "Unlimited" as the "origin" or "first-cause" of everything, that is, of the world-stuff everything is made of. The Greek words he used are *apeiron* and *archê*. *Apeiron* derives from *peras*, "limited," "bounded," or "finite"; the *a* is the alpha negative (as in the English words *amoral* and *atheist*). Hence *apeiron* translates as "not limited," "not bounded," or "not finite." The Greek word *archê* refers to the original substance or ultimate source material something derives from and returns into when it perishes.

THE BOUNDLESS

Thales, you'll recall, thought everything is made of water, but Anaximander criticized this idea, arguing that, on logical grounds, it can't be true. The universe cannot be made out of any one thing such as air, water, or fire, because these substances possess antagonistic qualities that would lead to mutual annihilation. Fire is hot and dries things; water is wet and makes everything moist. So if you put these opposites together they would annihilate each other, just as—to use a modern simile—matter would annihilate antimatter. So the world, Anaximander held, cannot be composed of any of the substances we experience.

"Of what substance," then, is the cosmos constructed? For Anaximander it is *apeiron*, the "boundless," the "unlimited." Unlimited how? Unlimited in the number of ways it can manifest itself or in the number of substances it can change into. Anaximander was thinking of a substance more ultimate than anything known to sense experience, something that can be transmogrified or reshaped into something else, something that can become oceans and rocks and clouds, as well as green leaves and sentient organisms.

Anaximander reached this conclusion not from empirical observation but by means of logical inference. The boundless, after all, is beyond experience; we can't perceive it. But we do experience the manifestations of apeiron in infinite ways as material substances. Anaximander is an empiricist in the grand sense of the word: He attempted to look at the world and account for what he saw. But (like modern physicists) he had to postulate the existence of something beyond experience to account for what is within experience, as we do, for example, when we posit the existence of gravity.

MOTION AND CHANGE

How does Anaximander account for the motion and change that effect the infinite material manifestations of the Boundless? He theorizes that an interaction of opposites produces motion and change; examples are such qualities as dry and moist, hot and cold, and light and dark. When things get too dry, the pendulum swings back and they become moist again, too moist and they begin to dry. Things get too hot and start to cool down, too cold and they begin to warm up. Opposites, therefore, are not merely qualities but dynamic forces.

The world, therefore, is not a thing but a process. Everything is in a state of becoming and perishing, of coming to be, disintegrating, and dying. Cosmic cycles manifest in all existence. Living things have evolved, apparently, from primitive animal forms, only to go through their appropriate life cycle and perish. From the fossil fish Anaximander found in the mountains of Asia Minor he inferred the existence of long-term alternating land-water cycles. Consequently, life, like physical matter, is created by and is imprisoned in an "alternation of opposites." Even gods are born and die.

NATURE

Anaximander contends that this eternal round of coming to be and passing away follows the dictates of necessity. It belongs to a determined natural order of things; the

[Anaximander holds that all derives from the boundless] And this arché is eternal and does not grow old, and it surrounds all the worlds.

HIPPOLYTUS

On Anaximander *Evidently when he sees the four elements changing into one another, he does not deem it right to make any one of these the underlying substance, but something else besides them.*

SIMPLICIUS

[Anaximander teaches that] Motion is eternal, and as a result of it the origin of the worlds was brought about.

HIPPOLYTUS

On Anaximander *And he does not think that things come into being by change in the nature of the element, but by the separation of the opposites which the eternal motion causes.*

SIMPLICIUS

On Anaximander *Living creatures came into being from moisture evaporated by the sun. Man was originally similar to another creature—that is, to a fish.*

HIPPOLYTUS

process could not be other than it is. The *apeiron*, or something within it, stimulates the interaction of opposites, causing things to come into existence and vanish again out of existence. Birth and death, natural processes, happen by "moral necessity." But this determinism doesn't make it all right: He thinks it unfair that, after but a day, a flower must perish and return to what it was created from. Whenever anything perishes, that it should have to pay a price for its existence is unjust. When the moist evaporates into the dry, its perishing is unfair, as proven by the fact the dry must return the favor and become moist again.

COSMOLOGY

Anaximander developed a picturesque cosmogony. Looking at the heavens, he speculated that countless worlds exist, being born and dying like everything else. "There are always some worlds in process of coming to be, others in process of passing away."[9] According to Aëtius, Anaximander believed the stars are small circles of fire, compressed by air that "breathes out flames from little openings in the air."[10]

In the beginning, Anaximander postulated, a great sphere emerged out of some primordial condition that was capable of producing heat and cold, perhaps out of the waters or from vapors. The sphere was like a great marble column that broke into sections, and its drums became the Sun, Moon, and stars.

On Anaximander *Anaximander said that the first living creatures were born in moisture, enclosed in thorny barks; and that as their age increased they came forth on to the drier part and, when the bark had broken off, they lived a different kind of life for a short time.*

AËTIUS

The Earth is also a cylinder shaped like a drum, its depth one-third its breadth. This Earth-drum is suspended in the sky, equidistant from forces in all directions. (This idea makes Anaximander the first philosopher/scientist to articulate the concept of space vis-à-vis cosmologies that have the Earth floating in water or bouyed up by some medium.) This Earth-drum has two faces; the top face displays a curved surface, and we humans live on it.

Anaximander envisaged this flat Earth-disk as the center of a revolving universe of turning circles. Each circle has the appearance of a giant wheel composed of an inner and outer rim of a hard shell-like substance, and between the rims a fierce fire flares. We see the Sun, Moon, planets, and stars through the shell-rims, punctured with "breathing" holes." Each heavenly body is a part of a different-sized concentric wheel. The Sun's wheel is twenty-seven times larger than the Moon's wheel. The whole system has a daily rotation, but each wheel has its own proper rotation period.

The sea, Anaximander reasoned, was left over from primal waters whose surface the Sun evaporated, and evaporation generates the winds. The "vapors and exhalations" produced during early times also initiated the motions of the Sun and Moon. Some of the leftover moisture settled in depressions in the Earth's surface and became lakes and seas. They eventually will dry up, Anaximander believed, since they continue to be evaporated by the Sun.

On Anaximander *Further [Anaximander] says that in the beginning man was born from creatures of a different kind; because other creatures are soon self-supporting, but man alone needs prolonged nursing. For this reason he would not have survived if this had been his original form.*

PSEUDO-PLUTARCH

ORGANISMS

One of the really nagging questions would-be empiricists face has to do with the origins of life-forms—us. Whence living things? What does it mean to be alive? What is the relationship of inert matter to life? Anaximander's answers are innovative and courageous. Animals "come-to-be from vapors raised by the Sun," and humans evolved over a long stretch of time from some quite different animal, probably a fish.[11] Anaximander was puzzled by his observation that human infants require prolonged care. Clearly humans didn't spring instantly into existence from another animal; they must have evolved gradually. But how this happened he couldn't quite imagine. The best he could figure was that human beings might have been transmogrified out of the bodies of fishes (at that time we may have resembled a fish), and "after birth they were reared in the way sharks are reared until they became capable of protecting themselves; and that eventually they were cast ashore so that they had to learn to live on dry land."[12] He thought the first humans must have been generated in moisture and possessed a "prickly skin" that eventually dried and cracked off, after which we gradually adjusted to new skins.

ANAXIMENES: THE WORLD IS AIR CONDENSED AND RAREFIED

The third Milesian philosopher was Anaximenes. He was the son of Eurystratos and lived from about 588 BC to about 524 BC, dying during the sixty-third Olympiad. His compositions were written in a local Ionian dialect "in a plain [readable] style, without affectation."[13] Anaximenes' mind seems not to have ranged over the cosmos with the same sweep as his two predecessors; he concentrated mostly on just two questions: What is the world made of? and What causes motion?

Air, so, what is the world made of? Air, reasoned Anaximenes. The Greek word is *aêr,* and he used it much as we would use it today to mean the lower levels of the atmosphere that enclose the Earth. He argued that this "basic air-stuff" (*archê*) is always in motion and is the cause of change via air condensation and rarefaction. A modern analogy might liken the process to the "high" and "low" of a weather front: "Low" is rarefied air, and the winds rush in; "high" is condensed air, and the winds blow outward and away. Such highs and lows alternate endlessly, rarefaction to condensation and back, causing motion in the air.

According to Anaximenes, highly rarefied air first becomes "ether" (Greek *aither,* the bright, clear sky of the upper atmosphere) and then bursts into fire. Fire is rarefied air. Condensed air first becomes clouds, then water, then all the other heavier substances—earth, rock, and so on. All the world's particular "things" are thus composed of air. Even the gods and spirits, although nonsubstantial, are airy.

It is tempting to imagine Anaximenes walking along the beach at Miletus and pondering the clouds forming over the gulf; they are composed, he said, of "felted" air. The word "felted" he adopted from wool shearers. Wool fluffed up with wool combs is "felted" into fleecy tufts. Similarly, felted air becomes the fleecy white cumulus clouds of spring.

In its still and stable state, air is imperceptible and appears to be "nonsubstantial." As a nonsubstance *aêr* was easily associated with *pneuma,* another Greek word that meant "air"—but a blast of air like a wind, a gentle breeze, or the air we breathe; in this latter sense it was associated with "soul" and "spirit." Anaximenes' "air," therefore, has close connections with the spiritual and the processes of life. As long as we live and breathe in air, we are alive. Hence, air is life itself, or at least the essence of life.

Anaximenes wondered about a few other things, if we can believe the later records. The Earth is a very big hunk of condensed air shaped like a tabletop, resting on lighter air, "like a lid," Aristotle records; and "this air, having no room in which to change its position, thickens and becomes a mass pressing against the Earth, like the water in a clepsydra [water clock]."[14] The Earth is a part of the eternal cosmic cycle of alternations—condensation and rarefaction; it too will perish someday.

MILESIAN LEGACY

The Milesians asked formidable questions, and this is perhaps their lasting contribution. They symbolize those who refused to believe what others unquestioningly

On Anaximander *[Anaximander declares] that originally men came into being inside fishes, and that having been nurtured there—like sharks—and having become adequate to look after themselves, they then came forth and took to the land.*

PLUTARCH

All changes are condensation and rarefaction.

ANAXIMENES

On Anaximenes *Anaximenes and Diogenes make air, rather than water, the material principle above the other simple bodies.*

ARISTOTLE

On Anaximenes *[Anaximenes] too makes motion eternal, and says that change also comes about through it.*

SIMPLICIUS

On Anaximenes *Anaximenes . . . said that infinite air was the principle, from which the things that are becoming, and that are, and that shall be, and gods and things divine, all come into being, and the rest from its products.*

HIPPOLYTUS

On Anaximenes *[Air] differs in its substantial nature by rarity and density. Being made finer it becomes fire, being made thicker it becomes wind, then cloud, then (when thickened still more) water, then earth, then stones; and the rest come into being from these.*

SIMPLICIUS

On Anaximenes *Anaximenes determined that air is a god, and that it comes into being, and is measureless and infinite and always in motion. . . .*

CICERO

Wherever it is possible to find out the cause of what is happening, one should not have recourse to the gods.

POLYBIUS

believed. They asked scientific questions, or tried to, and evolved scientific answers as best they could. Of course, they could not then work with concepts and make distinctions that today we take for granted. These include the separation of the experiential from the real, the distinction between sense empiricism and logical constructions, the analysis of substances into elements, and the mathematical formulation of basic physics supplemented by field theories that account for action-at-a-distance. We recognize, and we understand and honor, the limitations of time and place, with the unsettling awareness that our own limitations may turn out to be of a magnitude similar to theirs—something we can never be sure of. With hindsight we can see that the Milesians were moving in the direction of a scientific empiricism; but, again, that "movement" was not an element of their consciousness.

The Milesians were the first thinkers of record to employ the art of critical thinking, a rational stance quite distinct from passive acceptance of prevailing ideas. The Greek word that "critical" and "criticism" derive from is *krino*, "I judge" or "I place under judgment." When doing critical work, the intellect focuses on an idea, holds it up to the light, looks at it from various angles, weighs it, judges it, and then makes a decision about its truth value or validity and its usefulness.

Both directly and by implication Thales criticized the prevailing mythic system of his day. Anaximander criticized Thales' notion that everything is made of water, arguing that the opposites would annihilate each other. Anaximenes criticized his teachers when he held that everything is created from air. This critical-dialectical spirit helped clear the way for subsequent philosophical and scientific thinking. After further development by a number of presocratics, and after it had passed through the immaculate brain of the Athenian gadfly Socrates, this new enterprise—soon called *philosophia* by Pythagoras—was ready for the panoramic reflections of Plato and Aristotle.

ENDNOTES

1 Diogenes Laërtius, *Lives of Eminent Philosophers* (Boston: Harvard University Press, Loeb Classical Library, 1995), I. 22–44 (pp. 23–47).
2 Aristotle, *Politikê*, 1259a, 9.
3 Herodotus, *The Persian Wars*, I.75.
4 Herodotus, *The Persian Wars*, I.74.
5 Aristotle, *De Caelo*, 294a, 28.
6 Aristotle, *Metaphysics*, 983b, 7.
7 Aristotle, *De Anima*, 405a, 19.
8 Simplicius was a Neoplatonist writing c. AD 540.
9 Simplicius, *Commentaria*.
10 Aëtius was a Greek writer flourishing ca. AD 100.
11 Hippolytus, *Regutatio*, I.6.
12 Plutarch, *Moralia*, 730E.
13 Diogenes, *Lives*, II.3.
14 Aristotle, *De Caelo*, 294b, 14.

CHAPTER 3

THE IONIANS

A quirky Ephesian, suffering from a high IQ, develops (and mystifies) scientific speculation; a wise old Ionian minstrel talks about God and becomes the first critical theologian; and a demythologizing philosopher/scientist speculates on the seedy composition of matter and explains why great stones fall from the sky.

DRIVEN AND BOTHERED

The fragmentary records suggest that critical philosophy had begun with the Milesian hylozoists in the first half of the sixth century BC. Driven by wonderment, bothered by ignorance, and nourished by the emptiness of conventional answers, these first inquiring intellects had begun asking questions about the puzzling paths of the Sun, Moon, planets, and stars; about fossils and time (very disturbing!); about life and human origins; about the causes of motion and change; and much more. The questions they asked were significant, rather than the answers they gave, for neither they nor anyone else had much confidence in the answers. Of course, the general Ionian populace continued to adhere to the old ways and live their lives uncritically by the same unexamined ideas and customs. They met in the agora to gossip and tell stories of gods' and goddesses' shenanigans; they dropped by Artemis's temple to pay respects to the virgin huntress. They blamed Ceres for bad crops and Hermes for bad news, and they gave thanks to Zeus if the thunder squall didn't wash their ships onto shore. All in all, everything was normal and it was business as usual.

But a sufficient supply of puzzled intellects breathed the heady atmosphere of unleashed curiosity; they continued to wonder, deeply and seriously, about what was really going on in the world. When they looked carefully, what they did *not* find was Apollo driving his fiery chariot across the sky or Athena backing the Greeks in battle, as Homeric epic had pictured them. Mythmakers and poets could continue to assume that our lives were manipulated by the Fates or contentious deities, but when critical minds looked carefully at *experience*, they found nothing of the sort.

In the second half of the sixth century BC, three more philosophers from the Ionian coast continued Milesian speculations. Heraclitus of Ephesus and Anaxagoras of Clazomenae reasked questions about nature, and Xenophanes of Colophon exploded some of the anthropomorphic assumptions we humans dearly love.

You can't step into the same river twice.
HERACLITUS

Change is here to stay.
BUMPER STICKER

The sun is new each day.
HERACLITUS

Much learning does not teach understanding.
HERACLITUS

HERACLITUS OF EPHESUS

ORACULAR EPIGRAMS

°Transliterations of his name vary; the Greek is Hêrakleitos.

Heraclitus° was one of those thinkers thoroughly dissatisfied with the accepted accountings of things; in fact, he seems to have been disenchanted with everyone's opinion of everything. He lived twenty-five miles north of Miletus and was aware of the Milesians' speculations, and although he asked many of the same questions, he had a very different way of viewing the world and arrived at quite different answers.

Paradoxically, we know more *and* less about Heraclitus than about any other early Greek thinker, more because we possess a richer collection of extant fragments than for other presocratic philosophers, less because he is so difficult to understand. Euripides once gave Socrates a copy of a treatise by Heraclitus and asked his opinion of it. Socrates replied, "The part I understand is great stuff, and I assume the difficult material is equally good; but it needs a Delian deep-diver to get to the bottom of it."[1] When Heraclitus does express himself clearly, he is one of the most quotable of all the ancients. For example, ponder these aphorisms:

> Time is a child playing at checkers;
> Man's character is his fate;
> There awaits us at death what we neither expect nor think;
> You can't step into the same river twice;
> Seekers after gold dig up much earth but find very little gold;
> Much learning does not teach understanding;
> Nature loves to hide;
> Unless you expect the unexpected, you will never find the truth;
> The sun is new each day;
> Physicians cut, burn, stab, and rack the sick, and then demand a fee for doing it;
> Although it is better to hide our ignorance, this is hard to do when we relax over wine;
> Bigotry is the sacred disease;
> A foolish man is aflutter at every word;
> One man is worth ten thousand if he is first-rate;
> Dogs bark at everyone they don't know;
> All things come in due season.[2]

These "oracular epigrams" are among the more intelligible maxims from the stylus of Heraclitus. The preponderance of his thoughts, however, are more elusive; indeed, one of the epithets for him was "Heraclitus the Obscure." Here is a sampling. What might he have meant by them?

Eyes are more accurate witnesses than ears.

HERACLITUS

A likeness of Heraclitus of Ephesus (c.540–c.480 BC). (It is not known if this bronze head, recovered from the sea, is a portrait of an actual individual; however, it bears a strong resemblance to other extant figures of Heraclitus and displays the characteristics of the Ephesian skeptic.)

> Soul is the vaporization of which everything else is composed;
> A dry soul is the wisest and best;
> Here too [in a cooking fire] are gods;
> The way up and the way down are one and the same;
> It is wise to acknowledge that all things are one;
> The sun will not overstep his measures;
> God is day and night, winter and summer, war and peace, satiety and want;
> It is one and the same thing to be living and dead, awake or asleep, young or old.

These are seductive utterances; no doubt they were rich with substance. Heraclitus may have deliberately used ambiguity as a literary technique to force his listeners to wrestle with the multiple meanings he had hidden in his statements. No wonder he was called "the Obscure"!

IN THE HISTORY OF PHILOSOPHY

Heraclitus is remembered (1) for teaching that everything is in a state of motion and change; (2) for concluding that the world's essence is fire; (3) for locating cosmic order in the *logos*/reason; (4) for his unique concept of the *psychê*/soul; and (5) for his view of the world as in an eternal state of conflict.

It is weariness to keep toiling at the same things so that one becomes ruled by them.
HERACLITUS

THE MAN

Heraclitus flourished during the sixty-ninth Olympiad—504 BC to 500 BC. He was born about 540 BC, the son of an affluent Ephesian named Blosson; he died about 480 BC. As Blosson's oldest son he inherited the prestigious position of *basileios* (governor) of Ephesus, a post that included the duties of chief priest of the Eleusinian mystery cult; but he renounced his claim to the position in favor of his brother.

In fact, it seems Heraclitus wanted as little association as possible with the political and public life of Ephesus, for when citizens once asked him to develop a set of laws for the city, he declined on the grounds that further laws were fruitless because their foundation—the city constitution—was so bad. Heraclitus escaped the busy metropolis by going to the temple of Artemis a mile north of the city, where, on the marble steps at the base of the great fluted columns, he would play knuckle-bones with the boys. Asked once why he wasted his time in such trivial pursuits, he burst out, "This shouldn't surprise you. Isn't this a better way to pass the time than getting caught up in your political games!" "He was wonderfully precocious from his boyhood," Diogenes Laërtius tells us, "for when young he would say he knew nothing, but when he grew up he said that he knew everything."

This one thing is wisdom, to understand thought, as that which guides all the world everywhere.
HERACLITUS

Heraclitus wrote one book, titled *On Nature*, a work still extant in the time of Socrates. In it he divided his reflections into three sections: "Universe," "Politics," and "Theology." It seems to have been a disparate collection of notes and aphorisms. Quite possibly he suffered from bouts of depression and never completed his work, so it reads like a necklace of pearls carelessly strung together. Later readers thought he wrote obscurely on purpose to appear formidable so that no one would tackle his ideas unless he or she had the intelligence to understand them. We know Heraclitus didn't take pains to explain himself; readers either understood him or they didn't. If they didn't, they weren't up to his level; if they did, then further explanation was unnecessary.

People must fight for the law [nomos] just as they would for their city walls.
HERACLITUS

"Sometimes, however, he writes with penetrating clarity," Diogenes observed, "so that even the dullest can grasp his meaning and feel themselves stirred and challenged by it. For pithy profundity his exposition has no equal." His book became famous and made him a cult hero to a sect of followers called the Heracliteans.

There is little question that Heraclitus was gifted with one of the lofty intellects among history's great minds, that he suffered from a high IQ, as a modern quip has it. Diogenes frequently refers to his *megalophrosynê*, his "greatness of mind" (though the ambiguous word can mean "magnanimity" and "nobleness," as well as "pride" and "arrogance"). Heraclitus despised the ignorance of the masses, who, he said, "are unaware of what they are doing after they awake, just as they forget what they did while asleep." "What sort of mind or intelligence do they have? They believe popular folktales and follow the crowd as their teachers, ignoring the adage that the many are bad, the good are few." He also showered other thinkers with caustic comments. Hesiod, he said, was a popular teacher, but he really didn't "know night from day." "Hesiod distinguishes good days and evil days, not knowing that every day is like

Human nature has no real understanding; only the divine nature has it.
HERACLITUS

every other." "Much learning does not teach understanding; else would it have taught Hesiod and Pythagoras, Xenophanes and Hecataeus." Homer should have been "taken out and flogged" for his anthropomorphisms. Pythagoras developed "intellectual mischief into an artform." And because they exiled his friend Hermodorus, "the worthiest man among them," the Ephesians should be taken out and hanged, "every last man of them," and allow the city-government to be run by adolescent boys, who would do a much better job.

Of his last years we know very little. Diogenes (repeating earlier sources) says that "Eventually, becoming a hater of mankind, he retired into the mountains and stayed there living off grass and roots, a mode of life that made him ill of dropsy." Several accounts report that he returned to Ephesus quite sick, and finding that the doctors were of no help, as a last resort he plastered himself with cow dung, which, as it dried, might draw out the moisture from his body and leave his soul dry and pure. "To souls, it is death to become water," he had said. "A dried-out soul is the wisest and best." But nothing worked, and he died the next day. He was sixty years old.[3]

EPHESUS

In Heraclitus's time the city of Ephesus was one of the great metropolises of the Mediterranean world, a bustling seaport with a protected harbor set deep into the mountains of the Ionian coastline. From here commercial and naval vessels sailed to other seaports, such as Phoenicia, Alexandria, and Carthage, as far west as Sicily and Italy, and throughout the Aegean. The principal cargo carried to-and-fro was ideas. Ephesus lay at the edge of the great frontier where the Eastern and Western worlds were accosting one another, and people were abandoning the old ways of thinking in favor of new, better, and bigger ideas.

Like Miletus, Ephesus was a shining white-marble city visible from far out to sea. It was situated in a picturesque valley between low mountains. The wide Street of the Curetes descended from the east, lined even in Heraclitus's day with temples, public baths and gymnasia, theaters, and colonnades and walkways where every enterprise was carried on. In addition to patricians' homes, auditoriums, and state markets, a well-known brothel whose location was pointed out by a sign chiseled into the stone pavement, there to assist sailors just off the ships in the harbor. A few blocks farther north was the amphitheater, as large as the famous theater in Epidaurus, used for public assemblies. In Heraclitus's day political rallies, city business, and a variety of public orations took place here; in Saint Paul's time five centuries later the events involving Demetrius the Silversmith occurred in these precincts.[4] Still today the multitiered amphitheater is the setting on summer evenings for dramatic performances.

On the harbor side of the Marble Way was the expansive Tetragonos Agora displayed goods from the entire known world. "Everything was sold in the agora," a modern archaeologist writes. "Craftsmen engaged in their work there. Durable products and perishable goods were found there. Finely woven cloths, spices, herbs and perfumes were set alongside slaves for sale. Coppersmiths made their copper bowls there, potters made their amphorae and dishes, jewellers made jewels of all sorts, bracelets, necklaces, brooches, rings and other things, and these not only for Ephesians. The great metropolis of Asia Minor was a choice market for the citizens of [the whole world]. The money-changers also did good business."[5]

Leading westward from the amphitheater was the Arcadian Way, thirty-five feet wide, lined with colonnades, paved with mosaics, and flanked on either side by arcades housing a variety of shops and businesses. This street led directly to the harbor gate. It possessed a rarity for the ancient world: street lighting.

God is day-night, winter-summer, war-peace, satiety-famine. But he changes like [fire] which when it mingles with the smoke of incense, is named according to each man's pleasure.

HERACLITUS

The thinking faculty is common to all.

HERACLITUS

How can anyone hide from that which never sets?

HERACLITUS

A mile north of the city, the famed temple of Artemis was counted later as one of the Seven Wonders of the World. The all-marble building, four hundred feet long, boasted a hundred giant fluted columns and a marble roof; it was an impressive sight that could be seen from as far as the island of Samos. Artemis (or Diana) was the Huntress, the patron goddess of Ionia, related to all the earth mothers and love goddesses of Asia Minor: Cybele, Magna Mater, Aphrodite, Venus, Isis, and Ishtar.

EVERYTHING FLOWS

Heraclitus's philosophy can be distilled into three or four major concepts, none of which jump out with congenial clarity; they come to us as cryptic propositions we must wrestle meaning from. Socrates was right: To make sense of Heraclitus, we must be "deep divers."

Heraclitus's most fundamental observation is that everything in the world is in a state of change, and he expresses this notion with the lovely Greek words *panta rhei*, "everything flows." "Everything flows and nothing abides; everything gives way and nothing stays fixed." Heraclitus negates the received assumptions that some things are eternal: eternal verities, eternal deities, or (as the Milesians had argued) eternal substances. Heraclitus denies them all. Everything in the world is changing. Everything is in motion. Nothing endures. Nothing is forever. My lifetime, for example, is brief and my memory is short. I am permitted to live with the *illusion* that some things remain the same. I may look in the mirror this morning and rest secure that appearances are the same as I remember them from yesterday or last week; but . . . after a year, or ten years, or fifty? Time has its way. Likewise, my garden looks the same for a day or so, but after the passing of another winter? And what of the universe, the Milky Way, our Sun, the Earth, and "old ocean's gray and melancholy waste"—these endure, do they not? Only until the next oil spill, ozone hole, viral outbreak, solar flare, misguided meteorite, galactic collision, or final extinction of the flame in the all-engulfing cold of a darkening universe. Everything is changing, following its own inner logic and its own schedule. Nothing is exempt. Everything flows. *Panta rhei*.

What is the "force" or motive power that drives this ceaseless motion? Like Anaximander, Heraclitus reasoned that everything flows between opposites such as hot and cold, light and dark, and moist and dry. Everything oscillates eternally between poles that establish the limits of motion and change. Each member of a pair contains its opposite, but these opposites are not separate poles; rather, they are identical in some paradoxical fashion. One is never found without the other; each implies the other. Darkness and light flow into one another; they interpenetrate, as do wetness and dryness, heat and cold, and up and down. "The way up and the way down are one and the same," Heraclitus says.

FIRE

A second question arises: If "everything flows," what is it that is flowing? The Milesians had answered that the changing "thing" is water, air, or the Unlimited. But Heraclitus said no, permanent substances don't exist: air and water also flow and change. Rather, the universe is in some mysterious way an expression of fire.° Fire is not a "substance" at all, but a moving field of shimmering hotness. Fire itself is change and reveals to us the essential nature of the world: ever changing, coming into being, and fading away. "This universe always has been, is, and always will be an ever-living fire," he wrote, "kindling itself by regular measures and going out by regular measures."

As for the rest of mankind, they are unaware of what they are doing after they wake, just as they forget what they did while asleep.
HERACLITUS

Everything flows and nothing abides; everything gives way and nothing stays fixed.
HERACLITUS

°*See* pyr *in lexicon.*

Does this mean the universe is *nothing but* a dancing flame, without form or pattern? Not at all. Order does exist. Sunrises and sunsets repeat endlessly, in that order. The seasons arrive annually, right on time. In April flowers bloom for a day, then die and scatter seeds. Sheep beget sheep, and sparrows' eggs keep on producing baby sparrows, not crows. A time and a season exist for everything, as ordered.

The flow of things, therefore, is not chaotic or capricious. We live in a true *kosmos*,° as the Greek word implies. Were it not a cosmos, it could not be understood by the human intellect. Heraclitus borrows the notion of law from its legal context and applies it to nature. A law exists that dictates nature's operations in such a way that they will promote justice and stability. It must be inherent in the primal stuff (archê) that makes up the world-fire. This law is not an abstract "idea," as it was for Pythagoras, Plato, and modern science. Heraclitus believed it to be concrete and immanent in nature itself, a real entity. However faint this insight, it appears to be an early glimpse of the idea of natural law.

°See kosmos *in lexicon.*

REASON

Character for man is his destiny.
HERACLITUS

°See logos *in lexicon.*

Several other themes found in the fragments of his book are significant to Heraclitus. One is the notion of the *logos*.° The Greek noun is burdened with a bewildering variety of intended meanings: "word," "reason," "order," "intelligence," "wisdom," "principle," "account," "discourse," "statement," "conversation," "explanation," and "law." (For perspective, make a list of the meanings commonly given to *word* in English.) Heraclitus adopted *logos* to symbolize universal reason. Whether he believed this reason to be real, as Plato later argued, is not clear. What is clear is that Heraclitus was convinced that all humans could exploit and make use of it and that it was something to be cherished. It can offer an individual guidance on how to think and live. "Men should speak with rational awareness and thereby hold on strongly to that which is shared in common, as much as a city will defend its laws—or even more!" Most of us, however, don't make very good use of it. "Although this Logos is eternally valid, yet men are unable to understand it—not only before hearing it, but even after they have heard it for the first time." We humans, Heraclitus seems to say, should be able to recognize reason when we come across it, but so often we are blind to it. "We should let ourselves be guided by what is common to all. Yet, although the Logos is common to all, most men live as if each of them had a private intelligence of his own." Reason is available and permeates our being, yet most of us persist in acting irrationally. "Although intimately connected with the Logos, men keep setting themselves against it."

SOUL

I sought for myself.
HERACLITUS

The concept of soul (*psychê*) is also central to Heraclitus's thinking. All humans possess soul; it is the locus of intelligence and understanding. But soul is found in different amounts in different people. We can possess a lot of soul or just a little, in the same way we may have much understanding or very little. "Soul has its own inner law of growth." How much soul one possesses is judged as a moral matter an individual can exercise some control over. Great people will develop much soul, lesser people will develop less soul, and the amount of soul people develop is related to the amount of moisture in their systems. "Souls are vaporized from what is moist." That is, souls can become lighter by giving up water, heavier by adding water. Unfortunate souls weighted with surplus water can become saturated and soggy. Souls have a perverse appetite for this condition, notes Heraclitus. "Souls take pleasure in becoming moist." When a soul becomes too moist, very little soul is left. "It is death to souls to become water." By all means, says Heraclitus, "a dry soul is wisest and best."

The drier the soul, the better its chance of becoming the pure fire that bestows life and intelligence. (It is ironic that Heraclitus died of dropsy, a malady that floods the tissues and cavities of the body with lymphatic liquid.[6])

CONFLICT

A peculiar Heraclitean fragment reads, "People do not understand how that which is at variance with itself agrees with itself. There is a harmony in the bending back, as in the cases of the bow and the lyre." When interpreted in the light of his other ideas, Heraclitus seems to say that conflict and strife are essential elements of the cosmos. Some philosophers—notably Pythagoras—held that opposites will eventually evolve into a harmony, but this is not Heraclitus's view of things. The world is driven by opposites, and these opposites are necessary to the operations of the world; they will never balance out into a harmony. His metaphor for this idea is the bow and lyre. Tension between strings and frame is essential for the instrument to exist and perform. Without tension, a bow would not work to shoot an arrow; and a lyre's strings, if not drawn taut, could not produce musical sounds.

A man's character is his guardian divinity.

HERACLITUS

This translates into a view of the world as a cosmos of eternal conflict. Opposites have to be opposites; their polar identities are never lost in their operations. "It should be understood," Heraclitus says, "that war is the common condition, that strife is justice, and that all things come to pass through the compulsion of strife." Without strife and tension no world would exist. "Homer was wrong in saying, 'Would that strife might perish from amongst gods and men.' For if that were to occur, then all things would cease to exist."

That which is in opposition is in concert, and from things that differ comes the most beautiful harmony.

HERACLITUS

THE AGONY OF NOT KNOWING

It is a temptation to read more into the Heraclitean fragments than is really there, yet this may be inevitable since so many of his statements are richly ambiguous. If a statement can be interpreted in a half dozen ways, then it's virtually impossible to know with certainty what was in his mind. Indications are that he intended to imply several meanings simultaneously, a deliberate use of language that clashes with our modern need for clarity and precision. It is an expression of a poetic mentality.[7] Dogmatism, therefore, has no place in our interpretations. With Heraclitus, perhaps more than with any other presocratic thinker, we must settle for uncertainty.

The unlike is joined together, and from differences results the most beautiful harmony, and all things take place by strife.

HERACLITUS

As one ponders the Heraclitean fragments, one senses an exceptional and curious intellect wrestling with the perennial questions we ask about the world but unable to make sense of it all. His complex, fertile mind picked up hints, gathered ideas, and tried to make meaningful connections. Yet Heraclitus didn't have sufficient information to allow him to see what he wanted to see. His statements express anger, a bitterness born of acute frustration; it is the anguish of a mind that can't break through to clarity. As he looked at the world, he *saw* much, and he could push back the shadows some short distance. Yet he remained surrounded by darkness, and he knew it. In that knowing lies his suffering and nobility.

Take the matter of Oneness, for example. Heraclitus sensed that everything is connected, and he saw some of the connections. In one remarkable fragment, he says, "It is by disease that health is pleasant, by evil that good is pleasant, by hunger satiety, by weariness rest." In almost a modern sense, he seems to have been aware that objects/events in the world are not good or evil in themselves but that "good" and "evil" are subjective evaluations of things and events. We appreciate good health more when we contemplate times of sickness. But Heraclitus just may be saying something more: that evil is not real. It's not merely that by contemplating evil, we are reminded to enjoy good things, but that things are evil or good because, and only

The Temple of Artemis, with its hundred gleaming white marble columns, was one of the Seven Wonders of the ancient world. On its steps Heraclitus escaped from the hubbub of the city, played knucklebones with the boys, and denounced the Ephesians for political corruption.

because, we evaluate them that way. It was more than wordplay when Shakespeare later wrote, "There is nothing either good or bad, but thinking makes it so."[8]

This subjectivity of valuation is indicated by another fragment; Heraclitus writes, "Sea water is at once very pure and very foul: it is drinkable and healthful for fishes, but undrinkable and deadly for men." In still another fragment he says, "To God all things are beautiful, good, and right; men, on the other hand, deem some things right and others wrong." "Right" and "wrong" are human creations. He seems to imply that the responsibility for such value judgments lies with us, and we must cease attributing them to the gods, the Fates, or any other external causal agencies.

XENOPHANES OF COLOPHON

WANDERING MINSTREL

On Xenophanes When Empedocles remarked to him that it is impossible to find a wise man, "Naturally," he replied, "for it takes a wise man to recognize a wise man."

DIOGENES LAËRTIUS

The first known thinker to treat theological matters philosophically was from Colophon, a small Ionian city some fifty miles north of Ephesus. Xenophanes, son of Dexios, was a modest man, one writer says of him, though he had the audacity to satirize Homer, criticize Thales and Pythagoras, attack prevailing religious ideas, and call into question the divinity of the Sun and Moon. He was an inquiring intellect, a singer, poet, and satirist. Another writer says Xenophanes "did things his own way even though he differed from all who preceded him." Still another records that he went "against customary opinion" and exemplified the ever-widening spirit of his time.

However, at some point his irritating thoughts upset the Colophonese, and he was banished from his native city, for what exact cause we don't know. Perhaps he criticized his fellow citizens; he is on record as having scolded them for strolling in the agora adorned in purple garments, outlandish hairstyles, and perfume—deplorable lifestyles they had adopted from the Lydians. His self-appointed role as culture critic must not have endeared him to his compatriots.

In any case, he traveled thereafter, living for a time in Sicily and then at Elea in Italy and visiting the Aegean islands and Athens. Wherever he traveled he was admired for his wit and wisdom. One retort has been preserved for us: When the Sicilian philosopher Empedocles commented that these days it's nearly impossible to find a wise man, Xenophanes replied, "Naturally, for it takes a wise man to recognize a wise man."

Xenophanes journeyed among the Mediterranean cities and islands as a wandering minstrel, singing at banquets and festivals, reciting his poetry, and discussing ideas. His verse was partly in dactylic hexameter (epic verse), partly in iambic (elegiac verse). With unusual sensitivity, his word pictures are marked by acute perceptions of immediate experience.

Homer and Hesiod have attributed to the gods all things that are shameful and a reproach among mankind: theft, adultery, and mutual deception.

XENOPHANES

> While sitting at the fireside in the winter, at ease on soft couches, well fed, sipping tasty wine, and nibbling tidbits, it is then that a host may duly inquire of his guest: "Who are you among men, and whence do you come? How old are you, friend? How old were you at the time of the Mede invasion?"
>
> Now the floor is swept, hands and cups are washed clean. An attendant places woven garlands on our heads, another passes around a vase of fragrant ointment. The mixing bowl stands brimful of good cheer, and more wine in jars is at hand, delicious and with delicate aroma, never failing. Incense gives forth a sacred fragrance, and there is water, cold, refreshing, and pure. Golden-brown loaves are before us, with cheeses and rich honey, set out in abundance upon the princely table. At the center is an altar decked with flowers on all sides. Song and mirth fill the hall.
>
> Men who are about to make merry should first honor the gods with hymns composed of well-told tales and pure words. After they have poured a libation and have prayed for the power to do what is right—that, indeed, is the first business in hand—then there is nothing wrong in drinking as much as a man can hold without having to be taken home by a servant, unless of course he is very old. The man to be praised is he who, after drinking, can still express thoughts that are noble and well arranged. But let him not repeat those old hackneyed tales of Titans or Giants or Centaurs, nor those of violent civil broils: there is nothing to be gained from all that. But it is always good to give heedful reverence to the gods.[9]

For everything comes from earth and everything goes back to the earth at last.

XENOPHANES

WONDERER

Xenophanes' inquiring mind speculated on the parade of natural events in the world around him. He wondered about the rainbows that "cause appearances of violet, red, and yellow-green." He wondered about waters and winds. "The great sea is the begetter of clouds and winds and rivers" because, he reasons, "blasts of wind could not come-to-be within the clouds and blow forth from there if it were not from the great sea; nor could there be rivers, nor any rain from the sky without it." In a halting way, Xenophanes sought causal explanations. The Sun is an amalgam of numerous bits of fire "massing together," he says, and is formed anew each day from the vaporous ocean it descends into at sunset. An infinite number of suns and moons exists. The Earth, he said, is slowly sinking into the sea. He wandered in the marble quarries of Syracuse and Paros, found fossils of fish and snails, and concluded they were created when the Earth was under the sea; subsequently, the Earth emerged out

And she whom they call Iris, she too is actually a cloud, purple and flame-red and yellow to behold.

XENOPHANES

of the sea and dried. "We are all sprung from earth and water. All things come from the earth, and they reach their end by returning to the earth at last." Eventually the Earth will again sink into the sea and become mud. Humanity will be destroyed, but sometime thereafter a human race will arise again. Thus an eternal oscillation occurs of the Earth's rising from the sea and sinking back into the sea, causing great cycles of life and death. Similar cycles must take place on other worlds.

ANTHROPOMORPHISM

However, it is not for his scientific curiosity that Xenophanes is remembered in the history of philosophy but as a "critical theologian" or, more broadly, as a philosopher of religion. The first to point out the fallacy of anthropomorphic thinking, he observed what today we take as a commonplace: that we create our deities in our own likeness.

> The Aethiopians say that their gods are snub-nosed and black-skinned, and the Thracians that theirs are blue-eyed and red-haired. If only oxen and horses had hands and wanted to draw with their hands or to make the works of art that men make, then horses would draw the figures of their Gods like horses, and oxen like oxen, and would make their bodies on the model of their own.[10]

As for certain truth, no man has seen it, nor will there ever be a man who knows about the gods and about all the things I mention. For if he succeeds to the full in saying what is completely true, he himself is nevertheless unaware of it; and Opinion [doxa, mere seeming or appearance] is fixed by fate upon all things.

HERACLITUS

The gods, he held, do not possess human characteristics; nor are they "persons" who intrigue with one another and strive for dominance. The gods could not be ruled over and ordered around, for if they could be they would not be gods.

God does indeed exist, Xenophanes says, but he is "not at all like mortals in body or in mind." Rather, God is universal being. He is One. He sees all over, thinks all over, hears all over. He has no particularized organs as we do, such as eyes and ears, or legs to move about. "It is not appropriate to his nature to be in different places at different times." Rather, he "always abides in the same place, not moving at all." God is all mind and thought, and he is eternal.

Without toil [God] sets everything in motion by the thought of his mind.

HERACLITUS

So when we sculpt or paint the gods and goddesses to look just the way we do—as in marble statues and vase paintings—we have only projected our personal human qualities onto the deities. Many centuries later Spinoza was to pen a similar refrain: "A triangle, if it could speak, would in like manner say that God is eminently triangular, and a circle that the divine nature is eminently circular; and thus would every one ascribe his own attributes to God." Through the centuries this very human habit has been ridiculed and parodied, and occasionally appreciated, never more delightfully than in Carmen de Gasztold's *Prayers from the Ark*, whereby a variety of animals present their take on the higher order. "The Prayer of the Little Ducks" nicely reveals this "egomorphic" tendency which characterizes not just humans but all creation. *"Faites qu'il pleuve demain et toujours."*

> Dear God,
> Give us a flood of water.
> Let it rain tomorrow and always.
> Give us plenty of little slugs and other luscious things to eat.
> Protect all folk who quack
> and everyone who knows how to swim.
> Amen.[11]

Let these things be stated as conjectural only, only similar to reality.

HERACLITUS

Xenophanes was an eclectic philosopher who had skeptical doubts about nearly everything. He was an attractive and cheerful soul. He lived a long life, to the age of at least ninety-two, as he himself tells us: "By now it is sixty-seven years that my thoughts have been tossed restlessly up and down the land of Hellas; and when that period of wandering began [with his exile from Colophon] I was already twenty-five years old, *if*"—he adds thoughtfully—"*if* I am remembering such bygone details rightly."[12]

ANAXAGORAS OF CLAZOMENAE

BORN TO STUDY THE STARRY SKY

Anaxagoras of Clazomenae today would be thought of as an astrophysicist. Asked once why he had been born, he replied, "In order to study the Sun, the Moon, and the starry sky." On another occasion, when someone chided him for his lack of patriotism, asking why he seemed to have no concern for his country, he replied, with a sweeping gesture toward the heavens, "Careful, friend, it is my true country that I am concerned with."

Anaxagoras's home city of Clazomenae is nestled on a peninsula jutting into one of the great protected harbors of the world, the Gulf of Izmir (Smyrna in ancient times) in Turkey. It was a busy seaport, founded by colonials from Achaea in the ninth century BC. In 546 BC, as Cyrus the Great of Persia was threatening all of Asia Minor, citizens transported the city to an island in the harbor where it could maintain safer perimeters. There it flourished and became a center for sea travel, its ships putting in at all the cities of the Aegean and the eastern Mediterranean basin. For a time it competed with Phoenicia for commercial supremacy. Governed by the Athenians for a while, Clazomenae absorbed the vibrant lifestyle and culture of the western metropolis. Alexander the Great marched through this region in 324 BC on his way to conquer the world, and he constructed a bridge to connect the island-city to the mainland (it still can be seen). The city moved back to the mainland and was renamed Chytrion (Chytrium in later Latin). Its prosperity never waned but continued through Roman times.

IN THE HISTORY OF PHILOSOPHY

Anaxagoras is honored (1) for being among the first to demythologize the heavens; (2) for his image of the cosmos as a great vortex; (3) for concluding we live in a bio-cosmos containing other worlds with life-forms; (4) for his theory that the constituents of matter are invisible particles or "seeds"; and (5) for his belief that motion and order result from the operation of *nous*/mind.

THE MAN

Anaxagoras was born at Clazomenae in the seventieth Olympiad (c. 500 BC) and died there at the age of seventy-two (about 428 BC); he flourished about 460 BC. His father Eubulos was wealthy, so Anaxagoras obtained a good education. When criticized by his relatives for not taking better care of his inheritance, he said, "Here, you look after it!" and gave it all away.

He was about twenty when he came to Athens to study philosophy and remained there for thirty years. It appears he was invited to Athens because of his already-acclaimed brilliance in philosophy and science, and he soon became one of the bright lights in the intellectual circle around Periklês, where he came to know the leading artists and thinkers of his day. As a dedicated research scientist, Anaxagoras guarded his time and refused to get involved in the petty concerns of the Athenian social scene. In this Periclean sanctuary he was highly respected for his creative ideas and built an illustrious career. His most noteworthy talent was an ability to popularize science for ordinary citizens.

On Anaxagoras *He says that plants are like animals in feeling pleasure and pain—an inference which he draws from the fact that they shed their leaves and let them grow again.*

ARISTOTLE

On Anaxagoras *Now it is the opinion of Anaxagoras that the possession of these hands is the cause of man being of all animals the most intelligent.*

ARISTOTLE

We give the name Iris to the reflection of the sun on the clouds. It is therefore the sign of a storm, for the water which flows round the cloud produces wind or forces out rain.

ANAXAGORAS

°*For the rationale behind this charge, see pp. 102ff.*

It is the sun that endows the moon with its brilliance.

ANAXAGORAS

On Anaxagoras *Anaxagoras agrees with Leucippus and Democritus that the elements are infinite.*

ARISTOTLE

Diogenes Laërtius may have captured something of his personality and wit in Anaxagoras's well-remembered one-liners. When asked if the Lampsakene hills would someday be submerged into the sea, he answered, "Yes, it's just a matter of time." When someone expressed a fear of dying in a foreign country, Anaxagoras told him, "The descent to Hades is about the same from whatever place we begin it." After he had been sentenced to death for impiety, he quipped, "So? Long ago nature already comdemned me to death, and my judges too!" We are told that his children were somehow killed and that he laid them to rest with his own hands; he said, "I always knew that my children were born to die."[13]

It was Anaxagoras who first demythologized the heavens, but his innovations brought him considerable trouble. He had the gall to say he believed the Sun was "a mass of red-hot metal." For this a charge of impiety ("atheism")—the equivalent of treason—was brought against him. (The same charge was later lodged against Protagoras, Socrates,° and Aristotle—"impiety" seems to have been a ready weapon for defenders of the status quo.) Periklês' adversaries, possibly even Thucydides, his outspoken opponent, may have motivated the accusation. Imprisoned for a time, Anaxagoras escaped execution, possibly through the graces of Periklês, who, according to one account, "came forward and asked if anyone held anything against him in his public life." When no one spoke, Periklês said, "I am his disciple [supporter], so don't you dare drum up false charges against him just so you can put him to death. Release him!" He was released. But the charges against the sensitive man had destroyed his reputation, and he sought asylum in Lampsakos, a seaport across the Aegean on the Hellespont; there he spent the last fifteen years of his life as a much-honored citizen. When asked whether he missed Athens, he answered, "No, but I'm sure they miss me." At his request the magistrates of Lampsakos proclaimed an annual holiday for schoolchildren in the month he died and placed an inscription over his grave:

> Here Anaxagoras, who in his quest
> Of truth scaled heaven itself, is laid to rest.

STONES IN A VORTEX

Anaxagoras held that the Sun, Moon, planets, and stars are all "stones in the sky"—very large stones; the Sun, he says, is as large as the Peloponnesus—and occasionally these stones become red hot and fall from the sky. The playwright Euripides, who had been a pupil of Anaxagoras, wrote of the Sun as "a golden lump of earth."

Even among the more sophisticated this idea was thought absurd, and its author was judged to be not a little eccentric. Then in 467 BC a large meteorite fell on the island of Sicily, and news of the event went a long way toward vindicating the young scientist's views and bringing him a modicum of respect. In the eyes of the populace, however, his demythologizing of the heavens remained a threat. The average Greek *knew* that the heavenly objects were the "bodies of the gods," not big hot rocks in the sky.

How did the stones get up there? Anaxagoras's reasoning led him to the belief that the universe is a great vortex. At the beginning of time, he speculated, all the matter in the universe was set in a spiraling motion that generated a cosmic vortex. As this vortex spins, the heavy particles drift toward the center while the lighter particles move to the outside. Since the Earth is made of very heavy material, it rests at this system's center. The great stony masses—the Sun, Moon, planets, and stars—are pushed to the outer reaches and held there by the speed of their outward motion (we call it centrifugal force). Meteorites are smaller hunks of stone that, when they lose speed, fall back to Earth.

OTHER WORLDS

Anaxagoras concluded that "many worlds must exist," formed in just this fashion. Other vortices must exist, they would naturally generate other worlds, and on some of these worlds life must have arisen. Whole ecologies more or less like ours may have developed. Long before the fantasies of science-fiction writers and the speculations of exobiologsts, Anaxagoras painted the picture of a biocosmos where we humans are not alone.

> We should recognize the possibility that men may have been formed, as well as other organisms that possess souls; and that such men may perhaps dwell in cities and cultivate their fields just as we do, and that their earth yields them vegetable life of all kinds, the most useful of which they harvest and take home to supply their needs. In other words, it may be that the separating and individuating process goes on not only in our own world but elsewhere too.[14]

SEEDS

Anaxagoras's notions about physics were also innovative and influential. Diogenes noted, "Just as gold consists of very fine particles that we call gold-dust, he held that the entire universe is composed of similar microscopic bodies that contain parts homogeneous to themselves." [15] That is, all substances are made up of invisible "seeds" that contain various amounts of everything that exists. "In everything there is a portion of everything else," and all substances are rearrangements of these seeds' specific contents. Each seed contains some rock, earth, metal, bone, air, blood, and so on. As the seeds mix, like particles aggregate and become one of the known substances—rock, earth, wood, or whatever. Each particular thing in the world, generated from such mixtures of seeds, is perceived and identified by us according to its predominant element.

The dense and moist and cold and dark [elements] collected here, where now is Earth, and the rare and hot and dry went outwards to the farthest part of the Aether.

ANAXAGORAS

MIND

Mind, however, is a different story. Mind *(nous°)* is not just one more substance that mixes with everything else. Rather, mind is the "force" that binds everything together and initiates motion. In the beginning, Anaxagoras says, mind started up cosmic motion.

°*See* nous *in lexicon.*

> Mind took charge of the cosmic situation, so that the universe proceeded to rotate from the very beginning. At first the rotation was small, but by now it extends over a larger space, and it will extend over a yet larger one. Both the things that are mingled and those that are separated and individuated are all known by Mind.

No Thing comes into being or passes away, but it is mixed together or separated from existing Things.

ANAXAGORAS

And Mind set in order all that was to be, all that ever was but no longer is, and all that is now or ever will be. This includes the revolving movements of the stars, of the sun and moon, and of the air and aether as they are being separated off. It was the rotary movement that caused the separation—a separation of the dense from the rare, the hot from the cold, the bright from the dark, and the dry from the moist.

When Mind first set things in motion, there began a process of separation in the moving mass; and as things were thus moving and separating, the process of separation was greatly increased by the rotary movement.[16]

This is a new picture of the universe. It has a structure (the vortex) that, from a distance, points in the direction of modern galactic astronomy.

Anaxagoras's far-ranging intellect seems to have pondered everything. "At the beginning of time all the stars moved in the sky as they would in a revolving dome,

Originally everything was squeezed together without differentiation; then came Mind (Nous) and set them in order.

ANAXAGORAS

In everything there is a portion of everything except Mind; and some things contain Mind also.

ANAXAGORAS

On Anaxagoras *When one man (Anaxagoras) said that reason (Mind) was present—as in animals, so throughout nature— as the cause of order and of all arrangement, he seemed like a sober man in contrast with the random talk of his predecessors.*

ARISTOTLE

with the celestial pole, which is always visible, directly overhead; then sometime later the pole moved off center and assumed a tilted position."[17] He concluded that the Moon shines by light reflected from the Sun: "It is the sun that puts brightness into the moon." The Milky Way, however, is produced by the reflection of starlight and not by the Sun's illumination. Winds arise when the Sun's heat thins the air, causing it to move from one place to another. Rainbows are glimmers of the Sun reflected in the clouds; but this beautiful sight, he warns, should not be interpreted as an omen, as it always had been, but rightly may be seen as the harbinger of a storm that may "produce wind and pour forth as rain." Living things originally were produced from heat, moisture, and some sort of earthy material; only later did they reproduce of their own accord.

ENDNOTES

1 Diogenes Laërtius, *Lives of Eminent Philosophers*, II, 22; see also IX, 12.
2 Unless otherwise indicated, aphorisms are quoted from Philip Wheelwright, *The Presocratics* (The Odyssey Press, 1966), Chapter 3; though in this list, Fragments 1, 10, and 11 are free translations.
3 Diogenes, *Lives*, IX.3–4.
4 Acts 19:23–41.
5 Dr. Ü. Önen, *Ephesus: The City's History through Art* (Akademia, Izmir, 1983), p. 48.
6 Diogenes, *Lives*, IX.3–4. The irony is even reflected in dropsy's etymology: *dropsy* derives from the Latin *hydropsis*, which comes from the Greek *hudropsis* and ultimately from *hudor*, "water." In his *Meditations* (III.3) Marcus Aurelius adds a note on Heraclitus's death: "Heraclitus, after endless speculations on the destruction of the world by fire, came to be filled internally with water, and died beplastered with cowdung."
7 It is also akin to the Eastern use of language where the genius of the Chinese and Japanese mind is in suggesting ideas and images with poetry, anecdote, and haiku.
8 *Hamlet*, II.ii.259.
9 Wheelwright, *The Presocratics*, pp. 34–6.
10 Translation by Arnold J. Toynbee, *A Study of History*, vol. 7 (Oxford: Oxford University Press, 1954), p. 469.
11 Carmen Bernos de Gasztold, *Prayers from the Ark*, trans. Rumer Godden (Viking, 1962), p. 59.
12 Wheelwright, *The Presocratics*, p. 36, frag. 24; also Diogenes, *Lives*, IX.19.
13 Diogenes, *Lives*, II.10–13.
14 Wheelwright, *The Presocratics*, p. 164, frag. 27.
15 Diogenes, *Lives*, II.8.
16 Wheelwright, *The Presocratics*, p. 163, frag. 20.
17 Diogenes, *Lives*, II.9.

CHAPTER 4

PYTHAGORAS OF SAMOS

A mystic and mathematician discovers the language of nature and lays the first stone in the foundations of Western science; he establishes a monastic cultus and becomes the father of liberation therapies; and his epistemic legacy is enormous but very mixed.

THE LANGUAGE OF NATURE

When it comes to name recognition, Pythagoras heads the list of early Greek thinkers, thanks to a famous theorem: The sum of the squares of the sides of a right triangle is equal to the square of the hypotenuse. (Diogenes Laërtius tells us Pythagoras was so elated when he discovered this formula that "he made a thank-offering to the gods."[1]) But to which right triangle does his formula apply? To this triangle etched in wax, or to that one drawn on a whitewashed board, or to the angle scribed by the marble cornerstone? It applies, of course, to all right triangles—past, present, and future, anywhere in any universe. Pythagoras created an abstract formula with universal application. As Plato would later say, he discovered a universal truth.

Pythagoras actually found that physical nature is precisely ordered and that its order can be apprehended and symbolized with abstract mathematics. He "discovered" physics, and insofar as the acquisition of knowledge is concerned, Pythagoras was one of the most important human beings in history. He found the key to how the world works. But as a man, in addition to being a mathematician, Pythagoras was a physicist, philosopher, astronomer, teacher, coach, biologist, monastic, administrator, engineer of sorts, culture critic, visionary, feminist, ecologist, ethicist, statesman, physician, psychotherapist, mystic, musician, theologian of sorts, personal guru, and cult leader—all of which indicate Pythagoras was an exceptional human being with a powerful mind, a zest for life, and a passion to understand the world.

Pythagoras introduced weights and measures into Greece and developed theories explaining the elements, heat and cold, light and darkness, and the cycle of seasons. He realized that the morning star and evening star are the same, that the Sun lights the Moon, and that the Earth is spherical. He attempted to explain the functions of the brain, senses, veins, and arteries. He discovered musical intervals and tells us he actually heard "the music of the spheres." He broke with tradition and forbade the killing of living things; one must worship "only at an altar unstained with blood." During his heyday he was enormously popular; "not less than six hundred people attended his evening lectures."

On Pythagoras *When Leon the tyrant of Phlius asked him who he was, he said, "A philosopher," and he compared life to the Great Games, where some went to compete for the prize, others went to sell their wares, but the best went just as spectators.*
DIOGENES LAËRTIUS

On Pythagoras *There lived among them a man of superhuman knowledge, who verily possessed the greatest wealth of wisdom.*
EMPEDOCLES

Pythagoras of Samos (c.570–c.497 BC)

IN THE HISTORY OF PHILOSOPHY

Pythagoras is most remembered (1) for discovering that mathematics is "the language of nature," and from this insight (2) inferring that the world is made of numbers; (3) for proving, therefore, that physical nature is accessible to the human mind; (4) for his belief that the world is driven by opposites that will finally become harmonious; (5) for teaching that each human soul also can achieve "cosmic harmony"; (6) for his belief that souls, both human and animal, are eternally immortal through repeated reincarnations; (7) for insisting women must be educated on a par with men.

THE MAN

In life some grow up with servile natures, greedy for fame and gain, but a philosopher seeks the truth.
PYTHAGORAS
(ATTRIBUTED BY
SOCRATES)

So many legends swirl around Pythagoras it is difficult to separate fact from fiction. Born about 580 BC, he was the son of an affluent gem engraver and landowner named Mnesarchos, we are told. Legend declared him the son of Apollo, but this claim was made by (or for) so many cult figures that if we accepted it, paternity in the Greek world would become universally suspect. He flourished during the sixtieth Olympiad (540–536 BC).

Pythagoras was by birth a Samian. Samos is a picturesque island in the eastern Aegean Sea off the coast of Ionia. The pride of the island's people was the temple of Hera, famed for its beauty, so lovely the Ephesians, only a few miles away on the mainland, became jealous and decided to build an even larger temple to rival Hera's. Much of Samos was covered with pine trees, groves of olives and figs, rich vineyards, and grain fields. The island is small enough that Pythagoras could travel the length or breadth of it by donkey in a day, so the populace composed a community in which everyone knew everyone. All faces were familiar, and a spirit of friendliness prevailed of the sort that is lost in the anonymity of bustling cities.

Friendship is equality.
PYTHAGORAS

We would dearly like to know something of his formative years, but they are a virtual blank. He had brothers, and he apparently received the finest education available in gymnastics, music, mathematics, and what was known of the natural sciences. While still a youth he traveled to the island of Lesbos to study with a famous teacher, Pherekudês of Syros; then he returned to Samos to study with Hermodamas. Trained to think and see as a scientist, Pythagoras possessed a restless urge to know about everything. "While still young, so eager was he for knowledge, he left his own country and had himself initiated into all the mysteries and rites not only of Greece but also of foreign countries."[2] He apparently visited Egypt, learned the language, and studied astronomy, geology, and theology. He gained entrance to the sacred sanctuaries and learned something of the secret doctrines taught by the Egyptian priests.

While Pythagoras was traveling, the tyrant Polycrates seized the government of Samos. Ruthless toward enemies and friends alike, Polycrates was, nevertheless, a patron of the arts and spent vast sums on public works and on beautifying the island. He built a powerful navy, used largely for piracy. When Pythagoras returned home about 532 BC, he found the new regime repressive, so he and some three hundred followers emigrated westward to southern Italy and settled at a health spa known as Crotona, a Greek colonial port town on the Gulf of Tarentum famed for its medical school and its victories in the Olympian Games. For the rest of his life Crotona was his home. About 525 BC he established one of the great schools of antiquity. Pythagoras involved himself in local politics and composed a constitution for Greek expatriots; according to Diogenes, "so well did they govern the state that its constitution was in effect a true aristocracy (government by the best)."[3]

> *Let no swallows nest on your roof.*
> Pythagoras

Pythagoras was married to a Croton woman named Theano, who also wrote. She appears to have been unusually independent and to have expressed her own thoughts. Asked how long it took for a woman to regain her purity after having sex, she replied, "With her own husband she was pure instantly, with any other man never." Diogenes reports, "She advised a woman going to make love to her husband to let go of her shame when she takes off her clothes, and then when leaving him to put it back on along with them." When asked what "it" was in that statement, she answered, "What they mean when they called me a woman."[4] Theano was obviously more liberated than her husband, who advises a man to have sex with a woman only "when you are prepared to lose what little strength you have" because, he says, "sexual pleasures are always harmful and not healthful, though they are less harmful in the autumn and spring than in winter, and terrible in the summer."[5]

Pythagoras and Theano had a daughter and a son. The daughter, named Damo, "he entrusted with the custody of his secret memoirs, solemnly charging her never to give them to anyone outside the sacred community; and although she could have sold them for a considerable sum of money," Diogenes tells us, "she considered her father's wishes more valuable than gold and was willing to risk poverty to keep her word, even though she was a woman." The son, Telauges, became a respected teacher and succeeded his father as head of the Pythagorean community.

Pythagoras wrote at least three books: *On Education, On Statecraft,* and *On Nature* (and perhaps many others whose authorship is uncertain). The opening words of the latter treatise contain a comment of the sort many a writer, with less courage but better reason, has backed away from: "Now by the air I breathe and by the water I drink, may I never suffer blame for this work!"[6]

The Sanctuary

Pythagoras's school at Crotona was a learning institution and a sanctuary for the cultivation of the spirit. Housed in a sprawl of buildings extensive enough to accommodate hundreds of students, members adhered to strict rules and took vows of loyalty; they were sworn never to reveal the community's secret doctrines to outsiders. Property was shared ("Friends have all things in common"); they ate meals together, wore a distinctive white garb, and became known and admired for their

> *Assist a man in lifting a burden, not in laying it down.*
> Pythagoras

quiet lives, modest behavior, and solemn decorum. As Pythagoras's reputation spread, Porphyry tells us, "he won many followers—both men and women—from the city itself as well as many foreign princes and chieftains from the surrounding countryside."[7]

Members were divided into two groups: "outsiders," called "Acousmatics" ("merely hearers"), who studied in silence during a five-year probationary period; and "insiders," called "Mathematicians" ("true learners"), who were admitted to the cult's secrets and permitted to listen to the teachings of Pythagoras himself. Women were admitted along with men, and Pythagoras saw to it they received the same basic education—philosophy, mathematics, music, and art—though, in addition, they were given vocational training in the care of the home and family.

If we can believe later historians, it is not difficult to reconstruct a day in the life of the Pythagorean community.

> To strengthen their memory the students began each day, on first waking up, by recollecting in order the actions and events of the day before; after that they tried to do the same for the preceding day, and so on backwards as far as they could go, taking care to make the order of recollection correspond with the order in which the events had actually occurred. For they believed that there is nothing more important for science, and for experience and wisdom, than the ability to remember.[8]

This practice was probably connected to the Pythagorean belief that learning is recollection, remembering truths acquired by the soul during previous lifetimes; their daily mnemonic exercises doubtless were designed to perfect memories that could better apprehend this continuing knowledge.°

Each member then went on a solitary morning walk. "They performed their morning walks alone and in places where there was appropriate solitude and quiet; for they considered it contrary to wisdom to enter into conversation with another person until they had rendered their own souls calm and their minds harmonious."[9] Solitude and silence were supremely valued, and they set aside time for both at intervals throughout the day. This early morning stroll helped each to maintain his or her personal harmony and to ward off the world's stressful demands.

Then members attended classes. They studied and discussed the subjects they were taking, the doctrines of the cult, and the regulations that governed their living together. After another walk at midmorning, they devoted an hour or so to health care. They would "compete at wrestling in the gardens and groves or at high-jump with leaden weights in their hands, while others would practice the art of pantomime."

They lunched on bread and honey. Afternoons were filled with more studies. Toward evening they enjoyed a promenade, two or three together, walking along the streets or through the countryside. They marched in cadence, "walking in graceful rhythm together" to maintain a sense of harmony in everything they did. "After walking they bathed, and then assembled in a place where they ate supper in small groups, no group being of more than ten. Supper was regularly preceded by appropriate libations and sacrifices, and was brought to a close just before sunset." Supper consisted of maize, bread, raw and cooked vegetables and herbs, some meat, and a small amount of wine.

After the evening meal, libations of wine and water were offered to the gods. Animal sacrifices were prohibited by the Pythagoreans on the belief that animals and humans alike share "the privilege of having a soul."° In fact, reports Porphyry, Pythagoras believed "the soul is immortal" and "changes into other kinds of living things"; he taught, therefore, "that all living things should be regarded as akin."

°*So also for Plato; see pp. 145f.*

Above all, have respect for yourself.
                    PYTHAGORAS

In this world sunrise comes before sunset.
                    PYTHAGORAS

°*A notion also shared by Plato and Aristotle, but, unlike Pythagoras, the idea did not lead them toward ecological concerns or vegetarianism; see pp. 145 and 186; see also Plotinus, pp. 247f.*

Although they worshiped only Apollo the Life-Giver, they also honored other gods and daemons, and their ceremonies included magical rites and divination.

Evening was a social time, but not for idle chatter. They read and discussed in groups, the younger members reading what the older members selected. As the evening drew to a close, more libations were offered, and one of the elders gave a short talk or homily. At bedtime, they donned "pure white night-garments" and slept in "pure white beds."

"After going to bed do not allow sleep to close your eyelids until you have first examined all your actions of the day, asking yourself: Wherein have I done amiss? What have I omitted that ought to have been done? If you find on reflection that you have done anything amiss, be severe with yourself; if you have done anything good, rejoice."[10]

Membership in the community required no assent to doctrinal beliefs or performance of rituals; rather, the goal of the communal life was to ennoble one's entire existence and make it a spiritual harmonium.

"By such disciplines," we are told, "the Pythagoreans sought to arrange their lives entirely for the purpose of following God. They held that all things are possible with the gods, and that one ought to seek benefits only from the divine Lord of all."[11]

Blessed are the men who acquire a good soul; for if it is bad they can never be at rest, nor ever keep the same course two days running.
PYTHAGORAS

Hovering over the community was the philosopher himself, the power and final authority, a felt presence, a god incarnate—a Christ figure. A tall man, Pythagoras always dressed immaculately in a white robe. Some of his followers were convinced he worked magic and performed miracles. Aristotle reported that some Crotona citizens considered him a manifestation of the Hyperborean Apollo "come down from the far north," and once, "when he was disrobed, his thigh was seen to be made of gold."[12] He lived simply, eating little more than bread and honey and some vegetables, with a little wine. He loved music, mathematics, and astronomy, and all three became elements of his personal mysticism, as well as important subjects in his school's curriculum. "Of course the only altar at which he worshipped was that of Apollo the Giver of Life, behind the Altar of Horns at Delos, for thereon were placed flour and meal and cakes, without the use of fire, and there was no animal victim"—so writes Aristotle, relayed by Laërtius.

Behave one to another as not to make friends into enemies, but to turn enemies into friends.
PYTHAGORAS

TEACHINGS

Pythagoras's philosophy touched on every aspect of daily existence, and his pronouncements became the beliefs of the sacred community. He avoided long discourses and taught with short, often cryptic, aphorisms, knowing that the human memory better retains one-liners than extended lectures. Many of his teachings were preserved in epigrammatic form, as pearls his followers set to memory. Later writers give us long lists of them; they read like spiritual exercises or thoughts for the day. "Don't stir the fire with a knife. (Meaning, don't needle the tender self-esteem of someone who is puffed up with his own self-importance.) "Don't sit down on your bushel." (Pay attention to, and plan for, your future, just as you do your present; the bushel represents one day's rations.) "Don't eat your heart." (Don't waste time worrying about life's unavoidable problems and pains; also, don't waste your life trying to solve problems that don't exist.) "When you go abroad don't turn around at the frontier." (Don't turn back in the middle of a journey. Also, if you're ready to die, then proceed on into your next life; don't let your roots in this life hold you back.)

Do not turn back in the middle of a journey.
PYTHAGORAS

Many more exist. Some are lovely and not at all obscure: "Assist a man in lifting a burden, not in laying it down." "Above all have respect for yourself." "Friendship is equality." "Reason is immortal, all else is mortal."

Reason is immortal, all else is mortal.
PYTHAGORAS

But some of his aphorisms are cryptic, and we wonder what they could have meant. "Don't allow swallows to nest on your roof." "Don't engrave God's image on the circle of a ring." "Don't wipe up a mess with a torch." "Don't commit a nuisance toward the sun." Ambiguity always has been a trademark of spiritual gurus, who allow listeners to bring their own interpretations to carefully chosen words. Still, we wish we had some clues.[13]

MUSIC

One story tells of Pythagoras passing by a blacksmith shop and hearing the rings of hammers pounding on the anvils inside. The heavy blows produced a variety of pitches. Going inside to watch, he observed that heavy hammers created the lower notes and lighter hammers the higher notes. He already had experimented with the measuring of weights and knew that the weight of any object can be broken into fractional units and described mathematically. Now he saw the correlation between the pitch of the sounds and the mathematical notations for describing the sounds.

By all accounts Pythagoras loved music, and it is likely he was a musician. He had experimented apparently with stringed instruments—the monochord or the lyre—and had discovered that harmonic intervals are determined by the length of the vibrating string and can be expressed in precise ratios with abstract numbers.[14] By stopping down a string at various points, he could measure the two vibrating segments and determine their ratios. He found that a ratio of one to two gave off sounds one octave apart. A ratio of two to three sounded an interval of a fifth, three to four sounded a fourth, and so on. All musical sounds could be reduced to, and described by, numbers.

MATHEMATICS

Next it dawned on Pythagoras that, like hammer heads and vibrating strings, all natural objects may have their own vibrations and that the entire universe of matter-in-motion may have a mathematical structure. Everything is vibrating, he concluded, as though the world is a great orchestra and every material object is an instrument in that orchestra, giving off its own musical pitch. Anvils, bells, cymbals, pounding drums, the tinkle of porcelain shattering, the sculptor's chisel ringing against marble, the boom of a volcano erupting, and even the planets orbiting through the night skies—everything vibrates and makes music. If this is indeed true, then everything in the world follows the rules of mathematical logic and can be described with abstract numbers.

Before Pythagoras, pure abstract numbers were unknown. Legend has it that Pythagoras learned the rudiments of mathematics in Egypt, but only as they applied to practical problems such as parceling out irrigation plots or measuring quantities of water lifted from ditches along the Nile. Pythagoras took another step of great significance. Two candles plus two candles equals four candles, but "two plus two equals four" is an abstract equation that applies not just to candles but to all conceivable objects in the universe. An abstract formula, therefore, is a universal truth because the universe is made of matter, and matter obeys mathematical rules.° The formula $2 + 2 = 4$ has been severed from all particular objects/events; it is pure logical form and provides absolute certainty. Here is the origination of the powerful stream of thought in Western philosophy that only from abstract logical constructions can we attain certain knowledge.°

This was Pythagoras's first great discovery: mathematical abstractions. In the later words of Galileo, he had found that "the book of Nature is written in the

°This insight had a great impact on Galileo when he looked through his telescope and began to realize what "universal" really meant.; see Vol. II, p. 21.

°This belief is the soul of Plato's philosophy and the beginning of the rationalist tradition in the West; see pp. 152ff.

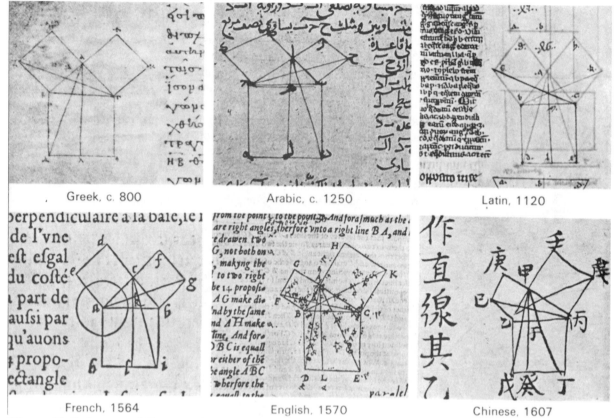

Greek, c. 800   Arabic, c. 1250   Latin, 1120

French, 1564   English, 1570   Chinese, 1607

Discovered by Pythagoras and Chinese mathematicians about 500 BC, the Pythagorean Theorem has been continually rediscovered and testifies to the human impulse to render thinking coherent and meaningful. Best grasped as a diagram, it says that the square of the long side of a right triangle equals the sum of the squares on the short sides. Above is the Theorem as it appeared in Euclid's Elements *c. 300 BC, followed by five translations.*

language of mathematics." One implication of this discovery is that the human mind can understand the natural world. We humans have rational intellects; if the world is mathematical and if our minds can do mathematics, then a match can be made. The structure of the cosmos is comprehensible.

Pythagoras's breakthrough launched him into a lifelong love affair with mathematics and geometry and led to numerous discoveries. He discovered several geometric theorems, the most famous still bearing his name—the Pythagorean Theorem. He also worked with square roots and found that the square root of two is an inexpressible number. (Its unwelcome existence became one of the secrets of the Pythagorean cult, since incommensurables weren't supposed to exist. The records tell us that one of their members, a man named Hippasus, was excommunicated for betraying its existence to the outside world.)

[The Pythagorean Theorem] The square on the hypotenuse of a right-angle triangle is equal to the sum of the squares on the sides enclosing the right angle.

HARMONY

Another inference drawn by Pythagoras is that all the vibrations of the cosmos are (or could be) harmonious. "They [the Pythagoreans] supposed the whole heaven to be a *harmonia* and a number," Aristotle wrote. Like Anaximander and Heraclitus, Pythagoras had theorized that the world is driven by pairs of opposites, and he had

Virtue is harmony.

PYTHAGORAS

listed an even ten pairs: limit and unlimited, one and many, odd and even, light and dark, good and bad, right and left, straight and curved, male and female, square and oblong, and rest and motion. But Pythagoras's schematic differs significantly from that of the earlier scientists.° Where Anaximander's opposites are eternally in conflict and Heraclitus's opposites lose their identities in each other, Pythagoras's pairs can be, and eventually will be, reconciled into a harmony. Just as the strings and woodwinds in an orchestra play music by literally vibrating together, the cosmic symphony's separate sections play together in universal harmony. Some parts of the cosmos have not yet achieved harmony, but the Sun, Moon, planets, and stars have achieved it; and those who listen carefully can perhaps hear "the music of the spheres." Pythagoras coined the phrase, and he claimed that, on occasion, he had heard the heavenly music.

See pp. 29 and 37.

Aristotle remained skeptical. The Pythagorean argument had been that small moving objects on Earth make sounds, so objects as large as planets and stars must also make sounds, big sounds. So why don't all of us hear these sounds?

> They explain this by saying that the sound is in our ears from the very moment of birth and is thus indistinguishable from its contrary silence, since sound and silence are discriminated by mutual contrast. What happens to men, then, is just what happens to coppersmiths, who are so accustomed to the noise of the smithy that it makes no difference to them.[15]

Aristotle thinks all this is nonsense. Their argument is presented with "grace and originality," but it is still untrue.

The love of friends is just concord and equality.

PYTHAGORAS

Moreover, in the Pythagorean scenario of opposites, the first-named of each pair is good, the second bad; so a moral element is implied in nature's operations. In some sense the cosmos embodies a struggle between good and evil (though not, it seems, between Good and Evil; the moral forces were never personified into warring spirits as in the Zoroastrian-Western worldview). Obviously, the more the good forces in each pair can win over the bad forces, the greater the harmony prevailing in the world.°

See pp. 220ff.

NUMBERS

The Ionian scientists had speculated that the ultimate stuff (*archê*) all things are made of is a substance of some sort, such as water, air, fire, or, for Anaximander, the "boundless." But the Pythagoreans, with a new insight into nature's physical operations, concluded that the cosmos is made of numbers. And why not? If the cosmos is mathematical, what provides the *substance* of mathematics? Numbers. As the Pythagorean thought of them, these numbers are not just mental ideas, nor were they mathematical points. They are real; they are things, and they occupy space. They are "actual constituents of perceptible things," Aristotle says, somewhat baffled by the notion: "They [the Pythagoreans] even construct the entire visible universe out of numbers—not numbers in the abstract, but spatially extended units of magnitude."[16] "They supposed the elements of numbers to be the elements of all things, and the whole heaven to be a musical scale and a number."[17]°

Note that even modern mathematicians tend to do the same; see Vol. II, pp. 521ff.

One reason the Pythagoreans thought of numbers as concrete entities is that, at that point in time, they possessed no abstract numbering system. Notational systems such as Roman numerals and Arabic numerals were yet to be invented. In the sixth century BC, someone who wanted to refer to numbers arranged pebbles or other small objects into a recognizable design. Someone who had access to a stylus and papyrus, wax tablet, or whitewashed board symbolized the numbers with points or dots. In this fashion, when the Pythagoreans thought of *four,* they represented the number by arranging four pebbles or marking four dots either in a row or in the shape of a square. If they thought of the number six, they thought (visually) of two rows of three. By convention, each number had its own shape.

The number ten, called the "Decad," was special to the Pythagoreans and represented perfection. It was revered for its mystical and magical properties. Written as a triangle, it was called the *tetraktus* and contained all sorts of hidden secrets. Starting with the single point at the top of the triangle, each line could be generated by adding one—1, then 2, 3, and 4, which added up to 10, the perfect number. The four numbers generate the four basic geometric shapes: the point (from one), line (from two points), plane (from three points), and tetrahedron (from four points). The lines/rows of the triangle alternately represent masculine and feminine numbers (odd are masculine, even are feminine). Furthermore, the ratios of each adjacent line represent the octave, fifth, and fourth intervals in musical harmony. So sacred was the figure that those joining the community took an oath on it never to reveal the secrets of the brotherhood: "I swear by Him who reveals Himself to our minds in the tetractus, which contains the source and roots of everlasting nature"—that is, the secret of immortality.[18]

COSMOLOGY

The idea that the universe is a coherent system—as the Greek *kosmos* implied—and not a collection of random events, was not a new idea; but the Pythagoreans gave it new meaning. All the bodies in the heavens behave like the strings of a perfectly tuned lyre following the laws of mathematics. Their movements are intelligible, describable, and predictable.

To the Pythagoreans, the number of heavenly bodies was an obvious number: It must be ten.° The five planets were visible enough in their nightly visitation; add the orbits of the Sun, Moon, and the starfield, and these total eight. To complete the complement, they counted the Earth as a planet and hypothesized the existence of a "Counter-Earth" orbiting on the opposite side of our Earth, where it never can be seen. These ten heavenly bodies revolve around a central fire that also remains invisible to us for the same reason: The Earth in its orbit maintains the same side toward the fire, turning once on its axis during each revolution.

°This idea later will be monstrously abused; for instance, see Vol. II, p. 17.

Pythagorean contribution to cosmology and astronomy was considerable. They believed the Earth is a sphere—not the flat disc or drum the Milesians pictured—that orbits a faraway center. Aristotle makes the significant observation that "Most people think that the Earth lies at the center of the universe, . . . but the Italian philosophers known as Pythagoreans take the contrary view. At the center, they say, is fire, and the Earth is one of the stars, creating night and day by its circular motion about the center."[19] This is a giant step away from a geocentric scenario, though not quite a heliocentric theory. Another fifteen hundred years passed before Copernicus, who drew on Pythagorean ideas, described, from empirical observation, an Earth that orbits the Sun.

THE SOUL

Pythagoras was not only a scientist and mathematician but also a mystic and redeemer. He sought the secret of living for himself and his followers, and he developed one of history's earliest coherent and intellectually respectable "ways of liberation."

The key to both his cosmic and his therapeutic systems was harmonia, "harmony." Any functional system is in a state of harmony if all its parts "vibrate" together. If all moving parts function properly, then the system runs "harmoniously" and can perform whatever purpose it was designed for. And metaphorically—though the Pythagoreans did not consider it a metaphor—just as the cosmos is composed of

The most momentous thing in human life is the art of winning the soul to good or to evil.

PYTHAGORAS

Pythagoras was remembered by his fellow Samians for many centuries. They named the harbor city of Pithagorian for him and as late as the third century AD struck this coin to honor him.

°*Pythagoras's teaching is significantly similar to countless other later "ways of liberation," Western and Eastern, pointing to a universal problem in the human condition and a human need; see Vol. II, pp. 529ff.*

°*The Greeks believed the foundation of all ethics lies in harmony with oneself; see pp. 186ff.*

many parts that vibrate in harmony, the individual human soul, a sort of minicosmos, can enjoy a state of harmony when all its parts work together. Most of the time our souls, imprisoned in the physical body, juggling a blend of opposites, and coping with stresses, have a difficult time getting it together. But the good news is that mere mortals, in this lifetime, can achieve harmony in their souls.°

Pythagoras taught that this lifetime is but a short interlude in a long journey of the soul. Each soul is reincarnated repeatedly into material form, and during each incarnation the body (Greek *soma*) again becomes the prison of the soul *(sêma)*. After each lifetime the soul descends to Hadês, where it undergoes a purging of its sin; then it returns to Earth and once more becomes reincarnate in its prison-house.

Therefore, the goal of life is to put a stop to this round of rebirths, the "Wheel of things" as Pythagoras phrased it. This can be achieved by striving for a virtuous life, which to the Pythagoreans meant harmony of soul, a soul in tune with itself and with the cosmos.° The truly harmonious soul will not return for rebirth but will become forever a part of the divine world-soul.[20]

How can this harmony be achieved? First, through meditation on cosmic harmony. We can become absorbed into the cosmic vibrations and partake of their harmony. Intellectual meditation on the music of the spheres can assist us in identifying our soul with the cosmos. Second, by living a well-balanced life (a healthy diet, exercise, good habits), we can keep the soul's components properly attuned. This was the raison d'être of the Pythagorean community: to provide a closed environment free of stress, with time for quietude, and where healthful habits and routines could be practiced.° Thus "the music of the spheres" and the harmony of the soul can become one.

FINAL DAYS

Pythagoras lived to at least age eighty or possibly even ninety. The end came when the local populace of Crotona became incensed at the political activities of the Pythagoreans, who were authoritarian in their elitist philosophy of power, believing that only those with true knowledge (the Pythagorean variety) should be allowed to rule. They believed that aristocracy was the only viable form of government. The Crotonans were decidedly democratic and perceived the cult as a threat. One account tells us that mobs stormed the monastery, burned it, killed a large number of its members (forty, by one report), and drove away the rest. Pythagoras was forced to flee but "was caught as he tried to escape; he got as far as a certain field of beans"— the Pythagoreans had a taboo against having anything to do with beans—"where he stopped, saying he preferred capture rather than cross it, and be killed rather than prate about his doctrines; and so his pursuers cut his throat."[21] The date was about 497 BC.

While he was alive his influence was enormous. "Throughout Italy Pythagoras made many into good men and true." After his death the Pythagorean community endured for "nine or ten generations" and then vanished from history.[22]

ENDNOTES

1 Diogenes Laërtius, *Lives of Eminent Philosophers*, trans. R.D. Hicks (Loeb Classical Library, Harvard University Press, 1925), VIII.12.

2 Diogenes Laërtius, *Lives of Eminent Philosophers*, VIII.2; for Diogenes as historian see p. XXX.

3 Diogenes, *Lives*, VIII.3.

4 Diogenes, *Lives*, VIII.43.

5 Diogenes, *Lives*, VIII.9.

6 Diogenes, *Lives*, VIII.6.

7 Quoted from Philip Wheelwright, *The Presocratics* (The Odyssey Press, 1966), p. 218 (T23). Porphyry was a Neoplatonist writer and historian who flourished c. AD 275. His choice of words here may be incorrect, but his testimony to the popularity of the Pythagorean movement is undoubtedly accurate.

8 Quoted from Wheelwright, *The Presocratics*, p. 220 (T24). Facts and quotations are from Iamblichus, a Syrian Neoplatonist who flourished c. AD 325 and wrote a *Life of Pythagoras*; for such details he is considered generally reliable.

9 Wheelwright, *The Presocritics*, p. 220.

10 Quoted from Wheelwright, *The Presocratics*, p. 229. This meditation from "The Golden Verses" was probably not penned by Pythagoras himself, but its teaching reflects the great mystic's spirit.

11 Quoted from Wheelwright, *The Presocratics*, p. 220 (T24); from Iamblicus, *Life of Pythagoras*.

12 Diogenes, *Lives*, VIII.11.

13 Diogenes, *Lives*, VIII.13.

14 Diogenes, *Lives*, VIII.17–18.

15 The monochord was a one-stringed musical instrument with a sound-box and a movable bridge; it was often used for the study of musical tones and intervals.

16 Aristotle, *De caelo* 290b 12.

17 Aristotle, *Metaphysics* 1090a 20.

18 Aristotle, *Metaphysics* 985b 28.

19 Quoted from Wheelwright, *The Presocratics*, p. 204.

20 Aristotle, *De caelo*, 293a 18.

21 These striking similarities to Hindu and Buddhist doctrine can hardly be coincidental.

22 Diogenes, *Lives*, VIII.39–40.

23 Diogenes, *Lives*, VIII.45.

CHAPTER 5

THE ELEATICS

Two logicians from Italy disturb the Athenian establishment with their logical conundrums; they initiate the rationalist tradition and stimulate the growth of logic and metaphysics; they influence all subsequent thinking about space, time, and motion; their paradoxes still challenge logicians and mathematicians today.

THE PANATHENAIC CONFERENCE

Parmenides introduced thought to replace imagination [phantasias].
TIMON OF PHLIUS

On Zeno *The paradoxes of Zeno of Elea are objects of beauty and charm, and sources of intense intellectual excitement.*
WESLEY SALMON

°*For more on Plato's reconstruction of what went on at the conference, see pp. 155ff. and Plato's* Parmenides, *126A–136E.*

Do not let custom, born of everyday experience, tempt your eyes to be aimless, your ear and tongue to be echoes. Let reason be your judge. . . .
PARMENIDES

In mid-August of the year 450 BC an auspicious meeting of minds took place in Athens when several prominent philosophers gathered to exchange ideas. Two of these men were Italian logicians who had traveled to Athens to attend the Great Panathenaea, a festival of lavish splendor held every four years in honor of the goddess Athena. One of them was a dignified white-haired scholar named Parmenides, the other his handsome young disciple Zeno. Eloquent and charismatic, Parmenides left an indelible mark on the philosophic community because of both his sharp intellect and his nobility of character. Zeno came off as something of a pedantic logic chopper, but they appreciated him nonetheless.

A third personality at the meeting, a very young Socrates, nineteen or twenty years old, later reminisced: "Parmenides seems to me, in the words of Homer, a man toward whom one feels reverence tinged with awe. When I was but a youth and he was a very old man I conversed with him, and he struck me as having a wonderful depth of mind. I fear that perhaps we fail to understand what he said, and even more to understand his reasons for saying it."[1]°

The Eleatic tradition, originated by Parmenides, is marked by some very distinctive aptitudes and operations: Its modus operandi was formal logic. "The school of Elea is of unique historical importance. It represents the first all-out attempt in the western world to establish pure reason, with its demands of logical consistency and relatedness, as the sole criterion of truth."[2] Flourishing first at Elea in southern Italy, Eleaticism was revived a half century later by disciples who lived at Megara, a town a day's walk west of Athens.

The essence of Parmenides' doctrine is the belief that the knowledge we attain through deductive reasoning is superior to any knowledge we obtain through the senses. This idea, rooted in Pythagoreanism, laid the first foundations of Plato's Idea-ism, Aristotle's logic, and the entire Western tradition in metaphysics, mathematical logic, and rationalist epistemology.

The Panathenaic meeting, as reconstructed by Plato in his dialogue the *Parmenides*, was already under way when Socrates came into the room. Zeno was reciting some of his paradoxes. Socrates listened and then began to question Zeno.° His sole purpose, he tells Socrates, is to shield his mentor against his critics. The subject matter of Zeno's arguments are duplicates of Parmenides', but his one-liners are accessible in ways Parmenides' convoluted eristics are not.

At length Parmenides tells Socrates at the meeting that Socrates is still too young to do good logic ("philosophy has not yet taken hold upon you"), but he assures him that he is on the right track. "When you were speaking to [Zeno] I was pleased with you, because you would not discuss the doubtful question in terms of visible objects or in relation to them, but only with reference to what we conceive most entirely by the intellect and may call ideas."[3]

Socrates then asks Parmenides to demonstrate his major doctrines in logical form. He hesitates: "Oh my! That is a great task, Socrates, to impose upon a man of my age," for it will be a "fearful ocean of words I must swim through."[4] But he finally agrees, an interlocutor is selected, and the dialectic begins. The subjects of the ensuing cycles shift, but they all connect with the principal Eleatic idea that reality is a motionless One.°

The discussion of motion is typical of all thirty-two cycles of argument in the *Parmenides*.

"Well, then," Parmenides says, "let's see whether it [the One] can be either at rest or in motion."

"Yes, let's," replies Aristoteles, the interlocutor for this part of the dialogue.

"Because if in motion it would be either moving in place or changing; for these are the only kinds of motion there are."

"Okay."

"But the One, if changing into something other than itself, would no longer be the same One."

"That's right, it couldn't be."

"Then it's not in motion by changing into something else."

"Apparently not."

"But what about its moving in the same place?"

"What about it?"

"If the One moved in a place, it would either have to revolve in the same spot [as circular motion] or pass from one location to another."

"Yes, it would have to."

"And something that revolves must rest upon a center and have other parts which revolve about its center; but what if it has no center and no parts? Is there any possible way it could revolve?"

"Obviously not."

"But does it change its place by moving into one place at one time and another place at another time? Can it move in that way?"

"I guess so, if it moves at all."

"Did we not find [in previous arguments] that it [the One] could not be in anything?"

"Yes."

"And is it not still more impossible for it to come *into* anything?"

"I don't understand why."

"If anything comes into anything, while it is still on the way in, it must be not yet in it; nor yet is it still entirely outside of it, if it's on the way in. Isn't that right?"

"Sounds right."

°*For this exchange between Socrates and Zeno, see Plato's* Parmenides, *127D–130A.*

On Zeno *Zeno's arguments, in some form, have afforded grounds for almost all theories of space and time and infinity which have been constructed from his time to our own.*

BERTRAND RUSSELL

°*This "One" is a fictional entity, like an irrational number in mathematics, used for the sake of logical argument.*

The heart when left to itself misses the road.

PARMENIDES

The Panathenaea was a much-loved festival of great antiquity celebrated in Athens every fourth year in honor of the goddess Athena. Highlight of the festival was a parade along the Panathenaic Way to Acropolis during which the crowds could listen to recitations of

poetry, judge musical contests, and watch marching troops and torch races. In the year 450 BC Parmenides and Zeno traveled from Italy to attend the festival at which time they met Socrates and dazzled the Athenian philosophers with their logic.

"Now if anything goes through this process, it can be only that which has parts; for a part of it could be already in the other, and the rest outside; but that which has no parts cannot by any possibility be entirely neither inside nor outside of anything at the same time."

"Okay."

"But is it not still more impossible for that which has no parts and is not a whole to come into anything, since it comes in neither in parts nor as a whole?"

"Clearly."

"Then it does not change its place by going anywhere or into anything, nor does it revolve in a circle, nor change."

"Apparently not."

"Then the One is without any kind of motion."

"Right. It would be motionless."[5]

Parmenides goes on to other subjects but returns later to pick up the argument of motion and takes a "both/and" approach.

"Must not the One be *both* in motion *and* at rest?"

"How is that?"

"It is doubtless at rest if it is in itself; for being in One, and not passing out from this, it is in the same, namely in itself."

"Yes, it is."

"But that which is always in the same, must always be at rest."

"Of course."

"Well, then, contrary-wise, must not that which is always in other be never in the same, and being never in the same be not at rest, and being not at rest be in motion?"

"True."

"Then the One, being always in itself and in other, must always be in motion *and* at rest."

"That must be our conclusion."[6]

There remains but one word to express the true road: Is.

PARMENIDES

And so on! . . . through thirty-two cycles of dialogue (sixty-six pages in the Loeb edition). Parmenides was trying to entrap his opponents with word games, to out-maneuver them to prove that our arguments, even the most rigorous of them, are, in the final judgment, worthless. They can be used to prove any point one wishes, and therefore they prove nothing. (How else could we interpret his statement that "the One is all things and nothing at all"?) When he tells Socrates that Socrates needs more training, he was saying, as it were, "All this is but a game; no truth can be found in it. Indeed, such a thing as truth exists, but your logic, *at the level at which we commonly move,* is helpless to attain it. Logic is a wonderful system of thinking, and it is of great value in ascertaining the truth; but one must be very skilled, highly trained, and sophisticated in its use, before it will serve as the instrument of the truth that is its true promise."

All Parmenides' arguments are fallacious, and from his day to ours students of logic have had a field day wrestling with them. But this just may be the point. Common sense warns us not to take these Eleatic doctrines literally or too seriously. Aristotle later wrote that an Eleatic logic that refuses to pay attention to what the senses tell us "seems next door to madness when one considers the facts." Literalness here insults common sense, and we can be sure these men knew this. Could a bright human being so totally deny the immediate facts of experience—motion for instance—and still retain a modicum of sanity? In our mind's eye we can see Parmenides and Zeno in the lecture hall in Athens, after their disquisition is finished, being honored, teased, upbraided, questioned—and laughing with their fellow critics when they are asked how, if no motion exists, they made the long trip from Italy and how it is they are standing there talking, gesturing, and arguing. It is hard to imagine that, on such an occasion, they could maintain a long-faced defense of their imaginary theses.

It is also important to note that the spirit of the Panathenaic meeting, as Plato reported it, was one of jovial commaraderie as the participants sparred with their verbal weapons. Uptight they were not, as they would have been if they really felt trapped in contradictions with grave consequences. They were having fun; they played with tongue in cheek and twinkle in eye. It's an "elaborate *jeu d'esprit*."[7] Parmenides especially was deft at these logical maneuvers, and this intellectual agility fascinated Socrates and Plato. Their wrestling was in earnest, for these are serious thought problems in logic, and their obsessive tenacity and determination to see through the fog paid off in subsequent centuries in ways they could not have foreseen. But they all sensed that their logic had enough "play in the gears" to warn anyone against betting their philosophic dollars on a shaky paradox or fuzzy definition. The dialectics Socrates practiced during the next fifty years were, in spirit, very like these word games of the Eleatics; he, too, played through his conversations with a mischievous twinkle. But when in time people took his dialectics seriously and interpreted the mind traps as personal threats—as happened with philosophically naive politicians, lawyers, and businessmen who also suffered from an underdeveloped sense of humor—then egos were bruised and, inevitably, it led to the deadly hemlock.°

°*See pp. 104–107.*

IN THE HISTORY OF PHILOSOPHY

The Eleatics are remembered (1) for arguing that, in the pursuit of truth, the senses are useless since pure reason alone can attain the truth; (2) for trying to prove with logic that time, space, and motion don't exist; (3) for teaching that being is One; (4) for inventing logical metaphysics; (5) for their logical paradoxes (from Zeno especially).

PARMENIDES OF ELEA

THE MAN

Parmenides was born about 515 BC in the city of Elea (now called Castellammare) on the southern coast of Italy. Italian by birth, he was Greek by heritage, for Elea was a Greek colony settled some twenty years earlier by Phocaean Greeks driven from Corsica by Carthaginian invaders. Beyond the fact that his father was a wealthy man named Pyres, we know nothing of his background.

While still a youth Parmenides came under the influence of Pythagorean philosophy through a poor but highly respected teacher named Ameinias. His hometown was some two hundred miles from Crotona, and it is likely he visited and perhaps studied at the Pythagorean compound. He might even have met the venerable philosopher himself. We are told, however, he soon rebelled against his Pythagorean mentors and began to develop his own monistic philosophy.

THE POEM

Besides Plato's reconstruction of the meeting in Athens in 450 BC, Parmenides' teachings are known to us from a poem entitled *On Nature*, some 160 lines of which are extant. He composed it in dactylic hexameter, the epic meter of *The Iliad* and *The Odyssey*; and by placing his poetic lines into the mouth of a mythical Goddess, he lent prestige to a composition that otherwise might be deemed prosaic.

His poem is divided into three parts: (1) a prologue, (2) "The Way of Truth," and (3) "The Way of Popular Opinion." In the dreamlike prologue Parmenides is transported to the palace of the Sun. "Along this road I was carried—yes, the wise horses drew me in my chariot while maidens led the way. . . . The handmaidens of the sun, who had left the realms of night and had thrown back their veils from their faces, were driving the chariot speedily toward the light." Thus, Parmenides establishes a metaphor for picturing his intellectual journey: he moved from darkness into light, from illusion and falsehood to truth.[8] When they reach the palace, the gates are unbolted and flung open. "The Goddess greeted me kindly, and taking my hand in hers she spoke these words: 'Welcome, my son, you who come to our abode with immortal charioteers at the reins! It is no evil fate that has set you on this road, but Right and Justice have brought you here. . . .' " This unnamed Goddess of wisdom tells Parmenides he must learn both the Truth and "the opinions of mortals which lack true belief"—that is, uncritical popular opinions.

In the second part of the poem, "The Way of Truth," the Goddess begins her instruction. After a preliminary skirmish—"Never shall it be proven that not-being is"—she launches into the heart of the Parmenidean philosophy.

I will tell you of the two roads of inquiry which offer themselves to the mind. The one way, that It Is and cannot not-be, is the way of credibility based on truth. The other way, that It Is Not and that not-being must be, cannot grasped by the mind; for you cannot know not-being and cannot express it.

It is necessary both to say and to think that being is. For to be is possible and not-to-be is impossible. . . .

There remains, then, but one word by which to express the [true] road: *Is*. And on this road there are many signs that What Is has no beginning and never will be destroyed: it is whole, still, and without end. It neither was nor will be, it simply is—now, altogether, one, continuous. . . . I shall not allow you to say or think of it as coming from not-being, for it is impossible to say or think that not-being is. . . .

Necessarily therefore, either it simply Is or it simply Is Not. Strong conviction will not let us think that anything springs from Being except itself. . . . Thus our decision must be made in these terms: Is or Is Not. . . .

Moreover it is immovable, held so in mighty bonds. And it is without beginning and end, because both creation and destruction have been driven away by true belief. . . .

Thinking and the object of thought are the same. . . .

Since there has to be limit, Being is complete on every side, like the mass of a well-rounded sphere, equally balanced in every direction from the center. . . . The All is inviolable. Since it is equal to itself in all directions, it must be homogeneous within the limits.

Thought and being are the same.[9]

In the third part of the poem, "The Way of Popular Opinion" (or "Belief" or "Appearance" °), only a few fragments of which have survived, the Goddess tells

You must learn all you can about everything, whether it be the truth or mere fashionable notions about things, because only then can you judge between the two and know what a vast difference there is.

PARMENIDES

Never shall it be proved that not-being is.

PARMENIDES

°*See* doxa *in the lexicon.*

Parmenides that although he has learned the truth about things through logical reasoning, it is also important that he learn the opinions of common mortals. "Learn about the opinions of men," she advises, "in order that your knowledge of such matters may not be inferior to theirs." The Goddess proceeds to present a summary of Pythagorean cosmology and biology. "You shall come to know the nature of the sky, and the signs of the sky, and the unseen works of the pure bright torch of the sun and how they came into being. You shall learn the nature of the round-faced moon and its wandering works. You shall know also the encompassing empyrean, whence it arose, and how Necessity grasped and chained it so as to fix the limits of the stars." [10] She reveals that the Moon "shines at night with a light that is not her own." She comments on men and women, love and genes ("seeds of love"), boys and girls. All these ways are popular opinion only, she warns, and there is no truth to be found in them.

BEING IS ONE

Parmenides then builds on a major Pythagorean theme. The world is made of numbers, and the human mind, in its rational mode, can think in mathematical terms. The rational mind can know the rational world. The conclusion—momentous for Western thought—is that the human mind can know reality. Parmenides proceeds to develop, with rigorous logic, a coherent conceptual scheme that apprehends the structure of the world.

Parmenides' logic leads him to a black-and-white concept of being. Reality simply is. What exists exists, and what doesn't exist doesn't exist. He intends this as more than tautological silliness, for the truth is that we all seem to assume, in our confused attempts to comprehend the world, that nonexistence does in fact exist. (At least we talk as though it does. Just ask any uncritical person if space exists and see what answer you get.) Parmenides believed this is a significant issue and argues that space cannot exist, for reality is composed of what exists, not of what doesn't exist. He adds that what is real not only exists but also must exist and that whatever does not exist also cannot exist. This categorical mode has no shades of gray.

Parmenides then argues that all reality is one thing; no spaces, empty places, voids, or interstices exist. It is "complete on every side, like the mass of a well-rounded sphere, equally balanced in every direction from the center." Parmenidian reality is a great spherical world that extends equally in all directions and is completely filled.°

Parmenides further argues that nothing can be created out of nothing, that something cannot be created out of nothing, that nothing can be created out of something, and that something cannot be created out of something. (What is *is*, remember, and it cannot be something other than what it is.) Reality is therefore eternal; it has no beginning and no end.

So, if reality has no spaces, no chinks that would permit small parts of reality to shift and move, then, Parmenides argues, we must conclude that motion also cannot exist. The mistaken belief that motion exists is a popular idea we derive from sense, but, he argues, it is necessarily false. Without space motion is impossible, and reality contains no space. Reality "is immovable," Parmenides says through the Goddess, "held so in mighty bonds. . . . Remaining always the same and in the same place by itself, it stays fixed where it is. . . . For strong Necessity holds it in bonds of limit, which constrain it on all sides; Natural Law forbids that Being should be other than perfectly complete." Within the Parmenidian sphere of reality, therefore, motion and change are fictions.

On Parmenides The Way of Truth is the first philosophical demonstration in history.
REGINALD E. ALLEN

Whatever is other than being is not-being; not-being is nothing whatever; therefore being is one.
SIMPLICIUS

All the usual notions that mortals accept and rely on as if true—such as coming-to-be and perishing, being and not-being, change of place and variegated shades of color—these are nothing but names.
PARMENIDES

°*See* plenum *in the lexicon.*

If something doesn't exist, then it's not in motion.

PARMENIDES

Think about it. Isn't it true that space is a necessary existent for something to move (to move *into*, to move *around in*, to move *through* and *out of*)? Things move only in space, don't they? If a given volume is completely filled, could movement occur? Aren't these obvious truths, and hasn't Parmenides succeeded in making his case? Perhaps we want to argue that things do move, and this proves space "is." But what is meant by "space"? Isn't space a region of emptiness, a place where something might have been but isn't? By definition space is a volume of nothingness. But how can "nothing" exist? "Something" can exist, but "nothing" cannot exist, obviously. And isn't this the point Parmenides is making?'

Parmenides' other arguments are similar in form. Can something come from nothing? When we try to be precise, when we do not allow out-of-sequence jumps, pulling of rabbits out of hats, and creating of universes *ex nihilo* or out of vacuum fluctuations, then in no way, logically, can something derive from nothing. Then could nothing derive from nothing? (Could space derive from space?) Of course not; the question is nonsense. Can something derive from something? Not if that first something is a plenum and motion and change cannot occur. Can nothing derive from something? What could such a question possibly mean?

According to Plato's testimony, Parmenides presented these kinds of arguments in his lectures and debates. His reasoning has fallacies, some of them blatant, some subtle and elusive. Parmenides warns that even in statements that seem absurd, hidden twists and turns may render them worthy of our attention.

A case in point: Parmenides writes that "thought and being are the same." Whereas Bishop Berkeley later argues that "to be is to be perceived" (*esse est percipi*),° Parmenides argues contrariwise that to be perceived is to be. If one can perceive an object in the mind, then it necessarily has to exist.

°See Vol. II, pp. 122ff.

For example, I picture in my mind's eye a bouquet of flowers on my coffee table. My senses tell me no such bouquet of flowers is there. If Parmenides is saying, "Sorry, if it's in my mind's eye, then the real object must be on the table whether my senses detect it or not," then he's wrong, and the statement is absurd. In my imagination I can see a million things—unicorns, mermaids, time travelers—that don't in fact exist.

Thinking and being are the same.

PARMENIDES

But perhaps Parmenides is arguing that if I have the picture of a bouquet of flowers in my mind's eye, then the *possibility of its existence* is logically necessary. But can't I create a mind picture of a floating city that cannot exist because it defies the fundamental laws of physics? Perhaps Parmenides is trying instead to make the point that it's impossible for me to think of something as *not existing*. Can I picture the nonexistence of a bouquet of flowers? Probably not. What I seem to do is to picture in my mind a bouquet of flowers to which I then add the *idea* of nonexistence. But I also can create pictures of nonexisting things (like unicorns) and add the idea of nonexistence to them. So the fact that I can think of something does not logically imply real existence.

Consider one step more. Parmenides also says, "Thinking and the object of thought are the same." Plato later argues that all our ideas—including bouquets, unicorns, and mermaids—are mental copies of Ideas that exist in the real world, that the objective Idea and the subjective idea are the same, the only difference being that the idea in the human mind is derivative. If I have in my mind's eye an image of a bouquet of flowers, it means, necessarily, that the bouquet exists in reality; but it exists, Plato was convinced, not as a material thing but as Real Idea. Parmenides therefore appears to be a pre-Platonic idea-ist smoothing the path for Plato's Theory of Real Ideas. But then we are puzzled by the fact Plato depicts Parmenides as fairly annihilating Socrates' arguments for the doctrine of Real Ideas.°

°See pp. 145f., 152, and Plato's Parmenides, 130A–135E.

What comes clear, finally, is that Parmenides engaged in eristic argumentation as a form of intellectual recreation; it was a semantic wrestling match with a bevy of wrestlers working over ideas tossed into the ring. Parmenides was an elegant player. A life or death duel at sunrise it was not; nor did he care about correct conclusions, although he harbored strong convictions about a few subjects—for instance, that the world of material objects is not "reality" and that our senses can be trusted as a source of information. The dialectic process was what mattered.

This method of treating ideas through public dialectic was a delight to the Greeks, and Parmenides, Zeno, and later Socrates and his followers carry it off with impressive skill. But too often less sophisticated debaters failed to see it as a fructifying game and took it seriously, with a consequent loss of truth, honesty, and life. The philosophic payoff has lasted for more than two millennia and, despite a few setbacks, has made the world of intellect a playground for the growth of ideas. We are today still riding the crest of a wave originated by the Eleatics and Athenians.

PARMENIDES' LEGACY

Though Parmenides differed with Pythagoras in his arguments against motion and plurality, his teaching is close to Pythagorean doctrine. The Pythagorean insight was to recognize that the mind can create abstract mathematical concepts and thereby free itself from having to refer to singular realities.° But rather than numerical abstractions, Parmenides traded in conceptual abstractions, such as being and nonbeing, possibility and impossibility, motion and motionlessness, change and changelessness, finite and infinite, filled and empty, past and future, and so on. Such abstractions, like Pythagoras's pure numbers, have universal applicability.

°See pp. 52ff.

Human beings, of course, have been thinking with abstractions for many millennia. What we find in these early Greeks is a bold awareness of the nature of abstract thought: They fixed it, analyzed it, talked about it, and understood for the first time what humans have been doing all along.

Bertrand Russell points out that "What makes Parmenides historically important is that he invented a form of metaphysical argument that, in one form or another, is to be found in most subsequent metaphysicians down to and including Hegel. He is often said to have invented logic, but what he really invented was metaphysics based on logic."[11]

Parmenides placed serious difficulties in the way of doing science, a budding discipline in the presocratic era. He argued vehemently against trusting the senses, held that motion in a plenum is illogical, believed that all is One, and taught that singular objects can't exist. Therefore, a generalized abstract science created from observing objects in motion was rendered impossible. Not until Aristotle again honored single objects/events and established the rules of induction could science recover from this Parmenidean regression.

It is interesting that Parmenides and Heraclitus were metaphysical opposites: Heraclitus said everything moves, Parmenides said nothing moves. In the long history of Western science, it turns out that Heraclitus was very right and Parmenides was very wrong. If Parmenides had limited his observations to mathematical forms, he would have been correct, since logical constructions, including mathematics and geometry, *are* eternal and thus do not change. The Eleatics made the mistake of applying abstract ideas to the real world before Galileo and Newton showed them how, but then Galileo and Newton might not have seen the truth of physical nature without the Eleatics.

Parmenides' assumptions prevented his making the distinction between the subjective realm of thought (what goes on only in minds) and the realm of real objects/events (what goes on "out there" apart from our minds). But this critical distinction was still far in the future. The clear separation of the mental from the real wasn't established until the advent of the English empiricists of the seventeenth century, so it can't fairly be held against Parmenides that he didn't see what was not seen in Western thought for another two thousand years.

ZENO OF ELEA

THE MAN

Parmenides' devoted follower also was born in Elea and lived there all his life. Zeno lived from about 490 BC to 430 BC and was active during the seventy-ninth Olympiad (464–460 BC). Laërtius calls him "the son of Teleutagoras by birth but of Parmenides by adoption." A prominent citizen in his city-state, he was invited to draw up a code of laws for his government. "He was a truly noble character both as philosopher and as politician," and "his extant books are brimful of intellect." Aside from his one journey to Athens, we know nothing of his adult life. His death apparently resulted from his part in an attempted coup against the tyrant Nearchos. When arrested and asked about his accomplices who helped him smuggle arms, he named some of the tyrant's close friends. Then he told Nearchos he must whisper a secret, was allowed to come close, and bit off the tyrant's ear. He wouldn't let go until they stabbed him to death.[12]

THE LOGICIAN

Zeno's friendship with Parmenides began while he was still a young man, and he stayed close to the great thinker all his life, playing essentially a supporting role. When he accompanied Parmenides to Athens for the Panathenaea, he was about forty years old, and his reputation already had been established from a book he had written early in life containing his dialectical arguments. When his Athenian hosts invited him to lecture, he displayed incisive intellect and skill as a debater. Plato admired Parmenides, but he seems to have considered Zeno something of a nuisance because he specialized in proving others wrong but could make no positive contribution of his own. (Plato wasn't at the Panathenaic meeting, of course; he wasn't born for another twenty years. So it is likely he reflects the opinion of Socrates, who must have been his principal source of information.)

Plato is referring to a form of argument called a *reductio ad absurdum*; its aim is to begin with a statement from one's opponent and, by developing its implications, show that it leads to absurd or false conclusions. The argument takes this form: "Suppose what you say is true, then your argument implies thus and so, which is contradictory. Therefore your statement is false." Zeno is credited with inventing this argument and was apparently the first to use it as a formal technique in writing and lecturing. In the hands of the wise, the goal of the reductio argument was not victory but truth; in lesser hands, it was commonly used to win at all costs, usually at the expense of truth.

Zeno's book contained forty reductio arguments of the kind he presented at Athens. Only a few have survived. If we can believe Plato's account of the meeting, Zeno was candid in stating the motive behind his work. "Actually the purpose of my writings has been to support the argument of Parmenides against those who try to make him look foolish by deriving absurd consequences from his doctrine that all is one. What my arguments are designed to do is turn the tables on those who believe in plurality; I try to show that on close examination their thesis involves more absurd consequences than the doctrine of the One. In just that argumentative spirit I wrote my book when I was a young man."[13]

Zeno of Elea (c. 490-430 BC)

[The moon], as she wanders around the earth, shines at night with a light that is not her own. . . . She is always gazing towards the rays of the sun.
PARMENIDES

On Zeno *If I accede to Parmenides, there is nothing left but the One; if I accede to Zeno, not even the One is left.*
SENECA

THE PARADOXES

Zeno's paradoxes are miniversions of Parmenides' longer arguments, and for these alone he is remembered in the history of philosophy. Several of them deal with place and space. "If place existed, it would have to be in something, that is, in a place," and this in turn would have to be in another place, which would have to be in another place, ad infinitum—which is absurd; therefore place doesn't, and cannot, exist.

Aristotle thought he could make short work of this argument. "It is not hard to solve Zeno's difficulty that if place is something it must be *in* something; . . . for the vessel is not part of its contents." Today, however, we would make a distinction between thought and reality: Place is not *something* "out there"; it is merely an idea in our mind that we use to specify the location of something. An idea doesn't have to be located anywhere—in fact *cannot* be located anywhere—except in our head. What we call "place" is an item of experience, not an event of the real world.

Another of his reductio arguments, which is a summary of Parmenides' similar argument, has to do with space. If space *is*, he says, it will be in something, for everything that *is* is in something, and to be in something is to be in space. Space, then, will be in space, which will be in another space, and so on ad infinitum. Therefore, space does not exist.

A critic might ask: does whatever exists have to exist in space? What about ideas, pain, love, and dreams? Don't they exist? Of course they exist . . . in our [spaceless] experience. Space is our mind's concept for the volume of nothingness between objects.

Zeno also developed a general reductio argument against the possibility of motion. If something moves, then it must move either where it is or in some other place where it is not. But obviously it can't move where it is, and certainly it can't move where it is not. Therefore, it can't move.

He made a similar point with the paradox of the arrow. At any instant, Zeno argues, an arrow in flight occupies a space equal to itself and therefore is at rest. This holds true of the arrow at any instant of its alleged flight through the air. At every instant it is at rest, and one can't derive motion from a series of rest-stops, no matter how many. Therefore motion doesn't exist.

We don't know whether Zeno was aware of the word traps in the construction of his reductio paradoxes, as in this one: "[A]n arrow in flight occupies a space equal to itself . . . and therefore is at rest." Of course the arrow—or any object whatsoever—always occupies a "space equal to itself" whether it is in motion or not. It does not follow that because it occupies such an equal-to-itself space, that it has to be at rest.°

Moreover, it may be that equating the material arrow with a "space equal to itself" is a conceptual event only and not a representation of anything real. The space we picture the arrow occupying is a figment of mind. As stated above, space is merely our mind's concept for the (unperceived) nothingness between objects. It is not *something* that *something else* can be *in*.

Aristotle labeled Zeno's conclusion to the arrow paradox patently false, "for time is not made up of instantaneous moments." The twentieth-century philosopher Henri Bergson, who did considerable work on problems of time and space, reveals the fallacy of Zeno's paradox in a quite different way. He suggests we use our empathetic imagination to place ourselves *inside* the arrow and identify with the arrow's "experience" or "point of view." From this perspective, then, what is your judgment about static "instants" or "rest-stops" or mathematical points?°

In Zeno's paradox of the racetrack, a runner cannot reach the end of the raceway until he has reached the halfway mark; but he can't reach the halfway mark until he has first reached the halfway mark to the halfway mark, and so on, ad infinitum. The conclusion, therefore, is that the runner can never begin the race, and motion is an

If anything is moving, it must be moving either in the place it is or in a place it is not. However it cannot move in the place it is, and it cannot move in the place it is not. Therefore it cannot move, movement is impossible, and motion doesn't exist.

ZENO

If space is, it will be in something, for everything that is is in something, and to be in something is to be in space. Space, then, will be in space, which will be in another space, and so on ad infinitum. Therefore, space does not exist.

ZENO

On Zeno's argument against motion *It is difficult to think of any other problem in science or philosophy which can be stated so simply and whose resolution carries one so far or so deep.*
WESLEY SALMON

°"Isn't 'in flight' just such a word trap since it implies motion? If an arrow is in flight how could it be 'at rest'?"— Kay Kaylor, copyeditor.

°For Bergson on Zeno's arrow, see Vol. II, pp. 435ff.

illusion. Zeno is right: The runner *must* go halfway before he can go any farther, *but*, having gone halfway, he can keep on going, can't he?

Zeno's most famous argument is the story (originated by Parmenides) of a footrace between Achilles and a tortoise. If the tortoise, given a handicap, begins the race some distance ahead of Achilles, then by the time Achilles reaches the point where the tortoise *was*, the tortoise will have moved ahead some distance. Again, when Achilles reaches the point where the tortoise *was*, the tortoise will still be ahead, though the distance between them is closing asymptotically, and so on ad infinitum. Therefore, since the distance between them is forever closing, Achilles can never overtake the tortoise. Therefore motion does not exist.

As Zeno sets up this paradox, his conclusion is correct: Achilles can never overtake the tortoise. That's the last word on the matter. No problem exists. A problem arises only because we *want* Achilles to overtake the tortoise because we are convinced that's how it would be in "real life." So, if you *want* Achilles to overtake the tortoise, then you must set up the problem in terms of their relative speeds in a given period. Achilles usually wins.

It may not have been obvious to Zeno that it takes *time* for an object to travel distance, any distance; and a specific instance of motion, such as Achilles' racing the tortoise, must be analyzed in terms of the time units required to cover so many distance units. Both space and time are required for the perception of motion, and any attempt to confine motion to just space or just time eliminates motion per se from the equation. Hence, Zeno's paradox is deceptive: He attempts to treat the problem of motion from an epistemic frame of reference from which the treatment of motion has already been eliminated.

ENDNOTES

1 Plato, *Theaetetus*, 183B.
2 Philip Wheelwright, *The Presocratics* (Odyssey Press, 1966), p. 90.
3 Plato, *Parmenides*, 135E.
4 Plato, *Parmenides*, 137A.
5 Plato, *Parmenides*, 138C–139A.
6 Plato, *Parmenides*, 145E–146A.
7 Taylor's term, referring to Plato's dialogue. A. E. Taylor, *Plato: The Man and His Work* (Meridian Books, 1956), p. 351.
8 Parmenides is not the only writer to picture the darkness of his early ways so he can take pride in his later illumination; St. Augustine pursues this methodology throughout his *Confessions*. See pp. 298ff.
9 Wheelwright, *The Presocratics*, pp. 95–100.
10 Wheelwright, *The Presocratics*, p. 99.
11 Bertrand Russell, *History of Western Philosophy* (George Allen & Unwin, 1946), p. 67.
12 Diogenes Laërtius, *Lives of Eminent Philosophers*, IX, 25–9.
13 Plato, *Parmenides*, 128E.

CHAPTER 6

EMPEDOCLES OF AKRAGAS

An imaginative Sicilian doctor develops an influential cosmology; he wrestles with the problem of human origins and creates a colorful prevision of the "survival of the fittest"; he laments the tragic state of knowledge in the general populace and decides he doesn't belong in this world.

UNDERCURRENT

We often remember a philosopher for one or two striking ideas, but then, as we read through his writings, we find that his deeper thoughts and concerns lay elsewhere. For example, we honor Pythagoras for his famous theorem about the sides of a right triangle, but his life as lived was one long passionate search for a mystical knowledge that, when shared with his followers, would create in them a spiritual harmony that could ennoble their existence. Similarly, Socrates is popularly memorialized for his oration at the Symposium and for his sage remarks at his trial and just before his execution, but he spent his days seriously preoccupied with the insidiousness of everyday thinking and with helping others improve their thinking skills. Plato is best known for his so-called doctrine of Real Ideas, but he focused his life passions on humanity's beastly behavior toward fellow humans and on his own calling to supply citizens with more benevolent ideas to live by. We rightly celebrate these thinkers' ideas for their impact on Western thought, but our reductionistic remembering is likely to make us miss what these people were all about.

Empedocles of Akragas is just such a case. He is usually remembered, and deservedly, for his physical cosmology and his prevision of a sort of evolutonary "natural selection." But as we read through the extant materials, we discover he was obsessed with other thoughts. Our fragments from him are few, granted, and much can be lost in translation and through the selective interests of later interpreters. Still, we get from his writings clear impressions of a man troubled by more than divine discontent. Empedocles was distraught by the human condition itself.

A recurring theme is the brevity and unsatisfactoriness of human existence. "The life of mortals is so mean a thing as to be virtually un-life; their doom is swift, they are blown away and vanish like smoke." He interpreted life and experience through his own magisterial vision of cosmic process. The present Age of Strife, he says, is "a land without joy, where bloodshed and wrath and agents of doom are active; where plagues and corruption and floods roam in the darkness over the barren fields of Atê." What he beholds is almost beyond endurance. "Ah, wretched unblessed race of mortals! Such were the strifes and groanings out of which you were born." Since

By love we perceive love, and hate by dreadful hate.

EMPEDOCLES

Pay heed and I will tell you the first-principle of the sun; moreover I will explain the sources from which everything that we now behold has sprung—earth, billowy sea, moist air, and giant sky that binds all things in its embrace.

EMPEDOCLES

*Empedocles of Akragas
(c. 484–c. 424 BC)*

I too am now a fugitive from heaven and a wanderer, because I trusted in raging Hate.
EMPEDOCLES

One vision is produced by the two eyes.
EMPEDOCLES

What is right may properly be uttered even twice.
EMPEDOCLES

Empedocles believed in the transmigration of souls, he concluded that his current existence was an unfortunate descent, and it puzzled him. "From what high place of honor and bliss have I fallen, so that I now go about among mortals here on earth?" He tells us that, at his birth, "I wept and mourned when I discovered myself in this unfamiliar land."[1]

Another sad theme, filled with frustration and anger, can be heard through some of his utterances: how pitiful is our understanding of everything and how much the mortal masses stop their ears from hearing the truth. "It is hard for men to accept [the truth], for they are hostile to beliefs that challenge their ways of thinking." Men tend to "let countless trivialities blunt the precision of their thoughts." Each of us complacently "forms opinions according to what he has chanced to experience as he drifts about, yet each vainly boasts of knowing the general nature of things. Such universal matters, however, are beyond the reach of sight and hearing, and even beyond the mind's grasp."[2]

These are hardly petty or peripheral undercurrents. Such obsessions determine the way we experience life and play a major role in the creation and selection of the ideas we live by. Yet often they go unnoticed as we concentrate on a thinker's more visible intellectual contributions.

Empedocles reflected on the cosmic panorama and attempted to construct a coherent model of the world that would explain the origins of the creatures inhabiting it. To do this he drew on every possible source of information. "Meagerly scattered among the body's members are the means of acquiring knowledge," he says, but adds that "many are the evils that burst in and blunt the edge of attentive thought." "Come now, with all your powers discern how each thing manifests itself, trusting no more to sight than to hearing, and no more to the echoing ear than to the tongue's taste: rejecting none of the body's parts that might be a means to knowledge, but attending to each particular manifestation."[3] This is an all-inclusive sort of empiricism. Empedocles seems to have broken deliberately with his teacher Parmenides, whose all-out rejection of sense-data clearly offended him. His cosmic vision may be a speculative creation that is more poetic than logical, but his basic impulse was to understand the world, and this requires respectable empirical foundations. His insistence on employing the total experience of mind and body to know the world made him a precursor of Aristotle and later empiricists more than of Plato and thinkers in the idealist tradition.

IN THE HISTORY OF PHILOSOPHY

Empedocles is remembered (1) for his passion to explain the world; (2) for his dynamic cyclical cosmology consisting of four "roots" (fire, earth, air, and water) and two forces (Love and Strife); (3) for his attempt to account for the origins of living things through "natural selection"; (4) for his belief that the soul is on a continuous journey through reincarnation; and (5) for his outspoken advocacy of democracy and freedom.

THE MAN

Empedocles was born in the city of Akragas (Agrigentum in later Latin) on Sicily, "that island of the three-sided coastline," Lucretius later wrote, "sprinkled by the salt spray of the green Ionian Sea."[4] Legend had it that the lush Sicilian soil was sacred to the goddesses Demeter and Persephone, to whom Zeus had given the island. Near its geographic center was the place where the "wide-pathed earth yawned" and Pluto caught up Persephone in his golden chariot and "bore her away lamenting" into the dark world of the dead. From the volcanic fires of Mount Aetna, her grieving mother lit her torches and began a search for the missing maiden.

Born about 490 BC, Empedocles flourished during the eighty-fourth Olympiad (444–441 BC). The son of Meton and grandson of a famous horse breeder who had won a race at Olympia, he came from an illustrious family prominent in the island's political life. Of his family, we know only that he had a brother named Callikratidês, an unnamed sister who once burned two of his poems, and a son named Exainetos; a wife is never mentioned. He studied with Pythagoras, but the Pythagorean community expelled him after he published a poem revealing some of the order's closely guarded secrets (they then passed a law against trusting poets). For a time he lived with the Ionian minstrel Xenophanes and seems to have been impressed with his thinking about the gods. He was also a pupil of Parmenides, deriving from him the idea that nothing is ever created or destroyed. It seems Anaxagoras inspired him to turn to investigating nature.

Empedocles was wealthy by inheritance, and "since many of the maidens of the city had no dowry he drew from his considerable wealth and bestowed dowries upon them."[5] Among the Akragantines, his fame rested on his glorified reputation as a healer, diviner, miracle worker, and raiser of the dead. In one story, he brought to life a woman who had not breathed for a month. He promised his disciples that they, too, could perform such miracles. "Thou shalt bring back from Hadês a dead man's strength."

Legendary anecdotes attest to his power to control the natural elements, and he promised to teach how. "Thou shalt arrest the violence of the unwearied winds that arise and sweep the earth, laying waste the cornfields with their blasts; and again, if thou so will, thou shalt call back winds in requital. Thou shalt make after the dark rain a seasonable drought for men, and again after the summer drought thou shalt cause tree-nourishing streams to pour from the sky."[6] One story (with probably a kernal of truth) tells that he actually performed what he promised his students. To halt the spread of a plague devastating the populace, he diverted the winds sweeping down the canyons above Akragas with leather bags made of ass-skins. (Homer told a similar story of Aeolis bottling up the winds with bags of oxhide.) Another account relates that when a pestilence struck the city of Selinus, Empedocles directed that two clean streams be diverted into the polluted river to clear its waters. The plan seems to have worked; the Selinuntines "prayed to him as though he were a god" and issued a coin to commemorate the event.

If we are reading him correctly, Empedocles detested autocratic rulers who expected unthinking obedience from a docile citizenry. A strong advocate of democracy, he believed people should be expected to operate on knowledge and a free exchange of ideas. "What is lawful is not binding only on some and not binding on others," he wrote.[7] Diogenes Laërtius notes that "it was Empedocles who persuaded the [Akragantines] to put an end to their factions and cultivate equality in politics."[8] Aristotle tells us Empedocles was such a champion of freedom that he actively opposed any form of restrictive legislation. Once he was offered the kingship of Akragas, but he refused, saying he preferred living a simple life.

Keenly sensitive to pain, Empedocles applied his knowledge of science to alleviate human suffering. Galen, the Hellenistic physician, considered him the founder of medicine in Italy. We know he established a school of medicine, developed a flourishing medical practice, and "great throngs" came to be healed. "Some merely want

On Empedocles The vitality of [his] scientific imagination . . . is enough to assure Empedocles of an honored place among the early contributors to the development of natural science in the western world.

PHILIP WHEELWRIGHT

But he [God] is equal in all directions to himself and altogether eternal, a rounded Sphere enjoying a circular solitude.

EMPEDOCLES

The Agrigentines live delicately as if tomorrow they would die, but they build their houses well as if they thought they would live for ever.

EMPEDOCLES

On Empedocles [His] physiology passes over into psychology without a break. (It is clear that as a doctor Empedocles would have practiced psychosomatic medicine.)

CHARLES H. KAHN

[This world is] the joyless land where are Murder and Wrath and the tribes of other Dooms, and Wasting Diseases and Corruptions and the Works of Dissolution wander over the Meadow of Disaster in the darkness.

EMPEDOCLES

Here were the Earth-Mother [Chthoniê] and the far-seeing Sunshine-Nymph [Hêliopê] . . . and Harmony with her serious countenance . . . and lovely Infallibility and dark-eyed Uncertainty.

EMPEDOCLES

Growth and Decay, Rest and Waking, Movement and Immobility, much-crowned Majesty, and Defilement, Silence and Voice.

EMPEDOCLES

According as men live differently the thoughts that come to their minds are different.

EMPEDOCLES

oracles," he complained, but others, "who have long been suffering from painful diseases, want me to help them with real remedies."[9]

Of the original 5,000 lines of Empedocles' two principal works, only some 450 lines have survived. *On Nature* is a scientific treatise dedicated to his favorite disciple Pausanias, who was also a physician; *Purifications* deals more with religious matters; a rhapsode performed it at the seventy-first Olympiad. It begins with a solemn invocation: "O Kalliopeia, immortal Muse, if when looking down on ephemeral things you have ever deigned to notice my endeavors, stand by me once again, I pray, while I utter a worthy discourse about the blessed gods."[10] Empedocles wrote both books in elegant Greek hexameters and laced his poetry with striking imagery and metaphor. Because of this colorful style, it is often difficult to interpret him. An annoyed Aristotle later wrote that a reader can access his cosmology only "if one studies Empedocles critically in order to get at his real meaning and not be put off by his obscure language."[11] Of course, poets always bother those who strive for clarity. Elsewhere Aristotle cautions: "Metaphors are poetical and so his expression [calling the sea 'the sweat of the Earth'] may satisfy the requirements of a poem, but as a scientific theory it is unsatisfactory."[12]

Stories of Empedocles' death illustrate the power of myth that commonly surrounds great figures. At least five versions exist. The most likely account tells us that when he visited the games at Olympia, his numerous enemies at home blocked his return, so he remained in the Peloponnesus and died there. Another tells us that after celebrating a feast during which he performed a resurrection miracle, he disappeared from the Earth—accompanied by an "exceedingly loud voice" calling his name and "a light in the heavens and a glitter of lamps." Laërtius relates a third tale that he deliberately ended his life by leaping into the fiery lava of Mount Aetna to prove he was a god.[13] (His friend Pausanias, who should know, said the story was false.) Another story claimed he broke his thigh in an accident and died of complications; still another said he hung himself from "a tall cornel-tree" and "his soul went down to Hadês." After duly recording all these legendary non-events, Laërtius concludes his account with "That's enough of that!"

Empedocles, blessed with a bright mind, saw much that others did not see; some would say too much, for it seems to have convinced him he was (at least) on the edge of divinity.

> Hail, friends! You who inhabit the great city looking down on the yellow rocks of Akragas and extending up to the citidel; who exercise yourselves with good works, offering a harbor to worthy strangers and being ignorant of meanness: I greet you. I come among you no longer as a mortal but as an immortal god, rightly honored by all, and crowned with fillets and floral garlands.[14]

On another occasion he asked his listeners to remember him after he was gone.

> In the course of time there come to earth certain men who are prophets, bards, physicians, and princes; such men later rise up as gods, extolled in honor, sharing hearth and table with the other immortals, freed from human woes and human trials.[15]

While he was alive on Earth, he is confiding to us, he was one of these immortals. These statements require context. Empedocles accepted the Pythagorean doctrine of reincarnation, according to which a soul can become incarnate innumerable times. The idea was religiously significant in a very personal way. Like Shakyamuni Buddha,° Empedocles claimed to be aware of his own past existences: "In the past I have been a boy and a girl, a bush, a bird, and a dumb water-dwelling fish."[16]

Statesman, scientist, philosopher, poet, medical doctor, surgeon, rhetorician, teacher, spiritual healer, mystic—as both thinker and human being Empedocles was unlike anyone else of his time. As colorful as he was charismatic, he promenaded wearing a royal purple robe with a golden band across his shoulders or around his waist, bronze shoes, a luxuriant growth of dark beard, and a Delphic wreath on his head and attended by a train of youths and maidens who had garlanded him with ribbons and fresh foliage. Eloquent in speech in a world of impressive speeches (he "invented" rhetoric or oratory, Aristotle tells us), he uttered his words as though they were revelations. "Come now, hearken to my words," he wrote; "learning will enlarge your mind."[17] More than master teacher and renowned healer, Empedocles' image of himself was that of a prophet.

°The Buddha, in the legendary Jataka tales, recalled 547 previous lifetimes; the similarity to Empedocles' claims is remarkable if not significant. See also pp. 56 and 146 for Pythagoras' and Plato's similar beliefs.

PHYSICS AND COSMOLOGY

Although Empedocles was driven by an unstoppable curiosity about everything, his philosophical contributions were mostly in physics and biology. Everything that exists has existed from all eternity, he wrote; no beginning of things occurred, and no end will occur. "They are fools," Empedocles wrote, "who suppose that what formerly Was Not could come into being, or that What Is could perish and be utterly annihilated," for "it will always be, no matter how it may be disposed of." On this Parmenides seems to have convinced him.[18]

Also on a second idea he agreed with his Eleatic mentor: Empty space doesn't exist.° The Parmenidean sphere is completely filled; it is a plenum. "In the All there is nothing empty." Whatever the universe is composed of, it is so tightly packed that it couldn't possibly hold any more. But this fact, to Empedocles, did not eliminate the possibility of motion, as it did to Parmenides, who had argued that any volume of matter so tightly packed that no interstices exist in it could not permit motion. Empedocles thought of the constituent elements as extremely fine bits of solid matter that move within the plenum and intermingle, thereby producing with their varied mixtures all the particular things that exist. Like Aristotle and Epicurus, he seems to have concluded that the existence of motion is the most obvious thing our senses tell us, and we had better not go against this perception.

Creation, therefore, involves merely the rearrangement of elements already existing. Mixed in different proportions, these ingredients produce objects and systems.

[From the four elements] come all things that were and are and will be; and trees spring up, and men and women, and beasts and birds and water-nurtured fish, and even the long-lived gods who are highest in honour.

EMPEDOCLES

°See pp. 65ff.

MIXTURES

Four basic elements—Empedocles calls them "roots"— make up the world—fire, earth, air, and water. In his poetic fashion he wrote: "Pay heed and I will tell you the first-principle of the sun; moreover I will explain the sources from which everything that we now behold has sprung—earth, billowy sea, moist air, and giant sky that binds all things in its embrace."

But these elements are not the source of their own driving power; they are merely the ingredients, the passive stuff that is moved. So what moves them? Empedocles postulated two forces, Love and Strife, that provide the impetus for the elements to mingle. Like attraction and repulsion, these are opposite forces; they provide the push and pull of the cosmos and keep the four elements in constant motion. "These two forces, Strife and Love, existed in the past and will exist in the future; nor will boundless time, I believe, ever be empty of the pair."[19]

The four elements, driven by the two forces, are locked in an eternal power struggle and produce a four-stage cosmic cycle. In one stage the repulsive force is

Hear, first, the four roots of things: bright Zeus, and life-bearing Hera, and Aidôneus, and Nêstis who causes a mortal spring of moisture to flow with her tears.

EMPEDOCLES

And all creatures, both animals and birds, were tame and gentle towards men, and friendliness glowed between them.

EMPEDOCLES

dominant, and the four elements, repelling one another, separate out into themselves. Strife, as it were, pushes the elements apart—all earth together here, all water together there, and so on. During this stage of separated elements, no objects or complex systems can exist.

But eventually Strife begins to give way to Love, igniting a mingling of elements. In this second stage, as the elements mix, all the objects and organisms we behold in our experience begin to emerge, and we think of this as creation. "Thence have sprung all the things that ever were, are, or shall be—trees and men and women, beasts and birds and water-dwelling fishes, and even such honored beings as the long-lived gods."[20]

But nothing lasts forever. As the attractive force of Love prevails, the four elements gradually become homogenized. When the mixing is complete, all particular objects and organisms are dissolved into nothingness. The all is One.

> Two-sided is the coming-to-be of perishable things, and two-sided is their passing away. The uniting of all things both creates and destroys; while the contrary phase involves both growth and scattering as things become divided [in the process of individuation]. And this thoroughgoing interchange never ceases: at times all things are united by the power of Love, while at other times they are repulsed and borne apart by the hostile force of Strife. Thus in so far as their nature consists in growing out of many into one and then being parted asunder again out of one into many, they are changeable and have no lasting life; but in so far as they never cease from continuously interchanging, in that respect they are unalterable as they continue on their course.[21]

LIVING ORGANISMS

The cycle never stops. No discrete things can exist during two of the stages of the cosmic cycle—when the elements are fully blended or fully separated. All that exists is the one mixture or the four elements. But during the other two stages, when the elements are moving to or from the polar extremes, infinite mixtures create particular objects. It must not be assumed the second and fourth stages are the same. The force of Love generates stage two; it is an auspicious time when all creation is blessed and happy and good things happen. By contrast, Strife where the generation of particulars does occur just as in stage two, is a time of troubles for all creation. The Age of Strife is "a land without joy, where bloodshed and wrath and agents of doom are active; where plagues and corruption and floods roam in the darkness over the barren fields of Atê."[22]

Aristotle interpreted this cosmic cycle to mean that "Love is the cause of good things and Strife of evil things. Thus one might truly say that in a sense Empedocles was the first to speak of evil and good as first-principles."[23] °

Do you not see that you are devouring one another in the thoughtlessness of your minds?

EMPEDOCLES

°*Empedocles' Love-Strife cosmology invites comparison with the Chinese Yang-Yin system and the Vishnu-Shiva (Preserver-Destroyer) system of Hindu Bhaktism. In these systems, significantly, the pairs are primarily metaphysical forces driving the world and are only secondarily, or in popular misinterpretation, principles of Good and Evil (as in the Ahura Mazda-Ahriman dualism of Zoroastrianism). Aristotle may have overstated Empedocles' Good-Evil interpretation of the Love-Strife operation.*

BIOLOGY

During the two stages when elements mingle, a very special creation takes place. Empedocles wrote: "Now I shall go back again over the pathway of my verses already set forth, drawing a new word out of the old. . . .[For] as the mingling went on, innumerable kinds of mortal creatures in great diversity of forms were produced and scattered forth—a wonder to behold!"[24]

The vision in Empedocles' mind was of animal and human body parts all generating separately, floating, as it were, in the mists of creation—fingers, ears, feet, heads, tails, and whole assemblages of parts joining in hideous fashion:

> There sprang up on the earth many heads without necks, arms wandering unattached to shoulders, and eyes straying about in want of foreheads.

Isolated limbs were wandering about. Many creatures were born with faces and chests turned in different directions. There were offspring of oxen with faces of men, while on the other hand there were human offspring that had the faces of oxen. And there were creatures in which the masculine and feminine natures were combined, the result of which was sterility.[25]

This scenario must have seemed outlandish even to Empedocles, but he reassures us it is "no trifling or foolish tale." His vision was a serious attempt to speculate on the origin of living things. Obviously, in this picture the wrongly attached body parts cannot survive; they are not functional systems. Only in the rare instances when the parts happen to come together in a functional arrangement can the organisms hope to survive. The odds are against it, but on that rare occasion when it happens twice in the same species, and one organism is male and one female, then reproduction can commence and an entire species can proliferate on its own.

Empedocles, therefore, must be credited with developing a shadowy glimpse of an evolutionary event based on chance and natural selection. Lowest in his evolutionary scale are plants, still sufficiently advanced to feel pleasure and pain, possess intelligence, and gather knowledge. Higher on the scale are animals and human beings, whose parts, largely by chance, have joined together into operational systems. When these fortuitous events did in fact occur, then life-forms could survive and reproduce—the survival of the fittest. Aristotle did not miss the significance of this scenario: "Certain things have been preserved because they had spontaneously acquired a fitting structure, while those which were not so put together have perished and are perishing, as Empedocles says of the oxen with human faces."[26]

REINCARNATION

While the material body is a mingling of the four basic elements, Empedocles came to believe that the soul is composed of a mixture of air and fire. As a practicing physician, he undoubtedly had witnessed the death of patients, and from the events he perceived at death, the cessation of respiration and the loss of body heat, he inferred that the soul infusing the body is a combination of air and fire. This is an empirical observation found almost universally in humankind's less sophisticated philosophies and religions. These associate, or identify, the human soul with air and/or fire.

Empedocles taught that the soul is immortal and that, though the body elements separate out, birth and death are merely events in the soul's continuing journey. "There is no birth in mortal things, and no end in ruinous death. There is only mingling and interchange of parts, and it is this that we call 'nature.'"[27] As an expedient he speaks of birth and death in a conventional way, but we must reconceive both events. "When these elements are mingled into the shape of a man living under the bright sky, or into the shape of wild beasts or plants or birds, men call it birth; and when these things are separated into their parts men speak of hapless death. I follow the custom and speak as they do."[28] But in truth what we call birth and death are only milestones in nature's ongoing process of mixing and unmixing of elements and in the soul's separating out from the body elements.

In this round of rebirths certain souls are especially unfortunate, either because they have committed grave sins or because they were born in an Age of Strife. Such a condemned soul, he wrote,

> must wander thrice ten thousand seasons shut off from the abode of the blessed, during which period he is reborn in all sorts of mortal shapes exchanging one grievous kind of existence for another. The force of air swirls him into the sea, the sea spits him out on to dry earth, the earth tosses

Heads without bodies,
Trunks without limbs.
Falling down awful heights of
Air . . .

EMPEDOCLES

Alas, oh wretched race of mortals,
direly unblessed! Such are the
conflicts and groanings from
which you have been born!

EMPEDOCLES

On Empedocles *Empedocles was*
of the opinion that sex plays a role
in the makeup of plants.

ARISTOTLE

On Empedocles *Anaxagoras,*
Democritus and Empedocles all
maintained that plants display
perception and intelligence. (But
such views should be rejected as
unsound.)

ARISTOTLE

It is by chance that men have come
to have conscious thought.

EMPEDOCLES

Happy is he who has acquired the
riches of divine thoughts, but
wretched the man in whose mind
dwells an obscure opinion about
the gods!

EMPEDOCLES

For by now I have been born as boy, girl, plant, birds, and dumb sea-fish.

EMPEDOCLES

And having looked at (only) a small part of existence during their lives . . . every man preens himself on having found the Whole.

EMPEDOCLES

him into the beams of the fiery sun, and the sun flings him back again into the eddies of air. All seize him, and all reject him.

Then he adds, sadly: "Such a man am I, alas, a fugitive from the gods and a wanderer at the mercy of frenzied Strife."[29] But this is not the end for such a life; Empedocles' vision of human life and destiny is filled with hope. "In the course of time there come to earth certain men who are prophets, bards, physicians, and princes; such men later rise up as gods, extolled in honor, sharing hearth and table with the other immortals, freed from human woes and human trials."[30] He says he will be one of these immortals. Empedocles would have understood the folk spiritual that laments, "This world is not my home." "There was among them a man of rare knowledge, highly skilled in all kinds of wise words, possessing the utmost wealth of wisdom." But, he adds, they knew him not.[31]

ENDNOTES

1 Frags. 2, 121, 124, 119, 118. All quotations from Empedocles are Philip Wheelwright's translations. A poet in his own right, Wheelwright captures better than any other translator I know the beauty of Empedocles' poetry. See Wheelwright, *The Presocratics* (The Odyssey Press, 1966), pp. 126–43.
2 Frags. 114, 110, 2.
3 Frag. 3.
4 Lucretius, *De rurum natura*, I.712.
5 Diogenes Laërtius, *Lives of Eminent Philosophers*, VIII.73.
6 Diogenes, *Lives*, VIII.59, frag. 111.
7 Frag. 135.
8 Diogenes, *Lives*, VIII.72.
9 Frag. 112.
10 Frag. 131.
11 Aristotle, *Metaphysics*, 985a.5.
12 Aristotle, *Meteorology*, 375a.24.
13 Diogenes, *Lives*, VIII.69.
14 Frag. 112.
15 Frag. 146.
16 Frag. 117.
17 Frag. 17.
18 Frags. 11, 12.
19 Frag. 16.
20 Frag. 21.
21 Frag. 16.
22 Frag. 121.
23 Aristotle, *Metaphysics*, 985a.5.
24 Frag. 35.
25 Frags. 57, 58, 61.
26 Aristotle, *Physics II*, 8, 198b.
27 Frag. 8.
28 Frag. 9.
29 Frag. 115.
30 Frags. 146, 147.
31 Frag. 129.

CHAPTER 7

THE EARLY GREEK ATOMISTS

Two scientists ponder the perennial question of what the world is made of; they give a penetrating analysis of matter that presages the assumptions of modern science; one becomes known as "the father" of atomic theory; he sharply distinguishes between knower and the known; his commonsense ethic of moderation invited a book-burning from Plato.

THE ATOMISTS

His likeness appears on the Greek hundred-drachma currency note and on the ten-drachma coin. Athenian streets are named for him, and the national road going northward from Athens passes the Democritus Nuclear Research Laboratory. These are appropriate honors, for the recipient is the philosopher-scientist Democritus, who, along with his teacher Leukippos, first inquired seriously into the nature of physical matter. Other presocratics—Empedocles and Anaxagoras among them°— °See pp. 45f. and 75ff. had made cursory attempts to understand what "matter" is, but their analyses were elementary compared to the dazzling speculations of Leukippos and Democritus. These two men were analytical geniuses whose detailed theory of atoms is impressive even today. Leukippos initiated this line of inquiry, and Democritus then developed Leukippos's ideas into a coherent system of physical philosophy. This system has influenced all subsequent scientific thought and leads directly to modern atomic physics and chemistry. For his brilliant work Democritus is honored as the "father" of atomic theory.

*Do not try to understand
everything, lest you thereby be
ignorant of everything.*
                    DEMOCRITUS

*[Both Leukippos and Democritus]
hold that the elements are the full
and the void; they call them being
and not-being respectively. Being
is full and solid, not-being exists
no less than being.*
                    ARISTOTLE

*Nothing exists except atoms and
space.*
                    DEMOCRITUS

*[The Atomists Leukippos,
Democritus, and Epicurus] said
that the first principles were
infinite in number, and thought
they were indivisible atoms and
impassible owing to their
compactness. . . .*
                    ARISTOTLE

*[Leukippos and Democritus] say
that the atoms move by mutual
collisions and blows.*
                    DIOGENES LAËRTIUS

°*See pp. 98ff.*

*Nothing occurs at random, but
everything for a reason . . .*
                    DEMOCRITUS

This school of inquiry is called "Atomism," and the philosophers who probed physical matter are known as "Atomists." The central idea of Atomism is that matter is composed of microscopic particles of one universal substance and that the infinitely varied arrangements of these particles produces everything existing in the material universe. These Atomist doctrines "bear a striking similarity to the more complex and empirically documented theories of modern science. It is thus as the progenitors of modern science that the atomists are usually and justly praised and evaluated."[1]

These first Atomists addressed the two existential VSQs ("Very Stubborn Questions") that already had been formulated by the Milesians: What is everything made of? How does the world work? But speculative philosophy during its first creative period had thought itself into a spate of contradictions and cul-de-sacs, a state of affairs that disgusted Socrates. He confided (according to Xenophon's *Memorabilia*) that after his own youthful pursuit of *physiologia* he became disenchanted with nature altogether and turned to the study of humanity. "He considered those who worry about such things foolish" and observed that "they are disposed toward one another like madmen." Among those who ponder "the nature of the universe,"

> some think that being is one only, others that it is infinite in number; some that everything is always in motion, others that nothing can ever be moved; some that everything both comes into being and perishes, others that nothing ever could come into being or perish.[2]

To be specific, Heraclitus had argued that physical matter is in continuous motion, and, therefore, change is the most fundamental characteristic of nature; "permanency," he said, is a figment drummed up by the mind. Then Parmenides countered that everything is permanent and nothing changes; instead, "motion" is an illusion of the mind. Thinkers in all camps were aware that inconsistencies existed but were convinced that, in any case, their arguments were the valid ones.

Socrates reacted to this frustrating condition by turning away from nature, and for the rest of his life he concentrated on "human things."

> He himself always enquired into the human things, what is piety, what is impiety, what is noble, what is shameful, what is just, what is unjust, what is moderation, what is madness, what is courage, what is cowardice, what is a state, what is a statesman, what is rule over human beings, what is a ruler over human beings, and concerning other things of which those knowledgeable he considered *kaloikagathoi*, while those ignorant could justly be called slavish.[3]°

Whatever reasons Socrates had for abandoning the field, the Atomists veered in the opposite direction. They intensified their attempt to understand nature and succeeded in constructing a systematic explanation of the totality of physical reality.

IN THE HISTORY OF PHILOSOPHY

Leukippos and Democritus are usually considered together since their teachings can't be securely separated. These Atomists are therefore known (1) for inventing the "atom" as the ultimate particle that makes up physical matter; (2) for concluding that space exists and is just as real as matter; (3) for teaching that reality is therefore composed solely of "atoms and the void," that is, of indivisible particles and space;

(4) for reasoning that humans are "cut off from reality," that is, that the real is inaccessible to human perception but that (5) the human intellect can know something of reality by reflecting critically on sense data; (6) for a mechanistic view of a value-free universe that is devoid of teleology and meaning; (7) for laying the foundations of a "humanism" in which individuals must create their own meaning and value; (8) for their belief that countless other worlds must exist created by the same vortical forces that produced our world; (9) for concluding that immortality can't exist since the soul's atoms disperse at death; (10) for their cheerful ethic of moderation (*sôphrosynê*°)

°*See lexicon.*

LEUKIPPOS AND DEMOCRITUS

In a lifetime of more than a century and through some seventy-two books, Democritus developed an innovative philosophy addressing questions about matter, motion, cosmic beginnings, human origins, knowledge, and living the good life. His wide-ranging interests are reflected in the titles of his books: *A Minor Attempt to Order the World, Description of the World, On Human Nature, On Reason, On the Senses, On Tastes, On Colors, On Logic, Causes of Celestial Phenomena, On Magnets, On Geometry, Numbers, A Description of Light Rays, On Rhythms and Harmony, On Beauty within Verse, On Song, On Painting, On Tranquillity*, and many more, including several books on travel. He wrote in a graceful style the ancients considered equal in its beauty to the Platonic dialogues. Apart from fragments preserved by Aristotle, who alludes to him extensively, and an array of reactions from later commentators—especially Epicurus, who adopted his system in its entirety—his extraordinary literary labors all have been lost.

But Democritus must share the honors, for his teacher Leukippos (*Leucippus* in Latin°) stands behind him and is undoubtedly the actual founder of atomic theory. But Leukippos is a virtual nonentity; we know little more than his name. If we turn to Laërtius for information, we get: "Leucippus was born at Elea, but some say at Abdera and others at Miletus. He was a pupil of Zeno"—and that's it. Our best guesses are that he flourished in the latter half of the fifth century BC and was perhaps a dozen years older than Democritus. He and Democritus are both associated with Abdera, and Leukippos apparently founded a school there about 440 BC. He studied at Elea or at least was influenced by the Eleatics, especially by Zeno's paradoxes of space. As for his philosophy, except for one brief fragment—"Nothing happens at random (by chance); everything that happens has a cause"—we know only bits and pieces from Theophrastus, Aristotle, and late Greek sources. It is obvious Aristotle respected him (and wrote a book on him entitled *On Democritus*, now lost) and possessed sufficient material to allow him to critique a few of his ideas. Leukippos wrote several books, among them *On Mind* and *A Major Attempt to Order the World*, but they are all lost.

One of the Atomists' most important contributions was the revolutionary notion that "what is not" exists, that "space," which must be defined as "nothing," must exist along with "something," that is, physical matter. The Eleatics had argued that space can't possibly exist, not merely because it is "nothing" but because if it did exist, then it would have to exist in space because everything that exists must exist in space.° Therefore, they concluded, space cannot exist. But the Atomists' argument was equally airtight. If space doesn't exist, then motion can't exist, because to move, something must have space to move in. Without space, motion is a logical impossibility. Since motion is an undeniable fact of our experience, then space also is undeniable. Therefore, space (even if defined as "nothing") must exist. "The All includes

Some men, with no understanding of how our mortal nature dissolves [at death] but keenly aware of the ills of this life, afflict life still more with anxieties and fears by making up false tales about the time that comes after the end.

DEMOCRITUS

°*Usually spelled "Leucippus." Latins used c to transliterate the Greek kappa, indicating that the Latin pronunciation of c was given a hard k sound; today the original sound of the spoken Greek can be preserved only by spelling his name "Leukippos."*

The man who is enslaved by wealth can never be honest.

DEMOCRITUS

It is noble to prevent the criminal; but if one cannot, one should not join him in crime.

DEMOCRITUS

Virtue consists not in avoiding wrong-doing, but in being without any wish for it.

DEMOCRITUS

°*See pp. 65ff.*

Medicine heals diseases of the body, wisdom frees the soul from passions.

DEMOCRITUS

We are pupils of the animals in the most important things: the spider for spinning and mending, the swallow for building, and the songsters, swan and nightingale, for singing, by way of imitation.

DEMOCRITUS

Refrain from crimes not through fear but through duty.

DEMOCRITUS

In power of persuasion, reasoning is far stronger than gold.

DEMOCRITUS

We know nothing truly about anything.

DEMOCRITUS

the empty as well as the full," as Diogenes puts it. In this way the Atomists set the stage for a centuries-long brain-boggling conflagration that has produced fire and smoke but little light. The nature of space remains an unsettling problem to this day.

Theophrastus says Leukippos was the first to hold

> that *what is* is no more real than *what is not*, and that both are alike causes of the things that come into being; for he laid down that the substance of the atoms was compact and full, and he called them *what is*, while they moved in the void which he called *what is not*, but affirmed to be just as real as *what is*.[4]

Aristotle attributes to Leukippos several other "atomist" ideas, such as that sense experience must be trusted for a knowledge of the world; reality consists solely of atoms and the void; each atom is a plenum and is therefore indivisible; and "by their clustering together they cause things to come into existence; by disengaging they cause things to perish"; and "when they touch and grasp one another they produce phenomena."[5]

Diogenes confirms that Leukippos also developed an influential cosmogony. He was "the first to establish atoms as *archai* (first principles)," out of which whole worlds are created "when these bodies chance to fall into empty space and become entangled with one another." The increased clumping of atoms (by contraction, we would say, due to gravitation) produces the stars. Stars are ignited "by their rapid motion." The Earth was produced in this way. As the atoms collected together and formed a spinning vortex, the lightweight atoms moved to the outside of the vortex, heavy ones moved to its center, and the Earth was formed. "The Earth is held steady [in orbit] as it is whirled about the center" and is "shaped like a kettledrum." Since the Earth tilts toward the south, Leukippos concluded that the Earth's northern regions "are forever snowed on and chilled and frozen fast." "Just as the world comes into existence, it also grows, comes to an end and is destroyed, all through some force of necessity, the nature of which," Diogenes complains, Leukippos "doesn't make very clear."

DEMOCRITUS THE MAN

Whatever role Leukippos played in creating the Atomist scenario, it was Democritus who developed Atomist physics into a coherent system and gave it to the world. Democritus was born at Abdera in Thrace, northern Greece, during the eighteenth Olympiad—about 460 BC. His father, Hêgêsistratos, was affluent and influential. One account (from Diogenes quoting Herodotus) says that his father once entertained King Xerxes of Persia; the royal entourage included "certain Magians and Chaldaeans" from whom, "while he was still a boy," Democritus "learned about theology and astronomy."[7] Through them he may have glimpsed distant horizons that aroused in him a curiosity about the larger world. He had two older brothers, and when he received his share of the family inheritance (more than a hundred talents, one talent worth some sixty pounds of gold), he chose to receive it in cold cash rather than property so he could finance his passion for travel; and, we are told, he used it all up in traveling. "I am the most widely traveled man of all my contemporaries, and have pursued inquiries in the most distant places; I have visited more countries and climes than anyone else, and have listened to the teachings of more learned men."[8] Democritus spent five years learning geometry from the "rope-knotters" (priests) of Egypt; he studied with Chaldaeans in Persia and with gymnosophists in India and visited the Red Sea and Ethiopia.

He was still young when he came to Athens, and, although he apparently tried to remain anonymous—"because he despised fame"—it was not long before he became well known in intellectual circles. For "truly Democritus was versed in every department of philosophy, for he had trained himself both in physics and in ethics, nay more, in mathematics and the routine subjects of education, and he was quite an expert in the arts."[9] He also acquired a popular reputation for fortune-telling and weather forecasting, for which the Athenian populace deemed him worthy of sacred honors. By contrast, Plato was so disenchanted with his theories that he threatened to burn all the books he wrote.° Plato knew Democritus's theories well, but, although "he alludes to almost all the early philosophers, he never once mentions Democritus, not even when it would be natural to controvert him, obviously because he knew that he would have to match himself against the prince of philosophers."[10]

Democritus also gained a legendary reputation for psychic sensitivity. The story was told that he was once visited by the famed physician Hippocrates, who brought along his maidservant. Democritus greeted the young lady with "Greetings young Maiden," but when he saw her the next day he hailed her with "Greetings Mistress." For "as a matter of fact," Diogenes (who loved gossip) notes, "during the night the girl had been seduced." The story apparently was told to demonstrate Democritus's clairvoyant ability.

Democritus made significant contributions to mathematics and geometry. One of the problems that occupied him is preserved in fragment 155.

> If a cut were made through a cone parallel to its base, how should we conceive of the two opposing surfaces which the cut has produced—equal or unequal? If they are unequal, that would imply that a cone is composed of many breaks and protrusions like steps. On the other hand if they are equal, that would imply that two adjacent intersecting planes are equal, which would mean that the cone, being made up of equal rather than unequal circles, must have the same appearance as a cylinder; which is utterly absurd.[11]

Of his long adult life we know nothing. Democritus was living at home in Thrace when he felt death approaching. According to one account, his sister was perturbed that if her brother died she might not be able to participate as planned in an annual religious festival, the Thesmophoria, in honor of the goddess Demeter. Considering her wishes, Democritus sustained his life with medications for three days while she performed her ritual obligations. Then, the celebrations complete, "he let his life go from him without pain, having then, according to Hipparchos, attained his one hundred and ninth year of life."[12]

ATOMS AND SPACE

It is ironic that the two most influential presocratic physical philosophies—Eleaticism and Atomism—fought a battle over the existence or nonexistence of . . . nothing! The irony becomes even more astonishing when one tracks the debate's subsequent history and realizes how productive it has been.

Parmenides had argued that space doesn't exist and had built his system on the basis of this assumption. Once the Eleatics started down this road, it became obvious that this assumption eliminated the possibility of motion. But Democritus listened to his senses and made the simple observation that motion exists, which means space also must exist, for without space for objects to move in and through the Eleatic doctrine would be correct: No motion could exist. Motion necessarily implies the

Untimely pleasures result in displeasure.

DEMOCRITUS

People are fools who hate life and yet wish to live through fear of Hades.

DEMOCRITUS

°*A very significant disagreement in the history of philosophy; see pp. 85f.*

Life is not worth living for the man who has not even one good friend.

DEMOCRITUS

It is the mark of the divine intellect to be always calculating something noble.

DEMOCRITUS

The cause of error is ignorance of the better.

DEMOCRITUS

Men have fashioned an image of Chance as an excuse for their own stupidity.

DEMOCRITUS

Democritus posed the question: "If a cut were made through a cone parallel to its base, how should we conceive of the two opposing surfaces which the cut has produced—equal or unequal?" How would you go about solving Democritus's conical conundrum, by logical analysis or by empirical observation?

On Democritus *Democritus . . . calls space by these names—'the void', 'nothing,' and 'the infinite,' while each individual atom he calls 'hing' [i.e., 'nothing' without 'not'], the 'compact' and 'being.'*

SIMPLICIUS

existence of matter and space. Therefore, "nothing exists just as much as something," Democritus says.

So all existence is made up only of atoms and space. (Leukippos had called atoms and void the two "basic elements" of nature.) The entire cosmos and everything in it—including the gods, our minds and souls, the Sun, the stars, and this world and possible other worlds—are composed of atoms that move about in space.

Atoms, Democritus says, are very small particles of solid matter, so small that they are never seen (they are "microscopic" long before microscopes). Atoms differ from one another only in size, shape, and rotation; these three qualities are infinite in their variety. Each atom is so solid, so fully packed with matter, that it cannot be cut or divided. The name "atom" (coined probably by Leukippos) is composed of the Greek alpha-negative *a*, meaning "not," and *tomos*, "cut"—hence, "not cuttable." Each atom is a complete little world in itself, ungenerated, indestructible, irreducible, unchangeable, and indivisible.

As these atoms move about, Aristotle wrote, "they tend to get ensnarled and interlocked. . . . When these substances remain joined for some time, it is explained by the fact that they fit snugly and so catch firm hold of one another; for some bodies are scalene while others are sharply hooked, some are concave, others convex, and there are numerous other differences." Iron atoms, for example, are hooked and jagged, giving iron its roughness and strength. Democritus theorized that atoms "cling together and remain in certain combinations until they are shaken apart and separated by outside forces."[13] When like atoms come together, they produce elemental substances such as water and air; when unlike atoms come together, they produce compounds, mixtures, objects, and systems. Water atoms, round and smooth, roll over one another (like ball bearings or small beads); this imparts to water its liquid quality, its wetness.

These atoms are eternally in motion, colliding, rebounding, and joining. They are without beginning or end, as is their motion. Democritus did not address the original source of the motion or its direction; Epicurus later pondered the problem of direction and concluded that, since he lived on a flat Earth, all atoms fall vertically because of their weight.

The reason he[Democritus] gives for atoms staying together for a while is the intertwining and mutual hold of the primary bodies; for some [atoms] are angular, some hooked, some concave, some convex, and indeed with countless other differences; so he thinks they cling to each other and stay together until such time as some stronger necessity comes from the surrounding and shakes and scatters them apart.

SIMPLICIUS

EPISTEMOLOGY

We cannot see atoms, of course. We instead perceive gross clusters of atoms, Democritus theorized, and when enough atoms cling together, we then perceive not the atoms but such qualities as colors, sweet and sour, hot and cold, roughness and smoothness. But since atoms are all composed of the same substance, these qualities we experience are clearly not properties of atoms themselves. Atoms are necessarily devoid of qualities.

Where, then, are the familiar qualities of experience located? Are they in any way real—that is, are they in some way intrinsic to atoms? Or are they the products of subjective operations? Democritus theorized that the atoms produce qualities in their clustering. Qualities are in some sense real; they inhere in the clusters, and the mind does not produce them. But how do the clusters create such a great variety of qualitative experiences? By their varied shapes and arrangements. Round and soft atoms produce in us sweet tastes. Sourness is produced in us by atoms that are "angular, tiny, thin, and twisted. By its sharpness it slips in and penetrates everywhere, by its angular roughness it draws the parts [of the tongue] together and binds them." All qualities of experience are thus properties not of atoms but of clusters of atoms.

A century later Theophrastos (Aristotle's successor as scholar of the Lyceum) added his interpretation.

> As for other sensory qualities [Democritus] argues that none has objective reality, but that all of them are effects of our sensuous faculty as it undergoes alteration; it is bodily alteration that produces images. Nor does he regard hot and cold as having an objective nature; they are merely a matter of configuration [of the clusters of atoms]. What we experience as qualitative change within ourselves is the effect of incoming atomic configurations being massed together so as to produce intensity of effect. What is massed together [on entering our sense organs] prevails [as a conscious experience].[14]

It follows that our senses are not trustworthy for knowing reality because (1) what is truly real can't be perceived; the atoms, that is, are invisible; and (2) what we receive from our senses are perceptions of qualities not intrinsic to the atoms. Since nothing exists in reality but atoms in space, reality is inaccessible to human perception. "By this criterion man must conclude that he is cut off from reality."[15] So Democritus may have made the earliest attempt to distinguish "appearance" from "reality" as two separate realms of events.

If our senses cannot give us trustworthy knowledge of the real world, then how can it be achieved? Democritus wrote of two kinds of knowledge:

> the one genuine, the other obscure. Obscure knowledge includes everything that is given by sight, hearing, smell, taste, touch. . . . Whenever [an investigation reaches the point where] obscure knowledge can no longer see the objects because of their smallness, and also cannot hear or smell or taste them nor perceive them by touch [the investigator must then have recourse] to a finer means of knowing.[16]

This "finer means" is the rational intellect. It has its own handicap, to be sure, since it must work with raw material the senses provide, an inescapable condition. Democritus illustrates the point with a short exchange between the intellect and the senses:

INTELLECT: It is by convention that color exists, by convention sweet, by convention bitter.

One must learn by this rule that man is severed from reality.
DEMOCRITUS

It is shameful to be so busy over the affairs of others that one knows nothing of one's own.
DEMOCRITUS

I would rather discover one cause than possess the kingdom of Persia.
DEMOCRITUS

Each man is a microcosmic universe.
DEMOCRITUS

SENSES: Ah, wretched intellect, you get your evidence only as we give it to you, and yet you try to overthrow us. That overthrow will be your downfall.[17]

How is perception of objects possible? Democritus's rational speculations developed a theory (drawing on ideas from Leukippos that will later be elaborated in detail by Epicurus)° that objects give off continuous physical images that move instantly through the air and compress the air in front of the eye, leaving the real object's imprint on the fluid within the eye. He argued that "vision is produced by the impact of these images upon the eyes."[18] From these filmy pictures, we then can develop a trustworthy understanding of nature's component matter, as well as its behavior. Therefore, to summarize, Democritus was convinced that knowledge of the world is a possibility, but it can be achieved only when the intellect reflects critically on the incoherent data the senses provide.

SOUL, FIRE, AND LIFE

All living things have souls, and, like everything else, souls are composed of atoms, Democritus says. Soul atoms, especially fine, round, and smooth, are so small they can penetrate aggregates of larger atoms and diffuse themselves throughout the body cluster. (Aristotle likens this theory to a story of how Daedalus once brought to life a wooden statue of Aphrodite by pouring mercury into it.) "Democritus declares that the soul is a sort of fire or heat," he says. "For the atomic shapes are unlimited, and those which are spherical he says make up fire and soul. They are like the so-called motes in the air which show themselves as sunbeams entering our windows. Such seeds taken all together, he says, are the constituent elements of the whole of nature."[19] These spherical atoms, as both fire and soul, set everything in motion. "He reasons that soul and mind are the same thing," Aristotle notes. "Since the shape which is most susceptible of motion is the spherical, it is of this shape that the atoms of mind and of fire consist."[20] When breathed in, they invade the body's tissues, thereby providing life and consciousness to the organs and to the organism as a whole. They perform different functions in different organs, enabling the brain to think thoughts, the heart to feel anger, the liver to feel desire.

When the quantity of soul atoms diminishes, the deficiency first lowers consciousness into sleep (we breathe in the soul atoms slowly and shallowly when sleeping), then into a coma, and finally into death. Soul atoms are constantly replenished as we inhale; when we die the renewal ceases, and our soul atoms disperse again into the atmosphere. Democritus concludes, quite reasonably, that the soul cannot be immortal.°

COSMOLOGY

The universe composed of atoms and space extends infinitely in all directions. At some time in the distant past, Democritus says, large masses of atoms accumulated in a great vortex. In a whirling maelstrom, the atoms collided and clumped together, and as they revolved around the center, the lighter atoms retreated "out to remote space." Atoms differentiated "as though they had been passed through a sieve." The heavier atoms sank to the vortex center and clustered together, and "this is how the Earth came into being." Other great blobs of atoms spun around in the whirling vortex and became the stars and other heavenly bodies, the Sun the farthest away and the Moon the nearest.

Since the cosmos is infinite, this vortical process must have occurred many or perhaps an infinite number of times. Our world cannot be unique. Countless other

---

Men find happiness neither by means of the body nor through possessions, but through uprightness and wisdom.

DEMOCRITUS

°See pp. 234ff.

One should emulate the deeds and actions of virtue, not the words.

DEMOCRITUS

Pleasure and absence of pleasure are the criteria of what is profitable and what is not.

DEMOCRITUS

°Compare Aristotle's conclusion on immortality, p. 186.

worlds must necessarily exist at the centers of an infinite number of vortices. Some of these worlds may possess suns and moons, and some, with sufficient water, may even sustain life.

ETHICS

Although we remember Democritus primarily for his atomic physics, he also pondered ethical problems and developed an innovative ethical system. His physics implies a mechanistic world with everything happening because it must; every event has a cause and effects a predictable result. It comes as a surprise, therefore, that he developed an ethical system that assumes free will and teaches moral responsibility, though it is not entirely clear how he arrives at his conclusions. He may have inferred the idea of freedom from the slipperiness of the all-penetrating soul atoms. In any case, he held that we humans can make meaningful choices, and the goal we should aim at is a life of well-being and cheerfulness. "Cheerfulness is experienced by men when pleasures are tempered and life becomes a harmonious existence." Central to Democritus's thinking is the time-honored belief in temperance, discretion, and self-control (*sôphrosynê*), so important to all Greek ethics. "Moderation multiplies our pleasures and increases our pleasure." The good life is to be achieved by avoiding pain and seeking pleasure—not the sensual pleasures, which, he says, are short lived and self-defeating, but the soul's more ethereal pleasures. A sense of well-being is not dependent on wealth, social standing, or any worldly achievements but on enriching the soul, cultivating the long-lasting pleasures, and meditating on noble thoughts. To accomplish this, one must be wise, and wisdom, Democritus would have said, is the capacity to distinguish actions that will enrich the soul from those that cannot.°

THE ATOMIST LEGACY

The philosophical significance of Democritus's work resides principally in three of his insights: (1) in his sharp distinction between the knower and the known; (2) in his mechanistic, value-free worldview; and (3) in his foundations for a philosophic humanism.

First, he made it clear we do not perceive the true realities. Only atoms and space are real, and neither possesses the familiar qualities of experience, such as colors, hot and cold, and sweet and sour. Hence the real world and the world of human experience are separate and distinct realms of activity. If this scenario is accurate, then it follows that our senses are, at face value, untrustworthy, and our pursuit of the truth about reality must proceed beyond sense experience. Appearance never can be a final guide as to what is "out there" in the world. With this, Democritus set in place the foundation stone for the development of all the empirical sciences. Today, the heaviest burden weighing upon modern investigation is still the problem of finding ways to move beyond both perception and static intellectual structures to an ever more precise knowledge of (in Feynman's words) "what in hell's going on out there."

Second, Democritus attempts to account for everything as the result of the interactions of atoms and space. Since "atoms and the void alone exist in reality," the world is a stage on which actions and events are played out "according to necessity." No gods exist to push matter around, and no logos or Mind energizes cosmic ingredients to assume structure and order; the world is not surging toward the future, driven by some intrinsic urge to better itself; and no value priorities, as precious as they are to us humans, exist to instruct atoms in the best ways to tangle. Atomic

Magnanimity consists in enduring tactlessness with mildness.

DEMOCRITUS

°*Epicurus dedicated his life to the development of the pleasure-pain ethic; see pp. 238ff.*

If any man listens to my opinions, here recorded, with intelligence, he will achieve many things worthy of a good man, and avoid doing many unworthy things.

DEMOCRITUS

If one oversteps the due measure [sôphrosynê], the most pleasurable things become most unpleasant.

DEMOCRITUS

One should choose not every pleasure, but only that concerned with the beautiful.

DEMOCRITUS

People are fools who live without enjoyment in life.

DEMOCRITUS

There are two sorts of knowledge, one genuine, one bastard (or obscure). To the latter belong all the following: sight, hearing, smell, taste, touch.

DEMOCRITUS

Sweet exists by convention, bitter by convention, colour by convention; atoms and Void (alone) exist in reality.

DEMOCRITUS

On Democritus *Everything happens according to necessity; for the cause of the coming-into-being of all things is the whirl, which he calls necessity.*

AËTIUS

It has been demonstrated more than once that we do not discover by direct perception what the nature of each thing is or is not.

DEMOCRITUS

For all men, good and true are the same; but pleasant differs for different men.

DEMOCRITUS

By convention there is sweet, by convention there is bitter, by convention hot and cold, by convention color; but in reality there are only atoms and the void.

DEMOCRITUS

The great pleasures come from the contemplation of noble works.

DEMOCRITUS

Cheerfulness is created for men through moderation of enjoyment and harmoniousness of life.

DEMOCRITUS

interactions involve no wrongs and rights, no good ways and bad ways to combine. Everything just is. This is precisely the worldview of modern science, but it was completely abandoned with the demise of Atomism; the ascendence of Platonism, Neoplatonism, and the religious idealisms of the Dark Ages; and Scholasticism. In the third century AD an angry Christian bishop named Hippolytos also reacted to Democritus, saying, "This man ridiculed everything—as if all human concerns were absurd!" Only with the work of the seventeenth-century critical philosophers, and especially Galileo, did this recognition return to enable empirical exploration of the world to get back on track. Two thousand years was a long halftime in what could have been a rousing good game.

Third, it also was two millennia before the seeds of a rich humanism could bear existential fruit. If meaning and values were not to be found in the impersonal oscillations of physical events, then, obviously, they must be "human things." Values turn out to be human, not cosmic, concerns. The seasons arrive, leaves fall, and life ceases but turns green again (hopefully) with the advent of spring, and human life proceeds with its rounds of birth and death in a similar way. If the value of a human life is of no more interest to the Great Machine than the falling of a leaf, then it rests with humans alone to give their lives value. Goodness, Truth, and Beauty may not characterize atoms, but they can be vital qualities of a human existence that possesses capacities for experiencing the good, the true, and the beautiful.

Moreover, this Democritean humanism makes a rare offer to individuals to exploit their uniqueness. Democritus recognized individual differences to a degree not found with any other early thinker and that was anathema to Socrates and Plato. He noted that experiences such as sweet, bitter, cold, and hot cannot exist in nature because "they don't appear the same to all living creatures, but rather that what is sweet to us is bitter to others, and to still others sour or pungent or astringent." He goes on to point out that people's bodily condition, which changes with age, also affects how they experience reality.

Is it any wonder, then, Plato was ready to pile the books high and light the torch? With blood and many tears he had labored to construct a universe humans were at home in and to which they could be intimately connected in a mysticism of intellect. When humans had thoughts, they would be thinking Real Ideas embedded universally in the structure of the world. Above all, Plato said, humanity should strive to become one with the "form of the Good," implying that values are built into the nature of things. Moreover, the world is in its essence mind (or spirit), not matter.

Furthermore, Plato followed Socrates in despising Sophist relativism. Democritus's recognition that perceptions vary from person to person would have smelled to him like the Sophistic teaching that "man is the measure of all things." Socrates and his pupil both spent their lives seeking the abstract and the universal, which alone qualified to be called knowledge. Individual differences were anathema to both men.

Lastly, what could have upset Plato more than Democritus's teaching that the goal of life is pleasure and that the rational intellect's proper role is to calculate how to obtain the greatest pleasures?

Plato was dissuaded from carrying out his threat only because Democritus's writings were so widely circulated they couldn't be collected for a book-burning.[21]

ENDNOTES

1 Drew A. Hyland, *The Origins of Philosophy* (G. P. Putman's Sons, 1973), p. 285.
2 Xenophon, *Memorabilia*, 1.1.14.
3 Xenophon, *Memorabilia*, 1.1.16.

4 John Burnet, *Early Greek Philosophy*, 4th ed. (1930), pp. 333ff, in *The Greek Philosophers*, by Rex Warner (Mentor, 1958), p. 47 .

5 Aristotle, *On Generation and Corruption*, 235a, 23.

6 Diogenes Laërtius, *Lives of Eminent Philosophers*, IX.30–33.

7 Diogenes, *Lives*, IX.34–49.

8 Philip Wheelwright, *The Presocratics* (Odyssey Press, 1966), p. 186, frag. 299.

9 Diogenes, *Lives*, IX.37.

10 Diogenes, *Lives*, IX.40.

11 Wheelwright, *The Presocratics*, p. 183.

12 Diogenes, *Lives*, IX.43.

13 From Aristotle's lost work *On Democritus*, preserved by Simplicius, in Wheelwright, *The Presocratics*, p. 187.

14 Theophrastus, *On the Senses*, I.61, in Wheelwright, *The Presocratics*, pp. 197f.

15 Wheelwright, *The Presocratics*, p. 182, frag. 2.

16 Wheelwright, *The Presocratics*, p. 183, frag. 11.

17 Wheelwright, *The Presocratics*, p. 183, frag. 125.

18 Diogenes, *Lives*, IX.44.

19 Aristotle, *On the Soul*, 406b, 15, 404a, 1, in Wheelwright, *The Presocratics*, pp. 188f. (T13).

20 Aristotle, *On the Soul*, 405a, 5, in Wheelwright, *The Presocratics*, p. 190 (T16).

21 I have here followed Drew Hyland's analysis of the question "Why should Plato have found the atomists' philosophy so distasteful?"; see his *Origins of Philosophy*, p. 285.

THE
GOLDEN AGE
OF
GREEK
PHILOSOPHY

THE SEARCH FOR
THE TRUTH OF THINGS

PART

2

CHAPTER 8

SOCRATES OF THE AGORA

Sophist educators bring education to the general public; they teach the relativity of everything and give a new twist to truth, morality, and legal theory; the "wisest man in all Hellas" goes for a higher truth, offends about everyone, defends himself at a famous trial, and pays the price.

WHERE TO BUY GROCERIES

Xenophon tells of the time he came across Socrates in the narrow, winding streets of Athens. Socrates stopped him and asked, "Where does one go to buy groceries?" Xenophon gave him directions but was then asked, "And where does one go to learn to become an honest man?" When no answer was forthcoming, Socrates beckoned: "Come with me, and I'll show you."[1]

Socrates was put to death with a cup of hemlock almost twenty-four hundred years ago, yet he is remarkably contemporary in spirit, his concerns are as vital as ever, and his courage still inspires. His appearance alone remains intriguing. Aristophanes says he walked like a "proud marsh-goose" and rolled his eyes while speaking. Plato says his gaze reminded him of a bull. Menon tells him to his face, "Your looks and the rest of you are exactly like a flatfish, and you sting like a stingray." In his Symposium Xenophon has Socrates saying, "My flat nose flares so as to receive smells from all sides." Some thought he was ugly, and the story was told that once in battle with the Thebans at Delium he helped save the day by glaring at the enemy. To his face Theodorus told him that, "with his snub nose and protruding eyes," handsome he is not. He resembled a satyr, Alcibiades says, or the figures of Silenus found in the stone-carvers' shop windows: broad face, round mouth, thick lips, heavy beard, wisps of gray hair fringing a balding dome—all set atop a robust, stocky torso that was built like an ox and as strong as two, but with a budding paunch that, he confessed, he wanted to reduce by dancing. Alcibiades was making a nobler point, however: Socrates is like the little statues of the Silens that, "when their two halves are pulled open, are found to contain images of the gods inside."

This was the man who could outwrestle the strongest athletes, outfight the hardiest foot-soldiers, outdrink the dippiest wine bibbers, and outthink the brightest minds of Hellas.

On Socrates There is, he said, only one good, that is, knowledge, and only one evil, that is, ignorance.

XENOPHON

Socrates of the Agora (469–399 BC), playing midwife, gave birth to the intellectual tradition in the western world.

THE SOPHISTS

Socrates' life and calling must be viewed against the background of the intellectual climate of the late fifth century BC. While he was still a young man, a new movement arose in Greek education, and it was in terms of this movement, and against it, that all three great Athenian philosophers—Socrates, Plato, and Aristotle—defined themselves. The leaders of this movement, called Sophists, were itinerant teachers, offering courses in a wide range of practical arts and skills. They would arrive in a city, rent a lecture hall, publicize a course they wanted to offer, enroll students, collect fees, and, for a few weeks, lecture their students through the course. Then they would move on to the next town. Sophism was an honorable profession, and many of the Sophists were able minds and good teachers. "If he comes to me he will learn that which he comes to learn," the Sophist Protagoras assured his clients.

The Sophist movement had arisen to fill a vacuum. One cause of that vacuum had to do with the bankruptcy of the presocratic enterprise. Early attempts at serious philosophic inquiry had focused on the nature and operations of the physical world, but they had apparently come to nought. To the first critical scientific questions about nature, too many conflicting answers had been arrived at, and they mutually canceled out. Presocratic thinking, therefore, had undermined confidence in the human intellect's ability to gain a foothold in the operations of nature. Socrates himself, well versed in the natural sciences, had given up on them, and Plato concluded that knowledge of nature could never be anything but "a likely story." The resulting skepticism was well summarized in the teaching of the Sophist Gorgias: "Nothing exists," he said, "but if it did exist, we couldn't know it; and even if we could know it, we couldn't communicate it."

The changing needs of Greek education and the needs of a general populace living in a democracy also fostered the Sophist movement. In the sixth century BC, education was limited to the noble and affluent and aimed at producing political and military leaders who could defend the state. To this end young men were taught to fear the traditional gods, obey the laws, and develop themselves physically and morally. When a young man was age sixteen, the state took charge of his education and prepared him for full citizenship. He learned its laws, attended public debates and jury trials, and undertook a program of vigorous physical training. At age eighteen he was presented to the state as a candidate for citizenship and, if accepted, was given spear and shield and an oath of loyalty. At this point his "higher education" began, consisting of two years of intensive military training and service in the field.

All this changed almost overnight. With the defeat of the Persian army at the Battles of Marathon (490 BC) and Plataea (479 BC) and the annihilation of Xerxes' navy at Salamis (480 BC), the threat of war receded and the need for military preparedness came to an end. A "Golden Age" began that lasted for more than a half century and witnessed spectacular achievements in architecture, ceramics and sculpture, drama, coinage, commerce, engineering, and myriad other arts. Everyone experienced new freedoms and opportunities. Gymnastics for personal development largely replaced physical training for the military. New forms of literature replaced older patriotic epics. The seven-stringed lyre and traditional chorus gave way to new musical instruments and forms. New courses were introduced into schools' curricula at every level. Inevitably, higher education became humanized and was perceived increasingly as an accessible channel for vocational training, business opportunity, and personal pleasure and fulfillment.

The Sophists entered this educational vacuum with a new goal: to teach the practical arts. Instead of pursuing grandiose dreams of comprehending the cosmos, they taught courses in rhetoric—how to speak clearly and persuasively; in grammar—how to speak and write good Greek; and in eristics—how to conduct and win arguments in public debates and courts of law. Obviously, if citizens became involved in litigation, the ability to defend their case before a jury of peers could make the difference between winning and losing, or—as with Socrates—between life and death.

I myself know nothing, except just a little, enough to extract an argument from another man who is wise and to receive it fairly.

SOCRATES

With regard to the gods, I cannot feel sure either that they are or that they are not, nor what they are like in figure; for there are many things that hinder sure knowledge, the obscurity of the subject and the shortness of human life.

PROTAGORAS

Learning requires both natural endowment and self-discipline. It has to begin when one is young. It does not take root in the soul unless it goes deep.

PROTAGORAS

On Protagoras *Protagoras was the first to declare that there are two opposing sides to every question, and he was the first to build arguments on that basis.*

DIOGENES LAËRTIUS

The Sophists taught the art of how to succeed in life and how to be a responsible free citizen of a democracy. Free citizens run for office, and for this they need the ability to speak clearly and knowledgeably. The Sophists were convinced success required a full liberal arts education, and this some of them tried to provide. Their curriculum included courses in literature, mathematics and geometry, architecture, drawing, political science, oratory, and music.

The names of some thirty of these wandering Sophists survive, and their cosmopolitanism is striking; they came from the far reaches of Hellas. Protagoras, the greatest, was born and raised in Abdera in northern Greece. Gorgias, his pupil, was a native of Leontini on the western Mediterranean island of Sicily. Prodicos was from Ceos, an Aegean island in the Cyclades, while Hippias came from Êlis in southern Greece. Thrasymachos was from Chalcedon in Asia Minor. But all cultural roads led to Athens, so it became the Sophist movement's center of operations.

Nothing exists; but if it did, we couldn't know it; and if we could know it, we couldn't communicate our knowledge of it.

GORGIAS

SOPHISTRY

Attitudes toward the Sophists changed drastically during the fifth century BC. In the sixth century "sophist" referred to poets, seers, and sages—those who symbolized practical wisdom, such as the "Seven Sages of Hellas." Soon after 450 BC, during the Sophist movement's heyday, the word came to mean one who professed knowledge of a specialized subject. *Sophos* meant skilled in a chosen field; and a *sophistês* was one who had mastered his craft or art and taught it professionally. The word carried with it overtones of honor and respect, somewhat like our modern use of the term "professor."

By the end of the century, however, "Sophist" was no longer a title of respect. The Sophists had fallen into disrepute and *sophist* had come to mean shallow, argumentative, quarrelsome, and dishonest; more than that, it carried the connotation of one who would defend any point of view for money and therefore lacked moral backbone. This is *sophistry* in its worst sense, and it still carries this meaning today: using one's reasoning ability to engage in devious, petty, and self-serving argumentation.

Why did the meaning of *sophist* undergo such a change? A variety of causes have been cited. The Sophists became too closely associated with the affluent classes and abandoned the average citizen who couldn't pay their exorbitant fees; they also became associated with shady deals connected with lawyers and law courts. They specialized in arguing all sides of a case or all sides of a moral issue without taking a stand on what was legally just or morally right, and they "corrupted" the youth of Athens by teaching them to question tradition and to critically judge society's ideas and values. Socrates and Plato castigated them for taking fees and thereby prostituting themselves to the highest bidder.

[Prodicos described the Sophist as being] on the borderline between a philosopher and a politician.

EUTHYDEMUS

All these indictments were valid and contributed to the Sophists' bad reputation. They came to represent a viewpoint devoid of content—all form and no substance. They taught their students to speak well, not to think well. Whether in the Olympic games or in law courts, winning was the only criterion of virtue, or success; whether the game was honestly played wasn't a consideration. "Justice is merely the advantage of the stronger," Thrasymachos said; might makes right, and no further dialogue can occur about the question of fairness under the law. Likewise in ethics, all is relative: Whatever a society holds as morally right or wrong *is* right or wrong for that society; no universal "truth" exists for judging and nullifying any society's moral values. In fact, no universal truth exists about anything. Everyone must be judged on his performance style: Does he *project* the right image? Does he *appear* self-confident in the debate? Do his arguments *sound* persuasive? Does he *deliver* the poem well? Does he *appear* to be honest and moral? Is he *perceived* as an upright, law-abiding citizen? Does he *seem* sincere? Perception was everything, and appearance was the only virtue.

Whatever the causes of this intellectual emptiness, by Socrates' time "Sophist" was no longer the honored profession it had been. Socrates said the Sophists have "lots of color but no truth." He wanted nothing to do with them and took pains to avoid identification with them. If to most Athenians Socrates bore the appearance of a Sophist, however, they can be forgiven. He argued like a Sophist, often becoming punctilious in cutting to the fine detail of a dispute, quite beyond the average citizen's intellectual capacities; and it seemed to casual listeners that, like the Sophists, he could take any side of an issue and back his opponent into a corner.

Resemblances notwithstanding, Socrates and his biographer Plato were keenly aware of the gulf that distanced them from the Sophists. Socrates charged no fees. He sought the truth. To them values are *not* relative. One idea is *not* as good as another. Winning is *not* everything: Virtue lies not in winning but in preserving one's self-respect and integrity in the process of playing the game. It is more important to *be* honest than merely to *appear* honest. It is more important to *think* clearly than to *speak* eloquently. Truth is neither relative nor limited to what one society or another *believes* to be true. Goodness, truth, and beauty exist—not just various opinions about them.

Socrates didn't entirely succeed in distancing himself from the Sophists. About 423 BC Aristophanes—a devoted follower who later turned against Socrates—staged a play called the *Clouds*. In it Socrates appears as a sizzling Sophist with his own "think tank" ("The Thinkery") and band of followers, engaging in obscene dialogue and exhibiting his familiar banter and quirks. Aristophanes mocked Socrates "for making the worse appear the better reason." Clearly Socrates was well known to the audiences who saw the play, and in their minds they took for granted his close association with the Sophists.

> On Socrates . . . *two things may be fairly ascribed to Socrates— inductive arguments and universal definition, both of which are concerned with the starting-point of science.*
>
> ARISTOTLE

PROTAGORAS

By all accounts Protagoras of Abdera was the first who declared himself a professional moneymaking *sophistês* (he charged a hundred minae for one lecture course). He wrote voluminously, though none of his work survives. The range of his learning was widely respected. Among his lost books were *The Art of Winning Arguments*, *On Wrestling*, and *On Mathematics;* works on ethics (ambition, virtue, moral evil); a book of quotable sayings; and his most significant work, *A Book for Legal Advocates, with Opposing Sets of Arguments.* He was a speaker of impressive eloquence, even though, at times, he could be long-winded. Plato was convinced that beyond his glibness his thinking was not profound, but then Plato was not naturally predisposed to appreciate anything connected with the Sophists. Still, generations of students sat spellbound at his oratory and admired his financial success; he amassed a fortune from teaching and writing.

Diogenes Laërtius tells a charming story of him, quite in character even if apocryphal. Protagoras attempted to collect a fee from a student he had made an agreement with: He would collect only if the student won his first case. "But I haven't pleaded my first case yet!" "Very well, then," Protagoras answered, "I will sue you, and if I win you will have to pay me by the judgment of the court, whereas if you win you will have to pay me by the terms of our agreement." So, the master's logic

> *Man is the measure of all things: of things that are, that they are; of things that are not, that they are not.*
>
> PROTAGORAS

[Plato has Protagoras saying] I claim that whatever seems right and honourable to a state is really right and honourable to it, so long as it believes it to be so.

THEAETETUS

triumphs. But that wasn't the end of the story according to Apuleius, who adds the following: "Whatever the outcome of the suit," the student countered, "I am freed of having to pay what you demand. For either I win the case and thus am cleared by the court's decree, or I am beaten and thus am cleared by the terms of our original bargain."[2] (The teacher had taught and the student had learned.)

The major motif of Protagoras's teaching was summarized in lines that opened one of his works (now lost): "Man is the measure of all things: of things that are, that they are; of things that are not, that they are not." Plato recorded what he thought Protagoras was saying in his dialogue the *Theaetetus*. The following exchange is between Socrates and a brilliant young mathematician named Theaetetus (who, later in his career, became a teacher on the staff of Plato's Academy).

> SOCRATES: Well, he [Protagoras] means something like this, doesn't he—that particular things are for me just what they appear to me to be, and are for you just what they appear to you to be. For you and I are men.
> Theaetetus: Yes, that is surely what he means.
> SOCRATES: Then, since so wise a man is not likely to be talking nonsense, let us pursue his meaning. It is sometimes the case, isn't it, that one of us feels cold while the other, although blown by the same wind, does not? Or that one of us feels mildly chilly while the other feels very cold?
> THEAETETUS: That is true.
> SOCRATES: And when such a situation occurs are we to describe the wind itself as cold or not cold? Or shall we accept Protagoras' solution, that it is cold for him who feels it cold and is not cold for him who does not feel it so?
> THEAETETUS: The latter, I should think.
> SOCRATES: And it does in fact sometimes appear cold to one observer and not cold to another simultaneously?
> THEAETETUS: Yes.
> SOCRATES: In the case of qualities like warm and cold, do "it appears" and "it is perceived" have the same meaning?
> THEAETETUS: Evidently so.
> SOCRATES: Protagoras means, then, that perception is always of something existent, and that the knowledge which it imparts is infallible?
> THEAETETUS: That seems clear.[3]

This dialogue contains one of the first treatments of the relativity of sense perception. Protagoras makes the critical distinction between the real and the experiential. When we say "It is cold" or "It is beautiful," Protagoras recognized that we aren't referring to any real object (despite the "it," which in English appears to refer to something "out there") but only to our *experience of* the object. "In this room I experience cold" (while you may experience hot); "When I look at this painting, I experience beauty" (while you may not)—and no contradiction of claims occurs. My perception, Protagoras is saying, is "true" for me, yours is for you, and that's the end of the matter.

But Protagoras carried this idea beyond sense perception. Later in Plato's dialogue, Protagoras is made to defend his own doctrine.

> My position, then, is that whatever seems right and admirable to a particular city-state is truly right and admirable—during the period of time in which that opinion continues to be held; and that it is the wise man's task, when the people are afflicted with unsound beliefs, to substitute others so that they seem true and therefore *are* true. . . . It is in this sense, and in this sense only, that some men are wiser than others; which does not affect the truth of the proposition that there is no such thing as thinking falsely.[4]

As far as it goes this relativism is true, of course. Societies do indeed live by different cultural, moral, and esthetic values, and they serve a useful pragmatic function in the culture that embodies them: They promote stability, continuity, and unity in the society; they provide a rallying point for group loyalty and defense; and shared values and assumptions make communication possible.

Sophistic teaching was firmly grounded on this relativism, and this doctrine was what so aroused Socrates' wrath.

SOCRATES: THE WISEST MAN ALIVE

THE GOLDEN AGE

With the appearance of Socrates in the latter half of the fifth century BC, a nobler attitude toward life and truth began to flourish. Socrates spent a lifetime teaching young men in their homes and conversing with ordinary citizens in the Agora, the crowded, busy marketplace just below the Acropolis. He attempted to get Athenian youth to realize that everyday thinking is too loose and shabby to solve the important problems of life. His pupil Plato carried on this Socratic tradition in his Academy two miles northeast of the Agora. Plato aimed at laying intellectual and moral foundations so that Athenian youth could rise to the demands of statesmanship: The world can have no peace, he believed, until statesmen are philosophers or philosophers become statesmen. Then Plato's pupil Aristotle taught for twelve years in his Lyceum a mile south of the Agora. He taught his students to search for the truth of things not primarily to make them statesmen, but because this is what would keep them human and lead to *eudaimonia*—"happiness."

With these three gifted men, what has been called the Golden Age of Greek philosophy emerged. It would not be wrong to say these three thinkers together rescued Greek philosophy from a decadent Sophistry and gave it to the world.

IN THE HISTORY OF PHILOSOPHY

One cannot help but feel a bit giddy when trying to state succinctly "what Socrates means"; he has meant so many different things to different people. Nevertheless, it is probably safe to say he will remain immortal (1) for inspiring Plato to pursue philosophy and philosophical writing; (2) for his trial and last hours, during which he demonstrated a courage derived from a lifetime practice of philosophy; (3) for "defining" philosophy as the search for wisdom through the pursuit of truth; (4) for believing that mature thinkers should delight in playing with ideas, an exciting enterprise he believed is the only path to knowledge and wisdom; (5) for a "Socratic method" that lets others talk until they reveal the truth to themselves; (6) for practicing "midwifery" whereby he helped others give birth to their own ideas; (7) for teaching an ethical individualism that required an individual to think for himself; (8) for insisting that if we know what is right, we will do what is right, and that this begins with knowledge of oneself; (9) for a "Socratic transcendence" that demands rising above the shabbiness of everyday thinking to a nobler contemplation of thought and feeling, as demonstrated by Socrates in the *Symposium*.

THE MAN

In the fourth year of the seventy-seventh Olympiad (469–468 BC), on the sixth day of Thargelion, Socrates was born in Athens. There he was raised, there he lived, and there he died in the first year of the ninety-fifth Olympiad (399 BC) at the age of seventy. He seems never to have travelled beyond the city walls except to fight with the

For man, the unexamined life is not worth living.

SOCRATES

(Inscribed on the Wall at Delphi) Gnothi Seauton: *Know thyself.*

My dear Criton, why should we pay so much attention to what "most people" think? The really reasonable people, who have more claim to be considered, will believe that the facts are exactly as they are.

SOCRATES

On Socrates *Xenophon's Socrates is bound to come across as one of those people who tell you how to live your life. This is particularly annoying when, like Socrates, they are "right."*

ROBIN WATERFIELD

Athenian army. His mother was a midwife named Phainaretê, his father a sculptor named Sophroniscos. Socrates followed in the footsteps of both: By trade he was a stonemason and sculptor, but his true calling, he said, was to be a midwife like his mother and help others give birth to their ideas. The comic poet Aristophanes adopted this metaphor and poked fun at Socrates: a midwife, yes, but too often he presided at miscarriages. Socrates already had employed the metaphor to chastise his pupils who became dropouts: "The offspring they brought forth with my help they have reared badly, and they lost them because they valued impostures and images more than the truth."[5]

Of his youth we know nothing. We have one passing note from Plutarch that an oracle told Socrates' father to "let the boy do whatever comes into his mind and do not restrain him, but give him his head, not bothering about him except to pray on his behalf to Zeus Agoraios and the Muses."[6] (But what father hasn't prayed for divine assistance in handling his headstrong offspring?)

Recent scholarship has suggested that we may in fact have some knowledge of Socrates' earlier intellectual development providing we take seriously Aristophanes' caricature of him in the *Clouds* and his own statement in Plato's *Phaedo* that attest to a dramatic change in his thinking that probably occurred during his early forties.[7] In contrast to the presocratic philosophers, Socrates turned to human concerns and by doing so wrought a revolution in philosophy. He "first called philosophy down from heaven," according to Cicero, "set her in the cities, introduced her into men's homes, and compelled her to investigate life and customs, good and evil."

All indications are that during his earlier years Socrates was dedicated to studying the natural sciences, which he had learned from his teacher Archelaus and from the works of Diogenes of Apollonia. Although Aristophanes was a close friend to Socrates, he satirizes Socrates unmercifully as a fuzzy-minded Sophist and half-baked practitioner of the physical sciences. This picture of Socrates coincides with his own recollections in the *Phaedo*, where he confides it was "glorious" to know the causes of things, to understand why things are generated and decay, and why things exist at all. But in the end, he says, after investigating everything in heaven and on Earth, "I came at last to decide that I was by nature not fit at all for this investigation."[8] From that time on Socrates devoted his energies to analyzing human problems and to the practical application of insights to the lives of his students and the people in the Agora he talked with each day.

About midlife he was married to Xanthippe, a woman remembered (quite unfairly because of Xenophon's harsh portrayal of her) as a shrew. More than likely, she was a conventional, if assertive, hausfrau and mother, making do with Socrates' constant absenteeism. Living with Socrates would have been enormously difficult, and her complaints are understandable since Socrates (like all Greek husbands) spent virtually all his time away from home in the company of young men, partying, working out, and philosophizing. Nor was he much of a breadwinner. A contemporary poet commented that Socrates had "thought everything out but ignored the problem of how to provide himself with funds." The records clearly indicate they had an adversarial marriage. Socrates said he endured Xanthippe just so he could develop self-discipline. Diogenes Laërtius recalls the time when Xanthippe "tore off his cloak in the Agora and his friends urged him to hit her back." Socrates replied, "Oh sure, so that while we scrap you can cheer us on with 'Go to it, Socrates! Another right to the jaw!' or 'Right on, Xanthippe!' No way," he said. She once told him "he suffered unjustly," and he retorted, "Why, would you have me suffer justly?" Once when Xanthippe scolded him and then drenched him with water, he said, "Did I not say that Xanthippe's thunder would end in rain?" The young Alcibiades once remarked that

I am that gadfly which God has attached to the State, and all day long and in all places am always fastening upon you, arousing and persuading and reproaching you.

SOCRATES

On Socrates By showing that what is without intelligence is without value, [Socrates] was appealing to people to take pains to be as intelligent and helpful as possible.

XENOPHON

I am a sort of bag full of arguments.

SOCRATES

Xanthippe's scoldings must be intolerable. Socrates replied, "I've got used to it, as one does to the constant rattle of a windlass. And after a while you don't mind the cackle of geese." "Perhaps," responded Alcibiades, "but geese furnish me with eggs and goslings." "And Xanthippe," Socrates reminded him, "is the mother of my children."

Socrates and Xanthippe had three sons, Lamprocles, Sophroniscus, and Menexenus.[9]° At the time of Socrates' death, the oldest was about age seventeen, and the youngest was still "in arms" when brought to visit his father in prison.

A LIFE OF DIALECTIC

Socrates believed the only path to knowledge was through discussion of ideas, so he spent his life conversing with followers in their homes and with friends and bystanders casually encountered in the marketplace. Diogenes says he engaged "keenly in argument with anyone who would converse with him, his aim being not to alter his opinion but to get at the truth." Socrates said he hoped to continue this trade even in Hadês° to find out "who is wise and who pretends to be wise but isn't." His dialogues were brilliant, entertaining, stimulating, and intimidating. He rarely closed a conversation without his listeners' becoming aware that they really didn't know, quite, what they were talking about.

Socrates spent nearly half a century carrying on dialogues very like the following exchange with one of his pupils. Here Socrates has asked the young Euthydemus whether he knows what "morality" is and whether he can judge accurately what acts are morally right and wrong.

"Look here," said Socrates, "shall we write an R here and a W there, and put down whatever we think is a right thing to do under R and what we think is wrong under W?"

"Sure, why not?"

Socrates wrote the letters as he had suggested, and then said, "Is there such a thing in human life as telling lies?"

"Of course there is."

"On which side shall we put that?"

"Obviously under Wrong."

"Is there such a thing as deception?"

"Certainly."

"On which side shall we put that?"

"That too under Wrong."

"What about doing harm?"

"That too."

"And enslaving?"

"That too."

"And shall we list none of these under Right, Euthydemus?"

"No, that would be shocking."

"Well now, suppose that a man who has been appointed to a military command reduces a wicked and hostile city to slavery, shall we say that he is acting wrongly?"

"No, of course not."

"Shall we not say that he is acting rightly?"

"Certainly. He's doing his job."

"And supposing that, in fighting against them, he deceives them?"

"That is right too."

"And if he steals and plunders their possessions, shall he not be acting rightly?"

"Certainly," said Euthydemus. "I thought at first that you were asking about these actions only in relation to friends."

°It is not certain they were all Xanthippe's sons. A tradition exists that Socrates had two wives, Xanthippe and Myrto, daughter of Aristides the Just, and that Sophroniscus and Menexenus were sons of Myrto. Because of the wars, Athens suffered a shortage of men and had passed a decree permitting male citizens to marry one woman and have children by a second, and "Socrates accordingly did so," Diogenes says. See Diogenes Laërtius, Lives of Eminent Philosophers, II.26; see also II.36–37.

°Hadês, of course, is not the "hell" of Judeo-Christian theology. The Hadês of Greek myth is the "world below" where Pluto, Lord of the Underworld, with his Queen Persephone, reigns and presides over the judgment and punishment of wicked souls.

It is very inconsistent for a man who asserts that he cares for virtue to be constantly unfair in discussion.

SOCRATES

Socrates spent his entire life in the Agora, according to Xenophon, "for early in the morning he used to go to the walkways and gymnasia, to appear in the Agora as it filled up, and to be present whenever he could meet with the most people." Doing little more than carrying on conversations, he gave birth to ideas and inspired others to give an account of their thinking. Then he was charged with treason, tried in the Heliaia, imprisoned in two small cells at the southwest corner of the Agora, and executed there with poison hemlock in the spring of 399 BC.

On Socrates *He used to express his astonishment that the sculptors of marble statues should take pains to make the block of marble into a perfect likeness of a man, and should take no pains about themselves lest they should turn out [to be] mere blocks, and not men.*

DIOGENES LAËRTIUS

Nothing is what it appears to be.

SOCRATES

I am a most eccentric person and drive men to distraction.

SOCRATES

"So perhaps all the things that we have put under Wrong ought to be put under Right too."

"Well, it rather looks like it."

"Now that we have settled that, shall we revise our definition and say that it is right to do this sort of thing to enemies, but wrong to do it to friends, and that to the latter one should be as straightforward as possible. Is that what you wish?"

"Very much so," said Euthydemus.

"Well then," said Socrates, "supposing that a general sees that his forces are downhearted and issues a false statement that help is approaching, and by this falsehood restores the morale of his men. On which side shall we put this deceit?"

"Under Right, I think."

"And supposing that someone has a son who needs medical treatment but refuses to take his medicine. If the father surreptitiously gives him the medicine in his food and by this deceptive artifice restores him to health, where should we put this example of deceit?"

"I think in the same category—under Right."

"Well now, supposing that someone has a friend who is in a state of depression, and is afraid that he might take his own life; and supposing that he covertly or openly removes a sword or some other weapon from him—in which column should we put this?"

"Surely this ought to go under Right too."

"Do you mean that we ought not always to deal straightforwardly even with our friends?"

"Of course we shouldn't," said Euthydemus. "I'm revising my earlier statement, if that's all right."

"Well, that's much better than putting things in the wrong categories," said Socrates. . . .

"Well, Socrates, I've lost confidence in my answers. Everything that I said before seems to be different now from what I thought then."[10]

By the time Socrates leads his companions down such a dialectical path, it is obvious the simple-minded judgments of everyday life are inadequate for establishing clarity, communicating effectively, and solving our moral problems. Such conversations were always exploratory on Socrates' part, and the student was left confused so that, if he was intellectually alive, he would be forced to resolve that confusion by working through the problem, perhaps painfully, and coming to more honest answers. This is the method of a great teacher. Those who could learn learned, while those who still doggedly held to simplistic thinking were hurt, defensive, angry, and vengeful—in that order. Diogenes says Socrates "would take to task those who thought highly of themselves, proving them to be fools."

To all this Lord Bertrand Russell comments wryly: "Certainly, if he practised dialectic in the way described in the *Apology*, the hostility to him is easily explained: all the humbugs in Athens would combine against him."[11]

THE AGORA

Socrates spent much of his adult life in the Agora, a bustling marketplace only a block long on the north side of the Acropolis. It was a gathering place for Athenian citizens, and here they bought, sold, and traded; carried on the politics of governing; engaged in religious activities; and, above all, talked. (The word *agora* derives from the Greek verb *agoreuein*, "to speak" to a crowd, "to address," "to harangue"—to talk.") The poet Eubulus describes the minicosmos of the Agora: "You will find everything sold together in the same place in Athens: figs, witnesses to summonses, bunches of grapes, turnips, pears, apples, givers of evidence, roses, medlars, porridge, honey-combs, chick-peas, law-suits, beestings-puddings, myrtle, allotment-machines, irises, lambs, water-clocks, laws, indictments."[12] Once, after pondering such a variety of goods, Socrates' response was typical: "How many things there are that I don't need!"

Xenophon tells us Socrates was always a part of the crowds and that he loved it, "for early in the morning he used to go to the walkways and gymnasia, to appear in the Agora as it filled up, and to be present wherever he would meet with the most people." The Agora was Socrates' spiritual and intellectual home. On one rare occasion when he ventured outside the city walls of Athens, his friend Phaidros teased him: "How very strange you are, sir. You talk like a tourist rather than a native. You apparently never set foot in the country or go outside the city walls." Socrates doubtless smiled at his companion when he replied, "Forgive me, my dear friend. I am, you see, a lover of learning. The people in the city have something to teach me, but the fields and trees won't teach me anything."[13]

Here in the Agora Socrates participated in the public and political life of the young democracy. Meetings were held in the New Bouleuterion, and the members adjourned to the Tholos for breaks and meals. The Tholos was the temporary place of residence for those on duty in government. In the year 406–405 BC Socrates served a term as president of the Boulê, the council that readied legislation for the Assembly. But Socrates confesses a certain ineptness in practical politics, for when it came time for him to take a vote for the first time he didn't know how and was laughed at. He faced one serious crisis during his tenure in office. Athens suffered enormous losses of men and ships at Arginusae that year, and the angry citizens proceeded to condemn the nine commanding generals as a group, not individually as required by law. Xenophon tells us that Socrates, "serving in the Boulê and having sworn the bouleutic oath [that he would uphold the law], and being in charge in the Assembly, when the People wished to put all nine generals to death by a single vote contrary to the laws, [Socrates] refused to put the vote. . . . He considered it more important to keep his oath than to please the People by doing wrong."[14] Life under the Thirty tyrants was equally dangerous. In the *Apology* Socrates himself° tells us that he and four other citizens were summoned to the Tholos and ordered to arrest a citizen, Leon of Salamis, and bring him in for execution so they could confiscate his property. Socrates

Bad men live that they may eat and drink, whereas good men eat and drink that they may live.

SOCRATES

°That is, as Plato remembers and reconstructs the account; for the nature of Plato's dialogues, and their dependability, see pp. 138ff.

flatly refused to obey the order and went home. "Perhaps I would myself have been put to death because of this if the regime had not soon been overthrown."[15]

Socrates' criticism of his culture and his government never ceased. "It would be a strange thing if a cattleman killed off his herd and failed to admit he was a rather poor keeper of cattle; it's even stranger when a governor of a polis kills off the citizens he's sworn to protect and fails to perceive himself as a pretty bad guardian."[16]

Socrates lived nearly a half century in the environs of the Athenian Agora, teaching and illustrating his belief that "the unexamined life, for man, is not worth living."

THE TRIAL

In the spring of the year of Laches (399 BC), three men brought charges against Socrates. He was summoned to appear before the King Archon in the Royal Stoa of the Agora to hear the formal charges read by the prosecutor Melêtos:

> This indictment and affidavit are sworn to by Melêtos, the son of Melêtos of the dêmê Pittheus, against Socrates, the son of Sophroniscos of the dêmê Alopekê. Socrates is guilty of refusing to recognize the gods recognized by the state, and of introducing other new divinities. He is also guilty of corrupting the young. The penalty demanded is death.[17]

King Archon then had the charges written on a whitened wooden tablet and posted on a public notice board attached to the pedestal of the monument to the Eponymous Heroes. In Athens lawsuits were a private matter; the state never brought a suit against anyone, and no professional lawyers existed. Individuals only could bring lawsuits against other individuals. In this case Melêtos, a pious conservative, was merely a front; the men behind the charges were Lycon (about whom we know nothing) and Anytos, a distinguished Athenian leader in the democratic party. Lycon and Anytos had been roused to anger and were apparently backed by other politicians, craftspeople, and Sophists who felt hurt by Socrates' unsparing intellect. "Anytos," Diogenes tells us, "could not endure to be ridiculed by Socrates, and so in

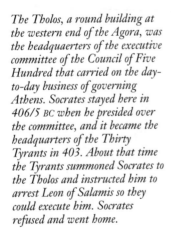

the first place stirred up against him Aristophanes and his friends" who then "helped to persuade Melêtos to indict him on a charge of impiety and corrupting the youth."[18] °

If Xenophon's later report is accurate, Socrates' response to all this was casual—he talked about everything but the trial. Hermogenes, an ardent supporter, said to him: "Really, Socrates, ought you not to be considering your defense?" He replied, "Don't you think that my whole life has been a preparation for my defense?"[19] Consequently, he prepared no speech for the trial and spoke extemporaneously.

What exactly were the charges brought against Socrates? They were (1) religious heresy, and (2) corrupting the young men of Athens. The first charge contained two points: Socrates refused to acknowledge the state-approved deities, and he introduced new deities. The first point is not that Socrates taught unorthodox *beliefs;* Athenian society had no such thing as "orthodoxy" other than a vague public consensus that always supported political correctness. Theoretically, citizens could "believe" whatever they wished. But *public practice* was another matter; it was the patriotic duty of all citizens to perform the approved rites and ceremonies connected with Athens' gods and goddesses. Athenians knew that their polis was protected by the deities it was dedicated to, and every citizen had a civic responsibility to support and maintain that connection so that divine protection would continue. Any threat to this relationship was a punishable offense. So Socrates was accused of undermining the welfare of the state, hence the welfare of all the people, by not supporting the mutual bond between Athens and its patron gods. In fact, no grounds existed for this charge. Plato, Xenophon, and Aristophanes gave abundant testimony that Socrates could commonly be seen at public shrines paying homage to the officially approved gods of the polis. The truth is that Socrates was a very religious man—in his own original way. But, as has been true in other times and places, allegations alone are sufficient to create the assumption of guilt.

The second part of the first charge makes more sense. The charge of "introducing new gods" is almost certainly a reference to Socrates' *daimonion,* a divine inner voice that, he claimed, spoke to him and warned him against doing things that could prove to be detrimental. The daimonion's modus operandi is illustrated in a humorous anecdote Plutarch recorded. Socrates and some young friends were walking along a street to Andocides' house when he fell into a sort of trance. He changed his course and turned onto another street, while his companions laughed at him and went straight on. "As they were passing through the marbleworkers' quarter past the lawcourts a flock of pigs ran some of them down and covered the others with dirt." Socrates had been warned by the intuitive voice he called his "sign."[20]

The Athenians had a problem with this. It was not that Socrates spoke to a deity but that a deity—a very private and personal deity, not accessible to anyone else—spoke to him; this inner voice, and not the state, guided Socrates' behavior in matters of conscience. In Athens individuals belonged to the state, and it did not tolerate nonconformist behavior in religious affairs and in other matters affecting it.

In regard to the second charge, Socrates was living, and teaching others to live, a life of extreme individualism. He was teaching young men to think for themselves and, following his own example, to criticize everyone and everything in the pursuit of clarity of thought and truth. To Athenians who already knew what to think, how to think, and, without thinking about it, what was right and wrong—since their society supplied them with the right answers, right assumptions, and right values and attitudes—this individualism was dangerous in the extreme. Moreover, Socrates was passionately preoccupied with questions of ethics and justice, precisely the areas where an uncritical populace had already made up its collective mind. Justice and

°We know nothing more of Lycon, but Diogenes (Lives, VI.10) notes that Anytus was later exiled, Melêtos was executed, and Antisthenes the Cynic was held responsible for both.

Then we shall have to start our inquiry about piety all over again from the beginning; because I shall never give up of my own accord until I have learnt the answer.

SOCRATES

No evil can happen to a good man, either in life or after death.

SOCRATES

I was really too honest a man to be a politician and live.

SOCRATES

morality were matters for the state to decide, not for maverick noncomformists to undermine with subversive seed cultivation.[21]

Therefore, in the context of the Athenians' assumptions about the nature of the state, and given their fear of individualism, Socrates was almost certainly to be found guilty as charged. In fact, judged by these narrow criteria, he *was* guilty as charged.

Inevitably, it was to be an emotionally charged trial. In the *Apology* Socrates says, "I have incurred a great deal of bitter hostility; and this is what will bring about my destruction, if anything does."[22]

The Athenian system was a young experiment in democracy. Each year a roster of six thousand names was compiled from which juries were selected as need arose. Each jury of 501 citizens was probably a fair cross-section of the free male Athenian society, between 2 and 3 percent of the total citizenry. Private citizens bringing suit had to argue their own cases, and defendants had to defend themselves.

The trial of Socrates was held in the Heliaia, the most important of Athens' courts, a large square marble building at the Agora's southwest corner. Jurors and spectators crowded together on wooden benches and listened, first to the prosecution's arguments. Water clocks timed the speeches. When Socrates took his turn, he denied the validity of the charges, saying he only had sought the truth, and requested the prosecution to produce the "corrupted youth" as evidence.

Plato was present at the trial. He listened to Socrates address the jurors and later recorded the tragic events in the *Apology*, a masterpiece of world literature. Socrates attempted to defend himself against the frivolous charges; then, found guilty and the prosecution having asked for the death penalty, he made the customary counter-proposal; lastly, condemned to death, he delivered a farewell address to the court.

These had to be terror-filled hours for Plato as he watched the conviction and sentencing of his beloved teacher by (to him) a pop-culture assortment of unsophisticated citizens wholly unqualified to think rationally about the fundaments of responsible citizenship, such as justice, honesty, and virtue, voting their fashionable fears and biases. He must have felt powerless to do anything about what was happening. A later account says that at one point Plato mounted the platform and tried to speak. "Though I am the youngest, men of Athens, of all who ever rose to address you—"; but the judges shouted him down and ordered him off the stage.

In his defense Socrates notes he had gained a reputation for "wisdom." He tells of the time when his old friend Chairephon went out to Delphi and asked the priestess of Apollo if anyone wiser than Socrates existed. The Pythian priestess delivered her famous oracle: No, none is wiser. "Socrates possesses more wisdom than any other man in all Hellas." Socrates was astonished when he heard this. "Wisdom! What wisdom! . . . I certainly have no knowledge of such wisdom, and anyone who says that I have is a liar and wilful slanderer."[23] He tells the court that, though initially puzzled by the idea, he began to ponder it. "When I heard about the oracle's answer, I said to myself 'What does the God mean? . . . I am only too conscious that I have no claim to wisdom, great or small; so what can he mean by asserting that I am the wisest man in the world?"

example

Socrates says he thought about the matter for some time and then decided to put it to a test. He would seek out others who were supposed to be wise and ask them point-blank if they were wise. So he went to a politician. The results? "I formed the impression that although in many people's opinion, and especially in his own, he appeared to be wise, in fact he was not." The politician even considered it rude that Socrates would ask him such a question. So, Socrates concludes, he was wiser than this politician in being aware of how much he didn't know, while the politician really believed he knew a lot.

The Delphic Oracle. Oracles were an integral part of Greek religion. The oracle at Delphi was a national institution that came to embody the entire corpus of traditional wisdom that the gods had to teach. There the Pythian priestess, hovering over fumes from the omphalos, *answered questions that guided the destinies of both individuals and nations.*

Socrates persisted, he tells the court, even though he was making himself unpopular. He sought out some poets and by querying them on their works tried to find wherein their wisdom lay. He found that "the very fact that they were poets made them think that they had a perfect understanding of all other subjects, of which they were totally ignorant. So I left that line of inquiry too with the same sense of advantage that I had felt in the case of the politicians."

Then he sought out some skilled craftspeople. They also failed the test, for "on the strength of their technical proficiency they claimed a perfect understanding of every other subject, however important." So, after these "empirical" examinations, Socrates had to conclude he was, after all, the wisest man in all Hellas, for he knew one thing, one vitally important thing, that no one else seemed to know: He knew what he didn't know. So Socrates accepted Apollo's verdict: Real wisdom belongs to God, human wisdom is really worthless, and the only truly wise man is one who knows he doesn't know.

At one point in his defense, Socrates presages the outcome:

> Please do not be offended if I tell you the truth. No man on earth who conscientiously opposes either you or any other organized democracy . . . can possibly escape with his life. The true champion of justice, if he intends to survive even for a short time, must necessarily confine himself to private life and leave politics alone.[24]

The speakers finished and a vote was taken: 281 guilty, 220 not guilty. If only 31 jurors who had voted him guilty had voted for his innocence, we might never have heard of Socrates. But by a narrow margin, his peers (did Socrates have peers?) found him guilty. The same body of jurors then set the penalty, each side having suggested an appropriate punishment. The prosecution asked for a sentence of death. It is likely his accusers never really wanted the death of the gadfly-sage, but intended to manipulate him into a plea of self-exile.

But Socrates' response is ambiguous and puzzling, and the records don't allow us to interpret his response with much confidence. (Xenophon's Socrates is arrogant and inappropriate; Plato's Socrates is lovable and inappropriate.) Whether he took a courageous stand or foolishly mocked his prosecutors depends on how one views the records; it may be that both judgments are valid (or it may be that our opinions on the matter are insignificant, or just insensitive). Since he felt he was guilty only of

If you see a man fretting because he is to die, he was not really a philosopher [but a philosôma, *a "body lover"].*

SOCRATES

I know nothing except the fact that I know nothing.

SOCRATES

On Socrates Socratic moral inquiry is inquiry about reality.

R. E. ALLEN

teaching the truth—a contribution of enormous value to Athens—he suggested he be supported at public expense for the rest of his life. Panicked at Socrates' inappropriate response, Plato (according to his own account) urged Socrates to offer a fine of thirty minae (instead of one mina), so he wouldn't seem to be mocking the court; Plato promised to give security for it. The switch in the vote indicates how the citizens' jury reacted to Socrates' counter-suggestion: for death 361, for acquittal 140.

According to Plato, Socrates ended his case by reassuring his jurors: "Wherefore, O judges, be of good cheer about death, and know of a certainty that no evil can happen to a good man, either in life or after death, and that he and his are not neglected by the gods. . . . The hour of departure has arrived, and we go our ways—I to die, and you to live. Which is better only God knows."[25]

LAST HOURS

After his conviction Socrates was housed in the state prison on the Street of the Marble-Workers only a stone's throw to the southwest of his beloved Agora. The prison had eight cells arranged on either side of a walkway, a courtyard, and a guard tower. Though the rooms were not large—Socrates' two cells were each fifteen feet square—neither were they terribly cramped, and his visitors were comfortably accommodated on benches around the walls.

Carrying out the sentence was delayed by the ritual purity requirements of a religious festival that officially ended with the return of a sacred boat from the temple of Apollo on the island of Delos. Held up by bad weather, the boat was delayed for a month. Then one day Criton,° an old friend, came to the prison to announce the boat's impending arrival. Criton once more urged Socrates to consider escaping from his casually guarded cell. Plato reconstructed their conversation in the *Crito*; the gist of it was No![26] In his argument with Criton Socrates imagined that the personified Laws of Athens came to him and told him he was bound by contract to obey them, and escape would be a dishonorable breach of that agreement.°

The next day, an hour or two before the end, Socrates left his friends in the primary cell and proceeded to the adjacent inner chamber to bathe—to spare his friends the task of caring for his body later. After he finished bathing, Xanthippe and his youngest son (possibly all three sons) were ushered into the inner chamber, where he spoke with them and Criton. Then the family was sent away, and Socrates returned to his friends in the main cell. At least a dozen of his friends were with him. Fellow Athenians included Apollodoros and Critobolos and his father; Hermogenes, Epigenes, Aeschines, and Antisthenes; Ctesippos the Paianian and Menexenos; and Menon and the youth Phaidon. Some "foreigners" (non-Athenians) also attended: Simmias the Theban, Cebes, and Phaidondes; and Eucleidês and Terpsion from Megara. Plato was not present because he was ill. Socrates sat on the edge of his bed rubbing his leg (the leg iron had just been removed). He reflected aloud on the relation of pleasure and pain. The conversation naturally turned to death and the question of immortality. Only two possibilities exist, he believed: nonexistence or a happy state where he could continue to ask questions without fear of reprisal. "In another world I shall be able to continue my search into true and false knowledge. . . . In another world they do not put a man to death for asking questions—assuredly not!"[27] He said he was not really sure what awaited him in the next life.

Then he was ready. About sunset the guard came in to ask Socrates' forgiveness and to tell him the time had come. His friends urged him to delay one more hour, long enough to have one last meal with them. He declined and told the guard to prepare the poison. Shortly a cup of hemlock juice was brought to him. Socrates asked,

---

Now it is time that we were going, I to die and you to live; but which of us has the happier prospect is unknown to anyone but God.

SOCRATES

Well, really, Crito, it would be hardly suitable for a man of my age to resent having to die.

SOCRATES

°The n ("movable nu") in Greek is commonly dropped from word endings, so Platon *becomes* Plato, Menon *is* Meno, *and* Phaidon *is shortened to* Phaido, *which, when the diphthong* ai *is transliterated into Latin as* ae, *becomes* Phaedo. *Traditional spelling of Plato's dialogues is without the* n, *a practice I have followed; but, for the names of individuals (e.g.,* Menon *and* Phaidon*), I have retained the* n *to distinguish the man from the dialogue (except for* Plato, *where tradition was too strong to resist).*

°See p. 140.

You bury only my body, not me.

SOCRATES

"Did you make enough to allow a libation to the gods?" The guard answered No, only enough for him.

Socrates took the cup, gave a brief prayer, and drank. He walked around the room, waiting for a feeling of heaviness in his legs. Then he lay down and promptly scolded his friends for their noisy weeping. "It is for this sort of thing that I sent the women away," he chided; "One ought to be allowed to die in peace." When the numbness reached his abdomen, he suddenly aroused and said to Criton, "Remember to pay a cock to Asclepius!"—presumably, to make an offering to the god of health and healing. He lay down again, and shortly he shuddered. He was dead.[28]

"This is the end of our comrade," Plato would later write, "a man, as we would say, of all then living we had ever met, the noblest and the wisest and the most just."[29]

On Socrates All in all he was *fortunate: he lived without working, read without writing, taught without routine, drank without dizziness, and died before senility, almost without pain.*

WILL DURANT

WHAT SOCRATES WAS ALL ABOUT

It is difficult to know whether Socrates "believed" anything at all or to decide what his "philosophy" might have been, if he had one. Diogenes Laërtius may be half right when he tells us Socrates didn't teach philosophy but rhetoric. In subsequent centuries, *epigonoi* being what they are, the "philosophies" of both Plato and Socrates were completed, crystalized, and canonized into what became known as "Platonism." But just as Plato was not a "Platonist," Socrates was not a "Socratic" (or a "Platonist"!). Socrates wasn't into believing; he wasn't into finalized thoughts. He was into thinking about ideas, into asking anyone who came within range, each day from dawn to dusk to dawn, something like, "What does that mean? You talk about 'courage' and 'beauty' and 'virtue' with such an air of authority that, clearly, you really think you know what you're saying. Let's explore these ideas you talk about so freely and see. When you speak, say, of 'courage,' what *exactly* do you mean? Is courage just one thing or do many varieties of courage exist? Give a clear definition of 'courage'— either the word or the living quality that distinguishes a courageous person."

SOCRATIC MIDWIFERY

To understand Socrates we need do little more than take him at his own word as recorded by Plato in the *Theaetetus*. "I am the son of a noble and husky midwife," he tells us, and he followed in his mother's footsteps—he, too, is a midwife. "But my calling differs from that of a midwife, for I care for men who are in labor, not women, and I tend their souls rather than their bodies." Real midwives have an easier time of it, he notes, for women, unlike his young men, don't give birth to false children.

With the metaphor of midwife Socrates makes three points. (1) His craft is important because it cares for the soul. "The greatest thing about my art is this, that it can test in every way whether the mind of the young man is bringing forth a mere image, an imposture, or a real and genuine offspring." (2) It is not his job to develop a "philosophy" of his own. "I have this in common with the midwives: I am sterile in point of wisdom, and the reproach has often been brought against me, that I question others but make no reply myself about anything, because I have no wisdom in me. This is a just reproach; and the reason I do it is this: the god compels me to act as midwife, but has never allowed me to bring forth. I am, then, not at all a wise person myself, nor have I any wise creations—no offspring of my own, born from my own soul." Elsewhere he confesses, "I myself know nothing, except just a little, enough to extract an argument from another man who is wise and to receive it with an open mind." (3) "Those who associate with me, although at first some of them

This art [midwifery] both my mother and I received from God, she for women and I for young and noble men and for all who are fair.

SOCRATES

seem very ignorant, yet, as our acquaintance advances, all of them to whom the god is gracious make wonderful progress. . . . And it is clear that they do this, not because they have ever learned anything from me, but because they have found in themselves many fair things and have brought them forth."[30]

As noted earlier, the essence of Socrates' "method" is to let others talk until they reveal the truth to themselves. He is, therefore, not a teacher in the usual sense, if by "teacher" we mean one who emplaces content into the mind of another; he is, rather, a teacher in the grand sense of leading others to draw out of themselves whatever their capacities allow. The fact that so many of Plato's dialogues end with no closure indicates Socrates was quite serious when he employed the midwife metaphor to describe the nature and purpose of his philosophic conversations.

Socrates did have some convictions, of course, some ideas he really did "believe"; but these were not substantive doctrines. With all his heart he believed in the value of truth, and he believed in the power of human reason to find the truth. One of the loveliest brief monologues in all literature is found in the *Meno*, where he affirms his faith in philosophy—the *search* for wisdom:

> I cannot state categorically that everything I have said in my arguments is true. But there is one thing I do know: That it is truly possible to find out what we don't know and in doing so we will become better human beings, more courageous and more fulfilled. For this I would be willing to fight to the end in both word and deed.[31]

Other "beliefs" he held, and lived by, are that the human being has a "soul" that is the essence of the rational experiential self, that this soul is eternal and indestructible, that the cultivation of the soul is the one supreme purpose of human life, and that the soul's fulfillment lies in its apprehension of Goodness and Beauty. These are about the only "beliefs" in Socrates' repertory. These he was committed to; they guided his every move in his life. They are "if-then" methodological beliefs: If one lives a life by these ideas, then he or she will have attained "beauty in the inward "soul"; beyond this, nothing is to be sought, nothing to be attained.

Ruins of the temple of Apollo at Delphi as a visitor sees them today. At the front (far end) stood the omphalos *("navel") and sacred tripod from which the priestess announced her oracles in response to questions from pilgrims who came to ask guidance from Apollo.*

ERISTIC DEBATE

If we can trust the subtler details of Plato's memory, the early Socrates was influenced by some of the debate methods of the Sophists, which he adopted for his own use. To accomplish their educational goals, the Sophists introduced debating techniques that are as familiar to us today as they were to the people of Athens. We know them as the adversarial techniques practiced by lawyers in the courtroom, by politicians campaigning for office, by legislators debating on the floors of Congress, and in college classes listed under titles such as "Speech Communication 140: Argumentation and Debate" ("especially recommended for political science, pre-law, criminal justice, and speech majors"). The Sophists called it "eristic debate," or simply "eristics." (The Greek noun *eris*, meaning "debate," carried strong adversarial connotations: "strife," "quarrel," "contention"; and it also could refer to domestic "discord," "quarrel," "wrangling," and "disputation." The goddess named Eris was a sister of Arês, the god who incites to war, and the talent ran in the family.)

As all good teachers do, the Sophists developed teaching techniques for drilling students and exercises for use in practicing their skills. As in today's psychodrama or role-playing, they had students take sides in debates and defend a particular viewpoint, then had them reverse roles to defend the other side. An extreme form of these teaching games, called "elenctic" debate (from the Greek *elenchos*, "cross-examination," "confutation," "disproof," with connotations of "to disgrace" and "to put to shame"), aimed at annihilating the other side's arguments.

The early Socrates engaged in just this kind of elenctic exchange with his interlocutors. In the dialogues he leads them down one path and then another, proving each time that their arguments are invalid. We may feel uncomfortable as we read him in action, for we sense a lack of empathy and often feel sorry for Socrates' inept opponents who haven't a ghost of a chance against the master logician's incisive intellect. No wonder Socrates was considered a Sophist. He talked like one, debated like one, discoursed on the same subjects, and gave his opponents a rough time just as they did.

But profound differences arose between Socrates and the Sophists, especially as brought out in the later dialogues. The Sophists, like all good lawyers, taught their students to take any side of an argument and build their case; and the truth, whatever that was—all truth was relative anyway, according to the Sophists—played no part in their forensic exchanges. This was anathema to Socrates. To teach that in the practical affairs of daily life, the truth was irrelevant—or that no truth exists—was a dangerous idea to be countered with all one's strength. A wise intellect cherishes the truth and grows in grace as it draws ever nearer to a knowledge of it.

So Socrates had a hidden agenda behind all his conversations, and this helps us understand why he was so popular (with young lions who could listen and hear) and unpopular (with Athenians who could not understand him). While the Sophists were convinced truth was irrelevant, Socrates demonstrated that dialectic could be carried on with a far nobler purpose. Debating just to win at logic games or word games, and to stroke one's ego, is absurd when, dedicated to the pursuit of truth, it can become a precious tool for the human soul to attain its worth and societies to know peace.

THE SEARCH FOR DEFINITIONS

In his search for clarity and truth, Socrates always had a game plan. Watch what happens in the following exchange from the dialogue called the *Lachês*. Socrates and two distinguished military leaders, Lachês and Nikias, are spectators at a show-and-tell demonstration of how a soldier can fight in full armor. Attending the program with them are two other men who are concerned about giving their sons the education they themselves did not get. So they all set about discussing educational theory. The

What is the depth of misery other than to desire bad things and to get them?

SOCRATES

[Socrates says approvingly that] Cebes is always on the hunt for arguments, and won't believe straight off whatever one says.

SOCRATES

issue in this case is whether valor can be taught, so the conversation turns to the definition and nature of "valor" or "courage," virtues essential to "manliness" (with overtones—the Greek word is *andreios*, meaning "manly" and "masculine," with connotations of "strong," "vigorous," "macho," and sometimes "stubborn").

"Then, Lachês, suppose that we first set about determining the nature of courage, and in the second place proceed to enquire how the young men may attain this quality by the help of studies and pursuits. Tell me, if you can, what is courage?"

"Indeed, Socrates, I see no difficulty in answering; he who does not run away, but remains at his post and fights against the enemy—he surely is a man of courage."

"Very good, Lachês; and yet I fear that I did not express myself clearly; and therefore you have answered not the question which I intended to ask but another."

"What do you mean, Socrates?"

"I will try to explain."

Socrates cites the example of Scythian soldiers who are known to employ flight and retreat as strategies, and wouldn't they be men of courage, too? Of course, replies Lachês. There are really many types of courage, Socrates suggests, in many different life situations. "And all these are courageous?" "Very true," Lachês agrees.

"Now I was asking about courage and cowardice in general. And I will begin with courage, and once more ask, What is the common quality, which is the same in all these cases, and which is called courage? Do you now understand what I mean?"

"Not over well," replies a puzzled Lachês.

Socrates tries several more times to get from Lachês a universal *definition* of courage, and not merely a list of examples. Lachês tries but never quite manages it. Maybe courage is "a sort of endurance of the soul," he says, or perhaps a "wise endurance." At one point Lachês confesses: "I fancy that I really do know the nature of courage; but, somehow or other, she has slipped away from me, and I cannot get hold of her and tell her nature." So they call in the other old soldier, Nikias.

"Come then, Nikias, and do what you can to help your friends, who are tossing on the waves of argument. . . ."

"I have been thinking, Socrates," says Nikias, "that you and Lachês are not defining courage in the right way; for you have forgotten an excellent saying which I have heard from your own lips. . . . I have often heard you say that 'Every man is good in that in which he is wise, and bad in that in which he is unwise.'"

"That is certainly true, Nikias."

"And therefore if the brave man is good, he is also wise."

Socrates seems almost elated. "Do you hear him, Lachês?"

"Yes, I hear him, but I do not very well understand him."

Socrates is more confident: "I think that I understand him, and he appears to me to mean that courage is a sort of wisdom."

"What can he possibly mean, Socrates?"

"That is a question which you must ask him. . . . Tell him then, Nikias, what you mean by this wisdom; for you surely do not mean the wisdom which plays the flute?" Of course not, Nikias replies. Maybe "courage is the knowledge of that which inspires fear or confidence in war, or in anything."

But Lachês cuts in with "Surely courage is one thing, and wisdom another."

"That is just what Nikias denies," says Socrates.

"Yes, that is what he denies; but he is so silly."

Socrates undoubtedly smiled at this. "Suppose we instruct instead of abusing him?"

But Lachês and Nikias set to bickering like the two proverbial old maids, and several times Socrates, playing the role of mediator, then father, then psychotherapist, has to put the discussion back on track. "I must beg of you, Nikias, to begin again," he says.[32]

But there the matter rests. The question of exactly what "courage" is remains unanswered, and the modus operandi of the *Lachês* is typical of many of the early Socratic dialogues. In the *Lysis*, an attempt is made to define "friendship," but this discussion, too, goes off track, and in the end no definitional clarity is achieved. In *Ion* the subject is "artistic inspiration." In the *Hippias Major* it is "beauty." In the *Charmides* Socrates and his interlocutors try to define "temperance." In the *Euthyphrô* Socrates tries in vain to elicit a definition of "piety" from the self-proclaimed expert in all things religious, who assures Socrates he knows what he's talking about; but as the dialogue proceeds it becomes clear Euthyphrô has not the foggiest insight into what piety might be. At one point a frustrated Euthyphrô gripes that he just doesn't know how to explain things to Socrates: "Whatever statement we put forward always somehow moves round in a circle," he complains. To which Socrates replies, "Then we must begin again and inquire what piety is. . . . and this time tell me the truth."

Since so many of the dialogues end without resolution, it is clear Socrates' purpose in conversing (and Plato's in writing) is to say that the goal of critical dialectic is the activity of attempting to think clearly and not the achievement of definitive results. He designed every move in these semantic chess games to edge the discussion forward *toward* a universal definition of some word or concept with the ultimate goal of clarity and honesty of thought. Undoubtedly, the final lesson we are supposed to carry away is that Socrates should be our role model: We are urged to shock ourselves awake, just as he did, to become wisely aware of what we don't know, and to do something about it.

Socrates seems to have later abandoned this extreme form of confutational debate. When Plato's writings are positioned in a general chronological sequence, it can be seen that Socrates himself changed and grew during his fifty-year career. In the style of the Sophists, his earlier exchanges were deliberately confrontational and adversarial; he engaged in sharp elenctic exchanges, and untold numbers of his fellow citizens felt the sting of his brilliance. The Athenians loved to debate, but Socrates was better at the art than anyone else; he could always win. (In the *Symposium* Alcibiades complains that "he conquers every one in discourse—not once in a while . . . but always!") He wielded this weapon indiscriminately and applied it fearlessly to politicians, military leaders, artisans, businesspeople—he was an equal-opportunity practitioner. "He would take to task those who thought highly of themselves, proving them to be fools," Diogenes wrote.[33] The bright young men who understood him could roll with the punches and turn his relentless pushing into a priceless time of learning, but adult citizens who had their complacent egos cut to size came to fear him. In truth, of course, he was right: We all engage in sloppy thinking.

But these sharp exchanges all fade away, according to Plato's middle and late dialogues. Socrates seems to have matured to the point of abandoning elenctic demolition, as though he developed greater empathy with the feelings of others and realized that *as an educational technique*, eristic confutation doesn't work; it only polarizes and brings on a rigidification of defenses. Thereafter, he was much less confrontational and carried on gentler, more positive conversations with his friends. He continued to play chess in his conversations, and, like a champion chess player, he saw possible moves well ahead of others. Yet one senses honest exploration occurring in some of the dialogues with his friends; their joint efforts to achieve clarity are sincere. We find no reason not to take Socrates at his word when he tells us he, too, was searching for answers. "For I am not clear-headed myself when I make others puzzled, but I am as puzzled as puzzled can be, and thus I make others puzzled too."[34]

In the *Meno* by the young soldier Menon asks Socrates what he would tell someone asking about definitions of color and figure. Socrates answers:

Every man is good in that in which he is wise, and bad in that in which he is unwise.

SOCRATES

> If my questioner were one of these clever fellows [like the Sophist debaters], who just chop logic and argue to win, I should answer him, "I have said my say; if I am wrong, it is your business to take up the argument and to refute it." But if we were friends, like you and me now, who wished to have a talk together, you see I must answer more gently and more like friends talking together.[35]

Plato has Socrates several times confess he has grave doubts about adversarial dialectic, and Socrates forbids the teaching of it to students because, he says, its early practice demoralizes the young.[36]

SOCRATIC TRANSCENDENCE

All this constitutes what is loosely known as "Socratic method," but what Socrates was really doing involves still more. In the dialogue known as the *Lysis*, while taking a stroll around Athens' walls, Socrates is waylayed by some young friends and asked to give them advice on the best way for a young man to sweet-talk someone he likes into an affair. But Socrates turns the "advice" into an exploration of the meaning of true friendship, and what gradually emerges from the exchanges is that Socrates' understanding of "love" is a far cry from the irrational sexual passions driving the young men. Again and again the discussion goes off track and they must start over, but in the process of leading his listeners along these exploratory paths, he moves them light-years away from their petty preoccupations and coy clichés. They come to an understanding of friendship founded on empathetic concern for the well-being of the other person and on the growing of two souls together in the pursuit of mutual goals.

This pattern occurs repeatedly throughout the dialogues. In the *Hippias Major* Socrates and Hippias set out to define the lovely Greek word *kalos*, "beauty." Hippias suggests that perhaps anything gilded with gold is beautiful or that maybe we call something beautiful when it is useful to us. After these puerile attempts, Socrates elevates the discussion toward an understanding of the essence of beauty that all things share.

In the *Charmides*, Socrates and his friends turn their attention to the defining of *sôphrosynê*, a quality especially precious to the Greeks: "moderation" or "temperance." Charmides suggests it might mean good behavior or perhaps a sort of modesty or deference, or perhaps it means minding one's own business. But Socrates links sôphrosynê to self-knowledge and goes on to show that a person who possesses sôphrosynê would have, above all else, a clear knowledge of what he knows and what he doesn't know. Ultimately, a knowledge of what is finally Good must be added to this kind of self-knowledge; only this will hoist our sails and steer us straight to the noblest and best in human life.

In the *Euthyphrô* Socrates gradually leads the middle-aged religious "expert" away from his complacent belief that he knows what "piety" is toward a realization that statements about right and wrong are worthless until clear criteria for making value judgments are established. Similarly, in the *Meno* Socrates leads two well-known Athenians, Menon and Anytos, through a long series of explorations of "virtue." While Menon argues that many virtues exist and gives examples, Socrates guides him on with ever deeper questions about "virtue"—whether virtue can be taught, when and how the soul learns about virtue, and whether anyone ever desires bad things. In the end they never clearly define "virtue," but the conversation has risen from fuzzy commonsense assumptions to the view that virtue is something truly divine, for it is a gift of the Gods.

In the *Gorgias*, Socrates and three well-known Athenians, all Sophists, set out to define "rhetoric," the art of persuasion. While the interlocutors defend the imminent practicality of teaching rhetoric, because it helps people defend themselves, Socrates proceeds to reveal the empty inversion of rhetoric philosophy. What is important to the rhetorician is not what you are, but what others think you are. You live life in terms of others' perceptions, so, to enable you to manipulate and control their perceptions, you put on a variety of masks that become your façades against the world. The truth of what you are becomes irrelevant and is lost. In this dialogue the Sophist Gorgias argues that rhetoric is the supreme art form because it empowers individuals to make everyone else do their will. It is a skill that enables an ignorant person to persuade an ignorant audience that he or she really understands an issue; therefore, it is the key to political success. A second participant, Polus, argues that the goal of rhetoric is to humor the prejudices of a patron or client. A third Sophist, Callicles, stresses that those who are powerful have a natural right to dominate the weak, and rhetoric makes that possible.

The *Gorgias* is one of the first great writings in all literature to mount an attack against the destructive dishonesties of the practical. It is an exposé of the sham and shallowness of "the real world." To these sophistic arguments Socrates replies that he and the Sophists are lovers of two very different mistresses. A wise man knows that what you are is important, not what others think you are. The dialogue contrasts game-playing with honesty, empty form with serious substance, and the truth with relativistic opinion. Just as medicine is for healing the body, true morality is a prescription for healing the soul.

Whenever the soul tries to examine anything in company with the body, it is plain that it is deceived by it.

SOCRATES

The most striking example of Socratic transcendence is found in the *Symposium*. A young playwright, Agathon, has just had a prize-winning tragedy performed in the Theater of Dionysos, and a gathering of his friends takes place in his honor. For the evening's entertainment someone suggests they all give speeches on love in honor of Eros, the God of Love. Phaidros begins the program with a speech on sexual passion as a cosmic force that makes all generation possible. When Pausanias speaks, he points out the difference between earthly and heavenly love and praises the latter as a higher kind of eros. Eryximachus elaborates on good and bad eros and the role of opposites in nature. Aristophanes presents a now-famous mythical tale of the human race's androgynous origins and accounts for our longing for the "lost half" of our selves. Agathon lists the tender qualities of the god Eros and how he can be trusted as the source of health and healing among humans.

Then it is Socrates' turn. Saying that when he was a young man he heard a speech about Eros given by a priestess from Mantineia named Diotima, who "was wise in this matter and in many others," he proceeds to unfold the story of "who and what sort of being is Eros." He is not a god, Diotima told him, for gods are perfect. Rather, he is a spirit existing somewhere "between a mortal and an immortal." He also "stands midway betwixt wisdom and ignorance." Like us humans, he is imperfect and incomplete; therefore, he is always striving and growing, yearning and reaching, and hungering for beauty and wisdom. Eros can be our hero and role model, for he, too, must struggle, take risks, muster up courage, and at times fail if he is to achieve happiness through wisdom. Like us he is never truly at peace with himself because he sees what he must still become. Ignorance and error drag down the human soul and prevent its reaching its spiritual goal; the antidote to this condition is knowledge and wisdom. What does the soul long for? For happiness (*eudaimonia*)—for its own sake and forever. We lust after happiness, desiring it with all our being. In this we are all lovers.

Diotima led on: Love focuses always on beautiful things. But why? "What is the [nature of] the love of the lover of beautiful things?" "What will he have who gets beautiful things?" Why do we yearn so deeply for this love? "Let me put it more clearly," Diotima said. "All men are pregnant, Socrates, both in body and in soul: on reaching a certain age our nature yearns to beget." We want to hold in our embrace all that is beautiful, to possess it and to procreate with it. "It is a divine affair, this engendering and bringing to birth." "The mortal nature ever seeks, as best it can, to be immortal"; and this immortality can be achieved only by generating offspring, be they children of the body or children of the soul. The physical body is mortal, but the soul is immortal. Because we are all "in love with what is immortal," a man's body seeks a woman and by begetting children can achieve immortality, but those with "pregnancy of soul" look to the things the soul can bring forth. What are these things? Our artworks, architecture, sculpture, poetry and plays, music, books, constitutions and laws, flower gardens, homes, honesty, integrity, happiness—all these are the beautiful products of the soul's pregnancy.

As a midwife, I attend men and not women, and I look after their souls when they are in labor, and not after their bodies: and the triumph of my art is in thoroughly examining whether the thought which the mind of the young man brings forth is a false idol or a noble and true birth.

SOCRATES

But I have still more, Diotima told Socrates, and, even though she had her doubts Socrates could understand, "you on your part must try your best to follow." True philosophers can ascend higher yet, but they must go it alone. Ideally, she said, we must begin in youth to see all the beauty we can, in beautiful bodies and in all things with physical beauty. Then we will take the next step and "set a higher value on the beauty of souls than on that of the body," thereby seeing beauty in everything: in flowers, sunsets, poems, paintings; in books, laws, constitutions, histories, good governments, moral principles; and in dreams, hopes, yearnings, relationships, sharing. When our sensibilities are thus awakened, we then will be open to all beauty, wherever it is to be found. No longer do we see only this or that particular object of beauty; now we see beauty itself, and with this we have attained a beautiful soul. The sight of every beautiful thing in the world is precious, because it resonates with our soul's innate and prior knowledge of beauty from a previous life. In our present life single beautiful things stimulate the soul and enable it to "recollect" its knowledge of universal beauty.

Then Diotima said to Socrates: "Give me the very best of your attention."

> When a man has been thus far tutored in the lore of love, passing from view to view of beautiful things, in the right and regular ascent, suddenly he will have revealed to him, as he draws to the close of his dealings in love, a wondrous vision, beautiful in its nature; and this, Socrates, is the final object of all those toils.

This is a sudden ineffable vision of Absolute Beauty, eternal and unchanging. It exists "ever in singularity of form independent by itself, while all the multitude of beautiful things partake of it." The soul, at last, has attained what is real: the form of the Beautiful. Even more, this soul is no longer an observer peering at a beautiful object; it has become so immersed in the Beautiful that it has merged with it. It has *become* Absolute Beauty. It has become one with the form of the Good, which cannot be spoken of: It only can be experienced in a glorious silence.

This is a human being's highest achievement—to live in contemplation of Pure Beauty. Transcending the beauty of material objects, "he is almost able to lay hold of the final secret." "Beginning from obvious beauties he must for the sake of that highest Beauty be ever climbing aloft, as on the rungs of a ladder . . . so that in the end he comes to know the very essence of Beauty. In that state of life above all others, my dear Socrates," Diotima said, "a man finds it truly worthwhile to live, as he contemplates essential Beauty. . . .[H]e is destined to win the friendship of Heaven; he, above all men, is immortal."

Socrates tells all this to his friends at Agathon's party—the words of love he heard from Diotima of Mantinea—and, he says, "I am persuaded of their truth. Being persuaded of them, I try to persuade others, that in their attainment of this end human nature will not easily find a helper better than love."[37]

ENDNOTES

1 Diogenes Laërtius, *Lives of Eminent Philosophers*, II.48.
2 Philip Wheelwright, *The Presocratics* (Odyssey Press, 1966), pp. 246–8.
3 Wheelwright, *The Presocratics*, pp. 241f.
4 Wheelwright, *The Presocratics*, p. 243.
5 Plato, *Theaetetus*, 150 E.
6 Plutarch, *de genio Socratis*, 20.
7 See Vander Waerdt's article "Socrates in the Clouds" in Paul A. Vander Waerdt, ed., *The Socratic Movement* (Cornell University Press, 1994), pp. 48–86.
8 Plato, *Phaedo*, 96a–b.
9 Diogenes, *Lives*, II.26; see also II.36, 37.
10 Xenophon, *Memoirs of Socrates*, 4.2.12–1.2.20, in *Conversations of Socrates*, trans. and ed. Hugh Tredennick and Robin Waterfield (Penguin Classics, 1990), pp. 182–4.
11 Bertrand Russell, *A History of Western Philosophy* (George Allen and Unwin, 1946), p. 112.
12 Mabel L. Lang, *Socrates in the Agora* (American School of Classical Studies at Athens, 1978), p. 9.
13 Xenophon, *Memorabilia*, I.i.10; and Plato, *Phaedrus*, 230.
14 Xenophon, *Memorabilia*, I.ii.32.
15 Plato, *Apology*, 32 C, D.
16 Xenophon, *Memorabilia*, I.ii.32.
17 Plato, *Apology*, 24 B.
18 Diogenes, *Lives*, II.38.
19 Xenophon, *Socrates' Defence*, 1–2, in *Conversations of Socrates*, trans. and ed. Tredennick and Waterfield, p. 41; see also Xenophon, *Memoirs of Socrates*, 4.7.10–4.8.8.
20 Plutarch, *de genio Socratis*, 10.
21 Robin Waterfield in the introduction to Xenophon's *Defence of Socrates*, in *Conversations of Socrates*, trans. and ed. Tredennick and Waterfield, pp. 29–40.
22 Plato, *Apology*, 28 A.
23 Plato, *Apology*, 19 E.
24 Plato, *Apology*, 31 D.
25 Plato, *Apology*, 41 B.
26 Plato, *Apology*, 41 A.
27 Presumably, Socrates drank a concoction of liquid infused from the leaves and roots of the spotted hemlock *(Conium maculatum)*, an alkaloid neurotoxin. Today considerable knowledge is available about the symptomatic reactions to hemlock poisoning, and it is virtually certain both Plato and Xenophon sanitized their accounts. See William B. Ober, M.D., "Did Socrates Die of Hemlock Poisoning?" in the *New York State Journal of Medicine* (©the Medical Society of the State of New York, February 1977).
28 Plato, *Phaedo*, 118.
29 Plato, *Theaetetus*, 149 A–151 D.
30 Plato, *Meno*, 86 C, D
31 Plato, *Laches*, 190 C–199 E, in *The Dialogues of Plato*, by Benjamin Jowett, vol. 1 (Oxford: The Clarendon Press, 1892), in *Readings in Ancient Western Philosophy*, by George McLean and Patrick J. Aspell (Appleton Century Crofts, 1970), pp. 89–96.
32 Diogenes, *Lives*, II.38.
33 Plato, *Meno*, 80 A.
34 Plato, *Meno*, 75 B.
35 In connection with the "eristic" style of debate practiced by both Socrates and the Sophists Plato's dialogue The *Euthydemus* is of special interest since the work is a humorous parody on the adversarial word games such giants as Zeno, Protagoras, and Gorgias employed but that, in the mouths of lesser practitioners, became petty ego games. The *Euthydemus*, comments W. R. M. Lamb, its translator for the Loeb series, is pure comic satire. "In the main it is a relentless exposure of the 'eristic' or disputatious side of the higher education which was fashionable at Athens toward the end of Socrates' life." See *Plato II* in the *Loeb Classical Library* (1924; reprint,: Harvard University Press, 1967), p.375.
36 Plato, *Symposium*, 201 C–212 C.

CHAPTER 9

THE SOCRATIC LEGACY

COUNTER-CULTURE PHILOSOPHIES

Socrates' personality and intellect inspired faithful disciples, as well as angry opponents; Cynics loved the man but protested that he failed to value the individual; Cyrenaics also loved him but said he missed the joys of living; others adopted limited Socratic ideas and went their various ways.

COUNTER-PHILOSOPHIES

During Socrates' lifetime numerous counter-movements had begun to spring up as protests against his philosophy, especially his apotheosis of intellect, denigration of sense, and dualistic notion of reality. He had spent his entire career challenging others' ideas, so inevitably his ideas, too, were challenged. Of course, Socrates and the Sophists had long been working over each other's ideas. Besides the fact that dialectical disagreement and elenctic argumentation were assumed aspects of philosophy since its presocratic beginnings, the human ego's paranoid cantankerousness let no idea fly away free. It's safe to say that no doctrine was ever promulgated without some critic dissecting it and finding it wanting. After Socrates every epigonos felt an urge to add to or modify the great thinker's teachings or to attach himself to some congenial idea and run with it. While Socrates still wandered through the colonnades of the Agora, several counterculture thinkers had glommed onto some specific but limited aspect of his teaching and developed it into a distinct, more or less coherent, philosophy. They all considered themselves faithful disciples and heirs of Socrates. So, counter-philosophies were rife all during the Golden Age, challenging the Socratic search for truth as a doomed enterprise and a misguided use of the philosophic intellect.

RISE OF THE HOUND-DOG PHILOSOPHERS

One aspect of Socrates's life was that of an ascetic culture critic. He criticized his fellow Athenians, blasting their arrogant self-righteousness and trashy values. He dressed in simple but sometimes ragged clothing, went barefoot, and scoffed at material pleasures. Though he didn't beg, he gave little thought to providing money for himself and family. So, a growing collection of antiestablishment and often brilliant outsiders emulated this side of Socrates' life.

One such group of social antagonists called themselves Cynics. The name derives from the Greek word *kuôn*, "dog" or "hound," with some interesting cognate forms: *kunikos*, "doglike"; and the descriptive adjective *kuneos*, "shameless," "insensitive,"

It is better to be a beggar than to be uneducated; the one needs money, the others need to be humanized.

ARISTIPPOS

I needed wisdom, so I went to Socrates.

ANTISTHENES

Why then do you live, if you do not care to live well?

DIOGENES

"invulnerable," "not embarrassable." Diogenes, the Cynic movement's articulate spokesman, "described himself as a hound-dog of the sort which all men praise but no one will go hunting with." Plato once called him a dog, and Diogenes replied, "That's right. Try to get rid of me and I'll find my way back home every time." When Diogenes died, a pillar capped with a marble statue of a dog marked his grave.[1]

The Cynic philosophy originated with an Athenian named **Antisthenes.** He lived from about 446 BC to 366 BC and was therefore a contemporary of both Socrates and Plato. "From Socrates he learned his hardihood," Laërtius tells us, "emulating his disregard of feeling, and thus he inaugurated the Cynic way of life." He greatly admired Socrates and became his disciple, commuting by foot from the city of Piraeus each day to listen to him. Antisthenes let his beard grow and wandered the streets of Greek cities with just one garment, a staff, and a leather pouch for carrying his food. Socrates once observed his torn robe and said to him, "I can see your vanity showing through that hole in your cloak." He was nicknamed Haplokuôn, just a "Plain Hound-Dog." Wielding the dialectical weapons of a Socrates, he taught, harangued, defended, and argued; and every argument, we are told, he would win. His many writings indicate a wide-ranging intellect: *On the Nature of Animals, On the Procreation of Children, On Justice and Courage, On Freedom and Slavery, On Belief, On Truth, On Talk, On Education, On Life and Death, On Music, On Pleasure, On the Use of Wine*—and many others. (Timon the Skeptic said he wrote too much.)[2]

Antisthenes was a culture critic; he went about criticizing everybody and everything—but always with a point, and often a sharp point, for he specialized in bursting ego balloons. For example, the Athenians believed the aristocentric claim that they had sprung from the earth and were, therefore, the salt of the earth. Antisthenes observes that such a claim put them on genetic par with "ground snails and wingless locusts," for they also came up out of the earth. "It is very strange," he says, "when we can separate the husk from the corn and the weak from the strong in war, but we never keep evil men from getting into politics." "When states can no longer distinguish good men from bad men, they will perish."[3]

If all laws were repealed, we [philosophers] would go on living just as we do now.
ANTISTHENES

The most secure stronghold lies in wisdom; it never crumbles away and is never destroyed or betrayed.
ANTISTHENES

There is nothing to hinder a man living extravagantly and well.
ARISTIPPOS

Antisthenes of Athens (c. 446–366 BC), founder of The Cynic movement in Greek philosophy.

The Cynics taught that the goal and purpose of life is to be—not wealthy, not admired, not erudite but—happy. The final human bliss, Antisthenes says, is "to be able to die happy." And the fundamental requirement of happiness is the ability to live a good and decent life; virtue alone ensures happiness, providing one possesses the courage to live it. (He says it requires "the strength of a Socrates.") The goal each of us should aim at is to learn to live in honesty and joy. This is a virtue that can be learned.[4]

The Cynics, outsiders by choice, deliberately alienated themselves from the insinuations of the culture they were born and raised in. They cultivated indifference toward society's values so that they could develop their own. The wise person is not enslaved by custom and "what others think"; his wealth lies in his freedom from all the trammels of "civilization." "A wise man will be guided in all his social behavior not by laws but by the law of decency." Antisthenes loathed those who displayed "a store of words and learning" about moral matters but failed to practice them. The moral life, and the good life, demands a courageous adherence to this simple principle, despite inevitable misunderstandings and criticisms. "It is the noblest of privileges to do good things and be criticized," Antisthenes says. Someone once told him he was widely admired. "Oh my!" he said, "what have I done wrong?"[5]

Accomplishing this autonomy requires reconditioning our feelings toward others' opinions. We must master our needs and desires and limit them to basic essentials; the result is a personal declaration of independence from the world. The most important lesson Antisthenes learned from Socrates, he says, was "to disregard feeling"; for if we are sensitive to the harsh criticisms and put-downs of others, then we become so concerned with what others think that we lose sight of who and what we truly are.° A virtuous life is possible only when we achieve freedom from the unempathetic judgmentalism of others. The Cynics' philosophic stance might be put thus: "Why should I spend my life defending myself against your misterpretations of what I said? What I say is what I say, and if you misinterpret it, that's your problem. If you ask me what I mean, then I'll explain. Of course it's hard not to get entangled in the emotional tugs-of-war when you understand very clearly what is right or just at a particular moment and others disagree. But why should I have to prove myself to others over and over? What a waste of my life! We argue, to be sure, but argument is a teaching technique, not the be-all and end-all of living. The focus of our philosophy is to live, not to be understood and accepted by others—or to keep them happy."

The goal of the philosophic life, therefore, is to develop an awareness that enables an individual to make intelligent choices. Along with their rejection of society, the Cynics also taught that academic subjects and the intellectual life as such are irrelevant to living a good life. Plato's lectures, Diogenes says, "are a waste of time."[6]

The Cynics had an epistemology of sorts, derived mostly from the Sophists. They were thoroughgoing individualists, and their individualism colored their epistemology as well. They thought Plato's doctrine of Real Ideas absurd because it lumped together the world's real solid objects into arbitrary abstractions and thereby lost their unique qualities. The Cynics believed all groupings—classes of things, herds of animals, flocks of birds, an audience of people, any collection of objects—are merely mental constructions created when the mind focuses on analogies and similarities. Such collections are not real. Each object, unique within itself, is what it is, and its "essence" belongs to it alone. The Cynics went so far as to declare all "synthetic" judgments invalid. To say, for example, "the sky is blue" brings together the sky (one thing) and blueness (quite a different thing) into an unholy marriage, for the sky is sky, and blue is blue; the uniqueness of each should be left to stand by itself. This logic applies especially to statements about human behavior. To say "Diogenes is a dog" links two incompatible ideas to form an illegitimate union, for "Diogenes" is a unique singular object with its own essence, and so also is "dog." So, the Cynics attempted to devise an epistemology that would allow unique objects to be themselves.

The Cynics may represent history's first attempt on the part of self-esteemed individuals to transcend the cultural patterns they were born and raised with and to recognize that the assumptions and values of one's society may not work for the fostering of a successful life. They were therefore the first philosophic individualists, and they have had counterparts in every culture and every century where the individual person's worth is appreciated.

Antisthenes waged war with a wise but acidic tongue. To a new student he said, "Come with a new book, a new pen, and new tablets; and if you have brains, bring them too." When someone complained of losing his notes, he advised, "Next time inscribe them on your mind instead of on paper."[7]

Diogenes of Sinôpe was by far the most famous of the Cynics. This is the renowned Diogenes who "lit a lantern in broad daylight and said, as he went about, 'I am looking for an honest man.' " Details of his life are sketchy. Originally a banker in Sinôpe (a Greek colony on the Black Sea), he seems to have been caught counterfeiting the coins of his home city and was exiled. On a voyage to Aegina he was captured by pirates, taken to Crete, and sold into slavery, after which he became a philosopher. We are told that, while on the auction block, he saw a well-dressed buyer in the audience and said, "Sell me to that man. He needs a master." When his friends tried to ransom him, he declined the offer, saying that "lions are not slaves to those who feed them." So, he became the overseer of a large household in Corinth and administered it with such excellence that his owner Xeniades "used to go about saying, 'A good spirit [daimôn] has taken up residence in my home.'"[8]

Diogenes settled on the Cynic lifestyle after watching a mouse. The tiny creature never worried about where it would sleep, it was not afraid of the dark, it ate simple food and only what it needed, and it adjusted to whatever environment it found itself in. Diogenes chose to emulate this simple life and "used any place for any purpose, for breakfasting, sleeping, or conversing."[9]

Diogenes is the superlative example of a philosopher who lived his philosophy in daily life; to know the man is to know his philosophy. He really didn't care what others thought of him. Someone once said to him, "People laugh at you." His reply: "I couldn't care less. Jackasses also laugh at those people, but just as they don't mind the jackasses' laughing, so I don't care about their braying at me."[10]

Diogenes focused his criticism on the common hypocrisies of daily life. "Musicians tune the strings of their instruments so they are in harmony but abandon their souls to disharmony." "Astronomers gaze at the heavens but fail to see what is right before their eyes." "Eloquent politicians talk up a storm about justice but fail miserably to practice it." "Grammarians criticize the writings of Homer but fail to correct their own." "Even the preachers who denounce the vices of wealth love it all the same." When he saw some sheep protected by leather jackets while the owner's children went without clothes, he said, "It's better to be the man's ram than his son."[11]

Religious hypocrisy especially irked Diogenes. When he saw some priests having a man arrested for stealing a bowl from the temple, he observed, "The big thieves are leading away a little thief." Some Athenians once told him he really ought to be initiated into the mysteries so that he could enjoy special privileges in the next life. "That's ludicrous," he said. "Are you telling me that men of true virtue will be mired forever [in Hadês] while evil men will dwell happily in the Isles of the Blest—just because they have been initiated?!" Diogenes was aghast when he saw devotees

Only the wise man knows who are worthy to be loved.
ANTISTHENES

I came to Socrates for education and to Dionysius for recreation.
ARISTIPPOS

Excellence is cultivated not by voracious reading but by useful reading.
ARISTIPPOS

I am a citizen of the world.
DIOGENES

On Diogenes He is a Socrates gone mad.
PLATO

Diogenes the Cynic.

praying to the gods for health while they were gorging themselves on the unhealthy viands left over from their temple offerings. In their prayers, he said, people ask for the wrong things rather than what is truly good—wisdom and virtue.[12]

He confessed he was proud of the human race when he reflected on the expertise doctors, philosophers, and navigators exemplify; but when he watched the fraudulent dream-mongers and psychics at work or the empty conceits who went about puffed-up because of their affluence, then he thought we are the silliest of all the animals.[13]

He was also sensitive to the ironies and contradictions of our lives. "For some people, despising pleasure is itself the greatest of pleasure; they derive more pleasure from despising pleasure than from the pleasures themselves!"[14]

Musicians tune the strings of their instruments but leave their own souls in dissonant discord.

DIOGENES

Like Socrates he was no respecter of persons; ordinary citizens, the great and powerful, and fellow Cynics were all treated with equal disrespect. He excelled at "pouring scorn on his contemporaries," Laërtius says. He called himself "a spy on the greedy." He often had exchanges with Plato. For instance, Plato had given a famous definition of Man as a "two-legged animal without feathers." So, Diogenes plucked the feathers from a chicken and brought it to the lecture hall, saying, "Here, Plato, is your Man." (As a result, we are told, Plato redefined Man as "a featherless biped with flat fingernails.") On another occasion he offered Plato some dried figs, and Plato (who had a reputation for loving figs and olives) ate them all. "I said you could share them," a disgruntled Diogenes griped, "not that you could eat them all!" Once when Plato was asked what he thought of Diogenes, he said, "He is a Socrates gone mad."[15]

Diogenes transcended society and culture. "I am a citizen of the world—a cosmopolitan," he said. To him social conventions commanded much less authority than "natural rights." Diogenes likened his free life to that of the Gods, implying that his standards transcended conventional social ethics, as well as local laws and customs.[16]°

°*And you thought this was a modern metaphor! See Laërtius's Lives, VI. 34–35.*

The picture commonly painted of Diogenes is of a ragged, unkempt beggar sitting in the shadow of his "jar" surrounded by dogs, shaking "the middle finger" at passersby,° and asking Alexander the Great to step aside because he was blocking the sunlight. (This "jar" he lived in was a giant *pithari*, a "wine-jar," actually a huge ceramic storage vessel for grain, tipped on its side.) This picture is not inaccurate, but it misses the point of what Diogenes was all about, and we do him great injustice when we paint him as a boorish misfit. For the man was gifted with an insightful mind and lots of common sense, and he used his extraordinary intellect to see deeply into human behavior. He saw what others didn't seem to see: dishonesty, deception, confusion, entanglements, and manipulations—inauthentic game-playing at all levels.° In a word, Diogenes was gifted with the ability to spot the hypocritical and to point it out, which made him bitterly disliked by some but enormously popular to others. Despite his sharp tongue and his rejection of society, most Athenians loved him. When a vandal broke the jar he lived in, the Athenians gave him a new one. And even Alexander the Great remarked, "If I were not Alexander, then I would like to have been Diogenes."

°*"We've upgraded our standards," Bill Maher says, "up yours." (The Cynics live on!)*

It is impossible for society to exist without law.

DIOGENES

°*Modern Existentialists attempt to capture this quality with the word "inauthenticity"; see Vol II, pp. 471, 474f.*

So, in his own life Diogenes made every effort to escape the traps of hypocrisy and to adhere to a lifestyle that allowed him to be his own man without having to defer to the petty expectations of others. This he did by ridding himself of property; like Antisthenes he possessed only a cloak and a leather bag for carrying his food. He begged (once begging from a stone statue "so he could get used to being refused"), slept anywhere he found himself, and resided in a very public place in the Athenian Agora. This way he could live a life of simple honesty, preserve his "seeing" as an observer, and play the role of a disengaged critic. He expressed what he saw

Diogenes the Cynic (404-323 BC) at home in his pithari *surrounded by his family, holding the lantern used in his search for an honest man.*

eloquently and pointedly; like his teacher Antisthenes, "he could easily vanquish anyone he liked in argument," and he had "a wonderful gift of persuasion." Once a father in Aegina sent his younger son to Athens for a brief sojourn, but he became enthralled with Diogenes and decided to stay. The father then sent his elder son to find the younger son, but he, too, became enamored listening to Diogenes and never returned. Finally the father went to Athens to search for both, and he also stayed: "He was just as much attracted to the pursuit of philosophy as his sons and joined the circle—so magical was the spell which the discourses of Diogenes exerted."[17]

Diogenes was, among other things, an intellectual's anti-intellectual. His listeners included political leaders, academics (such as Plato), Sophists (such as Gorgias), poets, and rhetoricians; many came great distances to hear him. His writings include a *Republic, The Art of Ethics, On Wealth, On Love, On Death, Letters,* and seven tragic plays.[18]

"You are an old man," he was told, "so take a rest." "What!" he replied. "If I were running a race in the stadium, would you tell me to slow down just as I was approaching the finish-line?" He died at Corinth at age ninety—on the same day Alexander the Great died in Babylon—and was buried by the gate leading to the Isthmus. He was honored with a bronze statue inscribed with "Time makes even bronze grow old, but thy glory, Diogenes, all eternity will never destroy." This was in the 113th Olympiad, about 323 BC.[19]

LATER CYNICS

Antisthenes had said that "virtue is the same for women as for men," and women also chose to live the life of the Cynic. We know of a woman named **Hipparchia** who was converted to Cynic doctrine. "She fell in love with the life and teachings of Cratês [a pupil of Diogenes, whom she married], and adopting the same dress, went about with her husband and lived with him in public." Once scolded for forsaking a

Bad men obey their lusts as servants obey their masters.

DIOGENES

For some, despising pleasure is itself most pleasurable; they derive more pleasure from despising pleasure than from the pleasures themselves.

DIOGENES

woman's role (such as weaving and sewing), she replied, "Are you telling me that I'm ill advised if, instead of wasting my time spinning cloth, I spend it on education?" Hipparchia lived about 300 BC.[20]

The Cynic philosophy continued to be taught from the time of Socrates through the sixth century AD by a congeries of rebels who shared a common attitude toward life and the world.

RISE OF THE CYRENAIC HEDONISTS

It is a proverbial fact that students see their teachers differently and resonate with different ideas. Had you been able to ask Antisthenes, Aristippos, and Eucleidês to give an account of their beloved teacher, the Cynic would have praised Socrates' courageous protests against society, the Cyrenaic would have hailed his recognition that humans are pleasure-seeking animals, and the Megarian would have admired the logical mind that could outargue every Sophist. These different descriptions, obviously, seem to be of three different people. That Socrates could be the well-spring for such varied perspectives testifies to his breadth and complexity.

Aristippos of Cyrene was the founder of another of the lesser Socratic schools, and it was the pleasure-loving side of Socrates that attracted him. Born in Cyrene in North Africa, he was in his twenties when Socrates' fame lured him to Athens. "I needed wisdom," he said, "so I came to Socrates." But he had only a few years with his teacher before Socrates was given the hemlock. Aristippos was away in Aegina at the time and didn't witness the execution, but he later said, "I want to die the way Socrates died." He lived from about 435 BC to 356 BC and was contemporary with Plato, Antisthenes, Diogenes, and other members of the Socratic circle.[21]

Aristippos came from an affluent Cyrenean family. Well bred and schooled in the social graces, he was a handsome, friendly, quick-witted, eloquent, easygoing, and decent young man. Everyone liked him. He was comfortable in any social situation; when asked what philosophy had done for him, he answered, "the ability to be at ease with everyone." He loved the good life and saw no reason why people shouldn't enjoy the beautiful, the pleasant, the joyful—all the things that can make our lives happy. Though he enjoyed the luxury of material things, he could take them or leave them, knowing that, in themselves, they are of no value; they are only instrumental goods for achieving pleasure. Plato once said to him, "You are gifted with the ability to flaunt your robes or to wander in rags with equal poise."[22]

He traveled much and was once shipwrecked on the island of Rhodes and taken captive by pirates (he tossed all his money overboard, saying, "It's better for the money to be lost for the sake of Aristippos than for Aristippos to be lost for the sake of the money"). He lived in Sicily, then Athens, and finally settled in his home city of Cyrene to found a school of philosophy, and there he taught for most of his life. He wrote a three-volume history of Libya and a work containing twenty-five dialogues, some of them titled *To Those Who Have Been Shipwrecked*, *To a Beggar*, *To His Friends*, *A Letter to his Daughter Arêtê*, *To Laïs Concerning the Mirror*, and *To Those Who Blame Him for His Love of Old Wine and Women*.[23]

Aristippos's philosophy has been considered the purest hedonism in all of Western thought.° Human life has but a single goal: pleasure—not virtue (*aretê*), not happiness (*eudaimonia*), not tranquility (*ataraxia*), not honor (*timê*), not temperance (*sôphrosynê*), not numbness (*apatheia*)—none of these lovely end goals esteemed by other philosophers. Pleasure and pain govern all living things, Aristippos says; we seek the first, and we avoid the latter. Pleasure (in all its forms) is good; pain (in all its forms) is bad. Pleasure is always good, no matter when, where, or how it's achieved;

Those who pursue an education but stop short of studying [philosophy] are like the suitors of Penelope; they found it easier to woo the maidservants than to marry the mistress.

ARISTIPPOS

°*But see the antinomian Gnostics, p. 220.*

I want to die the way Socrates died.

ARISTIPPOS

and whatever gives us the most pleasure is the most desirable, just as whatever gives us the most pain is the most undesirable.

Socrates had taught that virtue is the highest good and that happiness is a by-product of one's moral character. Aristippos agreed that virtue can lead to pleasure but emphasized that virtue, in itself, has no value at all. Virtue's only value is that it can lead to pleasure. And happiness? We all want to be happy, so we tell ourselves, but what we call happiness is merely the sum total of all our pleasures. Happiness does not exist apart from pleasure.

Pleasure belongs only to the present moment. The goal of a healthy human is to learn to enjoy to the fullest—purely, simply, and intensely—the "now" of our experiential present. Aristippos "derived pleasure from whatever was present at hand, and refused to dream of pleasures which, at that moment, were not present." Pleasure in the living present is the only and final good.[24]

While believing pleasure is everyone's goal, Aristippos's Cyrenaics recognized that individuals experience pleasure in their unique ways; one person's pleasure never exactly matches another's. What is pleasant for one may indeed be neutral or even painful for another and vice versa. (The taste of lemon is painful to me, pleasant to you; I like olives, and you don't.) They also recognized that some individuals are more sensitive than others to both pleasure and pain. Yet pleasure and pain are egalitarian levelers. Whether one is rich or poor, slave or free, male or female, highly esteemed or ignoble, all these things are irrelevant to the experiencing of pleasure or pain. As the Cyrenaics looked around them, it was obvious the rich were not happier than the poor or the poor happier than the rich.[25]

Because of this individuality, a generalized "knowledge" cannot be built upon sense experience, so Cyrenaic epistemology remained rudimentary. "The senses don't always tell us the truth," they said. "They disallow the claims of the sense, because they don't give us any kind of dependable knowledge." What things are in themselves we can never know. All we can "know" are the images, sensations, and feelings that objects/events produce in us experiencers, but this is all we need to know for the proper guidance of our lives. Like the Cynics, the Cyrenaics rejected any notion that abstract universals are real; the mind's abstractions are only ideas that bring together chance similarities. For example, when I think of abstract "animal," my mind supposedly links together whatever mice, lions, elephants, and hedgehogs have in common. But what do they have in common? Very little. Nothing of significance, Aristippos would have said. So the notion of a universal "animal" is a useless concept; it refers to nothing at all that is real. It is merely a name. [26]

The bodily pleasures are the most gratifying, Aristippos taught. Emotional pleasures are good, of course, but the physical pleasures are the more intense and give us the greatest satisfaction. Socrates had extolled the so-called higher pleasures of mind and spirit, but Aristippos thought this was nonsense (literally). Mental pleasures are good, but they don't compare with physical pleasures, just as mental pain is nowhere near as severe as physical pain. Memories of past pleasures are also good, but they fade, and the expectations of future pleasures—which may never materialize—pale in comparison to the present's intense physical pleasures. So our goal must be to learn to live, as much as humanly possible, in the present moment. "It is quite enough if we learn to enjoy each single pleasure just as it comes."[27]

Philosophy, for Aristippos, is the "science" that helps us make wise choices. Through rational planning we can find ways to maximize our pleasures in quality, quantity, and intensity. "The wise man will have an advantage over others, not so much in choosing pleasures, but in being able to avoid pain." When asked how an

It is quite enough if we learn to enjoy each single pleasure just as we experience it.

ARISTIPPOS

The real advantage accruing to the sage will lie, not in his choice of good and pleasant things, but in his ability to avoid evil and painful things.

HEGESIAS

educated person differs from the uneducated, he replied, "exactly as horses that have been trained differ from wild horses." Those who don't include philosophy in their education, he says, "are just like the suitors of Penelope" who won over the maid-servants "but were completely unsuccessful in wooing the mistress."[28]

But this matter of securing pleasures is not as simple as we might wish. Two things make it "a really bothersome business." First, some people's minds get confused, and they fail to seek pleasure at all. They either can't recognize pleasure or they feel so guilty when they experience pleasure that they make every effort to avoid it. Some actually seem to enjoy forms of pain. "Watching the imitation of suffering in a tragic drama can be pleasurable, while experiencing the real thing is painful."[29]

Poverty and riches have no relevance to pleasure; for neither the rich nor the poor as such have any special share in pleasure.

HEGESIAS

But, second, certain pleasures often lead to painful consequences, and the resultant pain may far outweigh the pleasure. For this reason Aristippos was a pragmatic realist when it came to calculating consequences. For example, flaunting society's laws and customs will frequently call down criticism, ostracism, and punishment, and the resulting pain will far exceed whatever pleasure the flaunting brought. So the Cyrenaics usually went along with popular notions of right and wrong, not because the values in themselves were right or wrong but because swimming against such "politically correct" canons would bring on unnecessary pain. They taught that "nothing is just or honorable or base by nature, but only by convention and custom." As one travels from one city-state to another, as did the Sophists, it would be expedient to take those "conventions and customs" seriously and be a "law-abiding citizen" (or visitor), even though the laws and customs may differ. We do not lose our autonomy when deliberately honoring the values of others, and it does reduce the amount of pain for everyone.[30]

The Cyrenaics also taught that selfish motives drive all behavior, that all our actions, however "unselfish" or altruistic they may appear, will in some way bring pleasure to ourselves in the doing. "The wise man will be guided in all he does by his own interests." We even make friends from selfish motives, but that doesn't lessen the value or the pleasure for either party to the friendship.[31]

The records indicate Aristippos lived his philosophy. He loved good food, talk, and wine, and he loved women. For a time he lived with Laïs of Corinth, "the most beautiful woman who ever lived" (according to a later writer) and the most famous courtesan of her time. When criticized for his behavior, he replied, "What's the problem? I'm the one who possesses Laïs, not she me!" "Abstaining from pleasures is no virtue," he said. "What is important is the mastery of your pleasures so they don't bring you down and lead to pain and suffering." On another occasion someone scolded him for living with a courtesan. Aristippos asked him, "Would you move into a house in which someone has lived before?" "Yes." "Would you sail on a ship on which others have sailed?" "Of course." "Then what difference does it make whether the woman you live with has, in the past, lived with many or no one at all?"[32]

He once was accosted by a courtesan who told him she was carrying his child. Annoyed by the charge, he retorted, "You don't know that! If you had been running through a thicket of thorny reeds, would you be able to go back and point out the exact thorn that pricked you?"[33]

The Cyrenaic philosophy is a thoroughly commonsense philosophy that average citizens easily could understand. It is not deeply intellectual, yet in their inclusion of sensation and feeling along with critical ideas, they make some strikes the more dedicated rationalists consistently missed. Their reading of "selfish" motives behind altruistic behavior is very close to today's beliefs; so is their analysis of the pain/pleasure calculus, their recognition that no action is "honorable or base by nature" but only by society's convention, and their denial that "there is anything in itself that is naturally pleasant or unpleasant"—these are seminal insights Plato, Aristotle, and others missed. Their strength lay in their simple pragmatic realism, as in, "They affirmed that allowance should be made for errors, for no man errs voluntarily, but under constraint of some suffering." They taught that "we should not hate other people, but try to teach them better." They counseled one to make no distinction between pleasures but to seek them all—wisely. The Cyrenaics thus gave practical guidelines for living to citizens who could make no sense at all of sophisticated academic debates.[34]

LATER CYRENAICS

Aristippos said that the greatest gift he ever gave his daughter **Arêtê** was "not to value anything she can do without," and we can assume she adopted a lifestyle similar to her father's. On Aristippos's death she became the head of the Cyrenaic school. She wrote some forty books, produced distinguished pupils, and earned from the Cyreneans the lovely title "The Light of Hellas."[35]

Each subsequent Cyrenaic made modifications to Aristippos's teachings. The next significant Cyrenaic, **Hegesias,** colored the philosophy dark. He began with Aristippos's notion that pleasure and pain rule our lives but concluded that life holds far more pain than pleasure. The experiencing soul, he reasoned, is trapped in a physical body that, in the normal course of living, is subject to all kinds of painful disturbances, and somehow fate sees to it that we suffer them all. To exist at all, therefore, means to suffer, and "happiness cannot be realized" in this life.° Philosophy's primary function is to assist individuals in avoiding pain. One should strive to achieve a state of invulnerability to life's unsatisfactoriness, but the one way to insure freedom from pain is through suicide. Hegesias is most remembered, therefore, for advocating suicide, and he was nicknamed Peisithanatos, "the Death-Persuader." This Hegesian version of Cyrenaic philosophy had moved very close to Stoicism and was ready to be syncretized with it.[36]

> *To exist is to suffer (the first of the Four Noble Truths).*
>
> THE BUDDHA

Annikeris—the man who ransomed Plato from slavery°—was a brighter light in the Cyrenaic school, although he nudged the philosophy toward popular tastes and promoted ideas the average citizen could grasp more easily. He argued that we don't "accumulate" pleasures; all we can do is to make the most of each pleasure as it enters our experience. One of our deepest pleasures, he says, comes when we sympathize with another's enjoyment and even when we sacrifice ourselves for someone we care for.[37]

°See p. 135.

> *The goal of living for the wise man should be to live without pain of body or mind.*
>
> HEGESIAS

The last noteworthy Cyrenaic was **Theodôros,** nicknamed "the Atheist" because he said the gods don't exist. "He considered joy and grief to be the supreme good and evil of one's life; the first is achieved through wisdom, the latter is brought on by thoughtlessness." He was nicknamed Theodôros "the Cheerful." One of his teachings, as recorded by Laërtius, is especially interesting: "Theft, adultery, and sacrilege would be allowable at appropriate times, since none of these acts is by nature base, if once you have removed the prejudice against them, which is kept up in order to hold the foolish multitude together." Although it requires fairly sophisticated semantics to untangle the complexities of what Theodôros is saying, the statement shows considerable insight. All actions, he is saying, are neutral in themselves; no human engagement is inherently good or bad. And all evaluations—good or bad, virtuous or evil, moral or immoral—are value judgments made by valuers. And sometimes—"at appropriate times"—these actions can be evaluated in different ways, as good rather than bad, moral rather than immoral, depending on the concrete circumstances. In certain situations, stealing might be justifiably seen as a virtue (Jean Valjean of *Les*

> *We must not hate men, but teach them better.*
>
> HEGESIAS

Misérables comes to mind, stealing to feed his family). Evaluations are not intrinsic qualities but always have a social context, and this social context determines the parameters for optional evaluations. Theodôros also shows insight in noting that people employ accepted ("politically correct") evaluations for social control.[38]

Like Aristippos, Theodôros loved to argue and seems to have specialized in insulting humor, for which, one account says, "he was condemned to drink the hemlock." He was expelled from Athens once and from Cyrene twice. After Theodôros, Cyrenaic teachings were largely absorbed into Epicureanism, which then blossomed and carried on a vigorous hedonist tradition.[39]

EUCLEIDÊS AND THE MEGARIAN LOGICIANS

Another member of the inner Socratic circle was struck with Socrates' genius for logical argument and refutation. **Eucleidês of Megara** birthed a school of logic in his hometown and produced influential disciples. Megara had been a strong city-state one (long) day's walk to the west of Athens, and it had alternated as friend and enemy to the Athenian polis. In 432 BC the Athenians, under Pericles, passed a decree forbidding the Megarians from entering any port in the empire or trading. Eucleidês was forced to make clandestine trips to Athens (dressed as a woman, one account says) to listen to Socrates. He was present at Socrates' execution, and Plato and other followers of Socrates took refuge in his home in Megara during the dangerous days after the execution. We are familiar with Eucleidês from his role in Plato's *Theaetetus* and *Phaedo*. No doubt Plato and Eucleidês got into many arguments over the problem of defining knowledge while Plato was staying with him, and for years the nature of Eleatic logic continued to haunt Plato.° Eucleidês wrote six dialogues, among them *Phoenix*, *Crito*, *Alcibiades*, and a *Discourse on Love*. (Everyone, it seems, wrote a discourse on love!)[40]

To say Eucleidês possessed an aptitude for logical computation would be an understatement. He doubtless had been impressed with Socrates' elenctic exchanges when the great debater demolished his opponents' arguments, so he revitalized this logical tradition: "The wrangling Eucleidês inspired the Megarians with a frenzied love of controversy," a later writer says. Versed in Parmenides' logical techniques, he joined them with Socratic ideas. Socrates (via Plato) had elaborated on the idea that Goodness was just one thing, although we see its different manifestations and call it by various names—honor, wisdom, God, love, mind, and so on. Parmenides had argued that Being was just one thing and that all single things manifested that Being, though we call them by different names—tree, rock, bird, star, Socrates, and so on. Eucleidês seems to have decided that the Socratic One (called "the Good") and the Parmenidean Being were the same. Hence, only Goodness truly exists, and anything opposing the Good cannot and does not exist.[41]

This notion became the cornerstone of what was known as Megarian Eleaticism, and the Megarians were famed for their logical games. "Have you stopped beating your father?" was a favorite question. "How many hairs must a man lose to be bald"? Eubulides "the Arguer" (Eucleidês' successor) asked. "How many grains of something does it take to make a heap?" "If I don't have something, can I lose it?" "If I tell you that I'm lying, am I telling the truth?"

The most noted of Eucleidês' followers, **Stilpon,** bested everyone in "ingeniousness and sophistry" so that almost all of Greece "was led away by him to join the Megarian school." All of Stilpon's property was once plundered when an enemy force occupied Megara. When the offer came to restore what he had lost, he replied that he had lost nothing, for he possessed only his education, speech, and knowledge—and no one had taken those away. Stilpon focused his criticism on Plato's

---

The world is my home country.
THEODÔROS

°*See pp. 157f. and Chapter 5 on the Eleatics.*

On Eucleidês *He argued that the supreme good is really one, even though we call it by many names such as wisdom, God, Mind, and so on.*
DIOGENES LAËRTIUS

On Eucleidês *Anything that contradicted the Good he rejected, arguing that it has no existence.*
DIOGENES LAËRTIUS

Men of worth are friends.
ANTISTHENES

notion of Real Ideas. When Plato said "Man exists," he obviously was not referring to any single man; and on the assumption that only individuals have true existence, Plato was, therefore, not referring to anything. So also if I say that ten thousand years ago "fig existed," then the single fig I'm eating now can't possibly be the same fig. What I'm eating, therefore, is not a fig.[42]

Eucleidês influenced Zeno of Kitium, the founder of Stoicism. Several other Megarians became epigonoi—Bryson, Polyxenus, Diodoros, and Philo—all of them minor by comparison, but contemporaries admired them nevertheless. The Megarian school endured until shortly after 300 BC.

Virtue is a weapon that cannot be taken away.

ANTISTHENES

RECYCLED

The Socratic legacy was developed primarily by the greatest thinkers of the time—Plato and Aristotle. Though the two differed on some fundamental issues, they handled Socrates' gift with such power that the protest philosophies were overshadowed by comparison and remained relatively minor systems, limited in their popularity. But after Aristotle the great tradition did begin to falter, watered down by lesser lights, and many of these counter-culture systems became the philosophic seeds for Epicureanism, Stoicism, and other syncretistic second-generation philosophies. Later, these systems provided ideas that were absorbed into a variety of amalgams such as the Skeptics, Eclectics, and the noetic° systems—Gnosticism, Neoplatonism, and the medieval Christian theologies. Nothing philosophical ever seems to have been lost; virtually every idea was recycled, transmogrified to serve different worldviews, frequently bastardized, but always given new life.

°*See lexicon.*

ENDNOTES

1 Diogenes Laërtius, *Lives of Eminent Philosophers*, VI.33, 40, 78. In this chapter only, except in endnotes, Diogenes Laërtius is referred to as Laërtius to avoid confusion with the Cynic.
2 Diogenes, *Lives*, VI.2, 8, 15–18.
3 Diogenes, *Lives*, VI.1, 6, 5.
4 Diogenes, *Lives*, VI.11.
5 Diogenes, *Lives*, VI.11, 8.
6 Diogenes, *Lives*, VI.2, 24.
7 Diogenes, *Lives*, VI.3, 5, 4.
8 Diogenes, *Lives*, VI.41, 74, 75, 74.
9 Diogenes, *Lives*, VI.22.
10 Diogenes, *Lives*, VI.58.
11 Diogenes, *Lives*, VI.27, 28, 41.
12 Diogenes, *Lives*, VI.45, 39, 28, 42.
13 Diogenes, *Lives*, VI.24.
14 Diogenes, *Lives*, VI.71.
15 Diogenes, *Lives*, VI.24, 43, 40, 25, 54.
16 Diogenes, *Lives*, VI.63, 71.
17 Diogenes, *Lives*, VI.38, 43, 32, 49, 23, 75, 74, 75–76.
18 Diogenes, *Lives*, VI.80.
19 Diogenes, *Lives*, VI.34, 76–78.
20 Diogenes, *Lives*, VI.12, 97, 98.
21 Diogenes, *Lives*, II.78, 76.
22 Diogenes, *Lives*, II.68, 67.
23 Diogenes, *Lives*, II.77, 83–85.
24 Diogenes, *Lives*, II.66.
25 Diogenes, *Lives*, II.86–93.
26 Diogenes, *Lives*, II.93, 95.
27 Diogenes, *Lives*, II.90, 91.
28 Diogenes, *Lives*, II.95, 69, 79.
29 Diogenes, *Lives*, II.90.
30 Diogenes, *Lives*, II.92.
31 Diogenes, *Lives*, II.95, 91.
32 Diogenes, *Lives*, II.75, 74.

33 Diogenes, *Lives*, II.81.
34 Diogenes, *Lives*, II.94, 95.
35 Diogenes, *Lives*, II.72.
36 Diogenes, *Lives*, II.93, 94.
37 Diogenes, *Lives*, II.96–97.
38 Diogenes, *Lives*, II.98, 99.
39 Diogenes, *Lives*, II.101.
40 Diogenes, *Lives*, II.108.
41 Diogenes, *Lives*, II.107, 106.
42 Diogenes, *Lives*, II.113–120.

CHAPTER 10

PLATO OF ATHENS

Crushed by the death of his teacher, the greatest of idealist thinkers seeks a transcendent truth that will unite all people and enable them to live in peace; he documents the life and mind of Socrates and continues the dialectic tradition; he founds the first great institution for higher learning; at the end of a long life he despairs that the world will ever be improved.

THE MAKING OF A PHILOSOPHER

SHATTERED DREAM

Plato was born on the seventh of Thargelion, the birthday of Apollo, in the eighty-eighth Olympiad—May 29, 428/7 BC. This was the best of times to be born, and the worst of times; best because he lived through the last great days of Athenian democracy and reaped the Golden Age's rich harvest in art, architecture, drama, and intellect; worst because he had to endure years of chaos and tragedy from continuous warring between Athens and her neighbors, from an unbelievable reign of terror under vicious oligarchs, and from the ravages of plague and famine. But through it all he sustained his idealism and continued to plan for a career in public life—until, after the fall of Athens in 404 BC and the execution of his teacher in 399 BC, his world came crashing down around his shoulders.

Both heritage and training fostered Plato's dream of a career in politics. On his father's side he traced his lineage to the old kings of Athens and on his mother's side to Athens' greatest lawgiver Solon. His stepfather Pyrilampes was a political leader close to Pericles, Athens' noblest ruler who presided over the young democracy's glorious years. Thus Plato was raised on Periclean politics. He also had watched his uncle Charmides and his mother's cousin Critias involve themselves in heated debated of public policy. Add to all this the fact that he had known from birth a gregarious spirit named Socrates who believed that any citizen worth his salt would be eager to participate in the public affairs of his polis. No wonder Plato developed great insight into political affairs; he lived behind the scenes, and he saw it all.

So Plato took for granted that he was destined for a career in government. Given the finest education available; having listened to the Sophists lecture citizens about laws, courts, and how to survive the rigors of democracy; and inbued with the assurance he would do great things, Plato tells us he was "full of eagerness for a public career." Late in life, near his eighties, Plato wrote a long letter reflecting on these early years. "In the days of my youth my experience was the same as that of many

People are always getting into arguments in which they utterly refuse to consider the other point of view; that is, they falsely believe themselves to be wise.

SOCRATES

Plato of Athens (429–347 BC), idealist philosopher and biographer of Socrates.

On Plato *The safest general characterization of the European philosophical tradition is that it consists of a series of footnotes to Plato.*

ALFRED NORTH
WHITEHEAD

On Plato *Over the centuries, a special, almost mystical aura has surrounded Plato, the pupil and interpreter of Socrates, as perhaps the strongest spiritual presence in the Western world before the coming of Jesus of Nazareth.*

WILLIAM HARLAN HALE

others. I thought that as soon as I should become my own master I would immediately enter into public life." Except for a precocious passion for writing poetry and despite his disillusion with politics from about age 29, he seems never to have wavered from his calling to public service.

But in 404 BC all this began to change. In that year the young democracy came unraveled. After a battle in which Athens lost her fleet and thousands of her best fighters were executed, she submitted to Sparta at any price. Athens was allowed to write up a new constitution and established an oligarchy called the Thirty, under the leadership of Plato's uncle Charmides. At some point Critias and Charmides invited Plato to take part in their revolutionary activities; "indeed they invited me at once to join their administration, thinking it would be congenial." He seriously considered the invitation, "for I imagined that they would administer the State by leading it out of an unjust way of life into a just way." But, Plato says, he waited and watched. He was soon horrified at what he saw. The new leaders began almost immediately to purge the city of anyone favoring democracy, arresting and executing, indiscriminately and without trial, any citizen with unpopular views and those whose property and wealth they wished to confiscate. On one occasion Socrates and four others were ordered to arrest an innocent citizen, Leon of Salamis. Socrates summarily refused to obey the outrageous orders and got by with it, probably because Critias was a former pupil.

"So when I beheld all these actions and others of a similar kind," Plato wrote, "I was indignant, and I withdrew myself from the evil practices then going on." For a year and a half the lawless violence continued, making Athenians look back longingly on the war years as a "golden age" of comparative peace. Then Critias was killed in battle, the Thirty were deposed, and a democracy of sorts was returned. For three years, under Sparta's command, social and economic conditions stabilized, and Plato, battered but not broken, thought again of a possible political career. "Once again I was really, though less urgently, impelled with a desire to take part in public and political affairs."

Then in the spring of 399 BC Plato's beloved mentor, whom he calls "of all men the noblest and the wisest and the most just," was indicted on the "most unholy charges." The man behind it all, a leader of the restored democracy, Anytos, charged Socrates with corrupting young minds and denying the officially approved deities of Athens. An otherwise able leader, Anytos shared the narrow-gauged fears of Athenian patriots who regarded Socrates as a dangerous freethinker undermining the established ideas and values that sustained the social order; they were genuinely alarmed that he was teaching their youth subversive attitudes. So Socrates was tried, found guilty, sentenced to death, and, a month later, executed with a cup of poison hemlock.° Plato was ill and did not witness the tragedy, but details were transmitted to him, and the horror of what had happened shattered his faith in human beings, confirmed his fear of democracy, and ended his dream of a political career. He was about twenty-nine years old.

With the death of his master, Plato's disillusionment was complete; the execution of Socrates turned him from a man of action into a man of thought. His original aspiration was to be a political reformer and effect change in the world by shaping public opinion and by fashioning new and better laws, but after the events of 399 BC he lost all hope of reforming the world through political means. "As I advanced in years it seemed more and more difficult to me that the affairs of state could be managed rightly." He saw that the fundamental ideas and values of the Athenian society were terribly flawed, and a much more fundamental change must occur before social and political reform: People must learn how to think, and they must undergo a revision of values based on the truth about human life, its nature, and its worth. Plato had the intellect to see clearly where the problem lay, and he had the motivation to think through the elemental foundations of human thought to lay bare the truth and then to establish a school that was in toto dedicated to the education of the future leaders of Athens, teaching them how to reason and how to go for the nobler values that would change the world. In other words, if Plato couldn't change the world directly, he would do so indirectly: He would launch an educational program to produce young leaders wise enough to create a revolution in human thought. "For the classes of mankind will have no cessation from evils until either the class of those who are right and true philosophers attains political supremacy, or else the class of those who hold power in the States becomes, by some dispensation of Heaven, really philosophic."[1]

IN THE HISTORY OF PHILOSOPHY

Plato is most remembered (1) as the principal biographer of Socrates (thus immortalizing Socrates' life, ideas, trial, and death); (2) for composing the Dialogues that have had immense influence on thought, language, and literature; (3) for recording (and perhaps developing) Socrates' dialectical (conversational) method for doing philosophy; (4) for his (or Socrates') rebuttal of sophistic thinking and method; (5) for preserving in *The Symposium* Socrates' encomium on love; (6) for the theory of Real Ideas (notably in the allegory of the Cave); (7) for his innovative ideas in egalitarian education that he practiced in the Academy; (8) for his threefold division of human nature; (9) for his (or Socrates') exploration of the concept of justice in the *Republic*; (10) for his political theories developed in both the *Republic* and *The Laws* and for his attempt to put them to the test in practical politics at Syracuse

To understand Plato is to be educated.

EDITH HAMILTON

°See pp. 102–107.

We must make every effort to determine the truth of these matters, mustn't we?

SOCRATES

On Plato *Plato, with his speculative vision, gave the West a tradition it has never lost and a goal it has never realized.*

ROBERT S. BRUMBAUGH

THE MAN

Historians have been enormously troubled trying to decide whether Plato was primarily an historian or a playwright, and a similar quandary applies to our traditional information *about* him. It is so fraught with gossip, legend, and even myth that it's difficult to sift historical fact from the wild stories told about him.[2] One Plato scholar concludes that "there may be more anecdotes preserved about Plato than about any other ancient personality," though both Socrates and Alexander the Great come in as close seconds.[3]

No state nor any individual man can ever become happy unless he passes his life in subjection to justice combined with wisdom.

PLATO

Born in Athens, in the *dêmê* (district or neighborhood) of Collytos, he was christened Aristocles after his grandfather; his athletic trainer later nicknamed him Plato (Greek *platôn*, "broad-shouldered," "stocky"). His father was named Ariston, his mother Perictione (although myth soon made him a son of Apollo and born of a virgin; one account says that when Perictione became pregnant, Apollo appeared to Ariston in a dream and told him not to have sex with his wife until after his [Apollo's] son's birth). "Possibly Plato is the first historical person, as distinct from the Greek

A seated Demos *(People of Athens) being crowned by a personified Democracy. A 4th Century BC relief sculpted as a political statement against tyranny and for democracy. Whatever was commanded by the authority of the Demos had the force of law.*

heroes of Homer and Hesiod, said to be the progeny of a union between a mortal woman and a divine father."[4]

Plato had two older brothers, Adeimantos and Glaucon, and a younger sister, Potone. His father apparently died while Plato was still quite young, and Periictione then married her uncle Pyrilampes, and together they had a son, Antiphon. (Pyrilampes had a son, Demos, by an earlier marriage.) So, Plato had a full complement of parents, stepparents, siblings, and half siblings and seems to have been raised with the normal range of experiences typical of a well-to-do Athenian youth.[5] Pyrilampes vanishes from the records after the battle of Delium in 424 BC (Plato would have been about four years old). Periictione was apparently still alive a half century later; she likely would have been in her late eighties or nineties. (About 366 BC Plato mentioned having to care for her, while griping he also had to care for four of his grandnieces.)

Little is known about Plato's youth. He didn't formally enroll in any institution (as Aristotle could a few decades later), but he was well educated and excelled in such subjects as mathematics, music, and rhetoric; before he was twenty, he apparently won recognition for writing all genres of poetry—lyric, tragic, comedic, and even erotic epigrams. Numerous uneven traditions claim he also painted. We also know he was exceptionally robust, took prizes in athletics, and may have taken part in several Panhellenic games. He met his civic duty to his polis as a soldier in the army, fighting in three battles against Sparta and once was decorated for bravery.

Socrates long had been a family friend, becoming an associate of Plato's uncle Charmides in 431 BC; so from his birth Plato was acquainted with the great philosopher's spirit and dialectics. About 407 BC, when Plato was nineteen or twenty, he had matured, he tells us, to the point when he began to "listen" seriously to Socrates, and he fell in love with philosophy, calling it a "precious delight." He already had studied Heraclitean philosophy with a teacher named Cratylus; he knew about Pythagoras and was fascinated by his mystical ideas, and he had spent some time at Megara studying Zeno's notions about logic.

Plato's student years were doubtless spent in the Athenian Agora's immediate environs, close to his teacher, who, it seems, was always found conversing with students in their homes or with public figures in the busy marketplace. Where Plato lived and spent his nights we don't know, probably in private homes near the Agora or possibly in his parents' home, at least part of the time. During the day he would have taken his meals with other students and with them spent most of his hours watching and listening to Socrates, exchanging with bystanders, and practicing his own analytical and dialectical skills. He would have been intimately familiar with the religious life of Athens and visited the temples in the Agora and on the Acropolis. Equally familiar would have been the shops and shrines along the Panathenaic Way, which came down from the Acropolis's north slope and led to the Dipylon Gate, where it forked. The western road led to the sacred shrines of Eleusis and the Greek countryside, and the eastern road led to the olive groves of Academus.

MEGARA

Plato was about twenty-nine when Socrates was put to death. Many of Socrates' friends and followers found themselves in danger in the days following his execution and fled for their safety. They were not merely associated with him in his supposed subversion; they believed in, and had been expounding, the same ideas he was executed for.

Plato attempted to shake the nightmare, leaving Athens immediately and staying with a friend and fellow student, Eucleidês, at Megara, a town one days' walk to the

Truth heads the list of all things good. Let anyone who intends to be happy and blessed be its partner from the start.

PLATO

Human nature involves, above all, pleasures, pains, and desires, and no mortal animal can help being hung up dangling in the air (so to speak) in total dependence on these powerful influences.

PLATO

west. Eucleidês had been present at Socrates' execution and no doubt shared the anguish of the event. Raging, saddened, frustrated, possibly depressed, and forced to reappraise his loyalties and his plans for the future, Plato determined at some point that there was one thing he would not allow to happen He would not let them succeed in silencing Socrates. Empowered by fury and a sense of colossal injustice, he began to write. For the next twelve years, wherever he happened to be, he worked on a series of dialogues all designed to preserve Socrates' thought and personality. At the end of this time, the angers had cooled, and Socrates was immortal. The world will have long forgot who Anytos was, or Melêtos, or Lycon, but through Plato's dramatic skill and dedication to his teacher, Socrates will live on in the mind and heart of any reader who takes up the dialogues to read the story of one of history's greatest lives and most tragic events.

THE PYTHAGOREANS OF TARENTUM

But my dear Crito, why should we pay so much attention to what "most people" think? The really reasonable people, who have more claim to be considered, will believe that the facts are exactly as they are.

SOCRATES

Plato's stay at Megara was brief, and he probably returned to Athens, watched the corrupt machinations of government, and pondered what had truly gone wrong within and between the humans who behaved this way. The records (too legendary to be very dependable) tell us that during these years he did some traveling, probably to Egypt (his writings indicate some familiarity with Egyptian religion and customs), possibly to Cyrene in North Africa, and, more certainly, to Italy and Sicily. In Cyrene he may have visited the renowned Pythagorean geometer Theodorus (who figures in the *Theaetetus*), a friend of Socrates. More firmly established in the records is a visit, around 388 BC, to the Pythagorean center at Tarentum in southern Italy and to Sicily. In Tarentum he was befriended by Archytas, a strong and decent man then in the process of forming a school of higher learning; Plato may well have begun to contemplate establishing his own school and wanted to see the Pythagorean model firsthand.

Archytas, like Theodôrus a brilliant Pythagorean mathematian, had gained considerable fame for his work in acoustics and musical theory. He elaborated on Pythagoras's doctrine that all phenomena, both natural and human, can be described with numbers, and he attempted to provide an empirical foundation for Pythagoras's theories. Much of Plato's mature philosophy rings with the sounds of Pythagoras, and this visit no doubt strengthened Plato's interest in mathematics; he later insisted that mathematics serve as the cornerstone of his own educational program at the Academy.

SICILY

If you ever inject truth into politics, you have no politics.

WILL ROGERS

Following his stay at Tarentum, Plato proceeded to Syracuse, a Greek colony on Sicily's eastern shore. This was the first of three visits that occurred about 388 BC, 367 BC, and 361 BC; he was involved with Sicilian affairs for more than thirty-five years. He probably first came to Syracuse at the invitation of the powerful military governor, Dionysios I, and had in mind the tantalizing possibility of putting some of his political thoughts to work. However, a subtext in the records hints that Plato and the tyrant didn't hit it off at all. Several stories record conversations between Plato and Dionysios when the philosopher was anything but tactful.[6] Plato seems to have been offended by the lifestyles of the affluent Sicilians he observed in Syracuse, finding the court life phony, empty, and meaningless, and he expressed himself perhaps too brusquely. In the *Republic*, for example, Glaucon once asks Plato, "Then you would not approve of Syracusan dinners, and the refinements of Sicilian cookery?" "I think not!" Plato answers. One account has Plato telling Dionysios that a tyrant (such as Dionysios!) is the most cowardly kind of ruler. When an angry Dionysios asked why he came to Sicily, Plato answered "To look for a good man." Dionysios retorted, "Even the gods haven't yet found such a man!" When Dionysios told Plato he was sure the philosopher would have many bad things to say about him when he got back to Athens, Plato answered that he had better things to talk about.

Sometime later when Plato was set to leave Syracuse in the company of a Spartan naval commander there on state business, Dionysios secretly instructed the commander to kill Plato or sell him into slavery. Plato was clamped in irons and transported to the island of Aegina, was offered for sale as a slave, but a friend named Annikeris ransomed him and he made his way back to Athens. We are told Annikeris declined repayment when some of Plato's other friends raised money for him.°

Dionysios the Elder died shortly thereafter, and his son Dionysios II succeeded him. Dionysios the Younger was thirty years old, uneducated, inexperienced, and unprepared for his tasks, which, besides governing, included the military defense of Sicily against the aggressive inroads of the Carthaginians. The strong man behind the new ruler, his brother-in-law Dion, had worked closely with Plato twenty years earlier during his first visit. Apparently Dion, fearing for his country, had the idea of inviting Plato once again to Syracuse to undertake the job of educating his problematic brother-in-law. Plato was skeptical about achieving any success, but he was willing to try. He had a better chance this time of applying his ideas to the real world than during his first visit. Equally important, perhaps, he hoped he might make a serious difference in preserving Greek culture in the west, which the barbarians from Carthage were about to devastate. Dionysios II urgently needed enough strength to repel the invaders and establish a constitutional monarchy linking the cities of western Sicily into a federation. With luck Plato might transmogrify this unserious upstart, who found himself at a momentous point in historic time, into a statesman. So, with misgiving, Plato accepted the invitation and sailed westward for the second time.

Since his first voyage to Syracuse, Plato had established his school and gained fame as an educator throughout Hellas, so his return occasioned a state celebration. Treated like royalty, he was transported by the new tyrant himself in a chariot when he arrived in his trireme. This time he stayed for more than a year. Plato, now firmly committed to the belief an education in science and mathematics was essential to developing character and competence, designed a liberal arts course of study for the young Dionysios, based on geometry, that would improve his critical skills and make him a more thoughtful, discerning leader. Dionysios apparently took to it, and geometry became the fashionable topic of conversation at the court, whose floors, we are told, became dusty from numerous people drawing geometric diagrams in the dirt and sand outside. Plato made some effort also to win Dionysius's wife to his course of study.

But the experiment in practical politics didn't work. Dionysios II was too weak willed and undisciplined, and his paranoid suspicions of Dion's motives soon led him to believe that Dion and Plato were hatching a plot against him. Dionysios forced Dion into exile, and a deep breach developed between the tyrant and his philosopher guest. Plato had to return to Athens, whence he continued a friendly correspondence with Dionysios, working toward a reconciliation between him and Dion. The cause was hopeless after Dionysios (failing to heed Plato's advice) confiscated Dion's money and forced his wife (also Dionysios's aunt) to marry another man.

Still trying to bring a resolution to hostilities and work toward establishing good government, Plato made a third and last trip to Syracuse six years later, when he was sixty-seven. Several other illustrious thinkers accompanied Plato this time, among them Aristippos and Aeschinês. While there he assisted in drafting a constitution for a confederation of the Greek-Sicilian cities. A story (which may be apocryphal) tells that on this occasion Dionysios gave Plato a huge endowment of eighty talents

Didn't we say that ignorance is a misfortune whoever suffers from it?

SOCRATES

°*Another account says he was about to be executed at Aegina when someone mentioned he was a philosopher; they released him forthwith.*

Madness comes from God, whereas sober sense is merely human.

SOCRATES

For human life intellect is far, far better than pleasure.

SOCRATES

(upwards of a half-million dollars); if the story is true, Plato may well have used the money to start his own school. Once again, Plato seems to have been in physical danger, this time from Dionysios's bodyguards; he was allowed to leave Sicily only when his friend Archytas intervened.

THE ACADEMY

After he returned to Athens from his first trip to Sicily, following "the miserable story of events in Syracuse," Plato seems to have suffered a serious illness due to the rigors of the long voyage. When well again, he gathered a few students around him and began to teach. Soon he launched into establishing a school dedicated to the study of ethics and politics. The founding of the Academy dates from about 387 BC, when Plato was around age forty, the midpoint of his life; and he spent the next forty years there till his death in 347 BC.[7]

Plato most likely began teaching students in his home, or in a local gymnasium, before any formal establishment of a school. His home first, and then his school, located on the outskirts of Athens about a mile northwest of the Dipylon Gate in the vicinity of the Kerameicos, was built on several acres of public land purchased for Plato by his friends. The site contained olive trees, statues, and a temple named for the legendary Attic hero Academus, who was buried there—hence its name. One legend described how Helen, a daughter of Zeus, had been kidnapped by Theseus; when her brothers came to rescue her, Academus disclosed to them her whereabouts. For this good deed the Academy was always spared whenever the Lacedaemonians invaded Greece. The grounds, eventually walled in, contained fountains, walks, lecture halls, classrooms, and a shrine of learning—a sort of chapel Plato himself built, dedicated to the worship of the Muses, Zeus's nine daughters who were the inspiring spirits of "music," which included all the arts and sciences.

A free soul ought not to pursue any study slavishly; . . . Do not, then, my friend, keep children to their studies by compulsion but by play.

PLATO

Philosophy was an umbrella that contained geometry and arithmetic and any other "thinking" discipline; in the *Timaeus* he writes of young men "devoting themselves to geometry or any other form of philosophy." Plato often referred to philosophy as the "loftiest music." In Greece inscriptions were commonly placed over the entrances to sanctuaries and temples; over the Academy's gate were inscribed the words "*AGEOMETRETOS MEDEIS EISITO*" "Let no one ignorant of geometry enter here." Plato had a strong affinity with the rational sciences and believed study of them leads the mind away from the world of the senses into the realm of universal truth. "God geometrizes," he said. Later, when prescribing principles for educating children, he wrote: "No single branch of a child's education has such an enormous range of applications as mathematics; but its greatest advantage is that it wakes up the sleepy ignoramus and makes him quick to understand, retentive and sharp-witted; and thanks to this miraculous science he does better than his natural abilities would have allowed."[8] Furthermore, he was convinced the study of these formal disciplines fosters the "knowledge of law and order, measure and symmetry, uniformity and regularity, harmony and rhythm" and is a major help in "the art of living."[9] Diogenes the Cynic once satirized Plato's love of geometry, insisting that he could see solid objects but had a hard time seeing abstractions; Plato replied to the effect it requires a very special eye to perceive the truth.

Strictly speaking, it is not instruction but provocation that I can receive from another soul.

RALPH WALDO
EMERSON

Plato's Academy was the first institution of higher learning in the Western world. Two other famous schools antedated Plato's: the Pythagorean school at Crotona, founded perhaps as early as 520 BC, and the school of Isocrates in Athens, dating from about 390 BC. But neither of these earlier institutions were liberal arts institutions. Pythagoras's school was primarily a closed sanctuary for cult members engaged in a mystical belief system; Isocrates' school was a vocational institution designed to train young men in the art of political rhetoric, and Isocrates himself, who was famed for his polished oratory, despised the philosophic subtleties of Plato's approach to education. The Academy soon achieved a wide reputation for its competence in legal and political matters, and city-states throughout Hellas sought academicians as advisors in constitutional law.

In contrast to these other schools, the Academy was dedicated to character formation based on knowledge and truth. It did not aim to indoctrinate young people with trendy obsessions, with trivial issues, or with a populace's myopic preoccupations, which Plato had observed as ethically bankrupt and pragmatically unworkable; it did not try to teach them to manipulate public opinion through sweet-sounding oratory and persuasive rhetoric, as did the Sophists. Its aim was to effect in-depth changes in human character, to create people with noble qualities, to produce young men and women dedicated to the Good and to Truth and Beauty, and to prepare a new generation of intelligent, rational, and wise leaders who could be clear, courageous, and strong in their principles. Plato believed the hope of the world rested with men and women of courage and character dedicated to the service of mankind. All this he summarized in his most famous lines: "Until philosophers are kings, or the kings . . . [become] philosophers," the human race will not rest from its troubles. This vision of education's power and purpose is one of the noblest legacies of Greek thought; it has guided the West for two and one-third millennia and remains a dream whose realization lies still far in the future.

The central idea of Plato's pedagogical philosophy was the "dialectic," the search for truth through a continuous living exchange of ideas. Socrates employed this method, and Plato carried on the dialectic tradition. Socrates left nothing in writing because he was convinced that only in the immediate back-and-forth trading of ideas could people gradually approach the truth. On more than one occasion Plato condemned writing as a means of conveying true knowledge. In the *Phaedrus* he has Socrates pleading that only spoken words under the guidance of divine inspiration and love can attain depth and clarity; the truth must be "written on the soul of the hearer to enable him to learn about the right, the beautiful and the good."[10] This was the method used by Plato and his staff in the Academy—living—dialogue, not dull lectures.

Plato's founding of his Academy meant that after years of wandering, he had found his calling and settled on his life's work: He would educate future leaders, and he would write. At the time of Plato's birth in 428 BC, young men wanting an education had to seek out a wandering Sophist, pay him huge fees, and sit in on his lectures; by the time of Plato's death in 347 BC, students came from all quarters of the Greek world to enroll in the Academy. There they were taught mathematics and geometry, astronomy, music, zoology, probably physiology and anatomy, ethics, politics, athletics, dialectic and rhetoric. Plato never charged any fees from his students. We know from his utopian *Republic* that women could become guardians of the state, so it's no surprise Plato admitted women into the Academy on a par with men. The names of two of his women students have been preserved for us: Lastheneia of Mantinea and Axiothea of Phlius. An interesting story relates that, to be accepted by the male students, Axiothea was compelled to disguise her femininity, so she dressed as a man.[11]

This marks the beginning of the liberal arts university with a fixed location, a staff of teachers, and a well-developed curriculum; and all institutions of higher learning in the Western world directly descend from Plato's Academy. Plato's school lasted until it was forcefully closed in AD 529 by the Byzantine emperor Justinian, who, as a

On Plato *Antiphanes said humorously that just as, in a far northern city, words froze into ice as they were spoken, and were heard in the summer when they thawed, so the words spoken by Plato to his students in their youth were finally understood by them only in their old age.*

WILL DURANT

The direction in which education starts a man will determine his future life.

PLATO

Astronomy compels the soul to look upwards and leads us from this world to another.

PLATO

devout Christian, looked on it as a bastion of paganism. It thus flourished for more than nine hundred years.

LATER YEARS

The details we would like to have of Plato's later years are lacking from the records or enshrouded in anecdotes. After the founding of his school, he seems to have spent the next twenty years developing and administering the institution, and writing little. After that, until his death in 347 BC, he apparently lectured only occasionally at his school, having turned over the reins of leadership to others.

His third mission to Syracuse, when he was sixty-seven, had proved fruitless, and, after attending the Olympic games in the western Peloponnese in July of 367 BC—attracting much attention as a celebrity—he returned to Athens. Between 360 and 347 BC he composed the remainder of his dialogues and was working on his big book of the *Laws* at his death. On his eighty-first birthday, one account tells us, Plato was invited to a wedding celebration (possibly at the marriage of one of his grandnieces—the eldest was about to marry her uncle Speusippos); he attended, danced into the night, became tired, and asked leave to lie down to rest. He died in his sleep, while listening to music, in the first year of the 108th Olympiad—347 BC. Another account, from Cicero, tells us he died at the age of eighty with "pen in hand," leaving his *Laws* "in the wax," still unfinished. Copies of some books of poetry by Sophron were found beside him in his bed. He was buried near his Academy in the Kerameicos; his tomb could still be seen four centuries later, and was then lost to history. Said to have been inscribed on his grave were the lines:

> Asclepius cured the body: but to make men whole
>
> Phoebus sent Plato, healer of the soul.

PHILOSOPHY IN THE DIALOGUES: FIRST PERIOD

HISTORICAL RECONSTRUCTION

Socrates had spent his life dialoguing—not writing, not reading (although he was very well read); but talking through ideas in living conversations. So, after his death, when Plato wanted to create a written record of his teacher's methods and ideas, the dialogue form was a natural vehicle. Plato was not the first to employ this form; Homer and the playwrights had made use of it, and when Socrates visited the workshop of Simon the Cobbler in the Agora, this leatherworker jotted down some of Socrates' chatter in dialogue form. But Plato gets credit for developing the technique into an effective literary form for philosophic inquiry and for raising it to a new level of artistic brilliance.

Time has dealt lovingly with Plato's writings; virtually all have survived. The traditional corpus contained 36 books, and we have them all. This is in happy contrast to Aristotle's works, of whose 551 books only about 30 survive.

An obvious anachronism exists in all of Plato's dialogues: Their settings take place from twenty to eighty years earlier in an Athens long gone and with characters long dead. Some of his scenes are set when Plato was just a child, some even before he was born. The *Protagoras*, for instance, written about 390 BC, is set while Pericles was still alive and at the helm of his polis before the beginning of the Peloponnesian War and before Plato's birth. The *Republic*, written after 390 BC, is set in an Athens still at war with Sparta, before 413 BC, and while Plato was in his early teens. With the greatest gap, the *Parmenides*, written about 367 BC, describes a famous meeting with Eleatic

Knowledge that is acquired under compulsion has no hold on the mind.

PLATO

On Plato *Plato is philosophy, and philosophy Plato.*

RALPH WALDO EMERSON

logicians that occurred in 450 BC, some eighty-three years earlier, when Socrates was only about twenty.

Plato's Socratic dialogues are therefore historical reconstructions. His word pictures are dramatic creations, never intended as meticulous depictions of actual occurrences. They are reported as actual dialogues—whence their charm; but they are masterpieces of literary artistry based on distant memories, jogged probably by personal notes and by exchanged reminiscences with others who were eyewitnesses or had hearsay information about such past events.

So Plato's writing career spans a half century, while he changed and grew, matured in his thinking and craftsmanship, wrote voluminously, and then experienced an apparent time of disillusionment. When his writings are placed in a rough chronological sequence, one can discern at least three stages in his work, while Plato underwent changes in mood and style, in opinions about education and teaching methods, in his attitudes toward the natural sciences, and in his philosophic priorities and concerns. He moved from an apologetic Socratic period, spending his energies defending and explaining Socrates, to a more positive philosophic period while he attempted bravely to find his own answers to the world's problems as he saw them. Then, finally, he experienced a severely pragmatic period, where, in the *Laws*, he became an authoritarian lawgiver exhibiting little residual interest in the discussion of philosophic ideas.

Plato was an unusually sophisticated Greek intellectual. Like Socrates, he was a searcher, not a believer; he avoided rigidity, final solutions, and bottom lines, resisting closure on any question. It follows that any search for, or expectation of finding, a tight coherence in his philosophy is not likely to succeed. That is, a "Plato's philosophy" or a "Platonism" per se does not exist, and never has, however deeply such a notion is embedded in certain Western traditions. This is the case for two reasons. (1) In his earlier writings Plato's primary purpose was to record and illustrate the dialectic style of his teacher, whose goal was to subject society's ethical thinking to rigorous examination. Plato's intent was to promulgate the machinery of Socrates' *method*, which was essentially to ask questions and carry on searching conversations with other thinkers to lay bare the fallacies in our thinking that cause us such trouble.°

Plato's great Socratic dialogues demonstrate philosophic dynamics; in every dialogue the issues are left open ended, without definitive answers. Near the end of the *Phaedo*, for instance, Plato has Cebes, a young Pythagorean scientist, confessing his discomfort with this freewheeling kind of exploration, but Socrates reassures him: "If you are at all puzzled about what we have been saying, don't hesitate to speak. Go through it and see if you think it might be improved; and take me with you through it again if you think I can help you any more at all in your difficulties."[12] Only in his later writings does Plato become somewhat systematic in developing philosophic content, and even then he fails miserably to tie up loose ends.

(2) The "Plato's philosophy" prevailing in Western tradition is the product of the worshipful devotion of later Platonists. Followers experiencing a strong resonance with Plato inevitably asked every question they could think of about what he thought and then tried to answer them all, thus fleshing out "Platonism" into an organized system. Platonic system-building began soon after Plato's death and continued without letup for the next twenty-three hundred years.

Plato's first-period dialogues were all probably written between the death of Socrates and the founding of the Academy—between 399 BC and about 387 BC, while Plato was in his thirties and early forties. Written for the literate layperson, their primary purpose was to memorialize Socrates—to salvage his reputation, condemn his misguided accusers, and immortalize his genius for pursuing the truth.

We'll never be able to examine pleasure adequately without also considering pain.

SOCRATES

°*See pp. 101–103, 107–115.*

I know nothing except the fact that I know nothing.

SOCRATES

°See elenchos in lexicon.

They are strongly adversarial; Socrates employs sophistic debating techniques, by which he gradually annihilates the arguments of his opponents; he demonstrates that their thinking, contrary to their own complacent belief they know what they are talking about, is really very fuzzy and fallacious.° They deal primarily with ethical and political questions and show no interest in the natural world or the physical sciences. Plato's famous theory of Real Ideas is virtually absent.

The **Apology** is Plato's eloquent reconstruction of the events and speeches at Socrates' trial. It contains the ever-inspiring account of courage and intelligence displayed by a great human spirit, and it records one of Socrates' most useful themes: that wisdom consists in knowing what one doesn't know.°

°See pp. 106–107.

The **Crito** purports to be a record of a conversation held while Socrates was in prison awaiting execution. In the darkness of early morning, his dear old friend Criton awakens him in the prison cell, tells him he will be executed the following day, and urges him to escape, pointing out that the jailer has been bribed, his friends are willing to ransom him, and "there are plenty of places where you will find a welcome." Back and forth, the two old men debate the immediate possibility of escape. Criton's° recurring argument is, in effect, What will people think of us, your devoted friends, if we don't succeed in persuading you to escape? To which Socrates gives a firm reply: Who cares what others think? Reasonable people will see the facts for what they are and understand why one has to do what he has to do.

The central philosophical problem of the *Crito* has to do with an honest citizen's relationship to the state and to the legal system of laws regulating it. The moral dilemma is, Should a good and decent "law-abiding citizen" obey the laws of his society if charged with a crime when he is, in fact, innocent? The answer Socrates gives is that although he is innocent of all he is charged with, the state, the court, and the laws constitute a legally valid governing system and a responsible citizen must

The Indictment: Socrates is guilty of corrupting the minds of the young, and of believing in deities of his own invention instead of the gods recognized by the State.

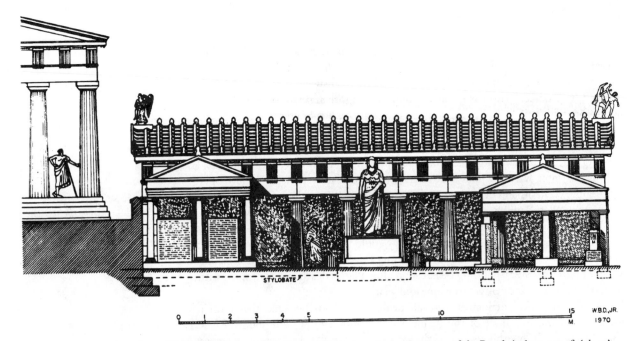

STYLOBATE

0 1 2 3 4 5 .... 10 15   W.B.D.,JR.
                                        M.   1970

The Royal Stoa, a relatively small building that housed the Laws of Solon, was the headquarters of the Royal Archon, one of Athens' principal magistrates. Socrates was summoned here to appear before the Archon for the preliminary examination that led to his execution. It was located at the north end of the Agora.

abide by its verdicts, even when it makes a mistake. The legal system, and indeed society itself, would crumble if individuals were permitted to decide for themselves whether or not they should obey the laws. Socrates knows the state made a mistake, but that's not the point: The state operated legally, and it is a citizen's duty, therefore, to obey its mandates. He had promised to obey; he must keep his word. Besides, a philosopher's goal should be to care for his soul, to live honorably, and not to take too seriously the vicissitudes of this mundane existence.

"So give it up, Criton, and let us follow this course, since God points out the way."

In the **Lachês** the conversationalists attempt to define "courage" ("valor," "manliness") and discuss whether such a virtue can be taught.° In the **Iôn** a professional rhapsode, or reciter of poems, insists the poet is a sophistic artist who in his own clever way develops a skill to impress and teach, but Socrates argues that true poets are not self-made "artists" but prophetic channels of "divine dispensation and possession." Their forte is not to teach but to empathize and inspire.

In the **Hippias Major** Socrates and a learned scholar from Êlis attempt a definition of the lovely Greek word *kalos*, "beauty." Hippias tries to answer by giving examples of beautiful things, but Socrates maneuvers for a definition, not a list. At the conclusion of the exchange, the question is left unresolved. The dialogue's real point is that all too often we think we know what we're talking about when we don't. Once again, with this dialogue, we are urged to shock ourselves awake and become aware of what we don't know.

The **Hippias Minor** is a study in ethical paradox. In it Socrates argues that the best human beings are those of intelligence and power who can deliberately do either good or evil, just as they choose, versus the blundering dolts who accidentally do only good. The final note is characteristically Socratic: "In discussing such matters I go astray" and "can't even agree with myself," implying he will have to keep on searching to find the truth of the matter.

In the **Charmides** Socrates, just back in Athens from a battle against the Spartans, has gone to a wrestlers' gymnasium to check on the "spiritual health" of the young men. There he is introduced to Charmides (Plato's uncle), a bright and handsome young man who exhibits wonderful *sôphrosynê* ("moderation," "temperance"). So another conversation ensues while Socrates pursues a definition, but without conclusion.°

In the **Lysis** Socrates is taking a stroll around the city walls of Athens and is waylaid by some young friends and lead him into another palaistra (wrestling school), where he is invited to give them advice on the best way for a young man to make points with someone he likes. One of the older young men is physically attracted to the handsome Lysis and wants to make a conquest, so Socrates is invited to give them all pointers on how to initiate an affair with the object of one's affections. But Socrates guides their minds to nobler concerns by discussing the essence of true friendship (a subject more fully explored in the later *Symposium* and *Phaedrus*).

The **Euthyphrô** is a strange story set in the northeast corner of the Athenian Agora. There in the Royal Stoa Socrates encounters Euthyphrô, a middle-aged man who, for the sake of "piety," is there to indict his aged father on a murder charge. Socrates is taken back by Euthyphro's intentions and quickly intuits the man's naive complacency. "Do you mean to say, Euthyphro, that you think that you understand divine things and piety and impiety so accurately that, in such a case as you have stated, you can bring your father to justice without fear that you yourself may be doing something impious?" But Euthyphro considers himself an expert in such matters and assures Socrates he knows exactly what he's doing. Thus Plato sets the stage for exploring the meaning of "piety" and "impiety"; the dialogue, that is, seeks definitions. As the exchanges proceed, it becomes clear Euthyphro has not the

It is very inconsistent for a man who asserts that he cares for virtue to be constantly unfair in discussion.

SOCRATES

°*See* andreios *in lexicon.*

°*See* sôphrosynê *in lexicon.*

foggiest notion about what piety might be. Socrates leads him down one blind alley and then another. At one point Euthyphro gripes that he no longer knows how to explain things to Socrates. "Whatever statement we put forward always somehow moves round in a circle," he complains, and that's how the dialogue ends. "Do you not see that our statement has come round to where it was before?" Socrates asks. "Then we must begin again and inquire what piety is. . . . and this time tell me the truth."

Nowhere in this dialogue or in any other does Socrates give the answer to a questioner. He is a kind of guru, a pathfinder, a cosearcher; he discerns where the other person is and from there leads him gently toward insight and clarity. He consistently respects each person's pace and groping; he never ridicules, though so often he has good reason to do so. Socrates' modus operandi was to allow others to talk until they had revealed the truth to themselves.

The *Euthydêmus* is a humorous parody of eristic word-games as employed by such Sophistic giants as Zeno, Protagoras and Gorgias, and sometimes Socrates, but that become petty ego trips in the mouths of lesser practitioners. Time and again we discover that Plato possessed a marvelous sense of humor and delighted in writing parody and irony.

The *Protagoras* is the record of the central disagreement between the Sophists and Socrates. At issue are the fundamental ideas and values citizens blindly assume while living their daily lives. Socrates saw clearly, and rightly, that a democratic society is founded on the assumption citizens have an understanding of the fundamental principles of a successful society, the classical human "virtues" such as justice, honesty, truth, decency, and so on. But as he talked and listened to everyday Athenians, he actually discovered they had not the vaguest understanding of the foundational principles of ethics and politics.

The focus of the *Protagoras* is, therefore, ethical and educational; it explores the question "Is virtue teachable?" The Sophists repeatedly make the claim that virtue (*aretê*) can be taught and *they* are its true teachers. In this dialogue Protagoras contends aretê is "the proper care of one's personal affairs, so as best to manage one's own household, and also of the State's affairs, so as to become a real power in the city, both as speaker and as a man of action."[13] The Sophists say they stake out the sphere of all things practical, boasting they do not waste their time in useless philosophical speculations. Their concerns are purely expedient: how to develop the skills of daily survival— "street smarts." Socrates agrees with them that it is very important to be practical in our cogitations and says he also disdains cosmic speculations. But he insists that in-depth education in virtues such as courage, justice, temperance, holiness, truth, and wisdom are the most practical of all. This, he holds, is the true purpose of education— to develop character (virtue) so that citizens can live a moral existence and not merely be trained to play the expedient, self-centered games of "the real world."

PHILOSOPHY IN THE DIALOGUES: THE MIDDLE PERIOD

THE MASTERPIECES

The Plato history best remembers is found in the second-period dialogues, above all in the literary classics the *Symposium* and the *Republic*, where we find a brilliant flowering of his dramatic skill and a maturing of his philosophic ideas. In these middle-period writings Plato has Socrates virtually abandoning the earlier adversarial exchanges in which he specialized in annihilating others' ideas.

In these dialogues Plato's own philosophical ideas are fully developed. The theory of Real Ideas is filled out and applied to problems in ethics, epistemology, esthetics, psychology, politics, and government. The search for clear definitions continues, and there are substantial explorations in the philosophy of language. Although there is a sensitive description of a nature scene in the *Phaedrus*, there is still no appreciation of nature or interest in the physical operations of the natural world. The identifying Platonic doctrines receive full development in these dialogues: the eternal indestructibility of the soul, learning as recollection, knowledge as virtue, and the rational mind and not the senses as the only source of knowledge. All in all, the middle dialogues have an excitement, an aliveness, a creativity, and a loftiness not found in the less mature early period and that begin to wane in the later writings.

The setting for the **Meno** is somewhere in Athens about 402 BC. Socrates engages two well-known men in a conversation about one of his favorite topics—virtue (aretê). Plato wrote this dialogue not too many years after Socrates' execution, and it is with enormous black irony that he chose these particular men as Socrates' interlocutors. Menon is familiar to us from Xenophon's *Anabasis*, where he comes across as an especially loathsome character. A wealthy young man from Thessaly in northern Greece, he, about a year after this supposed dialogue, went to Asia Minor (now Turkey) to join the rebellious Cyrus, who was fighting against his brother, the Persian king Artaxerxes II. "He was in the bloom of his youth," Xenophon says, "when he got command of the [Greek] mercenaries," some fifteen hundred strong, that he brought with him to Asia Minor. To him "simplicity and truth were just foolishness." He had but two obsessions: money and power. "As others pride themselves on godliness and truth and honesty, so Menon prided himself on his power to deceive, to fabricate falsehoods, to mock at his friends." He was treacherous, double dealing, arrogant, and barely civilized. When the rebel armies were defeated, Menon was captured by the Persian king, confined for a year, tortured, and then executed.[14]

The other lead-second in the *Meno* is the political leader Anytos who, some three years hence, will instigate proceedings against Socrates and lead to his execution. So Plato here indulges in two wonderful ironies touched with bitterness and humor: He depicts Menon, of all people, discussing virtue, and then he brings in Anytos, who proved in his indictment of Socrates that he had completely missed the fundaments of truth and goodness. To cap it all off, at the end of his dialogue, Plato has Socrates telling Menon that he must now go and teach Anytos about virtue "so he may be more gentle." Menon, the corrupt, would you believe, is to go teach Anytos, the closed-minded bigot, about *virtue!* Menon and Anytos were well known to Athenians, and giving them roles in which they explore the niceties of virtue were ironies lost on no one.

In the dialogue Menon jumps right in with an old Sophist conundrum (already dealt with in the *Protagoras*): "Can you tell me, Socrates—can virtue be taught?" Do we get virtue by nature or nurture, he asks, or from some other source? Socrates' initial response contains not a little insulting humor: Such a profound question proves that Thessalians, heretofore known only for their love of money and horses, also must have brains!

Menon argues that countless virtues exist—different virtues for different people in different situations; virtue must be judged in the context of concrete settings. He proceeds to give examples. But Socrates is not happy with a grocery list of virtuous items. "I was looking for one virtue and found a whole swarm," he says. He insists that all virtues must have a common essence, else we could not even have the concept of virtue, and he wants to know what that one thing is.

In no case is it just to harm anyone.

SOCRATES

But before they can come to any agreement, the discussion veers off into another direction. The question: Does anyone ever desire (and will) bad things?

"Don't you think, my dear fellow, that everyone always desires good things?"

"No, I don't think that at all," Menon says.

"Are you saying, then, that some people desire bad things?"

"Yes."

"Is this because they think the bad things are really good, or because they still want them even when they recognize that they are bad?"

"Both, I think."

"Do you really think, my dear Menon, that anyone, knowing the bad things to be bad, still desires them?"

"Certainly."

"Do those who think that the bad things benefit know that the bad things are bad?"

"No, I don't think that."

"Then," Socrates says, "it is plain that those who desire bad things are those who don't know what they are, but they desire what they thought were good whereas they really are bad; so those who do not know what they are, but think they are good, clearly desire the good. Is this not so?"

Menon concurs. "Well, it seems like it."

A conclusion, finally: "Then nobody desires bad things." Everyone always wants what is good, and if they ever actually want what is bad, it is only because they have made a mistake and think it is really good. And we all make this mistake because we don't know ourselves well enough. So, above all else, Socrates urges, "Know thyself." The goal of philosophic thinking is to come to know ourselves better and thereby be able to distinguish what is truly good from what only appears, in our ignorance, to be good, when it is really bad.

The conversation then moves to another of Socrates' favorite notions: that the soul is eternal and carries with it from one life to another a fundamental knowledge of abstract universal truths. "Since the soul is immortal and often born, having seen what is on Earth and what is in the house of Hadês, and everything, there is nothing it has not learned; so there is no wonder it can remember about virtue and other things, because it knew about these before . . . for seeking and learning is all remembrance."

Menon wants to know what he means by this—that all learning is remembrance. Socrates proceeds through a lengthy "proof" of the notion by asking Menon to call over one of his servants. "I'll prove my case in him," Socrates says. So, the boy comes over, and Socrates puts him through a series of questions about geometry. To simplify the dialogue somewhat: Socrates asks, in effect, what are two plus two? The boy answers, "four." This proves the point, he thinks, and Socrates is elated: The boy had not been told the answer, and he had not learned it by experience—but somehow he knew it. He went inside himself and came up with a correct bit of knowing—the right answer. Socrates presses the point: For anyone to learn, all it takes is someone to ask the right questions to stimulate the memory. "To get knowledge out of yourself is to remember, isn't it?" Socrates asks, but if one is not remembering things picked up in the present life, then, clearly, the memory is of things from a past life. Therefore, the soul is eternal and is the carrier of knowledge.

They return to the original question—"Can virtue be taught?"—and Socrates concludes that virtue originates "neither by nature nor by teaching; but by divine allotment unawares to those to whom it comes." That is, a man is virtuous "by divine dispensation." And there the discussion ends because, he says, we haven't yet decided what virtue really is . . . and "now it's time for me to go."

On Socrates *It is a Socratic paradox that "doing as one likes" is not power or freedom unless one likes the good.*

PAUL SHOREY

It must also be admitted, my friend, that men who are harmed become more unjust.

SOCRATES

Three of the subjects dealt with in the *Meno* are further developed in other dialogues.

(1) By this time, after watching Socrates put so many of his companions through the mill searching for definitions, it is quite clear he operated on the assumption that definitional "essences" exist as real entities. That is, such a thing exists as an "essence" of virtue, an "essence" of beauty, an "essence" of "valor," and so on. When beauty, for example, is seen in a dozen different concrete instances, all these instances of beauty have an essence in common, and Socrates is attempting to clarify and define this universal essence. Nor is he defining "words." He is attempting to define something that exists in the real world, to capture its essence with the mind. Epistemologically, Socrates is exhibiting the belief that the human mind can know reality, and know it accurately, but that "reality" must be apprehended with the intellect, not with the senses. Such things as beauty, courage, and wisdom he believed to be real qualities, not merely subjective experiences or concepts. We experience beauty in a rose because the rose is beautiful. We experience beauty in the human body, in a beautiful piece of music, and in a sunset because each and every object/event "out there" possesses the quality of beauty.

So in the *Meno* is found an early statement of the doctrine of Real Ideas (the "Theory of Forms"°), which became the centerpiece of "Platonism." Socrates' attempts at definition in the earlier dialogues rest on this belief that the *ideas* of beauty, moderation (*sôphrosynê*), the Good (*kalos*), and so on are universal "forms" whose qualities become the source of the particular corresponding qualities in the concrete objects of experience. The beauty of the hyacinth, the beauty of Sophocles' *Oedipus* trilogy, and the beauty of panpipes at sunset are not different beauties, for the essence of beauty is one, and definitions (by definition!) must be descriptions of this essential oneness.

In the *Meno* these Real Ideas are the ultimate constituents of reality and human knowledge, and they are the basis for ethical judgment. Plato further developed the theory of Real Ideas in the *Republic*, the *Phaedo*, the *Timaeus*, and the *Parmenides*.

(2) Socrates and Plato both apparently taught that virtue is knowledge and knowledge is virtue. If we know what is the right thing to do, they believed, then we will do it; and if we do what is wrong, it is because we did not know what was right. For no one desires bad things, and when we will ourselves toward bad things, it is because we mistake the bad for the good. And why do we make such a mistake? Because we don't know ourselves well enough. That is, the better we know ourselves, the better we will know what is good for us, and the fewer miscalculations we will make; and knowing more certainly what is good for us, we will proceed to will what is good. So Socrates' argument returns, repeatedly, to the fundamental Socratic/Platonic admonition of the Delphic oracle to "Know thyself." Hence, knowledge is the ethical remedy for bad behavior.

(3) Both philosophers, it seems, accepted the notion of the soul's immortal indestructibility, and herein lies the grounding for their theory of knowledge, also established in the *Meno*. All true knowledge is the soul's remembering (*anamnesis*) of abstract ideas from a previous existence. We can perceive particular objects/events with our senses—a red rose, a beautiful song, a right triangle, a sad story—but a mere perception of particulars is not "knowledge." True knowledge derives from the soul's (mind's) "perception" of universal abstract essences, and these are known by the intellect, not the senses. The particulars of sense experience are not to be scorned, for particulars "stimulate" the soul's memory and make it remember the Real Ideas brought forward from its previous life. Note, however, that Plato's mood seems to change regarding the value of the senses: In the *Phaedo* they are devalued in

Do you think it right to speak as having knowledge about things one does not know?

SOCRATES

°*See* eidos *in lexicon.*

He who cannot give and receive a rational explanation of a thing is without knowledge of it.

PLATO

He who lives well is blessed and happy, and he who does not the contrary.

SOCRATES

the extreme (see later), but in the *Symposium* and elsewhere they are praised as the triggers of our memory of Absolute Truth.

Plato's **Gorgias** is a play in three "acts," each a dialogue between Socrates and a Sophist on the relationship between the art of rhetoric and living the good life. While the interlocutors defend the imminent practicality of teaching rhetoric, because it helps people defend themselves, Socrates proceeds to reveal the empty inversion of rhetoric philosophy. The rhetorician believes that what is important is not what you are but what others think you are. In effect, you live your life in terms of others' perceptions; to enable you to manipulate and control the perceptions of other people, you put on a variety of masks that become your façades against the world. Gorgias argues that rhetoric is the supreme art form because it empowers one to make everyone else do his will. This skill enables an ignorant man to persuade an ignorant audience he really understands an issue; therefore, it is the key to political success. A second participant, Polus, argues that the goal of rhetoric is to humor the prejudices of a patron or client. In the third cycle Callicles of Acharnae presents a strong argument that those who are powerful have a "natural right" to dominate those who are weak.°

°See the debate on this issue in the Republic, *I.338ff.; and cf. Nietzsche's similar doctrine, Vol. II, pp. 292ff.*

The *Gorgias* is one of the first great writings in all literature to mount an attack against the destructive dishonesties of the practical; it is an exposé of the sham and shallowness of "the real world." To all these sophistic arguments Socrates replies that he and the Sophists are lovers of two very different mistresses. A wise man knows that what you are is important, not what others think you are. The dialogue contrasts game-playing with honesty, empty form with serious substance, and relativistic opinion with truth. Just as medicine is for healing the body, true morality is a prescription for healing the soul.

The **Cratylus** purports to be a discussion of the origins of language, especially the names of things; it is a first attempt to deal with the rudiments of semantics and is a fascinating dialogue to anyone interested in beginning attempts to deal with symbols and meaning. The **Menexenus** (which may not be by Plato) contains a funeral speech written by Aspasia, the wife of Pericles, and reported by Socrates and is probably designed to deliberately expose the shallowness of conventional oratory and its disregard for the truth. The famous **Symposium,** a literary masterpiece on friendship and love, deals only in passing with traditional philosophic issues—the natural sciences, music, and medical science are excoriated, and the doctrine of Real Ideas is mentioned briefly. Yet this dialogue is philosophical in a wonderful sense: It deals with our ultimate questions about the meaning of life, and it presents Socrates' own sublime answers.

The **Phaedo,** subtitled *On the Soul,* covers as many philosophic issues as any of Plato's dialogues (with the possible exception of the *Republic*); it tells us more about Socrates' beliefs and feelings than any other work.

In a small prison cell on the Agora's southwest corner, Socrates spends his last hours on Earth talking with his family and friends. While most of those present grieve and weep, Socrates remains upbeat through it all, discoursing amiably. "The man seemed happy to me," recalls a puzzled Phaidon. This setting in the cell, just before the hemlock, is most appropriate for the subject Plato now has Socrates addressing: the soul's eternal continuity.

°Phaedo *or* Phaidon; *see marginal note, p. 106.*

Plato's dramatic account of the scene is narrated by a young man named Phaidon° who is traveling home from Athens to Elis in the Peloponnese. Phaidon has overnighted with friends in the small town of Phlius, and since he has firsthand knowledge of Socrates' execution ("I was there," he says), his hosts are eager to listen. Although Phaidon was still in his late teens, he already had been captured in the

Now it is time that we were going, I to die and you to live; but which of us has the happier prospect is unknown to anyone but God.

SOCRATES

war with Sparta, sold as a slave, and ransomed by a friend of Socrates, after which he became Socrates' disciple.

Socrates begins: "Indeed, it is perhaps most proper that one who is going to depart and take up his abode in[the next] world should think about the life over there and say what sort of life we imagine it to be. After all, what better way for us to spend the time till sunset?"

What does Socrates believe will happen to him after the hemlock? "I hope I shall find myself in the company of good men, although I would not maintain it for certain." He states that those who spend their lives practicing philosophy have in fact been practicing for death, although it would be understandable, when death finally approaches, for even philosophers to squawk about it. At this Simmias, another young questioner, laughed but then apologized: "I don't feel like laughing just now, Socrates, but you made me laugh!"

At death, Socrates says, "the body separates from the soul, and remains by itself, apart from the soul; and the soul, separated from the body, exists by itself apart from the body." He proceeds to a lengthy denunciation of the physical body's pleasures and their seductive urgings, for our love of the senses deflects us from the truth.

So, whence this truth? "Do we say there is such a thing as justice by itself, or not?"—and, by extension, goodness, truth, beauty, temperance, love, and so on?

"Of course!" replies Simmias.

"And did you ever see one of them with your eyes?"

"Never," he says.

"And would he do that most purely who should approach each with his intelligence alone, not adding sight to intelligence, or dragging in any other sense along with reasoning, but using the intelligence uncontaminated alone by itself, while he tries to hunt out each essence uncontaminated, keeping clear of eyes and ears and, one might say, of the whole body, because he thinks the body disturbs him and hinders the soul from getting possession of truth and wisdom when body and soul are companions—is not this the man, Simmias, if anyone, who will attain to reality?"

"Nothing could be more true, Socrates."

The point of the philosophic life, therefore, is to prepare for death, which is "a freeing and separation of the soul from the body." "Those who rightly love wisdom are [always] practising dying, and death to them is the least terrible thing in the world, . . . [so] that when you see a man fretting because he is to die, he was not really a philosopher, but a philosôma—not a wisdom-lover but a body-lover."

As the *Phaedo* investigation proceeds, Socrates spells out in great detail, and with beguiling clarity, the framework for a classic psychological dualism that pervaded Western thought for more than two millennia.

"Now come," he says, "in ourselves one part is body and one part soul—right?" He already has established that the body undergoes changes, while the soul part is unchanging; so he concludes that the body can be "quickly dissolved," while the soul is "wholly indissoluble or very nearly so." The immortal soul is a prisoner in the mortal body, for "it is dragged by the body towards what is always changing, and the soul goes astray and is confused and staggers about like one drunken because she is taking hold of such things." "But the soul, the 'unseen' part of us, which goes to another place noble and pure and unseen like itself, a true unseen Hadês, to the presence of the good and wise God, where, if God will, my own soul must go very soon—shall our soul, then, being such and of such nature, when released from the body be straightway scattered by the winds and perish, as most men say? Far from it, my dear Simmias!"

Of the many more thoughts Socrates had on the matter, one is poignant: "If the soul is immortal, she needs care, not only for the time which we call life, but for all time, and the danger indeed would seem to be terrible if one is ready to neglect her. . . . she should become as good and wise as possible. . . . For when the soul comes to Hadês she brings with her nothing but her education and training." Truly, places of punishment, as well as rewards, exist for the soul after it has stood trial "before the judges" and has been found to have been purified (freed from the body) or unpurified (indulged in the multitude of available sins connected with the body). Any souls "who are thought to be incurable because of the greatness of their sins . . . these the proper fate throws into Tartaros whence they never come out." "But the soul which has passed through life purely and decently finds gods for fellow-travellers and leaders, and each soul dwells in her own proper dwelling place."

The ***Republic*** is Plato's masterpiece. To any reader who has lived with the five-hundred-page dialogue, it endures as an awe-inspiring literary and intellectual achievement. Philosophically, *everything* is found in the *Republic*—epistemology, ethics, politics, psychology, educational theory and practice, plus a running social commentary and continuous scrutiny of human nature (which underscores the foolishness of our attempts to pidgeonhole great writing into simplistic categories). The *Republic* contains Plato's mature political philosophy.

The subtitle of the *Republic* is *On Justice*, and no matter how far afield the discussions wander (and they wander far), Plato always returns to a dialectical analysis of the meaning of justice.° But why? Why did he devote hundreds of pages to the analysis of just a single idea? Because, first, it's not a single idea but a very complex and difficult one; second—and this must be related to his troubled experience with the earlier breakdown of order and decency in Athens—his singular overriding lifetime passion was to find an answer to why we humans behave toward each other the way we do and to find a remedy to our savagery. That is, he wanted to work out how to create a political climate that provides the conditions for civilized human beings to live the kind of happy lives they were meant to live.

Plato consistently reveals his distrust of unredeemed (uneducated) human nature. In Book II Glaucon (Plato's brother) plays devil's advocate and argues that a just man is just only because he is forced into it, not because of his true nature, and not because he wants to be. "We will catch the just man in the very act of resorting to the same conduct as the unjust man because of the self-advantage which every creature by its nature pursues as a good for itself." To illustrate, he tells the story of Gyges' gold ring.[15] Gyges was a shepherd serving the king of Lydia. He came into possession of a gold ring, which, to his delight, made him invisible when turned a certain way. So he entered the palace undetected, seduced the king's wife, killed the king, took over the kingdom, and so on. The point the story makes is that no human beings have such pure character that we can resist exploiting others if we can do so and get away with it. The so-called just man and the unjust man would behave in exactly the same manner, so that "no one is just of his own will but only from constraint," for justice never serves an individual's personal interests. If we did act from pure motives, we would be pitied as fools.

This view of human nature, writ large, permeates Plato's political and ethical thought. To capture the darkened condition of contemporary politics, Plato develops the parable of the ship captain and sailors. In this story the strong and burly captain is a little blind and a bit deaf, and his knowledge of navigation also is not up to snuff. So, crew members wrangle and conspire about taking over the ship, even though none of them possesses the skills for the job, which they say are not important anyway. Each sailor protests that, qualified or not, he has a *right* to be captain. So they mutiny, drug the captain, tie him up, and "take command of the ship, consume its stores and, drinking and feasting, make such a voyage of it as is to be

Morality, said Jesus, is kindness to the weak; morality, said Nietzsche, is the bravery of the strong; morality, says Plato, is the effective harmony of the whole.

WILL DURANT

°*Very important, for "justice" does not mean justice; see dikaiosynê in lexicon.*

On Plato *Plato advised drunken people to look into a mirror.*

DIOGENES LAËRTIUS

Democracy—a charming form of government, full of variety and disorder, and dispensing a sort of equality to equals and unequals alike.

PLATO

expected from such a lot." For their captain they install the one who led the mutinous revolt or whoever displays the most seductive rhetoric. They haven't a clue about what running a ship requires; they don't see that safe sailing. They haven't a clue about what running a ship requires; they don't see that safe sailing demands training, experience, and special sensitivity to such things as "the time of year, the seasons, the sky, the winds, the stars, and all that pertains to his art." End of story. Plato concludes his parable by saying he is really talking about the political incompetents actually in power in Athens and elsewhere.[16]

Plato's lifelong preoccupation was the problem of how to create the ideal state. One thing he was sure of: "Unless either philosophers become kings in our states or those whom we now call our kings and rulers take to the pursuit of philosophy seriously and adequately—political power and philosophic intelligence—while the motley horde of the natures who at present pursue either apart from the other are compulsorily excluded, there can be no cessation of troubles for our states, nor, I fancy, for the human race either."[17]

So in his search for quality leaders Plato distinguishes the "philosophic from the unphilosophic soul." Does any real difference exist, Socrates asks, between "the blind" and those who can "fix their eyes" on "the laws of the beautiful, the just and the good"?[18] His answer, of course, is that the difference is like night and day; only philosophers understand the true nature of justice and are qualified to become guardians of the state.

The character of the philosopher/guardian must be "the spirit of truthfulness, reluctance to admit falsehood in any form, the hatred of it and the love of truth."[19] He will be obsessed with "pleasures of the soul," not the body; wealth and material things "others may take seriously, but not he"; he will not have a narrow or petty soul; he will "seek integrity in all things human and divine"; and he will not be "a lover of money, or illiberal, or a braggart or a coward, or ever prove unjust or a driver of hard bargains." He must be, of course, intelligent, "quick to learn," and knowledgeable; he will have good judgment and a "sense of proportion."° "When men of this sort are perfected by education and maturity of age, would you not entrust the state solely to them?"[20] Cities fortunate enough to have such guardians will be ruled by "waking minds" and not "ruled darkly as in a dream by men who fight one another for shadows."[21]

Justice alone fills the heart of the philosopher/guardian, and Plato spends the better part of the *Republic* searching for a definition of justice, "a thing more precious than much fine gold." The discussion begins with the vague statement that perhaps "it is just to render to each his due," but this is rejected. Then Socrates and his interlocutors consider that maybe justice means "to do good to friends and evil to enemies," but with admirable insight into human behavior Socrates leads on to show that doing evil to someone only makes that person worse, and, besides, a just man never treats anyone unjustly. Then Thrasymachus, burning with self-righteous anger, says "I affirm that justice is nothing else than the advantage of the stronger," but this notion, too, fails finally to satisfy. Considerably later, Socrates concludes that "having and doing of one's own and what belongs to oneself would admittedly be justice."[22] Justice, that is, means that all individuals in a society—"child, woman, slave, free, artisan, ruler, and ruled"—should perform the task they are best at, their specialty, their work, their calling; "to do one's own business and not to be a busybody" is to stay in one's place, not to intrude into the space of others and not to try to be something one is not. Should everyone observe this rule, then a city-state would be coordinated, harmonious, efficient, stable, and peaceful. Justice would prevail.

Can you name any other type or ideal of life that looks with scorn on political office except the life of true philosophers?

SOCRATES

°Compare Nietzsche's vision of the Übermensch, Vol. II, pp. 292f.

The partisan, when he is engaged in a dispute, cares nothing about the rights of the question, but is anxious only to convince his hearers of his own assertions.

PLATO

The height of injustice is to seem just without being so.

SOCRATES

This description of justice is founded on the picture of the city-state as a living organism, with individuals as fully functioning components of that living system. Justice in the individual means the heart, the lungs, the brain, the circulatory system, the arms and legs, and so on all performing their specialized function and working together to enable the total organism to function as a whole, efficiently and harmoniously. In Plato's utopian state the individual belongs to the state and lives for it; the state does not exist for the individual. The living biological organism is healthy when all its organs function properly, each doing its own work; and the city-state, likewise, is healthy when all its component organs perform the function they were meant to perform and coordinate harmoniously for the good of all.

Virtually all the philosophic elements in Plato's thinking are bound together in his famous **allegory of the Cave**.[23] The story can be sequenced into five parts: (1) the setting; (2) the experience of the prisoners; (3) the experience of one who has had his chains removed and has turned to see the light; (4) the attitude of the still-darkened prisoners toward someone who has been "enlightened"; and (5) Plato's interpretation of the allegory.

(1) Plato imagines humankind dwelling in a cavern deep underground, where they witness a great shadow play. The entrance to the cavern, opening to the light, is wide but quite distant, so everyone lives in darkness. Above the entrance, on a ledge perhaps, is a great fire that lights this nether world; in front of the fire is a sort of raised wall, along which imitations of familiar objects (such as animals, people, trees, etc.) are carried back and forth, casting shadows on the cave's rear walls.

(2) The people who live in the cave have been chained in their places from childhood; they cannot turn their heads to look toward the entrance. All they have ever seen are the shadows dancing on the walls in front of them. Moreover, as the bearers of the imitation figures talk among themselves, their voices echo from the back walls, so the living shadows appear to move in stereo. These prisoners live in a shadow world. They have spent their lives looking at the shadows, naming them, talking about them, organizing their experiences around them, and making sense of them; the shadows give their lives substance and meaning. The shadows are their reality, and, inevitably, they *believe* this is the only world existing.

(3) What would happen should one of the prisoners be unchained and made to look toward the fire? He or she would at first be blinded, and the imitation objects that had been casting the shadows would look blurred. Then he would undergo a cognitive crisis, forced to relate the solid objects to the familiar shadows and to decide what was real and what was not. This would be a painful and perhaps prolonged adjustment; his eyes would hurt, and at first he would want to return to the shadows since they would be easier to see, and they would make more sense to him.

But then, suppose this individual was compelled to walk toward the entrance to the cave, where he was drawn out into the sunlight. There "the brilliance would fill his eyes and he would not be able to see even one of the things now called real." He would at first be "distressed and furious"; then gradually he would look at the solid particular objects spread before him—the trees, animals, people, lakes, mountains, stars, and Moon. How different these all would be from the shadows of his earlier experience. Then, lastly, he would see the Sun; he would come to realize, through reasoning, that the Sun alone is truly real and is the causal wellspring of all that exists, from the Earth and its seasons to all the forms of goodness and beauty. He would possess, now, a synoptic awareness of his previous shadowy life, the delusional half-life of the imitation objects, the derivative semireal objects of the world; he would at last see the true relationship of all these things to the Ultimately Real, the Sun itself. He would rejoice in his seeing.

(4) But he also would feel pity for the darkened state of his fellow prisoners. If he should return to the shadow world, what would he find? He would, first, shudder to think that he had once lived in this shadow world of illusions, convinced a meaningful life could be found here. Also, before his eyes had become adjusted to the darkness, he would be pitied for his blindness and ridiculed for looking at the Sun and ruining his eyesight. And if he tried to tell the still-darkened prisoners what he had seen, or if he attempted to free them of their chains, they might even try to kill him for his false reports and for threatening the stability of their secure lives.

(5) Plato then explains his allegory. His interpretation spreads over many pages of the *Republic* and can be illuminated by passages from other dialogues.

(a) "The world of our sight is like the habitation in prison, the firelight there to the sunlight here, the ascent and the view of the upper world is the rising of the soul into the world of mind." Now, if this interpretation of the world is correct—he adds, sincerely it seems, that "God only knows" whether it's really true—there are some things he's sure of.

One is that those who have seen the light—those who have, while living, been "transported to the Isles of the Blest"[24]—will find it very difficult to return to the world of humanity and be subject to the darkened ways of thinking that characterize mundane existence. "Those who have reached this height are no longer willing to occupy themselves with the affairs of men, for their souls ever feel the upward urge and the yearning for that sojourn above."[25] And should he try to move in the world, then he is going to seem inept, awkward, impractical, and not "with it"—bereft of "common sense" and "street smarts"—a fool, "compelled to struggle in law courts or elsewhere about shadows of justice; in the evil world of men he will be seen to be a great fool."[26] When he fails to take for granted what everyone else is sure of; when he sees through the arbitrariness of society's trashy values and loose assumptions; when he sees local ideas writ large into absolute and universal claims; when he doesn't laugh at what is funny to everyone else; when he wants to talk about moral issues that, to everyone else, are settled and nondiscussable; when he wants to question dangerous ideas that, to everyone else, are normal ideas "everyone knows"—then he will, at least, arouse phobic reactions or, at most, be ostrasized or terminated as an undesirable deviant too unpatriotic and depraved to live among normal folk.

In a passage in the *Gorgias* where Plato, with thick irony, has the Sophist Callicles haranguing Socrates with precisely the attitudes briefly described in the allegory of the Cave.

> Philosophy, you know, Socrates, is a charming thing, as long as a man indulges in it moderately in his younger days; but if he continues to spend his time on it too long, it will be his ruin. . . . It is a fine thing to partake of philosophy just for the sake of education, and it is no disgrace for a lad to follow it; . . . but when I see an elderly man still going on with philosophy and not getting rid of it, that is the gentleman, Socrates, whom I think in need of a whipping. For . . . this person . . . is bound to become unmanly through shunning the centres and marts of the city, in which, as the poet said, "men get them note and glory."[27]

(b) But however much the enlightened soul longs to remain outside the Cave, he must return to the darkened prisoners to try to turn their heads toward the light; he must assume "the care and guardianship of the other people." Moses must return to

Egypt to lead the Children of Israel to the holy mountain. The sannyasin must demonstrate to others the way to God. The Zen ox herder, having found the Bull/self, is drawn back to the world of men. Victorious from his Satanic temptations, Jesus must cross the Jordan to proclaim the Reign of YHWH. Zarathustra must descend from the mountains to bring sight to the world of the blind. Having achieved *bodhi*, the Buddha must bring the Four Noble Truths to all living things; and the boddhisattva must return to the world to guide others along their path of suffering.

It is painful to have one's opinions set right.

EURIPIDES

Plato: "Down you must go then, in turn, to the habitation of the others, and accustom yourselves to their darkness; for when you have grown accustomed you will see a thousand times better than those who live there, and you will know what the images are and what they are images of, because you have seen the realities behind just and beautiful and good things. And so our city will be managed wide awake for us and for you, not in a dream, as most are now, by people fighting together for shadows, and quarrelling to be rulers, as if that were a great good. But the truth is more or less that the city where those who are to rule are least anxious to be rulers is of necessity best managed and has least faction in it; while the city which gets rulers who want it most is worst managed."[28]

"For the truth is, my friend," I said, "that only if you can find for your future rulers a way of life better than ruling, is it possible for you to have a well-managed city; since in that city alone those will rule who are truly rich, not rich in gold, but in that which is necessary for a happy man, the riches of a good and wise life."[29]

(c) The Cave is the setting for further treatment of Plato's doctrine of Real Ideas. Any and every circle I draw on the chalkboard or on paper will be a near miss, a rough approximation, an imperfect circle, but our geometric calculations are based on perfect circles (or perfectly straight lines, squares, triangles, or whatever figure). The visible world is therefore imperfect, always, and perfect ideas are found only in the realm of thought. Three roses are fleeting specifics—tomorrow they will be gone; but both the number "three" and "rose" are eternal ideas that will last forever. Thought, therefore, is more real than anything in this material world of appearances and perpetual near misses. For Plato the study of mathematics and geometry is the discipline that helps students to learn to think in abstractions.

°See p. 37.

Today our knowledge of physics shows Plato to be right. Near the Earth or any other massive body, objects are set in motion by gravity, and universal mathematical formulas can describe their motions. Material objects, therefore, are always in motion and change (Plato adopts the notion of "everything flowing" from Heraclitus°); they are ephemeral, unstable, and uncapturable—not quite real. But the "laws" we can develop in our minds, based on the repeated patterns we observe in nature, are unwavering, dependable, graspable, and eternal—and represent the very real. All true knowledge, Plato would argue, is therefore made up of these univeral ideas captured by the mind.

Plato takes a further giant step. These universal (abstract) ideas we experience in our minds derive from some "place" (location) that exists "out there" in the realm of the real. Ideas, that is, are real, not merely experiential phenomena produced by the neurons in our brains. An order of reality truly exists, like a sci-fi "parallel universe," where Ideas exist as "things in themselves," independent of any minds thinking them; and the ideas we find in our heads are copies of, and derive from, the Real Ideas existing in that objective realm. They, and they alone, are eternal and real; the material world is an ever-changing world of instability and flux and fleeting, ungraspable phenomena, not to be bothered with, not deserving of our time and attention.

This has been called Plato's "two world" theory, for these Real Ideas are the patterns, the templates, the shapers or molders of all things in the world of matter. A coffee cup, for instance, derives its coffeecupness from the Real Idea of "coffee cup," the book from the Real Idea of "book," the tree from the Real Idea of "tree," and so on. What any single thing is, is derived from the Real Idea that makes it so. This world of perception, therefore, is an imperfect copy of the perfect Real World of abstract Ideas. All true knowledge, by definition, is made up solely of our minds' becoming aware of the universal abstract ideas derived from the real realm of Real Ideas.

It follows that true philosophers spend their life seeking and contemplating, that is, making use of, the universal abstract ideas; they bother little, if at all, with material things; they give them only a passing nod. Ideas provide us with understanding of what things are and why. Observation of particulars may tickle our senses, but if we want an understanding of how the world works, they are almost useless. ("Almost" because some sense objects can be "provocative of thought" and "tend to awaken reflection.")

The Cave explains that the growth of the soul in awareness means the turning away from the shadows to behold, gradually, the light of the Real Ideas, "the conversion of the soul itself from the world of becoming to essence and truth."

(c) The Cave allegory also contains Plato's philosophy of education, and true education, he contends, is not at all what most people think it to be. "What they aver is that they can put true knowledge into a soul that does not possess it, as if they were inserting vision into blind eyes." Not so, Plato says. True education is a process of drawing out, not putting in. The true educator turns the soul of a student from the unreal to the real, from the darkness of unknowing toward "the most brilliant light of being." Our eyes by nature have no trouble seeing sense objects, but true education is the turning of the head away from sense objects so that the soul can see what the eyes cannot see. The darkened soul "does not look where it should." Socrates, therefore, is the ideal model for an educator: Rather than lecturing a content into his listeners, he framed questions that would draw out what they already knew or could find out for themselves, and he let them talk until, of their own accord, they could see.

So, the purpose of education is to bring about "a conversion and turning about of the soul from a day whose light is darkness to the veritable day—that ascension to reality."[31] Plato outlines the courses of study that "would draw the soul away from the world of becoming to the world of being."[32] The studies most conducive to "the awakening of thought" are mathematics, geometry, and astronomy. "The qualities of number appear to lead to the apprehension of truth." Mathematics is a study that "plainly compels the soul to employ pure thought with a view to truth itself." Plato scolds astronomers who look up at the stars, for "if anyone tries to learn about the things of sense, whether gaping up or blinking down, I would never say that he really learns, for nothing of this kind admits of true knowledge." True knowledge "can be apprehended only by reason and thought, not by sight." Pure astronomy is correctly taught only when it challenges the soul/mind to see the eternal patterns in the motions of heavenly bodies.[33]

Plato advocated universal education. The state, not the family, must take charge of the young and provide for everyone twenty years of education, and at the end they are given screening tests. Those who don't pass automatically will become farmers, workers, and businesspeople. Those who pass will be given ten more years of education, and at thirty they will take another screening test; if they fail they will become soldiers and live together in a military commune. Those who pass the second test will then be given five years of "graduate" study in philosophy. Then at age thirty-five those who have survived this intensive period of higher education will be thrust back into the real world to find out through practical experience what the problems of life and society are all about and to learn how to apply theory to real problems. After fifteen years of immersion in the real world, at age fifty, "those who have survived the tests and approved themselves altogether the best in every task and form of knowledge must be brought at last to the goal." They automatically become the guardians of the state.

Plato's educational goals are broadly twofold: (1) to develop the masses into obedient and conforming citizens capable, as best each person can, of serving the state and achieving personal fulfillment within their allotted role; and (2) to produce qualified rulers, the guardians, who can rule wisely and justly. To achieve the first, Plato institutes censorship, eugenics, control of marriage and procreation, and state control of education and the rearing of children. To achieve the second goal, guardians are prohibited from owning property and money; they cannot marry or have families. Their greatest responsibility is to render existential judgments in all cases brought before them; they are not bound by abstract law or legal precedent and will render judgments after taking into account the unique conditions in each case. Guardians can be of both sexes, "for you must not suppose that my words apply to the men more than to all women who arise among them endowed with the requisite qualities."[34]

I think a man's duty is . . . to find out where the truth is, or if he cannot, at least to take the best possible human doctrine and the hardest to disprove, and to ride on this like a raft over the waters of life.

SOCRATES

Plato defines "justice" in a society as everyone staying in his or her place. But how do the rulers get the masses to "stay in their place"? Plato concocts the "noble lie"—reluctantly, he has Socrates saying, not sure he can "find the audacity or the words" to perpetrate such a myth that he expects the uncritical masses to believe. For they are to be told that they were fashioned down in Mother Earth. "All of you in the polis are brothers, but God fashioned those of you who are fitted to rule with gold in your natures, and you are therefore the most precious; in the helpers he mixed silver, and then iron and brass in the farmers and other artisans." Each class of human being will mostly breed to kind, but if a "golden father should produce a silver son" or a "golden son spring from a silver father," then he shall have freedom to move up or down, "according to his true nature." "Do you think we can get them to believe this myth?" Perhaps. The first generation might resist belief, but subsequent generations will accept it.

The founders are mandated to discern the bright and promising youth and to educate them, to compel them to make the soul's ascent and to see the good. Plato prescribes every detail of their upbringing, including purer forms of music, poetry, and the sciences, all of which promote depth and sensitivity. Aesthetic sensibility and moral feeling are fostered together. Young boys and girls will be provided with an environment filled with beauty, and this will lead them unconsciously to be sensitive to all that is morally beautiful and good.

The occasion for the ***Phaedrus*** is during one of Socrates' rare excursions outside Athens' city walls. He encounters a younger friend, Phaidros, and they settle down to talk about love on the banks of the river Ilissos. The nature scene (so unusual in Plato's writing) is idyllic. "It is indeed a lovely spot for a rest," Socrates says. "What a lovely resting place," Socrates exclaims, "filled with delightful sounds and fragrances. This plane tree is tall and spreading, and the agnus castus, in full bloom, is thick and shady, and we can bathe our in the cool spring that flows under the tree. The figurines and other offerings indicate that this is a place sacred to the river god Achelous and to the Nymphs. We can enjoy the gentle breeze and chirping cicadas, and the grass will be a soft pillow under our heads. This is the very essence of summer!"[35]

So they spend hours talking. On leaving, Socrates, still impressed with the setting, utters a now famous prayer: "Beloved Pan, and all ye other gods who haunt this place, make me beautiful within, and grant that whatever happens outside of me will help my soul to grow. May I always be aware that true wealth lies in wisdom, and may my "gold" be so abundant that only a wise man can lift and carry it away. For me that is prayer enough.[36]

The overall purpose of the *Phaedrus* is to show that rhetoric is merely empty chatter unless it is founded on truth, and to be founded on truth requires that empathy and love inspire all philosophic dialectic. It deals broadly with three subjects, with only a semblance of continuity between them: love (Socrates repeats his performances found in the *Symposium* and the *Lysis*); rhetoric and truth (a continuing preoccupation of Plato's, the theme of the *Gorgias*); and the superiority of living dialogue over the written word (a treatment unique to the *Phaedrus*).

After Phaidros reads a speech on love, Socrates says he can do better, and he proceeds to do so; but then he is embarrassed to realize that he has merely repeated an encomium on physical love. ("Anyone of good birth and breeding . . . would think that he was listening to men brought up among the scum of a sea-port," he So he makes a second speech, raising love to the status of a divine inspiration in the soul's search for knowledge of the Good. Plato makes extensive use of myths in the *Phaedrus:* the charioteer and his horses, to illustrate the conflict of the soul, elaborated more fully in the *Republic;* the procession of the Gods and the soul's descent; and the myth of the cicadas, reincarnate human beings who report to the Muses on song, dance, and things philosophic.

> *Human Nature involves, above all, pleasures, pains and desires, and no mortal animal can help being . . . in total dependence on these powerful influences.*
>
> PLATO

PHILOSOPHY IN THE DIALOGUES:
THE LATER PERIOD

In Plato's later dialogues, written during the last twenty years of his life, Socrates recedes into the background; the great teacher is no longer the lead debater (except in the *Philebus*). In his last book, the *Laws*, Plato himself replaces Socrates as the principal speaker.

These dialogues have been called "upper division" or "graduate" textbooks; Plato designed them for his sophisticated colleagues and students. In them Plato is more concerned with substance (philosophy) and less with form (dramatic dialogue); he wants to inform his readers, not entertain them. Here are found extended treatments of some of the perennial problems in epistemology, politics, and metaphysics. Except for a fascinating critique by Parmenides, the doctrine of Real Ideas almost vanishes, as though Plato has taken it as far as it will go or lost interest in it. He initiates careful work in grammar and semantics; for the first time, in the *Timaeus*, he shows an interest in natural science and cosmogony. Then, finally, he wrote the *Laws*, revealing a depressed attitude toward life and the possibility of improvement.

The **Parmenides** (subtitled *Concerning Ideas* in ancient times) is an amazing work and surprising, for it doesn't feel like the Plato we've been reading in the earlier dialogues, and the formal nature is so extreme that we're taken back. No one doubts its authenticity, and it succeeds in demonstrating the dialogue's apparent purpose: to show that Plato can do formal logic with the best of them.

In the year 450–449 BC a gathering occurred in Athens of three of the age's greatest intellects—Socrates and the Eleatic logicians Parmenides and Zeno.° The two

> *Whenever the soul tries to examine anything in company with the body, it is plain that it is deceived by it.*
>
> SOCRATES

°For more on Parmenides' role at this meeting, see pp. 58–61.

great Eleatics had come to Athens for the Panathenaea festival, and they lodged near the Kerameicos in the home of Pythodoros (a pupil of Zeno, later a general in the Peloponnesian War). Present at the meeting were a very young Socrates (about twenty years old), Adeimantos and Glaucon (Plato's older brothers), Antiphon (Plato's half brother), Antisthenes the Cynic, and Aristoteles (later to become one of the infamous Thirty tyrants). Other nonparticipating listeners also may have been present.

But the dialogue is a retrospective set some fifty years later, after Socrates' death. The narrator, Kephalos of Clazomenae, has come to Athens to learn the true story of that famous meeting from Antiphon, who often heard the story from Pythodoros. They find Antiphon at home in the dêmê Melitê and persuade him to tell them the story.

"Parmenides was quite elderly at the time," Antiphon recalls, "about sixty-five years old, very white-haired, and of handsome and noble countenance; Zeno was at the time about forty years of age," tall and good-looking. Antiphon recounts the conversation, beginning with Zeno, who has just read aloud several of the paradoxes he was already famous for. The young Socrates questions Zeno.

"Zeno, what do you mean by this? That if existences are many, they must be both like and unlike, which is impossible; for the unlike cannot be like, nor the like unlike? Is not that your meaning?"

"Yes," Zeno says. "You follow the arguments with a scent as keen as a Laconian hound's . . . these writings are meant to support the argument of Parmenides against those who attempt to jeer at him and assert that if the all is one, then many absurd results follow which contradict his theory." So, his thesis, Zeno tells them, is designed "to oppose the advocates of the many and give them back their ridicule with interest, for its purpose is to show that their hypothesis that existences are many, if properly followed up, leads to still more absurd results than the hypothesis that they are one."

Socrates gloms onto the argument and suggests that if Zeno had adopted the concept of Real Ideas, then the supposed contradiction vanishes, for things could "participate" in the Ideas of "like" and "unlike" at the same time. Parmenides and Zeno "paid close attention to him and frequently looked at each other and smiled, as if in admiration of Socrates." Parmenides then asks Socrates if he is the author of this doctrine of Real Ideas and the participation of objects in these Ideas. "Do you think there is such a thing as abstract likeness apart from the likeness which we possess, and abstract one and many, and the other abstractions of which you heard Zeno speaking just now?"

"Yes, I do," Socrates says.

"And also," Parmenides says, "abstract ideas of the just, the beautiful, the good, and all such conceptions?"

"Yes," he replies.

"And is there an abstract idea of man, apart from us and all others such as we are, or of fire or water?"

"I have often," he replies, "been very much troubled, Parmenides, to decide whether there are ideas of such things, or not."

"And are you undecided about certain other things, which you might think rather ridiculous, such as hair, mud, dirt, or anything else particularly vile and worthless? Would you say that there is an idea of each of these distinct and different from the things with which we have to do, or not?"

With wonderful candor, Socrates says he often equivocates, feeling sometimes the absurdity of such an idea, but at other times accepting the notion that Real Ideas exist for everything. "Then when I have taken up this position, I run away for fear of falling into some abyss of nonsense. . . ."

[Socrates says approvingly] Cebes is always on the hunt for arguments, and won't believe straight off anything anyone says.

SOCRATES

"You are still young," Parmenides says, "and philosophy has not yet taken hold upon you, Socrates, as I think it will later."

The arguments continue through many exchanges, and eventually Parmenides succeeds in casting doubt on the entire concept of Real Ideas. Time and again Socrates is backed into a corner by the great logician, who finally admonishes him with the words, "You try too soon, before you are properly trained, to define the beautiful, the just, the good, and all the other ideas. . . . Exercise and train yourself while you are still young in an art which seems to be useless and is called by most people mere loquacity; otherwise the truth will escape you. . . . When you were speaking [with Zeno] I was pleased with you because you would not discuss the doubtful question in terms of visible objects or in relation to them, but only with reference to what we conceive most entirely by the intellect and may call ideas. . . ."

As the great logician continues to explain what he means, it finally becomes clear to us readers that Parmenides is the noblest of minds seeking the truth *as formal logic can reveal it;* he cares deeply that our thinking be logically clear, whatever the outcome or answer. This and other dialogues (especially the *Theaetetus* and *Sophist*) reveal that Socrates and later Plato have the greatest respect for Parmenides and continue to be haunted by his purely logical approach to truth, which, at this auspicious meeting of minds, he demonstrated with awesome brilliance.[37]

The ***Theaetetus*** is a moving 125-page document dealing with problems in epistemology. Reading it, one gets the feeling that Plato has poured his heart and soul into it, for he concentrates on a lifelong obsession: the epistemological foolishness of Sophism, specifically the brand of Sophism taught by Protagoras. The dialogue is one long attempt to find a true definition of knowledge. "What do you think knowledge is?" Socrates asks. He makes the point often that we may have knowledge of specific things, such as shoes, clouds, and birds, or even specific abstractions such as a sense of beauty on looking at this poppy or that feeling of courage after having watched a child rescued from drowning. But none of this can be true knowledge if we don't have a clear understanding of the universal abstract essence-idea of knowledge.

Theaetetus is a brilliant young mathematician who has been wounded in battle (probably in the year 369 BC), has contracted dysentery, and is dying. The dialogue opens with two of Socrates' friends, Terpsion and Eucleidês, discussing the tragedy. Eucleidês recalls that Socrates had once met Theaetetus and was much impressed with him. (Theaetetus, by the way, bore a striking resemblance to Socrates with his "snub nose and protruding eyes.") Eucleidês was present at the original meeting and took notes, so this dialogue, written about 368 BC but set shortly before Socrates' death, is Plato's reconstruction of the conversation that supposedly occurred between Socrates, Theaetetus, and a third man, Theodorus, also a mathematician.

Protagoras and the other Sophists had maintained that each person possesses a private reality, that this private experiential reality provides an accurate knowledge of what is truly real "out there," and that this is all that exists: No reality exists beyond one's personal perception. "Whatever each person perceives, that is real for that person. . . . All perception, then, is perception of what really exists; it can rightly be called knowledge; and therefore it can't be false."

Protagoras had taught that "Man is the measure of all things, of such things as white, or heavy and light; and each person possesses within himself the criterion for making such judgments; when his concepts coincide with his perceptions, then he concludes that whatever his senses tell him is true, and that in fact is true."[39] °

This analysis is anathema to Socrates (and Plato) because it makes the senses the criterion of truth, so Socrates goes to work on the Sophist doctrine. "Isn't it true that

On Plato *The Parmenides is the worst specimen of empty logic-chopping in all literature, and the bravest example in the history of philosophy of a thinker irrefutably refuting his own most beloved doctrine—the theory of Ideas.*

WILL DURANT

Intellect rules the universe.

SOCRATES

°See pp. 94–97.

sometimes when the wind blows one person will feel the wind to be cold and another won't? Does that mean that the wind itself is cold or not cold? Or shall we go along with Protagoras and conclude that the wind is cold to one person, not cold to the other, and that's all there is to it?"[40]

The notion that no reality exists beyond personal sense perception is totally unacceptable. Socrates argues that "we are all quite capable of having false perceptions, so that it is not true at all that whatever a man thinks he is perceiving, he is in fact actually perceiving." The truth, he says, is that "nothing is what it appears to be."[41]

Pain is the disruption of an organism and pleasure its restoration.

SOCRATES

But the Sophists went far beyond perception; they taught the relativity of all judgments and opinions. If an individual, a state, or a society believes something, then that belief, for that individual or group, is true. Protagoras says (according to Plato), "I hold that whatever is judged by a state to be right and of value is truly right and of value to it, just as long as it continues to believe this to be so."[42] All judgments, beliefs, and opinions are relative to the person or persons who believe them.

Socrates seems baffled that a bright thinker could hold such a notion: "Protagoras even agrees that those who believe that he is wrong are right!" "Since he grants that all opinions are true, he even concedes that those who disagree with him and think that his position is false are correct. Doesn't this force him to conclude that his own opinion is false when he grants that others are correct when they hold that his opinion is false?" Only an idiot would say, "You're right when you say I'm wrong, and I'm right when I say that."[43]

°*See* doxa *in lexicon.*

Socrates counters this relativism by saying that just as we are capable of having false perceptions, we are also prone to having false opinions°; so, a lengthy exchange ensues while they analyze how we form opinions, both true and false. Socrates defines opinion as "talk that has been carried on in the silence of one's own self."[44]

The question "What is knowledge?" is never clearly answered in the *Theaetetus;* in fact, Socrates complains, "our talk has been badly tainted with unclearness all along." The closest they come to an answer is to note that true knowledge is "a function of the soul," for "it alone and by itself is engaged directly with realities." The body's senses give us perceptions and sensations; but then the soul goes to work on these sense-given raw materials, and "slowly and with difficulty, with hard work and wrestling," genuine knowledge is attained. The senses perceive only individual objects, but the soul sees "what all things have in common." True knowledge, therefore, is the product of our immediate sense experience combined with our subsequent rational reflection on it. We call this process education.

The *Theaetetus* offers to us many delightful asides. For example, we have Socrates' description of his life as a midwife. "I am the son of a noble and dedicated midwife" he says, "but my craft differs in being practiced upon men, not women, and in tending their souls in labour, not their bodies." Then he says, "We must use this science of midwifery to deliver Theaetetus of the thoughts about knowledge with which he's pregnant."[45] °

°*See pp. 107ff.*

°*See p. 24.*

Plato recounts the story of the early philosopher Thales' falling into a ditch. "Take the case of Thales," he says. "While he was studying the stars and looking upwards, he fell into a pit, and a neat, witty Thracian servant girl jeered at him, they say, because he was so eager to know the things in the sky that he could not see what was there before him at his very feet."[46] ° Plato proceeds to use the story as a metaphor for the dangers that threaten "all who pass their lives in philosophy," warning that they will appear ridiculous "not only to Thracian girls but to the masses in general"; for they will be seen as fools with their heads in the clouds, quite out of touch with the concerns of the "real world."

The *Theaetetus* contains Socrates' beautiful summation of the origins of philosophy.

> THEAETETUS: Yes, Socrates, I stand in amazement when I reflect on the questions that men ask. By the gods, I do! I want to know more and more about such questions, and there are times when I almost become dizzy just thinking about them.
> SOCRATES: Ah, yes, my dear Theaetetus, when Theodorus called you a philosopher he described you well. That feeling of wonder is the touchstone of the philosopher, and all philosophy has its origins in wonder. Whoever reminded us that Iris[the heavenly messenger] is the offspring of Thaumas[wonder] wasn't a bad genealogist.[47]

In the *Theaetetus* we also find Socrates reflecting on his meeting with Parmenides during the Panathenaea in 450 BC. "For I met him when I was very young," he recalls, "and he seemed to me to have a wonderful depth of mind. I'm still haunted that we may not have understood his words and what he meant by them."[48] °*See p. 58ff.*

Plato applies Socrates' admonition to "Know thyself" to a variety of specifics. For instance, "It is very inconsistent for a man who asserts that he cares for virtue to be constantly unfair in discussion; and it is unfair in discussion when a man makes no distinction between merely trying to make points and carrying on a real argument. In the former he may jest and try to trip up his opponent as much as he can, but in real argument he must be in earnest."[49]

Plato (via Socrates) continues his attack on the shallowness of lawyers. "Those who have knocked about in the courts and the like from their youth up seem to me, when compared with those who have been brought up in Philosophy and similar pursuits, to be as slaves in breeding compared with freemen."

In the *Theaetetus* Socrates puzzles briefly over the conundrum of dreaming and wakefulness. "The question is, what proof could we offer if we should be asked whether, at this very moment, we are asleep and our thoughts are just a dream, or whether we are truly awake standing here talking with one another. . . . It is up for grabs whether we are awake or asleep and dreaming."[50] The famous epigram by the Chinese Taoist sage Chuang-tzu is even more succinct: "Once upon a time, I, Chuang-tzu, dreamt I was a butterfly, fluttering hither and thither, to all intents and purposes a butterfly . . . suddenly, I awoke. . . . Now I do not know whether I was then a man dreaming I was a butterfly, or whether I am now a butterfly dreaming that I am a man." [51]

The setting for the **Sophist** is the spring of 399 BC. An anonymous pupil of the great Eleatic logician Parmenides joins a small gathering of philosophers in Athens, and in the ensuing exchanges we are shown that the Megarians, who consider themselves the inheritors of Eleatic rigor, are really off track and don't represent the spirit of Socrates. Pure methodological logic follows, applied ultimately to the doctrine of Real Ideas; they try to work out the relationship of the Ideas to one another and to real objects. A. E. Taylor writes that the *Sophist* makes an enormous contribution to both logic and metaphysics; it "definitely originates scientific logic."[52]

The purpose of the **Politicus** was to explore (again) the question of what kind of government is the best and to apply a Parmenidean-style logic to the definition of "statesman" to find out what theory of government is best supported. The setting and participants in the *Politicus* are the same as in the *Sophist*, except that a young student of mathematics named Socrates is the principal interlocutor.

Plato is still convinced here that the perfect form of government would be ruled by one man (or woman) qualified by his depth of knowledge and his ability to do,

Are we to say that the universe . . . is controlled by irrationality, randomness and chance? Or are we to say the opposite, as our predecessors did, that it is governed by intellect and the coordination of a wonderful reason?

SOCRATES

always, what is good and right; and his entire being would be dedicated to making the souls of his citizens healthy and whole. In any case of litigation brought before him, this one wise ruler would examine the unique combination of factors and render a judgment based on that situation alone. But being realistic, Plato says that no one man, no matter how brilliant and wise, can possibly inform himself fully on every case; therefore, general laws must be enacted in a society and applied as wisely as possible to the individual case.

Through logical analysis, the *Politicus* explores three forms of government: monarchy, oligarchy, and democracy. Plato's analysis is thorough, and his grasp of social ethics is not that unrealistic. If a monarch governs by constitutional law, it is the best; but if a monarchy goes bad, it is the worst, for it becomes a "tyranny." If an oligarchy (rule by a few) is constrained by law, it can work with a modicum of justice; but if it goes bad, then—like the monstrous Thirty in Athens—it can bring disaster. If a democracy is governed by law, it is the least bad, though it is the weakest and most inefficient; but when it goes bad, then mob rule results.

The key to a workable polity is education, both for the statesman and for the populace. Plato employs the metaphor of the woven cloth to represent two basic kinds of people: action-oriented extraverts (not his term!) and thought-oriented, artistic introverts. The wise statesman, through education, will find a way to weave these two temperaments together, warp and woof, to create a balanced and stable society. Marriages should be strictly regulated so that these extreme temperaments don't perpetuate themselves; all types should be urged to intermix to produce greater unity and therefore a peaceful society.

Like the *Parmenides*, the **Timaeus** comes as a surprise. It too doesn't *feel* like Plato—the style and vocabulary are alien, and it ushers us into a world that Plato has heretofore defined as off-limits to the human intellect. The *Timaeus* is the only dialogue devoted to cosmogony and the natural sciences, and what comes as a shock is that Plato has time and again assured us that it is impossible to acquire dependable knowledge of the natural world. But, despite his misgivings, sometime late in his career he felt a need to summarize his own best speculations on the origins and structure of the entire cosmos and its contents. So, in the *Timaeus* we find Plato, first of all, laying the epistemological foundations of a "probable" physics and then describing in strange detail the creation of the universe and the origins and condition of all living things, including humans. Along the way he includes theories regarding the elements, causality, time, motion (and "soul," the cause of motion), perception, and reality (the Real Ideas, his metaphysics).

On Plato *To explain the wonders of the world he preferred imagination to observation.*
    WOODBRIDGE RILEY

But the dialogue begins with a seemingly irrelevant story—the famous myth of Atlantis. The setting for the narration is 422–421 BC in a home in Athens. Timaios is a middle-aged Pythagorean mathematician and astronomer from Locri in southern Italy; also present are Socrates, Critias (Plato's uncle), and Hermocrates, a general from Syracuse. Critias recounts the story of Atlantis, which, we are told, has survived only in the annals of Egypt. The story is given very briefly: Some nine thousand years earlier the federation of Atlantis arose on an island somewhere to the west of the Pillars of Heraklês. This ruthless kingdom had conquered much of Europe and North Africa with the intent "to enslave by one single onslaught." But despite their wealth and military might, the Atlanteans were defeated by the noble prehistoric Athenians "who stood pre-eminent above all in gallantry and all warlike arts" and who thereby saved all the nations from slavery. Sometime later great earthquakes and floods devastated the island in a single day and night, and "Atlantis was swallowed up by the sea and vanished."[53] There the story ends, to be taken up again in a subsequent dialogue, The *Critias*, where Plato tells of the great wars between the

Athenians and Atlanteans—all to make a point about the power of nobility and truth in the life of a civilization.

The direction of the dialogue then changes. Timaios presents a lengthy lecture summarizing all knowledge of the natural world. He begins by laying the epistemological foundations for a science of nature: the difference between being and becoming, a doctrine that runs through almost all Plato's writings.[54] Plato has found that these two terms precisely describe two different worlds—human thought (Being) and human perception (Becoming). (1) Human thought in its abstract form deals with universal and unchanging ideas (we're back to mathematics and geometry: two plus two is an eternal and unchanging idea), and these ideas correspond exactly to the Real Ideas that exist in, and shape, the universe, Or, more correctly, these ideas in our heads are identical to those Real Ideas.

But (2) our perceptions represent a forever-changing world of material objects. The winds blow; ice melts; mountains erode; the Sun, Moon, and planets change their positions; and bodies of all living things are in a condition of motion and change. As noted earlier, nothing remains the same from one moment to the next; nothing is solid, stable, or continuous. Indeed, because physical substance is forever becoming something other than what it is, its existence is not fully real, and "being" should not be ascribed to it. It is ephemeral and evanescent; it therefore eludes apprehension by the rational mind and can't be described.

To say that intellect regulates the universe does justice to the order we perceive in it, in the sun, moon, stars and the whole vault of heaven.

PROTARCHOS

Two of Plato's dialogues, the Timaeus *and the* Critias, *contain the famous story of Atlantis, a ruthless kingdom that in a single day and night "was swallowed up by the sea and vanished." Plato's sole reason for telling the story was to illustrate cosmic justice: bad guys lose, good guys win. The evil Atlanteans were out to enslave all nations, but the noble Athenians, "who stood pre-eminent above all in gallantry and all warlike arts," defeated the Atlanteans and saved the world from slavery. This painting by Sir Gerald Hargreaves (1949) is an example of how a myth takes on a life of its own and is endlessly embellished to serve the human craving for mystery and fantasy.*

The fallout from all this is that the truth can be found only in pure rational thought; the senses are never to be trusted as a source of dependable knowledge. The rational human being (the "philosopher" as philosopher) will trade only in these eternal ideas that are universal truths. Consequently, education's purpose is to "draw the soul away from the world of becoming to the world of being."[55]

Despite his misgivings about our knowledge of nature, Plato proceeds to speculate. The universe was created by a great Architect called the "Demiurge." "It is plain that he fixed his gaze on the Eternal"; that is, he used the Real Ideas as a template for creation. "He created order out of disorder." Because reason is better than nonreason, order is better than disorder, and living things better than nonliving, this world he created is "a Living Creature endowed with soul and reason owing to the providence of God."[56] Only one such universe exists, made in the image of its Maker. After constructing heaven, he created time, days and nights and months and years. "Time, then, came into existence along with the heaven, to the end that having been generated together they might also be dissolved together, if ever the dissolution of them should take place."[57] Then he created the Sun and Moon and the "five other stars"; it is the wanderings of these planets "that constitute Time."[58]

All this, of course, is theological myth, not philosophy, and the resemblance to creation stories from the great religious traditions is striking. It seems that Plato exhausts his resources and has to fall back on his own creative logic and mythical tradition to complete the scenario, for he says, "to discover and declare their origin is too great a task for us." So, he summarizes the origins of the rest of the gods as offspring of Gê and Uranus, Cronos and Rhea, Zeus and Hera, and so on.[59]

Pleasure arises when harmony is being restored.

SOCRATES

The long narration explains motion and rest; the four elements in detail—fire, air, water, and earth; and the human senses and the nature of sense perception—hot and cold, hard and soft, heavy and light, above and below (fascinating! He knows the Earth is round and that "above" and "below" are terms relative to one's position).[60] Then he turns to the creation of human beings and the causes of human experience (pleasure and pain, tastes, smells, hearing, perception of colors)[61]; human anatomy (chest, heart, bones, skin, hair, nails)—"those who were constructing us knew that out of men women should one day spring . . . and would need for many purposes the help of nails"[62]; and finally he gives a lengthy list of diseases and their causes, first of the body then of the soul.[63]

In the course of the hundred-page narration, Plato touches on several interesting subjects. He occasionally speaks of women. He reiterates his ideas as stated in the Republic that "the occupations assigned to them, both in war and in all other activities of life, should in every case be the same for all alike."[64] But his general attitude toward women is more negative. A man who has failed in this life will be reincarnated and "changed into woman's nature at the second birth"; then if he fails as a woman "he shall be changed every time, according to the nature of his wickedness, into some bestial form after the similitude of his own nature."[65] He reiterates his doctrine near the end of the dialogue: "All those creatures generated as men who proved themselves cowardly and spent their lives in wrong-doing were transformed, at their second incarnation, into women."[66]

At the very end of the lengthy dialogue there is a brief discussion of the origins and physiology of sex. The gods who were in charge of creation at the time, he says, decided to give men and women different natures. Then "they bored a hole into the condensed marrow which comes from the head down by the neck and along the spine" and "endowed the part where its outlet lies with a love for generating by implanting therein a lively desire for emission." In the male "the nature of the genital organs is disobedient and self-willed, like a creature that is deaf to reason; and it attempts to dominate all because of its frenzied lusts."[67] In women this obsession expresses itself differently. When the womb is not fulfilled with fruit "beyond the due season, it is vexed and takes it ill; and by straying all ways through the body and blocking up the passages of the breath and preventing respiration it casts the body into the uttermost distress, and causes, moreover, all kinds of maladies; until the desire and love of the two sexes unite them."[68]

After reading the *Timaeus*, one feels he has experienced Plato's all-inclusive world-view. Plato's speculations ring like a mystical theology generated by a superlogical mind that is out of its element but still yearning, for whatever reason, to flesh out a coherent description of the World. It is a breathtaking blend of rigorous logic and occult imagery as outlandish as the most primitive tribal mythology. Plato no longer asks questions; he no longer seeks. He just wanted to put down, for the record, all his life's ponderings about the world and human beings. He wanted to be a cosmologist, paleoanthropologist, biologist, physicist, and theologian. But Plato was a poor observer of the world, and his mind was colored by an anti-empirical bent. He may have intuited that in his time scientific model-building was not yet possible because of insufficient observations. Nevertheless, although he did tell the story, it was with reluctance, and no wonder: A "likely story" it is not.

Is all this philosophy? One may have doubts. If we could ask the question of Aristotle, he would undoubtedly answer, "Yes, of course it's philosophy. But it's *bad* philosophy. Plato tries to describe the world without having looked at the world. He does his best to weave a coherent fabric, even bringing in mathematics and geometry to give it logical structure. But he fails to examine critically his starting points, his beginning assumptions, his *archai;* and since his assumptions are flawed, the systems he builds, no matter how coherent logically, are inevitably flawed also."

As of the twentieth century, what Plato attempted to do has in fact been done. Pick up any good textbook in physics or astrophysics (not those written for the "liberal arts major" or the "educated layperson" but one that includes mathematical descriptions). The pages are filled with abstract ideas (formulas, equations) that are unchanging, eternal, and universal, and such ideas are virtually identical to the Real Ideas Plato spent so much time describing. In this sense, therefore, Plato's contribution to Western thought is momentous. He did in fact lay the foundations for a movement toward the intellectual apprehension of the dynamic operations of the universe.

The ***Critias*** (an incomplete dialogue) contains a much fuller elaboration of the myth of Atlantis found in the the *Timaeus*. It is a detailed description of Athens in ancient times and of the Athenians, "the noblest and most perfect race amongst men"[69]; it tells of a true "Golden Age," when kings were just and people were happy. These great kings, descendants of the gods, accomplished marvels of engineering and government. Plato clearly planned to complete the story by recounting the wars between the two great kingdoms, climaxing with the victory by the Athenians—because they were a noble people—over the Atlanteans. The story was doubtless supposed to rise like a crescendo, but before the account reaches the great wars, it ends abruptly.

The motivation for the dialogue seems to have been the idea that great things can be achieved by science and technology when, and only when, the heart of a people is just and right. This kind of utopian vision, so close to Plato's heart, attempts to depict things as they might be by describing things as they might have been. Once again, we have the eternal dream of human beings that righteousness will prevail in this world of sin and suffering; that societies will come to their senses and realize that material obsessions will always, in the long run, bring defeat; and that all "progress" lies in the souls of humans and their potential for peace through moderation and

On Plato *It is very difficult for the historian to allow Plato to be Plato.*

PENA KABENGELE

Don't move something bad when it's okay where it is.

GREEK PROVERB

decency. Plato never could let go of this vision; nor could he let others solve the world's problems. Throughout his long life of watching the behavior of human beings, two things were clear to him: first, that this world is self-destructive because of its petty obsessions with false goals and, second, that human beings can attain the dream of a world of goodness and happiness, providing they get back on track and pursue the true goals of a noble life—Goodness, Truth, and Beauty.

The *Critias* is a kind of connecting link between the *Republic* and the *Laws*. It also might be thought of as a sequel to the *Timaeus*, designed to further expound Plato's political theory. The setting for the dialogue is the same as for the *Timaeus*.

The **Philebus** explores a theme that runs through all of Greek life and literature: For a human being, what is "the good life"? What should an intelligent, wise, vibrant, and aware human being concentrate on to find the highest fulfillment in this lifetime? Debaters of the issue rather naturally fell into three camps. *Honor:* Should one work toward ever greater acclaim by others (through civic-mindedness and public service, the social graces, concern for fashionable issues, respectable affluence)? *Pleasure:* Should one strive to maximize pleasures (with "wine, women, and song," men, physical beauty, art and music, gardens, scenery, poetry)? *Intellect:* Should one develop the life of the mind (through education and knowledge, literature and science, intellectual companionship and intelligent dialectic in the pursuit of truth)?

In the *Philebus* Socrates debates the merits of pleasure versus intellect with Protarchos, a "young friend" who has been a pupil of the Sophist Gorgias. (The title character Philebos is little more than a bystander.) The dialogue, written late in the 350s BC, is Plato's bold effort to describe how he believes a human being ought to live. In the later *Laws* he wrote, "Human Nature involves, above all, pleasures, pains and desires, and no mortal animal can help being hung up dangling in the air (so to speak) in total dependence on these powerful influences. This is why we should praise the noblest life [because] it excels in providing what we all seek: a predominance of pleasure over pain throughout our lives."[70] In the *Philebus* he wrote, "We'll never be able to examine pleasure adequately without also considering pain"; so, this dialogue is a long, probing (and often convoluted) analysis of pleasure and intellect and what works best to escape pain and give a human being a fighting chance at fulfillment.

Plato discusses pure and impure pleasures, the intensity of pleasure, whether pleasure is "merely" escape from pain, true and false pleasures, and whether pleasures are ends in themselves or are instrumental to achieving telic goals. Then he analyzes intellect and knowledge; he discusses practical knowledge that deals with the material world, the purity and precision of "educational" knowledge, the world of pure thought, and dialectic as the search for universal truth as found in Real Ideas.

Then, lastly, he returns to what constitutes "the good life" and concludes that both intellect and pleasure are essential to a fulfilled human being. Plato never wavers: "For *human* life intellect is far, far better than pleasure." But a *complete* human is *both* a rational *and* sensual animal, so we must allow ourselves to indulge in selected pleasures on the provision they don't interfere with the rational life.

After the meanderings of this hundred-page work, Plato ends with the basic proposition stated by Socrates in the first lines of the dialogue: "Philebus says that for all living creatures the good is enjoyment, pleasure, delight and whatever is compatible with them. But my contention is that they are not the good, but that reason, intellect, memory—not to mention their cognates, correct belief and true calculation—are far better than pleasure for all creatures capable of attaining them; they offer the greatest benefit for all those who, now or in the future, are able to attain them. Isn't this, Philebus, more or less what each of us is saying?"

On the Philebus *The Philebus, as Plato's most deliberate and thorough attempt to describe the good life, may be regarded as the canonical Platonic text on the subject of the way men ought to live.*

ROBIN WATERFIELD

The best way to educate the younger generation is not to rebuke them but patently to practise all your life what you preach to others.

PLATO

"Absolutely, Socrates."

The *Laws* is Plato's last work, written during the decade prior to his death; parts of it may have been left unfinished or unrevised. Why Plato was driven to write two massive utopian treatises—the *Republic* and the *Laws*—might seem puzzling at first. We assume that, in some way, he felt he had not yet accomplished what he wanted or that he had to do something more. But the puzzle fades when we note the differences between the two books. The utopia-polis of the *Republic* is a picture of the ideal state; in it Plato establishes the theoretical principles for running a successful state. In that state the purpose of law is "to produce happiness in the city as a whole, harmonizing and adapting the citizens to one another by persuasion and compulsion, and requiring them to impart to one another any benefit which they are severally able to bestow upon the community."[71] Then, in the *Laws*, Plato accedes to the "real world" and provides the specific guidelines, prescriptions, and penalties for handling the harsh realities of a very, very imperfect humanity. He insists (in the *Republic*) that his dream of a well-ordered state, though difficult, is "not altogether a day-dream" but "is in a way possible."[72]

Still, much of this late work doesn't read like the earlier Plato. If one knew nothing of him and had never read any of his other dialogues, the city-state of the *Laws* undoubtedly would be judged a strange and obsessive dream written by a dismal misanthrope who distrusted everyone and everything; by a self-indulgent authoritarian who hated life, hated the body, hated women, hated most men, hated pleasures, hated music, and hated art; by a fearful escapist who endured this world and longed for the next; and by an elitist who found the masses unenlightened, untrustworthy, unsavory, unlikable, and resistent to all that is intelligent and good. The *Laws* contain little that cannot be found in his other dialogues, especially in the *Republic*; but these later naked prescriptions strike us as extreme, and Plato's authoritarian attitudes appear to us moderns—conditioned to a moderately successful democracy—as paranoid and negative. In any case, the author of the *Laws* is not the inspiring, open-minded, humorous, and loving Plato we have come to know from the *Symposium*, *Phaedrus*, *Phaedo*, and other Socratic dialogues. We are very fortunate to have the *Republic* to put the legalistic content of the *Laws* in perspective.

Perhaps the most striking fact in the *Laws* is Plato's abandonment of any interest in discussing ideas. Dialectical philosophy has vanished. He silences any residual curiosity about the world with his overpowering practical need to dictate and control. When he does approach philosophical subjects, he merely makes dogmatic pronouncements about the "correct view" and goes on. The *Laws* is a severely judgmental work that has lost the spirit of Socratic exploration, with its excitement and joyous insight.

The *Laws* is a long discussion between three old men. The lead is an "Athenian Stranger," never identified by name but whom we assume is Plato himself (playing the role Socrates plays in the earlier dialogues), who delivers one continuous lecture (for 530 pages), punctuated by assents and occasional questions from two companions, Cleinias, a Cretan, and Megillos, a Spartan. The three are on a pilgrimage from Knossos to a shrine of Zeus in south-central Crete. The journey is "quite a long way, and the tall trees along the route provide shady resting-places"; so, they frequently rest and talk.[73]

By the time he wrote the *Laws*, Plato had concluded that no existing society can be reformed gradually through conventional political machinery. A successful city-state must be built from scratch. So Plato chooses an insular valley on the island of Crete and begins to dream-build his utopian state. "Let's construct an imaginary community," he says, "pretending that we are its original founders."[74] He names it Magnesia. It is to be a small self-contained and self-sustaining agricultural polis, lim-

[One will] become a genuine lawgiver only if he designs his legislation about war as a tool for peace, rather than his legislation for peace as an instrument of war.

PLATO

On Plato *The growing boy or girl is to live in an environment of beauty, and the appreciation of the beauty of the environment is expected to lead insensibly to appreciation of whatever is morally lovely and of good report in conduct and character.*

A. E. TAYLOR

ited to 5,040 citizens. Isolated from the rest of the world, it forbids trade and travel (so new ideas can't creep in) and has no harbor (to discourage tourists and eliminate the corrupting presence of sailors who spend their time looking for *pornai*). A certain number of aliens are allowed residence, but their green card is limited to twenty years. Free citizens may own slaves. "Your slave will be a difficult beast to handle," he wrote, and must be strictly controlled. The welfare of foreigners and slaves is of little concern to the Magnesians (or to Plato).

Plato's goal in this polis-state is to regulate every detail of citizens' lives, including their thoughts, feelings, attitudes, and behavior. In attempting this he seems (to us) petty, prudish, and intrusive; respect for personal space and privacy is nonexistent. For example: "A pregnant woman should go for walks." "You should always prefer to marry somewhat beneath you." "Children should never be conceived when the parents' bodies are in a state of drunken relaxation."

Plato's political philosophy is rooted in his personal experience and in his assessment of human nature. He had learned from his involvement in the chaotic affairs in Athens that unredeemed human nature cannot be trusted. The masses he found hopelessly recalcitrant; only a few of the best men and women (the *aristoi*) really can think and understand. "Among the masses you'll always find a few, but only a few, of the special human beings with whom it's worth your time to associate."[74] This fundamental dichotomy colored everything in Plato's life and writing. He is upbeat in the *Laws* when it comes to working with the intelligent and educable; he is a pessimist when dealing with the hoi polloi. For the benefit of the former, he discourses on the intent behind the laws; for the latter, he legislates in black and white and simple rules because he believes the benighted masses have little capacity for understanding right from wrong or for handling complexities. So he prescribes the simplest commands with matched penalties: This is right, and that is wrong; do this, don't do that; and if you do thus and so, then this will be the penalty. This sounds more like a tyrant than a philosopher, or, even worse, Plato has become the lawyer he has spent so much time loathing.

Several clear-cut principles or beliefs underlie the establishment of the Magnesian utopia.

(1) All law is to be grounded on principles derived from the philosopher's vision of the Good. "Plato fervently believes that certain eternally valid norms exist, laid down for man by divine fiat; that these norms are ascertainable and leave no room for others; that real 'freedom' is to obey this divine law, and to do otherwise is to be a slave to one's passions; and that a man's education must therefore train him in this obedience."[75]

(2) Since these norms are complete and immutable, no deviation or change of them or from them must occur; any change would necessarily be away from perfection and would therefore be evil. In the arts, for example, "Change, we shall find, is extremely dangerous. . . . We must do everything we possibly can to distract the younger generation from wanting to try their hand at presenting new subjects, either in dance or song."[76]

(3) Citizens belong to the state. "Education must be compulsory for 'one and all' (as the saying goes), because they [children] belong to the state first and their parents second." When young citizens set out to find a marriage partner, "we should seek to contract the alliance that will benefit the state, not the one that we personally find most alluring." Then "the bride and groom should resolve to present the state with the best and finest children they can produce." This he calls "supervised procreation." "Everyone is to have the same friends and enemies as the state."[77]

Virtue and great wealth are incompatible.

PLATO

Soul resides within this visible spherical body [the Sun] and carries it wherever it goes, just as our soul takes us around from one place to another.

THE ATHENIAN (PLATO)

On Plato *The Laws offers the surrender of a dying Athens that had completely lived to a Sparta that, ever since Lycurgus, had been dead.*

WILL DURANT

(4) Freedom of thought or individualism must not exist. Children, for example, must be molded "like wax while it is still supple" and conditioned to correct behavior and unthinking obedience; they must understand they exist for the sake of the state and any display of individualism will be severely punished. "The vital point is that no one, man or woman, must ever be left without someone in charge of him; nobody must get into the habit of acting alone and independently."[78] "We must condition ourselves to any instinctive rejection of the very notion of doing anything without our companions; we must live a life in which we never do anything, if possible, except by combined and united action as members of a group." "This is what we must practice in peacetime, right from childhood—the exercise of authority over others and submission to them in turn. Freedom from control must be uncompromisingly eliminated from the life of all men, and of all the animals under their domination."[79]

To control the flow of ideas, censorship and severe restriction on contact with the outside world are necessary. "No young person under forty is ever to be allowed to travel abroad under any circumstances." When sports contestants travel outside to attend games, on their return "they are to tell the younger generation that the social and political customs of the rest of the world don't measure up to their own." When foreign visitors are allowed entrance, officials must "take good care that none of this category of visitor introduces any novel custom."[80]

(5) Religion is of the utmost importance. The mandatory credo of all Magnesians will be (a) the gods exist; (b) they are concerned with human behavior; and (c) they cannot in any way be swayed by prayer or sacrifice to favor our petty requests and let us off the hook. All worship is to be at public shrines. "The possession of shrines in private houses is forbidden." If private shrines are discovered, the offenders will be punished "until the shrines are removed"; but if an adult should persist in his worship of "gods not included in the pantheon of the state," then "he must be punished by death for sacrificing with impure hands." In light of the fact that his beloved mentor had been put to death for impiety, Plato's rules on impiety are astonishing. "If anyone disobeys and introduces any different hymns or dances in honour of any god, the priests and priestesses, in association with the Guardians of the Laws, will have the backing of sacred and secular law in expelling him. If he resists expulsion, he must be liable to a charge of impiety for the rest of his life at the hands of anyone who wishes to bring it." Should subjects persist in their impiety after reconditioning (sent "to live with sensible people"), they must be "punished by death."[81]

(6) For both the individual and society, the cultivation of the soul is of supreme worth; hence, the conquest of the body and its obsessive longing for pleasure is a primal concern. "Right from their earliest years we're going to tell [our children] stories and talk to them and sing them songs, so as to charm them, we trust, into believing that this victory [the conquest of the body] is the noblest of all." "If they win this battle, they'll have a happy life—but so much the worse for them if they lose." "The appetite for pleasures, which is very strong and grows by being fed, can be *starved* if the body is given plenty of hard work to distract it. We'd get much the same result if we were incapable of having sexual intercourse without feeling ashamed: our shame would lead to infrequent indulgence, and infrequent indulgence would make the desire less compulsive." "Respect for religion, the ambition to be honoured, and a mature passion for spiritual rather than physical beauty—'Pious wishes!' you'll say; 'sheer moonshine!' Perhaps so. But if such wishes were to come true, the world would benefit enormously."[82]

(7) Plato has much to say about women, but what he gives with one hand, he takes back with the other. "In so far as possible, in education and everything else, the

The pursuit of money should come last in the scale of value.

PLATO

In a higher world it is otherwise; but here below to live is to change, and to be perfect is to have changed often.

JOHN HENRY NEWMAN

The male genital organs are disobedient and self-willed, like a creature that is deaf to reason; and they attempt to dominate everything because of their frenzied lusts.

PLATO

Spite is a painful condition of the soul.

SOCRATES

female sex should be on the same footing as the male." A legislator "mustn't just regulate the men and allow the women to live as they like and wallow in expensive luxury." The proper punishment for a soldier who turns coward would be to change him from a man into a woman: "[T]hat would be the most appropriate punishment for a man who has thrown away his shield." But since that's not possible, then, "like the woman he is by nature," he must be dishonored by stripping him of all the freedoms and privileges that make a man a man. The female half of the human race, Plato says, "is inclined to be secretive and crafty, because of its weakness." "You see, leaving women to do what they like is not just to lose half the battle," because "a woman's natural potential for virtue is inferior to a man's, she's a proportionately greater danger, perhaps even twice as great."[83]

CODA: PHILOSOPHER AND HUMAN BEING

Often a reader of Platonic literature comes across the statement, or the sentiment, that it would have been better if Plato had ceased writing sometime after the *Republic* and before the *Laws*. Such a statement is understandable, for (to us moderns) he almost succeeds in negating a life heretofore dedicated to Goodness, Truth, and Beauty; he almost eclipses the wealth of insight and inspiration he had labored so long to bequeath to the world. In the *Laws* he leaves us with images, ideas, and attitudes that are anathema to us; we can't quite get them out of our mind. And because all us humans are paranoid (Plato was right!), we become obsessed with the negative and find it difficult to refocus on the "dear delight" that is Plato and philosophy.

But wider considerations suggest another perspective. When we say we wish he hadn't written the *Laws*, we are in fact speaking not of Plato but of ourselves, saying we don't want to deal with what life itself often does to us as human beings. Spare us, we ask. Don't make us have to deal with these depressive truths. However, if we could manage to switch our concerns away from ourselves and ask *Plato* about his last years, we would hear a different answer. What would *he* say should we tell him that, on the basis of the *ideas* in the *Laws*, we have concluded that he ended his days as a miserable misanthrope, depressed by failure and discouraged by life?

All wise men proclaim in unison that intellect is the king of heaven and earth.

PLATO

"I have lived a full and productive life. I have worked at what I love—writing and teaching—mostly writing. I have been surrounded by loving colleagues, and I have become the proud teacher of some of the best men in all Hellas. My school is thriving, and it is famed for the right reasons: It has provided the opportunity for young men and women to pursue the Truth and thereby to live happy and productive lives."

And this, in fact, is what we find *behind* the *Laws*. A hater of humankind, a depressed escapist? Not quite. He still believed with all his heart that human nature is redeemable; he had the highest respect for bright people who have tended their souls. He still believed justice can be achieved, and that a stable state is possible. He still believed in education as the key to a happy society. His lifelong ideals were intact; he still worked diligently for "peace, respect for others, good laws, justice in full measure, and a state of happiness and harmony among the races of the world."[84] And the Athenian stranger—if in fact this is Plato—is still full of life; he is so filled with ideas that, for more than five hundred pages, he can't stop talking!

You Greeks are always children: there is not such a thing as an old Greek. . . . You are young in soul, every one of you.

EGYPTIAN PRIEST TO
SOLON

Plato's gift to civilization is incalculable. He raised a million questions and, with the help of his master, forced us to think about a myriad things we would have been blind to had we remained hypnotized by belief and "opinion." "Socrates asked questions but did not answer," we are told, "for he admitted that he did not know." So also for Plato. And though Plato attempted to find some answers, by and large he failed, so we are still stuck with the questions, which we must answer in our own time in our own way. "The purpose of all education," he wrote, "is the provocation of thought." The goal of Socrates' dialectic was to assist others in the development of their reasoning abilities. In all this both men are among the world's great success stories.

Perhaps Plato's greatest gift is his having written so much that is so wrong. Anyone who writes thousands of pages is going to make thousands of mistakes. These he made partly because of a lack of empirical data but also from bad logic, bad judgment, and invalid epistemic assumptions. His psychology is inadequate. His physics is almost nonexistent, as is his chemistry, astronomy, and cosmology ("he substitutes imagination for hard data"). His sociology is very poor, his comparative anthropology lacking. His metaphysics is necessarily unempirical and useless. His epistemology is confused in the extreme, as are his semantics.

But all this is merely petty carping when compared with his positive achievements. To be sure, critical evaluation of his ideas has been, is, and will forever be required for our creative use of Plato and for our progress and growth. He would of course find this completely in order; this is what *he* spent *his life* doing. But Plato's life-story is another matter, and the final judgment must be that it was a life well lived in difficult times, like ours. Not that he was *trying* to live a full life, for that, like the search for the Tao, doesn't work. "Do you think that a mind habituated to thoughts of grandeur and the contemplation of all time and all existence can deem this life of man a thing of great concern?"[85] The words are Socrates' but the sentiment Plato's. "I think a man's duty is . . . to find out where the truth is, or if he cannot, at least to take the best possible human doctrine and the hardest to disprove, and to ride on this like a raft over the waters of life."[86]

ENDNOTES

1 Plato, *Epistle* VII 326; Plato, *Republic* V.473D.
2 Virtually everything said or recorded about Plato must be taken with a degree of skepticism; every fact claim is a matter of probability, high or low, and nothing more. Myth and legend about him began even before his death and continued to accumulate for the next thousand years. They include stories of his virgin birth as the son of Apollo; see Alice Swift Riginos, *Platonica: The Anecdotes Concerning the Life and Writings of Plato* (E. J. Brill, 1976).
3 Riginos, *Platonica*, p. 7.
4 Riginos, *Platonica*, p. 13.
5 Apollo had quite a few sons (not to mention daughters); among them were Alexander the Great and Pythagoras. So Plato seems to have had numerous, even countless, half siblings.
6 Several versions of the conversations betweeen Plato and Dionysius I exist, none of which may be historical. Although they may have been fabricated to show that Plato was not a submissive lacky to the tyrant but could hold his own, they may contain an essential truth about Plato's attitude and about the relationship between the two men.
7 A. E. Taylor, *Plato: The Man and His Work* (1926; reprint, Meridian Books, 1956), p. 9.
8 Plato, *Timaeus*.
9 Plato, *Timaeus*.
10 Plato, *Phaedrus*, 278A; see also Plato's *Seventh Letter*, 344A.
11 Knowledge of these two female students is from Diogenes Laërtius, quoting an earlier source, Dicaearchus, who was a student of Aristotle, writing in the late fourth century BC. For more, see Diogenes Laërtius, *Lives of the Ancient Philosophers*, III.46. Another account says both women were students of Speusippus and adds that Speusippus was in love with Lastheneia. Still another says Axiothea was converted to Platonism through her reading of the *Republic*.
12 Plato, *Phaedo*, 85A.
13 Plato, *Protagoras*.
14 Xenophon, *Anabasis*, II, in *Anabasis: The March Up Country*, by W. H. D. Rouse (Ann Arbor Paperbacks, 1964), pp. 56f.
15 Plato, *Republic*, II.359C–360D; the gold ring was Gyges' or "his ancestor's"; the text has a variant.

16 Plato, *Republic*, VI.488A–E; see also I.332E; Plato's *Politicus*, 302Aff., 299B; *Euthydemus*, 291D; and *Laws*, 758A, 945C.
17 Plato, *Republic*, V.473C–D.
18 Plato, *Republic*, VI.484B–C.
19 Plato, *Republic*, VI.485C.
20 Plato, *Republic*, VI.485B–487A.
21 Plato, *Republic*, VII.519E–521B.
22 Plato, *Republic*, I.331E–354C, for the lengthy discussion; see also IV.433A–434C.
23 Plato, *Republic*, VII 514Aff.
24 Plato, *Republic*, VII.519C.
25 Plato, *Republic*, VII.517C.
26 Plato, *Republic*, VII.517E.
27 Plato, *Gorgias*.
28 Plato, *Republic*, VII.520C–D.
29 Plato, *Republic*, VII.521A.
30 Plato, *Republic*, VI.509D–511E.
31 Plato, *Republic*, VII.521C.
32 Plato, *Republic*, VII.521D.
33 Plato, *Republic*, VII.527Dff., 529B–C.
34 Plato, *Republic*, VII.540C.
35 Plato, *Phaedrus*, 230.
36 Plato, *Phaedrus*, 279.
37 Plato, *Parmenides*, 127D–136C.
38 Plato, *Theaetetus*, 152C.
39 Plato, *Theaetetus*, 178B.
40 Plato, *Theaetetus*, 152B.
41 Plato, *Theaetetus*, 158A.
42 Plato, *Theaetetus*, 167C.
43 Plato, *Theaetetus*, 171A–B.
44 Plato, *Theaetetus*, 190A.
45 Plato, *Theaetetus*, 150B, 184A–B.
46 Plato, *Theaetetus*, 174A–B.
47 Plato, *Theaetetus*, 155C–D.
48 Plato, *Theaetetus*, 183E–184A.
49 Plato, *Theaetetus*, 167E.
50 Plato, *Theaetetus*, 172D.
51 Plato, *Theaetetus*, 158B–C.
52 Taylor, *Plato*, p. 392.
53 Plato, *Timaeus*, 90B.
54 Plato, *Timaeus*, 27D–29A, 50Bff., 52Dff.
55 Plato, *Republic*, VII.521D.
56 Plato, *Timaeus*, 29B–C.
57 Plato, *Timaeus*, 38B.
58 Plato, *Timaeus*, 38C, D; see 47A–B.
59 Plato, *Timaeus*, 40E–41A.
60 Plato, *Timaeus*, 62E–63E.
61 Plato, *Timaeus*, 44Dff.
62 Plato, *Timaeus*, 76E.
63 Plato, *Timaeus*, 82Aff., 86Bff.
64 Plato, *Timaeus*, 18C; see also *Republic*, 416Dff.
65 Plato, *Timaeus*, 42B–C.
66 Plato, *Timaeus*, 90E.
67 Plato, *Timaeus*, 90B.
68 Plato, *Timaeus*, 91C.
69 Plato, *Timaeus*, 23B.
70 Plato, *Laws*, 732.
71 Plato, *Republic*, VII.519E–520A.
72 Plato, *Republic*, VII.540D.
73 Plato, *Laws*, 625.
74 Plato, *Laws*, 951.
75 Trevor J. Saunders, *Plato: The Laws* (Penguin Classics, 1970), p. 270.
76 Plato, *Laws*, 797f.
77 Plato, *Laws*, 783, 955.
78 Plato, *Laws*, 942.
79 Plato, *Laws*, 942.
80 Plato, *Laws*, 950, 951, 966.

81 Plato, *Laws*, 919, 799, 909.
82 Plato, *Laws*, 840, 841.
83 Plato, *Laws*, 805, 806, 944, 781, 780.
84 Plato, *Laws*, 713f.
85 Plato, *Republic*, VI.486A. Note Marcus Aurelius's reference to this passage in his *Meditations*, VII.35.
86 Plato, *Phaedo*, 95B.

CHAPTER 11

ARISTOTLE OF STAGIRA

The first great empirical philosopher develops theories about motion, ethics, happiness, esthetics, politics, an Unmoved Mover, and much more; he lays the foundations of virtually all the sciences; and he creates a coherent empirical worldview that influences Western thought for the next two millennia.

MACEDONIA

For one swallow does not make a summer, nor does one day; and so too one day, or a short time, does not make a man blessed or happy.
ARISTOTLE

Aristotle is the third of the great Athenian philosophers of the Golden Age. The first, Socrates, wrote nothing; he made his impact through a living influence on all who knew him. After his death, his disciple Plato adopted his method and spirit, and he in turn passed the torch on to Aristotle, a young man with an encyclopedic mind

Aristotle (384–322 BC), the first great empirical thinker in the western tradition.

and a passion to understand the world. Socrates' two followers produced an astonishing corpus of written material. In fifty years of writing, Plato wrote 56 books, most of them with Socrates as protagonist. Aristotle was even more prolific; during thirty-eight active years he produced a total of 551 books. These three thinkers, together, created a new consciousness in Western thought.

Aristotle worked in Athens, but he was not an Athenian. He was a Macedonian, and his lifetime coincided with the rise of the Macedonian empire. Macedonia's King Philip II had long had his eye on "the Athenian harbors and dockyards and war-galleys and silver-mines" (Demosthenes' words), and in August of 338 BC he defeated the Athenians at the Battle of Chaeronea and absorbed the crown jewel of Hellas into his dream of empire. A century earlier the kings of Macedonia had established themselves as royal patrons of the best in Greek culture, initiating a tradition that lasted for two hundred years. In the fourth century the Macedonian kings maintained close ties with the Athenian universities and used the services of educators, scientists, geographers, engineers, economic and political advisers, and leading creative minds in literature, the arts, and philosophy.

Thus, long before Aristotle's birth, and even before Philip's conquest, Macedonia had absorbed the shining achievements of the Greek spirit. To be sure, the Macedonian passion for action—love of fighting, hunting, public contests, horsemanship, and Bacchic festivals—remained alive; but in the more sophisticated urban centers and at the royal court, development of the total person had become an assumed ideal.

Though Aristotle was born in a small Greek settlement just across the Macedonian border in Thrace, he moved all his life among influential Macedonians.[1] He spent his youth at the king's court, and later, as a famed educator, he was summoned by King Philip to become tutor to his son Alexander. After Aristotle moved to Athens, many of 'his closest associates were Macedonians. Nikanôr, the Macedonian commander in Piraeus, was his sister's son; and Antipater, Alexander's Macedonian regent in Athens, was a close friend Aristotle named as executor of his will. No wonder the Athenians thought of Aristotle as a resident alien living in their midst.

IN THE HISTORY OF PHILOSOPHY

Aristotle's influence on the Western intellect is second to no other philosopher, both when he has been correctly interpreted and when he has not been. He is remembered principally (1) for his invention and elaboration of the rules of logic (induction and deduction); (2) for his interpretation of heavenly phenomena; (3) for his scientific approach to biology, from which he derived the belief in *entelecheia*; (4) for his tripartite analysis of the human psyche; (5) for his ethics of *eudaimonia*; (6) for his theory of good government; (7) for his concept of poetry as *mimêsis* and *katharsis*; (8) for his metaphysical analysis of the four *aitia*, "causes"; (9) for his theory of motion and the Unmoved Mover.

THE MAN

Aristotle's parents, Nikomachos and Phaistis, were living in Stagira on the Chalkidic peninsula when he was born sometime between July and September in 384 BC. One of three children, he had a sister Arimnestê and a brother Arimnestos. Both parents, of noble lineage, could trace their descent from Asklepios, the god of medicine. Nikomachos was close to the Macedonian king Amyntas III (Alexander's grandfather), serving as his physician at the royal court in Pella. This new capital city, still surrounded by marshes and open fields, was the garrison of the most powerful army in the world; it witnessed the visits of foreign emissaries and unending military preparations. Aristotle and the crown prince Philip became close friends. His

On Aristotle *It was Plato who formulated most of philosophy's basic questions—and doubts. It was Aristotle who laid the foundation for most of the answers.*

AYN RAND

On Aristotle *There is no future for the world except through a rebirth of the Aristotelian approach to philosophy. This would require an Aristotelian affirmation of the reality of existence, of the sovereignty of reason, of life on earth—and of the splendor of man.*

LEONARD PEIKOFF

Children and fools ask questions that no sensible man bothers to discuss.

ARISTOTLE

Democracy arises out of the notion that those who are equal in any respect are equal in all respects; because men are equally free, they claim to be absolutely equal.

ARISTOTLE

perceiving eyes may have seen too much during these years, for he developed a strong dislike of princes and court intrigues.

Both his father and mother died within a few years, and the orphaned youth was sent back to Stagira to be cared for and educated by a man named Proxenos. We have no firm knowledge of his brother and sister, but since we find that Arimnestê was soon married to Proxenos, we can speculate that all three children may have been sent back to Stagira together. Aristotle must have performed brilliantly in his studies for, at age seventeen, he was accepted as a student in Plato's Academy in Athens.

STUDENT

Aristotle arrived at the Academy in the late spring of 367 BC (shortly after Plato's second departure for Sicily) and remained there for twenty years. No details of his life during this period are known. We can safely assume it was a time of intellectual maturation. We know he was in love with learning and had a passion for books—qualities that inspired Plato, likely with teacherly affection, to dub him "the Brain" and "the Bookworm" (more literally, he was called *ho Nous*, "the Mind," and *ho Anagnostês*, "the Reader") and to refer to his home as "the Reader's House." Aristotle began to collect books and eventually built a large library of his own.

As a student his curious mind must have been involved in all aspects of the Academy's program. Above all, the school was an institution for teaching political science and was designed to produce statesmen. Aristotle would have lived in or near the Academy, located a couple miles outside Athens on the north side. There he would have strolled the grounds and routed himself along the Panathenaic Way to the Agora. We can suppose he often traversed the Street of the Marbleworkers talking or dickering with craftspeople, merchants, and the city's political leaders.

ASIA MINOR

In the minds of his students, Plato seemed immortal, but in 348 BC the great educator died and his school entered into an uneasy transition. Little doubt exists that Aristotle was close to election as the Academy's new head, but instead Plato's nephew Speusippos succeeded to scholarch, likely without formal election. Violent anti-Macedonian uprisings also occurred in southern Greece at this time, ignited by the Macedonian capture of Olynthus, a powerful maritime city-state on the Chalkidic peninsula, in August of 348 BC. So, in the spring of 347 BC, at age thirty-nine, Aristotle departed the Academy and with two companions, Theophrastos and Xenocrates, traveled to Asia Minor. There they were invited to live at the court of their old friend Hermias, who by this time had become a vassal of the Persians and appointed ruler of two city-states in the Troad. They settled in the newly built city of Assos.

Aristotle organized a small circle of like-minded thinkers to explore politics and ethics. The gathering was not an organized school but a sort of think tank for Hermias designed to help him further Greek rule and culture in Asia Minor. Aristotle taught, wrote, reflected, and continued to develop his ideas, still along Platonic lines.

LESBOS

After two years at Assos Aristotle and his friends transferred to Mytilênê, the capital of the offshore island of Lesbos. Theophrastos was from Eresos, a small town on the island's southwestern side, and may have been instrumental in their turning to Lesbos to pursue research and (quite possibly) to find sanctuary.

You don't know a man until you have consumed a peck of salt with him.

ARISTOTLE

In everything, as the saying goes, the first step is what counts. First beginnings are hardest to make and as small and inconspicuous as they are potent in influence, but once they are made, it is easy to add the rest.

ARISTOTLE

On Aristotle *There I beheld the Master of those who know. . . .*

DANTE

All things desire God.

ARISTOTLE

The hills and valleys of this northern Aegean island were graced with rich grain-fields and vineyards, olive groves, and stands of virgin pine forest. Occupying the island's center was the giant Pyrrha lagoon, one of the lovely places where Aristotle and his companions gathered specimens and carried on zoological investigations. Sites where he conducted research are mentioned in his writings: Twelve place-names identify locations in Macedonia and Thrace, thirty-two in Asia Minor and around the Troad, and six at the Pyrrha lagoon. Repeating their efforts at Assos, they set up a school of sorts to teach and, increasingly, to explore the natural sciences. Aristotle's writings in biology reveal a detailed knowledge of the marine biology of this part of the world, and from this time on the metaphors and paradigms guiding Aristotle's philosophical speculations derive largely from biology.

CROWN PRINCE

In the winter of 343–342 BC, when Aristotle was forty-two, King Philip sent him an invitation to return to Pella to supervise the education of his son Alexander, then thirteen years old. The young prince—blond, tousle-haired, bright, sensitive, nervous, excitable, and competitive—was proving unmanageable. Knowing well it would be a test of skill and patience, Aristotle accepted, proceeded to the capital, and settled again at the court where he was raised. But Philip decided the royal court was not the best place for serious study, so he located Aristotle at Mieza, a quiet village in the foothills of the Bermius range twenty-five miles southwest of the capital. There, in the country atmosphere of vineyards and orchards, along shady avenues lined with stone benches, Aristotle took up the task of transforming the flighty future king into a civilized animal. Alexander brought with him a dozen or so of his young friends; Aristotle tutored them all. Philip admonished his son to study diligently. Pay close attention to what Aristotle taught, he said, "so that you may not do a great many things of the sort that I am sorry to have done." The course of study Aristotle gave the young men included Homer and other poets, geometry, astronomy, and rhetoric and debate.

Here is one of those events so annoying to historians, a relationship history judges to have been momentous with possibilities—but that we know nothing about. Here were two men with great stores of energy and sense of vocation and, as the Greeks would say, with *kairos*—the perfect moment in time to affect each other's destinies—and *nothing* of this event survives in the records. Our imaginations are free to create scenarios ad infinitum. Despite the age difference, the two strong personalities undoubtedly impacted each other. They differed so profoundly that it seems too much to hope they understood each other. Alexander was a man of action, Aristotle a man of thought. Alexander sought power and glory; Aristotle wanted only to understand the world. Alexander dreamed (as did his father) of molding the known world into a single empire, while Aristotle was convinced any political unit larger than a city-state was unworkable. Alexander advocated a fusion of races; Aristotle considered all non-Greeks slaves by nature, barbarians bereft of intellectual light. He later wrote, in his *Politics*, that "those who are sprung from better ancestors are likely to be better men, for nobility is excellence of race."[2]

Alexander must have wondered how any man as bright as Aristotle could spend so much time reading and reflecting when so much must be done; to the crown prince his teacher must have seemed pedantic, punctilious, and prissy. And Aristotle must have felt, at times at least, that Alexander was a hyperactive adolescent too impatient for reflection, too inexperienced for serious politics, too hot blooded for ethics, and impervious to the subtler lessons of life—a young prince eager to return to the hunt, the games, the boys, and the girls and quite unripe for wisdom.

Life itself is not enough, even if it brings external happiness; only the good life, the life of a philosopher, is worth living.

ARISTOTLE

To be a philosopher is better than to make money, but it is not more desirable for a man who lacks the bare necessities of life.

ARISTOTLE

We should nowhere be more modest than in matters of religion.

ARISTOTLE

The lonelier I am, the more of a recluse I become, the greater is my love for myths.

ARISTOTLE

To learn is a natural pleasure, not confined to philosophers, but common to all men.

ARISTOTLE

It is this simplicity that makes the uneducated more effective than the educated when addressing popular audiences.

ARISTOTLE

To be conscious that we are perceiving or thinking is to be conscious of our own existence.

ARISTOTLE

We cannot overstrain man's nature.

ARISTOTLE

God and nature create nothing that does not fulfil a purpose.

ARISTOTLE

Their years together at Mieza must have marked them both, and the records hint that Aristotle and Alexander never quite let go of each other. While campaigning against Darios in Asia, Alexander was informed that Aristotle had published some of the ideas he had taught the young men at Mieza. Alexander sent a furious letter to Aristotle complaining that he thought these ideas were special and private, and he resented their becoming the common property of hoi polloi. We also have reports that Alexander, as he moved eastward across Persia and into the Indus valley, set his troops to gathering information about, and actual specimens of, exotic flora and fauna that were dispatched back to Athens for Aristotle's gardens and museums. (Probably from such reports Aristotle wrote fascinating descriptions of the elephant and ostrich, neither of which he was ever likely to have seen.[3]) On the tragic side, Aristotle's nephew Kallisthenes became the official chronicler of Alexander's march into Persia, but at a banquet one evening the tactless young historian, in a drunken stupor and angry at attempts to deify Alexander, refused to pay homage to the king. He was soon implicated in an assassination plot and executed. Alexander wrote a letter to Antipater, his regent and Aristotle's good friend in Athens, saying he was out to punish not only Kallisthenes but also "those who sent him to me and those who now harbor in their cities men who conspire against my life." After receiving such threats, Alexander's paranoia led him to believe Aristotle was in on the plot to kill him.

But in 342 BC, Aristotle's singular concern was his commission to prepare the crown prince to be a successful monarch of the Macedonian kingdom. He wrote dialogues and treatises that Alexander could use as textbooks, among them *On Monarchy* and *On Colonies*, both now lost. In addition to teaching him rhetoric, oratory, grammar, and literature, he was to instill in him the principles of good governance and to make him humane in his assessments, intelligent in his policies, and moderate and mature in his decisions.

INTERIM YEARS

On King Philip's expansive agenda was an invasion of the Persian empire, and to this end he had been negotiating with Hermias for the use of his Trojan cities as Macedonian bases. Hermias was still a Persian vassal, and in 342–341 BC the Persian overlords discovered that Hermias was playing both sides. They captured him by trickery, tortured and mutilated him, and then crucified him. Impaled and dying, he somehow managed to get a final message out to his friends, saying he had not betrayed them and had done nothing unworthy of a scholar and a gentleman. He went to his death refusing to implicate Philip. Aristotle, still at Mieza when he heard the news, wrote an elegiac tribute to his lost friend and later set up a statue at Delphi in his memory.

After Hermias's death Aristotle married Hermias's niece Pythias. Aristotle later wrote that the ideal marriage age for a man is thirty-eight and for a women eighteen; whether this comment should be construed as autobiographical is uncertain. Now began the happiest years of Aristotle's life. The couple bore two children: first a daughter named Pythias after her mother and then a son named Nikomachos after Aristotle's father.

But sometime during these years Pythias died. Aristotle subsequently memorialized her in a grand funeral ceremony in Athens, much like those the Athenians gave when they honored their goddess Demeter at Eleusis. We have no details of her death, and we don't hear of their daughter again until Aristotle mentions her in his will. At a later time (probably while in Athens) a young lady named Herpyllis became an important part of Aristotle's life. Herpyllis was originally a slave girl who then became chief servant or head maid in charge of Aristotle's household (she originally may have been Pythias's handmaid). She became Aristotle's companion and lover. (The early traditional biographies describe her variously as a *therapaina*, a waiting maid; a *hetaira*, a concubine or companion; and a *pallakê*, a concubine or mistress.) Aristotle's will revealed what she meant to him personally.

In 339 BC Philip was ready to begin his campaign against Persia and left his son as regent in Macedonia. Aristotle's service at the royal court came to an end, so he returned to Stagira and settled in a house inherited from his father. Theophrastos joined him. We know nothing of Aristotle's activities during this period of three or four years. In 336 BC Philip was assassinated, and the crown prince became king of Macedonia, known henceforth as Alexander the Great.

THE LYCEUM

In the spring of 334 BC, as Alexander set off to conquer Asia, Aristotle returned to Athens, by then under Macedonian control. Why he returned at this time is not known, but Speusippos had just died and Xenocrates, Aristotle's friend and fellow scientist from Mytilênê, had been chosen to head the Academy.

One of Athens' three public gymnasia or meeting halls was located a mile southeast of the Acropolis on the city's southern outskirts, and Aristotle began to lecture there to a small group of students. Called the Lyceum, this public gathering place included a shady garden, covered walkways, and a gymnasium on the grounds of a temple dedicated to Apollo Lyceus—Apollo the Light-Giver. It had been long used by local and itinerant Sophists and teachers, including Socrates, and it continued to be open to the public. As Aristotle's popularity increased and his following grew, he rented more land and buildings. Not a citizen, he possessed no property rights and couldn't purchase property in his own name. Later, during the administration of his successor Theophrastos, the Lyceum's first true scholarch, extensive real property was acquired, buildings constructed, and a formal school became institutionalized.

In contrast to Plato's Academy, which stressed mathematics and geometry, the Lyceum from its inception was a center for scientific research and the teaching of scientific method. Aristotle found that to be a scientist, he also must be a collector and curator, so he and his students conducted their own fieldwork and developed research collections. On the Lyceum grounds Aristotle built up a zoo and botanical garden, and inside the buildings he created laboratories and a library. His lecture room contained one or more sofas, a three-legged table, a bronze statue, a bronze globe, and presumably couches and writing places for the students. His "blackboard" was a white board, a *leukôma*, or a wooden tablet covered with gypsum, on which he wrote and made diagrams.

Aristotle was fifty when he began lecturing in the Lyceum, and for a dozen years he directed research programs, taught, and wrote. He seems to have been a superb administrator and delegator. He assigned his students to collecting information in virtually every field, from the biology of animals and plants to the ethical behavior of barbarian tribes and the constitutions of Greek city-states—enough hard data to fill a library and assure that both teacher and students always would have sufficient research material to draw on for their studies.

Aristotle also lectured as he wandered the grounds of the park and under covered walkways, just as he had at Mieza. His students soon came to be known as Peripatetics, the "Strollers" (from *peripatos*, "school," but with the connotation of "discussions while walking around"). During morning hours he lectured on technical subjects; in the afternoon he presented open-air lectures to the public on popular topics, such as education, rhetoric and grammar, mathematics and geometry,

To perceive is to suffer.
ARISTOTLE

We cannot learn without pain.
ARISTOTLE

Without friends no one would choose to live, though he had all other goods.
ARISTOTLE

Alexander the Great (356–323 BC), pupil of Aristotle and king of Macedonia at age 20.

statecraft, ethics, poetry, drama and literature, and the art of living the good life. He spent his evening hours engaged in conversations or writing.

CHALKIS AND EXILE

In the summer of 323 BC a virtual hell broke loose in Athens when Alexander died unexpectedly in the palace of Nebuchadnezzar in Babylon, probably from malaria and too much drink. By late October riots had spread throughout the city. The citizens of Athens, long restive and ripe for rebellion, and stirred by the patriotic oratory of Demosthenes, unleashed pent-up angers against their conquerors and, because of his close associations with Macedonians, against Aristotle. He was officially accused of "atheism" or "impiety"—introducing new gods into the Athenian pantheon. Some remembered that Aristotle had set up a statue at Delphi as a memorial to Hermias, and since Hermias was a eunuch, to honor such a man as a god offended the pious citizens of Athens. They also may have remembered the "religious" funeral performed for his deceased wife. But these were only excuses. The true cause of the charges was his Macedonian connections. In any case, "impiety" was a standard accusation: Anaxagoras, Protagoras, and Socrates had been so charged.

Beauty is the gift of God.
ARISTOTLE

Aristotle watched the gathering storm and decided to withdraw lest—as he put it in a letter to Antipater—the Athenians "would outrage philosophy a second time." A half century earlier they had sinned against their noblest citizen and put him to death; Aristotle would not stay around for a recurrence. He retreated to his mother's landholdings in Chalkis on the island of Euboea, twenty-five miles north of Athens; there a Macedonian garrison would protect him. He wrote a letter to Antipater (the Macedonian regent in Athens) complaining that "in Athens the same things are not proper for a stranger as for a citizen; it is difficult to stay in Athens." Aristotle was tried in absentia and stripped of his honors. When he heard about it, he wrote to Antiphon, "About the voting at Delphi and their depriving me of my honors, my feeling is that I am sorry, but not extremely sorry."

Education is the best provision for old age.
ARISTOTLE

LAST WILL

During his time in Chalkis Aristotle wrote his will, and this precious document reflects the man's character. "All will be well," he says, but just in case something should happen to him, "Aristotle has made the following arrangements." His friend Antipater is to be principal executor, though his nephew Nikanôr, the oldest male family member , is to take charge of his estate when he arrives back in Athens from a lengthy and apparently dangerous trip abroad. Nikanôr is to care for Herpyllis, the slaves, and all his property; he is to marry his daughter Pythias when she is old enough; and he is to look after his son Nikomachos just as "if he were the father and brother." (Nikomachos was Aristotle's legitimate heir and inherited everything not otherwise disposed of.) Herpyllis is to be given special care. "The executors and Nikanôr, in memory of me and of the steady affection which Herpyllis has borne towards me, shall take care of her in every way, and, if she desires to be married, shall see that she be given to someone worthy of her, and me." She is also to be given a considerable sum of money from the estate and three handmaids of her choice (in addition to the two she already has). If she decides to live at Chalkis, she is to be given "the lodge by the garden," and if she chooses to live at Stagira, then she is to be given his father's house; whichever she chooses is to be fully furnished. His slaves and servants are to be compensated. "None of the servants who waited upon me shall be sold, but they shall continue to be employed; and when they arrive at the proper age they shall have their freedom, if they deserve it." Then he makes a final request: "Wherever they bury me, there the bones of Pythias shall be laid beside me, in accordance with her own instructions."[4]

Aristotle had tolerated the exile in Chalkis for barely a year when he died from stomach disease, probably from a gastric ulcer or cancer of the stomach. It was September or early October in the year 322 BC. He was age sixty-three.

FAMILY

As Aristotle had willed, his daughter Pythias married Nicanôr, the son of Aristotle's sister Arimneste, but Nicanôr died not long afterward, and Pythias was then married to Procleus, but he too died sometime before 300 BC. After these misfortunes, and probably still in her thirties, Pythias married a well-known physician named Metrodorus, and they had a son whom they named Aristotle. Theophrastos became scholarch of the Lyceum and, always a close friend of the family, gave special loving care to this young man, Aristotle's grandson, allowing him to associate and study with the older students in the Lyceum even though he was too young to belong to the *koinonia* of scholars. "The oldest of them shall pay every attention to him, in order to ensure for him the utmost proficiency in philosophy"—this from Theophrastos's will.

Aristotle's son Nikomachos was legitimate and therefore covered in the law after Aristotle's death. An extant Arabic version of Aristotle's will says "As to my estate and my son there is no need to be concerned about provisions in this will." Theophrastos, who had become Nikomachos's guardian, cared for and educated him. But Nikoma-chos also died young, probably when only four or five years old, just a few years after Aristotle. We have no further knowledge of Herpyllis.

PERSONAL

Any attempt to recover Aristotle's physical likeness remains problematic. Eleven busts exist, but they are all replicas of earlier works, and the earliest of these was sculpted some 350 years after his death; however, it may be a copy of an original statue Alexander set up in his teacher's honor. We know he was wealthy from an inheritance from his father and from substantial remunerations from King Philip. The biographical tradition tells us Aristotle was often the butt of satire because "he was conspicuous by his attire, his rings, and the cut of his hair."[5] He apparently

We should behave to our friends as we would wish our friends to behave to us.

ARISTOTLE

Men cling to life even at the cost of enduring much suffering, seeming to find in life a natural sweetness.

ARISTOTLE

Without friends no one would choose to live, though he had all other goods.

ARISTOTLE

There was never a genius without a tincture of madness.

ARISTOTLE

gave the appearance of an aristocratic gentleman, slender and with fine features. However, a hostile tradition (such a tradition exists for almost every great historical figure) described him as having small eyes and spindly legs and speaking with a lisp.

We are on firmer ground when we seek to recover the man's character. Aristotle was, above all, a scholar. Though not a recluse, he enjoyed the scholar's quiet life and the adventures of the mind; only philosophers (that is, educated people) can fully enjoy life, he believed, and all the evidence indicates that, despite the inevitable tragedies, he enjoyed life. "Life is by nature good," he once wrote. "Men cling to life even at the cost of enduring much suffering, seeming to find in life a natural sweetness."

Also a tireless worker, he read and wrote continually, devoting his life to his quest for knowledge. Before Aristotle, people did not widely collect books and spend large amounts of time reading. Students heard books; they didn't read them. But Aristotle had a large library in his home, his own property, and after his time it became commonplace for private citizens to amass personal libraries. Aristotle's mastery of the intellectual history prior to his time testifies to his voracious reading.

Aristotle's passionate search for the truth is legendary. "Those who deny truth should be punished!" "The least initial deviation from the truth is multiplied later a thousandfold." "The study of the truth is difficult because it is such a huge target and no one can focus precisely on just what he wants to hit; but, on the other hand, it is easy because it's a target too big to be entirely missed."

Truth, for Aristotle, meant being an honest and careful empiricist, meaning that the truth of things could be found only by looking carefully at the world and drawing conclusions from observation and evidence. "Facts prove," he says. "Theoretical speculation must be based on facts gained by experience, as in astronomy, for example." He was a constant critic of the earlier philosopher-scientists for their failure to look and to see: "They did not seek explanations that conformed to observed appearances," he complains. The logical shenanigans of the Eleatics especially incensed him: "Although their opinions appear to follow logically in a dialectical discussion, yet to believe them seems next door to madness when one considers the facts." To this day scientists remain indebted to Aristotle for his understanding of scientific method. For example: "Such appears to be the truth about the generation of bees, judging from theory and from what are believed to be the facts about them; the facts, however, have not yet been sufficiently grasped; if ever they are, then credit must be given rather to observation than to theories, and to theories only if what they affirm agrees with the observed facts." In stressing the importance of observation, Aristotle undoubtedly reacting to the noetic abstractions of Plato.

Aristotle, aware he was a link in the golden chain of a long line of intellectual workers, remembered to pay his debts. All discovery is the result of "previous labours that have been handed down from others, advanced bit by bit by those who have taken them on." Furthermore, he knew that nothing is really new: "These and many other things have been invented several times over in the course of ages, times without number; for necessity is the mother of inventions."

He was an intellectual. "All men by nature desire to know," and "all men love thinking and knowing most of all." "To learn is a natural pleasure, not confined to philosophers, but common to all men." Knowledge is intrinsically joyful. "To demand that knowledge must be useful is the act of one completely ignorant of the distance that separates things good from things necessary." And he adds, "Education is the best provision for old age."

But Aristotle was also practical, firmly grounded—"down to earth" is the happy English metaphor. He advises us to listen to "the undemonstrated sayings and

---

All men by nature desire knowledge.

ARISTOTLE

Men have a sufficient natural instinct for what is true; things that are true and things that are just have a natural tendency to prevail over their opposites.

ARISTOTLE

Theoretical speculation must be based on facts gained by experience.

ARISTOTLE

opinions of experienced and older people, or to people of practical wisdom, not less than to [scientific] demonstrations; experience has given them an eye, and they can see things right." "It is by the practical experience of life and conduct that the truth is really tested." "We do not see men becoming good physicians from a study of textbooks." Likewise, his entire ethical philosophy is grounded in his experience of people, not derived from abstract ideas. "For the ordinary man the intellectual life is restricted to what is necessary for his life. The majority of mankind may well be pardoned for doing as they do; while they pray for happiness they are content if they can just live." "To be a philosopher is better than to make money, but it is not the highest priority for a man who lacks the bare necessities of life." And again: "The man who deviates a little from goodness should not be blamed; it is often necessary to choose the second best."

He was an idealist when it came to trusting human nature and human capacities. We have free will, he insists: "A man is the origin of his own actions"; therefore, we can will ourselves to choose the nobler path. "Men have a sufficient natural instinct for what is true; things that are true and things that are just have a natural tendency to prevail over their opposites."

But Aristotle was also a realist. His hopeful optimism is not blind; rather, it rests on his conviction that education can transform base human nature into something noble. "Intelligence is a gift of nature, but no one, by nature, is a wise man." "Educated men are as much superior to uneducated men as the living are to the dead." It is education that completes a man, or enables his soul to achieve its destiny: "The nature of man is not what he is born as, but what he is born for." Untamed nature, raw reptilian brains that indulge their emotions, usually choose the worst, not knowing the best. Among the uneducated "goodness is rare." "The avarice of mankind is insatiable; men always want more and more without end." "Most men obey necessity rather than argument, and punishments rather than the sense of what is noble." "Most men, while they wish for what is noble, choose what is advantageous." "Where absolute freedom is allowed there is nothing to restrain the evil which is inherent in every man." "We cannot overstrain man's nature," he warns.

Philosophy can ennoble and make possible the living of the good life. ("Philosophy," as Aristotle often uses the term, means "education" in a full "liberal arts" sense: learning as the transformation of character.) "Life itself is not enough," he writes, "even if it brings external happiness; only the good life, the life of a philosopher, is worth living." (An echo of Socrates' dictum: "For a human being, the unexamined life is not worth living.") "To the philosopher alone belong laws that are durable and actions that are right and noble. He alone lives with his eyes on nature and the divine, and like a good steersman, directs his life in dependence of what is eternal and unchanging, and lives his own master." It requires philosophy to distinguish the noble from the trivial and to assist us to let go of the trivial; without philosophy "All the things men think great are mere scene-painting."

He was awed by the world's mysteries. "Our grasp of the eternal things is but slight, nevertheless the joy which it brings us, by reason of their excellence and worth, is greater than that of knowing all things that are here below; just as the joy of a fleeting and partial glimpse of those whom we love is greater than that of an accurate view of other things." "For the student who is naturally of a philosophic spirit and can discern the causes of things, Nature which fashioned them provides joys which cannot be measured." "In all natural things there is something of the marvellous."

Aristotle was religious, but in his own way. "All things have by nature something divine in them." "All things desire God," he says, but "God" is not a personalized

It is by the practical experience of life and conduct that the truth is really tested.

ARISTOTLE

To enjoy the things we ought and to hate the things we ought has the greatest bearing on excellence of character.

ARISTOTLE

The least initial deviation from the truth is multiplied later a thousandfold.

ARISTOTLE

being like Athena or Apollo (Aristotle was too good a scientist to allow himself to personify nature). "Those who first looked up to the heavens and saw the sun race from its rising to its setting and beheld the orderly dances of the stars, looked for the Craftsman of this lovely design, and surmised that it came about not by chance but by the agency of some mightier and imperishable nature, which was God."

"Beauty is a gift of God," he wrote. He was sensitive to beauty in every form; it was for him the highest goal of a human life. "There cannot be anything prior to that which is eternally beautiful, and truly and primarily good." The final cause *(aition)* of nature itself drives every living creature toward its fulfillment, and for a human being that final fulfillment rests on the apprehension of beauty. Beauty, that is, is the goal of nature. "That which comes into being beautifully comes into being rightly."

Friendship is based on equality.
ARISTOTLE

Aristotle cherished his friends and devoted considerable space to a theory of friendship in his *Nicomachean Ethics* (Books VIII and IX). "Without friends no one would choose to live, though he had everything else." One learns to be a friend by being raised in a good family: "It is in the household that we find the origins and wellsprings of friendship, as also of political organization and justice." "We should behave toward our friends as we would wish our friends to behave toward us."

WRITINGS

It is of itself that the divine thought thinks . . . and its thinking is a thinking on thinking.

ARISTOTLE

Aristotle lectured on esoteric subjects to his students and on more popular subjects to the public. The written materials designed for his students were therefore technical and specialized, while those delivered to the populace were cast in an easy style. He wrote his technical works in the form of short treatises on specialized subjects and intended them for use as textbooks in the Lyceum's classrooms. Of these only about thirty survive. His popular works, some twenty-seven in all, were dialogues similar in form to Plato's; these were the works widely known in his time. These lost dialogues included titles such as the *Menexenus*, *Symposium*, *Politicus*, and *Sophistês*. The style was apparently finished and eloquent since Cicero later wrote of "the suave style of Aristotle. . . . A river of gold." Only a few quoted fragments survive from these popular works.

Aristotle divided his technical writings into two categories: theoretical works and practical works. The theoretical works include the sciences, metaphysics, and mathematics. The distinguishing characteristic of these theoretical works is the fact the subject cannot be other than it is. They are descriptions of unalterable facts. For instance, we might not personally like some datum of physics, for example—the law of gravity, say, after one has taken a tumble down the stairs; but our feelings about the matter are irrelevant; the law of gravity is what it is and cannot be other than it is; our disliking the Big Bang or $E = mc^2$ cannot change nature's operations in the slightest. So also for the "laws" of mathematics: Two plus two still equals four whether or not I succeed in balancing my checkbook.

By contrast, the practical subjects are those that are amenable to human volition. The subject matter of ethics, politics, and art are all products of human will and intellect and are therefore subject to our control. Since we created them, we can reshape them. If we don't approve of discriminatory laws, political practices, or the popular forms of music and dance, then we can, to some extent, take charge and bring about change.

Educated men are as much superior to uneducated men as the living are to the dead.

ARISTOTLE

Aristotle's extant writings have come down to us in a strange form. They are concise, abbreviated, disorganized, and condensed, like tortured lecture notes; in fact, they may derive from Aristotle's own notes or from notes his students took down, or they may be condensed outlines of his voluminous writings, designed to be placed in the Lyceum's archives. Fortunately, a good translation can make many of his passages delightful reading.

Among the thirty surviving technical writings are six treatises on logic; they include all his work on syllogisms, deduction, induction, and scientific method. We possess three treatises on the natural sciences, five treatises on biology, nine brief treatises on what we would call psychology, one treatise on metaphysics, two treatises on ethics (actually two versions of the same original book), and one treatise each on politics, oratory, and poetry.

EXPLAINING THE WORLD

Aristotle saw that an inquiring mind must make inroads into three great provinces of knowledge if our questions are to be answered. First, one must understand the knowledge-gathering instrument itself, the human intellect, and clarify the procedures it must follow for honest thinking; this Aristotle proceeded to do in six treatises collectively called the *Organon* ("Instrument of Thought"). Second, one must apply these rules of right thinking to every area of human experience where knowledge is sought; this he did in all his specialized treatises, such as *Physics, Meteorology, Psychology, History of Animals, Movements of Animals, On the Heavens, Ethics, Politics, Poetics*, and so on. Third, one must strive to see the whole by searching for the connections, commonalities, and essences that link the disparate pieces of information gathered through scientific explorations, and one must be able to understand the ultimate truth about the nature and dynamic operations of the cosmos, that is, to understand the whole of reality. This Aristotle accomplished in his *Metaphysics*, in *On Coming-to-be and Passing-away*, and in certain passages in his other works.

With this threefold program, Aristotle set the stage for the intellectual discovery of nature's secrets for the next two thousand years; and, in a very personal way, as best he could in his time and place, he accounted for virtually all the puzzling events of his own experience.

THE INVESTIGATION OF HUMAN THINKING

The first step required of a careful scientist is spelled out in six treatises of the *Organon*. These are the *Categories, Interpretation, Topics, Sophistic Reasonings, Prior Analytics*, and *Posterior Analytics*. ("Analytics" is Aristotle's term for "logic," so these latter titles might better be rendered *Logic before Observation* and *Logic after Observation*.) In Aristotle's system, logic is not one of the sciences; rather, logic provides the tools—the methods, skills, and insights—by which the sciences carry on their work. It was therefore thought of as a preparatory study to be mastered before performing one's scientific investigations. Aristotle's treatment of scientific method is found in the *Prior Analytics* and *Posterior Analytics*. In the *Posterior Analytics* he develops the rules of induction, a mode of reasoning that proceeds from particular facts to general principles. From just a few observed facts one can conclude that a general statement is probably true, and the more the observations that support the conclusion, the greater the probability it is true universally.

Aristotle applied the principles of induction in all his scientific writing. For example, the *History of Animals* is an impressive collection of facts about a variety of animal species, notably marine organisms, which he had observed, dissected, and doubtless diagrammed. He tells us he once broke open and examined a large number

In all natural things there is something of the marvellous.
ARISTOTLE

On Aristotle *His approach is remarkably sound, and no other ancient philosopher has so scrupulously and with such consistent purpose tried to free himself from prejudices and reach the truth.*
INGEMAR DÜRING

Nature does nothing uselessly.
ARISTOTLE

chick and birds' eggs and watched the progressive development of the embryo. He witnessed the gradual emergence of the different bodily parts and began to understand how the budding chick gets its nourishment from the yolk.

> If you wish, try this experiment. Take twenty or more eggs and let them be incubated by two or more hens. Then each day, from the second to that of hatching, remove an egg, break it, and examine it. . . . With the common hen the embryo becomes first visible after three days. . . . The heart appears like a speck of blood, beating and moving as though endowed with life; and from it two veins with blood in them pass in a convoluted course, and a membrane carrying bloody fibers from the vein-ducts now envelops the yolk. . . . When the egg is ten days old, the chick and all its parts are distinctly visible.[6]

If we were to perform a hundred such experiments, we would observe the same progressive development of the embryo, and we could infer a general principle about the development of all bird embryos from the observed growth pattern. In discovering a universal pattern, Aristotle moved away from particulars, and this ability to generalize by creating abstract principles is, according to him, properly called knowledge. By implication particular facts should not be thought of as knowledge, for if one possesses only singular observations, then the connections, relationships, and essences that are the proper subject of knowledge are missed, and one's ability to understand the world drops to zero.

But induction is only one side of the story. In another treatise, the *Prior Analytics*, Aristotle goes to the heart of his logic systems by stating the rules of deductive thinking. Deductive logic, he believed, is best expressed in the form of the syllogism. The syllogism exhibits perfect reasoning. A syllogism consists of three propositional statements: a major premise, a minor premise, and a conclusion. A true syllogism contains two premises only, and the conclusion is inferred from the premises, as in

The actuality of thought is life.
ARISTOTLE

All roses are red.
Summer Delight is a rose.

Therefore, Summer Delight is red.

Where the conclusion is correctly inferred, the conclusion is said to be valid (even though, as in this example, it also may be false because the major premise is false). Logic is the science of (or study of) valid inference.

Aristotle was the inventor of formal logic, the first thinker to attempt to reduce human reasoning to a set of rules. Whereas the presocratic philosophers turned their attention directly to nature's puzzlements, Aristotle, taking his cue from Socrates and Plato, first laid the foundations for thinking about the world by investigating the human mind that proposes to do the investigating.

°*Plato might be considered an exception to this statement. He did attempt to describe the cosmos but without observational data; hence the result is logical mythology. See pp. 159ff., on the* Timaeus.

THE COSMOS AND ITS CONTENTS

Aristotle then applied to the world the insights gained from his analysis of human thinking. Never before had a human being attempted to encompass all knowledge, and we stand in awe of his attempt.° His goal was to translate a capricious, mysterious multiverse into a beautifully organized, coherently meaningful universe. It was bedrock in Aristotle's faith that this could be done.

THE NATURAL WORLD   Aristotle's model of the universe is found in his *Physics, Mechanics, On the Heavens*, and *Meteorology*. A spherical shell, he reasoned, encloses the universe. As we stand on the Earth and look outward, that outermost shell carries the fixed stars and revolves on its own axis. Inside this outer shell are other, smaller revolving shells that carry the Sun, Moon, and the seven planets, and at the center of this universe rests the Earth, which all the spherical shells revolve around. Because the planetary orbits are so complex, Aristotle found he must postulate the existence of fifty-five shells to account for the motions he sees in the heavens.

He concluded that only one universe exists, eternal and indestructible, with no beginning or end. "For in the whole range of time past, as far as our inherited records reach, no change appears to have taken place either in the general plan of the outer heaven or in any of its parts."[7] Because it is perfect, it must be composed of some substance different from that of the Earth's objects, which are always changing and decaying. This celestial substance he calls ether. (This notion of heavenly perfection prevailed in Western thought for almost two millennia until in 1610 Galileo looked through his telescope and saw disfiguring spots on the sun; and the heavens were no longer perfect.)

Aristotle was sure that our Earth is at the center of the universe, far removed from the high first heaven. Since all objects, when flung into the air, fall back toward the Earth's center, the heavy Earth itself must occupy the lowest and central point in the cosmos. Compared with the heavens, the Earth is small. If one travels from Greece to Egypt, for example, then the relative positions of the overhead stars change, so one can deduce that the Earth is probably a sphere. This model gains support from the observations of lunar eclipses, when the Earth casts a rounded shadow on the moon, proving the Earth is a round ball. "Hence one should not be too quick to disbelieve the opinions of those who think there is no break between the regions beyond the Pillars of Hercules and the regions of India and that thus the ocean is one."[8] (This sophisticated inference was read by Columbus and encouraged him to undertake his voyages to the west.)

In his *Meteorology* Aristotle attempted to explain a great variety of physical events that occur in nature. Sound, he concluded, is a vibration of the air (this is the beginning of acoustics). Rainbows are seen when sunlight is refracted by moisture in the air (the beginnings of optics). He tried to explain the actions of water, oil, metals, and clay when subjected to heat and cold (the beginnings of chemistry). He predates Galileo in experimenting with falling bodies and correlating weight and speed, and he describes the physics of the lever (the beginnings of mechanics). He also accounts for meteors, the glow of the Milky Way, mist, snow, frost, dew, wind, thunder, and earthquakes.

ZOOLOGY   Aristotle felt a special love for zoology, and the results of his work are found in the *History of Animals, Parts of Animals, Reproduction of Animals, Locomotion of Animals,* and *Movements of Animals.* Acquainted with some five hundred and forty species of animals, he personally investigated the habits of, and probably dissected, about fifty of them. Among them were mollusks, octopuses, anemones, bees, and other marine animals and insects. He devoted much time to marine animals—his specialty—studying the habits of shellfish, crabs, lobsters, and cuttlefish. In his treatises, he investigates the bodies of mammals, oviparous quadrupeds, birds, and fishes and explores the functions of digestive organs, blood, the brain, the structure of bones, and sense organs, explaining why each of them evolved. He considers the head and trunk, describing the teeth, mouth, heart, lungs, liver, intestines, and limbs. He discusses the functions of the tongue and mouth in birds, snakes, crocodiles, and fishes, pointing out similarities and differences.

It is in zoology that Aristotle reveals his genius for classification. He makes methodical comparisons of animals and humans and finds striking similarities in anatomical design and function. He distinguishes between clear-blooded invertebrates (insects, testaceans, mollusks, and crustaceans) and red-blooded vertebrates (fishes, amphibians, birds, and mammals). He also distinguishes between oviparous

On Aristotle *Aristotle may be regarded as the cultural barometer of Western history. Whenever his influence has dominated the scene, it paved the way for one of history's brilliant eras; whenever it fell, so did mankind.*

AYN RAND

On Aristotle *All in all, the History of Animals is Aristotle's supreme work, and the greatest scientific product of fourth-century Greece.*

WILL DURANT

All natural bodies are organs of the soul.

ARISTOTLE

and viviparous animals. He was aware that whales and dolphins are not fish but mammals and that they must return to the ocean's surface to breathe.

On Aristotle *Linnaeus and Cuvier have been my two gods, though in very different ways, but they were mere schoolboys compared to old Aristotle.*

CHARLES DARWIN

Aristotle also possessed a clear sense of evolvement. While species do perpetuate their own kind, nature as a whole moves from the simple to the complex; it reveals a ladder of ascent from the low to the high. "Nature proceeds little by little from things lifeless to animal life, so gradually that it is impossible to detect the exact line of demarcation, or to tell on which side of it an intermediate form should lie. Thus, next after lifeless things in the upward scale comes the plant; and among plants one will differ from another in the amount of its apparent vitality. . . . Then in plants . . . there is observable a continuous scale of ascent toward the animal. In the sea there are things which it is hard to label as either animal or vegetable."[9] The world exhibits a majestic scale of being, from creatures at the bottom just barely existing to creatures at the top living rich and full existences; all living organisms have their place somewhere on this scale. The ape stands between the lower viviparous animals and human beings. All species reproduce their own kind, and each species, and every organism within each species, is designed to struggle to achieve the fullest realization of its species nature.

THE HUMAN ANIMAL

He who is unable to live in society, or who has no need because he is sufficient for himself, must be either a beast or a god.

ARISTOTLE

Aristotle then attempted to make sense of the human animal. Dissection of cadavers was not known in his time, so he learned about the human body largely by analogy with animal bodies. He investigated the social behavior of men and women and, through instrospection and empathy, studied our conscious experiences, such as pain, grief, aspirations, happiness, and beauty. The fruits of his research into what we would call psychology, social psychology, political science, sociology, anthropology, and even theology are contained in *On the Soul, Nicomachean Ethics, Eudemian Ethics, Politics,* and *Poetics.* Among his treatises on psychology are such works as *On Sleep, On Dreams, On Sensation,* and *On Memory.*

Intelligence is a gift of nature, but no one is a wise man by nature.

ARISTOTLE

Soul (*psychê*), for Aristotle, is the vital life drive found in all living things. In simpler organisms such as plants, one finds the **nutritive soul** whose function is to give each organism and each species its identity. This soul sustains it for growing, feeding, adapting, and reproducing, and it keeps each organism focused on achieving its natural end. Then, shared by all animals (including humans), the **sensitive soul** makes possible the higher sensitivities—feelings of emotion and memories that provide for struggle and adaptation. Humans alone possess the third kind of psyche, the **rational soul;** it enables humans to reason and thus to transcend the limiting conditions of lower organisms. Every living plant and animal is a unity of soul and body, which together create the functional system of the unique individual. At death this unity dissolves, for neither soul nor body can survive the dissolution.

All things have by nature something divine in them.

ARISTOTLE

The soul of an organism is, or at least contains, its *telos,* its end purpose. It provides the pattern of growth and development of each living thing from its inception as seed through its embryonic forms and growth phases into its adult stage. Aristotle developed this concept of purposeful growth from his observations of plants and animals; everywhere in nature things "know" precisely how to germinate and grow into whatever they are supposed to become. Every seed knows its appointed goal. No sprout or hatchling wants to die aborning; each organism pushes with all its being to grow into whatever it is destined to become. Becoming, Aristotle discovered, is the law of the world. Nothing just is. Driven by internal impulses, everything is in process of becoming something else.

Aristotle was so impressed with this discovery that he made it a cornerstone of his philosophy. His word for it is "entelechy" (*entelecheia,* "being complete"), the striving toward an appointed end-goal. It means that the kernel of corn is assured of growing into a corn plant and that the baby robin, with a little luck, will grow into an adult bird and reproduce more robins.

One obvious thing about the human animal is that it wants to be happy. Happiness (*eudaimonia*) is therefore the principal ingredient in the human entelechy. However much we can actualize ourselves in terms of worldly criteria, if we are not happy, then our telos is yet to be realized. "Every good thing is sought in order that, by possessing it, one may become happy." We so often believe that happiness can be achieved through material accomplishments, but in this we are misguided, Aristotle believed, for happiness can be attained solely through the soul's actualization.

Aristotle concluded that only a rational being can be happy. Anyone failing to nourish this unique human gift will forfeit happiness. "That which is proper for each thing is naturally the best and pleasantest for it. For man, therefore, the life of reason is best and pleasantest, since reason more than anything else *is* man. So too this life is also the happiest."[10]

But it takes more than rationality to make us happy. We must also live a moral life. Socrates may have believed that if we know what is right we will do it, but Aristotle is more penetrating. We must know what is right, of course, but we also must have the will to do it. Our wills are free, he believed; we can choose to act unjustly or we can choose to live nobly. "Virtue depends on ourselves and vice likewise. For where it is in our power to do, it is in our power not to do. Where we can say no, we can say yes." Living a moral existence can be effortless if we practice good habits.

> If then a man knowingly does things which must make him unjust, he will be voluntarily unjust. However, it does not follow that if he wishes it, he can stop being unjust and become just, any more than a sick man by wishing can become well. It may be that he is voluntarily sick through living incontinently and disobeying his doctors. At one time then it was open to him not to be sick, but not now when he has thrown away his health. Once you have flung a stone, it is too late to call it back."[11]

Making a commitment to live right is the first step, and practicing is the second. "We learn by doing," Aristotle wrote; "men become builders by building and lyre-players by playing the lyre. So we become just by doing just deeds, temperate by acting temperately, brave by behaving bravely."

GOOD GOVERNMENT

So the goal of living is the good life, the moral life, the life that can bring happiness. But human beings are not isolated cells pursuing happiness on a lonely island. We are social beings by nature and cannot live apart from others in community. "He who is unable to live in society, or who has no need because he is sufficient for himself, must be either a beast or a god."[12]

Since we humans are by nature gregarious and find we must join with others to achieve mutually agreed-upon goals, Aristotle opens his *Politics* with a description of various kinds of human communities. The family is the primary community, but several families usually combine to form a village, then several villages to form a state. "The state is thus a natural creation and man is by nature a political animal."[13]

Political leaders often believe that the state exists solely to prevent crime and promote business, but this shortsighted notion misses the state's primary function. By definition, the state must be "a community of well-being" designed to provide the conditions for achieving a "happy and honorable life." "Evils draw men together," Aristotle wrote, but once security and order have been achieved, the positive function of

That which comes into being beautifully comes into being rightly.
ARISTOTLE

Happiness, if not god-sent, comes as a result of virtue, study and effort.
ARISTOTLE

Who sole or first among mortals revealed it clear to sight, that man becomes happy if he becomes good.
OLYMPIODORUS

All the things men think great are mere scene-painting.
ARISTOTLE

The only stable state is the one in which all men are equal before the law.
ARISTOTLE

Law is order, and good law is good order.
ARISTOTLE

government is to make it possible for decent citizens to live a moral life. Individuals do not exist for the sake of the state—a Platonic idea Aristotle vehemently rejected; rather the state exists for the sake of individuals and their pursuit of happiness. "Political society exists for the sake of noble actions, and not of mere companionship."

The *Politics* is a critical review of a variety of models developed in the Greek city-states during the fifth and fourth centuries BC. What sort of government is best? Aristotle doesn't exactly equivocate, but having seen the ideal, he then bows to practicality and concludes that different kinds of political organization might be necessary for different kinds of people. He rejects as unworkable autocratic monarchies and oligarchies, communistic utopias, and popular democracies. The first two invariably lose the individual in the service of a dictator or a tyrannical minority, and democracy tends to degenerate into rule of the mob, which then imposes its mediocre ideas and values on the entire populace. It is true, he wrote, "the only stable state is one in which all men are equal before the law"; but in an all-inclusive democracy, people who are equal before the law invariably proceed to claim that they are also equal in aptitude, intelligence, and wisdom. "Democracy arises out of the notion that those who are equal in any respect are equal in all respects; because men are equally free, they claim to be absolutely equal."[14]

Aristotle concludes that the ideal state would be ruled by the noblest, ablest, and best-trained men or a small group of such men. Obviously, he says, "they should rule who are able to rule best." But no mechanism exists for assuring that such men will find their way to a ruling position. So, in the final analysis the best form of government would be a limited democracy with a large educated middle class creating and administering its laws. This kind of government, assuring liberty and equality to all free citizens (but not including women, slaves, artisans, or businessmen with a singleminded obsession with personal gain) is probably the most stable and long lasting. Such a class as a whole would be somewhat better educated, a little wiser, and perhaps less corruptible than an unruly mob or tyrannous autocrat. Therefore, with some reluctance, Aristotle concludes that "the best political community is formed by citizens of the middle class" who have sufficient time to participate intelligently in the affairs of government.

POETRY

It will come as no surprise that Aristotle is also the founder of literary criticism. In Book I of his little essay called the *Poetics*, he analyzes tragic drama, a literary art form much loved by Athenians. (Book II of his *Poetics*, long lost, was apparently a treatment of comedy.) Writing a century after the great tragedians Aeschylus, Sophocles, and Euripides and thoroughly steeped in literature, poetry, and drama, Aristotle attempts to apply his theory of knowledge to a mass of material in order to discover its nature and forms. We can be sure from his treatment of the emotional and esthetic life that Aristotle enjoyed reading and feeling a poem or seeing a stage performance of a play; but as a philosopher he sought something more: "Poetry is more philosophic and of graver import than history, since its statements are of the nature of universals, whereas those of history are singulars."[15]

Aristotle packed it all into one famous sentence: "Tragedy, then, is the imitation of an action that is serious, complete, and of a certain magnitude; in the form of action, not narrative, through pity and fear bringing about the proper purgation of those emotions."[16] The key words in this definition are imitation (*mimêsis*) and purgation (*katharsis*).

"Drama is the imitation of an action." Drama imitates life in one of three ways: It pictures things as they were or are, as they are said or thought to be, or as they ought

Neglect of an effective birth control policy is a never-failing source of poverty which, in turn, is the parent of revolution and crime.

ARISTOTLE

They should rule who are able to rule best.

ARISTOTLE

Political society exists for the sake of noble actions, and not of mere companionship.

ARISTOTLE

Man is by nature a political animal.

ARISTOTLE

to be. Humans are "the most mimetic of all animals," he wrote, and "the desire to imitate is instinctive in man from childhood."

Tragedy, too, imitates. The plot (*mythos*), "the soul of a tragedy," always tells a human story. "It has two parts—complication (nouement) and unraveling (dénouement)," and the latter always involves a reversal of fortunes. It is the story of a man of noble qualities who discovers that he or his situation is not what he thought; his downfall, from great heights, comes as he sees the truth to which he had been blind. We in the audience identify with the hero's predicament for we too have lived through tragedy. He doesn't deserve his fate, and we weep through his dreadful revelation, his courageous struggle, and his despair. With fear and pity we leave the performance feeling more honest and whole, our emotions having been cleansed of our petty preoccupations. We have lived vicariously through the particulars of one tragic life, but we have felt the essence of the human condition. Drained of our debilitating emotions, we can return to our daily tasks in a calmer, more rational manner, and in so doing we can also recover our humanness.

Beauty is truth, truth beauty.
JOHN KEATS

ULTIMATE QUESTIONS: METAPHYSICS

Having explored the world, Aristotle proceeded to wonder what is ultimately and finally going on. What patterns, essences, and operations can one discern? Can the human mind capture the Big Picture? We find his conclusions in his *Physics* and *Metaphysics*.

When Aristotle's works were edited by Andronicus of Rhodes about 60 BC, several of his technical treatises dealing with "essences" were placed on the shelf immediately after his writings on physics; hence, Andronicus called them "the works right after physics," in Greek, *meta ta physis—Metaphysics*. The book is composed of notes that were originally separate, fitted together without much continuity. While Aristotle's work on "physics" includes the sciences of physics, biology, and psychology, metaphysics is the study of the essence of things, their existence or mode of being. It is the search for all-embracing first principles that can answer the question How does the world work? Metaphysics asks, Why are things as they are? What causes them? What exactly are we asking when we ask what a thing is? What is substance or matter? Why does an object take a particular form? What is the nature of the motion that moves the cosmos and its contents toward their ends?

The whole is more than its constituent parts.
ARISTOTLE

THE FOUR CAUSES (1): MATTER AND FORM By Aristotle's time a long history existed of earlier attempts to explain motion and change, among them Anaximenes' alternation of condensation and rarefaction of air, Anaximander and Heraclitus's interactions of opposites, and Empedocles' balancing action of Love and Strife. Aristotle thought all these attempts were failures because they were concerned with but a single cause when in fact causality is much more complex.

Causation is the most fundamental mechanism of nature, and to account fully for the coming into existence of any object, four "causes" must be recognized. Aristotle's word for cause is *aitia*, meaning "what makes a thing what it is" or "the primary agent responsible for" the existence of an object/event.[17] The first step in understanding why an object is what it is to establish the identity of "the material out of which the object is generated"; this is the **material factor.** Second is the **formal factor,** "the form or pattern" of a thing, "what the thing is defined as being essentially."[18]

Once you have flung a stone, it is too late to call it back.
ARISTOTLE

Now, all things share matter and form. These are distinct factors; objects are made of matter and they have a form or shape. But though matter and form are distinct, they are never separate. Matter is never found in a "raw" state; it is always found in some particular shape or form. Matter without form or form without matter are, to Aristotle, Platonic fictions.

To give an example, here on my desk is a coffee cup. It is what it is because of its form, not because of its matter. Matter-wise, it is made of about the same ceramic material as the lamp in the corner, the brick in the fireplace, and the planter with petunias. Its matter, clearly, is not what gives it its identity as a coffee cup. Its identity comes from its form. It is a coffee cup because it shares a coffee-cup form with countless other coffee cups.

Aristotle thus arrives at "universals"—that is, universal forms. It turns out that when I refer to a coffee cup I'm not referring to a single object, but to a whole class of objects to which my particular coffee cup belongs. Should I wish to refer only to the object on my desk, then I would merely point to it. But when I refer to it as a "coffee cup" I am importing into the picture a preexistent universal concept (abstraction) which, when applied to the object on my desk gives it its identity. It belongs to a class of objects called "coffee cups." The universal concept tells me what it is.

The world may be made up of singular objects, but they are not unrelated singular objects. Every object shares certain characteristics with other objects. What our minds know very well, often intuitively, is that the individual objects of the world group themselves together into classes. The birds of the world don't appear to us as a huge collection of unconnected organisms; they present themselves to us in established groups the members of which connected by shared characteristics, and the human mind creates categories for relating these shared characteristics. The mind "sees" the characteristics that all birds have in common and creates a class called "bird" which it then utilizes to recognize all future objects that share these characteristics—feathers, beaks, anatomy, behavior, and so on. When I come across a new object that possesses these characteristics, my mind classifies the new object as "bird." Then, and only then, do I know "what it is."

But Aristotle presses the question: Why do the world's objects come in these related groups? Because, he says, the members of any particular class share the same form. All birds are birds because they share the form of "bird," and *this form is real*. It is neither a product of our minds' organizational processes nor of our capacity for creating abstractions. Our minds have apprehended a real entity that causes the world's objects to be related. Each single bird is real, but so is the form "bird" that connects and relates all birds into a single class.

All this is familiar from having studied Plato's Theory of Real Ideas (or "Forms").° But Aristotle differs sharply from his teacher on the location of the forms. Plato, always the more mystical, was convinced forms exist separate from matter. If, for example, all birds should become extinct (like their ancestors the dinosaurs), the bird's nonphysical form (and the dinosaur's form) would continue to exist, waiting for matter to once again take on that form. But for Aristotle, forms can exist only in conjunction with matter. He could never find a nonphysical bird form apart from a real, living, physical-looking bird. (Neither could Plato, for that matter, but not being an empiricist and not having to look at the world, he could continue to believe in bird form just as long as he had a need to.)

THE FOUR CAUSES (2): MOTION AND TELOS   The third and fourth causal factors are the **propelling factor** (usually called the "efficient cause") and the **telic factor.** The propelling cause is "the immediate source of change or of cessation from change." This is what we are most often referring to today when we speak of "the cause" of some object/event: The tree toppled be*cause* the wind blew it over; the oil slick occurred be*cause* the tanker ran aground; the dinosaurs went extinct be*cause* a meteor or comet struck the Earth. This is the causative factor that least interested Aristotle, partly because it is the most obvious and had been explored by earlier thinkers.

Poetry is something more philosophic and of graver import than history, since its statements are of the nature of universals, whereas those of history are singulars.

ARISTOTLE

Gourmands pray for the gullet of a crane.

ARISTOTLE

°See pp. 144f., 152.

The fourth factor is the telic factor, "the end *(telos)* or purpose for the sake of which a thing is done." Any attempt to "explain" a kernal of corn, for instance, would be woefully incomplete without a description of what the seed is "for," that is, without explaining why it exists at all. To say that it is a yellow seed with a pointy end and starchy flavor is to miss the function of its design—its reason for being. Steeped in biology, Aristotle could not escape the fact that "there is purpose . . . in what is and in what happens in Nature." To him it was unthinkable "that the front teeth come up with an edge, suited to dividing the food, and the back ones flat and good for grinding it, without there being any design in the matter."

In Aristotle's view the forms giving individual objects their identity are not static molds to which matter passively conforms. Rather, forms are active, dynamic shaping *processes*—not things. Each form contains within it a code that conducts a process of change toward a specific end.

Aristotle developed two more critical concepts—the potential and the actual. Imagine the sculptor Rodin working in his studio in Paris. At this moment in time in the 1890s he stands before a large chunk of white marble. Later there will exist a sculpture called *"The Thinker."* But before he begins the chipping and shaping of the marble, *"The Thinker"* is potentially in the marble—potentially but not actually. Though it is only through the mind and hands of a great artist that this potential can be realized, it is *form* that actualizes that potential into a particular object. Aristotle derived the idea of potential and actual from biology. All living things harbor within them a plan of growth and development. The olive seed is potentially an olive tree. The coconut is potentially a palm tree, but not an olive tree. The mature adult form of anything and a plan for getting there is embedded in the seed, and this plan resides in the form, not in the matter. This form in living things is also the soul (psychê).

Aristotle believed that the four causative factors fully account for the existence of the world and all its contents.

MOTION AND THE UNMOVED MOVER   It was Aristotle's treatment of motion that endeared him to medieval thinkers, for it climaxed with a momentous idea. In Book VIII of his *Physics* he first takes a shot at the Eleatics who had argued paradoxically° that motion doesn't exist: "That motion does exist is tacitly admitted by all who discuss natural science; for if there were no such thing as motion, they would be unable to theorize as they do about the making of the cosmos and the genesis and disappearance of things. . . ." Even with that, Aristotle was not finished with the absurdity of Parmenides and Zeno's assumptions: "To suppose that everything is constantly at rest, and to seek to establish this rationally with no reference to sense-perception, is a kind of paralysis of the intelligence. . . ."[19] Here Aristotle reaffirms that empirical observation should always take precedence over an abstract logic that can too easily lead us down a sterile path. A good physical scientist, he says, just assumes motion is the most fundamental aspect of the natural world.

Having dismissed the Eleatics, Aristotle proceeds with a definition of motion. All motion, he suggests, has a purpose; it is always going somewhere; it is in fact nature's way of proceeding from something to something else and always involves *entelecheia*, fulfillment. It is potential in process of becoming actual. Motion may be thought of as a polar movement from complete potentiality to complete actuality; once actuality has been achieved, motion will cease. Looked at in the context of the four causes, motion is the process by which form manifests itself in matter to produce some one particular object.

Now, "whatever is in motion must be moved *by* something." Aristotle was neither the first nor last to feel the baffling implications of this line of thinking, but his

Evils draw men together.
ARISTOTLE

I have gained this by philosophy: that I do without being commanded what others do only from fear of the law.
ARISTOTLE

°See pp. 69f.

A man is the origin of his action.
ARISTOTLE

The nature of man is not what he is born as, but what he is born for.
ARISTOTLE

undaunted intellect refused to back away from the problem. So, any object that is in motion is in motion because something else preceding it transferred its motion to it. Only motion produces motion. From this, logic immediately leads us to an infinite regress: If everything in motion is preceded by something else in motion that is preceded by something else in motion that is . . . then this series goes back and back to infinity. Our minds insist that there must have been a beginning, for the idea of an infinite regress is beyond the capacity of the mind to conceive or accept. "If then, every moving object is set in motion by some cause . . . and if where the source of the motion is another moving object there must be some original mover that is not itself moved by anything else; . . . we may conclude that the original mover, since it is not moved by anything else, is necessarily the cause of its own motion."[20]

So, we come to Aristotle's notion of an Unmoved Mover, for "in every case where objects are moved there is an original unmoved mover." Earlier philosophers, including Plato, had taught that time and motion are eternal, but Aristotle argues that it is not motion, but something else, that is eternal. "As motion exists always and unintermittingly, there must be something eternal—whether one thing or many— that is the basic producer of motion; and this prime mover must itself be motionless."[21] After considering whether several or even an infinite number of such first movers might exist, he reasons that just one must exist: "It is enough, then, that there should be one ultimate mover, which, being the first of unmoved entities as well as eternal, will be the 'originating principle' (archê) of motion in everything else."[22]

This is a mindblower. But perhaps his solution is not so outlandish after all—providing we can grant the validity of notions such as actuality and potentiality and ignore quantam theory. "This, when we stop to examine it, is a most reasonable conclusion," Aristotle says, for we find in our everyday experience real systems that appear to be self-caused. First, he notes, we are all unmoved movers. He wrote: "[E]very animal is self-moved . . . ; the 'originating principle' (archê) of the motion is in the moving things themselves. . . . Thus an animal taken as a whole is the source of its own motion."[23] Second, "force fields" exist in nature that behave as unmoved movers—magnets, for instance (though this is not an example Aristotle used°). A bar magnet lying on the table is quite motionless, but sprinkle it with a handful of iron filings and watch them move. They arrange themselves in patterns revealing lines of magnetic force. The magnet is therefore an unmoved mover. Aristotle's original mover can be thought of analogously as a self-moved living entity—a concept most congenial to medieval theologians who identified the Unmoved Mover with God.° Or we might speculate that God is like a Great Magnet with a force field powerful enough to produce all the motion in the universe. In any case, Aristotle's statement of the problem later attracted some of the best minds in the West, and during the Scholastic era his solution became dogma.

In revolutions the occasions may be trifling but great interests are at stake.

ARISTOTLE

The basis of a democratic state is liberty.

ARISTOTLE

°*Aristotle did know about magnets and Thales' speculations about them. See p. 28.*

°*See especially Thomas Aquinas, pp. 403ff.*

ENDNOTES

1 The section On Aristotle in Diogenes Laërtius, *Lives of Eminent Philosophers*, makes interesting reading; see Book V.1–35.
2 Aristotle, *Politics*, III, 13, 35.
3 Aristotle, *Parts of Animals*, I, 16 (elephant); III, 14 (ostrich).
4 Diogenes, *Lives*, V.11–16.
5 Diogenes, *Lives*, V.1.
6 Aristotle, *History of Animals*, VI, 2–3.
7 Aristotle, *Physics*, xxviii.
8 Aristotle, *Physics*, xxviiif.
9 Aristotle, *Nicomachean Ethics*, xxxi.
10 Aristotle, *Nicomachean Ethics*, xxxiv.
11 Aristotle, *Nicomachean Ethics*, xxxiii.

12 Aristotle, *Politics*, I, 2.
13 Aristotle, *Politics*, I, 2.
14 Aristotle, *Politics*, V, 1.
15 Aristotle, *Poetics*.
16 Aristotle, *Poetics*.
17 This treatment of the "four causes" follows the translation and interpretation by Philip Wheelwright, *Aristotle* (The Odyssey Press, 1951), pp. 25f.
18 Aristotle, *Physics*, II, iii.
19 Aristotle, *Physics*, VIII, iii, 1.
20 Aristotle, *Physics*, VIII, v.
21 Aristotle, *Physics*, VIII, vi.
22 Aristotle, *Physics*, VIII, vi.
23 Aristotle, *Physics*, VIII, iv.

PHILOSOPHY
AFTER
ARISTOTLE

IDEAS TO LIVE BY

PART

3

CHAPTER 12

THE DIS-INTEGRATION OF PHILOSOPHY AND THE RISE OF NOETIC THEOLOGY: 322 BC–AD 250

After Aristotle philosophy branches into separate movements; a mood of skepticism, eclecticism, and practicality overtakes all the great schools of philosophy; some syntheses are attempted; the independent sciences emerge; finally, noetic philosophy turns away from the world to seek answers in the realm of the mind.

DIS-INTEGRATION

I already knew the answer, so I didn't have to think.

LORI VILLAMIL

The death of Aristotle marked the end of the Golden Age of Greek philosophy. The sense of puzzled wonderment about "the moon, sun, and stars, and the beginning of the universe" and the confident assumption that the human mind could know the truth about such things—these critical philosophical impulses began to fade. Socrates had not taught philosophy as doctrinal truth but as a method for opening minds so that they could search for the truth; Plato carried on this Socratic style of inquiry when he established the Academy as a center for critical education. Similarly, Aristotle's search for knowledge had laid deep and wide foundations for an empirically sound, but very open, worldview, and he organized the Lyceum as a center for scientific research.

And the saying which thou sayest, back it cometh later on thee.

HOMER

So, for the great Athenian thinkers, philosophy meant, at its heart, the open-minded search for the truth, whatever that truth might turn out to be. Neither the Academy nor the Lyceum was designed as a cloistered community for the defense of dogmatic answers or a rehab retreat for comforting ideas, and the creation of soothing notions was the farthest thing from Socrates' mind.

As leaves on trees, such is the life of man.

HOMER

But by AD 250 it was almost as though these men had never lived. The Socratic spirit of free inquiry was gone. During this five-hundred-year interim the critical accomplishments of the Golden Age philosophers had been abandoned or transformed, and the stage was set for a thousand-year reign of the noetic° theologies.

°*The word noesis (whence "noetic") in Greek philosophy "usually refers to knowledge that is independent of sensation" or "the knowledge of reality had by the pure function of reason alone" (Peter Angeles). See lexicon.*

Historians of philosophy can't seem to find words strong enough to describe what happened to philosophy in this post-Aristotelian era. Philip Schaff, a church historian, speaking of Neoplatonism, judges it as "the last phase, the evening red, so to speak, of the Grecian philosophy."[1] Others have called it "the eclipse of philosophy," "the surrender of philosophy," and "the downfall of philosophy"; a time that witnessed "a medley of lesser systems" and "a decline of vitality"; and an age of "decay and dissolution," so that, for half a millennium, "philosophy lay dying."

There is some truth in all these judgments, depending on definition and focus. No subsequent scholarch of the Academy or the Lyceum shared the depth and breadth of Plato or the universal genius of Aristotle, and for centuries what passed as philosophy was largely a rehashing of their warmed-over thoughts. But critical philosophy was not dying. By AD 250 the grand tradition of philosophy had disintegrated,° and it was about to be suppressed for a millennium. But it was not dead.

We need better metaphors. The career of philosophy after Aristotle could be pictured as a great river branching into numerous continuing tributaries (some as rolling rivers, others as mere streams or tiny rivulets); or as a tree with limbs sprouting in diverse directions from a massive trunk (some limbs large, others just twigs). It could be described as a large university dividing into smaller autonomous colleges for specialized research and teaching (some with large faculties, others small and understaffed) or (with slightly less metaphor) as a body of accumulated Greek knowledge splitting—with *kairós* ("appropriate timing") and *anangkê* ("inevitability")—into various concentrated fields that thereafter represented different temperaments, values, and goals that human thought might legitimately focus on.

Could we, with hindsight, endow Aristotle with a prescience of things to come (strictly as artifact, since he did not believe in precognition), we might hear him, about 323 BC, pondering such thoughts as these: "It is no longer possible for any one individual to be a leader in all branches of learning. . . . No one can hope to contribute much to the clarification of ideas in logic who is not himself a logician, or to the clarification of ideas in physics who is not himself a physicist, and so on throughout the fields of specialized knowledge. It thus seems inevitable that there should [evolve] philosophical disciplines corresponding to the various branches of study and providing the frameworks upon which they may be studied and evaluated in and of themselves."°

At the end of this era, what has been described as the death of philosophy did in fact happen. But better metaphors would suggest that it was forced to slumber through a long winter of hibernation or put to sleep in a state of suspended animation to await an honorable awakening a thousand years later. For when its time did arrive in the thirteenth century, philosophy reawakened with vigor and clarity, ready to go to work again.

MAJOR BRANCHES OF POST-ARISTOTELIAN PHILOSOPHY

Early in the post-Aristotelian era, Greek philosophy began to branch into three major schools.

(1) The **pragmatic philosophers** argued that the job of philosophy is to help us live each day as nobly as possible, and this definition of philosophy was well represented in all three of the Golden Age thinkers. In the *Apology*, for example, Socrates had presented philosophy as the intellectual discipline that leads to wisdom that leads to the Good Life. So two new schools of philosophy, the Epicureans and Stoics, arose to teach philosophy as the discipline we all need to make our lives happy.

(2) The **empirical philosophers** insisted that the job of philosophy is to seek the truth about empirical realities, to push on to a better understanding of "the moon, sun, and stars" and everything else under the heavens, including all aspects of human

°*As employed in this chapter, dis-integrate and dis-integration (with hyphen) do not imply "to destroy" or "destruction" but the process of component elements separating (intact) from a previously integrated whole.*

Who knoweth if to die be but to live,

And that called life by mortals be but death?

EURIPIDES

Pliant is the tongue of mortals; numberless the tales within it.

HOMER

°*These "prophetic" words are quoted (with "have evolved" altered to "evolve") from Stephen Toulmin in the introductory article to "Philosophies of the Branches of Knowledge," in* The New Encyclopaedia Britannica *(1987 edition), vol. 25, p. 660.*

Vain is the word of that philosopher by which no malady of mankind is healed.

EPICURUS

life. This was a principal legacy of the presocratics (such as Anaxagoras and Democritus), and it had flowered gloriously with the empirical passions of Aristotle. This side of philosophy rapidly developed into fruitful specializations that eventually became the myriad scientific disciplines of Western civilization. All of today's empirical sciences are legitimate offspring of the Golden Age philosophers.

(3) The ***metaphysical/idealist philosophers*** continued to speculate in the tradition some of the presocratics (such as Pythagoras and the Eleatics) initiated and Plato developed. This line culminated in the noetic systems of Philo Judaeus, the Gnostics, the Neoplatonists, and the Christian theologians. This idealist tradition underwrote Judaic and Christian apologetics and became transformed into a variety of dogmatic bodies of doctrine, thereby inducing critical philosophy's winter of hibernation through the Dark Ages.

Since questions from the Golden Age thinkers had deeply probed these three philosophical concerns, centuries of epigonoi could thereafter devote their energies to finding answers to those questions. In time all three branches became great success stories in the intellectual history of the West. The pragmatic philosophers helped to sustain millions of devoted followers during late Greek and Roman eras and remained major belief systems as late as the sixth century AD. The scientific philosophers amassed a voluminous knowledge about nature and humankind until about the third century AD, when empirical investigations were suppressed by ecclesiastical and civil authorities. Afterward, all attempts to look at the world were put on hold for a thousand years. With the revitalization of Greek science in the thirteenth century, largely through the recovery of Aristotle's writings, foundation stones were soon in place for the building of a new reality structure. Lastly, idealist philosophy found itself shaped by a hyperactive Zeitgeist into a plethora of noetic systems aimed at creating comprehensive descriptions of the nonmaterial reality structure of the world, natural and supernatural; virtually all these "philosophies" were in fact noetic theologies supporting humanity's spiritual quest for belief.

THE PRAGMATIC PHILOSOPHERS

Within a generation of Aristotle's death, pragmatic philosophy made a powerful entrance onto the Athenian scene. To all who were struggling to develop coping power for facing the demands of daily life, questions designed to apprehend cosmic truth seemed less important, and questions of immediate practicality came front and center. What can I believe? How can I maintain peace of mind in a hostile world? How can I protect my integrity in a dishonest world? How can I hold onto even a semblance of nobility through pain and suffering? How can I live each day with hope and joy, knowing that I will soon, all too soon, cease to be? "For in only a short while" wrote Marcus Aurelius, "thou shalt be nothing but ashes and dry bones and a remembered name, or, quite possibly, not even a remembered name."[2] In the face of inescapable personal tragedy, how can I live the Good Life? Philosophic thought turned to the task of giving each individual a set of ideas and values that would enable him to better marshal his resources and make his way through each day.

These pragmatic thinkers, therefore, did not give high priority to gathering facts about physics, astronomy, and biology. The search for "objective truth" had become secondary; the search for a "truth for me" had become all-important. To be sure, those holding each set of beliefs were convinced, more or less, of their objective truth. But *believing* an idea to be true and attempting to *show* that an idea is true by

For just as there is no profit in medicine unless it expels the diseases of the body, so there is none in philosophy either unless it expels the malady of the soul.

EPICURUS

Those who do not attend closely to the motions of their own souls must inevitably be unhappy.

MARCUS AURELIUS

using empirical evidence and rational argument are two quite different attitudes toward the value and function of ideas.

Two philosophical movements were preeminent in addressing immediate survival questions—the Epicureans and the Stoics. Both were personal philosophies; they supplied each individual with ideas that would enable him to cope with the unsatisfactoriness of human existence. Both developed great ethical systems that were rooted in earlier cosmologies: Epicureanism appropriated Democritus's physics to explain the soul and immortality; Stoicism drew upon Heraclitus's notion of fire and the Cynics' idea of nature. So each philosophy was, in itself, a fairly coherent worldview. (The philosophies of Epicurus and Zeno the Stoic are dealt with in separate chapters.°)

What is the first business of one who practices philosophy? To get rid of self-conceit. For it is impossible for anyone to begin to learn that which he thinks he already knows.

EPICTETUS

°See Chapters 13 and 14.

RISE OF THE PHILOSOPHIC SKEPTICS

Early in the post-Aristotelian era, an important philosophical outlook or attitude arose in Athens that might well be called an antiphilosophy; though in practice it was pragmatic, it also behaved like an indelible dye that spread out to color every branch of philosophic reflection. This movement was philosophic Skepticism, and it was launched by *Pyrrhon of Êlis* (c. 360–270 BC) about 300 BC. At the same time that Zeno was pacing in the Painted Stoa and Epicurus was lecturing in his Garden, Pyrrhon was developing a philosophy of reasonable doubt that taught that Zeno and Epicurus were right—philosophy's goal is to make life happy. And the fundamental requirement for being happy, he said, is to stop banging one's head against a brick wall attempting to achieve the epistemically impossible. Philosophers always want to know the truth, but the truth, by its very nature, they said, is off-limits to the human mind. Given the alienation of subject from object, and considering the foibles of human reason, the wise man will abandon all attempts to find an objective truth of anything.[3]

Just as father and brother are relative terms, day is relative to the sun, and all things are relative to our mind.

THE SKEPTICS

But without the truth what is one to do? Pyrrhon had traveled eastward and studied with Indian Gymnosophists and Persian Magi, Diogenes tells us, and this led him to create a "most noble philosophy" that took "the form of agnosticism and suspension of judgement" (*epochê*°). Don't try to know the world; don't worry about forming precise ideas about anything. Nothing is, in itself, as we perceive it or judge it. We may speak of a beautiful painting or a valuable book, but beauty is not a quality of the painting and value is not a quality of the book. "He [Pyrrhon] denied that anything, in itself, is honorable or dishonorable, just or unjust"; we merely see things (evaluate things) that way, and societal customs and values largely shape the way we see and value things. "No single thing is in itself any more this than that." The upshot of all this is that human knowledge is really just an illusory, self-created batch of mind pictures that tell us nothing about the real world's true nature. We mustn't press our luck or arrogantly claim we know what any critical mind knows we don't know. Epistemic humility is the only appropriate stance of an aware intellect; arrogance is a confession of ignorance.[4]

Dogmatic philosophers are fools.

THE SKEPTICS

°See lexicon.

This brand of epistemic skepticism was not new; several presocratics had doubted we can attain an accurate understanding of what really goes on in the world. When Heraclitus said "everything flows and nothing abides," he seems to have been implying that nothing in nature stays still long enough for us to obtain a clear picture of it. "As for certain truth," he said, "no man has it." Anaxagoras wrote that "Through the weakness of the sense-perceptions, we cannot judge truth." Democritus concluded

We must not assume that what convinces us is actually true.

THE SKEPTICS

that "we really don't know anything about anything" since "it has been demonstrated more than once that we do not discover by direct perception what the nature of each thing is or is not." Parmenides and Zeno of Elea had played with the idea that everything our senses tell us is One Big Lie. In Socrates' time the Sophists were notorious for their no-knowledge declarations. Protagoras's dictum that "man is the measure of everything" implies that our understanding is entirely relative; whatever one believes to be true is true, for him. The ultimate statement of skepticism was given by Gorgias the Sicilian sophist: "Nothing exists; but if it did, we couldn't know it; and if we could know it, we couldn't communicate our knowledge of it."[5]

But the Skeptics went far beyond all previous doubting and massively documented what they believed they saw. "The Skeptics were forever engaged in undermining the dogmas of other schools of philosophy," Laërtius says. They did this by systematically collecting others' fact claims and value judgments and pointing out the anomalies, contradictions, and confusions in them. They organized these contradictions and used them as blasting powder against the dogmatic claims of others (especially the Stoics) to destroy their credibility. When "facts conflict," the Skeptics said, "the inevitable conclusion is that we are ignorant of the truth." Every statement that makes a claim to truth can be countered with its opposite, and all such statements, after destroying their opposites, "turn around and destroy themselves."[6]

The Skeptics never developed positive doctrines of their own. Because they focused on undermining others' ideas, the entire Skeptical enterprise may appear negative; but since much of what they undermined turn out to be (in history's long view) false fact claims and arbitrary value judgments, their contribution was essentially positive and their impact on philosophical thought in subsequent centuries was very great. They frequently were attacked by critics, who pointed out that if you say that the truth can't be known, you're contradicting yourself, for you're submitting at least one statement that you believe you know to be true. So the Skeptics went out of their way to avoid the criticism: They determined nothing, they said (including their determining that they determined nothing); they overthrew their own overthrowing; and they even refuted their own refuting. All their attacks on others were mere probabilities, not to be taken as dogmas. In fact, *everything* we think we know is a pragmatic probability and nothing more.[7]

The founder of the Skeptical movement had been earlier a starving artist (a painter) from the Peloponnesus. A very private man, Pyrrhon lived with his sister Philistia in Athens and (to the horror of politically correct Athenians) performed the chores of a homemaker (like dusting the furniture and carrying pigs to market). He stayed out of public life, though he was known to seek strangers on occasion, wander with them incognito, and carry on conversations. Though brilliant in debate with others, he enjoyed the company of his own mind more and was often seen talking to himself. He was much esteemed by the Athenians, who made him a gift of honorary citizenship, and his native city Êlis respected him so much the town council "voted that all philosophers be exempt from taxation." Like Diogenes the Cynic, Pyrrhon lived his philosophy; that is, he practiced skepticism. His distrust of the senses was so pronounced that if he saw a chariot bearing down upon him, he really didn't believe what his eyes and ears were telling him; he would ignore his senses and continue to stand in the middle of the street. From such disasters-in-waiting ("whether being run down by carts, falling off cliffs, or being bitten by dogs") he was by friends who followed him around looking after him. (A later Skeptic, Ainesidêmos the Academic, said all this was just gossip, for Pyrrhon really applied his skepticism only to questions of philosophy.) He was famous for his unflappable composure. Once, while he was sailing on a ship during a storm, other passengers were terrified, but Pyrrhon

We are accustomed to saying that there is no such thing as space, and yet we have no alternative but to speak of space for the purpose of argument.

THE SKEPTICS

The senses deceive, and reason says different things.

THE SKEPTICS

Every saying has its corresponding opposite.

THE SKEPTICS

The apparent is the Skeptic's criterion of knowledge.

DIOGENES LAËRTIUS

remained serene and pointed to a little pig on board that calmly went on eating; philosophers, he said, should emulate the little porker and remain unperturbed by the restless seas about them. He lived to be almost ninety years old. Since Pyrrhon left no writings of his own, our knowledge of him derives from later Skeptics, especially the noble and prolific Sextus Empiricus, who, though he wrote five hundred years later, appears to have given an accurate account of Pyrrhon and his thoughts.

THE "PYRRHONEAN PRINCIPLE"

The "Pyrrhonean principle" (as Ainesidêmos labeled it) is to focus on the phenomena of immediate experience and what the human mind proceeds to do with them. And what it does with them is to create contradictions, anomalies, and confusions, so the Skeptics each spent a lifetime exploring and exploiting those contradictions, organizing them, and using them as fuel for their attacks on all brands of dogmatists. "They would first show the ways in which things gain credence, and then by the same methods they would destroy belief in them."

In their systematic exposition of false claims, the Skeptics collected and organized commonly occurring "puzzlements" ("perplexities," "epistemic embarrassments") into ten categories. The first category contains a list of how living creatures differ in their experiencing. For example, they experience pleasure and pain differently; hawks are keen sighted, dogs keen scented; hemlock kills humans but nourishes quail; and so on. So, from all these variable "impressions" no dependable knowledge can be inferred.

The second category deals with the great variety of personal likes and dislikes. The third points out how the reports of our senses can differ from one another. The fourth describes how various mind and body states—such as illness, sleep, sorrow, hate, love—affect our impressions. The fifth notes the variety of differences in moral feelings, esthetic tastes, and customs one finds in different societies. The sixth relates how appearances vary with conditions ("purple shows different tints in sunlight, moonlight, and lamplight").

The seventh category deals with distances, relative positions, and locations and how they affect appearances. Distant objects such as the Sun appear small; rugged hills appear "misty and smooth"; and irridescent feathers on a dove's neck change color with the angle of reflected light. "Since, then, it is not possible to observe these things apart from places and positions, their real nature is unknowable." (This remarkable conclusion reads like a time warp; see below.)

The eighth category deals with quantities and qualities, the ninth with our varied responses to the familiar and the unfamiliar; the tenth focuses on the relativity of qualities and position (heavy and light, left and right, up and down, more and less, strong and weak) and the interdependency of certain concepts (such as father and son, night and day).

Such ubiquitous unresolvables led the Skeptics to challenge all truth-tests or criteria for establishing the truth of any fact claim. We have only two ways of judging the truth, they said: by "sensibles" (empirical observations by our senses) and by "intelligibles" (coherent reasoning). But "the senses deceive, and reason says different things." Look around: Everywhere "man disagrees with man and with himself." So, the conflicting claims we humans make call both criteria into question. Therefore, since no trustworthy criterion exists for determining the true from the false, no truth can be known. (The Stoics had held that certain ideas produce in us such "irresistible feelings" that we just know them to be true; but Skeptics replied that "we must never assume that what convinces us is actually true," for it really appears that people can be convinced by about anything.)

No single thing is in itself any more this than that.
PYRRHON OF ÊLIS

Some say the Skeptics' goal of life is a state of apathy [apatheia]; *others say it is a state of gentle peace* [praotêta].
DIOGENES LAËRTIUS

Nothing is good or bad by nature.
THE SKEPTICS

To every argument there is an opposite argument.
THE SKEPTICS

The Skeptics assaulted all criteria for making judgments, holding that they were arbitrary and relative, and they questioned the learning process. They adopted the Eleatic denial of motion and "coming-to-be and passing away." They decided causality has no real existence but is only an idea (and not a very useful one). And they concluded that nothing, "by nature," is good or bad, just or unjust.

WE MUST SUSPEND JUDGMENT

The Skeptics' central doctrine—the impossibility of our knowing the true nature of things—led them to several conclusions.

(1) If the truth is unknowable, then we must suspend judgment on the true nature of virtually everything. This dimly-lit world has no place for arrogant claims, authoritarian pronouncements, or closed minds. (No one disdained dogmatism more than the Skeptics.° "Dogmatists are fools," they said.) On all questions of what the real world is truly like—the claims the dogmatists argue about so heatedly—"we suspend our judgment because they [the claims] aren't certain, and we confine our knowledge to our impressions. We admit that we see, and we recognize that we think this or that, but *how* we see or *how* we think we simply don't know." All that we ever experience are appearances or impressions of objects, never the real objects themselves. "We perceive that fire burns," but of the physical processes involved in the burning, "we know nothing"—"so we suspend our judgment." "We perceive that a man moves and that he dies"—but of the mechanics of motion or the physiology of dying "we know nothing"—"so we suspend our judgment." Timon the Skeptic added, "I don't know whether honey itself is sweet, but I readily admit that it seems sweet to me"—in other words, we must accept, and live with, our experiences, whatever they may be, without knowing the reality itself.

(2) It follows that our lives must be lived—in fact, are lived, whether we know it or not—by probabilities only. "We recognize that it's day and that we're alive, and many other apparent facts in life." But beyond such mundane observations, no certain knowledge exists that would render our judgments and decisions anything but pragmatic expediencies.

(3) The fact we live in a contained subjective world led the Skeptics to the conclusion that all experiential claims are valid, and therefore we should take seriously everyone's reports about their private impressions. This insight could lead (though frequently it did not) to a greater empathy for others and a richer understanding of human differences.

(4) Lacking the possibility of knowing reality, it follows that no science is possible ("science" defined either as a method of inquiry into the real or as a body of objective knowledge about the real world). "Of the inherent properties [of physical matter] we know nothing."

(5) So, coming full circle: Not having to struggle mightily in the pursuit of truth (and no longer feeling compelled to argue about conflicting truth claims), we can achieve peace of mind. "Just as a shadow never leaves us, so tranquillity (*ataraxia*) follows suspension of judgment."

Pyrrhon's pupil **Timon of Phlius** tirelessly continued the skeptical tradition, largely through satire and poetry. His many writings included thirty comedies and sixty tragedies, dialogues, epics, *silli* ("lampoons"), satyric plays, and lusty poetry. As a satirist he spared no one and ridiculed the dogmatic philosophers with his parodies. Timon had but one good eye, so, of course, he was called Cyclops. A very private figure, he loved his gardens and had a (seemingly) happy marriage with children. A saying proclaimed that "some philosophers catch their disciples by pursuing them, but some (such as Timon) by fleeing from them." Like some other great writers, he was

We suspend our judgment because we are not certain about things; we confine our knowledge to our impressions.

THE SKEPTICS

°*Unless it was Voltaire, who said that "uncertainty may be uncomfortable, but certainty is ridiculous."*

On Timon *Among philosophers, some catch their disciples by pursuing them, some (like Timon) by fleeing from them.*

HIERONYMUS THE PERIPATETIC

What we object to is our easy acceptance of the picture of reality that sense phenomena give us.

THE SKEPTICS

undisciplined and disorganized, leaving his poems scattered about the room. When reading his compositions aloud for someone, he would read whatever pages happened to turn up and would worry later about whether it all made sense.[8]

Skeptic attitudes and ideas were massively absorbed into the Academy. *Arkesilaos of Pitanê*, a scholarch of Plato's Academy (see later, in connection with the Academy), became a major exponent of skepticism. Diogenes says (though incorrectly) that Arkesilaos "was the first to meddle with the system handed down by Plato." *Carneades of Cyrene* (c. 213–129 BC), scholarch of the New Academy, became the voice of the burgeoning skeptical movement. *Ainesidêmos of Knossos* rejuvenated Skepticism in Alexandria in the late first century BC; it was he who drew up the ten categories of contradictions and attacked causality.[9]

Much of what we know about the Skeptic school derives from the scholarly writings of *Sextus Empiricus*, writing (probably) in Rome near the end of the second century AD. Sextus was Greek and wrote in Greek. By vocation he was a doctor, but his passion was as a historian of ideas, and his works are valuable anthologies of information. Among them are *Outlines of Pyrrhonism*, *Against the Logicians*, and *Against the Ethicists*. Sextus attacks all attempts to create abstract generalizations from a limited number of empirical facts (all observational data are limited, he notes). We have no way of knowing that an abstract concept is universally valid unless we have investigated the whole universe. Every generalization is therefore only probable and nothing more. He continued the Skeptic obsession with contradictions and collected more to show that all the mental furniture of our philosophic systems are burdened with a cargo of paradoxes; these include the notions of cause, time, space, creation, coming to be and passing away, nature, and more. Mathematics, as universal generalization, is nonsense. As for what is right and moral, virtue and evil, just and unjust—just look at the conflicting beliefs and practices of humans everywhere. There is no such thing as a universal morality or esthetic. One simply cannot generalize. Like earlier Skeptics, Sextus annihilates all dogmatisms through suspension of judgment. But this suspension shouldn't for a moment cool our ardor for living. Nature intends that we use our minds and senses wisely. Social norms, laws, and customs are givens, and a wise person will not attempt to swim upstream against them; the accumulated wisdom of mankind is rich in probabilities, and we should avail ourselves of all of them.

All this makes Sextus sound like an early Existentialist. The gist of what he is saying is that we can be completely honest only when confronting the concrete realities of a specific situation and tailor-making our thoughts and decisions for that unique set of circumstances only. His nickname "Empiricus" is well given.

THE SKEPTIC LEGACY

The Skeptics were among the first to recognize clearly that, *at their place in time*, it was impossible to determine with any confidence what goes on in the real world; and, from our vantage point, we can judge they were correct. Without the sophisticated skills and measuring devices we have today, how could they understand nature? Without the abstract formulas of mathematics and geometry, physics was not possible. Without electron microscopes, mass spectrometers, telescopes, and charge-coupled devices to explore the very small (and the particles of "reality" are very, very small) and the very large (the Big Bang's residues are very, very big)—none of the understandings we now have in physics, biology, chemistry, and astronomy could have been attained. When the Skeptics pondered the mountain of contradictory claims "authorities" and "experts" made, they were forced—justifiably—to become agnostic. Though they overbuilt their case, their conclusions brought a fresh

The apparent is omnipotent wherever it goes.
TIMON OF PHLIUS

We perceive that fire burns, of course; but how it happens we don't know—we suspend judgment.
THE SKEPTICS

We don't deny that we see; we only say that we don't know how we see.
THE SKEPTICS

Not more one thing than another.
THE SKEPTICS

°*On the egocentric predicament, see Perry, Vol. II, pp. 338f.*

We determine nothing.
THE SKEPTICS

When we say "We determine nothing" we are not determining even that.
THE SKEPTICS

°*The Skeptics failed to make their case against causality, where David Hume later succeeded; see Vol II, pp. 140ff.*

It is in man's nature to care for all men.
MARCUS AURELIUS

honesty into the whole stagnant philosophic enterprise. "I don't know" can be a very powerful idea when it's true.

The Skeptics were the first to recognize the nature of the egocentric predicament and its implications for epistemology.° "What we [Skeptics] object to is uncritically believing that the appearance of something gives us a knowledge of the reality." We know only phenomena, and what knowledge we do possess of the real world is created by our minds on the basis of these phenomena. With this the Skeptics made a major contribution to future science and laid the foundations for a clear understanding of exactly how it is that we can come "to know" the contents of the real world. This was not quite the clear distancing of the experiential from the real; they failed to locate properties where they in fact are; but it was a beginning.

As noted earlier, the seventh category of "puzzlements" deals with "distances, positions, places and the occupants of the places." Distant objects appear to us small, and far-off mountains appear blue and without texture; at sunrise the sun is red, at midday white. (We might add that railroad tracks appear to intersect, roadways to narrow; mirages make flat things look lumpy, straight things bent.) "Since, then, it is not possible to observe these things apart from places and positions, their real nature is unknowable." All observations, the Skeptics are saying, involve an observer (as special relativity and quantum physics have shown), and the observer's position always affects the appearance of the reality (and maybe the reality itself, but that's still up for grabs among today's physicists). This insight renders our knowledge of the real precarious even in the early twenty-first century.

The Skeptics were apparently the first to recognize that we employ concepts indispensable to thought even though they may refer to nothing real (though we usually believe they do). For example, they attacked the notion of causality. A cause is relative to some effect; without an effect no cause exists. But relationships (as in "relative to") are "objects of thought only and have no substantial existence." They cited the analogy of the father and child: If no child exists, then no father exists. But just as the father-child relationship is a conceptual creation, they argued, so also is the so-called "causal link" between real objects. Some of the Skeptics attempted to bolster this weak argument by submitting that natural processes—such as "motion" and "coming-to-be"—don't really exist anyway, so the idea of cause is useless.°

Their recognition that "nothing is by nature good or bad, just or unjust" might be thought of as a first step in a long process of clarifying the status of values. Even though they argued that we can't know *anything* about the qualities of real objects, they were fairly sure that values don't inhere in the objects themselves. They failed, however, to see that values are located only in the minds and hearts of valuers, that values (evaluings) are only the abstract ideas and feelings that we evaluators make about the objects/events of experience.

The impact of skepticism on the intellectual history of the next few centuries was enormous. The Skeptics picked up on all previous murmurings against the senses, magnified Socrates' disinterest in nature's operations, downloaded the diatribes from Plato against the senses, recast the teachings of Parmenides and Zeno, who said our senses lie to us in a most heinous way. They put all this together, organized it, created a mass of arguments to defend their case, launched onslaughts against all arrogant claims to knowing, invoked an epistemic relativity, and produced a movement that discouraged several centuries of thinkers from investigating the world and life. If they had come first, they would have undermined virtually the entire life work of Aristotle.

So on the negative side the Skeptics' legacy was a mood of despair about the human mind's ability to acquire knowledge. On the positive side their legacy was their exposé of a host of untenable knowledge claims and their reestablishment of an epistemic honesty that had been lost in all the fashionable dialectics. This helped to clear the field for a sounder science to emerge.

WHAT HAPPENED TO THE ACADEMY?

After Plato's death in 347 BC, the Academy was led by a succession of scholarchs continuing into the sixth century AD. Historians have sectioned the history of the school into the Old, Middle, and Late Academies, and under each successive leader Plato's ideas underwent revision. His immediate successor, his nephew *Speusippos* (son of his sister Pôtônê), headed the Academy for eight years (347–339 BC). Of his 43,375 written lines only a few fragments survive, but the records are sufficient to tell us he couldn't quite convince himself Plato's Real Ideas were really real, so he sought to de-emphasize Plato's central doctrine. Influenced by the Pythagorean discovery that numbers describe the world's operations, he accepted that numbers were real entities (he called them "mathematicals"). He paved the way for later Neoplatonic philosophy by speculating that an immortal world-soul exists somewhere between the realm of real numbers and the realm of material objects. Thus, the first scholarch after Plato began the process of undermining the coherence of Plato's thoughts and took a first small step toward the treatment of Platonism as a body of doctrine and the abandonment of it as a method of inquiry.

The two female students enrolled at the Academy attended Speusippos's lectures, and rumor had it that he fell in love with Lastheneia.° Speusippos relinquished his leadership of the school to Xenocrates when he became crippled by paralysis; depressed by his condition, he finally committed suicide.[10]

The next scholarch, *Xenocrates* (formerly Aristotle's traveling companion), remained faithful to the larger structure of Platonic reality, though he reorganized and expanded certain details. During his twenty-five years as head of the Academy (339–314 BC), he went beyond Plato and Speusippos and applied the notion of Real Numbers to theological ideas. He introduced into Platonism a cosmic dualism between two principles that eternally oppose one another: "the One," which is the cause of unity, repose, and good things; and the Dyad ("the Two"), which is the cause of disunity, motion, and evil.° The interaction of these two principles produces three levels of reality: objects, Real Ideas, and "heavenly bodies" that mediate between the two.

Xenocrates had been a lifelong pupil of Plato, but a swift learner he was not; Plato once compared him to Aristotle, saying "the one needed a spur, the other a bridle." Strong willed, humble, and independent, he loved silence and solitude. He was exceptionally honest (Philip of Macedon once remarked that Xenocrates was the only man at his court he couldn't bribe). He had a majesterial appearance that Athenians deferred to as he walked through the Agora. Something of his gentle nature is revealed in a story (probably true) that a sparrow, fleeing a hawk, flew into the folds of his cloak; Xenocrates comforted the sparrow and sent it on its way, saying that "a suppliant must never be denied sanctuary."[11]

Thus, in both Speusippos and Xenocrates we witness a pattern of reorganization, augmentation, and reinterpretation of Plato's ideas. Later members of the Old Academy continued to add to or make substantial changes to original Platonism. *Polemon of Athens* (scholarch, 314–c. 276 BC) "used to say that we should exercise ourselves with facts and not with mere logical speculations." He seems to have recognized that the creative imagination, if cut loose from its empirical moorings, can float away into

While it is granted that a pure geometry is free to posit any axioms that it pleases, a geometry purporting to describe the real world must have true axioms.
STEPHEN TOULMIN

°See p. 137.

°Compare Xenocrates' dualism with the adversarial dualism of Mani; see p. 220.

[Cleanthes the Stoic charged Aristarchus with blasphemy] *for supposing the heaven to remain at rest and the Earth to revolve in an oblique circle, while it rotates, at the same time, on its axis.*
CLEANTHES THE STOIC

the blue. It is, he said, like one who has memorized a book on harmony but has no feeling for music. Plato, of course, would have disowned such a notion, saying that "empirical facts" are too shaky to be of any value.

Polemon was also remembered for his wild youth. Once, quite drunk, he burst into Xenocrates' lecture hall during the scholarch's lecture on temperance; though tipsy, he was enthralled as the great teacher, unmoved, kept on talking. This marked a turning point in his life, for "from the time when he began to study philosophy," he acquired great "strength of character" and "became so industrious as to surpass all the other scholars, and rose to be himself head of the school in the 116th Olympiad." He was known for his even temper, serene personality, and "simple austere dignity." While scholarch "he would withdraw from society and confine himself to the garden of the Academy, while close by his scholars made themselves little huts and lived not far from the shrine of the Muses and the lecture-hall."[12]

Cratês of Athens followed Polemon as head of the Academy. (Arkesilaos, the next scholarch, called Polemon and Cratês "remnants of the Golden Age.") By the time the so-called Middle Academy came into being with **Arkesilaos of Pitanê,** about 315 BC, the philosophic mood of Platonism had become one of skepticism, and Arkesilaos is the first of the Academic Skeptics. His position, influenced by Stoicism, was that sense perception is the criterion of truth (Plato would have seen bright red at this notion), but since all our senses deceive us, then accurate knowledge of the world is impossible (a conclusion Plato would have applauded). A wise philosopher, therefore, will hold back from supporting any proposition whatever; he will maintain an uncommitted attitude which the Skeptics labeled "hands off" or "abstaining," "suspension of judgment" (*epochê*). Arkesilaos was a lifelong foe of Stoic dogmatism and spent considerable time attacking their notion that one can be certain that a fact-claim is true by an "irresistible feeling" that it is true. He gained notoriety for arguing on all sides of an issue since, after all, the truth can't be known. A "science" of the physical world is not possible. A false perception, he said, may be just as seductive as a true one. Myth, opinion, and gossip may seem just as persuasive as fact, and no dependable criterion exists for separating the true from the false. All of us, from the wisest to the most foolish, are forever suspended in a zone of uncertainty between knowledge and false belief. All we are capable of is gathering "probable" information about the world that will serve us for intelligent decisions and actions.

A superb debater, Arkesilaos seems to have been talented at turning every discussion into an argument, which of course he would win. "In persuasiveness he had no equal, and this all the more drew pupils to the school, although they were in terror of his pungent wit. But they willingly put up with that; for his goodness was extraordinary, and he inspired his pupils with hopes." Arkesilaos, we are told, shunned politics and dedicated his life to the Academy.[13]

Subsequent thinkers of the New Academy escalated this skepticism. **Carneades of Cyrene** (c. 213–129 BC) followed Arkesilaos in teaching that no criterion for judging the truth is possible; what we so glibly call "truth" is only an "appearance of truth" or, at best, a matter of probability. We labor under a twofold handicap: Just as our senses deceive, so also does our logic; we think our reasoning is clear and valid when it is really shaky and one sided (just remember how persuasively the Sophists had argued on all sides of every issue). Carneades was especially unhappy with Stoic theology. The notion that the orderliness of nature proves the existence of an intelligent deity he called nonsense; whatever order does exist can be easily interpreted as a creation of nature itself. And the belief the cosmos was created for humanity's benefit is just plain silly, given the extent of disaster and pain it provides us.

Carneades, an industrious scholar, loved his books so much that he became a recluse while studying and would let his hair and nails grow long out of neglect. "His talent for criticizing opponents was remarkable, and he was a formidable controversialist." In 155 BC Carneades and the leaders of the Academy and Stoa were sent by Athens as special ambassadors to Rome to plea for a remission of a huge fine levied for their having plundered a neighboring state. While awaiting a verdict from the Roman senate, Carneades gave some public lectures that were so spellbinding to Roman youth that he was sent home lest he corrupt them all. He lived to be eighty-five years old.[14]

Subsequent leaders of the New Academy—notably *Philo of Larissa* (c. 140–c. 77 BC) and his pupil *Antiochus of Ascalon* (c. 124–69 BC; scholarch, 79–78 BC)—assimilated Stoic and Neoplatonic elements into the Platonic tradition. Antiochus accused Carneades of self-negation in his theory of probability, for he had said no criterion can exist for judging true from false but then went right ahead and talked about true and false. Philo answered by saying an absolute truth really exists but we can't know it; Antiochus again replied—stupid nonsense. The quarrel became bitter and endangered the Academy's reputation.

Academic skepticism was revitalized in Alexandria by *Ainesidêmos of Knossos* (late first century BC), who carried on, and embroidered, the analyses of his skeptical predecessors. Ainesidêmos attacked the knowledge claims of virtually everybody, especially the Stoics, building a strong evidentiary case that nobody knows anything for sure. He drew up an exhaustive list of ten categories of common contradictions.[15] For example, he pointed out that perceptions differ markedly from one person to another (such as how we experience pleasure and pain), indicating that our notions of external stimuli vary so much that we can't generalize about their nature. He noted that one man—Demophon by name, a servant of Alexander the Great—always melted in the shade and shivered in the sun. Humans and animals perceive reality so differently that we can't infer with any confidence what that reality is. Individuals and whole societies differ in their judgments of what is beautiful or ugly, true or false, and good or bad. "Nothing is good or bad by nature." From this epistemic relativity, it follows that what is truly "out there" and what is truly good and bad, ugly or beautiful can't be known. Nature sends too many mixed signals.

Then near the beginning of the third century AD, Plato was reborn (better, reincarnated) into Neoplatonism—a superheavy resurrection of Platonic ideas recast as a mystical religion. Plato's antiempirical bias reached its outer limits in the noetic theological speculations of *Plotinus of Alexandria.*°

The last scholarch of the Athenian Academy was *Damascius of Damascus.* In the year AD 529 the Byzantine emperor Justinian judged the Academy to be a stronghold of paganism and ordered it closed. Fearing for their lives, Damascius and six of his colleagues fled (or exiled themselves) to Persia and were given sanctuary at the court of the king Chosroes. These seven scholars, the most distinguished men in their field, hoped they would find a Platonic utopia where, as philosopher-kings, they could study in peace. In no time they were disillusioned and longed to return home. In AD 532 the Persian monarch negotiated a treaty with Justinian and included in it a stipulation that the exiles could return unharmed and be allowed to teach their beliefs without interference. So they returned, but the Academy was no more. It had endured for 916 years.

Thus, a very un-Platonic skepticism, an arbitrary eclecticism, and a noetic mysticism strongly colored the development of post-Platonic Academic philosophy. Plato's open-spirited passion to continue Socrates' dialectical search for the truth

The life of reason is alone free from magic.

PLOTINUS

°*Plotinus and Neoplatonism are covered in Chapter 15.*

and his insistence that the human mind could find an existing truth—these were all but forgotten.

WHAT HAPPENED TO THE LYCEUM?

On Aristotle *Aristotle's triumphant fulfillment of his inherited task was a climax from which the tide of speculation could only recede.*

G. R. G. MURE

°See p. 179.

On Strato *[His position on weights and motions] frees God from his great work and me from fear.*

CICERO

Aristotle was gifted with an awesome intellect. It was synoptic; he wanted to create a universe out of a multiverse. He had a prodigious memory and unbounded curiosity, and he turned his philosophic attention to virtually every known subject. We can judge, from our vantage point, that he succeeded in laying foundations for the sciences of physics, astronomy, and meteorology; taxonomy, biology, forensic pathology, and animal behavior; psychology, epistemology, logic, and esthetics; political science and ethics; and, finally, metaphysics—the philosopher's unified field theory for understanding the universe and its contents.

Perhaps the oft-repeated observation is true that Aristotle was the last human being to master the entire supply of knowledge that was available in a single time and place. G. R. G. Mure judges that "Aristotle's triumphant fulfillment of his inherited task was a climax from which the tide of speculation could only recede," and each successor at the Lyceum was "a lesser and a dimmer figure than the one before."[16]

The work of the Lyceum continued for almost eight centuries. The earliest of Aristotle's followers carried on his empirical scientific orientation but minimized theoretical speculation. His first successor after his death in 322 BC, was **Theophrastos,** his coworker and traveling companion; he reigned as scholarch for thirty-five years. Theophrastos followed Aristotle's thinking in all essentials but sought a greater unity in the many fields that Aristotle explored and made his philosophy even more empirical and less metaphysical; he made some major changes in Aristotelian logic. His field of specialization was botany; he wrote *On the History of Plants* (nine volumes) and *The Growth of Plants* (six volumes); all volumes have survived. He also wrote extensively on ethics. It has been conjectured that Theophrastos edited Aristotle's notes for a lecture course on ethics and named the work *Nicomachean Ethics* in memory of Aristotle's son Nikomachos.° Theophrastos gathered Aristotle's library of books and manuscripts and gave them to one of Theophrastos's students, Neleus of Skepsis.

In 288 BC Theophrastos was succeeded by **Strato of Lampsacus** (called "the Naturalist" because of his fascination for, and careful study of, all of nature). He presided over the Lyceum for eighteen years. Like Aristotle he was encyclopedic and "excelled in every branch of learning." He wrote voluminously; the names of many of his works are known to us, among them *On Justice, On Injustice, On Lifestyles, On Courage, On Sleep, On Dreams, On Colors, On Mining Machinery, On Enthusiasm, On Time, On Nonexistent Animals, On Animals in Folklore,* and *On the Future,* but none of his work survives. He did little to change Aristotle's ideas, though he, too, tended to minimize Aristotle's metaphysical teleology.[17]

Strato left the school to **Lyco of Ilium** ("since everyone else seems either too old or too busy"), and his bequest included "the furniture in the dining-room, the cushions and the drinking cups."[18] Lyco was scholarch for forty-four years but seems not to have taken his illustrious heritage all that seriously. His passions focused rather on his physical fitness, his soothing mellifluous voice (for a nickname they altered Lyco to Glyco, "Honey-voice"), and the education of young boys—"modesty and love of honor are essential equipment for boys just as spur and bridle are for horses."[19]

Eudemus of Rhodes, another of Aristotle's disciples, collected Aristotle's ethical teachings in a summation called the *Eudemian Ethics.* **Aristoxenus of Tarentum,**

called "the Musician," imported Pythagorean ideas into the Aristotelian system, especially the notion of harmony. Still another early member of the Peripatetic school, **Demetrius of Phalerum,** concentrated on the history of opinions.

During these years Aristotle's writings formed the basis for the Lyceum's curriculum. Neleus took the original books from Aristotle's own library to Skepsis, a town in the Troad, in Asia Minor. The king of Pergamon, Eumenes II, had plans to make his city a center of Greek culture, including a royal library to rival the one at Alexandria; for books to stock his new library, he dispatched investigators to scour the country. Fearing Aristotle's books would be seized, Neleus's heirs hid them in an underground cellar or tunnel. More than a century later, they were exhumed—moth-eaten and half ruined by dampness—and returned to Athens by Apellicon of Teos, a wealthy collector and book lover. He had them recopied, but much of the writing was illegible and the copiers, guessing at the words, introduced a multitude of errors into the texts.

As the Romans conquered Greece and the rest of the eastern Mediterranean, they transported to Rome whatever they could find from the great Hellenistic libraries. When the Roman general Sulla sacked Athens in 86 BC, Apellicon's entire library, including the Skepsis manuscripts, was carried to Rome. There a grammarian named Tyrannion added them to his collection of thirty thousand volumes and began to arrange and edit them. Finally, an Aristotelian scholar named **Andronicos,** who came to Rome from the island of Rhodes between 50 BC and 40 BC, gained access to the great collection of Aristotle's writings. Andronicos was a careful, honest, and highly respected scholar. "One of the happy coincidences of history [is] that this scholar, educated in a good Aristotelian tradition, happened to find in Rome a library rich in manuscripts of Aristotle's writings."[20] He edited all the books; collated them with other available manuscripts from Athens, Alexandria, and private collections; deleted material that had accumulated in the texts; restored readings; and arranged them in what he believed to be the original order, bringing together the works on logic and titling them the *Organon*. The books that came "after the works on physics" *(meta ta physica)* he called the *Metaphysics*, thereby coining one of the most famous words in Western vocabularies.

Andronicos must be credited with preserving the entire Aristotelian corpus which, after a thousand-year detour, could make its way to the West. He initiated the long tradition of Aristotelian apologetics and interpretation. After Andronicos Aristotelianism was thought of not as a method for scientific research but as a body of codified doctrines.

RISE OF THE INDEPENDENT SCIENCES

Alexandria had been a very special city since Alexander the Great laid its foundations and determined it would be just that. A seer had told him that the newly-planted city would be endowed with the "most abundant and helpful resources" and would become "a nursing mother to men of every nation."[21] Delighted with the omen, Alexander himself laid down the city's outlines. Striding along the isthmus extending into the Mediterranean with marking chalk in his hands, followed by surveyors and equestrian handlers, he designated the locations where he envisioned docks and streets, marketplaces, and temples dedicated to Greek and Egyptian deities. The city was to follow an axial-grid plan with a wide boulevard running east to west and streets intersecting at right angles; on the perimeter were to be fortifications. When Alexander ran out of chalk, his attendants brought him baskets of flour so that he

°See p. 175.

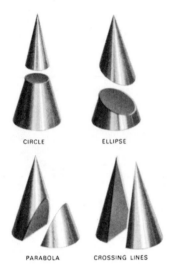

CIRCLE   ELLIPSE

PARABOLA   CROSSING LINES

HYPERBOLA

Archimedes (following Apollonius of Perga) found that a cone intersected by a flat plane results in a variety of interesting curves: a circle when the cut is parallel to the cone's base; an ellipse when cut oblique; a parabola when cut parallel to the cone's side; a hyperbola when the plane slashes vertically through the cone's center. These graceful curves were first described by Apollonius in his Conics; Archimedes further explored them in On Conoids and Spheroids. It turns out that these conic sections are the paths followed by projectiles, satellites, asteroids, comets, moons, and planets under the influence of gravity as they orbit planets, stars, and black holes.

could continue marking the city's lines, and, although seagulls ate most of the barley meal, the city still got built as Alexander planned it. The date of Alexandria's founding was April 7 of 331 BC.

On Alexander's death in 323 BC, his vast kingdom was split among four of his generals, and Egypt went to Ptolemy, a close friend since their boyhood together at Pella (and possibly at Mieza with Aristotle).° Ptolemy made Alexandria his capital, and under his patronage it rapidly grew into the great cosmopolitan city foreseen by the omen. The early Ptolemies (fifteen in all ruled) were passionate patrons of the arts and nourished an atmosphere of serious scholarship. They brought Greek language and culture to Egypt, and by 200 BC a vast library of Greek literature existed, including voluminous commentaries on the philosophers and classics.

Furthermore, merchants and businesspeople engaged in extensive international trade. The silk route with China opened, and Alexandrian ships sailed to faraway places such as the Far East and the British Isles. Alexandria became a hub of cultural influences from many nations, a melting pot of religions, philosophies, customs, and traditions. Greek life and thought was everywhere permanently changed. After Alexander's lightning-like career, the world at once became both larger and smaller. Ptolemy II founded a university, museum, and library, and Alexandria soon equaled Athens as a center of learning. The Museum, dedicated to the Muses, was designed after the Academy and Lyceum in Athens. The keepers of the Library labored to collect every existing Greek work, catalog them, select the best manuscripts for critical editions and commentaries, and make them all available for scholarly research. At its peak of fame the Library contained about a half million volumes (papyrus rolls); these were augmented about 33 BC when Mark Antony captured the Pergamon library and gave the entire collection to Cleopatra, who passed it on to the Alexandria Library. The Museum and Library had on their staff the greatest scholars, writers, and scientists of the Hellenistic era.

The world's first independent sciences arose in Alexandria. The presocratics and Aristotle had speculated about the operations of nature, but, under the impact of Plato's pessimism and the Skeptics' dismal predilections that nothing could be known about anything, three centuries of philosophic guessing had come up with— nothing. Such a gloomy nonepistemology was intolerable to more upbeat thinkers and goaded them into splitting from the grand tradition to go it on their own. So, the pessimism of the philosophers bore the optimism of the scientists. The mathematicians and naturalists connected with the Museum and Library at Alexandria created many of the new sciences.

Euclid of Alexandria (fl. c. 300 BC), the greatest mathematician and geometer of the ancient world, was a member of the Museum's staff and (probably) assisted Ptolemy in establishing the Alexandria Library. When asked by Ptolemy if an easier way to learn geometry didn't exist, he replied that "There is no royal road to geometry." He synthesized all mathematical knowledge accumulated to his time; his *Elements of Geometry* dealt with plane geometry, solid geometry, the theory of magnitudes, and properties of whole numbers. Then, ***Archimedes of Syracuse*** (c. 287–212 BC) studied at Alexandria under Euclid's successors. A distinguished mathematician, he demonstrated that theoretical physics could be developed outside the philosophic tradition. *On the Equilibrium of Planes* is an elegant treatise on physical phenomena. His work on the area of a circle and conic sections paved the way for the discovery of calculus. It was Archimedes who discovered that "a solid body, when weighed in fluid, will be found to be lighter than its weight in air by the weight of the fluid it displaced"—a discovery made when he got into a bathtub and noticed the displaced water splashing over the edge. He then, "without a moment's delay and

Pl. 94¹⁴–95⁵

14 ⲧⲁⲛⲧⲉⲣⲟ ⲁⲡⲉⲓⲱⲧ' ⲉⲥⲧⲏⲧⲱⲛ ⲁⲩⲣⲱⲙⲉ
   ⲛⲉϣϣⲱⲧ' ⲉⲩⲛⲧⲁⲩ' ⲙ̅ⲙⲁⲩ ⲛ̅ⲟⲩⲫⲟⲣⲧⲓ

16 ⲟⲛ ⲉⲁϥϩⲉ ⲁⲩⲙⲁⲣⲅⲁⲣⲓⲧⲏⲥ ⲡⲉϣϣⲱⲧ'
   ⲉⲧⲙ̅ⲙⲁⲩ ⲟⲩⲥⲁⲃⲉ ⲡⲉ ⲁϥϯ ⲡⲉϥⲫⲟⲣⲧⲓⲟⲛ

18 ⲉⲃⲟⲗ ⲁϥⲧⲟⲟⲩ ⲛⲁϥ' ⲁⲡⲓⲙⲁⲣⲅⲁⲣⲓⲧⲏⲥ
   ⲟⲩⲱⲧ' ⲛ̅ⲧⲱⲧⲛ ϩⲱⲧ' ⲧⲏⲩⲧⲛ ϣⲓⲛⲉ ⲛ̅

20 ⲥⲁ ⲡⲉϥⲉϩⲟ ⲉⲙⲁϥⲱϫⲛ ⲉϥⲙⲏⲛ' ⲉⲃⲟⲗ
   ⲡⲙⲁ ⲉⲙⲁⲣⲉϫⲟⲟⲗⲉⲥ ⲧ̅ϩⲛⲟ ⲉϩⲟⲩⲛ' ⲉⲙⲁⲩ

22 ⲉⲟⲩⲱⲙ' ⲟⲩⲇⲉ ⲙⲁⲣⲉϥϥⲛ̅ⲧ ⲧⲁⲕⲟ (77) ⲡⲉϫⲉ
   ⲓ̅ⲥ̅ ϫⲉ ⲁⲛⲟⲕ ⲡⲉ ⲡⲟⲩⲟⲉⲓⲛ ⲡⲁⲉⲓ ⲉⲧϩⲓ

24 ϫⲱⲟⲩ ⲧⲏⲣⲟⲩ ⲁⲛⲟⲕ' ⲡⲉ ⲡⲧⲏⲣϥ' ⲛ̅ⲧⲁ
   ⲡⲧⲏⲣϥ' ⲉⲓ ⲉⲃⲟⲗ ⲛ̅ϩⲏⲧ' ⲁⲩⲱ ⲛ̅ⲧⲁⲡⲧⲏⲣϥ'

26 ⲡⲱϩ ϣⲁⲣⲟⲉⲓ ⲡⲱϩ ⲛ̅ⲛⲟⲩϣⲉ ⲁⲛⲟⲕ'
   ϯⲙ̅ⲙⲁⲩ ϥⲓ ⲙ̅ⲡⲱⲛⲉ ⲉϩⲣⲁⲓ ⲁⲩⲱ ⲧⲉⲧⲛⲁ

28 ϩⲉ ⲉⲣⲟⲉⲓ ⲙ̅ⲙⲁⲩ (78) ⲡⲉϫⲉ ⲓ̅ⲥ̅ ϫⲉ ⲉⲧⲃⲉ ⲟⲩ
   ⲁⲧⲉⲧⲛⲉⲓ ⲉⲃⲟⲗ ⲉⲧⲥⲱϣⲉ ⲉⲛⲁⲩ ⲉⲩⲕⲁϣ

30 ⲉϥⲕⲓⲙ ⲉ[ⲃⲟⲗ] ϩⲓⲧⲛ̅ ⲡⲧⲏⲩ ⲁⲩⲱ ⲉⲛⲁⲩ
   ⲉⲩⲣ[ⲱⲙⲉ ⲉϩ]ⲛ̅ϣⲧⲏⲛ ⲉⲩϭⲏⲛ ϩⲓⲱⲱϥ'

32 [ⲉⲓⲥ ⲛⲉⲧⲛ̅]ⲣⲣⲱⲟⲩ ⲙ̅ⲛ ⲛⲉⲧⲙ̅ⲙⲉⲅⲓ

95 ⲥⲧⲁⲛⲟⲥ ⲛⲁⲉⲓ ⲉⲛ[ϣⲧⲏ]ⲛ [ⲉⲧ]

2 ϭⲏⲛ ϩⲓⲱⲟⲩ ⲁⲩⲱ ⲥⲉ[ⲛⲁ]ϣ ⲥⲟⲩⲛ
   ⲧⲙⲉ ⲁⲛ (79) ⲡⲉϫⲉ ⲟⲩⲥϩⲓⲙ[ⲉ] ⲛⲁϥ ϩⲙ̅

4 ⲡⲙⲏϣⲉ ϫⲉ ⲛⲉⲉⲓⲁⲧ[ⲥ ⲛ̅]ⲑⲏ ⲛ̅
   ⲧⲁϩϥⲓ ϩⲁⲣⲟⲕ ⲁⲩⲱ ⲛ̅ⲕⲓ[ⲃ]ⲉ ⲉⲛⲧⲁϩ

20 ⲡⲉϥⲉϩⲟ ('his treasure'): at first ⲡⲉϥϩⲟ ('his face') to which the second
   ⲉ was added. Correct is ⲡⲉϩⲟ

22 ⲙⲁⲣⲉϥϥⲛ̅ⲧ *sic; l.* ⲙⲁⲣⲉϥⲛ̅ⲧ

The Gnostic Gospel according to Thomas in Coptic script, discovered in 1945 in Upper Egypt. It contains 114 logia— Sayings of Jesus. Logion 77 reads: "Jesus said: I am the Light that is above them all, I am the All, the All came forth from Me and the All attained to Me. Cleave (a piece of) wood, and I am there; lift up the stone and you will find Me there."

transported with joy jumped out of the tub and rushed home naked," shouting all the while "Eureka! Eureka!"—"I found it!"[22]

Strato of Lampsacus (see earlier, in connection with the Lyceum), second scholarch of the Lyceum after Aristotle, became the tutor of Ptolemy's son. In addition to logic and ethics, he wrote on physiology and physics and was one of the first to set up controlled experiments to confirm scientific hypotheses. A careful observer of physical phenomena, he wrote on vacua, weights, acceleration, and falling bodies through space and time. He wrote a (now lost) work, *On Motion*. Cicero said his science "frees God from his great work and me from fear." Strato's labors carried on the tradition Aristotle initiated in his *Mechanics*.

The astronomer **Aristarchos of Samos** (c. 310–230 BC), a pupil of Strato, was also connected to the Museum. With his discovery that the Earth orbits the sun as a fixed center, he brought to a halt the perceived daily movement of the stars across the sky and the annual passage of the sun through the background of stars. His cosmology was Copernican two thousand years before Copernicus. **Ktesibios of Alexandria** (fl. c. 283–247 BC), a physician and engineer, wrote on mechanics, artillary machines, and pneumatics. He noted the elasticity of air and invented compressed air weapons, suction pumps, the thermometer, and the pipe organ.

Eratosthenes of Cyrene (c. 276–c.194 BC), friend of Archimedes and one of the most brilliant all-around scientists of antiquity (he was nicknamed "Pentathlos" to highlight his expertise in the many sciences), became director of the Alexandria

"Eureka! Eureka!"
ARCHIMEDES OF
SYRACUSE

Archimedes declared that it is possible to move any given weight with any given force, and if another world exists somewhere, and he could get to it, he could move it.

PLUTARCH

Library about 255 BC. It was he who first calculated the circumferance of the Earth by observing that at Aswan in Upper Egypt, at noon on the summer solstice, the sun's rays fell vertically, while at Alexandria (500 miles to the north) they fell at an angle of about 7° from vertical. He deduced that the Earth's circumference is about 25,200 miles. He also measured the Earth's tilt on its axis and worked on improving the calendar.

Herophilos of Alexandria (c. 335-280 BC), an anatomist, examined cadavers the government, for which he has been called "the father of anatomy." He wrote precise descriptions of the nervous, vascular, and digestive systems; of the brain, intestines (he named the duodenum), arteries and veins, and the circulatory system; and of the eye, liver, pancreas, genitals, and prostate gland. Using a water clock, he was the first to measure the pulse beat.

The great observational astronomer *Hipparchos of Rhodes* (died sometime after 127 BC) worked at Alexandria. He compiled the first star catalog of some 850 stars, discovered the precession of the equinoxes, and calculated that the tropical year was 1/330 of a day short of the accepted 365 1/4 days. He also laid the first foundations of trigonometry and wrote on physics in a lost work titled *On Bodies Carried Down by Weight*. *Vitruvius* (late first century BC) was a Greek scientist, historian of science, and architect. He argued that philosophy "explains the nature of things" and that many practical problems "cannot be remedied unless one has learned from philosophy the principles that govern natural phenomena."[23] In his *On Architecture* he explored the dynamics of virtually all natural phenomena, from fire to wind currents and from the retrograde motions of planets to devices for pumping water.

Celsus of Rome (b. c. 25 BC), called the Roman Hippocrates, was the greatest of Roman medical writers. He composed a scientific encyclopedia that treated agriculture, the military arts, rhetoric, law, and philosophy; it summarized all medical knowledge as of the first century AD and became a widely used medical text during the Renaissance. *Pliny the Elder* (AD c. 24–79) compiled a thirty-seven-volume encyclopedia, titled *Natural History*, with anthologized materials on astronomy, geography, zoology, botany, medicine, metallurgy, plants, and gemstones (along with myths, fairy tales, and magic). Pliny died in the eruption of Vesuvius in AD 79. *Heron of Alexandria* (fl. AD 62), a brilliant mathematician and engineer, developed the theoretical basis of machinery (wheel and axle, lever, pulleys, wedge, and screw). He also invented a surveyor's sighting instrument and a "steam engine" whose two steam jets rotated a glass sphere mounted above a boiler on an axial shaft.

Claudius Ptolemaeus (fl. AD 127–145), the famed Alexandrian geographer, astronomer, and mathematician, continued the critical spirit of Greek philosophy. He wrote the most influential early work on astronomy, the *Almagest*, describing, with elaborate and subtly persuasive arguments, the geocentric ("Ptolemaic") system that reigned supreme over cosmological theory till the fifteenth century, when the heliocentric ("Copernican") theory replaced it. In his *Optics* he used mathematics and experiments. In his *Geography* he continued the Greek interest in a scientific cartography, and in another work, the *Planisphere*, he explains the fundamentals of stereographic projection. Even in his *Tetrabiblos*, on astrology, Ptolemy's critical spirit can be found.

Galen of Pergamon (AD 129–199) was an experimental physiologist and the last great physician of the Hellenistic era. He compiled in 153 books all knowledge then available on medicine and biology. *Diophantus of Alexandria* (fl. c. AD 250) was a Greek mathematical genius. His *Arithmetic* carried forward Greek algebraic analysis and laid the foundations for its development in Islam. He was the first to use the plus

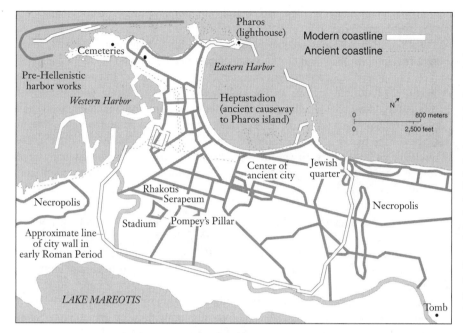

Pharos
(lighthouse)

Modern coastline
Ancient coastline

Cemeteries

Eastern Harbor

Pre-Hellenistic
harbor works

Western Harbor

Heptastadion
(ancient causeway
to Pharos island)

N

0   800 meters
0   2,500 feet

Center of
ancient city

Jewish
quarter

Rhakotis
Serapeum

Necropolis

Necropolis

Stadium

Pompey's Pillar

Approximate line
of city wall in
early Roman Period

LAKE MAREOTIS

Tomb

Within a century of its founding in 321 BC, Alexandria had become a center of scholarship and science; some of the most brilliant thinkers of antiquity—Euclid, Archimedes, Aristarchos, Claudius Ptolemy, Eratosthenes—were associated with its museums and library. This map shows the ancient city as laid out by Alexander, the western and eastern harbors, the lighthouse called Pharos (whose ruins have recently been discovered), and the Serapeum, one of the two world-famous libraries. After prolonged civil wars and deliberate burnings by Christians and Muslims, the museums and libraries were destroyed and Alexandria's greatness came to an end; the Dark Ages began.

and minus signs for mathematical operations; he develop a system of algebraic symbols to stand for an unknown quantity (as we use x) and for powers of the unknown (such as x^2 and x^3). **Pappas of Alexandria** (fl. AD 284–305), a prodigious and versatile mathematician and mechanist, wrote learned commentaries on Euclid and Ptolemy and collected volumes of past knowledge in the field of geometry and preserved it in his *Mathematical Collection*.

Latin science in the West was sustained by only a few bright lights. **Chalcidius** (first part of fourth century AD) conveyed to scientists of the Dark Ages the ideas of natural science from Plato, Aristotle, and the Stoics: these included Aristotle's theories of concentric spheres, prime matter, and the transmutation of elements. He also noted Heraclides' belief that the planets Venus and Mercury orbit around the Sun. Chalcidius's Christian Platonism that influenced the Medieval interpretation of the Greek thinkers.

These are but a few of the working scientists of the Hellenistic era; all were offspring of the empirical tradition, and especially of Aristotle. When the Romans succeeded in subduing the Mediterranean world, Greek science was absorbed by the practical-minded Romans, who promptly allowed it to stagnate since they had little interest in, or talent for, theoretical knowledge of any kind. After the fall of Rome, what little learning had survived was sanctuaried in monasteries, where, during the thousand-year blackout called the Dark Ages, monks continued to copy the few philosophical and scientific writings that had not been lost or burned.

On Aristotle [Aristotle's work is] the greatest synthesis of human thought and knowledge the world has ever known, before or since.

PHILIP WHEELWRIGHT

RISE OF THE NOETIC SYNCRETISMS

It is not surprising that Alexandria also produced the most influential philosophies and theologies of the age or that they were great syncretisms composed of disparate elements from diverse cultures, religions, and worldviews. Inevitably, the new systems reflected different ways of looking at, and valuing, life, and they perpetuated conflicting attitudes toward the nature and function of ideas. From Alexandria the syncretistic mentality and fashion spread to Rome and other cultural centers.

Two quite different kinds of syncretisms emerged from Alexandria's stew of ideas: syncretistic philosophies and harmonizing theologies.

(1) The philosophical syncretists created complex new systems composed of vast collections of doctrines from earlier philosophers. These synthesizers were still philosophers; they still sought the truth, if not through the Socratic tradition of exploratory dialogue or from an Aristotelian empiricism, at least through a putting together of the pieces of the great jigsaw puzzle in an attempt to see the Big Picture. They were still searchers, driven by a modicum of curiosity, asking questions that would lead them toward a better "seeing" of the whole. It was entirely a noetic, not empirical, use of intellect. The Neo-Pythagoreans and Plutarch represented this brand of syncretism.

(2) The religious harmonizing syncretists were theologians rather than philosophers whose goal was essentially the same as the philosophical syncretists—to apprehend the total picture of metaphysical reality. But they came from an entirely different place: They started with a firm and final knowledge of revealed truth and employed Greek philosophy only to explicate and defend their sacred, undoubted "first principles." They were not searching for the truth; they believed they already possessed it. Philosophy for them was essentially the logical enterprise of constructing coherent systems from elements derived from two different worldviews, one that was absolutely true, the other confined to a supportive role. Philo Judaeus, the Neoplatonists, and the medieval Christian theologians represented this form of syncretism.

THE SYNCRETISTIC PHILOSOPHERS

By the late second or early first centuries BC, the mystical ideas of Pythagoras began to reappear in Alexandria reclothed in Platonic, Aristotelian, Stoic, and Skeptical dress. About AD 50 *Apollonius of Tyana,* an ascetic sage (glorified into a mythical hero and miracle worker by the Empress Julia Domna), claimed to be a reincarnation of Pythagoras; he revitalized Pythagorean legends and preached a lifestyle of monastic purity and mystical contemplation. This Neo-Pythagorean eclecticism continued into the second and third centuries AD with the work of Neo-Pythagorean Platonists *Moderatus of Gades, Nicomachus of Gerasa*, and *Numenius of Apamea,* who effectively transformed Neo-Pythagoreanism into Neoplatonism and ended its career as an independent movement. About AD 300 a Syrian Neoplatonist named *Iamblichus,* who also considered himself a faithful Pythagorean, composed the final noteworthy synthesis of Pythagorean doctrine. Both Neo-Pythagorean and Neoplatonist syncretisms had enormous influence on Judaic and Christian theology.

The much-admired *Plutarch of Chaeronea* (c. AD 46–120) can be thought of as both Neo-Pythagorean and Platonist (we are reminded creative thinkers rarely can be classified with simple categories). He was a teacher and lecturer on philosophy credited with writing 227 books. Known primarily for his *Parallel Lives,* a collection of forty-four biographies of Greek and Roman heroes, he also wrote *Ethica,* which is some sixty morality tales in dialogue form, and a touching *Consolation* to his wife Timoxena on the death of their two-year-old baby girl. Life really does bring more pleasure than pain, he assured her, and lovely memories of their daughter outweigh the pain of losing her. Most of his work has survived. Though he traveled widely, he settled for a quiet life in a small town in northern Boeotia.

Plutarch studied at the Academy in Athens and maintained close ties with it all his life; his philosophical theology was a Platonism heavily influenced by Pythagorean, Aristotelian, Stoic, Epicurean, Cynical, and Skeptical doctrines—all syncretized and

As for our canonical authors, God forbid that they should differ.

SAINT AUGUSTINE

It is not by demonstration that they [the prophets of old] have advanced their statement, for they are witnesses of the truth beyond any demonstration.

JUSTIN MARTYR

The studies of philosophy are aids in treating of the truth.

CLEMENT OF ALEXANDRIA

colored by his own mystical temperament. His system was entirely noetic. God is transcendent, out of reach and out of touch. He alone is fully real; all other existences are less real than the ineffable God, who cannot be known by humans. But this distant deity does make himself known to humanity in small and studied revelations through lesser gods, angels, spirits, and even the gods of the Greeks and other religions. It was through these derivative deities that the material world was created.

Two world-souls also exist, one good, one bad (a dualism not unlike the Zoroastrian story of Good versus Evil, from which Plutarch's cosmology may have come). These cosmic forces are locked in eternal struggle with each other; good and bad spirits and good and bad humans are the foot soldiers fighting the never-ending battle. Humans possess a soul derived from both world-souls; the evil component is felt in the desires of the flesh, and the good component has its locus in the faculties of reason. The rational part of our soul soars upward at death to join the angels, while the lower part will likely become reincarnate in some bodily form.

Plutarch's ethics was central to his thinking. Since humans possess free will, we are responsible for our decisions, and our suffering is a consequence of bad decisions that allow our lower natures to determine our behavior. Not all our passions are bad, however, for they can be controlled and channeled according to reason; when we do this, the good world-soul within us scores a personal victory over the evil world-soul.

Plutarch's theology was a major step forward in developing Neoplatonism, which in turn influenced Judaic and Christian speculations for the next millennium. The soteriological framework of all these noetic theologies postulates the imprisonment of the human soul in an evil material body of sensual flesh, and the struggling soul must find release through obedience to spiritual promptings.

Faith is the pioneer of reason, and discovers the territory which reason explores.
PHILIP SCHAFF

THE HARMONIZING THEOLOGIANS

A sizable Jewish population lived in Alexandria almost from the day of its founding; Alexander himself assigned the district where Jews were to reside. During the third century BC Jewish scholars became deeply Hellenized and it was in Alexandria, as nowhere else, that Hebrew religion confronted the best in Greek thought and culture. Jewish intellectuals rapidly mastered the Greek philosophers and were struck by how often they encountered ideas and values familiar to them from their own Scriptures. But they faced a problem. Although the Greek philosophers were exciting and deserved serious study, the foundations of knowledge already had been firmly laid through revelation by YHWH/God in the Torah and by the Prophets; no additional truths remained to be sought. The Good Life Socrates described as the golden achievement of a rational life was really possible only through a faith-full acceptance of, and obedience to, God's truth; and man's reasoning faculty, left to follow its own inclinations, could be a useless and even dangerous instrument.

But for those with intellects, blind belief does not gratify; the problem remained. Upon reflection it looked to them as though the Greeks had received dark glimmerings of the light fully revealed to the Chosen remnant. From this insight it was but a short step to the inference that Greek thinkers were in fact influenced by the Hebrew Scriptures, and even that YHWH/God had revealed his doctrines to the Greeks, though in allegorical form. One Jewish scholar concluded that Moses had taught the alphabet to the Greeks; another decided that Moses had created the Egyptian civilization. Once these recognitions were established, it was only left for them to search through both secular philosophy and sacred Scripture to find hidden parallels, and then to employ rational analysis to clarify and defend the divinely given truths. The task of a philosopher, therefore, is to harmonize secular speculations with sacred facts.

Fides proecedit intellectum.
Faith must exist before one can understand.
SAINT ANSELM OF CANTERBURY

Thus the intellect was made subservient to faith, and philosophy became the hand-maiden of theology.

The most eminent figure in Alexandrian philosophy and literature was **Philo Judaeus** (20 BC–AD 40). Gifted with a synthesizing mind, and deeply versed both in Judaic literature and Greek philosophy, he spent a lifetime weaving strands of the two together, warp and woof, into a new philosophico-religious fabric. He drew largely from Plato and Aristotle, the Stoics, and Neo-Pythagoreans and some from the Skeptics. Little is known of his life aside from his belonging to a prominent Alexandrian family and, in AD 40, his heading a delegation to the Emperor Caligula to plea, on behalf of the Jewish community, that persecutions cease.

Philo's God is transcendent—totally, essentially, absolutely; he is so completely Other and Beyond that he must reveal himself to finite humans through nature, myth and allegory, and even polytheism and poetry. God is not good or beautiful or holy; he is *beyond* goodness and beauty and holiness, *beyond* all human concepts, apprehensions, and nomenclature. Nothing whatever can be said of God. All that can be said is to describe what God is not. "Eh-yeh," God said, "I am who I am"; beyond that—nothing. From this metaphysical nihilism began the Western tradition known as "negative theology." °

Such a totally transcendent deity did not—can not—create this essentially evil world, nor can he communicate directly with it. The World was created through the Logos and countless lesser logoi that function as intermediaries between the Other and the world of physical things; through them dark intimations of the Other are communicated to humans. God governs the World in two ways: through the laws of nature planted by the Logos into the original creation of matter, and by direct and immediate divine intervention into the concrete moment-by-moment situations of life.

Human beings are composed of a bit of the divine Logos imprisoned in a sense-driven body. This body, created of evil matter—like the Gnostics, who followed Plato, Philo located all evil in the amorphous, recalcitrant nature of matter itself—is the enemy of the spirit and isolates each human being from the divine. Thus, we humans are born into a condition already infected with an inclination toward evil. The goal toward which we must strive is to escape from prison. We accomplish this by with-drawing from the world, fixing our focus on God by meditating on him day and night, and seeking inner quietude through an ecstatic union with the ineffable Other.

Philo's harmonization of the massive accumulation of Judaic teachings with all of Greek philosophy was a gargantuan task requiring a synoptic mind, a prodigious memory, and a lifetime of rationalizing thought. What he was doing, in his own mind, was solving the mysteries a critical intellect discerned in Judaic Scripture and clarifying the truths of the Judaic heritage. All true knowledge, Philo wrote, is acquired under the immediate inspiration of God/Logos.

HEYDAY OF THE GNOSTIC THEOLOGIANS

Late in the first century AD, there arose a movement that was to challenge all the residual Greek philosophies, Greek religion, and a rapidly growing but embryonic Christianity; by the end of the second century, it was found throughout Egypt and Syria (where it originated), Asia Minor, north Africa, Gaul, and especially Rome. This new "-ism" possessed an epic myth answering every conceivable question about the cosmos and the human condition, and it supplied strong ethical guidelines for the conduct of daily life. From the Greek word for "knowledge," *gnosis*, it got its name: Gnosticism.

Credo quia absurdum est. *I believe because it is absurd.*

TERTULLIAN

For by doubting we come to inquiry, by inquiry we discover the truth.

ABÉLARD

°*This concept of an absolutely Other God is neither Hebrew nor Greek and stands as Philo's own contribution to Western theology. See "negative theology" in lexicon.*

Credo ut intelligam. *I believe in order to understand.*

SAINT ANSELM

Gnosticism was the most massive syncretism ever created by the human mind. It was like a great salad, or a whole festival of salads, concocted by very, very creative chefs. The ingredients varied. In one location it had more lettuce and less tomatoes; in another, more onions and radishes; in still another, more cucumbers, peppers, and lots of tomatoes but no radishes; and so on. No two salads were the same. They all looked like salads and tasted like salads, and they all nourished;° but the mixtures differed, as did the wild variety of garnishes and dressings used to flavor them.

Philosophically, Gnosticism drew heavily from Plato—the notion of aeons, dualism of the ideal world versus the material world, the fall of souls, sin arising from matter, and the soul as prisoner in the body; from Pythagoras—numbers as mystical symbols; from the Stoics—physics and ethics; and even from Homer and other Greek classics. But Gnosticism's dominant ingredients were religious ideas and images drawn from Zoroastrianism—cosmic dualism of Good and Evil, Light and Darkness, the Satan figure, and reification of abstractions; from Judaism—the Jehovah God, Apocryphal literature, and elements from the Kabbala; from Christianity—the doctrine of redemption, a Christ-figure, and they regarded Christianity as the supreme development of all religion; from a Buddhism that was gradually moving into western Asia—docetic appearances, asceticism; and from countless other, frequently local, sources. It was a highly complex system favored by intellectuals; it was never popular with the masses. In the later speculations of Basilides and Valentinus (c. AD 150), it became an epic myth spread out on an apocalyptic scale, a picture painted on a cosmic canvas than which nothing more grandiose could be imagined. And it was usually a true syncretism, not just a loose eclecticism, whose ingredients were blended together into a coherent story with a continuous plotline.

Gnosticism was a theology rather than a philosophy. Its literature is filled with visions, angelic messengers, demons, heavenly voices, talking animals, resurrections, miracles, healings, and punishments. It describes earthquakes and thunder and lightning to scare nonbelievers; supernatural lights, fires, winds, and waters obeying the commands of the righteous; serpents, tigers, leopards, and bears sicced on evildoers; martyrs crowned with roses and dusted with incense; and an abyss that swallows up antagonists. All this was interspersed with hymns, prayers, and long "theological" discourses.[24]

°. . . they all poisoned! said the church fathers.

We might speak of philosophy itself as being ancillary to Christianity.

ORIGEN

THE STORY

All the Gnosticisms shared a great teleocosmic drama . It begins with a supreme God called "the Deep" (*Bythos*), a vast eternal realm of Being beyond being, beyond all predications and human comprehension; he is completely transcendent, the wholly Other, the ineffable Absolute. Gnostic writings, therefore, contain voluminous descriptions of what he is not and thus contribute to the tradition of "negative theology."

The curtain rises on the epic drama when the Deep stirs and, out of his love, sends forth emanations, thirty in all. They are personified beings named Mind, Grace, Reason, Wisdom, Knowledge, Power, Truth, Life—all aspects or qualities of the Deep. These beings—called "Aeons"—form a halo of brilliant light around the Deep called the Pleroma ("fullness"), the divine realm. The farther the Aeons emanate from the Deep, the darker and weaker they become. Two of these Aeons play special roles in the unfolding drama: Anthropos ("Primal Man"), a primordial principle (somewhat like Plato's Real Idea of Man); and Sophia ("Wisdom"), the youngest and one of the most remote (number twenty-eight) of the Aeons so far created.

Then a great crisis rocks the Pleroma. Driven by a passion to reunite with the Deep, Sophia, in a single moment, crosses forbidden boundaries, plunges back into the Deep, and thereafter brings forth an *ektrôma*, a being "untimely born" (a "miscarriage" or sometimes translated as a "live abortion"), an amorphous substance (referred to by Moses when he wrote that "the earth was without form and void"). This is the Fall, and because of it Sophia suffers uncontrollable fear, anxiety, and despair.

Sophia's actions initiate a falling away from the divine realm. Like irreversible waves of radiation emanating from an exploding supernova, the falling cannot be stopped, even though all the Aeons attempt to stop it. Sophia and countless lower powers are expelled out of the Pleroma.

One of the descending beings, a loathsome monster called the Demiurge (Plato's "Demiurgos" described in the *Timaeus*), now proceeds to create the material universe, using the heavenly order as a template for the physical order. He creates seven spherical heavens and thus becomes the supreme Archon ("Lord," "Ruler") of the (physical) heavens and Earth. He is arrogant, sinister, manipulative, and malevolent. All physical matter created by this evil being is itself evil, and anything *made* of this evil matter is evil. The Demiurge is identified (in the Christian Gnosticisms) with the creator deity of the Old Testament. This ignorant world-maker thinks he is the one and only. "I alone am God!" he asserts. "NOT!" comes the reply. "Above you and before you and higher than you is Anthropos the Primal Man."

The seven lesser archons now become the creators of earthly humans, composed of body and soul, fashioned in their image from the substance of Primal Man. (These archons are the beings quoted in Genesis 1:26 who said "Let us make man in our image.") But Sophia, having been expelled from the Pleroma, and falling like a spark of light into the dark world of evil matter, secretly implants in each human soul a seed of pure spiritual substance called *pneuma* ("breath," "spirit"). Imprisoned in an evil body, the pneuma longs to return to its source.° Within each human being, therefore, a never-ending struggle will occur between the evil material body and the upward-reaching pneuma-spirit. The other archons fight to keep each seed imprisoned in its alien host.

°*This longing is called "epistrophe" by Plotinus; see what he makes of it, p. 273, and see lexicon.*

Sophia, too, cries out for redemption. So out of his compassion the Deep himself, urged on by the sympathetic Aeons, creates a last pair of Aeons who will be the agents of cosmic redemption. These are (according to Christian Gnostics) Christ and Holy Spirit. They comfort Sophia and remove the Untimely from the Pleroma. Then the thirty Aeons together send forth one more Aeon to be the spouse of Sophia. His name is Sotêr ("Savior"), or Jesus. After further sufferings, Sophia is purged of all her sin and is returned to the Pleroma as the bride of Jesus.

In us humans the longing of the pneuma-seed is not in vain. It can indeed be extricated from the evil body so that it can return to bathe in the Pleroma's pure light. The secret of this extrication is the possession of a special gnosis, a knowledge that saves. The content of this gnosis is a set of beliefs about the the nature of the human condition (as explained by the epic myth) and behavioral requirements inferred from the story. All those chosen as recipients of the redemptive gnosis become "Pneumatics" and begin a return journey that, after death, will carry the pneuma-laden souls through the seven spheres, past the gate-guarding archons, to reunite with the Pleroma and, perhaps, with the Deep. In Judaic/Christian forms of Gnosticism, this saving gnosis was first introduced in the Garden of Eden when the serpent brought the forbidden gnosis to Adam and Eve. The tyrannical Jehovah had mandated that men and women should remain ignorant and obedient, like children; but the good serpent, defying the mean-spirited autocrat, brought the precious gnosis to the first couple, whose eyes were then opened so that they could know life. This was the opening shot on the great battlefield of cosmic redemption. After Eden the revelations of sacred gnosis continued through Moses, the prophets, Jesus, and other channels, such as the Buddha and Zoroaster.

So the pneumatic spark in a human being is not of this world, though before a soul receives gnosis it will be unaware of its own existence; it is benumbed, asleep. But when awakened by knowledge, it becomes not merely aware of its longing but of how that longing can be satisfied.

Redemption is not merely personal but cosmic. As individual pneumatics return through the Pleroma to the Deep, a great reversal is initiated that climaxes with the fiery destruction of the physical world and a re-realization of the pristine state of divine nonexistence. Finally, God himself, the Demiurge, is saved. He returns to the eternal imperturbability of the Deep.

THE GNOSTICS

Outlandish in its imagery and implausible to a modern mind—or even to a mildly empirical mind—in its sweeping excursion into every nook and cranny of human experience, Gnosticism attempted to solve many of the perennial problems of philosophy and religion. These included questions about cosmogony and eschatology, the origins of evil, why we feel alienated and in need of redemption, the relationship of spirit and matter, directions for right living, and so on. To their satisfaction, the Gnostics answered them all.

As early as about AD 60, Saint Paul encountered Gnosticism and furiously attacked it. Christ is not merely one of the aeons, he wrote to the Ephesians (1:20–2:10), for God seated him "at his right hand in heaven, far above all primal powers, mighty authorities, battle forces, and angelic orders, and (above) all titles bestowed not only in the present existence (*aeon*) but also in the age to come." Paul was even more irate when he told the Colossians (1:12–23) that Christ and Christ alone *is* the pleroma—"the entire fullness (*plêrôma*) chose to dwell in him" (1:19); "it is in him that the fullness (*plêrôma*) of God's nature lives embodied" (2:9). Paul prayed that the Colossians would be filled with wisdom (sophia) and spiritual insight (*pneumatikê*). He said God has assured us we have been rescued from "the dominion of darkness" so that we may live in "the realm of light." God through Christ, not through some mythic Demiurge, created everything, including "kingly thrones, angelic orders, supreme powers (primal forces), authorities." Paul ends his letter (2:8) with the warning, "Take care that nobody but nobody exploits you through the pretensions of philosophy." °

Details of the epic myth varied in the different systems, both in its theological structure and its ethical inferences. The schools of Basilides, Valentinus, and Marcion were heavy on Christian elements. ***Basilides*** taught in Alexandria about AD 125 and claimed to be a disciple of the apostle Matthew. His followers developed a docetic (Greek *dokêsis*, "fanciful vision") theory of Christ's crucifixion, teaching that Jesus could not have had a physical body (since matter is evil) and therefore was not (could not have been) crucified. They said that on the way to Golgotha Simon of Cyrene exchanged places with the docetic Christ-spirit; he slipped in under the cross, carried it to the hill of crucifixion, and there provided the physical body needed for the cross.

Valentinus taught in Rome about AD 140, where he produced the most elaborate of the Gnostic systems and the one that most aroused the hatred of Christian apologists. A creative genius from Alexandria, he had moved within the church but, when slighted over for promotion, became disillusioned and moved to Rome about AD 140. He turned to Gnosticism and in his many volumes of theology put a Gnostic spin on virtually every orthodox Christian belief. Valentinus's brand of Gnosticism

°*See also 1 Cor. 12:8 and 1 Tim. 6:20.*

became the most influential of all the syncretistic salads, reaching its greatest popularity about AD 165. Tertullian, the Christian theologian from Carthage and one of the period's most remarkable thinkers, commented that Valentinus's version of Gnosticism "transmogrifies into as many shapes as a courtesan who daily changes her dress and then keeps fussing with it."

"God is all love," Valentinus said, "but love is not love except there is some object of affection." So the thirty Aeons were paired. The first pair, Nous (male) and Aletheia (female) ("Mind" and "Truth"), bring forth the heavenly Christ (m.) and the Holy Spirit (f.). This heavenly Christ first reveals to all the Aeons that a plan of redemption exists, at which the Aeonic choirs sing out with anthems of joy and thanksgiving. The Sôtêr figure also exists, created by all the Aeons together; in union with the redeemed Sophia, they form the final coupled pair. Finally, according to Valentinus, there is an earthly Christ, the Jewish messiah born of Mary (through whose body he moved like water through a pipe). The heavenly Christ descended upon the lower Christ at the baptism in the form of a dove to announce the arrival on Earth of the secret gnosis.

Most of the Gnostic cults were ascetic. They reasoned, quite logically, that if matter is evil and the body is composed of matter, then the proper attitude toward the evil body is one of contempt. So, they forbade meat, wine, and sensuous foods; prohibited sexual gratification within (or without) marriage; eschewed attendance at festivities; counseled the virtues of self-deprivation; and recommended strict self-control in everything—with the goal of denigrating the body to elevate the spirit. The ascetic Gnostics counted among their sects the followers of Marcion, Saturninus, Tatian, and Mani.

But a surprising number of Gnostic cults took a different, but equally logical, turn. If the body is truly evil, then a faithful pneumatic should attempt to conquer its cravings; and this is to be done not by avoiding those cravings but by mastering them. Sensuality is to be overcome, not repressed. The only way to accomplish this it to accept the human senses, let them lead, and attempt to gratify them to saturation, at which point they lose their power. It is no great thing, one Gnostic said, to bridle our lusts, but it is truly a great accomplishment when we can indulge them and not let them conquer us. "The flesh must be abused," preached **Nicolas of Antioch** (who is mentioned in Acts 6:5), and his Nicolaitans abused it with great relish. Of course, horrified church fathers interpreted their abusings as shameless immorality. In Revelation 2:6 and 15 John tells his readers in Ephesus and Pergamon "to hate the Nicolaitans just as I do" and repent "or else I'll come to you immediately and start a war against them with the sword of my mouth." The Gnostic libertines produced a vast literature, and their sects—Nicolaitans, Ophites, Simonians, Carpocratians, and Antitactae, among others—were found throughout the Roman Empire.

One other, and later, Gnostic religion came from the East and spread westward through the empire. In the third century AD a Persian philosopher and astronomer named **Mani** syncretized elements from Zoroastrianism and Christianity to produce a revolutionary quasi-Gnostic system. Mani came from an affluent family in Hamadan and was educated in Babylonia. While still young he experienced a revelation in which he was chosen to be the prophet of a new religion: "Mani, the apostle of Jesus Christ, by the providence of God the Father—these are the words of salvation from the eternal and living source"—the words that opened his scriptures. After initial successes in his preaching, he ran afoul of Zoroastrian priests and fled to India and China, learning Buddhism along the way. When he returned to Persia in AD 270, he was apprehended, tried, crucified, flayed, and hung by the city gate of Djondishapur.

The cosmic framework of Mani's Gnosticism was pure Zoroastrian dualism. The world is a great eternal battleground between the Kingdom of Light and the Kingdom of Darkness. In the beginning Satan and his dark demons launched an attack on the righteous kingdom, and in the resulting struggle the world was born, an unhappy mixture of darkness and light. Satan created Adam from evil matter but with a spark of spiritual light; he created Eve also, but she was given a smaller spark of light. (All men have a little more light than women, according to Mani.) Every human being is likewise composed of an evil body and soul but with a redeemable spirit within. The entire cosmos, including singular beings, is fighting to escape from the darkness into the light. The longing of the world-soul to escape its dark shackles is seen in every seedling that emerges from the darkened ground, in every rose that blooms and every plane tree that spreads its branches in the sun. The true Manichaean would never crush a flower, cut down a tree, or injure a living thing that, like himself, was struggling upward toward the light.

Just as the great goal of cosmic history is the separation of light from darkness, so the goal of life for a Manichaean is to free the spirit from the clutches of dark matter. This is accomplished through lifelong ascetic disciplines: practicing pure thoughts and words, holding to a vegetarian diet, releasing the self from all material things, revering nature, and avoiding all sensual gratification.

After Mani's death his teachings spread rapidly in Turkistan, Mesopotamia, and the Roman Empire as far as Italy and Spain. Both pre-Christian and Christian emperors continually persecuted his followers. Manichaeism everywhere possessed an effective organization under the leadership of Mani's successors: twelve apostles, seventy-two bishops, presbyters, deacons, and wandering evangelists. It continued to flourish into the sixth century AD. Its most prominent later disciple (for nine years) was the young Saint Augustine.° °See p. 303f.

In 1945 thirteen papyrus scrolls, still bound in leather, were discovered in the ruins of an ancient cliffside tomb near the town of Nag-Hamâdi, Egypt. They were the remains of a Gnostic library. Stashed in jars, preserved for sixteen centuries in the wonderfully dry sands of Upper Egypt, they apparently represented the work of a vibrant Gnostic community that spoke and wrote Coptic. Among the books was *The Gospel according to Thomas*, a Gnostic gospel containing 114 sayings and parables of Jesus, some of them familiar from the canonical gospels, some new and strange. Many have a decidedly Gnostic tone.

> Within a man of light there is light and he lights the whole world *(kosmos)*.
> When he does not shine, there is darkness. (Logion 24)

The Pharisees and the Scribes have received the keys of Knowledge *(gnosis)*, (but) they have hidden them. (Logion 39)

Jesus said: If they say to you: "From where have you originated?", say to them: "We have come from the Light, where the Light has originated through itself." (Logion 50)

Jesus said: I am the Light that is above them all, I am the All, the All came forth from Me and the All attained to Me. Cleave a (piece of) wood, (and) I am there; lift up the stone and you will find Me there. (Logion 77)[25]

Impact of Gnosticism

For the history of philosophy, Gnosticism is one of the most significant of the ancient philosophico/theological systems.

(1) It became a role-model for subsequent noetic systems, most notably Neoplatonism, the Judeo-Greek systems such as that of Philo Judaeus, and the Christian-

Greek theologies of Saints Augustine and Aquinas. Without Gnosticism to lay strong foundations for a noetic tradition, it is an open question (we are reminded that "history does not reveal its alternatives") whether the creation of such extreme nonempirical systems would ever have become fashionable.

(2) Gnosticism created a major crisis in the young Christian communities everywhere. So strong was its threat that the most vigorous ecclesiastical intellects devoted entire lives to the death-struggle against Gnostic ideas; and it was they, responding to Gnostic "heresies," that created what is known as the Old Catholic Church and brought about the development and crystalization of western catholic theology.

After Saint Paul's early attacks on Gnosticism, virtually every patristic father for the next two centuries joined the battle. The author of *Revelation* opposed Kerinthos in Asia Minor. Hippolytus of Rome attacked the Gnostics everywhere, scoured the Greek philosophic tradition for their sources, and wrote his *Philosophumena* against Basilides. In north Africa Tertullian wrote against Valentinus and the Carthaginian painter Hermogenes (noting that "he married more women than he painted"). Irenaeus of Lyons attacked the libertines ("I hate the deeds of the Nicolaitans") and fought long and hard against Valentinus, as did Justin Martyr in his *Syntagma against All Heresies*. Polycarp of Smyrna called Marcion "the first-born of Satan." Origen of Alexandria wrote vigorously against the followers of Valentinus. Saint Augustine wrote knowledgably against the Manichaeans (for nine years he had been one) in his *Contra Epistolam Manichaei* and *Contra Faustum Manichaei*.

Gradually, out of the fire and smoke of battle, a clearer Christian theology and a tightly organized ecclesia emerged. Since Gnostic theologians had tossed together the ingredients of the great salad and covered it with Gnostic dressing, Christian theologians carefully sifted through every detail of faith and Scripture for its truth or falsity. Thus, the distinction between orthodoxy (truth) and heresy (false teaching) was born, the first, of course, to be taught and the latter to be fought. In Alexandria Christian theologians (influenced by Platonism and the logos doctrine) labored on the doctrine of the incarnation, the Trinity, and Christology. The North African churchmen worked intensively on problems of human nature and salvation. Irenaeus worked to clarify the unity of God, creation of the world, incarnation of the Logos (against Gnostic docetism), the divinity of Christ, the resurrection of the body, the Antichrist, the millennium, and the end of the world. And so on ad infinitum.

By AD 200 the defense of the truth was complete. About AD 185 Irenaeus submitted that the Apostles preached with "perfect knowledge," and their written Gospels were therefore authoritative and final. That perfect knowledge, he said, had been transmitted down through a succession of bishops who were keepers of the sacred tradition and must be obeyed. Moreover, Irenaeus argued, the organized church is the depository of all Christian teaching "since the Apostles, like a rich man in a bank, lodged in her hands most copiously all things pertaining to the truth."[26] By AD 150 instruction in the true "apostolic teaching" was given to prospective members before baptism.

Thus, by about AD 200, largely in response to the Gnostic challenge, western Christendom had developed a definitive creed, a canon of authoritative scripture, and powerful episcopal leadership; with these formidable weapons, it had successfully defended its sacred heritage. Before the rise of Gnosticism, to be a Christian required only that one acknowledge Jesus as Lord and receive baptism. After the great battle, Christians were required to pledge their acceptance of the established creed, follow the approved scriptural canon (Old and New Testaments), and submit to the absolute authority of the bishops.

RETROSPECTIVE AND LEGACY

"A sense of wonder started men philosophizing," wrote Aristotle. "Their wondering is aroused, first by trivial matters; but they continue on from there to wonder about less mundane matters such as the changes of the moon, sun, and stars, and the beginnings of the universe. What is the result of this puzzlement? *An awesome feeling of ignorance*. Men began to philosophize, therefore, to escape ignorance. . . ."

Plato added that this "feeling of wonder is the touchstone of the philosopher, and all philosophy has its origins in wonder."

In 322 BC this sense of wonder was still alive and well. Freedom prevailed in the city-state of Athens just long enough for a serious exploration of the world to begin. For more than two centuries philosophers were upbeat about the possibility of understanding how the world works and finding the truth about our place in it. The puzzlements resulting from their investigations were mind boggling, but with the best minds of the age asking a billion questions, the shadows of ignorance had begun to recede.°

°Note the conditions that supported philosophical inquiry in the time of the presocratics and Socrates, pp. 23, 94–97.

By AD 250 all such inquiry had ceased. The best minds of the post-Hellenistic age had come to fear ideas that differed, so they spent their time defending an established set of beliefs beyond which there was nothing more to be discovered. Whereas in 322 BC the mental outlook among knowledgeable minds was one of humility and openness to learning, by AD 250 the mentality of the learned was defensive and closed to learning. Thoughts that didn't jibe with established parameters were fought off by attacks on those who thought them. Curiosity was punished. Questions were suppressed. Knowledge of this world had become unimportant; knowledge of the next world had become all important. Without new frontiers to explore, without the excitement of pushing back the dark horizons of ignorance and not knowing, human minds were plunged into a long age of stagnation. The millennial hibernation of critical thought called the Dark Ages had begun.

Why did this happen? In this chapter several lines of philosophic development have been traced. Doubtless others existed, but these are clear.

In the mainstream philosophies of the Academy and Lyceum no first-rate, fearless, creative minds emerged to hold on to the Socratic style of critical inquiry; philosophers largely spent their time rehashing the great ideas of earlier thinkers.

Then the pragmatic philosophers began to teach that philosophy's job was to make life not knowledgeable but happy, so they spent their intellectual lives working out systems of ideas (beliefs) for themselves and their followers to live by. The pursuit of objective truth fell by the wayside.

When the Skeptics came onto the scene with their denial that the human mind can ever know the true nature of the real world, their counsel of despair infected philosophical exploration for the next five centuries and discouraged the asking of theoretical questions that might have led to the discovery of true knowledge about nature and humanity.

A few diehard thinkers rejected both the skeptical influences and the fashionable noetic metaphysics and proceeded to look at the world anyway, but to do this they found it expedient to withdraw from the grand philosophic tradition and carry on special investigations in their own way. Though their empirical labors were to be wonderfully fruitful, their withdrawal left the field to the idealist philosophers whose subject matter was confined to the realm of the mind. The result of this refocusing was the creation of the great noetic synthesizing systems. In the speculative tradition of philosophy, the idealists were in, the empiricists were out.

What ensued, with seeming inevitability, was a battle of the great noetic systems. Without a real world to keep philosophic reflection anchored and against which ideas could be empirically checked, the battle became largely a power-struggle between speculative worldviews. With the advent of the religious harmonizers whose *archai* ("starting points") were revealed truths, philosophy was transformed into theology, at which point the power-struggle became one of pitting Ultimate Authorities against one another. No authority could be more ultimate than the One True God who revealed a special knowledge to a special chosen elect through a special revelation. With this, the harmonizers brought forth a new concept into the intellectual tradition of the West, the claim that the full truth was already known (it had been known all along) and that there was really nothing more to be sought. The Gnostic claim that only a select few were in possession of Knowledge (gnosis) encouraged an exclusivism of the elite, an aristocentrism that distinguished the elect from the not elect, the saved from the not saved.

By the time the great battle with Gnosticism ended, the weapons necessary for defending the truth of the Christian ecclesia against offending ideas were in place. Freedom to think creatively, freedom to explore the heavens and the Earth, had been laid to rest. Differing ideas were anathematized, differing points of view forbidden. "As for our canonical authors," Saint Augustine wrote, "God forbid that they should differ."[27]

Philosophy had become the handmaiden of theology. In Judaism, Christianity, and Islam, philosophy's role was "to justify the ways of God to man." "We might speak of philosophy itself as being ancillary to Christianity," wrote Origen of Alexandria. "The studies of philosophy are [merely] aids in the treatment of the truth," argued Clement of Alexandria. "The [Hebrew] prophets didn't have to justify their statements by [empirical] demonstration, for they are witnesses to a truth that is beyond demonstration"—so wrote Justin Martyr.[28]

Philo had reasoned that only one Truth can exist, and philosophy, when properly conducted, will always arrive at the Truth revealed in Scripture. But Tertullian, the first Christian father to write in Latin, responded with the declaration that faith and philosophy are incompatible. "What has the Academy to do with the Church?" he stormed; "What has Christ to do with Plato, Jerusalem with Athens?" Perhaps philosophy and faith could be compatible friends or, maybe, coworkers? Absolutely not, he said. "Let us have nothing to do with a Stoic Christianity, or a Platonist or dialectical Christianity. All curiosity is at an end after Jesus, all research after the Gospel. Let us have faith, and wish for nothing more." Christianity is to be believed, not intellectualized. *"Credo quia absurdum est,"* he wrote. "I believe because it is absurd" (referring to Christian truth and specifically to the doctrine that God sacrificed himself on the cross). "For Tertullian Christianity was a great divine foolishness, wiser than the highest philosophical wisdom of men, and in no way to be squared with existing philosophical systems."[29] °

°See pp. 288ff.

This mentality continued through the Dark Ages. *"Credo ut intelligam,"* declared Saint Anselm of Canterbury about AD 1100; "I do not seek to understand in order that I may believe, but I believe in order that I may understand, for of this I feel sure, that, if I did not believe, I would not understand." *"Fides proecedit intellectum,"* he said, "Faith must exist *before* one can understand." Even in orthodox circles, however, a few dissenters arose, such as Abélard, writing some two decades after Amselm, who insisted Anselm had it backwards: "It is by doubting that we come to inquiry, and it is by inquiry that we discover the truth." But Abelard was fighting a losing battle and lost considerably more than a philosophical argument.[30] °

°See pp. 350ff.

The mind-set of the Dark Ages has been summarized in a single sentence: "I already knew the answer, so I didn't have to think."[31] A "Dark Age" existed in each soul deprived of the light of learning.

In Arabia the religion of Mohammed was preaching a different attitude toward learning. Greek science was precious to Muslims, for they saw knowledge of the world as one more way to know Allah. Muslim intellectuals and scientists eagerly sought the writings of the Greeks and translated them into Syriac, Persian, and Arabic. By AD 900 the works of Plato and Aristotle and the classics of Greek mathematics, astronomy, and medicine were available throughout the Arabic world. Muslim astronomers built observatories so that they could check Greek predictions against empirical observations. The Arabs made innovative advances in virtually every field of inquiry.

In November of AD 1095 Pope Urban II called for a crusade against the Saracens, and shortly thereafter, and for the next two centuries, Christians encountered the literary riches of Islamic culture. As the Muslims withdrew from Moorish Spain, Constantinople, and the Holy Land, they left behind their precious books, which were recovered by eager monks and scholars who learned Arabic and translated the writings of the Greeks into Latin. By AD 1200 much of Greek philosophy and science was available in the West, and a reawakening of the spirit of critical inquiry began, though for another century philosophy was treated as a harmonizing discipline. What we call the Dark Ages only gradually passed into history. Intellectual ferment continued through the Renaissance and then, at the beginning of the seventeenth century, began to accelerate with the work of Bacon, Galileo, Brahe and Kepler, and then Newton and the new empiricists.

ENDNOTES

1 Philip Schaff, *History of the Christian Church*, vol. 2, *Ante-Nicene Christianity* (Scribner's, 1910; reprint, Eerdmans, 1950), p. 96.
2 Marcus Aurelius, *Meditations*, V.33.
3 Diogenes Laërtius, *Lives of Eminent Philosophers*, IX.61–108.
4 Diogenes, *Lives*, IX.61.
5 See pp. 96ff.
6 Diogenes, *Lives*, IX.74, 76.
7 Diogenes, *Lives*, IX.61, 103–108.
8 Diogenes, *Lives*, IX.109–116.
9 Diogenes, *Lives*, IV.28–45, 62–66; IX.78–88.
10 Diogenes, *Lives*, IV.1–5.
11 Diogenes, *Lives*, IV.6–15.
12 Diogenes, *Lives*, IV.16–20.
13 Diogenes, *Lives*, IV.22, 28–45.
14 Diogenes, *Lives*, IV.62–66.
15 Diogenes, *Lives*, IX.79–88.
16 G. R. G. Mure, *Aristotle* (Oxford University Press, 1932; reprint, Galaxy Book, 1964), p. 233.
17 Diogenes, *Lives*, V.58–64.
18 Diogenes, *Lives*, V.62.
19 Diogenes, *Lives*, V.65–74.
20 Ingemar Düring, *Aristotle in the Ancient Biographical Tradition* (Göteborg, 1957; reprint, Garland Publishing, 1987), p. 420.
21 Peter Green, *Alexander of Macedon* (University of California Press, 1991), p. 276.
22 Marshall Clagett, *Greek Science in Antiquity* (Collier Books, 1955), pp. 97f.
23 Clagett, *Greek Science*, pp. 97f.
24 Summarized from *History of the Christian Church*, vol. 2, *Ante-Nicene Christianity*, by Schaff, p. 451; quoting from *Die Apokryphen Apostelgeschichten und Apostellejenden* (1883), by R. A. Lipsius, vol. 1, p. 7.
25 *The Gospel according to Thomas*, estab. and trans. A. Guillaumont, H.-Ch. Puech, G. Quispel, W. Till, and Yassah 'abd al Masih (Harper and Row, 1959).
26 Irenaeus, *Heresies*, 3:41; quoted from *History of the Christian Church*, by Williston Walker (Scribner's, 1949), pp. 60–61.

27 Augustine, *City of God*, XVIII, 41.
28 Origen, *Epistle to Gregory*, Chap. 1; Justin Martyr, *Dialogue with Trypho*, Chap. 7.
29 Philo: Clagett, *Greek Science*, p. 165; Tertullian: Schaff, *History*, vol. 2, p. 823; Stephen Toulmin and June Goodfield, *The Fabric of the Heavens* (Harper and Row Torchbooks, 1961), p. 148; Williston Walker, *History of the Christian Church*, p. 68.
30 Anselm: Schaff, *History*, vol. 5, p. 602; Abelard: Schaff, *History*, vol. 5, p. 623.
31 Lori Villamil.

CHAPTER 13

EPICURUS OF SAMOS

Philosophy takes a pragmatic turn and becomes a search for ideas to live by; a profoundly curious Epicurus seeks explanations of everything and places all knowledge in the service of happiness; he establishes in Athens a third great school in which education is not a drudgery but a lasting joy.

THE ART OF MAKING LIFE HAPPY

In the year 306 BC a young philosopher from the island of Samos sailed to Athens with a dream of establishing a new school on the home court of the intellectual giants. His name was Epicurus, and the school he founded came to be known simply as "The Garden." Over the entrance to his modest plot of ground he placed the inscription "Guest, thou shalt be happy here, for here happiness is esteemed the highest good." He defined philosophy as the art of making life happy. For thirty-six years he taught a do-it-yourself philosophy based on trust in human nature, the enjoyment of life's simple pleasures, and the sanctity of friendship. Above all, he said, if we know ourselves and are always true to ourselves, then our days can be lived in peace and our years will be rich in happiness. He wrote, "Love goes dancing round and round the inhabited Earth, veritably shouting to us all to awake to the blessedness of a happy life."

Sadly, such an upbeat message was an open invitation to hostile attack; it was bound to bring down the philosophic establishment upon Epicurus and his followers, and they were forced to spend much of their time defending this irrational teaching. More than that, they sensed that such a joyous, life-affirming philosophy was destined to be grossly misinterpreted. They were right. For the next two thousand years "epicurean" came to stand for values and a lifestyle they would have nothing to do with.

When it is time to go . . . we will leave life crying aloud in a glorious triumph-song that we have lived well.

EPICURUS

IN THE HISTORY OF PHILOSOPHY

The fool, with all his other faults, has this also: he is always getting ready to live.

EPICURUS

Epicurus is remembered and eulogized (1) for establishing the third institution of education in Athens, known as "The Garden"; (2) for dethroning reason and placing human feelings at the center of the philosophic life ("pleasure is the alpha and omega of a blessed life," he said); (3) for adapting Democritean physics to the pursuit of happiness; (4) for teaching that *ataraxia* is the ground-state of a happy life; (5) for his (unfashionable) conviction that human nature is good; (6) for discovering a correlation between pleasure and health, pain and sickness; (7) for his belief that there are but two ontological fears (of death and of the gods) that disturb our lives; (8) for making the epistemic distinction between knowing subject and object known.

THE MAN

We must not spoil the enjoyment of the blessings we have by pining for those we have not.

EPICURUS

Epicurus was born on the beautiful Aegean island of Samos on the seventh day of Gamelion in the third year of the 109th Olympiad—early February of the year 341 BC. His parents, Neokles and Chairestratê, native Athenians, had been transplanted to the island a dozen years earlier as part of a mass colonial settlement, and as émigrés they were treated as second-class citizens. So, Epicurus was socially stigmatized all his life, for to be island-born was, in the eyes of urbane Athenians, to be backward and uncultured. Moreover, both parents practiced occupations considered socially degrading. His father was a teacher who for a time supervised his own school, and Epicurus assisted him. His mother was a bright woman who seems to have supplemented their income by visiting homes "to read charms" and perform rites of purification; a reluctant Epicurus accompanied her on her rounds. (It follows, of course, that he would develop a lifelong disdain for "every form of divination" and superstition.) Samian attitudes judged schoolteaching to be, for mature adults, a time-wasting occupation. A later (hostile) satirist named Timon ridiculed Epicurus with the epithet *grammadidaskalidês*, which translates to a distasteful "elementaryschoolmaster'sson." He also dubs him "a shameless pseudo-physicist" and "the most uneducated of mortals."[1] So, in society's eyes Epicurus started out with a triple handicap, and he never escaped the stigma of class prejudice. The Epicurean movement, throughout its long history, was more popular with the masses than with sophisticated society.

It is impossible to live pleasurably without living wisely, well, and justly; and impossible to live wisely, well, and justly without living pleasurably.

EPICURUS

Epicurus spent his childhood and youth on Samos. He received the traditional early education in grammar and classic poetry. By age fourteen he had delved into the physical theories of Democritus and confessed that he had fallen in love with philosophy. Gifted with an unstoppable curiosity, he was precocious in intellect, critical in discernment, and strong in his opinions. Once—he was only twelve or so—when his teacher was dictating a line from Hesiod about the generation of the cosmos "out of chaos," Epicurus asked what the passage meant. His teacher, irritated, responded that a pupil should be quiet and memorize what he's told; and, anyway, it wasn't his job to teach philosophy. Then, said Epicurus, "I'll have to seek out the philosophers if they are the only ones who know the truth about things." By the time he was eighteen years old, he was well grounded in the Platonic curriculum offered in the schools and had rejected everything he had been taught. He considered Plato's idea-philosophy too abstract and irrelevant to the inner life of human beings. But his love of philosophy was not to be extinguished, for Democritus had begun to speak to his curiosity about the operations of the larger world.

The truly free man is justified in having a good laugh at all men.

EPICURUS

At age eighteen (in 323 BC) Epicurus sailed to Athens to fulfill two years of required military service, but this was the wrong time to be in Athens. That summer Alexander the Great died in distant Babylon, and the Athenians chose the moment to revolt against their Macedonian overlords. After a bloody uprising came a bloody subjugation of Athenian rebels and the execution of their leaders. Samos was given a new military government and Epicurus's parents were evicted from their land and forced to take refuge on the Ionian mainland. So, after completing his cadetship, he joined his parents at Colophon. He detoured to the island of Rhodes to study Aristotelian philosophy, but he couldn't endure the teacher's petty cynicisms and, after but a few months, returned home. His parents provided support through his years of

Epicurus of Samos (341–271 BC)

schooling. He spent some time with another teacher studying Democritean philosophy, but again a falling out occurred between them, with not a little bitterness. The physics of Democritus was taught in a way that seemed academically irrelevant to Epicurus, and there was in it a skepticism that offended him.

Epicurus spent ten years at Colophon—his maturing years from twenty-one to thirty-one—studying philosophy and teaching rhetoric, the bread-and-butter occupation for so many philosophy teachers. He gradually differentiated his own ideas and concluded that the philosophic systems taught in the public schools were wrongheaded if not immoral. Plato's views largely dominated educational theory. Over the door to his Academy Plato had inscribed the words "Let no one enter here unless he is grounded in geometry"; and geometry had provided the paradigm for the search for universal truth. It had become a prerequisite in the public schools. Epicurus was acquainted with geometry, but he rejected it as worthless for solving the daily problems of life; we can study geometry till hell freezes fast and not be better human beings for it. It doesn't improve our moral judgment, make us more loving, or give us peace of mind.

Epicurus also rejected Plato's epistemic doctrine of Real Ideas. It seemed obvious to Epicurus that ideas are to be found in our minds, not "out there" in the world of objects/events. So Plato's definition of truth—attuning our mental concepts to Real Ideas—was, to Epicurus, so much nonsense. The truths that work for us and help us to live day by day are the only worthwhile truths.

There were other elements of the approved curriculum that angered Epicurus. One was how dialectic was taught. Dialectic, the study of communications skills and debating techniques, was a subject easily abused. The principal abuse, according to Epicurus, was that it taught a kind of insidious dishonesty by encouraging disputants to take sides on issues.° Taking sides, as we do in formal debate or as lawyers do in prosecuting or defending a case, seduces the mind into a narrow perspective that blinds us to the larger picture. As one "takes sides" or "takes a stand for what one believes," the mind inevitably strives to marshall facts and arguments to support that position; in so doing it fails to see and to value the facts and arguments that would support other positions, as there always are.

Vain is the word of that philosopher by which no malady of mankind is healed.

EPICURUS

Human nature is not to be coerced but persuaded.

EPICURUS

°See pp. 95ff., and 110ff.

°This became a major doctrine in Epicurus's ethics; see parrhesia in lexicon.

°The Jains of India teach an interesting doctrine that says there are officially 353 positions that can be taken on any issue, and there is therefore no justification for dogmatism until all 353 positions have been investigated. This doctrine in Jaina logic is called syād-vāda, the "perhaps method"; the proper response to any argument is "perhaps it is and then perhaps it isn't." Think how many arguments could be avoided with such a doctrine!

For just as there is no profit in medicine unless it expels the diseases of the body, so there is none in philosophy either unless it expels the malady of the soul.
                                    EPICURUS

The man at peace with himself is inoffensive to his neighbor also.
                                    EPICURUS

Epicurus judged that all adversarial games encourage self-deception. To counter such teaching, he developed a doctrine of absolute frankness,° a kind of dedication to the larger picture that prevents one from taking a dogmatic position, digging in, and erecting a walled fortress around it, then blindly refusing to see the facts and arguments supporting other positions. He discouraged his students from taking sides in any discussion and demanded they rise above "sidedness" and maintain a "disinterested" involvement. He thought individuals dedicated to growth would not allow themselves to get caught up in an egocentric argument and be pushed into defending a narrowed viewpoint. In the mundane world it seems normal to take one-sided stands on issues, for "everyone does it"; the simplistic two-value orientation pervades the mentality of an uncritical public. Epicurus saw through this artificial dichotomy and refused to have anything to do with it. Only by transcending the trap of one-sidedness and rising to the point where we can see, with openness and honesty, the truth of all positions, can we be sure we are on the appropriate path that leads to integrity and greatness.° The win-lose mentality was anathema to him. For centuries the Epicurean school fought the influence of the rhetoricians; it forbade any use of hyperbole, metaphors, or poetic figures designed to persuade. Epicurus taught his students to seek only the truth and never embroil themselves in parochial debates, even to defend Epicurean teachings. For this reason Epicurus reserved to himself the right to defend his philosophy and school from outside attacks.

By the age of thirty-one Epicurus had thought through the basic principles of his philosophy, but two essential things he had not yet achieved: techniques for successful teaching, and a mechanism or organization for making his ideas known.

Having completed his preparation at Colophon, he journeyed to the city of Mytilênê on the island of Lesbos to begin teaching, but his time there was brief and unhappy. He had developed a loving philosophy, but he was still angry and defensive, and he came across to the Mytileneans as an arrogant know-it-all. He seems to have projected an abundance of self-assurance (overcompensation?) and expected mass conversions to his opinions about life, ethics, gods, education, physics, and much else. His evangelical recruitment took place largely in public gymnasia, where young men in their teens engaged in athletic exercises. These gymnasia were open-air parks, surrounded by colonnades and trees, with enclosures for various forms of sports. The civil authorities who supervised the gymnasia judged Epicurus, with his peculiar philosophy and contentious manner, as a threat to the city's youth. Violence erupted on at least one occasion, and he was expelled from the precincts, barely escaping with his life.

The lesson he learned at Mytilênê seems to have been a turning point. His next teaching post was back on the mainland at Lampsakos, an industrial city on the Hellespont. There he began teaching a less intemperate doctrine. For some four years a repentent and regenerate Epicurus taught with mounting success and gradually gained a following of faithful friends, devoted disciples, and affluent admirers in high places.

His great dream, however, was to establish a school of philosophy in Athens that could operate as a center for the dissemination of his ideas. He had spent years studying canonical philosophies and concluded that they were nothing but sterile speculation; they had left him empty and angry, and he judged that others also shared his disappointment. Epicurus had worked out a philosophy that could bring bread to the hungry, one that could meet the needs of human beings desperately striving to survive the struggles of daily life. He felt a calling to share what he saw. At the completion of four successful years of teaching in Ionia, he had the financial support of the citizens of Lampsakos and at last could look westward to Athens.

THE GARDEN

So in his thirty-fifth year Epicurus sailed to Athens. Though still young, he was an experienced teacher; he had worked out his subject matter in detail, and the light of his vocation burned brighter than ever. He had come to the capital city not merely because it was the cultural center of the Hellenic world but because he wanted to get close to the wellspring of philosophy and challenge it at its heart.

With his proceeds he bought a house and a garden. The house was located just inside the city walls northwest of the Acropolis in a residential district called Melitê. If it was like the average Athenian dwelling, it contained two courtyards, perhaps two dozen rooms, and was enclosed by an unpainted clay brick wall. On entering through the front gate, one walked out into a larger courtyard where the men of the household lived and worked; it was surrounded by columns, a covered porch, and a dozen or so private rooms for sleeping and working. During daylight hours in good weather, most activities were carried on in this courtyard. At the back was a dining room, and through it one entered a smaller courtyard for women, flanked by a large room used by the master and mistress of the house, a dozen or so private rooms for sleeping and working, and a smoky kitchen (without a chimney!) where the women prepared food.

From his funds Epicurus also took eighty minas and bought a garden outside the city walls, perhaps a half-mile distance from his house. It was located northwest of the Dipylon Gate on the road leading to Plato's Academy. Compared to the Academy's extensive olive groves, it was not a large garden, but it was sufficient to meet his modest needs. It provided an arena for lecturing and enclosures where classes could meet.

The school's staff and students lived, worked, and slept in the main house. By modern standards it was crowded, but this was common in Greek households; extreme sociability was unavoidable in Greek society. Epicurus, the community's administrator, reserved for himself the unofficial title of "the Wise Man." The staff included several teachers and three administrative assistants who, among other duties, conducted individual study programs with students. In residence also were one or more literate slaves serving as secretaries and copiers of manuscripts.

I am gorged with pleasure in this poor body of mine living on bread and water.

EPICURUS

It is idle to seek from the gods what a man is capable of providing for himself.

EPICURUS

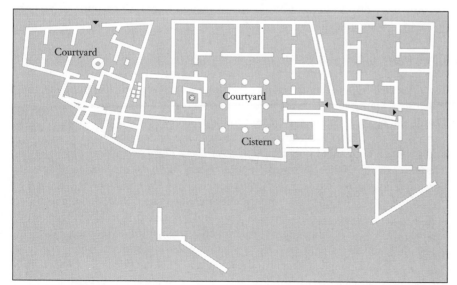

Private homes of "middle-class" craftsmen and merchants were modest in scale and furnishings. Epicurus bought such a dwelling just inside the city walls of Athens and turned it into a school to house his staff of teachers, students, and assistants.

°Compare with Pythagoras and Plato; see pp. 49f., and 137ff..

In a notable break with custom, women participated fully in the life of the school.° The majority of the women were former courtesans, and one of them, the beautiful Leontion, lived with Epicurus as a concubine and achieved considerable fame through her prolific and polemical writing. The lovely names of several of the women of the household are preserved for us by Diogenes: Mammarion, Hedeian, Erôtion, Nikidion, and Boidion.

Students of all ages were enrolled in the school. Some joined the household and lived with the staff; others lived at home and attended classes at the Garden. There were elementary and secondary classes, and more individualized advanced instruction for adolescents and adults. Epicurus's school was unfashionably egalitarian; it admitted everyone whether male or female, slave or free, rich or poor, Greek or barbarian. All it required was a pledge of loyalty: "I will be faithful to Epicurus for it was my free choice so to live."

The graded curriculum was designed to foster growth toward wisdom by incremental stages. Students of all ages deferred to and obeyed their superiors, but that superiority was to be gauged not by age or grade but solely by one's progress along the path to wisdom. Each student was to emulate the personal qualities of his more advanced peers; it was a pyramid of influence and respect, at the head of which stood Epicurus himself as the Wise Man.

Every living creature, the moment it is born, reaches out for pleasure and rejoices in it as the highest good, shrinks from pain as the greatest evil, and, so far as it is able, averts it from itself.

EPICURUS

Friendship was both a philosophic doctrine and a precious fact of life for Epicurus. He believed in and taught a friendship of all human beings. He judged an individual by the number of his friends; it was, he believed, a measure of one's capacity to love. Pleasure is the driving force to our lives, and the pleasure that derives from friendship is a superlative pleasure.

Epicurus didn't teach by lecturing, as was the universal practice in Greek higher education. He taught largely by informal conversation and by example. He wrote more than three hundred books in very lucid prose, including *On Love, On the Gods, On the Highest Good, On Fate, On Benefits and Gratitude, Theories on the Feelings*, four books *On Human Life*, and thirty-seven books *On Nature*—all now lost. Three long letters summarizing his philosophy and a collection of his sayings are preserved by Diogenes Laërtius in his *Lives of Eminent Philosophers*, written about AD 225. Some of Epicurus's aphorisms deserve a place among the treasures of Greek literature. An extensive library of Epicurean works, including fragments of his *On Nature*, was recently unearthed from the ashes of Herculaneum, where the eruption of Vesuvius had buried them in AD 79.

Pleasure is the beginning and end of the happy life.

EPICURUS

For thirty-six years Epicurus guided every detail of his school and became a much-admired, if controversial, light in the Greek world. He lived privately and unobtrusively. He steered clear of politics, stayed out of public debates, and protected himself from the harsh realities that could disturb his peace of mind. He was a much-loved father figure to his followers, to whom he was an incarnate symbol of health and healing. After his death several members of the original circle faithfully carried on the master's teachings and defended his philosophy. Colotês of Lampsakos wrote a book titled *Why the Doctrines of Other Philosophers Make Life Impossible*. Hermarchos of Mytilênê wrote polemical works against Empedocles, Plato, and Aristotle. Polystratos wrote a work which he entitled *On Unreasonable Contempt for Popular Opinion*. The Epicurean movement flourished under these and other literate successors; it spread rapidly through the Greek-speaking world, and during the Roman era it reached the empire's far corners. It remained a vigorous, life-giving philosophy for five hundred years. Its most noted apostle was the Latin poet Lucretius who expounded Epicurus's teachings in his long poem *De rerum natura, On the Nature of Things*.

Inevitably there also grew up a hostile tradition around Epicurus (as around every major thinker), recorded at length by Diogenes. One critic attempted to sully his name by publishing "fifty scandalous letters" Epicurus supposedly wrote. He was said to have sent pruriant notes to other men's wives and to have corresponded with many courtesans. His brother was said to be "a panderer." He held secret midnight meetings, spent lavishly on food, and gorged himself (so that he vomited twice daily). He called people names—"windbag," "ignoramus," "shyster," "fawning gold-bricker," "strumpet"; he named Democritus a master of stupid nonsense, called the students of Plato "Dionysian suckups," and accused Aristotle of selling drugs. Epicurus was easily angered, it was said, contentious, argumentative, a manipulator, and a flatterer; he knew nothing of philosophy and little about life. (How familiar this sounds: If you can't muster the intellect to criticize ideas, then attack the thinker.)

But after recording these hostile epithets, Diogenes, himself angry at such mean-spirited attacks, wrote, "All these critics are stark raving mad!" For the universal testimony of those who knew Epicurus was to his gentleness and "unsurpassed goodwill to all men." He was famed and appreciated for his gratitude—"gratitude to his parents, his generosity to his brothers [he had three], his gentleness to his servants . . . his benevolence to all mankind. . . . Friends indeed came to him from all parts of Hellas and lived with him in his Garden . . . where they lived a very simple and frugal life."[2]

What about Epicurus the man? Can we recover a reasonable picture of what he was like? On the principle that we praise in others the qualities we approve in ourselves (or that we aspire to in ourselves), some plausible estimations can be derived from his many and varied descriptions of the ideal "wise man."[3] Through reason and practice, this "wise man" will attempt to eliminate from his life all feelings of hatred, envy, and contempt. He will be aware of his feelings, to the point of becoming more emotionally sensitive even than other men. He will live his life seeking *ataraxia*, though if he experiences great pain he will cry and groan like anyone else. He will feel grief deeply, but he will not allow suffering to make him withdraw from life. Nor will he allow himself to become cynical. He won't fall in love or marry and have a family (though he might marry under certain conditions, presumably for companionship). He will not overly indulge himself in sexual matters. Women will be his friends on a par equal with men.

The "wise man" won't waste his time with politics, or become a tyrant. He will not bring lawsuits in the courts. He will take good care of his property and plan for the future. He will be fond of his country. As for his reputation, he will pay some notice to it so that others won't look down on him, but he won't put much stock in it. His financial condition will be of no concern at all. He won't beg. He will make money, but he will earn it solely through the exercise of his wisdom. "He will be grateful when he is corrected." He will be able to converse about music and poetry (though he may not be able to write either himself). He will pity his servants and not punish them outright. He won't bother with funeral rites. He won't try to manipulate others with polished oratory.

"He will be armed against fortune and will never give up a friend." "And he will on occasion die for a friend."[4]

The testimony of all who knew Epicurus was that he came very close to his own ideal.

One should heal his misfortunes by grateful recollection of friends who have passed on and by reflecting that what has once happened cannot be undone.

EPICURUS

Let nothing be done in your life which will cause you fear if it becomes known to your neighbor.

EPICURUS

If you would enjoy real freedom, you must be the slave of philosophy.

EPICURUS

EPICURUS'S PHILOSOPHY

Epicurus had no patience with philosophers who climbed into their ivory towers and lost themselves in speculative idealisms (Plato is one example) to the abandonment of practical ethics. Unless a philosopher demonstrates his concern for the plight of each struggling human being, he doesn't deserve to be called a philosopher. "Vain is the word of that philosopher by which no malady of mankind is healed," he wrote. Philosophy and medicine should be thought of as coworkers in healing. What would we think of medicine if it remained an abstract science? Would we not cry out that the purpose of medicine is to heal the body? So also for philosophy. "For just as there is no profit in medicine unless it expels diseases of the body, so there is none in philosophy either unless it expels the sickness of the soul."

°See lexicon.

Epicurus's reasoning is generally scholastic.° He used his knowledge of science to get where he already knew he wanted to go; or, as the mathematical genius Gauss once said, "I have had my solutions for a long time, but I do not yet know how I am to arrive at them." It is likely that Epicurus had arrived at his nuclear propositions by his early twenties; the rest of his life was spent clarifying the path by which he intuitively arrived at them.

He divided his philosophy into three parts. The first, called the Canon, introduced "the system" and contained his epistemology. The second, Physics, held his theories about nature, including what we would call physics, meteorology, and astronomy. The third was Ethics and dealt with psychology and the living of a happy life.

We are born once and cannot be born twice, but for all time must be no more. But you, who are not master of tomorrow, postpone your happiness: life is wasted in procrastination and each of us dies without allowing himself leisure.

EPICURUS

But no matter how far afield his mind wandered, Epicurus focused all his philosophic energies on "considerations which make for a happy life." Our one need, he wrote, is "untroubled existence." Knowledge of nature is important, but it has "no other end in view than peace of mind and firm conviction." His program had no place for self-deception and myth. Facing the stubborn facts of the world with complete honesty is essential to peace of mind; we cannot attain ataraxia if we allow ourselves to "fall away from the study of nature altogether and tumble into myth." To live a happy life we must be good (if amateur) scientists, for "if you fight against clear evidence you never can enjoy genuine peace of mind." But here Epicurus makes a critical distinction. "There is nothing in the knowledge of risings and settings and solstices and eclipses and all kindred subjects that contributes to our happiness"; rather, it is what happens to us while coming to terms with the truth of things as revealed to us by our own senses that restores and maintains the integrity of soul necessary for peace of mind.[5]

EPISTEMOLOGY

The greatest fruit of self-sufficiency is freedom.

EPICURUS

Epicurus's system was the first influential nonrational philosophy of the Greek world. He dethroned the god reason, and in doing so he swam upstream against the philosophical establishment. In Platonic philosophy reason is supreme; only Ideas are ultimately real, and they are to be known only by the rational mind. Similarly, Aristotle held that only through the exercise of the rational psyche do people become human. Epicurus inverted all this. He had listened to philosophers argue and was not impressed by the achievements of reason.

But if reason can't be trusted to lead us out of the woods, where can we find a valid criterion? "It is upon sensation that reason must rely when it attempts to infer the unknown from the known." Our perceptions and feelings are the criteria for truth; it is "from the plain facts of experience" that we must infer any knowledge of the real world, "for all our notions are derived from perceptions." Sensing is direct and immediate; it is not involved in reason (that subsequently creates ideas about our sensing) or memory (by which abstractions are formed). Sense is never in error and is irrefutable. Epicurus's entire philosophy can rightly be seen as an attempt to explain "the facts of feeling and sensation."[6]

Epicurus is therefore as convinced an empiricist as Plato was an idealist. Our senses and our feelings alone are how we establish truth. "Not even reason can refute the sensations, for reason wholly depends upon them." If I see a green tree, my senses aren't lying to me. I perceive what I perceive. *After* I perceive a green tree, I can intellectualize my seeing into a rational proposition and articulate it as "I saw a green tree." But in making such a fact claim, I may or may not be telling the truth; I may or may not have seen a green tree. By contrast, the raw sensations themselves simply are; if they give me green, then green I have—and the matter ends there. "All sensations are true," he wrote.[7]

To summarize: We must honor our sensations—both of sense and emotional feeling—as the source of the basic information we need for living the good life; they alone will tell us what is clear and true and what needs further work.

But granted that my senses are not lying to me, can I trust their perceptions to be accurate representations of the world "out there"? Do I have any basis for believing that the real world is truly as my faithful senses are telling me? Imagine that I'm sitting in my garden, looking at an orange-red Piñata rose. Obviously, Epicurus argues, something connects me (my visual sense) to that real object "out there" on the rosebush so that I may "see" the rose. I'm "in here" and it's "out there." Something, therefore, leaves the surface of the rose, moves through the "void" (space), covers the finite distance between the rose and me, and enters my eyes, and then I see. But what do I see? (Epicurus is in this instance thinking of light.) To answer this question, he carefully followed Democritus and hypothesized that real objects continuously give off copies or pictures of themselves. A subtle film of material, composed of very fine atoms, is emitted from the surfaces of objects and moves rapidly through space to impinge upon our sense organs. These atomic films are very thin and light, "far exceeding that of any object we see." They are adapted for "expressing the surface textures" of objects and preserving the qualities of the objects. The films are given off in very rapid motion. "Their velocities are enormous," he says. If they were not rapid and continuous, then we would see the images "flicker" (as we might see a motion-picture film being projected at, say, eight frames per second). But we don't see such a flicker, so the images must stream off objects so rapidly that our perception of an object such as the rose is continuous. Objects appear to us to be always there in a perfectly stable and enduring way. If these filmy pictures reach our visual perceptors undisturbed, then we will receive authentic images of real objects; if they are disturbed along the way, then we will receive distorted images. Our senses, therefore, can generally be trusted to tell us accurately about the objects/events of the real world. The shape of the object we see is truly the shape of the real object itself.[8]

But is this true for all the qualities attributable to the rose? What about colors, for instance? Color, Epicurus reasoned, is not a quality of the rose. Such qualities "must not be supposed to exist independently by themselves." The atoms (see below) that combine to create the rose also produce, in their many combinations, the colors we "see"; but these are temporary qualities lasting only as long as the atoms continue in their specific "rose" configuration. Colors are "real" in the sense that they are not created by the mind, but their existence is tied to the varied combinations of atoms.[9]

The same pattern exists for all the senses, says Epicurus. An object may produce noise, but without some medium existing between the noise-source and our hearing sense, we could not hear the sound. So, he postulates the existence of a "flowing stream" or "current" that passes from the object to our auditory senses. It is not the air itself "that is moulded into shape" by the noise, but "particles" of some sort that move through the air. Similarly, we could not smell were it not for the existence of "particles" that move from the emitting object, such as the rose, to impact our

If God listened to the prayers of men, all men would quickly have perished: for they are forever praying for evil against one another.

EPICURUS

Live unknown.

EPICURUS

olfactory senses. These particles, in size and shape, are just "the proper sort for exciting the organ of smell," some of them exciting our sense pleasantly, others disagreeably.[10]

In his epistemology Epicurus was very close to making two critical distinctions that occupied later philosophers.

(1) First, he began to discern that some of the qualities we perceive as belonging to real objects may be produced by our experiencing organs, the senses and our minds working together, and are not objectively real qualities at all (these are later dubbed the "secondary qualities"); while other qualities (the "primary qualities") more likely inhere in the real objects themselves. In Epicurus's view "Atoms have no colour . . . nor flavour nor sound nor cold nor heat," writes R. D. Hicks, the translator for the *Loeb Classical Library* volume, "in short no variable quality; . . . but the various qualities are due to the arrangement, positions, motions, and shape of the component atoms." [11]

(2) Closely connected with this insight is the precise *location* of the occurrence of objects/events as in either the real world "out there" or "in here" in our world of subjective experience. Epicurus did not in his time possess sufficient knowledge of physics, physiology, or psychology to make these distinctions clear; nevertheless they were important to him, he made what inroads he could, and he lay foundations for these most fundamental of epistemological principles.

Subsequent to receiving our perceptions and feelings, the mind creates general abstract concepts: *prolepseis*, "preconceptions" or "anticipations." A preconception is "a universal idea stored in the mind." It derives from our having seen an object many times; that is, my mind creates the general idea of "tree" after having seen many single trees. When I say "That is a tree" it implies that I have had some considerable previous experience with trees, that my mind has created from those singular experiences the abstract idea of tree, has stored this idea, and awaits my retrieval of it for use again when I see another tree and want to identify it. Abstract ideas are therefore necessary for an accurate understanding of what anything is, and along with our perceptions, they can be trusted. They can also be tested by what today is called the correspondence and coherence tests of truth. If a prolepsis corresponds to and coheres with further observed data, then it is true; but if further sense data conflict with it, or if no further data are found to support it, then it should be considered false. Epicurus therefore notes that, before declaring an idea true or false, we often have to wait for the acquisition of further sense data to support or falsify it.[12]

Epicurus taught a doctrine of innate ideas which, he said, precondition all living things, including animals, for experiencing the world around us. A child will point with his finger long before he can talk. Lion cubs at play will go through the motions of fighting long before they have teeth or claws. Young birds flex their wings before they are ready to fly. In us humans our capacity to distinguish colors is an example of nature's way of preparing us, ahead of time, to see and process color information. Similarly, he says, the concept of justice is an example of how nature prepares us with social ideas prior to our need of them.

NATURE AND PHYSICS

Epicurus was a keen observer of even the minutest details of the human and natural worlds, and it appears that his entire waking life was a continuous probing analysis of what he saw. Following the promptings of his wide-ranging curiosity, he delved into all things human—life, origins, thinking and knowing, language, ethics, selves, pleasures and happiness; he developed theories about virtually every natural phenomenon from earthquakes, winds, thunder, snow, and rainbows to the nature and

Live like a god among men.
EPICURUS

Steer clear of all culture.
EPICURUS

I know not how to conceive the good, apart from the pleasures of taste, sexual pleasures, the pleasures of sound and the pleasures of beautiful form.
EPICURUS

composition of comets, the Sun, the Moon, and "the wandering stars." Like Aristotle, he was a synoptic adventurer, fascinated by everything. He strove to understand the details while never losing sight of the whole; and he urges us, time and again, when we are focusing on the details of his philosophy, to keep always in mind the structure of the entire system, "for a comprehensive view is often required, the details but seldom."

What is everything made of?—he reiterates the questions of the presocratic scientists; and to answer his questions about the natural world, he turned to Democritus who becomes (as Cicero later puts it) "the fountainhead from which Epicurus derived the streams that watered his little garden." Epicurus adopted almost in toto the physics of the Atomists. "The whole of being consists of bodies and space." "Beyond bodies and space there is nothing which the mind can imagine as existing." The bodies are "atoms," small (we would say microscopic) material *archai* "out of which composite bodies arise and into which they are dissolved." They are solid (with no space in them); they are absolutely indivisible; and they differ only in their size, shape, and weight. Originally all these atoms fell vertically, parallel to one another, and perpendicular to the Earth. (He assumed the Earth was flat, so that "down" is the same direction everywhere; the motions of falling atoms are therefore parallel.) But if all atoms move with parallel motion, how can they ever cluster together to form objects?° To solve this problem Epicurus introduced the notion of "the swerve." Atoms deviate spontaneously from their vertical paths in random fashion. They collide with one another and cling together to form material objects. This is a spontaneous deviation, without cause; the when, where, and how of their clustering is unpredictable. Our world, therefore, is not a mechanistic cosmos, with the parts of the machine behaving according to natural law. Rather, it is a universe of spontaneity and freedom—no predeterminism and no destiny. This is true of all clusters of atoms, including human beings, but we alone can image a future and act on our vision. The feeling of being free is not an illusion but an authentic feeling that reveals to us the truth of our condition. Because we are free we are morally responsible for our actions.

Atoms, therefore, are "in continual motion through all eternity." Some of them vibrate or oscillate in place "when they chance to have become entangled or caught by masses of other atoms" that are clustered just right for entangling; other atoms collide and rebound to considerable distances from one another. They are all separated by space—"the void." "Both atoms and void exist from everlasting."[13]

Using these fundamentals of Democritean physics, Epicurus proceeds to "reason out" the universe. Space and time are both real, he wrote, and both can be understood by the "plain facts" of experience. "If there were no space, . . . bodies would have nothing in which to be and through which to move, as they are plainly seen to do." To understand time we need only to reflect on how we use the word "time" in daily conversation, as when we speak of the "time of day," of the time- duration of our feelings of pleasure or pain, of the length of time something is in motion or at rest ("I slept for an hour"). No time exists apart from what we mean in these particular contexts. Epicurus came very close to saying that time is only an experience of conscious organisms, not a "thing" of which qualities can be predicated.[14]

He then proceeds to apply his epistemological principles to an understanding of the natural world. He worked without myth and attempted to keep his speculations close to observed facts. "We are bound to believe that in the sky revolutions, solstices, eclipses, risings and settings, and the like, take place without the ministration or command of any being." "Where we find phenomena invariably recurring, the invariableness of the recurrence must be ascribed to the original interception and conglomeration of atoms whereby the world was formed."[15]

Peace of mind [ataraxia] and freedom from pain are pleasures which imply a state of rest; joy and delight are seen to consist in motion and activity.

EPICURUS

°*Modern cosmologists face a similar puzzle with the Big Bang theory. Evidence seems to indicate that the universe was perfectly smooth after the primordial explosion, so it is considered a major theoretical problem to figure out how that smoothness evolved into the clumpiness we now see in galaxies and stars.*

If there were no space, bodies would have nothing in which to be and through which to move, as they are plainly seen to do.

EPICURUS

There is nothing in the knowledge of risings and settings and solstices and eclipses and all kindred subjects that contributes to our happiness.

EPICURUS

The Sun, Moon, and stars "took form and grew by the accretions and whirling motions of certain [atomic] substances of finest texture." But what causes motion? Epicurus insists on "plural explanations" of all natural phenomena. The motion of Sun, Moon, stars and planets (1) may be due to "the rotation of the entire heavens"; or (2) the heavens may be stationary and the bodies move by some force "implanted when the world was made"; or (3) they may be due to "the obliquity of the heaven"; or (4) "it may equally be due to the contrary pressure of the air"; or (5) there may be an inadequate fuel supply in some part of the heavens [which, like a vacuum, pull the bodies inward]; or (6) maybe a "whirling motion was from the beginning inherent in these stars so that they move in a sort of spiral."

Epicurus is honest and a good scientist in his speculations, for he says, in effect, that we don't have sufficient sense information to be sure about the origins and movements of the heavenly objects, so he provides in every case all viable explanations that agree with "sense." Often "the facts invite us to give a plurality of explanations." He berates thinkers who give but a single accounting of nature and ignore other valid alternative explanations. "To lay down as assured a single explanation of these phenomena is worthy only of those who seek to dazzle the multitude with marvels."[16]

Thus he observes and attempts to explain "fiery whirlwinds," tornadoes and waterspouts; earthquakes, clouds, winds, storms, thunder and lightning (and why "lightning precedes thunder"; he gives seven possible explanations of lightning), hail, snow, ice, dew and hoarfrost. He also tried to explain rainbows, haloes around the Moon, how the Moon shines, phases of the Moon (perhaps due to "the rotation of the Moon's body"), the circumpolar motion of stars, the "wandering of certain stars" (planets), the regularity of orbits ("the divine nature must not on any account to adduced to explain this"), meteors, comets, solstices, solar and lunar eclipses, risings and settings, variations in length of nights and days, weather changes, and so on.

Epicurus reasoned further that other worlds must exist, in fact, "an infinite number of worlds, some like this world, others unlike it." Since atoms are infinite in number, "they have not all been expended on one world."[17]

His writings on nature are veritable textbooks on scientific method. He continually attempted to match his explanations to what his eyes and ears told him. He reiterates frequently that "exclusion of myth" and "holding fast to the facts" are the sole conditions for doing honest science.

ETHICS AND THE HAPPY LIFE

Epicurus founded his system of ethics on the recognition that there exists "two states of feeling, pleasure and pain, which arise in every animate being, and that the one is favourable and the other hostile to that being, and by their means choice and avoidance are determined." Throughout life we expend our energies seeking pleasure and avoiding pain.

He thought this simple insight so overpowering that he found it incomprehensible that any thoughtful person could disagree with it. "Every living creature, the moment it is born, reaches out for pleasure and rejoices in it as the highest good, shrinks from pain as the greatest evil, and, so far as it is able, averts it from itself."

Our feelings, therefore, provide all the necessary cues by which life can be lived. "He who has a clear and certain understanding of these things will direct every preference and aversion toward securing health of body and tranquillity of mind, seeing that this is the sum and end of a blessed life. For the end of all our actions is to be free from pain and fear, and, when once we have attained all this, the tempest of the

Our one need is untroubled existence.

EPICURUS

Let no one be slow to seek wisdom when he is young nor weary in the search thereof when he is grown old. For no age is too early or too late for the health of the soul.

EPICURUS

soul is calmed." "Pleasure is the alpha and omega of a blessed life. . . . It is the starting-point of every choice and of every aversion." It is our "first and native good." All our waking hours are dedicated to the gathering of pleasures, to increasing the number and quality of our pleasures, and, at the same time, to escaping from pain. "The cry of the flesh is *not* to hunger, *not* to thirst, *not* to shiver with cold." Pleasure and pain are intrinsic and need no justification. All pleasure increases the quality of life and makes us want more life; we must measure the quality of our life in terms of how pleasurable it is. Pain also is intrinsic; we never need to justify trying to avoid it. All creatures understand pain, and no creature ever seeks it; all organisms understand pleasure, and all strive to experience it. A happy life is determined by the degree of our success in avoiding pain.[18]

Epicurus also discerned a connection between pleasure and health on the one hand, and pain and sickness on the other. Pleasure restores; it is medicine for the healing of body and soul. Pain destroys; it dis-integrates both body and soul. Since, for Epicurus, body and soul coexist, the health of one affects the health of the other; one cannot have health of mind without health of body, or a healthy body without a healthy soul.

ATARAXIA

There is an aspect of pleasure that is seldom noted; Epicurus was apparently the first to work with it. He asked: If pleasure is to be equated with peak experiences, then how do we characterize the running ground-state during which we enjoy good health, quiet repose, and a sense of well-being? He answered: This ongoing ground-state, quite apart from peak moments of intense pleasure, is the deepest and highest pleasure of all. Other thinkers had argued that this continuous no-pain condition should be thought of as a neutral state devoid of both pleasure and displeasure. But Epicurus countered that, as long as body and soul are free of pain, then this enduring ground-state is the purist pleasure of all. His word for it, *ataraxia*, translates to "serenity" or "tranquility." Epicurus is suggesting that we should be always aware of this joyful experience and unceasingly appreciative of it. Of course, peak instances of pleasure insert themselves into our lives in a special way, and our enjoyment is naturally more intense during such times.

Evidence indicates that, although his Garden community ate abstemiously most of the time, they arranged a banquet periodically, perhaps once a month, during which they feasted with reasonable abandon; after a prolonged period of eating very little, the rare viands provided especially pleasurable delights to the senses; during leaner regimens they were to hold these moments in their memories as reminders of the precious pleasures that our senses provide. Nothing is wrong with peak pleasures; they enrich our lives. But quite apart from such peak moments, wise human beings stay in touch with their ongoing pleasureable ground-state and value it as the foundation for a happy life.

TWO FEARS

Epicurian doctrine held that two ontological fears disturb the ataraxia of our lives; both are superstitions based on false beliefs. The first is a dread of what might happen to us in the next life. We can imagine that a blissful heaven might await us, but all we can be sure of is that we can't be sure. Given the way most humans behave, a better guess is that we might find ourselves in Hadês, Tartaros, or another unpleasant place. We also experience other less imaginative but more authentic fears about death—a diffuse anxiety about abandoning loved ones, or an ineffable dread of the state of nonbeing.

On Epicurus *Epicurus describes virtue as the sine qua non of pleasure, i.e. the one thing without which pleasure cannot be.*
DIOGENES LAËRTIUS

The end of all our actions is to be free from pain and fear.
EPICURUS

The misfortune of the wise is better than the prosperity of the fool.
EPICURUS

*There do exist gods, and we can
know of them; but they are not
such as the multitude* [hoi polloi]
believe.

EPICURUS

Epicurus's answer to these fears is unequivocal. No afterlife exists; therefore, we have nothing to fear. The assumption of an afterlife is a false assumption. Death is "the privation of all sentience" and therefore, he says, "is nothing to us." This "makes the mortality of life enjoyable, not by adding to life an eternity of time, but by taking away the yearning after immortality." There can be no terror "in ceasing to live." "Foolish, therefore, is the man who says that he fears death, not because it will pain when it comes, but because it pains in the prospect." He doesn't submit this to be accepted on faith; rather it rests on scientific fact. Epicurus turned to Democritus and adopted his physics to provide a foundation for his no-afterlife doctrine. Nothing exists except atoms and space, Democritus had taught. No second order of reality exists—no supernatural, no abode of spirits, no mystical realm of Real Ideas. A human being is a compound of body and soul, to be sure, but both are composed of atoms, though soul atoms are of much finer quality than body atoms. Body and soul are born together, live a life together, and die together. At death body and soul disintegrate and the atoms of both disperse, so continuity of either is impossible. We have nothing to fear because the only thing we can possibly fear is unpleasant experience, and after death we have no experience.[19]

The second disturbing fear is of the gods and what they might do to us. This assumption, too, Epicurus taught, doesn't correspond with reality. The hovering intrusive gods of mythology don't exist. Epicurus doesn't deny the existence of gods; he concedes they do exist, but they dwell far away between the stars and are so absorbed in the fullness of their own existence that they take no interest in human affairs. No evidence exists to support the notion that divine spirits intervene in our lives. So, just as we have nothing to fear after death, so also we have nothing to fear in this life about the capricious gods.

*The flesh endures the storms of the
present alone, the mind those of
the past and future as well as the
present.*

EPICURUS

Epicurus, therefore, using reason and scientific fact, did his best to dispel what he perceives to be the deepest fears disturbing our sleep and upsetting the serenity of our lives. The wise have no reason not to enjoy the sense of well-being that nature guarantees to all of us. If we can let up from our striving, dispel the superstitious fears of gods and death, then we will find that ataraxia is a natural state.

FEELINGS

Wise individuals will be sensitively in touch with their emotional feelings and will trust them as a basis for what is good and what is bad. Along with the senses, feelings tell us what is pleasurable—hence, good for us; and what is painful—hence, bad for us. Nothing in Epicurean doctrine counsels indifference or callousness, as was the case with the Stoic *apatheia*.° Epicurean thinking encourages the individual to become aware of all his feelings; the consequence of this, says Epicurus, is that "he will be more susceptible of feeling than other men. . . ." Our capacity for pleasure, in both range and intensity, will increase through practice. Nor do we numb ourselves to pain, for such numbing would be a kind of dishonesty with the self. "Human nature is not to be coerced but persuaded, and we shall persuade her by satisfying the necessary desires as long as they are not going to be injurious."[20]

°See p. 251.

*No pleasure is in itself evil, but
the things which produce certain
pleasures entail annoyances many
times greater than the pleasures
themselves.*

EPICURUS

Using this pleasure-pain calculus Epicurus developed a theory of social ethics. Judgments of right and wrong should rightly have reference to the consequences they lead to; and the criterion by which such consequences are to be judged is their potential for producing pleasure or pain. Any action leading to pleasure for the individual or group is, by definition, moral, good, and (hopefully) lawful. Laws should be designed to protect and conserve pleasure-producing behavior. In a similar way, any action leading to painful consequences for the individual or group must be considered morally wrong. Pain is intrinsically bad; pleasure is intrinsically good. Only individuals who acknowledge, respect, and follow their feelings can be truly moral; and it follows that truly moral persons will respect and honor the pleasures and the pleasure-seeking behavior of others. This gives new meaning to the New Testament command to love others as we love ourselves.

HUMAN NATURE

Epicurus was one of the rare philosophers to hold that human nature is inherently good, a condition to be cherished and trusted. This upbeat assessment contrasted sharply with the prevailing Platonic psychology, which taught that the self is in a state of unresolvable conflict between reason and the pushy, headstrong passions. It also contrasts with later Pauline doctrine that describes the individual as trapped between the promptings of the spirit and the yearnings of the flesh. In the opinion of both Plato and Saint Paul, the body is a prison incarcerating the nobler self—*reason* for Plato, the *spirit* for Paul.°

°*Galatians 5:16–24.*

The just man enjoys the greatest peace of mind, while the unjust is full of the utmost disquietude.
EPICURUS

By contrast, Epicurus preached a faith in human nature that assures us we can live with ourselves without conflict or confusion. Our essential nature longs to be happy and whole, and our feelings are the revelations of this nature, and we can trust them too. They will always tell us what is bad for us—namely, pain, disharmony, and disease; and they will always tell us what is good for us—namely, pleasure, growth, harmony, and health.

Epicurus himself had an abiding faith in human beings. The individual, exercising free choice, can make decisions to move toward wholeness and ataraxia; there is no end to what one can accomplish. This life is it, and we should strive to live it well. It is a matter of commitment, making good choices, and practicing. Individuals in touch with their deepest nature possess the only instruction manual they need for living a full life.

Epicureanism was a do-it-yourself philosophy. Its program was designed to develop an enlightened awareness in mature individuals so that they will know the goal of life—pleasure; they will know how to discriminate between pleasure-producing goals and pain-producing goals; and they will know how to discriminate between the more lasting pleasures that produce ataraxia and the less fulfilling (but legitimate) short-lived pleasures that can produce enjoyment but can't affect our ground-state.

In the final analysis, Epicurus taught, each one of us is alone in our quest for happiness. No deities exist who can drop onto the stage, *deus ex machina*, and rescue us. "It is idle to seek from the gods what a man is capable of providing for himself." The same goes for our teachers or gurus: They provide us with inspiration and support, but in the end we must discover the path within ourselves. The individual who experiences his feelings with sensitivity, honesty, and trust will be the one who effectively takes charge of his life and finds the path to ataraxia. Two centuries earlier, and far away, another lonely soul had said similar words to his faithful disciples: "You must be your own lamps, be your own refuges. Take refuge in nothing outside yourselves. Go now, and diligently seek to realize your own nirvana."

PLEASURE AND HAPPINESS

It is upon sensation that reason must rely when it attempts to infer the unknown from the known.
EPICURUS

Epicurus's ideas in psychology can still impress. Pleasure turns out to be a complex affair, and the many aspects of pleasure develop gradually in each of us. As children our decisions are instinctive. A child chooses pleasure, of course, but does so by instinct and without reason. But as the years pass, awareness replaces instinct, and step-by-step we learn to choose our experiences. During childhood and youth we seek pleasures of a physical nature, especially the play routines that develop strength of body. But as we mature into adults with a modicum of wisdom, we learn how to design our lives with care and forethought; we can select and maximize the pleasures that bring the greatest satisfaction.

However, life rarely offers us simple choices. "We do not choose every pleasure whatsoever, but ofttimes pass over many pleasures when a greater annoyance ensues from them." Wise individuals calculate and weigh their pleasure/pain experience, for "not all pleasure is choiceworthy, just as all pain is an evil and yet not all pain is to be shunned." "It is, however, by measuring one against another, and by looking at the conveniences and inconveniences, that all these matters must be judged." Long-range pleasures are more desirable than short-range pleasures, and we may have to give up short-range pleasures to obtain longer-lasting pleasures. We also find we must endure pain to arrive at the pleasures we deem worthy of that pain, and, conversely, we often have to give up cherished pleasures to avoid the pain they would bring us. In contrast to the Cyrenaics, who urged never giving up an immediate pleasure for a hypothetical future pleasure that may or may not materialize, Epicurus urged wise individuals to survey the whole picture when exercising their judgment to maximize pleasure and minimize pain.[21]

GROWTH

Since humans are creatures of habit, we may have to practice all our lives to reorient our paths toward Epicurean wisdom. It may be for me a major tour de force to develop the habit of seeing a glass half full rather than half empty, but it is within my power to will that it be so. I *can* will myself to see the good things of life and to be grateful for them. Epicurus wrote forcefully of this pragmatic exercise and taught to his pupils the virtue of all-pervading gratitude. He fully practiced it himself. To be sure, for many of us, our orientation toward life is so depressed that, with Charlie Brown, it is a mark of progress when we learn to dread just one day at a time. But at some point the light dawns and we see that most of the things we spend our lives worrying about don't happen (and that their not happening bears no relation to our having worried about them).

Nature mandates that our bodies and souls, given half a chance, will naturally seek pleasure and avoid pain. But we commonly find our selves neuroticized by our social environment so that we seek pain instead of pleasure. We are often conditioned to believe we are bad boys and girls who deserve pain (punishment for *being* "bad," not *behaving* badly); on our own we therefore seek pain so that we "get what we deserve" (which tends to mollify our guilt and self-hate—which is experienced, relative to our bad feelings, as pleasure). Epicurus taught that all this can be changed. With faith in ourselves and trust in our basic natures, we can do an about-face. We can learn to appreciate how delicious the pure healing pleasures can be and come to want more and more of them.

Ataraxia is available to all of us just because we're human; it's ontological and absolutely democratic, guaranteed to all of us by nature. No special aptitude is required. It isn't offered just to the affluent, the privileged, or the socially correct. Nor is it a far-distant reward given after years of meditation or a state to be enjoyed only in the next afterlife. We can all enjoy the condition now, almost without effort. If we can let up from our striving, dispel the superstitious fears of gods and death, then we will find that ataraxia is a natural state. It requires only that we advise the controlling ego to cease its fearful manipulations and let our feelings become our guide.

Our canon is that direct observation by sense and direct apprehension by the mind are alone invariably true.

EPICURUS

To say that the season for studying philosophy has not yet come, or that it is past and gone, is like saying that the season for happiness is not yet or that it is now no longer.

EPICURUS

TRIUMPH

Epicurus died in his Garden in the second year of the 127th Olympiad (271–270 BC). He was 72. He had once written, "Even if under torture, the wise man is happy," and, finally, he was put to the test. Though in much pain, he dictated an affectionate letter to his friends in Lampsacus. "On this blissful day of my life, which is likewise my last, I write these words to you all. The pains of my strangury and dysentery do not abate the excess of their characteristic severity and continue to keep me company, but over against all these I set the joy in my soul at the recollection of the disquisitions composed by you and the rest." True to himself and his philosophy, he maintained the serenity and sweetness that characterized his life.

He left a will.[22] In it he expresses the hope that the lifestyle of his Garden might continue as best it can, and that "none of those members of the School who have rendered service to me in private life and have shown me kindness in every way and have chosen to grow old with me in the School should, so far as my means go, lack the necessities of life." He directed that his faithful slaves Mys, Nikias, and Lykon be freed and added "I also give Phaedrium her liberty." His house, Garden, and some money he left to the school; his books he left to his favorite disciple Hermarchos. He asked that funds be set aside to honor his family and to celebrate his memory monthly and his birthday annually. His final hours were a triumph of ataraxia over pain.

So we must exercise ourselves in the things which bring happiness, since, if that be present, we have everything, and, if that be absent, all our actions are directed toward attaining it.

EPICURUS

Pleasure is the alpha and omega of a blessed life.

EPICURUS

ENDNOTES

1 Diogenes Laërtius, *Lives of Eminent Philosophers*, X.3. See also (and thanks to) Norman Wentworth DeWitt, *Epicurus and His Philosophy* (University of Minnesota Press, 1954), p. 40.
2 Diogenes, *Lives*, X.7–11.
3 Diogenes, *Lives*, X.117–21.
4 Diogenes, *Lives*, X.120.
5 Diogenes, *Lives*, X.79.
6 Diogenes, *Lives*, X.32, 55.
7 Diogenes, *Lives*, X.31–2.
8 Diogenes, *Lives*, X.46–50.
9 Diogenes, *Lives*, X.68.
10 Diogenes, *Lives*, X.53.
11 Diogenes Laërtius, *Lives of Eminent Philosophers*, trans. R. D. Hicks (1925; reprint, Harvard University Press, 1995), vol. 2, p. 584n[a].
12 Diogenes, *Lives*, X.33–4.
13 Diogenes, *Lives*, X.43, 44.
14 Diogenes, *Lives*, X.40.
15 Diogenes, *Lives*, X.76, 77.
16 Diogenes, *Lives*, X.90, 93, 114.
17 Diogenes, *Lives*, X.45.
18 Diogenes, *Lives*, X.34, 128–9.
19 Diogenes, *Lives*, X.125.
20 Diogenes, *Lives*, X.117.
21 Diogenes, *Lives*, X.129, 130.
22 Diogenes, *Lives*, X.16–21.

CHAPTER 14

ZENO, MARCUS AURELIUS, AND STOICISM

A Cypriot businessman develops a new philosophy urging human beings to live according to Nature; then the noblest of the Romans writes his *Meditations* (to himself) and adapts Stoic doctrines to help him get through each day; he ponders the death of children, the brevity of life, the roles we play; and he dreams of a world brotherhood.

GOD AND NATURE

Stoic philosophy first saw the light of day around 300 BC when a dismal but loving philosopher named Zeno began to preach a seductively simple idea: "Live in harmony with Nature." Carefully interpreted, this idea provided its followers with the conviction that life can be lived as it was meant to be lived—nobly and in peace. During the five centuries Stoicism shaped the daily thoughts of Greeks and Romans, it functioned as a religious faith and produced some of the most admired lives ever to grace the pages of history.

This (in part) was what the logion meant. To live in harmony with Nature meant to live in harmony with God, for Nature is God. Out of his own being God created the material substance of the universe, and he is its soul (today we would say the laws of physics) that gives it order. Matter was thought of as the body of God, while the perfect order of Nature revealed the soul of God. No wonder then that the study of Nature—physics, astronomy, biology, and so on—was so important to the Stoics. To study Nature is to study God, with the goal of becoming more like God in every way.

Just as God is made up of matter and an ordering soul that turns the cosmos into a perfectly functioning system, so also the human organism is made up of matter and an ordering soul; it, too, by becoming like God, can grow into a perfectly functioning system. But, more, each human minicosmos is a fragment of the divine cosmos—it is not merely *like* God; it *is* God. It differs only in being a very small fragment, while God is the Whole. The goal of Stoic ethics, therefore, was to nourish and give strength to the God within each of us.

So the Stoics were mystics, and no one had ever felt closer to Nature. When they looked up at the night sky and beheld the orderly movement of the heavenly bodies, they saw God. When they pondered the diurnal cycle and the orderly return of the seasons, they saw God. When they looked within and observed, with awe, the orderly operations of the rational mind, they saw God. Closeness to God, therefore, required openness to, and submissiveness to, Nature, both without and within. Historically, this belief led to the serious study of the natural sciences, on the one hand, and a plumbing

We have two ears and only one mouth. Why? So we can hear more and talk less.

ZENO OF KITIUM

No one can be really good without an accurate knowledge of the Nature of the Universe and what makes him human.

MARCUS

into the depths of the human soul, on the other. In the realm of the sciences, the Stoics developed a worldview that included a complete cosmogony, cosmology, and eschatology; a physics that accounted for motion and change; and a biology that explained the nature of living things, human and animal. As for explorations within, the penetrating insights of a Seneca and an Epictetus, and the searching honesty of the meditations of Marcus Aurelius, are golden testimony to the power of Stoic faith.°

°*For the general character of post-Aristotelian philosophy, see pp. 196ff.*

IN THE HISTORY OF PHILOSOPHY

The Stoics are known primarily (1) for applying philosophy to life and, specifically, to the problem of finding a way to live nobly in the world without being destroyed by it; (2) for the doctrine of *apatheia*; (3) for mystical feelings that drew them close to Nature and for their belief that a successful life is to be found by living in harmony with Nature; (4) for the doctrine of "natural law"; (5) for teaching that God is within each soul; (6) for their teaching that God and Nature are one; (7) for their thoroughgoing materialism; (8) for insisting that abstract concepts are in the mind, not in the world; (9) for their dream of a world brotherhood in the framework of a cosmopolis.

What is the first business of one who practices philosophy? To get rid of self-conceit. For it is impossible for anyone to begin to learn that which he thinks he already knows.

EPICTETUS

ZENO AND THE STOA

Stoicism was founded by Zeno, a thirty-year-old entrepreneur from the city of Kition (Latin, *Citium*, now *Larnaca*) on the island of Cyprus. His lineage was Phoenician, and he was tall, thin, and dark, and, we are told, displayed a dismal countenance with a perpetual frown. Having been a very able businessman, he was wealthy when he sailed from Kition with a load of "purple"; but he was shipwrecked somewhere off the Piraeus port, lost everything, and thereafter made his way to Athens to become a philosopher. One day soon after arriving in Athens, he was sitting in a bookseller's stall reading about Socrates in Xenophon's *Memorabilia*. He asked the bookseller where such men spend their time. Just at that moment Crates the Cynic walked by. The bookseller pointed to him and said to Zeno, "Follow that man." He did; he became a pupil of Crates and, showing "a strong aptitude for philosophy," launched his career with the study of Cynic thought. (He mused that Fate had driven him to philosophy by means of "a prosperous voyage that ended in shipwreck.") Crates was not as extreme in his rejection of society as his teacher Diogenes, though he still lived the life of a mendicant sage. Like Zeno, he was initially wealthy, but he gave all his money away (or, by another account, threw it all in the ocean). He went about wearing a heavy cloak in summer and threadbare rags in winter, declaring that poverty and disrepute were his home country.

Eventually Zeno parted from Crates and studied with Stilpo the Megarian and Xenocrates, the scholarch of Plato's Academy. But, since Zeno was strong willed and idiosyncratic, it wasn't long before he developed his own philosophy and set up a school for teaching it in a stoa on the north side of the Agora. On the walls of this public portico hung large painted scenes from the Trojan War, so it was called the "Painted Stoa"—whence the name "Stoic." Here, for another thirty years, Zeno walked up and down in the crowded colonnade delivering discourses, haranguing bystanders, and dialoguing with students. He wrote more than a dozen widely read books, among them *Life according to Nature, Human Nature, On Emotions, On Law, On Greek Education, Homeric Problems* (five volumes; he was a literary critic), *Ethics, Republic,* and *On the Whole World*. None of his work survives. So admired was he by the

What fools these mortals be!
SENECA

Salvation in life depends on our seeing everything in its entirety and in its reality, in its Matter and its Cause: on our doing what is just and speaking what is true with all our soul.

MARCUS

Zeno of Kitium (c. 333–262 BC)

Athenians that they gave him honorary keys to the city walls and published a decree praising him for "exhorting to virtue and temperance those of the youth who come to him to be taught, directing them to what is best, affording to all in his own conduct a pattern for imitation in perfect consistency with his teaching"; they "crowned him with a golden crown," erected a bronze statue in his honor, and built him a tomb in the Kerameicos from public funds.[1] He died at ninety-eight, having "enjoyed good health without an ailment to the last." Exiting from the Stoa one day, he tripped and broke a toe, which caused excruciating pain. In anger and frustration he pounded the ground and cried out, "I come, I come, why dost thou call for me?" His time had come, he decided, so he held his breath "and died on the spot." [2°] This was about 263 BC.

Zeno taught and lived a life of personal independence and nonconformity, honesty, and humility. Early on he was thin skinned and sensitive to "what others think"; but he had to get over it, and with the help of Crates (who deliberately humiliated him in public to desensitize him) and Cynic apathy, it seems he did so. He liked to be alone and felt claustrophobic in crowds; he would sit on the end of a couch so admirers couldn't squeeze in on both sides, and at parties he would slip away unnoticed. He was on friendly terms with the king, Antigonos, who would drop by his home unannounced with a noisy entourage. When Zeno died, Antigonos mourned him: "What an audience I have lost"; and when asked why he admired Zeno so much, he said, "Because, although I gave him many generous gifts, they never made him conceited or mean-spirited."

Zeno's thinking was careful and precise. He could annihilate another's argument with dispatch and conciseness. Armed with a battery of quick retorts, in repartee he was unassailable. (Diogenes Laërtius, in his *Lives of Eminent Philosophers*, devotes several pages to popular anecdotes about Zeno, many of them puerile and shallow; but on careful reading something of Zeno's spirit comes through.) To a glib young chatterbox talking nonsense, he said, "We have two ears and only one mouth. Why? you ask. So we can listen more and talk less." When Crates once grabbed Zeno's cloak to drag him away from the Sophist Stilpo, he countered, "The only way to seize a philosopher, Crates, is by the ears. Drag me off by persuading me; but if you drag me physically, then my body may be with you, but my mind is still with Stilpo." When,

°Here begins a major Stoic doctrine, that individuals have a right to commit suicide when they judge that the time is right; this is a part of the larger Stoic belief that individuals should take charge of their own experience. Marcus Aurelius believed suicide is morally justifiable when it is no longer possible to live a fulfilled and virtuous life "according to Nature." Besides Zeno, other great Stoics who took their own lives were Cleanthes, Seneca, and Lucan. See Marcus's Meditations, III.1; V.29; VIII.47ff; X.22, 32.

You must live for another, if you wish to live for yourself.
                                    SENECA

It is only the present moment that a man lives and the present moment only that he loses.
                                    MARCUS

on another occasion, someone stumbled, he observed, "Better to trip with the feet than with the tongue."

He was gifted with great endurance and energy in an "iron frame." He was frugal, wore just a thin cloak as did the Cynics, endured the elements, and (perhaps for show) begged from passersby. He ate just little loaves of bread with honey, some dried figs, water, and a little wine (providing it had a "good bouquet"). To the Athenians he was a legend and a proverb: "More temperate than Zeno" was the saying. Austere and dignified (most of the time), he would surprise everyone by letting down at a drinking party. "Even lupines that are naturally bitter become sweet when they're soaked," he reminded them.

He was buried in the Kerameicos as promised, honored by the Athenians as the man who, in his nobility, had "scaled high Olympus."[3]

LOGIC AND EPISTEMOLOGY

Zeno's eclectic mind had surveyed philosophical ideas past and present, and he drew deeply from what he had read and heard. From Heraclitus he accepted the view of the ever-changing fire as the creative force of the world and the notion of a natural law (in the form of the *logos*) that orders the cosmos. From Socrates he obtained the starting point of his ethics—that knowledge is virtue; the pursuit of knowledge and the development of virtue are one and the same; and virtue is impossible without knowledge. From the Cynics he derived his cosmopolitan outlook, including the belief that all humans are bound by a universal law that has first calling over local laws and customs. From the Megarians he learned rigorous techniques for logical reasoning and elenctic debate. From Aristotle he adapted the notions of the potential and the actual. Zeno's principal contribution lies in his syncretizing these elements into a coherent worldview, fleshing it out, and applying it concretely to daily life.

The Stoics divided their philosophical endeavors into three categories: logic (including their work with language, grammar, communications, and a theory of knowledge), physics (bound up with their theology), and ethics—the science of how to live (including their psychology and politics).

The Stoics were the first to analyze the Greek language exhaustively, thereby creating linguistics, grammar, and semantics. They identified the parts of speech, explained cases and tenses, explored definitions and meaning, analyzed ambiguities and fallacies, and wrote about style in prose and poetry. In logic they concentrated especially on syllogisms and criteria for testing the truth of statements. One purpose drove all of this work: to enable one to recognize the truth. In their theory of knowledge, the Stoics rejected the idea realism of Plato and the form realism of Aristotle. All knowledge is rooted in sense perception. Just as sealing wax receives the seal's impression, the passive human soul receives imprints from the senses, which are then stored as images in the mind, available for subsequent processing. This first-stage datum of consciousness was called "an imprint," "an impress," and "a moulding." (Chrysippos referred to it as "the altering of the soul.") When several similar imprints have been received and stored away, the mind proceeds to generate from them general abstract concepts. It then arranges these concepts in a logical fashion to produce universals. This, the Stoics held, constitutes knowledge proper. The mind, therefore, deriving its substance from the senses, and only from the senses, can make accurate and trustworthy copies of real objects. But they are *only* copies; the Stoics were quite clear that ideas are produced by, and are found only in, the mind. Ideas are not real entities.

Not one of us is without fault . . . no man is found who can acquit himself.

SENECA

Nothing is but what thinking makes it.

MARCUS

Love of bustle is not industry.

SENECA

Thou has but a short time left to live. Live as on a mountain; for whether it be here or there matters not provided that, wherever a man live, he live as a citizen of the World-City.

MARCUS

Men do not care how nobly they live, but only how long, although it is within the reach of every man to live nobly, but within no man's power to live long.

SENECA

What is thy vocation? To be a good man.

MARCUS

I was shipwrecked before I got aboard.

SENECA

Truth, therefore, can be defined as the correspondence between a mental impression and the real object. But how can we be sure an idea is true, that it corresponds to reality? Not from thought, because we create a thought from our sense impression; we can't verify a thought impression's accuracy by another thought impression. Rather, verification is found in the intensity of feeling: If an idea impresses itself on the mind with an intensity we can feel, literally, then we can be sure the idea is true and represents accurately the real object. Awareness of an idea's truth can be an intuitive process or an active operation of reason that deliberately focuses on and clarifies the intense feelings by which true ideas make themselves known to us.

Stoic epistemology therefore gives to the mind (or the soul) a power Plato and Aristotle denied it. The mind is the sole creator of universal concepts; abstractions must be looked for and found only in the human thinking machine, not in a mystical realm of Real Ideas or as a shaping force that inheres in matter. This notion, called *nominalism*, continued to do battle for another two millennia with various doctrines whose collective purpose was to denigrate the mind's creative power. They argued that human ideas necessarily derive from a Great Mind that alone has the majesty and perfection to generate the awesome contents of human thought.

PHYSICS AND FAITH

The Stoics were thoroughgoing materialists; only matter, they concluded, is real. If something exists, then it's made of matter; if it's not made of matter, then it doesn't exist. This applied to everything—to physical objects, to the soul, to the gods or to God, to ideas, to numbers, and even to qualities of objects ("good" and "bad" and "red" and "beautiful" are material things). All is matter or nothing.

While only matter exists, the Stoics distinguished between coarse matter (which is passive) and fine matter (which is active). The distinction we commonly make between matter (roses, rocks, rain, etc.) and forces (gravity, ideas, emotions, etc.) is really a distinction between coarse and fine matter. Fine matter is so fine it can move in and through coarse matter like air currents. Thus, very fine soul matter moves throughout coarse body matter, animating it and imparting to it specific qualities and functions.

The human soul, composed of exceedingly fine matter, is a fiery breath diffused throughout the body. The fine matter of a human soul is identical with the fine matter God is composed of; hence, the human soul is divine and shares all the qualities of God. The more nobly we live by divine reason, the more we grow into Godlikeness or, better, into Godness. As the world operates by causal necessity, so also the human soul is not a free entity but a determined being following the causal laws of God/Nature. The only "freedom" derives from the fact an aware human being can know and understand the laws he is conforming to, whereas lower animals cannot. (If this notion seems puzzling, we can remind ourselves that no human is immune to the laws of physics, and even though we can study them in precise detail—as outlined in any physics textbook—we find we have to obey them just the same.) Human beings are blessed with a capacity to understand our world and our place in it. Humankind's highest obligation is not to struggle against Nature but to design a lifetime of action that will flow harmoniously along with the universal laws of God/Nature.

For an explanation of what matter is and how it operates, the Stoics turned to Heraclitus: Matter is made of (and driven by) fire, it is governed by the Logos, and it is God. The world, therefore, is several things at once. It is a dynamic rather than a static thing. It is in the process of becoming; following its own inner logic or groundplan, it is changing and growing—but not chaotically or randomly. It is a rational world, suffused through and through with the reason of the Logos/God who eternally organizes and directs all operations and rigidly determines all actions and events. Nothing irrational happens and nothing that is not part of a divine plan. Everything happens, that is, the way it must happen.

The cosmos, therefore, is a personal world; it is amenable to, and intelligible to, the human mind, and it is congenial to human aspirations. But more than that, the World is a great living Creature, a cosmic animal, a World-organism we can trust. When the Stoics thought of God, they thought of the living World; when they thought of the World, they thought of a living God. God was their name for the human mind's highest principle. The Stoics were sophisticated in their use of language. Any word could be employed in referring to God since the World-deity is ineffable; he is beyond human apprehension. He can be thought of as Zeus, Logos-Reason, Cosmos, Providence, Ether, Nature, World-Soul, Destiny, Fate, Mind, Matter, Fire; Fiery-Reason-of-the-World, Mind-in-Matter, Breath-of-the-World, and even Reason-Containing-the-Seeds-of-All-Things (*logos spermatikos*,° one of the Stoics' favorite phrases for God). When we think of the ordering function of physical laws, we can call him Providence or Divine Ruler. When we think of the deterministic operations of the world, we can call him Destiny or Fate. If we want to focus on the God who nourishes and looks after us, then we can call him Father Zeus or Life-Giving Air.

The words matter not; they are merely references to the variety of ways we experience God and, at best, terms symbolizing some limited aspect of the divine reality. The Stoic philosophy of language conformed to Greek usage of religious terms; the deities of the Greek pantheon long had been thought of as personifications of nature. Zeus, for example, symbolized the cosmos and the heavens. Apollo represented the sun, Artemis the moon. Athena was the upper air and Poseidon the waters of the Earth and oceans. Aphrodite symbolized the love and care of the world toward human beings.

This was a richly rewarding concept of nature. From the idea of an active World-reason following a perfectly engineered set of specifications, Stoics could think and feel themselves an integral part of a dynamic divine creative process. Give up and give in to the God within, who will lead each human soul along the path toward becoming a perfectly functioning system. However, individual objects or persons may not conform to the full potential of Nature's leadership. The sea winds may blow and distort the black pine on the cliff into a gnarled parody of the great tree that might have been. Or consider a bonsai maple: Is this eighteen-inch-high look-alike what the maple tree was destined to become? In a similar fashion, human beings can fall short of manifesting in their lives the promise of their natures. Still, to Stoics, nature and natural law are objects of their faith. Just as the black pine or maple seedling "knows" what it "wants" to grow into, so also each human being possesses within a full template for an unfolding life plan. We can meditate on this developmental life force, identify with it, and thereby better appropriate the rationalism of the Logos into our own life.

Stoicism was a universalist philosophy. Just as Nature has a universal law, all human beings should also have a universal law—one set of laws for all humankind. The fact that what is considered right in one city-state might be thought of as wrong in another was anathema to Stoics. They therefore dreamed of a "cosmopolis," a single city-state for all, where all humans could live and be judged by a single standard that would supplant all local laws and customs. This logic was followed to its noble

Whatever man thou meetest, put to thyself at once this question: What are this man's convictions about good and evil?

MARCUS

Let him who hath conferred a favor hold his tongue.

SENECA

°See lexicon.

A sacred spirit dwells within us, the observer and guardian of all our evil and our good . . . there is no good man without God.

SENECA

To the rational being only the irrational is unendurable.

EPICTETUS

Simple and modest is the work of Philosophy: lead me not astray into pomposity and pride.

MARCUS

conclusion: All humans are children of God and are therefore brothers and sisters. Wise Stoics will be citizens of the world; they will feel at home everywhere. This ideal became a cornerstone of Stoic thought and a driving force behind the Stoic world mission.

The living world, however, is not eternal. All things, even the gods, must come to an end. The world arose in the beginning when the primal fire condensed into air and water, and then the water condensed into solid earth. But all elements tend to return, by rarefaction, to primal fire. So, at the end of time the world will be consumed in a fiery conflagration, and afterward, through another series of condensations, it will be reborn to exist in every detail just as it did before. Stoic cosmology envisioned an endless repetition of identical worlds, conflagration to conflagration—the Eternal Return.°

There is no great genius without some touch of madness.

SENECA

°*The "Eternal Return" is a motif in Nietzsche's philosophy; see Vol. II, pp. 291ff. Note the similarity to the Götterdämmerung of Norse mythology and to Hindu cosmology.*

HOW TO LIVE

Ethics was considered "the divine part" of Stoic philosophy. All their labors in epistemology and physics were designed to support questions about human destiny and happiness. Humans were made to strive for happiness *(eudaimonia)*, and the key lies in realizing that everything happens because it must, so humans can achieve a satisfactory life only by choosing to "go with the flow" of what must be. This is virtue. Wealth, honor, and pleasure are false virtues. Only the virtue of living with Nature can bring happiness. Virtue is its own reward. True virtue lies not in action but in one's intention. No overt action can be evaluated as good or bad, only the intent that creates the action. For the Stoic, that is, virtue is found only in a good will. Evil is defined as deliberately living out of harmony with the laws of Nature.

A popular prayer (sometimes called "The Serenity Prayer") nicely captures one central idea of Stoic ethics: "God grant me the serenity to accept things I cannot change, courage to change things I can, and wisdom to know the difference." Starting from their deterministic assumption that everything happens as it must, and from the undeniable fact that much of *what happens to us* in life takes place without our bidding, the Stoic drew a logical conclusion: Why fret over events we can't

The good or ill of man lies within his own will.

EPICTETUS

One of the most striking buildings in Athens, the Painted Stoa was decorated inside with battle scenes painted on large wooden panels. The most eminent resident of the Painted Stoa was Zeno of Kitium who used it as an open-air classroom: "He used to discourse in the Painted Stoa," Diogenes writes. "Henceforth people came hither to hear him, and for this reason they were called Stoics."

possibly do anything about? Life is well supplied with recalcitrant givens. I have no say over when and where I was born; over my gender, race, and blood type; and whether I'm stocky or slender. I have no control over world events that engulf me—wars, economic downturns, holocausts. Tidal waves, earthquakes, volcanic eruptions, floods, and droughts are beyond my sphere of influence. Nor can I determine how other people think of me, feel about me, and treat me. Why should I allow such things to get to me?

From infancy on we develop vulnerabilities. We are taught to consider others' feelings, and we often develop a sense of pride in our own sensibilities. More than that, we often are taught we are responsible for the world's ills and that we can change anything should we set our minds to it. But, the Stoic tells us, vulnerability in this sense is not a virtue. Hurting because of the thoughtless actions of another is a weakness, not a strength. Personal growth lies in reconditioning ourselves to be invulnerable to everything we can't help. The Stoics had a thoughtful word for it: *apatheia*, which we can translate as "apathy" providing we know the word doesn't mean "listlessness." To become apathetic is to learn to be unheedful of all events that can hurt us and about which we are helpless to initiate change.

What, then, are we in charge of? Though we may have nothing to say about what happens to us, we are in complete charge of *how we respond* to what happens to us: Our thoughts, our feelings, our will, and our behavior are ours and ours alone. Whether I decide to get angry over an injustice or fearful over a stock market low is a matter of will—I can choose to feel pain, or I can react "stoically," accepting the fact of their existence calmly, not allowing such events to disturb the health of my soul.

Epictetus wrote: "Seek not that the things which happen should happen as you wish, but wish the things which happen to be as they are, and you will have a tranquil flow of life."[4]

LATER STOICISM

For more than two hundred years, Stoicism was the dominant philosophy of the Greek and Roman nobles and intelligentsia; then, during the first century AD, it spread rapidly among the masses and became a sort of "established" philosophy. Often eclectic and without a rigid orthodoxy, it was a flexible system that could adapt to meet a variety of human needs; over its long history it underwent considerable revision and change.

The history of Stoicism covers (1) Early Stoicism, as taught by Zeno and his two successors Cleanthes and Chrysippos; (2) Middle Stoicism, early Roman Stoicism as developed by the Rhodian scholars Panaetius and Posidonius; and (3) Late Stoicism, represented by the great Roman writers Seneca, Epictetus, and Marcus Aurelius. Early and Middle Stoicism are known to us only from brief fragments and comments from later writers; Late Stoicism is known from the Roman writers whose works have been preserved almost in full.

The Stoa, a thriving institution by the time of Zeno's death, was taken over by his pupil **Cleanthes** of Assos, who, with his mystical temperament, edged Stoicism nearer to becoming a religion. His brief *Hymn to Zeus* is all that survives from his writings. Zeno had commented that Cleanthes' mind was like a marble slab: It was difficult to write on it, but when finally inscribed it retained forever what was written thereon. On Cleanthes' death in 232 BC the Stoa came under the headship of **Chrysippos** of Tarsus, a prolific scholar who wrote more than seven hundred

We are mad, not only individually, but nationally. We check manslaughter and isolated murders; but what of war and the much vaunted crime of slaughtering whole peoples?

SENECA

Train thyself to pay careful attention to what is being said by another and as far as possible enter into his soul.

MARCUS

Apart from the will there is nothing good or bad.

EPICTETUS

Lead me, Zeus, and you, Fate, wherever you have assigned me. I shall follow without hesitation; but even if I am disobedient and do not wish to, I shall follow no less surely.

CLEANTHES

Of supreme importance to every living thing is keeping body and soul together and maintaining consciousness of its existence.

CHRYSIPPOS

It is a man's especial privilege to love even those who stumble.

MARCUS

°*This scenario is suggestively similar in detail to the beliefs of the Jains of India, who distinguish between "mundane" souls bound in sticky karma matter and "liberated" souls that ascend to the top of the world in blissful contemplation. See, for example, Hari Satya Bhattacharya,* Reals in the Jaina Metaphysics *(The Seth Santi Khetsy Charitable Trust, Bombay, 1966), Chapter 7.*

volumes, all now lost. Though Chrysippos's writing was pedantic and obscure, he made lasting contributions to logic and grammar; it was largely his Stoicism that influenced Western thought. Epictetus once wryly observed that "When a man is proud because he can understand and explain the writings of Chrysippos, say to yourself, 'If Chrysippos had not written obscurely, this man would have had nothing to be proud of.'" [5] He died in 205 BC. With the work of Zeno and his two successors, the coherent essentials of Stoic philosophy were complete.

Two scholars from the island of Rhodes represented the Middle Stoa. **Panaetius** (c. 185–109 BC) was born to a wealthy and influential family, studied at Pergamus—which boasted one of the great libraries of the ancient world, second only to Alexandria—then studied at Athens. Panaetius introduced Stoicism to the Roman world. He moved to Rome in 143 BC and began transforming Stoicism into a belief system congenial to aristocratic Romans, whom he influenced through his friendship with the younger Scipio (the general who destroyed Carthage). He humanized and softened Stoic doctrine, made it more accommodating to the world, and admitted the validity of worldly pleasures (which Zeno had denied). He emphasized gradual human growth toward Stoic wisdom through education and practice. He was elected as president of the Stoa and spent the last twenty years of life in Athens.

Posidonius (c. 135–51 BC) was Panaetius's most brilliant student. Nicknamed "The Athlete" (also a wrestler), he was a Syrian by birth. Philosopher, scientist, historian, and geographer, he traveled widely over much of the western empire, carrying on research and writing voluminously. (His history of his own times filled fifty-two volumes.) After settling in Rhodes, he became a magnet for Stoic studies and attracted the best scholars; he strongly influenced the development of Roman Stoicism, especially through his pupil and friend Cicero. He differed with Zeno in holding that human emotions are natural and good. Posidonius also gave the Stoic idea of immortality a new twist. While Zeno had suggested that only virtuous souls are immortal and Cleanthes had taught that all souls are immortal regardless of their virtue and Chrysippos was sure only virtuous Stoics would survive death and Panaetius had argued that a soul dies with the body—Posidonius, by contrast, taught that the good souls rise into the upper realms of the cosmos whence they came and will there live on as one with divine Reason, basking among the stars and contemplating the movement of the heavens. The sinful souls, caked with layers of earthy matter and heavy, hover near the Earth, where they can be repeatedly reincarnated into further existences.° [He agreed with most Stoics, both early and late, that the soul is not eternal but lives only until it is consumed in the fiery conflagration at the end of this world period. Another popular doctrine promulgated by Posidonius held that the Stoic world mission and the expansion of the Roman Empire are two sides of the same coin; the empire, as a representative of the universal God, must live up to its moral obligations to all people everywhere.

The Late Stoa is represented by some of the world's greatest writers. **Seneca** (4 BC–AD 65), born in Spain, was wealthy, eloquent, and influential. His writings include ten dramatic tragedies, dozens of treatises, homilies, and several books on the natural sciences. Banished to Corsica in AD 41 by the jealous Messalina, wife of the emperor Claudius, he was recalled in AD 49 (by Claudius's second wife Agrippina) to become tutor to the youthful Nero. In AD 65 his Stoic faith was put to the test. He was charged with complicity in a conspiracy against the emperor and ordered by Nero to end his life. Since the Stoics approved of one's right to take charge of the circumstances of one's death, rather than waiting for the decline of faculties and a doddering exit, Seneca opened his veins at the peak of his spiritual power, as he had been commanded. The moving events of Seneca's last hours were recorded for us in the Annals of Tacitus.[6]

Epictetus (AD 55–135) had been a Phrygian slave belonging to one of Nero's bodyguards; freed, he taught in Rome till AD 90, when the emperor Domitian expelled all philosophers from the city; after that he taught at Nicopolis in northern Greece. Epictetus addressed the masses rather than citizens of wealth and culture, for it is the poor, he said, who are in need of philosophy. Though he wrote nothing, his lectures have been preserved through the notes of one of his pupils, the historian Arrian. A theistic idealist, Epictetus taught that we are in charge of nothing but our own will. "Two maxims we must ever bear in mind," he said, "that apart from the will there is nothing good or bad, and that we must not try to anticipate or direct events, but merely to accept them with intelligence."[7] We must accept, he was saying, whatever we can't change. He also taught that human nature is essentially good but that moral teaching can make us better.

Marcus Aurelius wrote but a single work, the *Meditations*, but it was enough to make him one of the most loved of all Western philosophers. Marcus was a visionary statesman, an innovative legislator, and a brilliant commander of Roman legions that held the empire's borders against relentless barbaric invasions. He is most remembered in Western history for the sort of personal qualities that transform otherwise mundane souls into saints.

MARCUS AURELIUS OF ROME AND THE WORLD

PHILOSOPHER-KING

Marcus Aurelius (AD 121–80), the fourteenth emperor of the Roman Empire, was a devout Stoic layman whose philosophical life embodied virtually all doctrines of the Stoic tradition. He is an admirable example of one who lived his faith. Marcus was great because he succeeded in living in the world while refusing to compromise his ideals with the petty obsessions of lesser men; his Stoic philosophy—a set of convictions, carefully and rationally thought through, about how *he* should run *his life*—made this possible. His only writing was a sort of inner-life journal of random reflections we commonly call *Meditations* but that he referred to as *Things Written to Himself*. It was not a book of confessions, like Augustine's, designed to purge away the guilt of being human. In fact, the only noticeable guilt in Marcus is the divine discontent of chastising himself for sometimes accepting lower standards than he ought.[8] Rather, the *Meditations* was for Marcus a dialogue with his own soul; it was a way of wrestling with pain, clarifying problems, searching for guidance, and attempting to illuminate the path ahead. It was for him an ongoing exercise in self-discovery and a workbook for the practicing of good habits. We may fairly wonder whether Marcus could have carried the loads of his imperial office and survived the tragedies of a lonely life had he not had his journal for confiding his true thoughts and feelings.

THE MAN

He was born in Rome of an old Spanish family and named Marcus Annius Verus. While still a youth he lost both parents, but he remembered them gratefully. From his father, he wrote, "I learned modesty and manliness"; and from his mother, a woman of talent and culture, he learned "religious piety, generosity, and not only refraining from wrong-doing but even from thoughts of it." He dearly loved his mother (who was enormously wealthy) and from her learned, he says, "to be far removed from the ways of the rich."[9]

Gold is tested by fire, great men by adversity.

SENECA

On Seneca What more could a Christian say than this pagan has said?

SAINT AUGUSTINE

No thing great is created suddenly, any more than a bunch of grapes or a fig. If you tell me that you desire a fig, I answer you that there must be time. Let it first blossom, then bear fruit, then ripen.

EPICTETUS

Only the educated are free.

EPICTETUS

First say to yourself what you would be; and then do what you have to do.

EPICTETUS

Seek not that the things which happen should happen as you wish, but wish the things which happen to be as they are, and you will have a tranquil flow of life.

EPICTETUS

The Emperor Marcus Aurelius (AD 121–80)

Watch the stars in their courses as one that runneth about with them therein; . . . for thoughts on these things cleanse away the mire of our earthly life.

MARCUS

On Marcus *By nature a good man, his education and the moral training he imposed upon himself made him a far better one.*

CASSIUS DIO
(MARCUS'S
BIOGRAPHER)

He spent his childhood in a country home on the Caelium, one of the Seven Hills of Rome—"my Caelia," he called it. From there he could look northward and see the Forum, the Coliseum, the Circus Maximus, and the Palatine capped by the imperial palace. From his birth he lived and breathed the opulent atmosphere of the Eternal City.

At the age of six Marcus was endowed with a gold ring and a tunic and was initiated into the Order of the Equites. At seven he was enrolled in a religious guild whose duties included conducting state ceremonies for Mars, the god of war. During their processionals through the city streets, Marcus would have worn a breastplate covered by a military cloak and carried a short sword on his left arm and a shield or spear in his right; they paraded, danced, and chanted hymns to Mars in archaic Latin.

Marcus was given the best education possible, and it began with a thorough grounding in reading, writing, and arithmetic. He was always grateful for his education; he considered himself fortunate "to have enjoyed good teachers at home and to have learned that it is a duty to spend liberally on such things."[10]

At twelve his secondary education commenced with studying geometry, music, mathematics, and painting. To be educated in the Roman world meant a thorough acquaintance with Greek language and literature, so he was placed in the hands of one Greek and two Latin masters. He became fluent in both languages by reciting and memorizing long passages from the dramatists and historians. Marcus later wrote his thanks to Alexander the Grammaticus, who had taught him "to avoid finding fault and not to criticize in a carping spirit those who use outlandish expressions, solicisms, and an awkward style; but to use the right phrase to express oneself neatly and precisely."[11]

Marcus began his study of philosophy at age twelve, and while Stoicism eventually became his guide through life, at this tender age the doctrine of the antinomian Cynics captivated his young mind. His Latin biographer Cassius Dio tells us Marcus imitated these wandering mendicants who made a cult of the simple life: He "adopted the dress and a little later the habits of endurance of the [Cynic] philosopher. He followed his studies, clad in a rough Greek cloak. He slept on the ground, and it was only at his mother's insistence that he consented with reluctance to sleep on a little bed strewn with skins."

At fourteen the third stage of his education began. He assumed the *toga virilis*, a plain white garment indicating he was now an adult man and a full Roman citizen. He concentrated on studying oratory, which included philology, literature, and philosophy. He had three tutors in Greek oratory, one in Latin oratory, and one in law; altogether, this gave him a full university education in the liberal arts.

Marcus turned seventeen in April AD 138, and momentous events began to transpire. In January of that year the emperor Hadrian had chosen Marcus's uncle Antoninus to succeed to power, but Hadrian had chosen Antoninus on the condition he in turn adopt his nephew as his successor. Hadrian had monitored Marcus's development since childhood and admired the young man's brilliance and devotion to his studies. The emperor had made a pun on his name Verus, which in Latin means "true"; Hadrian nicknamed him Verissimus, "the truest" of all.

Thus Marcus became frightfully aware, while still sixteen, that someday—Fate permitting—he would have to assume the awesome responsibilities of running the Roman Empire. On the night of his adoption, he had a dream about his shoulders seeming to be made of ivory, and he feared he would not be able to bear the burden of governing the empire; but he awoke from the dream reassured his shoulders would be strong enough.

At age seventeen (that April), therefore, Marcus became heir apparent to the imperial throne. He became a quaestor, was designated consul of Rome, and was given the name Caesar. He enrolled in the college of priests and moved into the imperial palace. Life does go on in a palace, he later wrote, so "it should be possible to live the right kind of life even in a palace." But it wasn't going to be easy.

In the spring of AD 145 Marcus, then twenty-four, married a cousin, Annia Galeria, known in history as Faustina II. In his reflections Marcus thanks the gods for being blessed with a wife "so obedient, so affectionate, and so without affectations."[12] [All told, fourteen children were born to them, including two sets of twins.]

Marcus had to deal with the pain of death all his life. In AD 149 Faustina bore twin sons, and Marcus celebrated the event by issuing a coin showing busts of two small boys and bearing the inscription *Temporum felicitas*, "what a happy time!" But soon the coins showed Marcus and Faustina with one tiny girl and one baby boy, and, still later that year, new coins showed them, standing, with a little girl alone. Several times in his *Meditations* Marcus refers to grief from the loss of children. He wrote: "Others may pray, 'How may I not lose my little child!' But thy prayer should be: 'How may I not be afraid when I lose him.'"[13] He quotes Epictetus: "A man while fondly kissing his child should whisper in his heart: 'It just could be that tomorrow thou wilt die.' Ill-omened words! 'Not at all,' said Epictetus, 'nothing is ill-omened if it is a natural process. For it would also be ill-omened to talk of ears of corn being harvested.'"[14] Another son was born to Marcus and Faustina in AD 152, and the story was repeated. Coins first showed two little girls and an infant boy, but by AD 156 they depicted only two little girls with their parents.

Little wonder that Marcus reflected so often on our mortality; little wonder that the brevity of human life never left his consciousness. "How tiny a fragment of boundless and abysmal Time has been appointed to each man! For in a moment it is lost in eternity." "A little while and thou wilt have forgotten everything, a little while and everything will have forgotten thee." "A limit has been set to thy time, which if thou use not to let daylight into thy soul, it will be gone—and thou!—and never again shall the chance be thine." "Execute every act of thy life as though it were thy last." "Let thine every deed and word and thought be those of a man who can depart from life this moment."[15]

Look within [all things]. Let not the special quality or worth of anything escape thee.

MARCUS

Do not think yourself hurt and you remain unhurt.

MARCUS

Little indeed, then, is a man's life, and little the nook of earth whereon he lives.

MARCUS

For nothing is so conducive to greatness of mind as the ability to examine systematically and honestly everything that meets us in life.

MARCUS

This that I am, whatever it be, is mere flesh and a little breath and the ruling Reason.

MARCUS

Coins from the reign of Marcus Aurelius documenting loss of his children. Coins were minted to celebrate the arrival of his babies, but on later coins their likenesses have been removed. The loss of his children was the greatest grief of Marcus's life. This gold aureus, minted in AD 159, depicts Faustina the Younger with their three children.

[Think of] the times of Vespasian, and thou shalt see all these things: mankind marrying, rearing children, sickening, dying, warring, making holiday, trafficking, tilling, flattering others, vaunting themselves, suspecting, scheming, praying for the death of others, murmuring at their own lot, loving, hoarding, coveting a consulate, coveting a kingdom. Not a vestige of that life of theirs is left anywhere any longer.[16]

This awareness of the transience of life shadowed all Marcus's waking thoughts. It eased the pain; it enabled him to go on. No raging at the dying of the light. No burning and raving at close of day. Don't bang your head against the wall of impossibility. Be a Stoic: Change what you can; accept what you can't. It is Nature's way. "Behave not as though thou hadst ten thousand years to live. Thy doom hangs over thee. While thou livest, while thou mayest, become good."[17] At age twenty-five Marcus vowed his full devotion to studying Stoic philosophy—for as long as the world would let him. Throughout the rest of his life he alternated between carrying his worldly obligations—which he met energetically, resourcefully, and with much common sense—and nourishing his philosophical/spiritual life. When his duties became oppressive, he would return to his thoughts in stolen hours, late at night, in a tent pitched beside a battlefield and there, by candlelight, continue his reflections.

Marcus became emperor at age thirty-nine (on March 7, AD 161) and was titled "Imperator Caesar Marcus Aurelius Antoninus Augustus." Always uncomfortable with the power and public rituals his office required of him, he wrote (to himself), "Be careful that you don't become Caesarified" and "Don't let yourself be dipped in the purple dye!"[18] All who knew him testified that in his personal qualities—sincerity, discipline, morality, simplicity—Marcus was the same man as emperor that he was as a private citizen. But it was a struggle. "Keep thyself a simple and good man, uncorrupt, dignified, plain, a friend of justice, god-fearing, gracious, affectionate, manful in doing thy duty. Strive to be always such as Philosophy minded to make thee. Revere the Gods, save mankind. Life is short."[19] Marcus's likeness is familiar from coins and inscriptions. He had a handsome face, deep-set brooding eyes, and black curly hair and, as a warrior-emperor, was heavily bearded. Physically, he was not strong; he apparently suffered from digestive trouble, chest pains, and ulcers and had prolonged periods of illness; he was under the treatment of doctors most of his life. Marcus was dedicated to his work. "A man should do a man's work, as the fig tree does the work of a fig tree, the dog of a dog, and the bee of a bee." One of the highest ideals of human life is to be what we are, and this being is established for us; we must get in touch with it. "Consider each tiny plant, each little bird, the ant, the spider, the bee, how they go about their own work and do each his part for the building up of an orderly Universe. Dost *thou* then refuse to do the work of a man?"[20] In his younger years Marcus would arise as early as three or four o'clock so as to have hours to himself before the world intruded on his space; in his later years he slept little. He enjoyed boxing, fencing, and wrestling, both as participant and spectator. He also was a talented painter.

Those who knew him saw a modest, reserved, and serious man, thorough in all he did; he paid great attention to detail, almost to the point of perfectionism. His biographer Cassius Dio says that "he never said, wrote, or did anything as if it were an unimportant matter." His lifetime preoccupation with the condition of slaves, orphans, and minors tells us much about his character.

Marcus's presentiments of weighty responsibilituies more than came true. He spent most of his ruling years fighting back invasions on the northern frontier and quelling revolts. After defeating the Parthians in Syria in AD 161, his soldiers

A relief from c. AD 176–80 showing Marcus pardoning defeated barbarians.

A limit has been set to thy time, which if thou use not to let daylight into thy soul, it will be gone—and thou!—and never again shall the chance be thine.
MARCUS

Thou canst at a moment's notice retire into thyself. For nowhere can a man find a retreat more full of peace or more free from care than his own soul.
MARCUS

°*For example, see Arnold Toynbee's* A Study of History *(Oxford University Press, 1954), vol. 10, pp. 213–242.*

Execute every act of thy life as though it were thy last.
MARCUS

Rational creatures have been made for one another.
MARCUS

Those who do not attend closely to the motions of their own souls must inevitably be unhappy.
MARCUS

brought back a plague that swept the empire and decimated the Roman population. In AD 167–8, after Marcus had crossed the Danube pursuing invaders, Germanic tribes invaded Italy, and the mighty Roman Empire weakened and almost fell; but he finally defeated the invaders and secured the frontier. During these years invasions of Roman territory occurred in Egypt, Spain, and Britain. In AD 175 a trusted general in the east, hearing a rumor of Marcus's death, proclaimed himself emperor; though assassination soon ended the revolt, Marcus marched through the eastern states to secure them. While he was away Faustina died.

During times such as these, Marcus wrote *Things Written to Himself*, in Greek. It contains an intimate glimpse into one man's inner struggle to come to terms with the downside of life—and rise above it. Such thoughts have a timeless feel. The fact he wrote them during the heat of battle makes them all the more poignant.

The *Meditations* is divided into twelve books. The first book—but the last one written—is his tribute to family, friends, and teachers who had meant much to him. He thanks them all and notes what he learned from each. This is the book that has had such a profound influence on Western readers.° The other eleven books are his attempt to summarize the lessons he had learned from life. He wrote them not in the quiet of a palace library but amid his administrative and military responsibilities along the battle lines. Marcus composed Book Two, for example, while he was fighting the Quadi; he wrote Book Three at Carnuntum, a Roman outpost on the upper Danube frontier (some twenty miles east of Vienna), while he was conducting a campaign against the Marcomannic barbarians.

STOICISM IN LIFE

Marcus had to work out a philosophy to live by. His notebook shows just how desperately he needed the strength and support of meaningful beliefs. He first became acquainted with Stoic philosophy when he was age twelve, but the ideas lay dormant; at that age he had little use for them.

But sooner or later life makes philosophers of us all. In time he came to need a coherent set of ideas to render life intelligible, to help him accept what he must accept and change what he can change, and he had to accomplish this without losing either his integrity or his sanity. What was important was not whether he could find *the* answers—none may exist—but whether *he* could find answers that would work *for him*.

Marcus might have asked, first, whether one really has to live in the world. It's rough out there. Maybe there are gentler paths to follow. Perhaps better paths exist for others but not for Marcus. In another lifetime, he surely would have chosen some other life path so that he could meditate, reflect, paint, write poetry, compose music—so that he could tend to his spiritual life. But for all of us the time and place are given, and since Fate chose to birth Marcus in second-century Rome and endow him with Stoic ideas, this meant accepting the conditions and responsibilities assigned to him.

He reminded himself: "Men seek ways to escape from all this—in country retreats, by the sea, or getting away to the mountains; and you too long deeply for such things. But such a longing is not right for one who understands life, for it is always possible, instantly, to retreat into thyself, and there find peace and release from the cares of life."[21] The wise will not seek other forms of escape, though we all may want to, for we are all called to live "the life of the social animal" and be responsible to our fellow human beings, to whom we belong. But from the cruel pragmatics of "the real world" we all must flee. "When forced, as it seems, by thine environment to be utterly disquieted, return with all speed into thy self, staying in discord no longer than thou must."[22]

So, as Marcus saw it, *the problem* was finding a way to live in the world and not be destroyed by it. One *answer*, he reasoned, lies in making a deep and permanent distinction between what we can take charge of and what we can't, a distinction, that is, between our inner world that we can exercise a modicum of control over and the real world "out there" that we have little or no control over at all.

Clearly, we are not in charge of the world-out-there. The world of events is merely a stage, provided for us by the Fates, where we play out our lives. "All the world's a stage," Shakespeare later wrote, "and all the men and women merely players."[23] But we must understand clearly that we have little choice of the roles we play. Fate has cast us in our roles. Marcus, for instance, did not *choose* to be emperor or to marry Faustina; he did not *choose* to fight the Parthians or Quadi. No auditions, no tryouts, no callbacks occurred. Such events are the acts and scenes in the playing out of the drama, and while a few individuals are selected to play lead roles, most of us are merely spear-carriers. But once cast we all have a sacred duty to play our roles well, for this is how history will judge us.

Furthermore, Marcus saw, quite a few of the stage props supplied for our roles are also given and are quite beyond our control. We can't change the time and place of our birth, our parents, our genetic makeup, or the fact of aging and death. So why fret and fume and struggle over what we can't change?

We all should be actors playing our roles with consummate skill but without ever being caught up in the destructive passions of the dramatic plot. Marcus thought in terms of *apatheia*. The word derives from the Greek alpha-negative *a*, meaning "not," and *pathos*, "suffering," implying an indifference to painful events. Stoic apathy was a peaceful state of mind and body resulting from a deliberate detachment from the disturbing conditions of everyday life.

What we must do, Marcus reasoned, is turn to our inner world and take charge. Marcus saw the self metaphorically as a precious plot of ground and individuals as caretakers of their garden plot. Each must look after the garden, tend it, not let weeds grow, and keep the plants and flowers protected and nourished. "From now therefore bethink thee of the retreat into this little plot that is thyself. Above all distract not thyself, be not too eager, but be thine own master, and look upon life as a man, as a human being, as a citizen, as a mortal creature."[24]

This is the goal of life for Marcus: to protect and nourish the well-being of the self. The tranquility of our spiritual/emotional self should be a normal, natural ground-state that never leaves us. The wise one "will not go against the Divinity that is planted in his breast; but rather he will preserve his deepest inner self in tranquility. He will, above all, preserve his own autonomy and integrity, and not let anything alienate him from himself."[25]

LESSONS OF LIFE

Other themes of faith recur repeatedly in Marcus's reflections; while almost all are classical Stoic beliefs, his treatment of them made them intensely personal. One of the strongest is his sense of belonging to the World. Stoicism was the first great universalist philosophy of the Greek world, and Marcus found himself in complete harmony with the Stoic world vision. Just as the Roman Empire had expanded and dissolved traditional boundaries, so Marcus's Stoic inclusiveness rested, not on differences, but on the commonalities of human experience.

Marcus's all-inclusive thinking had three foci. First, he loathes pettiness and detests small minds and small souls; the antidote for the disease of narrowness is to think big. "Take a bird's-eye view of the world, its endless gatherings and endless ceremonials, voyagings manifold in storm and calm, and the vicissitudes of things

All that is in tune with thee, O Universe, is in tune with me! Nothing that is in due time for thee is too early or too late for me!
MARCUS

This must always be borne in mind, what is the Nature of the whole Universe, and what mine, and how this stands in relation to that.
MARCUS

Fret not thyself; study to be simple.
MARCUS

Let thine every deed and word and thought be those of a man who can depart from life this moment.
MARCUS

coming into being, participating in being, ceasing to be. Reflect too on the life lived long ago by other men, and the life that shall be lived after thee, and is now being lived in barbarous countries; and how many have never even heard thy name, and how many will very soon forget it, and how many who now perhaps acclaim, will very soon blame thee, and that neither memory nor fame nor anything else whatever is worth reckoning." "Thou hast but a short time left to live," he reflects. "So live as on a mountain; for whether it be here or there matters not provided that, wherever a man live, he lived as a citizen of the World-City." And for Marcus? "As Antoninus my city and my country is Rome; but as a man I belong to the world."[26]

Second, "It is in man's nature to care for all men." Dividing the human species into race groups, classes, or ethnic, nationalist, or language units creates needless artificial boundary lines. The human race is one. Reason, he held, is common to all, and it gives to everyone a sense of what is right and wrong; this being the case, a natural law inherent in all humans tells us how to live. "If so," he reasoned, "the Universe is as it were a state," and each human being is a fellow citizen of this World-city where "all other states are as but households."[27]

Third and most important, we must think big if we are to live right; we must be able to see ourselves in the truth context of the Whole. "He that knoweth not what the Universe is knoweth not where he is." "This must always be borne in mind, what is the Nature of the whole Universe, and what mine, and how this stands in relation to that." "First, I am a part of the whole Universe controlled by Nature; and second, I stand in some intimate connection with all other kindred parts." Marcus constantly dwells on the necessity of seeing the Big Picture. Think big, he was saying to himself; otherwise he will go off track, lose sight of who and what he is, and live by myths. "Watch the stars," he wrote, "for thoughts on these things cleanse away the mire of our earthly life." Playing on a Pythagorean theme, he meditated, "Look at the sky in the morning, that we may have in remembrance those hosts of heaven that ever follow the same course and accomplish their work in the same way, and their orderly system, and their purity, and their nakedness; for there is no veil before a star." This was the mystic in Marcus, and he felt it with a sense of urgency. "Yet now, if never before, shouldest thou realize of what Universe thou art a part." [28]

"It brings gladness to a man to do a man's true work," Marcus wrote; and "a man's true work" demands taking "a comprehensive view of the Nature of the Universe and all that is done at her bidding." Marcus's passion to see and understand the whole universe was sincere; he had an authentic synoptic mind. He dearly longed to know where he fit into the big picture, to give his life meaning in terms of the whole. But Marcus insisted that his belief system must be founded not on faith in mythic ideas; he was firm in knowing that his big picture must be honest, true to the world's stubborn facts, a belief system founded on truth. Others may counsel their souls into blind belief: Just believe, for, after all (it is said) everyone must have beliefs to live by. And Marcus, too, yearned to believe, but he was sufficiently honest as a thinker to insist that his beliefs be connected to reality. In other words, he refused to be a blind believer.

For this reason Marcus Aurelius deserves to be included with the Western philosophers, for though he belongs to the post-Aristotelian pragmatic turn in philosophy, he still wanted the philosophy he must live by to be founded on the truth. Marcus is an outstanding example of one who passionately wanted to find a philosophy to guide him through each day but who knew he must do it himself (for no one else's philosophy would do the job for him). He knew clearly that he couldn't indulge in blind belief in creating that philosophy; he must work it out on the firm foundation of the

Consider each tiny plant, each little bird, the ant, the spider, the bee, how they go about their own work and do each his part for the building up of an orderly Universe. Dost thou then refuse to do the work of a man?

MARCUS

For it is but the present that a man can be deprived of, if, as is the fact, it is this alone that he has, and what he has not a man cannot part with.

MARCUS

The soul takes its dye from the thoughts.

MARCUS

truth of things—not a partial piece of the truth, not a one-sided truth or a "selective" truth, and not a parochially biased truth but *the* truth, the *whole* truth, and *only* the truth. He wrote: "Salvation in life depends on our seeing everything in its entirety and in its reality, in its Matter and its Cause: on our doing what is just and speaking what is true with all our soul."[29] (Marcus would have been elated to live in our time, in the twenty-first century, having access to the abundance of empirical information for building his beliefs.)

It follows that Marcus, reflecting Stoic values, placed great emphasis on education and knowledge. He wanted to "see things in all their naked reality." "For nothing is so conducive to greatness of mind as the ability to examine systematically and honestly everything that meets us in life." He expressed a lifelong gratitude to philosophy for giving him knowledge and perspective. "All the things of the body are as a river, and the things of the soul as a dream and a vapour; and life is a warfare and a pilgrim's sojourn, and fame after death is only forgetfulness. What then is it that can help us on our way? One thing and one alone—Philosophy; and this consists in keeping the divine 'genius' within pure and unwronged, lord of all pleasures and pains, doing nothing aimlessly or with deliberate falsehood and hypocrisy." Elsewhere he says, "Simple and modest is the work of Philosophy: lead me not astray into pomposity and pride."[30]

As he applied these ideas to life, where did Marcus come out? "In each case therefore must thou say: 'This has come from God; and this is due to the conjunction of fate and the contexture of the world's web and some such coincidence and chance; while that comes from a clansman and a kinsman and a neighbour, albeit one who is ignorant of what is really in accordance with his nature. But I am not ignorant, therefore I treat him kindly and justly, in accordance with the natural law of neighbourliness.'"[31]

To summarize: (1) Though he moved within the frame of Stoicism, Marcus took full responsibility for working out a truth-philosophy for himself, knowing that no one else could do it for him; (2) he created his philosophy from the best facts ("scientific") as he knew them in his time; and (3) he infused this philosophy with the noblest values he could identify and apply to his life. Marcus Aurelius thus is a valuable role model for anyone in the process of developing a personal philosophy and struggling to apply it to daily living.

Another recurrent theme in Marcus's *Meditations* tells us much about the man, and it involves at least a paradox and at most a contradiction. First, Marcus believed that everything happens as it does because of causal "necessity." That is, like all Stoics, he was a determinist. "Has something befallen thee?" he wrote. "It is well. Everything that befalls was from the beginning destined and spun for thee as thy share out of the Whole." "Remember that, as it is monstrous to be surprised at a fig tree bearing figs, so also is it to be surprised at the Universe bearing its own particular crop." This determinism he applied, time and again, to human behavior. "Whatever man thou meetest, put to thyself at once this question: *What are this man's convictions about good and evil?* For if they are such and such about pleasure and pain and what is productive of them, about good report and ill report, about death and life, it will be in no way strange or surprising to me if he does such and such things. So I will remember that he is constrained to act as he does."[32]

Out of this Stoic determinism Marcus succeeded in accepting miscreant behavior in others to an unprecedented degree, for "to expect the bad not to do wrong is worthy of a madman; for that is to wish for impossibilities." This empirical observation on his part attests to his observational powers. Others do as they do, he knew, because they are determined ("by genes," we might say, or "by environmental conditioning");

In the way of Nature there can be no evil.

MARCUS

But my nature is rational and civic; my city and country, as Antoninus, is Rome; as a man, the world.

MARCUS

All the things of the body are as a river, and the things of the soul as a dream and a vapour; and life is a warfare and a pilgrim's sojourn, and fame after death is only forgetfulness. What then is it that can help us on our way? One thing and one alone—Philosophy.

MARCUS

A little while and thou wilt have forgotten everything, a little while and everything will have forgotten thee.

MARCUS

they do not act of their own free will. He therefore had a great capacity for acceptance of what others did. Even more, it led to empathy and forgiveness. At one point he wrote (to his soul), "Train thyself to pay careful attention to what is being said by another and as far as possible enter into his soul." "Look within. Let not the special quality or worth of anything escape thee." It follows that Marcus was one of the least judgmental of all Western philosophers. (He was critical when weighing ideas, of course, but not when evaluating people.) By temperament and by self-creation, he ceased to be a blamer. "If the choice rests with thee, why do the thing? If with another, whom dost thou blame? Atoms or Gods? To do either would be crazy folly. No one is to blame." With this empathetic understanding and consequent insight into human nature, and with a rare grace, he accepted the foibles of all human beings. . . .[33]

All that is rational is akin.

MARCUS

. . . except himself. Marcus did not accept that he, too, was determined. For himself he *assumed* free will and personal accountability. "Hear Epictetus," he reminded himself, "no one can rob us of our free choice." He clearly felt that he was in charge of his inner life, that he could there select and mold and create at will. "Efface thy impressions, saying ever to thyself: 'Now lies it with me that this soul should harbour no wickedness nor lust nor any disturbing element at all; but that, seeing the true nature of all things, I should deal with each as is its due. Bethink thee of this power that Nature gives thee.'" He assumed the freedom to choose to live according to Nature, and that it was wholly within his sphere of control to nourish the virtues he wanted to guide his life. *He* would choose how *he* treated others. "I am not ignorant, therefore I choose to treat another kindly and justly, in accordance with the natural law of neighbourliness." *He* alone would determine how *he* responded to life's inevitable downside. "Has something befallen thee? It is well. Everything that befalls was from the beginning destined and spun for thee as thy share out of the Whole." "'Ah,' you say, 'unlucky am I, that this has befallen me!' Nay, but rather, lucky am I that, though this has befallen me, yet am I still unhurt, neither crushed by the present nor dreading the future. . . . Does what has befallen thee hinder thee one whit from being just, high-minded, chaste, sensible, deliberate, straightforward, modest, free, and from possessing all the other qualities, the presence of which enables a man's nature to come fully into its own?" "Forget not in future, when anything would lead thee to feel hurt, to take thy stand upon this axiom: 'This is no misfortune, but to bear it nobly is good fortune.'" "Pass then through this tiny span of time in accordance with Nature, and come to thy journey's end with a good grace, just as an olive falls when it is fully ripe, praising the earth that bare it and grateful to the tree that gave it growth."[34]

It is in man's nature to care for all men.

MARCUS

These deterministic-behavioristic beliefs led Marcus to another guideline that went far in taking the sting out of the incessant criticisms heaped upon a Roman emperor: Since others can't help what they think, the proverbial "what others think" is unimportant; only what he himself thought was of final value, so both praise and hostile criticism are irrelevant to one's commitment to a noble life. "That which is praised is made neither better nor worse thereby," he wrote. "Does an emerald forfeit its excellence by not being praised? Does gold, ivory, purple, a lyre, a poniard, a floweret, a shrub?" We must not let ourselves be blown about by "others' opinions." "Be like a headland of rock on which the waves break incessantly; but it stands fast and around it the seething of the waters sinks to rest."[35]

We should not embrace the opinion of all, but of those alone who live in conscious agreement with Nature.

MARCUS

Dress not thy thought in too fine a garb.

MARCUS

LAST HOURS

Encamped in Vienna in the nineteenth year of his reign, while his army was holding back the Germanic invaders, Marcus was stricken ill; he sensed that death, an old invader long stayed, was near. He beckoned his son Commodus to his bedside and outlined strategies for holding off the Germanic invaders. He abandoned further food and drink. On the sixth day he rose from his couch, led Commodus outside his tent, and presented him to his armies as their new emperor. Then he returned to his tent, lay down, covered his head as if to sleep, and died. He was almost fifty-nine. The date was March 17 of the year AD 180. He had borne the burdens of empire, the loss of wife and children, the betrayal of trusted friends, the degradation of war, the stress of life, personal illnesses, and the spectre of death; yet through it all he had maintained his sensitivity, his decency, and his humanity.

His body was returned to Rome in a final triumphal march.

Enter into every man's ruling Reason, and give every one else an opportunity to enter into thine.

MARCUS

> *Man, thou hast been a citizen in this World-City, what matters it to thee if for five years or a hundred? For under its laws equal treatment is meted out to all. What hardship then is there in being banished from the City, not by a tyrant or an unjust judge, but by the very Nature who settled thee in it? So might a praetor, having commissioned a comic actor, dismiss him from the stage. 'But I have not played my five acts,' you protest, 'but only three.' Well, maybe so. But in life three acts often count as a full play. For he that is responsible for thy composition and, now, thy decomposition—it is he who will decide when it's complete. Thou art responsible for neither. Depart then with a good grace, for he also that dismisses thee is gracious.*[36]
>
> THINGS WRITTEN TO HIMSELF (XII.36), BY IMPERATOR CAESAR MARCUS AURELIUS ANTONINUS AUGUSTUS (REIGNED AD 161–80).

Pass then through this tiny span of time in accordance with Nature, and come to thy journey's end with a good grace, just as an olive falls when it is fully ripe, praising the earth that bare it and grateful to the tree that gave it growth.

MARCUS

ENDNOTES

1 Diogenes Laërtius, *Lives of Eminent Philosophers*, VII.10–11.
2 Diogenes, *Lives*, VII.28, 31.
3 Diogenes, *Lives*, VII.29.
4 Epictetus, *Discourses*, III.10.
5 Epictetus, *The Manual of Epictetus*, 49, in *A New History of Philosophy*, by Wallace I. Matson (Harcourt Brace Jovanovich, 1987), I, 158.
6 Tacitus, *Annals*, XIII.
7 Epictetus, *Discourses*, III.10.
8 Marcus Aurelius, *Meditations*, V.5.
9 Marcus, *Meditations*, I.2, 3.
10 Marcus, *Meditations*, I.4.
11 Marcus, *Meditations*, I.10.
12 Marcus, *Meditations*, I.17.
13 Marcus, *Meditations*, IX.40; see also I.8.
14 Marcus, *Meditations*, XI.34.
15 Marcus, *Meditations*, XII.32, VII.21, II.4, II.31, II.11.
16 Marcus, *Meditations*, IV.32.
17 Marcus, *Meditations*, IV.17.
18 Marcus, *Meditations*, VI.30; see also V.16.
19 Marcus, *Meditations*, VI.30.
20 Marcus, *Meditations*, V.1.
21 Marcus, *Meditations*, IV.3.
22 Marcus, *Meditations*, VI.11.
23 *As You Like It*, 2.7.144ff.
24 Marcus, *Meditations*, IV.7.
25 Marcus, *Meditations*.
26 Marcus, *Meditations*, IX.30, X.15, VI.44; see also I.7.
27 Marcus, *Meditations*, III.4, III.2.
28 Marcus, *Meditations*, VIII.52, II.9, X.6, VII.47, XI.27, II.4; see also XI.1.
29 Marcus, *Meditations*, VIII.26, XII.29.
30 Marcus, *Meditations*, IV.11, III.11, II.17, IX.29.
31 Marcus, *Meditations*, III.3.

32 Marcus, *Meditations*, IV.26, VIII.15, VIII.14.
33 Marcus, *Meditations*, XI.18, VI.53, VI.3, VIII.17.
34 Marcus, *Meditations*, XI.36, VIII.29, III.11, IV.26, IV.49, IV.48.
35 Marcus, *Meditations*, IV.20, IV.49.
36 Marcus, *Meditations*, XII.36.

CHAPTER 15

PLOTINUS OF ALEXANDRIA

The greatest of Neoplatonist thinkers transforms Plato's philosophy into a mystical theology; through meditation he ascends (four times) into the World Soul and leaves behind a pain-ridden physical body; his noetic theology tolls the death of Greek empiricism for the next thousand years.

MYSTICAL THEOLOGY

In the third century *anno Domini*, in Alexandria, Egypt, the brilliant mind and gentle heart of an extraordinary man birthed a great mystical theology. His name was Plotinus, and his "philosophy," Neoplatonism, is often judged as the Greek world's last great intellectual achievement. His philosophy, essentially a reincarnation of Plato's metaphysics transformed into a massive anti-intellectual system, was destined to have enormous appeal to aspiring souls who yearned for something more than what the rational mind, looking unsteadily at the world through deceptive senses, could promise. Plotinus's noetic speculations ended the search for an understanding of the world that characterized the presocratic and Athenian thinkers. After Neoplatonism, all vestiges of critical philosophy entered into a long hibernation, and faith began a thousand-year reign. This marked the beginning of the Dark Ages for philosophy.

SOURCES

The seeds of Neoplatonism had been sown early in the third century by an Alexandrian teacher named Ammonius Saccas, a man "unapproached in breadth of learning." He was honored as the "father" of Neoplatonism. Though famed in his time and held in high esteem by his contemporaries, he is a shadowy figure. According to Porphyry, he was originally a Christian but was converted to Hellenic religion (other accounts from Christians say he remained a Christian). His attempt to reconcile Plato and Aristotle became the basis for his Neoplatonism. Ammonius became the teacher of several eminent thinkers, among them Longinus, Origen the Christian theologian, and Plotinus. His disciples apparently derived the mystical element in all their teachings from him.[1]

Plotinus developed Neoplatonism into an influential cosmic mysticism. His student, Porphyry of Tyre, wrote his biography, and in it he tells us Plotinus was an impressive thinker whose thoughts are well known to us but that his exemplary life is almost impossible to reconstruct since "he could never be persuaded to talk about his ancestry, his parents, or where he was born." Earthly existence just wasn't important to

What do you feel when you see your own inward beauty?
PLOTINUS

No eye ever saw the sun without becoming sun-like, nor can a soul see beauty without becoming beautiful.
PLOTINUS

Plotinus of Alexandria (AD 204–70)

him. Our physical life on the material plane is not worth a fleeting thought since matter is not really real. Matter is the final, exhausted, orgasmic creation of a spiritual universe meditating on itself. Physical matter is itself evil and is therefore the source of all evil in the world. Plotinus, we are told, was terribly embarrassed to be found trapped in a material body. When urged to sit for a painter or sculptor, he refused. "Really now, isn't it enough to have to carry about this reflection in which nature has encapsulated us? Are you serious in asking me to leave behind a likeness just so later viewers can point to a bad image of a bad image and boast that they are looking at something of value?" Plotinus's portrait was painted after all, Porphyry confides; his friend Amelius arranged for an artist to sit in on his lectures, observe him surreptitiously, and paint a picture from memory; he "gave us an excellent portrait of Plotinus without his ever knowing about it." [2] To be sure, Plotinus possessed a zest for living, but that zest did not include living in this world. His whole being centered on the life of the soul and its longing to exit this physical world and become one with God.

Porphyry's brief (forty-two-page) biography of Plotinus documents his teacher's last six years. Porphyry was a keen observer and adoring disciple, and while his account is meager in external dates and events, it succeeds wonderfully in providing an intimate look into the great mystic's inner life. Add Porphyry's biography to Plotinus's own voluminous writings, and we have a remarkably clear view into the workings of both his impressive intellect and his mystical temperament. (Amelius, his chief assistant, was with him for twenty-four years, and he, too, made notes of Plotinus's lectures and anthologized them into almost a hundred volumes; but they are all lost.)

Mystical classics have neither birthday nor native land.
WILLIAM JAMES

Aristotle leads one up to acts of understanding with never a hint that there is anything beyond them.
PROCLUS

WRITING

Writing was an effort for Plotinus; he was a religious sensitive, not an academic scholar. He was also severely dysgraphic and dyslexic. His life was essentially verbal; he always taught orally, by informal lecture and discussion. When, at age fifty, he did commence writing at the urging of friends, he jotted down his notes in slapdash fashion, giving little attention to organization and continuity and none to style. With great concentration he would outline his thoughts in his head down to the last detail; then, when he sat down to write, the material came flooding out at one time and in a rush he would feverishly copy it all down. His thought was deep and intense, his writing terse and concise. But his handwriting was virtually illegible. "Plotinus could not bear to go back on his work even for one re-reading," Porphyry tells us, "and indeed the condition of his eyesight would scarcely allow it: his handwriting was slovenly; he misjoined his words; he cared nothing about spelling; his one concern was for the idea: in these habits, to our general surprise, he remained unchanged to the very end." On one occasion, his friend Longinus, the literary critic, received some manuscripts from Plotinus and found them filled with what he assumed to be scribal errors; he complained, "I would have thought that our friend Amelius would have corrected the copyists' mistakes, but I guess he was too busy." Porphyry assured Longinus that the manuscripts contained no such scribal errors: They were exactly as Plotinus had written them.[3]

As a result, the literary quality of Plotinus's work is the poorest of any major Western philosophical writer, and scholars have been pushed to their limits to produce a decent Greek text and translations. Porphyry posthumously edited Plotinus's writings and performed something of a miracle in assembling the vast collection of notes, arranging them into a semblance of order, and making the corpus intelligible. "Such revision was necessary," he apologizes with laconic understatement. He divided the hodgepodge of material into six groups, each containing nine monographs or treatises. From the Greek word for "nine," *ennea*, Plotinus's great book is called *The Enneads*, or *The Book of Nines*. "I put related treatises together in each *Ennead*," Porphyry informs us, "giving the first place to the less difficult questions." The influence of the *Enneads* on Western thought has been enormous, less on philosophy than on theology; in the Middle Ages it virtually became the bible of Catholic mystics. The Plotinian scholar Elmer O'Brien judges that Plotinus's ideas "molded Western thinking more than did those of a Plato or an Aristotle."[4]

In philosophy all truth is old, and only error is original.
WILL DURANT

IN THE HISTORY OF PHILOSOPHY

Some understanding of the Neoplatonic system is essential if one is to make sense of the next thousand years of philosophical and theological speculation. Christian doctrine from about AD 300 on through Augustine, the Middle Ages, High Scholasticism, and even some branches of modern theology is incomprehensible without an acquaintance with Plotinus's cosmic vision.

Plotinus is remembered in the history of philosophy (1) for transmogrifying Plato's philosophy into a coherent "Neoplatonic" worldview; (2) for defining reality as spiritual rather than material; (3) for his utter disdain of this world, the body, the senses, and all earthly pleasures; (4) for his triune vision of God as the ineffable One, derivative Mind, and World-Soul; (5) for the doctrine of "emanation"; (6) for teaching that life is a journey of the soul toward mystical union with God; (7) for the doctrine of "epistrophe," the longing of the soul to return to its source; (8) his picturesque belief in reincarnation and karma.

You would not seek Me if you had not already found Me.
BLAISE PASCAL

THE MAN

Plotinus was born "in the thirteenth year of Severus" (AD 204) at Lycopolis in Egypt. Genetically, his stock was probably Latin, having descended from recent emigrants from Rome. Religiously, he may have been a Copt, a native Egyptian Christian. He

Graecia capta ferum victorem cepit. Conquered Greece took captive her barbarous conqueror.
HORACE

must have received a good education, since he later evidenced a theoretical knowledge of arithmetic and geometry, mechanics, optics, and music, though he couldn't take time to go into these subjects deeply. He also studied astronomy but stayed clear of the mathematics. The works of the Greek philosophers he had read, but he tended to concentrate on a few favorite books and neglect the rest. His mind moved easily with abstract concepts, but he found it something of a nuisance to have to capture the rapidly moving flow of ideas in the static structures of language. If something was read to him, he grasped the meaning instantly, summarized its essence in his own words, and went merrily on. Concrete data he found uncongenial and bothersome, and empirical observation was to him a useless skill to be left undeveloped.

At the age of twenty-seven, Plotinus "was caught by the passion for philosophy," but he migrated from teacher to teacher and emerged "from all these lectures saddened and discouraged." Finally, a year later, at a friend's suggestion, he sought out Ammonius Saccas, famed for his depth of knowledge and a florid literary style. "Plotinus went, heard a lecture, and exclaimed to his comrade: 'This is the man I've been looking for!'" Something in the great teacher's personality or message captivated Plotinus, and he studied with him for eleven years until Ammonius's death in AD 242.

Plotinus had become interested in Eastern philosophies and wanted to study further "the Persian methods and the system adopted among the Indians." Since the emperor Gordian was just setting out on a military expedition against the Persians, Plotinus joined the campaign. Gordian successfully drove the Persians back across the Euphrates River, but then he was murdered in Mesopotamia by his own soldiers. In considerable danger, Plotinus escaped and made his way back to Antioch and then on to Rome.

He was forty when he arrived in the capital in AD 244. He set up quarters, opened a school, and taught there for the rest of his life. He lived in comfortable surroundings but maintained a simple, even ascetic, lifestyle. Porphyry tells us Plotinus moved in an ever-expanding circle of disciples, made lasting friends, and was loved and trusted by everyone. "He was gentle and was always at the beck and call of anyone having the slightest acquaintance with him. During his twenty-six years in Rome, during which he was frequently the arbiter in disputes, he never made an enemy of anyone."

Porphyry first came to know him in Rome in AD 263 and observed that Plotinus's home had become a sort of orphanage, with Plotinus the guardian of the children—"his house was therefore filled with lads and lasses." It had become a practice for older prominent citizens to bequeath their children and property into Plotinus's care, "feeling that with Plotinus for guardian the children would be in holy hands." "Until the young people take to philosophy," Plotinus said, "their fortunes and revenues must be kept intact for them." True to his trust, we are told, he took good care of them. Among his friends were numerous professional men and women, senators and their families, and even Emperor Gallienus and Empress Solonina.

Plotinus once asked the emperor to rebuild a ruined city in Campania and designate it as a special enclave for an experiment in politics. There, Gallienus would establish a utopian city-state governed by the political ideas in Plato's *Republic* and *Laws*; it was to be called "Platonopolis." Plotinus and his disciples would live there and make it a society where citizens could live a just and peaceful existence of the kind not possible, it seems, in the "real world." This is the only occasion when Plotinus is known to have shown an interest in political matters or, for that matter, interest in *any* affairs of this world. The emperor turned down Plotinus's request.

Plotinus consistently urged his followers to dissolve their worldly ties and concentrate on their spiritual lives. Once when a Roman senator, Rogatianos, studying

The philosopher goes the upward way by nature, the musician and the lover must be led by it.

PLOTINUS

To be in a natural state is good, even if one is not aware of it.

PLOTINUS

Plotinian philosophy resigned his position, gave away his property, and withdrew from the world, Plotinus "praised him very highly, holding him up as a model to those aiming at the philosophical life." Another follower named Serapion attempted to adopt Plotinus's philosophy but "was unable to free himself from the degradation of finance and money-lending."

Plotinus's vocation, therefore, was to supply his followers with a philosophy to live by, a philosophy that would reorient them away from the sensual-material obsessions of daily life so that they could concentrate on tending their souls and seeking a home in the next world. This was a prophetic calling. He was a monk counseling monkhood, an ascetic preaching asceticism, a mystic describing the joys of mysticism. He was an evangelist without being an evangelist.

MIND AND HEART

In Rome Plotinus devoted most of his time to teaching. His school was not rigidly organized but a loose collection of teachers and students associating informally in a supportive intellectual atmosphere. Plotinus would read passages from Plato, Pythagoras, Aristotle, or some other writer, quote commentaries on them, and then present his own analysis. In good Socratic fashion, the students would discuss what they heard. "He encouraged his hearers to ask questions," Porphyry notes, a practice that "led to a great deal of wandering and useless discussion."°

Plotinus's intellect grasped concepts swiftly and accurately. His repertoire was rich in knowledge, his "seeing" penetrating; when writing or speaking about others' ideas, he could cut through the clutter of excess verbiage and penetrate to the heart of the matter. When lecturing, he possessed an inner stimulation; his face became illumined with energy, and he radiated charm and warmth. He was "completely free from the staginess and windy rant of the professional speechifier; his lectures were like conversations. . . ."[5] "He generally expresses himself in a tone of rapt inspiration," Porphyry wrote, "and he states what he himself really felt about the subject and not what has been handed down by tradition." He was an excellent debater, a formidable opponent and a comforting advocate. Well versed in his predecessors' writings, he was quick to give credit, though what he finally wrote was always his own creation.

He was also unusually empathetic. "One day Origen came to the conference-room; Plotinus blushed deeply and was on the point of bringing his lecture to an end. When Origen begged him to continue, he said: 'A speaker's enthusiasm is dampened when he finds that his hearers have nothing more to learn from him.'" Porphyry noted his patience: "On one occasion I went on and on for three days asking questions about the soul's connection with the body, and he just kept on explaining it to me."

Plotinus was above all a mystic. Although he lived a life to serve others, he never forgot that his singular obligation was to assist the soul—his own soul, the only soul whose sacred stewardship he possessed—in its journey to God. Four times during the six years Porphyry knew him, Plotinus, in meditative trance, experienced union with God. This absorption into the ineffable One is the goal of human existence, he believed; it previsions the sublime state all worthy souls will achieve in the next life.

UNION

Never robust in health, Plotinus died after a long and painful illness. He was sixty-six. His disease—possibly leprosy complicated by other serious illnesses—was contagious, so to withdraw from his friends he retired to a country estate in Campania. Except for his companion and physician, Eustochius, he was alone. His last words,

The good man is always happy; his state is tranquil, his disposition contented and undisturbed by any so-called evils—if he is really good.
PLOTINUS

°*So what else is new?*

Homo sum; humani nihil a me alienum puto. *I am a man; I consider nothing human alien to me.*

TERENCE

addressed to his doctor, were "I am striving to give back the Divine in myself to the Divine in the All."

After his death, his friend Amelius consulted the oracle of Apollo "to learn where Plotinus's soul had gone." He received back his answer from the sacred oracle in majestic stanzas:

> I raise an undying song, to the memory of a gentle friend. . . .
>
> Man at first but now nearing the diviner ranks! The bonds of human necessity are loosed for you and, strong of heart, you beat your eager way from out the roaring tumult of the fleshly life to the shores of that wave-washed coast free from the thronging of the guilty. . . .
>
> Sleep never closed those eyes: high above the heavy murk of the mist you beheld them; tossed in the welter, you still had vision; still you saw sights many and fair not granted to all that labour in wisdom's quest.
>
> But now that you have cast the screen aside, quitted the tomb that held your lofty soul, you enter at once the heavenly consort: where fragrant breezes play, where all is unison and winning tenderness and guileless joy, and the place is lavish of the nectar-streams the unfailing Gods bestow. . . .
>
> O Blessed One, you have fought your many fights; now, crowned with unfading life, your days are with the Ever-Holy.
>
> Rejoicing Muses, let us stay our song and the subtle windings of our dance; thus much I could but tell, to my golden lyre, of Plotinus, the hallowed soul.[6]

Greatness of soul is despising the things here; and wisdom is an intellectual activity which turns away from the things below and leads the soul to those above.

PLOTINUS

THEOLOGY

Plotinus's friend Longinus once wrote that "while much of [his] theory does not convince me, yet I am filled with admiration and delight over the general character of the work, the massive thinking of the man, the philosophic handling of the problems; in my judgement investigators must class Plotinus's work with that holding the very highest rank."

Our present task is to understand this philosophy, and to do this several preliminary observations will be helpful. One point is that nowhere in the *Enneads* does Plotinus describe, with deliberateness and clarity, the cosmological structure of his world system. He merely assumes the structure and proceeds to explore in massive detail the soul's precarious journey from this world to the next. It is important, therefore, to outline his mystical thought-cosmos up front and in the simplest possible way.

His terminology also presents a problem. Plotinus was not the first or last philosopher to develop such a fresh vision of the world that it can't be captured with existing language. They must create a new vocabulary or—and it is very annnoying!—employ old words in new ways. Plotinus endowed such words as "soul," "mind," "nature," and "matter" with peculiar Plotinian meanings, and readers must be willing to give him space to redefine as he saw fit.

Soul is given beauty by intellect.

PLOTINUS

But in what sense is Neoplatonism a philosophy at all? Might it better be classified a religion, a theology, or something else? Plotinus thought of himself as a philosopher working in the classic philosophical tradition; in his mind he was the continuation and fulfillment of Pythagoras, Plato, the Stoics, and other Greek thinkers; he drew on them all for material for building his worldview. Lines he wrote such as "the *Timaeus* indicates" and "from a passage in the *Phaedo*" sound as though he is citing revealed scripture. Furthermore, he confronted many of the classic issues in philosophy and attempted to work out answers and implications—issues such as the dependability of sense perception, free will and moral responsibility, and the metaphysical status of Platonic forms. Lastly, his system appealed philosophically to some of the best intellects of his time, and they argued Neoplatonism in the same dialectical fashion as in the old days when the Athenians debated. In addition, he frequently sounds like the stereotypical philosopher: He employs philosophical jargon; he is pedantic, abstruse, and often irrelevant; and some of his passages elude all wrestlings to render them intelligible.

Plotinus was a synthesizer. He drew (selectively) on a wide range of philosophical sources, transmogrified them with a restless intellect, and molded them into a coherent worldview. Father O'Brien wrote: "It was Plotinus and no one else who detected the hidden virtualities of these very diverse doctrines, who separated them out from their context, refurbished them brightly in the large alembic of his mind, brought their latent potentialities to perfection, and expressed them finally in new formulae at once so penetrating and so suasive that it is small wonder so much of subsequent mystical speculation was willing to fall beneath his spell."[7]

Plotinus's fundamental concern was to elaborate the path for the human soul to pursue union with God. Plotinus himself lived an anguished existence here in the human condition; his deepest impulse was to find a way out of the pain. Life for him was very unsatisfactory, a condition just barely habitable (as it was, in a similar way, for the Buddha). The worldview he developed, spun out by the imaginative faculties of an unusually fertile mind, is a religious metaphysics. His cosmos was God; God was his cosmos. All things that exist derive from the overflowing Divine spirit, and the purpose of human existence is to journey upward to the soul's final absorption into God.

That's religion. Plotinus, however, was not an evangelist imploring sinners to submit to his authority in (blind) faith. He was too cerebral for that. He was committed to working out with the greatest logical coherence all the implications and problems connected with his religious assumptions, and he obsessed over wanting to share what he discovered as he pursued a better understanding of the elements and processes in his mystical vision. But he behaved more like a frontiersman blazing the way than a preacher of dogmatic beliefs. Although Plotinus was all intellect (like his first hypostasis), he honored both mind *and* heart, intellect *and* spiritual need.

And that's theology. Theology, by definition, is the attempt to give religious belief and experience intellectual clarity and justification; it is essentially apologetic. Since the world Plotinus lived in was not the observed or observable world, his description of "the world" turned out to be a noetic theological cosmology. Neoplatonism is, therefore, a theological system, and Plotinus is best thought of as a mystical theologian.

Two comprehensive questions employed in the academic study of religion can provide access to any complex worldview and give it structure and intelligibility; these questions work especially well with Neoplatonism. They follow: (1) How does the world work? (2) What is our (human) place in the scheme of things? That is, what world structure frames and gives body and coherence to that religion, and, within the parameters of that world structure, how is each individual counseled to seek and find salvation?

You must become first all godlike and all beautiful if you intend to see God and beauty.

PLOTINUS

HOW DOES THE WORLD WORK

The metaphor Plotinus used to attempt to comprehend the world draws on the idea of light. In his time and place, in north Africa, light was associated with candles,

Ugliness is matter not mastered by form.

PLOTINUS

Plotinus teaching in his school in Rome. From a late 3rd–early 4th century sarcophagus now in the Vatican Museum.

oil-burning lamps, fires in the stubble fields, and, of course, the ambiguous Sun. Pharoahs and unlettered fellahin alike recognized the Sun as the source of life. It nourished the fertile soil of the Nile's long green valley and separated all that was alive and good from the unforgiving sands of the desiccating desert. Amon-Rê was a Sun god, and in the counterreligion of Akhenaton the sun disk's rays radiated out to the ankh of life.

So, think of a cosmos bathed in spiritual light emanating from an all-pervading light source—a spiritual Sun. This Sun burns with a blinding incandescence, and its sole reason-for-being is to bathe the world with light and goodness. Its illumination penetrates outward in all directions to dispel the darkness of nothingness. The farther the light moves from its source, the dimmer it becomes, until, at its outer limits, its glow fades to nonexistence and darkness encloses all.

But note: (1) This is not a material light, of course; it is not electromagnetic radiation. It is a spiritual light illuminating a spiritual universe. But, like physical photons, this spiritual light shines most intensely near its source and dims with spiritual distance; it moves outward through a spiritual cosmos to dispel spiritual darkness. (2) This spiritual light is the only true reality; all else, including matter, is derived and imitative. Matter is merely an unreal manifestation of the real. (3) This Light is the source of all goodness. It is not merely something; it is a good something. Just as it is perfect Existence, it is also perfect Goodness. Thus, as light shines forth from the Light, it bathes the world with Reality and Goodness, qualities that dim and diminish with increased distance from the Source.

Matter is evil.

PLOTINUS

(4) Light emanates, we say, and the doctrine of "*emanation*" is a major theme in Plotinus's theology. This outflowing emanation of spiritual light possesses structure; it is a unity, but it is also composed of subparts (in Greek, *hypostasis*, or "derived essence," "that which is subsumed under"). The Light-Source is the godhead Plotinus calls simply the *One*. From this One emanates a first hypostasis—*Mind* (in

Greek, *Nous*, or "mind," "intellect"; the "location of ideas"). Then from Mind emanates a second hypostasis: *Soul* (*psyche* in Greek; the source of motion). Soul is the creative principle inherent in the One and Mind, the generative source of both human souls and the physical matter making up the natural world.

So the world is an eternal dynamic outflowing from the One/God. But in Plotinus's schema, a countermovement to the outflowing emanation occurs, and a lovely Greek word captures it: *epistrophê*, or "a wheeling about," "a turning about," "a return motion." The light is drawn to return to its source, the Light, and the derived hypostases and all created things feel this urge to return to the source of their being. For an analogy, picture the "closed universe" of present-day cosmology, whereby the galaxies and stars catapulted outward by the Big Bang are attracted by gravitational forces back toward a primordial fireball like that of their origin. All things harbor this impulse to return, but the farther they are from their source, the less it is felt, until, like the last faint vestiges of light overcome by darkness, it diminishes to the point where it hardly exists. Again, by analogy, think of the inverse square law of physics that describes the behavior of light and gravity. But, however dimly perceived, the epistrophic urge to return home exerts a magnetic pull, and all creation feels the irresistible draw back to the Source.

This, then, is an outline of Plotinus's imaginative worldview. The All-that-Exists is spiritual Light, and its two dynamic forces are emanation and epistrophe—an expanding out and a returning back. These are, again, like physical forces, but they are not such. The One overflows its *spiritual* boundaries and gives rise to Mind; Mind overflows its *spiritual* boundaries to give rise to Soul; and Soul overflows its *spiritual* boundaries to generate singular souls such as inhabit human bodies and to create physical matter. Nor are these successive events in time; one does not take place "before" or "after" the other. Nor do they occur simultaneously. They are supratemporal—out of time and beyond time altogether.

THE ONE

Plotinus's "the One," therefore, is the Light-Source that the world derives from. Though the One is the source of all being, it does not itself possess being: It is beyond being. It *is*, but it does not possess existence. In the language of later theology, it is the "ground of being" but not being itself. And it is the ultimate source of all that is.

Further, we can have no knowledge of it. Any merely human concept, and any word we might apply to it, is inapplicable; all anthropomorphisms would limit the unlimited, contain the uncontainable, qualify the unqualifiable. We can take a negative tack and spell out what the One is not: It is not matter, it is not darkness, it is not evil, and it is not even an "it." Thus, if we hedge it with sufficient images of what it is not, we might in a sense know something about it. But in truth we don't know anything of *it* as *it* really is.°

Plotinus was clearly aware of the contradiction involved in his concept of the One and was uncomfortable with it. If the One is so totally unknowable and unqualifiable, how, then, can he write about it or speak about it at all? His paradox really has no way out. "Strictly speaking," he says, "we ought not to apply any terms at all to It; but we should, so to speak, run round the outside of It trying to interpret our own feelings [sic, not ideas] about it, sometimes drawing near and sometimes falling away in our perplexities about It." And there he leaves the matter—and proceeds to write volumes about It.[8]

In sum, the One is the Godhead. It is the Light shining through the darkness from which all things are created. Its nature is to overflow and create. Like light, it

Matter is the cause of the soul's weakness and vice; it is then itself evil before soul and is primary evil.
PLOTINUS

Mind makes being exist by thinking it.
PLOTINUS

°*Plotinus's concept of the Other, the unexplainable, is from Philo Judaeus; compare his "negative theology" with that of Philo and Saint Thomas, pp. 215f., and 406.*

Thee, God, I come from, to Thee go.
GERARD MANLEY
HOPKINS

must shine or it would not be light. This emanation, in its overflowing, gives rise to the first hypostasis, Mind.

THE MIND

Although the One is pure unity, the first hypostasis involves multiplicity. The essence of the mind is ideas, and ideas are plural. So this emanation is composed of, or is, an infinite collection of ideas—just as Plato described it. The Mind is identical to Plato's Real Ideas. Plotinus adopted Plato's metaphysical scenario almost verbatim and absorbed it into his theological system.

Plotinus proceeded to develop the schematic. The ideas of this first hypostasis are the principles for creating all things. They are the forms, the patterns, the templates for shaping the things actually existing in the world; they provide the "blueprints" for "manufacturing" things. They are the patterns for creating abstract forms, however, not things themselves. Nature, and the patterns of nature, is shaped or imprinted with the forms; but Nature, it must be remembered, is an abstraction, and the "laws of Nature" are mental forms, not material things.

The Divine Mind also is the source of all other minds, and the ideas in other minds are derived from the Divine Mind. Thus, as Plato implied, to think rational thoughts is to think in tandem with God's thinking; indeed, it is to think his thoughts.

Although Mind feels the epistrophic urge to return to its source, its primal urge is—like the One—to overflow. So Mind, too, continues to emanate, and while emanating it gives rise to the second hypostasis, the Soul, or, better, the World-Soul.

THE WORLD-SOUL

The World-Soul is the agent of creation. Although Mind provides the idea templates that form all the things existing, nothing about Mind is aggressive or creative. Like an architect's blueprint, it is passive; it provides the pattern and structure (the "directions" or "guidelines") for creation, but it does not create. World-Soul provides the creative energy for the things of this world to come into being.

At the highest level of creation are human souls. Although mere mortal visualization is inadequate, the picture one gets is of individual finite souls breaking off or separating from the World-Soul, like drops of spray tossed from breaking waves moving over the surface of a vast ocean. Composed of the same "substance" as the immortal World-Soul, each single soul, human or animal, is also eternal and immortal. And just as World-Soul feels the urge to return to the source of its being, so each single soul feels a relentless, gnawing urge to return home. "This world is not my home" the gospel hymn sings to us, "I'm just a passer-through. / My treasures are laid up / somewhere beyond the blue." No human beings who tend their soul will possibly feel at home in this catastrophic condition we call life; they will feel the divine magnet tug on their soul, and sooner or later they will submit to it.

A second major operation of World-Soul is to create the material world. If anything in the Plotinian triad can be called "Creator," it would be World-Soul. It is the energy, the force, the power that generates matter, not ex nihilo but out of itself. Matter, if we may, is created from energy—spiritual energy.° Thus Nature, and all the things belonging to Nature, is the result of the overflowing World-Soul. But this universe of matter lies just at the edge of light: It is the final darkened creative act of a distant Divine Light. (Recall the Voyager II photograph of our Sun taken from the distant orbit of a very frozen Pluto.) Matter is thus gross, on the cusp between real and unreal, and being far from the source of Goodness, it is evil. It is the last orgasm of divine creation, and although it thereby can't be all bad, it is too far from the Light to be good. Matter and all things made of matter must be shunned as unworthy of the touch of an aspiring soul.

This, then is the theological structure of the world. It is a noetic vision and has nothing whatever to do with the empirical world. Nor does it relate in any way to traditional speculation about the gods or a personal God, as do the various Gnosticisms. If the gods exist—and Plotinus tacitly accepted their existence—they, too, must function within the framework of this cosmic structure.

WHAT IS OUR (HUMAN) PLACE IN THE SCHEME OF THINGS?

Toward what are we as individuals directed in this life? What should we be doing to achieve the true goal of our existence? What is the end (the *telos*) of life? These questions Plotinus answered in passionate detail, as only a highly imaginative intellect could answer them.

Our singular purpose in being here is to look after our soul and nurse it along its lifelong journey to God. We must disconnect from the world of trivial preoccupations; we must withdraw from the seductive environment of the senses that would detour our mind and body from the constant cultivation of our spiritual life. Our every effort is to become "uncontaminated by flesh and body." "Since it is here that evils are . . . and the soul wants to escape from evils, we must escape from here." Within us, after all, is an epistrophic urge to turn our face toward the light and have done with the darkness of a world where we are not at home. The good soul is "passionately in love with the invisible." "The common life of body and soul cannot possibly be the life of well-being. Plato was right in maintaining that the man who intends to be wise and in a state of well-being must take his good from There, from above, and look to that good and be made like it and live by it." We should listen carefully to our inner feelings and get in touch with that redemptive longing to return to our true home. This longing will not betray us; it will lead us ever higher; we will find ourselves edging toward the light.[9]

> By what means then can we escape? What path can we find to flee? We shall put out to sea, as Odysseus did when fleeing from the witch Circe. . . . He was not content to stay where he was though he had delights for his eyes and lived in the midst of much sensual beauty. . . . How shall we travel to this far land? Where is our way of escape from this world? We cannot get there on foot; feet only serve us in this world, like when we want to travel from one country to another. Nor will a carriage do the job, or a boat. Let go of such notions, and stop looking. Close your eyes and awaken another way of seeing—a way that everyone has but few use.[10]

What will happen to us should we decline to listen to the epistrophic calling and become mired instead by the temptations of sense? Reincarnation into this subterranean prison will capture and hold us, over and over again, until, out of our own free will, we decide to respond to the inner voice and move toward God. The soul is immortal, after all; it has no beginning and no end, and it existed before this lifetime and will continue to exist after it. So, it will be reborn time and again (in good Hindu fashion) into incarnate bodies—the form depending on the goodness of each previous lifetime.°

Our present life's quality depends in part on our soul's moral nature in its previous lifetime. Following Plato's tripartite division of the soul, Plotinus reasoned that the rational, the sensitive, or the vegetative element may dominate our soul. If our soul is qualified by sense, then it will respond to the vibrations of sense and take its cues from matter. Its natural tendency will be to move downward and away from the Light, and

Vision floods the eyes with light but it is not light that shows some other thing; the light is itself the vision.

PLOTINUS

The starting point is universally the goal.

PLOTINUS

The zest dies down when the speaker feels that his hearers have nothing to learn from him.

PLOTINUS

°*The similarity to the Indian systems (Hindu, Buddhist, Jain) is striking in both structure and detail, but Plotinus never seems to have developed the concept of karma, though his doctrine logically implies it.*

our soul will need greater courage if it is to prevail. The soul that lives close to sense and matter will be reincarnated at lower levels in the form of an animal or plant.

"In the heavens of our universe," Plotinus tells us, countless souls of various qualities exist who will be incarnated into different grades of earthly bodies depending on the moral tone of their previous existences. Those who have performed minimally "are men once more." Those who lived like animals will return as animals. Those who abandoned themselves to lust will return as wild, lustful animals. Those who lived the dumb life of vegetables (couch potatoes and cabbage heads come to mind) will return as green plants. As Plotinus puts it, "Those who in their pleasures have not even lived by sensation, but have gone their way in a torpid grossness—they will become mere growing things, for only or mainly the vegetative principle was active in them, and such men have been busy be-treeing themselves."[11] Those who "have loved song become vocal animals"—nightingales or song sparrows, perhaps. Statesmen will return as eagles. Idealistic visionaries will return as "high-flying birds." Social reformers will return as social insects—"a bee or the like." Those who have victimized others will return as victims. Murderers will return only to be murdered. Those who refused food to the hungry will return as starving wanderers. (Presumably, dull teachers will come back as hell-raising students, and analytic philosophers will return as wooden horses on a merry-go-round.)

The soul is a free agent: Out of its own free will it can make free choices. "The Soul, to whichever side it inclines, has in some varying degree the power of working the forms of body over to its temper. . . . the real determination lies with the souls, who adapt the allotted conditions to their own particular quality."[12] This is the way the cosmic system works. Life is a temporary imprisonment for all of us and not a happy existence. The soul who can't seem to get it right will be imprisoned time after time until it heeds the epistrophic urge and turns toward the Light. And not in vain: The final attainment, not at all beyond our grasp, is oneness with God. "The souls pass from body to body, entering into varied forms—and, when it may, a soul will rise outside of the realm of birth and dwell with the one Soul of all." All souls can be redeemed, but some souls will require an almost infinite amount of time before they can successfully struggle against the weighty downward drag of gross matter and begin their ascent.[13]

"We must break away toward the High: we dare not keep ourselves set towards the sensuous principle, following the images of sense, or towards the merely vegetative, intent upon the gratifications of eating and procreation; our life must be pointed towards the Intellective, towards the Intellectual-Principle, towards God."[14]

TOWARD THE LIGHT

How do we move toward the light? Plotinus wrote of a purification process for the soul to slough off the bonds of this world and concentrate on its ascent to God.

> The purification of the Soul is simply to allow it to be alone; it is pure when it keeps no company; when it looks to nothing without [outside] itself; when it entertains no alien thoughts . . . when it no longer sees in the world of image, much less elaborates images into veritable affections. Is it not a true purification to turn away towards the exact contrary of earthly things? . . .

> Purification is its awakening from the baseless visions which beset it, the refusal to see them; its separation consists in limiting its descent towards the lower and accepting no picture thence, and of course in the banning of all that it ignores when the pneuma [finer body, or spirit] on which it is poised is not turbid from gluttony

It is the business of virtue to raise ordinary nature to a higher level.
PLOTINUS

The gods must come to me, not I to them.
PLOTINUS

But if he does not know that he is healthy, he is just the same, and if he does not know that he is handsome, he is handsome just the same. So if he does not know that he is wise, will he be any the less wise?
PLOTINUS

Knowledge, if it does not determine action, is dead to us.
PLOTINUS

and surfeit of impure flesh, but is a vehicle so slender that the Soul may ride upon it in tranquillity."[15]

In his program of etherealization, Plotinus moved within the framework of his transmogrified Platonic vision. At each hypostasis, a particular type of contemplation leads the soul upward; at the mundane physical level, it is permissible to contemplate the sights and sounds of Nature.

> Who that truly perceives the harmony of the Intellectual Realm could fail, if he has any bent towards music, to answer to the harmony in sensible sounds? What geometrician or arithmetician could fail to take pleasure in the symmetries, correspondences, and principles of order observed in visible things? . . . Surely no one seeing the loveliness lavish in the world of sense—this vast orderliness, the Form which the stars even in their remoteness display—no one could be dull-witted, so immovable, as not to be carried by all this to recollection, and gripped by reverent awe in the thought of all this, so great, sprung from that greatness.[16]

It must be emphasized that, in contemplating Nature, we easily can be seduced away from the Light if we perceive merely the surface and sensual beauty of, say, stars, mountains, lakes, wildflowers, and beautiful people. True beauty is not to be found in sense perception but only in the mind. Beautiful *things* should lead us on to an appreciation of beautiful *forms* (beautiful blueprints), which, in turn, should lead us on to an appreciation of Mind (the Draftsmen who drew up the blueprints) and beyond that to the One.

> Admiring the world of sense as we look out upon its vastness and beauty and the order of its eternal march, thinking of the gods within it, seen and hidden, and the celestial spirits and all the life of animal and plant, let us mount to its archetype, to the yet more authentic sphere: there we care to contemplate all things as members of the Intellectual—eternal in their own right, vested with a self-springing consciousness and life—and, presiding over all these, the unsoiled Intelligence and the unapproachable wisdom.[17]

The vile and ugly is in clash, at once, with Nature and with God.
PLOTINUS

Individuals who, by nature or design, become philosophers are moving toward the Light, for they specialize in thinking God's thoughts. They no longer ponder the things of this world and are not seduced by them; these are below their vision as they look—and think—upward. Just as our finite minds are derived from the Divine Mind, so our finite thoughts can enter into God's thoughts and, leaving behind their finiteness, become absorbed into the infinitude of the Unlimited Mind.

Higher still, the Soul can ascend beyond Mind and contemplate the One, the Light itself.

Once there is perfect self-control, it is no fault to enjoy the beauty of earth.
PLOTINUS

> Let the great soul be conceived to roll inward at every point, penetrating, permeating, from all sides pouring in its light. As the rays of the sun throwing their brilliance upon a louring cloud make it gleam all godlike, so the soul entering the material expanse of the heavens has given life, has given immortality; what was abject it has lifted up; and the heavenly system, moved now in endless motion by the soul that leads it in wisdom, has become a living and a blessed thing. . . .[18]

This is an ecstatic state entered into, thoughtfully and carefully, through trance. In the brilliance of that light, all individual consciousness disappears; multiplicity is gone. The experience is integrated selfness—a Oneness, a Wholeness, a resting in a ground-state of joy. This soul now becomes beautiful.

Go back into yourself and look; and if you do not yet see yourself beautiful, then, just as someone making a statue which has to be beautiful cuts away here and polishes there and makes one part smooth and clears another till he has given his statue a beautiful face, so you too must cut away excess and straighten the crooked and clear the dark and make it bright, and never stop "working on your statue" till the divine glory of virtue shines out on you, till you see "self-mastery enthroned upon its holy seat."[19]

This state is not achieved, however, unless and until the One descends to illuminate the soul with a special light. Though the saintly soul will spend an earthly lifetime preparing for it, when it finally comes, it is a gift, . . .

By what is intellective, we are permanently in the higher realm; by our lower part, we are prisoners of sense.

PLOTINUS

so that we are left wondering whence it came, from within or without; and when it has gone, we say, 'It was here. Yet no; it was beyond!' But we ought not to question whence; there is no whence, no coming or going in place; now it is seen and now not seen. We must not run after it, but fit ourselves for the vision and then wait tranquilly for its appearance, as the eye waits on the rising of the sun, which in its own time appears above the horizon—out of the ocean, as the poets say—and gives itself to our sight.[20]

ENDNOTES

1 Porphyry, *On the Life of Plotinus and the Order of His Books*, 3.10ff. (See next reference.)
2 Virtually all we know about Plotinus comes from Porphyry's *Life*; it is included in the Loeb Classical Library of Plotinus's works, trans. A. H. Armstrong (Harvard University Press, 1966; reprint, 1989), vol. 1, pp. 3–87. (Short quotations from Porphyry's *Life* are not referenced here since his biography is brief and sources including it can be easily found.)
3 Porphyry, *Life*, 13.
4 Elmer O'Brien, S.J., trans., *The Essential Plotinus* (Mentor, 1964), p. vii.
5 Porphyry, *Life*, 18.5ff.
6 Porphyry, *Life*, 22.10–60.
7 O'Brien, *The Essential Plotinus*, p. 17.
8 Plotinus, *Enneads*, VI.9.3. In V.5.6 Plotinus expands on the problem: "It would be better not to use the word 'one' at all than use it here in the positive sense, for only confusion could come of that. The word is useful solely in getting the inquiry started aright to the extent that it designates absolute simplicity. But then even this designation must be promptly eliminated, for neither it nor any other designation can be applied to what no sound can convey, what cannot be known on any hearing. Only the contemplative knows it; and even he, should he seek to see a form, would know it not." (O'Brien, *The Essential Plotinus*, p. 18)
9 Plotinus, *Enneads*, I.6.7.20ff., I.2.1.1ff., I.6.4.20ff., I.4.16.10ff.
10 Plotinus, *Enneads*, I.6.8.
11 Plotinus, *Enneads* (trans. Stephen MacKenna), III.4.2.
12 Plotinus, *Enneads*, III.4.5.
13 Plotinus, *Enneads*, III.2.4.
14 Plotinus, *Enneads*, III.4.2.
15 Plotinus, *Enneads*, III.6.5.
16 Plotinus, *Enneads*, II.9.16.
17 Plotinus, *Enneads*, V.1.4.
18 Plotinus, *Enneads*, V.1.2.
19 Plotinus, *Enneads*, I.6.5 .
20 Plotinus, *Enneads*, V.5.8.

MEDIEVAL PHILOSOPHY

THE STRUGGLE BETWEEN BELIEF AND CRITICAL PHILOSOPHY

PART

4

CHAPTER 16

PHILOSOPHY DURING THE DARK AGES: ONE

PORPHYRY TO HYPATIA (AD 305–415)

Philosophy enters into a thousand-year winter of hibernation, during which the Theater of Intellect goes dark and Western civilizaton dies; noetic theologies have a field day; lesser lights make scattered attempts to reignite critical inquiry, but belief continues to blight reason.

DEVASTATIONS

After the promising speculations of the presocratic philosopher-scientists and the achievements of the Golden Age Athenian thinkers (the period from 585 BC to 322 BC), mainstream philosophy began to dis-integrate. As noted in Chapter 12, it split into a variety of schools of thought, and from 322 BC to about AD 200, each branch of philosophy tended to pursue, more or less, its own autonomous career. Then all critical activity faded, and a cold winter of anti-intellectual stagnation set in that lasted for a thousand years, when virtually no progress was made in philosophy or the sciences. With good reason, this era (from about AD 200 to AD 1200) has been traditionally called the "Dark Ages."°

This millennium witnessed the disintegration of civilization, the loss of critical intellect, the fading of the sciences, the erosion of the arts, and the conversion of idealist philosophy into noetic theology. From the third to the ninth centuries, education declined everywhere; schools vanished, libraries were destroyed, books became rare, and illiteracy was almost universal. Medical knowledge was lost, replaced by superstition and occultic "cures." The great highways were no longer repaired, while cities declined in population and ceased to be cultural centers. The entire social, political, economic, and military substructure of Greco-Roman civilization crumbled.

The causes behind this downward spiral are many, and although some can be captured in broad strokes, our generalized statements can never capture the human tragedy experienced by those who lived through these difficult times. For lack of alternatives, we are forced to create big inclusive mental packages—"the fall of the Roman Empire," "the Muslim conquest of Spain," "the devastation of the Italian countryside"—but all such abstract descriptions distance our imaginations and feelings from the concrete and the real; they fail, always and utterly, to recover the humanness in the now-experiences of living individuals.

The most visible cause of this devastation was the massive migrations of ethnic tribes from northern and eastern Europe and western Asia. These mass movements

°Some historians contend that "Dark Ages" is the wrong appellation for this era since occasional advances in the arts occurred. For critical philosophy, however, "Dark Ages" seems peculiarly appropriate. The Greek philosophers of the Golden Age who rejoiced in their freedom to think without fear would have, without hesitation, called this an age of darkness.

Adversity reminds men of religion.

LIVY
(ROMAN HISTORIAN,
59 BC–AD 17)

Death is not the greatest of evils; it is worse to want to die, and not be able to.

SOPHOCLES

of whole populations had been occurring since prehistoric times, when the Indo-Europeans (Aryans) irrupted out of the steppes of southern Russia and Germanic peoples descended from northern Europe and Scandinavia. They had reached the Roman frontiers by about 113 BC; fifty years later they were pushing into Italy, and by AD 200 they had reached the Black Sea and were plundering Mediterranean cities. For some two centuries, impelled by growing populations and a need for new land, they encroached on the Roman provinces in both the West and East. In the eyes of the shorter dark-skinned Romans, these barbarians appeared as tall gladiator-type giants with white skin, blue eyes, and blond hair, clad in animal skins and rough cloth; they were rude, quarrelsome, gluttonous, and loved fighting. They lived in forest villages and were devotees of a crude religion that assured them that warriors killed in battle would receive their reward by going to a mythic Valhalla where they could spend their lives in drunkenness. Justifiably, the Romans feared these fierce, uncultured invaders who knew nothing of poetry or literature and law or civility.

Then in AD 375 the Huns exploded out of central Asia, attacked the Germanic tribes, and pushed them across the borders farther into the Roman Empire. At Adrianople in AD 378 the Germans defeated the Roman legions, settled down, and began the Germanization of the empire. In AD 410 Alaric and his Visigoths blockaded the city of Rome. Germanic tribes known as Vandals, fleeing the hordes of Huns, descended on Spain, crossed the Strait of Gibraltar into North Africa, and set up a Vandal kingdom at Carthage. When, in AD 476, a Germanic general was declared king of Italy, the Roman Empire was no more. With the Lombards' occupation of the upper Italian peninsula in AD 568, the Germanic migrations came to an end, though incursions from the Slavs, Bulgars, and Magyars from southern Russia continued for another three centuries.

In the seventh century AD a young and vigorous Islam burst out of the Arabian peninsula and within a century had conquered North Africa, Egypt, Palestine, Syria, and Persia and had vanquished much of Europe from southern Gaul and Spain in the West to India in the East. Muslims with fiery swords and burning souls willing to die for Allah would have doubtless overrun Europe had not Charles Martel succeeded in

The innocent suffer—how can that be and God be just? That is not only the central problem of tragedy, it is the great problem everywhere when men begin to think.

EDITH HAMILTON

Purity of race does not exist. Europe is a continent of energetic mongrels.

H. A. L. FISHER
(BRITISH WRITER)

History . . . is, indeed, little more than a register of the crimes, follies, and misfortunes of mankind.

EDWARD GIBBON

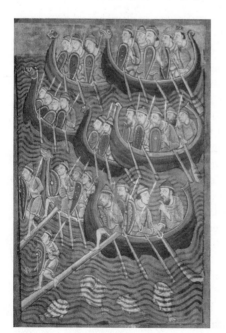

Vikings in longships invading England c. AD 1130 under the command of the Danes Hinguar and Hubba.

blocking their northward march at the Battle of Tours in AD 732; afterward, they settled in Spain and, for some three hundred years, Islamicized the Spanish culture.

Then a new devastation began when Norsemen raided a monastery on the Holy Island of Lindisfarne, England, in AD 793. For two centuries they terrified European populations. Wave after wave of Viking expeditions from Denmark and Norway swept over the British Isles, northern Europe, and the Mediterranean countries, reaching as far as Constantinople. Sailing in long ships, they looted the undefended monasteries and churches of coastal communities, then sailed up Europe's great rivers to plunder inland cities. The Vikings often sold captives to Arab slave traders. In England the Peace of Wedmore in AD 878 restored some stability, but King Alfred was forced to cede half of England to the rough invaders to achieve a peace.

LOSS OF LEARNING

With the fall of Greco-Roman civilization, the forces that had assured stability and security ended. The new rulers of the fragmented Roman world were ignorant and illiterate; they possessed no intellectual life and cared little for Greek and Roman culture, so the learning tradition was almost lost. Ignorance, superstition, lawlessness, violence, and anarchy reigned. Writing about AD 600, Pope Gregory described the chaos of his times:

> What is it that can at this time delight us in this world? Everywhere we see tribulation, everywhere we hear lamentation. The cities are destroyed, the castles torn down, the fields laid waste, the land made desolate. Villages are empty, few inhabitants remain in the cities, and even these poor remnants of humanity are daily cut down. The source of celestial justice does not cease, because no repentance takes place under the scourge. We see how some are carried into captivity, others mutilated, others slain. What is it, brethren, that can make us content with this life? . . . Let us then heartily despise the present world and imitate the works of the pious as well as we can.[1]

Many of the faithful knew that the world was about to end and hoped they would soon enjoy better conditions.

By AD 600 critical intellect was stilled in Christian Europe, and things only got worse during the next two centuries. The Benedictine authors of *L'histoire littéraire de la France* judged the eighth century the darkest, the most ignorant, and the most barbarous the world had ever seen. The leaders of most Western countries could only by a stretch be called civilized, and France's emperor Charlemagne himself could barely write. What learning remained was confined to clergy and monks, yet most of them were poorly educated; some priests didn't even know the Lord's Prayer and the Apostles' Creed. Superstition was great among priests, monks, and the laity; in popular imagination the world was peopled with witches, goblins, dragons, and demons. Virtually all understanding of natural phenomena disappeared, and countless supernatural occurrings were recorded. The number of new written works plummeted, especially during the seventh, eighth, and tenth centuries. The tenth century was dubbed the *saeculum obscurum*, the "time of darkness."

A prime cause of intellectual and cultural decay was the scarcity of books. Books were written on paper, and the availability of papyrus for making paper was cut off after the Muslims captured Egypt, so books were copied onto parchment (usually sheepskin), which was very expensive; they became valuable treasures, and copies of the Bible and other sacred books were chained to pulpits. Sheets of parchment

---

Atque ubi colitudinum faciunt pacem appellant. They create a desolation and call it peace.

CALGACUS
(CALEDONIAN TRIBAL CHIEF)

The wise learn many things from their foes.

ARISTOPHANES

Under coercion a man may sin except with respect to idolatry, incest and murder.

COUNCIL OF LYDDA
DECREE (132)

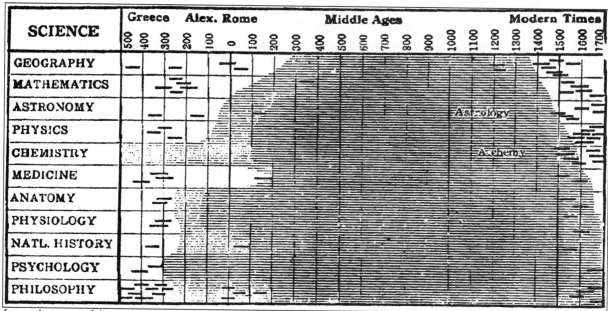

Loss and recovery of the sciences during the Dark Ages. Each short horizontal line indicates the life-span of a distinguished scholar in his field. The non-existence or ignorance of a subject during the Dark Ages is indicated roughly by the depth of the shading. When a philosopher or scientist (such as Aristotle) made major contributions to several fields his line appears in each of those fields.

containing Greek texts (which even the clergy could no longer read) were commonly scrubbed and erased so that they could be reused. Only with the introduction of cotton paper in the eleventh century and linen paper in the twelfth did book production again start to rise.

More devastating still was the deliberate destruction of libraries by both Muslims and Christians. The great Alexandrian library, called the Brucheium, had been destroyed during the civil wars in the third century AD; Christians, in AD 391, laid waste the nearby library in the Serapeum. After the Muslims subdued Egypt, one John Philoponus, a Neoplatonist Christian, implored the conquerers to save the half million volumes in the royal library. Caliph Omar gave his reply: "If these writings of the Greeks agree with the book of God [the Qur'ān], they are useless and need not be preserved; if they disagree, they are pernicious and ought to be destroyed." The scrolls were destroyed (whether by Muslims or Christians is uncertain), and the vast knowledge they contained—the best in Greek, Roman, Jewish, Persian, Babylonian, and Hindu literature—perished with them.

Attitudes toward secular learning were similar in the West. Pope Gregory established the official policy toward Greek philosophy: All remnants of "pagan" culture must be destroyed. Literacy in Latin he encouraged, however, because the Christian Church required it to conduct ritual and ecclesiastical affairs.

Whom the gods would destroy, they first make mad.
EURIPIDES

If God could make angels, why did he bother with men?
DAGOBERT RUNES

A hungry people does not listen to reason.
SENECA THE YOUNGER

THE THREE PHILOSOPHICAL TRADITIONS

The great Athenian philosophers had fairly covered everything in the field of intellect. Though Plato bent toward idealism and Aristotle toward empirical realism, they both unleashed their ferocious curiosities on the full range of human experience.

Aristotle especially embodied a philosophically healthy blend of observation, introspection, and speculation. But as knowledge accumulated, specialization became the order of the day. So, with the gradual dis-integration of mainstream philosophy after Aristotle's death, the three major tributarial streams—empirical, idealist, and pragmatic—all fared differently and followed different paths.

Empirical philosophy split from the mainstream philosophical tradition and gave birth to a multiplicity of hard sciences, notably in Alexandria. All these specialized sciences—mathematics and geometry, mechanics, geography, astronomy, chemistry, physics, biology and botany, physiology and medicine—leveled off in the second and third centuries AD when the pragmatic Romans gradually supplanted the Greek genius for abstract learning and when Christian teaching refocused reflection onto soteriological concerns.

Speculations about nature didn't entirely cease within Christendom, of course. Tertullian pondered botanical and metallurgical processes (but concluded they were invented by fallen angels). Bishop Ambrose of Milan said the heavens are composed of fire and water. Saint Augustine reiterated the Platonic idea that a "prime matter" exists that is "unshaped," incompletely formed. He also made astute observations regarding personality differences in twins. Even that most dedicated monastic Saint Basil noted that if insects are dipped into oil, they die, so he deduced that they breathe through pores located over their entire bodies.[2]

But "seeing" nature was relatively rare and studying nature almost nonexistent. A noteworthy exception to the first is found in the three Cappadocian Fathers—Basil the Great, his friend Gregory Nazianzen, and his brother Gregory of Nyssa. All three studied in Athens during the fourth century AD, where, Gregory Nazianzen confided, they avoided the street that led "to the public school and to the teachers of the sciences. . . . Our holiness was our great concern; our sole aim was to be called, and to be, Christians." Still, all three monks developed an unusual sensitivity to the beauties of nature. Gregory of Nyssa once wrote:

> When I see every rocky ridge, every valley, every plain, covered with new-grown grass; and then the variegated beauty of the trees, and at my feet the lilies doubly enriched by nature with sweet odors and gorgeous colors; when I view in the distance the sea, to which the changing cloud leads out—my soul is seized with sadness which is not without delight. And when in autumn fruits disappear, leaves fall, boughs stiffen, stripped of their beauteous dress—we sink with the perpetual and regular vicissitude into the harmony of wonder-working nature. He who looks through this with the thoughtful eye of the soul, feels the littleness of man in the greatness of the universe.[3]

To Gregory all beautiful things carry a spiritual message: They point our minds beyond themselves to the beauty of God. When Basil beheld the stars, he knew them to be "eternal flowers of heaven that raise the spirit of man from the visible to the invisible." After completing his studies in Athens, Basil found a place in Pontus in Asia Minor where nature's loveliness surrounded him, whence he wrote to his friend Gregory:

> A high mountain, covered with thick forest, is watered towards the north by fresh perennial streams. . . . On one side the stream rushes foaming down from the mountain . . . . Shall I describe to you the fertilizing vapors which rise from the moistened earth, the cool air which rises from the moving mirror of the water? Shall I tell of the lovely singing of the birds and the richness of blooming plants? What delights me above all is the silent repose of the place.[4]

In peace sons bury their fathers, but in war fathers bury their sons.
CROESUS
(LAST KING OF LYDIA)

I have well forsaken my residence in the city as a source of a thousand evils, but I have not been able to forsake myself.
BASIL THE GREAT

I have withdrawn myself, and have found rest to my soul only in solitude.
GREGORY NAZIANZEN

Such appreciation of nature was unusual in early Christian literature; no doubt very many others saw nature's beauty but didn't write about it because the subject was relatively unimportant and such preoccupations were not fashionable. Those who could still look at the world found that what they saw could richly nourish their spiritual lives. The silence of the wilderness captivated Basil (in the example), but he added that, no matter where he lived, "I have not been able to forsake myself. . . . for while I carry about with me the passions which dwell in me, I am everywhere tormented with the same restlessness, so that I really get not much help from this solitude."[5] He hungered for quietness in his own soul.

More commonly, the Christian Fathers saw in nature God's attempts to reveal to humans hidden messages about Christian truths and morals. The result was a long and enduring Christianizing of natural history, about which the Fathers often made known their opinions. They thought the habits of animals, for example, revealed a variety of theological doctrines; they even read Aristotle's investigations in biology in such a way as to embody and teach Christian morals.

In seeking to answer their spiritual needs, the best intellects of the time failed to develop a critical curiosity and to ask questions of the kind Aristotle would have asked: What are stars, and why do they move the way they do? What can we learn from the "design" and "order" of nature? What causes the vapors to "rise from the moistened earth?" Why do plants bloom? Why do seeds reproduce their own kind?

Aristotle would have agreed wholeheartedly that our spiritual lives must be nourished, but he would have insisted that the desire to know the truth of things also must be honored by unfettered intellects still driven by a passionate search for an understanding of the world. These two human concerns are not mutually exclusive, though if a suppressing Time Spirit is powerful enough—as it was during late Hellenistic centuries—it can cause us to forget this and to make the mistake of defining them as adversarial preoccupations.

The other two major streams of philosophy—the speculative idealist and the pragmatic—followed quite different paths. The *idealist tradition* Pythagoras, the Eleatics, and Plato developed was caught in midair by the brilliant minds of Philo and Plutarch, Gnostics such as Basilides and Valentinus, and, most notably, the Neoplatonists. This tradition was ripe to undergo a massive transmogrification of philosophy into theology under the alchemical aegis of the early Christian Fathers; afterward, it enjoyed a long career, virtually unchallenged, for a thousand years. This Greek idealist tradition led into, and thus became, the operational worldview of the Middle Ages.

The *pragmatic tradition* represented by Epicureanism and Stoicism, after enjoying wide success during Roman times, was rapidly phased out with the coming of Christianity and other mystery religions, such as Mithraism and the Egyptian cults of Isis and Osiris. Justin Martyr, for example, hated Epicureanism because it advocated pleasure as the greatest good; he was sure that had to be wrong, so he preached against it with the vigor of a disgruntled convert. Other Fathers disliked Stoicism because it denied immortality and was (as they interpreted it) either atheistic or pantheistic. So, Greek attempts to supply a pragmatic philosophy people could live by, and that would make them happy, were replaced by Christian doctrine that thereafter proceeded to function in the same pragmatic way—supplying beliefs for people to believe in, though with one nuclear difference. Happiness is not attainable in this life, so the pursuit of pleasures that deflect us from spiritual preoccupations should be abandoned so that we may concentrate on preparing ourselves for the next life, where an abundance of true fulfillments awaits us.

From all the evils of marriage, virginity is free.
GREGORY OF NYSSA

Change of place brings us no nearer to God, but where thou art, God can come to thee, if only the inn of thy soul is ready.
GREGORY OF NYSSA

The bread that you store up belongs to the hungry; the cloak that lies in your chest belongs to the naked; the gold that you have hidden in the ground belongs to the poor.
SAINT BASIL THE GREAT

A generous and noble spirit cannot be expected to dwell in the breasts of men who are struggling for their daily bread.

DIONYSIUS OF HALICARNASSUS (GREEK HISTORIAN, C. 20 BC)

Whoever wants to be a Christian should tear the eyes out of his Reason.

MARTIN LUTHER

THE SOURCE OF TRUTH

Beginning about AD 200, a single idea about the nature of truth took a commanding lead over all other philosophical first principles: Truth is found in divine revelation, not through human reasoning. This idea originated in religions of the Middle East; after conquests there by Alexander and Rome, it was but one of the transforming ideas that found an easy flow into the Hellenized West. The idea was adopted by Philo Judaeus in Alexandria and then passed on to Christian theologians. It was part of a package of ideas Alexandrian clergy developed; together they provided the framework for a new worldview that, with little alteration, was stamped on the religious beliefs of Greek Christians, Syriac Christians, Islamic and Jewish medieval thinkers, and Latin educators.

Along with the notion of truth by revelation, the other ideas in this package were (1) the conviction that philosophy exists to serve theology (as Philo famously put it, "philosophy is the handmaiden of theology"); (2) the belief that revealed truth and rightly reasoned truth will always agree (only one theologian, the irascible Tertullian, disagreed with this); and (3) recognition of the necessity of using both literal and allegorical interpretations of Scripture to provide a harmonious agreement between reason and faith. These ideas all appeared in Philo's writings, and Western theology was born from this conception of the relationship of truth and intellect.

Who has not the Church for mother can no longer have God for father.

CYPRIAN (BISHOP OF CARTHAGE)

PRAEPARATIO EVANGELICA

All during the first, second, and early third centuries AD, the zeitgeist shaped the doctrines and attitudes that were to characterize intellectual activity for the next thousand years. Philosophy as a critical activity was gradually phased out, and in one way or another Greek philosophy was seen to have been a preparatory program—a *praeparatio evangelica*—God instituted to pave the way for the coming of Christ's gospel. Devout Christian thinkers who called themselves "philosophers" and assumed the mantle of the Greek intellectuals waged the great spiritual battle against false teachings.

Christ as philosopher, between apostles. This marble relief is from a sarcophagus in Constantinople from c. AD 400.

Justin Martyr (c. AD 100–66) was the first Christian Father to define himself as a philosopher. The question "What can I believe?" drove his early life, and he explored every brand of philosophy searching for answers. Stoicism he tried first, but he rejected it because it taught him (he believed) that knowledge of God was unattainable. Then he studied Aristotelian doctrine but was offended by greedy teachers. Pythagoreans told him he must acquire a knowledge of music, geometry, and astronomy before he could understand things spiritual. Platonism came closest to meeting his spiritual needs with its counsel to meditate on Goodness, Truth, and Beauty as the true cosmic realities.

Then one day, during a walk along the seashore, he encountered a wise old Christian sage who told him that the Old Testament prophets had found the truth long before the Greek philosophers. Justin went to the Scriptures to read for himself and there discovered what he had been seeking: The truth must be known through revelation, not through reason.

With this metanoia his life mission became one of proving that reason always fails and that the true path to certitude is through faith. His calling to share this certainty colored the rest of his life: "Every person who can preach the truth, but does not preach it, will incur the judgment of God," he said. Evangelist though he was, he continued to wear the robes of a philosopher so that he would be more readily accepted in the role of intellectual apologist for his beliefs. As he took his early morning stroll, others would hail him with "Greetings, philosopher!"

Justin's essential message was this: Christianity is the only true philosophy. He drew on many of the Greek thinkers, especially Plato, whom he often quoted, and the Stoics. He concluded that whatever light the Greek thinkers possessed could be traced to the Hebrew prophets. From Neoplatonism he appropriated the idea of the Logos (as retheologized in the Gospel of John 1.1–18). This Logos was God's reason as it became incarnate in Christ; anything reasonable is therefore Christian, and all things Christian are reasonable. The Logos implanted seeds (*spermata*, the *logos spermatikos* of the Stoics) everywhere, among both Jews and gentiles, but especially among Greek philosophers and poets, who are God's "prophets" sent to prepare the Greeks for Christ. So, all who listened and lived according to the reasonable teachings of a Socrates or a Plato were really Christians, even if they didn't know it. "Christ was partially known by Socrates," he said.

Virtually all early Church Fathers adopted these structural ideas as elaborated by Justin; clergy defined and limited philosophy's role for the next millennium and then continued to shape theology in the West throughout the second millennium. Almost without exception, these early seekers were bright men who were well versed in Greek philosophy, literature, history, and poetry. The search for beliefs to live by was central to their seeking, and, to a man, they seem to have been unable to find that life-sustaining truth in intellect or reason.

Tatian of Assyria (AD 110–72) was Justin's pupil. He too had studied Greek mythology, history, and poetry—and found them empty. He went on to show that the Hebrew prophets were older and wiser than all the Greek thinkers. His methodology consisted mostly of sarcasm and ridicule:

> What great and wonderful things have your philosophers effected? . . . they let their hair grow long; they cultivate their beards; their nails are like the claws of wild beasts. . . . O man competing with the dog [the Cynic], you know not God, and so have turned to the imitation of an irrational animal. . . . philosophy is with you the art of getting money. . . . [Your doctrines] clash with one another. . . . One of you asserts "God is body," but the

A comprehended God is no God.
DIO CHRYSOSTOM
(GREEK SOPHIST)

Brother, you say there is but one way to worship and serve the Great Spirit. If there is but one religion, why do you white people differ so much about it?
CHIEF RED JACKET
(SENECA INDIAN CHIEF,
C. 1758–1830)

If the world goes against truth, then Athanasius goes against the world.
ATHANASIUS

So many men, so many opinions.
TERENCE (LATIN
PLAYWRIGHT, C.
190–159 BC)

Nothing evil was created by God; we ourselves have produced all the wickedness.
TATIAN (SYRIAN-
CHRISTIAN APOLOGIST,
HERETIC, FL. SECOND
CENTURY)

truth is: *He is without body*. You say "the world is indestructible," but the truth is: *The world will be destroyed*. You say "conflagrations will occur at various times," but the truth is: *Destruction will take place all at once*. You say "Minos and Rhadamanthus are judges," but the truth is: *God alone is Judge*. You say "only the soul is endowed with immortality," but the truth is: *The flesh is also immortal*. . . . O Greeks, what injury do we inflict upon you? Why do you hate those of us who follow the word of God, as if we were the vilest of mankind?[6]

From God, and through God, and unto God, are all things.

SAINT PAUL
(ROM. 11:36)

Theophilus of Antioch (died c. AD 181) agreed that elements of truth could be found in Socrates and Plato, but, he said, they had stolen them from the prophets and, anyway, the Scriptures contain whatever truths humankind needs to know. **Hermias "the Philosopher"** (end of second century AD), like many of the Church Fathers, ridiculed the dialectical Greek thinkers, whose conflicting views made it impossible to know what to believe; this proved, he said, Saint Paul's comment was true: "The wisdom of this world is foolishness in the eyes of God" (1 Cor. 3:19). In a book titled *A Mockery of Heathen Philosophers*, he wrote:

> I confess that I'm puzzled by [the teachings of the philosophers]. I am immortal, they tell me, and I rejoice; but then [they tell me] I am just a mortal who at death dissolves into atoms, and I weep. I am water, or I am air, or I am fire; then I am none of these. One tells me that I'm a wild beast, another that I'm a fish, another that I'm a brother to dolphins. So I look at myself and no longer know what I am—man, dog, wolf, bull, bird, serpent, dragon, chimaera. The philosophers would change me into all shapes of wild animals, from those that live on land or water to things that fly in the air. They would paint me either wild or tame, with or without speech, with or without a rational mind. According to them I should be able to swim, fly, creep, run, and sit. And then there is Empedocles who would make me into a bush![7]

It is extreme evil to depart from the company of the living before you die.

SENECA THE YOUNGER

This was a common criticism the Church Fathers leveled at Greek thinkers—that they could never agree on anything; and this, of course, made them look ridiculous in the eyes of those who were very clear on what they believed.

The last Roman theologian to write in Greek was **Hippolytus of Rome** (c. AD 170–235), one of the most learned scholars of his day. He thoroughly digested the Skeptical philosophy of Sextus Empiricus and wrote an extremely valuable history of Greek philosophy, the *Philosophumena*, whose purpose was to show that all heresies can be traced to the "pagan" thinkers.

Fere libenter homines id quod volunt, credunt. Men willingly believe what they wish.

JULIUS CAESAR

Alexandria long had been the wellspring for so many schools of thought. With the coming of Christianity, it was inevitable Alexandria would become a center of Christian intellectual activity. Near the end of the second century AD, a catechetical school supervised by the bishop of Alexandria was established there. Though its original purpose was to prepare "heathens" and Jews for baptism, it soon expanded its role to become a prestigious theological seminary housing a dedicated faculty of Christian scholars and theologians. Many of the preeminent Church Fathers were trained there.

Under the leadership of its two most esteemed heads, Clement and Origen, the Catechetical School had the principal goal of harmonizing philosophy with the Bible. Just as Philo had earlier harmonized Greek thought with Judaic truth, so these Fathers harmonized Greek thought with Christian truth. Adopting the central (and most threatening) doctrine of the Gnostics—that one is saved through the divine gift of a special "saving knowledge" (*gnosis*)—they taught that Christianity, not

Gnosticism, possessed the true gnosis. They saw Greek philosophy as a schoolmaster preparing the way for Christ. "Unless you believe," Isaiah 7:9 was (mis)quoted as saying, "you will not understand."°

Clement of Alexandria became head of the Catechetical School about AD 189. Thoroughly versed in Hellenic literature and culture, he found nothing in them that could satisfy his craving for secure foundations. Then, as an adult, he found a teacher, Pantaenus, who "filled the souls of his disciples with genuine, pure knowledge." So he embraced the truth of Christianity. Indeed, some truth could be found in Greek thought, he believed; he compared philosophy to a wild olive tree that faith can cultivate. "The studies of philosophy can assist us in our treating of the truth." Logic, for example, can be useful to make sure "that truth cannot be trampled under foot by the sophists." But all in all, while the Divine Logos brought some enlightenment to everyone in the world, the benighted Greek philosophers had introduced so much error into it that it had to be corrected under the pure light of revelation. "No faith without knowledge, no knowledge without faith," he said. The essence of Clement's teaching was that Christian faith can fully nourish the entire complement of human moral, spiritual, and intellectual hungers.[8]

Origen of Alexandria (AD 185–254) was elected as head of the Catechetical School at age eighteen. A genius with prodigious energy and an indelible memory, he prepared himself for his job by studying with Plotinus's famed teacher Ammonius Saccas and by devouring everything he could find in Greek philosophy. Through his prolific writing, he became a towering figure in the early Church ("he wrote more than other men can read," Saint Jerome said). In his exposition of Christian ideas, he drew heavily on the thoughts of Plato, Aristotle, Philo, Neoplatonists, and Gnostics. From the Gnostics he introduced into Christian thought the preexistence of the soul, the eternality of the world, and the final return of all things to God (the Church later condemned him for all of these after it had settled on correct doctrine). In his *Epistle to Gregory* he wrote that "philosophy is ancillary to Christianity":

> I would wish that you should take with you on the one hand those parts of the philosophy of the Greeks which are fit, as it were, to serve general or preparatory studies for Christianity, and on the other hand so much of geometry and astronomy as may be helpful for the interpretation of the Holy Scriptures.[9]

Origen became a one-man lighthouse, guru, and guide to all who could be persuaded to walk the path from heretical ideas to the Christian faith.

The first Church Father to write in Latin was **Tertullian of Carthage** (c. AD 150–220), the supreme controversialist of the early Church. "Tertullian was a rare genius," Philip Schaff, a church historian, wrote, "perfectly original and fresh, but angular, boisterous and eccentric; full of glowing fantasy, pointed wit, keen discernment, polemic dexterity, and moral earnestness, but wanting in clearness, moderation, and symmetrical development. He resembled a foaming mountain torrent rather than a calm, transparent river in the valley."[10] No one was more hostile to Greek rationalism than Tertullian; it was to him the source of all false doctrine, the "patriarch of all heresies." "With the adoitness of a special pleader," Schaff continues, Tertullian "entangles [his opponents] in self-contradictions, pursues them into every nook and corner, overwhelms them with arguments, sophisms, apophthegms, and sarcasms, drives them before him with unmerciful lashings, and almost always makes them ridiculous and contemptible. His polemics everywhere leave marks of blood. It is a wonder that he was not killed by the heathens, or excommunicated by the Catholics."[11]

°*Isaiah 7:9 reads, "If you do not hold fast, / Surely you shall not stand fast"* (it is verse in the Hebrew, not prose; *from* The Complete Bible: An American Translation), *referring to Isaiah's warning to King Ahaz to stand firm in battle against the Syrians in 734 BC. Martin Luther likewise lifted the passage from its context and misquoted it:* "Gläubet ihr nicht, so bleibet ihr nicht."

He is nearest the gods who knows how to be silent.

CATO THE ELDER

The most ignorant peasant under the Christian dispensation possesses more real knowledge than the wisest of the ancient philosophers.

TERTULLIAN

The Church Fathers considered heretical thinking the greatest threat they faced, and Tertullian was who established the Church's policy of zero tolerance: Heretical ideas have no right of appeal to holy Scripture. Tertullian argues this in *On the Prescription of Heretics*, where *praescriptio* is a legal term referring to a maneuver to block a plaintiff from being heard in court before the case's merits can be presented. (Note also the assumption here that false ideas can be supported from Scripture.) The Church alone, as the sole guardian of truth, was given the right of such rationalized appeal.

A common charge the Fathers made against the philosophers was that the prophets had given them the truth, but out of their conceit they had distorted it. In his *Apologeticus* Tertullian wrote that "the philosophers watered their arid minds" from the Scriptures, but because of their selfishness, "if they fell upon anything in the collection of sacred Scriptures which displeased them, in their own peculiar style of research, they perverted it to serve their purposes." Whatever truth the philosophers had discovered "devolved into uncertainty, and there arose from a few drops of truth a whole flood of arguments" (*argumentationum inundatio*).[12]

Saint Jerome (c. AD 340–419), the translator of the Bible into Latin (the "Vulgate"), though calling himself a philosopher, made it clear his beliefs were not up for critical analysis. His motto: "Read the ancients, test everything, hold fast to the good, and never depart from the catholic faith."

Saint Augustine of Thagaste (AD 354–430) had been an ardent searcher for a truth he could believe in and therefore knew the nausea of uncertainty. Addressing the Manichaean Gnostics (he had been one), he wrote:

> Those who do not themselves know of the pain it costs to find the truth, or understand the wear and tear of having to guard against error—such people will speak against you with hatred. But I, who, after enduring a long and wandering journey, came to know the truth, I will show toward you the same patience that my fellow-believers showed towards me during the time I was wandering about blind and half out of my mind.[13]

RECAPITULATION AND OVERVIEW

These, then, are some of the shaping ideas carried into the Dark Ages and that set the stage for Western philosophical and theological thought. By the close of the AD 300s, the Church Fathers had crystalized, codified, and canonized the structure of a new medieval worldview. They declared the foundation stones of this worldview—the truths of revelation—off-limits to critical evaluation. This worldview had no place for critical philosophy.

To summarize, the early Christian Fathers held these principal ideas about Greek philosophy and philosophers: (1) The Greek thinkers had received a partial truth from God and the prophets, but they had sullied and degraded it by their vanity; it degenerated into uncertainty. (2) The Greek philosophers disagreed with one another, argued over punctilious issues, and never settled anything. "Just take a look at all the voluminous writings of the philosophers," Saint Augustine wrote. "You almost never find any two of them saying the same thing." (3) Since nothing was certain with the philosophers, they offer no secure beliefs a seeker can trust and apply with confidence to daily life. (4) Secure foundations are found, therefore, not by using the rational intellect but by accepting the truth of God's revelation. (5) In the final analysis only faith is of value; though knowledge can assist faith, it is not essential to our salvation. (Should we wish to support our faith with knowledge, that's all right but not necessary.) (6) Therefore knowledge of the empirical world is of little interest to a faithful Christian. So wrote Saint Augustine:

> When one asks what we can believe about religion, it is completely unnecessary to probe into the workings of nature, as the Greek natural philosophers did; and it's nothing to be concerned about if a Christian is ignorant of such things as forces and the number of elements, or the motion, order, and eclipses of the heavenly bodies; . . . or about a thousand other things which those philosophers have either found out, or think they have found out. . . . Their so-called discoveries are often just guesses. It is enough for the Christian to believe that the only cause of everything, whether heavenly or earthly, whether visible or invisible, is the goodness of the Creator, the one true God.[140]

On Skepticism The Church of Christ detests these doubts as madness, having a most certain knowledge of the things it apprehends.

AUGUSTINE

CANDLES IN THE DARK

Throughout the thousand-year time of darkness, tiny bursts of light occurred (in the mind's eye, the metaphor of fireflies lighting the night seems unavoidable); these brave illuminations helped to keep alive the learning of the Greeks until, with the recovery of classical literature in the twelfth century, philosophy and science were awakened from hibernation and a rebirth of critical learning began again.

All the following individuals (in this and the next three chapters) tried to forge, and sometimes succeeded in forging, a link in the golden chain of the critical philosophical tradition. All were children of their times. "St. Augustine looked at Roman history from the point of view of an early Christian," Robin Collingwood, a modern historiographer, wrote. "Tillemont, from that of a seventeenth-century Frenchman; Gibbon, from that of an eighteenth-century Englishman; Mommsen, from that of a nineteenth-century German. There is no point in asking which was the right point of view. Each was the only one possible for the man who adopted it."[15]

We will find in the history of philosophy that Christian theologians always make philosophy subservient to faith and theology, and whenever reason threatens, they appeal to a higher source for their criteria for judging what is true; and critical philosophers, to the best of their ability, always challenge that appeal and ask for intelligent dialogue on the great issues burdening human existence. Throughout this dark period all intellects, both religious and critical, attempted to give intellectually respectable reasons in the defense of their beliefs. So, the undercurrent of dialectical tension never ceased and, unfortunately, frequently broke forth into blood and fire.

During this period the best intellects labored, not to create new thoughts but to preserve what the past had bequeathed to them by copying ancient manuscripts and hoarding the scrolls that came into their hands. The most brilliant creativity was channeled into the continuing task of harmonizing whatever seemed reasonable (to the individual thinker) with Scriptural truth.

The following thinkers are included here because they added something of value to the accumulating insight of the philosophical tradition—however slight that contribution might have been—or because they played a significant role in preserving Greek learning during times of widespread illiteracy, ignorance, and superstition.

°Numbers 4 and 6 were later altered by several of the Scholastic thinkers (notably Albertus Magnus and Roger Bacon) of the thirteenth and fourteenth centuries, who again had access to Aristotle's writings; see pp. 391f., and 427ff.

Dubito, ergo credo. *I doubt, therefore I believe.*

MARSHALL FISHWICK

PORPHYRY OF TYRE

Porphyry of Tyre was Plotinus's most dedicated disciple and a distinguished Neoplatonist. Almost singlehandedly he popularized Neoplatonist philosophy so that it

°Because Neoplatonism was such a pervasive philosophy throughout the Dark Ages, among both Hellenic and Christian thinkers, and took such varied forms, it might be helpful to review its cosmic framework; see pp. 271ff.

On Porphyry *He is the first systematic theologian in the history of thought.*
PETER BROWN

All that is human must retrograde if it does not advance.
EDWARD GIBBON

°See lexicon.

could meet the spiritual needs of ordinary people throughout the empire. His philosophy differed from Plotinus's in minor details.°

Extant writings, fragments, and bits of gossip hint that Porphyry was a fascinating individual, but little is known about his life. He lived from about AD 232 to sometime during Diocletian's persecution of Christians from AD 300 to 306. Born at Tyre in Syria, he studied philosophy in Athens and Alexandria, where, he tells us, he met Origen, the Christian theologian. Having heard exciting things of Plotinus, he journeyed to Rome in AD 263 and joined the informal collection of intellectuals around the charismatic teacher. He worked and studied diligently, soon damaged his health from overwork, suffered depression, and, at the suggestion of Plotinus, withdrew to the island of Sicily, where he lived for five years. Returning to Rome, he remained in the circle of disciples until Plotinus's death in AD 270. He became the next head of the school. Incidentially, "Porphyry" was a nickname; his Syrian name was Malcus, meaning "king."

Porphyry was a scholar of immense learning, interested in virtually every field of knowledge; he wrote erudite treatises on history, astronomy, philology, religion, and the sciences. All his life he had felt the weakness of a purely intellectual quest for God, so he dabbled in seances, Indian yoga, and other occult rites, hoping to find a "Universal Path" for freeing the soul. Late in life he married a widow, Marcella, who had seven (or perhaps eight) children. (This is the man who had "conceived a hatred of the human body.") A woman of some intellectual power, she was also interested in philosophy; for her he wrote a book, *To Marcella*, where, understandably, he counseled her to practice ascetic virtues and to continue to study philosophy.

In his own time Porphyry's most popular work was *The Return [to Heaven] of the Soul*. But later he was mainly remembered for two things: his work on Aristotle and his attack on the Christians. He wrote an introduction (*Eisagôgê* in Greek, often transliterated as *Isagoge*) to Aristotle's *Categories* and followed it with several commentaries. His *Eisagôgê* became the sole textbook of Greek logic in the Middle Ages, and with it Porphyry introduced the problem of universals° into the philosophical limelight, thereby setting the stage for a heated debate among the schoolmen of the ninth and tenth centuries. Porphyry asked three questions (derived from Plato and Aristotle's metaphysics): (1) Are universals real or merely abstract creations of the mind? (2) If they are real (as many argued), are they corporeal or incorporeal (with or without a material body)? (3) If they are both real and incorporeal (as most believed), do they exist only in objects (per Aristotle) or as separate "Real Ideas" (per Plato) apart from objects? These questions, seemingly academic and punctilious, were seen to have serious implications for certain Christian doctrines and were therefore considered crucial issues justifying the involvement of the age's best intellects.

Then he wrote *Against the Christians*. Before Porphyry, Neoplatonism and Christianity had coexisted in relative peace, both developing independently and without major interference with each other (Christian apologists were busy fighting off Gnosticism); but with Porphyry the two great noetic systems faced each other in direct conflict. To Porphyry philosophy's purpose was to ennoble the soul, to put it on the right path so that it could return to God. To this end he had earnestly labored over all the complex questions connected with the soul's redemption and return and had resolved them. But so had Christian thinkers. Their answers, however, were radically different. Conflict was inevitable, and Porphyry seems to have been the one who instigated the confrontation. With evangelical fervor, he wrote fifteen volumes of analysis and criticism of Christianity. He had done his homework; his writings show he possessed a thorough understanding of Christian doctrine.

Porphyry directed his attack at what he perceived as the lying leaders and misguided followers of a fanatical cult. His criticism was not of Christ's teachings—he found much good in them—or of Christ, whom he respected and ranked with the great sages. (The Neoplatonists eulogized Christ, Augustine noted, but tongue-lashed his followers.) He directed his wrath at the superstitious practices and outlandish writings of what popularly passed, among the masses, for Christian faith. The true philosopher, Porphyry held, turns his entire life toward the loftiest spiritual realms and never allows his soul to be mired in sensate forms of religiosity.

This focus on Christianity is a specific instance of Porphyry's much larger hostility toward all demeaning popularizations, whether of religion or philosophy. In his mind the blasphemous rites and crass anthropomorphisms of common cultic practices sullied the lofty realities of Neoplatonic spirituality. He wrote vehemently against the trappings of pop culture—magic, crude rites, divinations, exorcisms, and amulets and figurines the ordinary devotee put faith in. Even the Olympian gods, he said, were evil demons posing as good guys so as to insinuate themselves into humankind's prurient natures.

Just a few fragments of *Against the Christians* have survived as extracts in the writings of his adversaries. For centuries Porphyry was remembered only as the bitter enemy of Christianity. His work brought forth strong responses from very able Church Fathers; copies of it were burned, and in AD 448 an edict of the emperors Theodosius II and Valentinian condemned it. But, despite the harsh response, even some Christians recognized his genius. Saint Augustine called him *doctissimus*, the most eminent of all the "pagan" philosophers.

In a work titled *Chronika*, Porphyry wrote a world history from the sack of Troy to the death of Plotinus. He wrote *Life of Pythagoras*, now lost. *Sentences* is an exposition of Plotinus's teachings modified slightly by his own beliefs. *On Abstinence* advocates vegetarianism and asceticism and condemns pleasure, especially sexual. Porphyry was the first to define all pleasure as evil (Augustine knew Porphyry's writings well and on this point agreed with him°).

Porphyry's reflections contain very little philosophy. While Plotinus was an original, Porphyry, for the most part, reworked, codified, and defended Plotinus's theological ideas, transforming them into a religion for anyone. He does make some minor adjustments. In his *Sentences* Porphyry alters the master's notion of reincarnation, holding that the human soul will indeed be reincarnated but never as a lower, animal form of life. Not unlike Saint Paul's vision of the resurrected soul reclothed in a "spiritual body" (1 Cor. 15:44), Porphyry envisions the good soul rewarded in the next life with a very refined material body. His ethics is also a rehash of Plotinus's; matter produces evil because it is so remote from reality (the One). Porphyry's overriding concerns were pistological and evangelical: how to purify the soul so it can return to God and how to make the cosmological realities of Neoplatonism intelligible to everyone.

IAMBLICHUS OF CHALCIS

Like his teacher Porphyry, Iamblichus was an esteemed Neoplatonist from Syria. If Porphyry's Neoplatonism was a popularized version of Plotinus's system, then Iamblichus's revised version went over the edge. Rather than raising human beings to God, he brought the gods down to people and made the gods everyone's next-door neighbors.

In the history of philosophy Iamblichus is noted (1) for removing all vestiges of philosophy from Neoplatonism and making it into a mystico-magical system; and (2) for defining the business of philosophy as the attempt to render the gods

Truth is a torch, but a terrific one; therefore we all try to grasp it with closed eyes, fearing to be blinded.

GOETHE

Eloquence may set fire to reason.
OLIVER WENDELL
HOLMES

°See pp. 301ff.

Carpe diem, quam minimus credula postero. *Seize today, and put as little trust as you can in tomorrow.*

HORACE (ROMAN POET, 65–8 BC)

intellectually defensible. (Porphyry had defined philosophy as the discipline designed to save the soul.)

Iamblichus was born at Chalcis in Coele-Syria (now the Bekaa Valley of central Lebanon) about AD 250; he died about AD 330. He came from a well-to-do family, studied with Porphyry in Rome, and later taught in Syria. Those who knew him judged him a truly great man, as great as his teacher (except in his style of writing). Because his philosophy diminished intellectual values and brought polytheistic divinities front and center, he was dubbed Iamblichus "the divine." He believed in magic and ubiquitous evil spirits; he was famed for talking with the dead, performing materializing miracles, and (they said) for levitating.

Among his books, written in Greek, were *On the Egyptian Mysteries*, *On the Pythagorean Life*, *Exhortation to Philosophy*, *On the General Science of Mathematics*, and *Theological Principles of Arithmetic*. Besides these, only a few of his lesser works have survived. Lost are his writings on the soul and on Chaldean doctrine, as well as his commentaries on Plato and Aristotle.

Like Porphyry, Iamblichus complexified the cosmology of Plotinus. Picture a cosmos of spiritual light spreading across billions of light-years from Blinding Brightness to utter darkness, from Pure Spirit to inert matter, from Perfect Goodness to intrinsic evil. Plotinus had said this cosmos contains three principles: the One (the God beyond being and knowing), the Mind (the divine intellect filled with Real Ideas), and the Soul (the creative agent), out of which emanates the physical universe and living things.

> *To have doubted one's own first principles is the mark of a civilized man.*
>
> OLIVER WENDELL HOLMES

This is the Neoplatonic system's foundational structure, and each disciple proceeded to modify or add to it in some fashion. The One, Iamblichus said, is really Two, a One that is ineffable (completely unknowable), and a knowable One that creates the Mind. He then divided the Mind into two sets of three; the first (higher) set contains (is) the archetypes of ideas, and the second (lower) set contains (is) the ideas themselves. The Mind, working through the Soul, creates nature. All these entities are in truth gods performing their functions. The Mind, for example, is really a double set of triadic gods. The Soul, too, is a triad of sets of gods. The highest of the sets of Soul gods is "supramundane" and inaccessible to our world; the lower two "mundane" sets of Soul gods, which include the Greek gods, angels, evil spirits, and other divine messengers, interact with the world. We humans pray to, give offerings to, and ask favors of these. They have the power to interfere with the forces of nature and alter them for our benefit. These familiar spirits can assist the human soul in its journey of purification.

Yet, for Iamblichus, the soul's journey is long and despairing. To Plotinus the journey had not been so formidable. But for Iamblichus the distance from this world's darkness to the bliss of mystical union with the One (like having to cross billions of light-years of spiritual space) was increased to virtual impossibility. The human soul, still weighed down by heavy matter from its mundane life, must, as it were, "swim upstream" past evil demons and other spiritual obstructions. By itself the soul is helpless, but with the assistance of the gods, placated by the proper rites and ceremonies, the trip is not quite impossible.

In earlier days the more intellectual and spiritual elements dominated Neoplatonism. But with the mystical pop version of Porphyry and the numeral mysticism of Iamblichus, Neoplatonism was mutated into a religion cluttered with magical beliefs and practices.

> *General propositions do not decide concrete cases.*
>
> OLIVER WENDELL HOLMES

Iamblichus had considerable influence on the Academy in Athens, where, under Proclus, a brief resurrection of a more philosophical Neoplatonism occurred; but it was Aristotle who was revived, not Plato.

THE HERMETIC LITERATURE

In the third century AD, a group of anonymous treatises called the Hermetica became prominent and was later to have considerable influence on Arabic speculation and on Latin philosophy and science, especially during the late Middle Ages and the Renaissance, when they gave birth to a Christian Hermeticism. They purported to be works of divine revelation from the Egyptian god Hermes Trismegistos (or from a wise Egyptian priest called Hermes), hence their name. Composed as dialogues in Greek and Latin, their origins are unknown; some of them may date from as early as the first century BC.

One class of the Hermetica deals with popular subjects such as astrology, alchemy, magic, and medicine. Their purpose was soteriological: By means of such occult practices, people can discover a gnosis that can lead to salvation. (Some of the popular Hermetica may have Gnostic origins.)

Another later group of Hermetic treatises deals with theology and philosophy; they include the *Asclepius* and seventeen treatises known as the *Corpus Hermeticum* and represent a syncretism of elements from Platonism and from Persian, Judaic, and perhaps Christian theologies. These more philosophical treatises, along with the mystical, magical, and religious elements, contain speculations about astronomy, physics, embryology, botany, and medicine. They frequently refer to supernatural intervention in and control of natural processes. Our knowledge of nature is not from observation but is a gift from the gods or from God. This represents one of the first applications of divine revelation to purely scientific knowledge.

Very little is new in the philosophical Hermetica. Its Neoplatonic elements are a familiar Plotinian orthodoxy—Nous derives from the One as emanation of light, and Soul similarly derives from Nous. Between the divine Soul and evil matter is a buffer of air. The realm of physical matter, while amorphous, is still the creation of the First God and therefore can be called a Second God; humankind constitutes a Third God. Humans are made up of an evil physical body inhabited by a divine mind and soul that, on release, can return to the source of their being. That release, however, depends on whether we abandon the world of the thwarting senses and seek communion with God.

THE EMPEROR JULIAN

Flavius Claudius Julianus would have been a philosopher, but he had to give up philosophy to become emperor of the world. (He thus repeated, and understood, the anguish of Marcus Aurelius.) He was the first learned emperor since Marcus and felt at ease in cultured society. During his studies at Pergamum, Ephesus, and Athens, he had fallen in love with everything Greek. He was especially attracted to Neoplatonic philosophy and Mithraic religion. All his life he derived spiritual sustenance and comfort from philosophy.

Julian had been baptized and raised a Christian, and he outwardly continued to conform. He was the son of Constantius, a half brother to Constantine the Great, who had declared Christianity the established religion of the empire. But Julian's path to power had been a bloody one. His father, his older brother, and several other family members had been murdered by aspirants to the throne, all of whom were professed Christians. On becoming emperor in AD 361, he immediately declared his intention to rule as Marcus had ruled—as a philosopher-king. He issued an edict proclaiming freedom of religion. At the same time he made known his plan to replace Christianity as the state religion with a revitalized Hellenistic religion. Shortly thereafter, he began to expel Christians from official positions; suppression and persecution followed. Christian leaders were exiled and tortured, churches burned.

No one ever became extremely wicked suddenly.

JUVENAL

Vicisti, Gallilaee! You have conquered, Galilean!

THE EMPEROR JULIAN
(DYING WORDS)

The Emperor Julian (AD 331–363) wearing the robe of a philosopher.

Julian was a man of remarkable intelligence and ability, with a gentle scholarly temperament. Had conditions been different, he would have pursued a career in philosophy. He dreamed of an ideal political order on the scale of Plato's *Republic*, free of corruption, insuring peace for all its citizens. His small book *On the Gods* revealed his awareness that the mythic deities are merely symbols to assist the finite human mind to grasp the unthinkable realms of the divine. He personally inveighed against the trouble-making Christians in a work called *The Trickery of the Galileans*, now lost. A strange little book, the *Misopogon*, "Beard-Hater," was Julian's polemical reply to the Antiochenes who had ridiculed him by saying he thought he was a philosopher just because he sported a beard.

Julian was emperor for barely two years; in June of AD 363, during a battle in Persia, he took a spear through his liver. His religious revolution came to naught, except to earn him the eternal epithet of "Apostate." Within a generation the empire was once again officially Christian.

HYPATIA OF ALEXANDRIA

When Julian died of his battle wounds in AD 363, the army elevated Jovian, a Christian committed to the orthodox creed, as the next emperor. One of Jovian's first moves was to reestablish Christianity as the state religion. The next emperor, Valentinian, mandated a policy of religious freedom and mostly stayed out of ecclesiastical affairs, but he allowed soothsayers and magicians in Italy to be burned alive or beaten to death with lead-loaded straps. Under his son and successor Gratian, with the encouragement of Bishop Ambrose of Milan, "pagan"° temples were confiscated, priests and vestal virgins were banned from their offices, and the altar to the goddess of victory was removed from the senate building in Rome. Under Valentinian II suppression of both non-Christians and Christian heretics continued, and after a passionate speech by Ambrose, the emperor turned down a request by Symmachus for the restoration of the altar to Victoria. The next emperor, Theodosius I, was a devout Nicene Catholic; he took the further step of prohibiting all "pagan" rites, defining them as crimes against the state and subjecting practioners to severe penalties.

All various modes of worship which prevailed in the Roman world were all considered by the people as equally true; by the philosopher as equally false; by the magistrate as equally useful.

EDWARD GIBBON

Tempora mutantur et homines deteriorantur. *Times change and men deteriorate.*

LATIN PROVERB

°*This appears to be the first ever use of the word "pagan." The Latin plural* pagani, *meaning "peasantry" and, by association, "rude," "simpleminded," and "ignorant," was first employed in a law passed under Valentinian in AD 368 and became widely used during the reign of Theodosius. Earlier Latin terms used to refer to non-Christians were* gentes, gentiles, nationes, *and* Graeci. *The English word "heathen" derives from "heath" and is commonly given the same pejorative meanings.[16]*

Hypatia of Alexandria (c. AD 370–415), mathematician and Neoplatonist philosopher.

The general Christian populace, led by fanatical monks, had turned vicious against all things non-Christian, believing that the "heathen" gods were really evil spirits who dwelt in the "pagan" temples. In Alexandria, where Neoplatonic philosophy was still strong, violent confrontations, incited by Bishop Theophilus ("a bold, bad man," Edward Gibbon wrote, "whose hands were alternately polluted with gold and with blood"), occurred between Christians and "pagans." Temples throughout Egypt were destroyed, including the majestic temple to Serapis in Alexandria. Similar bloody outbreaks occurred in Gaul, where multitudes of temples were razed and replaced by churches and cloisters, and in Syria, where Marcellus, bishop of Apamea, led a band of armed soldiers and gladiators in destroying everything associated with "pagan" practices—temples, altars, statues ("idols"), and countless other ancient artifacts that had ministered to the lives of their devotees. The enraged "heathen" reacted by burning Marcellus alive.[17]

In AD 412 the young, assertive Church Father Cyril became patriarch of Alexandria and rapidly extended his control beyond the religious orders into the temporal realm. Even Orestes the governor was awed by the power the Christian bishop so swiftly acquired and was concerned especially by his use of the *parabolani*, members of a religious fraternity originally organized for charitable purposes but who had become unruly and dangerous. The parabolani evolved into a cadre of personal servants ready to obey the patriarch.

On assuming office, Cyril immediately began to carry out his plan to purify the Alexandrian Church by persecuting heretics and nonbelievers. He first attacked the Novatians (who advocated strict measures against lapsed Christians), appropriating their property and excommunicating them from church activities. Then early in AD 415 he attacked the Jews. Synagogues were leveled to the ground and property confiscated; some forty thousand Jews were driven from the city. Governor Orestes complained to the emperor, but no action was taken.

All heresies are forbidden by both divine and imperial laws and shall forever cease.

EMPEROR GRATIAN
(DECREE)

The fool and the wise man are equally harmless; it is the half-wise and the half-foolish who are most to be feared.

GOETHE

Revenge is always the delight of a little weak and petty mind.

JUVENAL

Only individuals can suffer and only individuals have a place in tragedy.

EDITH HAMILTON

The dignity and the significance of human life—of these, and of these alone, tragedy will never let go.

EDITH HAMILTON

Once when Orestes was passing through the streets in his carriage, some five hundred Nitrian monks attacked him. (Cyril had studied at the monasteries at Nitria.) Orestes was pelted with stones and bloodied. He later executed the leader of the stone-throwing monks, but Cyril ordered his body to be taken to the cathedral, where he was honored with eulogies befitting a martyr.

Also at this time in Alexandria, Hypatia, the most renowned thinker of the times, directed the Neoplatonist school. She lived from about AD 370 to March of AD 415. Her father Theon was an acclaimed mathematician and philosopher, and Hypatia followed in his steps. She was known for her remarkable brilliance, her beauty, and her eloquence. Her lectures were popular—she specialized in Platonic and Aristotelian philosophy—and she attracted numerous students, among them Synesius of Cyrene (later to become the Christian bishop of Ptolemais), some of whose letters to Hypatia are still extant. Because of her unique intellectual gifts, she had come to symbolize the light of Hellenic learning, and she was the first ever notable female mathematician in the Western world. She did creative work in philosophy, mathematics, and astronomy ("pagan" subjects, the Christians said). Her Neoplatonist philosophy was more intellectual and less mystical than that of Plotinus or the Athenian school. She wrote commentaries on Diophantus's *Arithmetica*, Ptolemy's *Almagest*, and Apollonius's *Conics;* all are lost. Synesius's letters record talks he had with her about how to construct an astrolabe and a hydroscope.

A rumor circulated among the populace that Hypatia was having an affair with Orestes and that she was instrumental in keeping the prefect and the bishop from reconciling. One day during Lent while Hypatia was proceeding through the streets in her carriage, she was seized by monks and enraged citizens, dragged to the cathedral, stripped naked, and murdered; then, with sharp-edged oyster shells, her flesh was flayed from her body and burned.

Following Hypatia's death, scholars, philosophers, educators, and scientists migrated to other cities. After seven glorious centuries, the greatness of Alexandria as a center of learning ended.

ENDNOTES

1 Philip Schaff, *History of the Christian Church* (Scribner's, 1910; reprint, Eerdmans, 1950), vol. 4, pp. 212f.

2 Augustine, *Confessions*, XII, iii (3); Basil, *Homilies on the Hexameron*, VII, 3.

3 Schaff, *History*, vol. 3, pp. 895ff.

4 Schaff, *History*, vol. 3 , p. 899.

5 Schaff, *History*, vol. 3, p, 900.

6 Tatian, *Oratio ad Graecos*, III, 1–48 in the *Ante-Nicene Library*, in Schaff, *History*, vol. 2, p. 729.

7 Schaff, *History*, vol. 2, pp. 741f.

8 Clement, *Miscellanies*, Book VI, Ch. 10, in *Greek Science in Antiquity*, by Marshall Clagett (Collier Books, 1955), p. 166; Schaff, *History*, vol. 2, p. 780.

9 Origin, *Epistle to Gregory*, Ch. 1.

10 Schaff, *History*, vol. 2, pp. 822f.

11 Schaff, *History*, vol. 2, p. 824.

12 Tertullian, *Apologeticus*, Ch. 47.

13 Saint Augustine, *Contra Epistolam Manichaei quam vocant fundamenti*, I.i.2.

14 Saint Augustine, *Enchiridion*, Ch. 9.

15 Robin G. Collingwood, *The Idea of History* (A Galaxy Book from Oxford University Press, 1956), p. xii.

16 Schaff, *History*, vol. 3, p. 61n.

17 Schaff, *History*, vol. 3, p. 65.

CHAPTER 17

PHILOSOPHY DURING THE DARK AGES: TWO

AUGUSTINE OF THAGASTE
(AD 354–430)

Peering out from his own impassioned world, the most brilliant intellect of
the Dark Ages analyzes and reflects on everything in Heaven and Earth; he
anguishes over his own depraved nature and develops a definitive soteriology for himself and the Latin West; he creates philosophy of history, ponders the mystery of time, and (long before Descartes) proves that he exists.

Saint Augustine is by far the most significant thinker of the Dark Ages. Prolific he
was, which accounts partly for his impact upon Western thinking; but the vigor of
his intellect, the humanness of his searching, the aliveness of his writing, and the
authenticity of his religious faith—these enduring qualities make him immortal, and
he possessed them all in superlative measure. In everything he did—however we may
interpret and evaluate his contributions today—the man was impressive.

*I desire to know God and the soul.
Nothing more? Nothing
whatever.*

AUGUSTINE

THE *CONFESSIONS*

Aurelius Augustinus was born on the 13th of November in the year AD 354; he died
seventy-six years later during the seige of his north African seaport city of Hippo, by
barbarian invaders known as Vandals, on August 28, AD 430.

At about the age of forty-five Augustine wrote his *Confessions*, an autobiography
covering the first thirty-three years of his life. By "his life" is meant his inner life.
The book contains none of the usual trappings of a life story: went there, did that,
wrote a book. Rather the work traces "the evolution of the heart." And it was *not*
written for us human readers. His *Confessions* is addressed to God, and since God,
supposedly, already knows the story, the book lacks any chronological narrative of
events. It is a worshipful hymn of gratitude and thanksgiving. Working with a patho-
logical burden of guilt, Augustine recounts the doings of his earlier life; he confesses
to his God the shameful events that resulted from his impulsive nature; he then gives
thanks to his Lord for having led him out of that depraved state and back to the path
of redemption. "Allow me, I beseech you, to wind round and round in my present
memory the spirals of my errors. . . ."[1]

Though formally addressed to God, the work was in fact written with his ascetic
colleagues in mind. Augustine is, by nature, a sharer, and his anguished journey from

Fecisti nos ad Te, et inquietum
est cor nostrum, donec
requiescat in Te. *Thou hast
made us for Thee, and our heart
is restless till it rests in Thee.*

AUGUSTINE

Verus philosophus est amator
Dei. *The true philosopher is the
lover of God.*

AUGUSTINE

Augustine of Thagaste
(AD 354–430)

If the thing believed is incredible, it is also incredible that the incredible should have been so believed.

AUGUSTINE

I have loved Thee late, Thou Beauty, so old and so new; I have loved Thee late!

AUGUSTINE

On Augustine *His mind was the crucible in which the religion of the New Testament was most completely fused with the Platonic tradition of Greek philosophy.*

JOHN BURNABY

sinful man to servant of God was one his fellow monks and priests could appreciate and identify with. So in the *Confessions* he plays the role of a guru and role model leading his brother monastics along the path of renunciation. He tells them what it was like to steal pears, be seduced by the theater, abandon a lover, and pay the price for his worldly loves. He tells them about his search for serenity and about his continuing doubts and struggles with the flesh. They would understand. In effect, he is saying, "if I can do it, then, with God's help, you can do it too."[2]

Augustine was obsessed, all his life, with the nature of his own inner experience and was acutely aware of the conflicts raging in his psyche. His *Confessions* has been called a hundred-thousand-word program of psychotherapy aimed at relieving the pain that was thwarting his will and short-circuiting his attempts to do what was right by driving him to do what was wrong. Augustine was "in therapy" throughout his adult life, both before and after the *Confessions*; and his autobiography clarifies, for him and for us, the events that brought on the drastic spiritual turnaround that took place when he was thirty-two in a garden in Milan. In the long, painful course of therapeutic self-examination he discovers, with astonishing insight, the processes that first tore his soul apart and then, with God's help and his mother's prayers, led him home. As he searched within, what he found, as he saw it, was the darkened, disobedient self that his mother had feared was lurking in her son, a sinful self that she had told him, a million times, by silent words and loving looks, to fear and to fight. What his inquiries into his soul revealed was a baby, then a child, then a youth, then a young man all driven by selfishness and greed, an original-sin-filled craving self manipulated by an unredeemed all-too-human nature.

So we have Augustine's inner-life story in the *Confessions*, and we have his outer-life story as recorded, shortly before his death, by a friend and fellow bishop named Possidius, in *A Life of Saint Augustine*. Along with Augustine's other books and letters, and records from others who knew him, these writings give us the fullest account ever written of one of the world's most probing intellects.

IN THE HISTORY OF PHILOSOPHY
(AS OPPOSED TO THEOLOGY)

Augustine is important (1) for his probing into the experience of time; (2) for his Cogito (predating Descartes's Cogito by 1,250 years); (3) for his creation of the philosophy of history; (4) for his ethical theory, which, though not innovative or in advance of the Greeks, has been enormously influential in the West. Above and beyond these contributions, and apart from his purely intellectual accomplishments in philosophy and theology, readers through the ages have found Augustine's richly lived life story to be a paradigm and a mirror that can reveal to us depths and heights, lights and shadows, follies and flights in our own lives, and offer us insights without end into the mind traps, moral confusions, and mystical yearnings that must be faced by each individual who finds himself or herself on "the hero's journey."

THE MAN

Augustine was birthed in the north African town of Thagaste (or Tagaste; today Souq Ahras in northeastern Algeria, about 45 miles from the Mediterranean coast, near the Tunisian border). He was the third child of a Roman citizen (a "devout pagan") named Patricius and a Christian woman of great piety named Monica. Their first child was a son, Navigius, the second a daughter who later became a nun in Augustine's diocese of Hippo. Some evidence has them belonging to the tribe of

Kabyles, a branch of the Berber race. (Today the Berbers are dark skinned, and this has led to the claim that Augustine was "black"; but the tradition is very strong that they were of "Latin descent," and Augustine's culture and connections are entirely with the Romans, not the tribes of the African desert.)

Patricius was a "little brown man with quick brown eyes." He was a full citizen of the Roman Empire with the right to wear the Roman toga. An energetic business-man, a landowner with vineyards, orchards, wheat fields, and slaves (but always struggling to meet financial needs and pay his taxes), he had little time for his family and was absent most of the time, away on business or enjoying the baths in the city.

Monica was a bright, passionate, and complex woman, long suffering, seemingly passive and quiet, but in her passivity and silence judgmental and controlling. She came from a middle-class Christian family of easy circumstances. Augustine was the third, last, and favorite child of the young Monica; she was twenty-three at the time of his birth. She wanted a classical education for her son, but wished far more that he share her faith. A devout orthodox Catholic—but imbued with much primitive north African myth and superstition—she was firm in belief and very clear in knowing what was wrong and right; she did her best to teach her son the tenets of her Chris-tian faith. "She loved to have me with her, as is the way with mothers, but far more than most mothers." If her son disobeyed "she acted as if she was undergoing again the pangs of child-birth." Whenever Augustine strayed, which, being headstrong, he did with great regularity, she reacted as if it was for her a deep and personal injury.[3]

"I have no words to express the love she had for me, and with how much more anguish she was now suffering the pangs of child-birth for my spiritual state than when she had given birth to me physically. . . . my pious mother would not fail to visit me every night [in my dreams], that mother who followed me over land and sea that she might live with me."[4]

By contrast, his father was a remote figure, but, from a distance, still influential in his son's life. He was forty-six when his youngest son was born. Augustine never felt loved or understood by his father and seems to have had no warm feelings for him. "He saw in me only hollow things." Nevertheless, Patricius was enormously proud of his son, very aware of his brilliance. With a "pigheaded resolve" he scraped together enough money to give his son a good education. When Patricius died in AD 372, Augustine (about eighteen at the time) noted the event with only the briefest comment.[5]

Augustine was raised in a family, and therefore (as the quip goes) he was abused. Sensitive as he was, he was deeply abused by the bitter tension between his parents. Patricius had affairs, which Monica endured with patience, but she crucified Patri-cius with her silence. She was a woman, wife, and mother of extraordinary power grounded in the unshakable conviction that she was always right. As for Augustine she was convinced that "the son of such tears could not be lost." It was his mother's voice, not his father's, that haunted him all his life. His father "could not cancel in me the rights of my mother's piety," Augustine writes, appreciatively; "For she tried earnestly, my God, that You should be my father, not him."[6]

Both parents were strong in their dreams for their son. Patricius was determined that his son should amount to something—perhaps as a lawyer or civil administrator who would make his father proud to be a Roman citizen. Monica was equally deter-mined that her son should amount to something—as a devout believer in the faith of Christ. Both, in their own ways, gave strong encouragement to Augustine's ambi-tious temperament.

Augustine was a precocious child, small of stature, with a quick intelligence and a nervous manner. He loved all kinds of play with the other boys, especially in com-

On Augustine *With this book* [City of God] *paganism as a philosophy ceased to be, and Christianity as a philosophy began. It was the first definitive formulation of the medieval mind.*
WILL DURANT

petitive games that he won. He hated school at first (he got the point easily, became bored, and let his attention wander; of course he was beaten for being bad). What education he did receive was shallow; he read little more than a few Latin classics and received only a smattering of history and nothing in the sciences. The sole purpose of his education, early and late, was "to learn the art of words, to acquire that eloquence that is essential to persuade men of your case, to enroll your opinions before them." This was in its basics a Sophist education, not the truth-seeking, liberal arts education of a critical philosopher. All his life Augustine had the facile ability to persuade himself and others with an *inundatio* of words. Whatever he wanted, he talked himself around it and toward it and into it and through it; no man ever used such a superabundance of words more effectively. With words he transformed his inner world and tried, to the best of his ability, to transform the outer world as well.[7]

YOUTH

I became to myself a wasteland.

AUGUSTINE

By the time he was twelve, Augustine had been thoroughly conditioned to the boisterous but fashionable misbehavior of his boyhood chums. "There was a pear-tree on a plot near our vineyard. . . . We had been playing in the fields long after night had fallen, as was our wicked habit. Off we went to shake down the fruit and carry it away: we filched great loads of pears, not to eat, but just to throw at pigs."[8] By his own testimony he was already into sex. Despite his mother's hovering presence, he had discovered girls and lived for little else than the next sexual encounter.

By his fourteenth year he was excelling in the humanities; his brilliance was evident and his teachers advised further study. So for his "secondary education" Patricius sent him away to Madaura, a college town twenty miles south of Thagaste. Monica was worried that her son would emulate his father. "She commanded me, and with much earnestness forewarned me, that I should not commit fornication, and especially that I should never defile any man's wife. These seemed to me no better than women's counsels, which it would be a shame for me to follow. . . . and I took pleasure to do it, not for the pleasure of the act only, but for the praise of it also; . . . and when I lacked opportunity to commit a wickedness that should make me as bad as the lost, I would feign myself to have done what I never did." So at Madaura, Augustine dedicated himself to his studies but also renewed his dedication to "the darksome ways of love." There, at fifteen, he was controlled by two passions: the enjoyment of his books and the indulgence of his senses.[9]

Who would not shrink back in horror and choose death, if he were given the choice between death and his childhood all over again?

AUGUSTINE

At sixteen he was back in Thagaste, waiting for his father to accumulate the means to pay for his schooling. He waited the better part of a year, with little to do— "a season of idleness" he called it. Adolescence had burst upon him and his rebellion against parental restraint had swelled to high tide (the metaphor is his: "I, poor wretch, foamed like a troubled sea, following the rushing of my own tide"). Monica was still worried about women and communicated her fears to him; Augustine gave her quite enough reason to be fearful (but she would have been fearful even if he hadn't). Earlier, at the baths, Patricius noticed that his son had entered puberty; he went home and told Monica, who "was startled with a holy fear and trembling." We can speculate that Monica's anguish at her son's opportunistic conquests was an echo of her experience with Patricius; she displaced onto her son a long-suppressed fury at her husband's infidelities. Augustine later commented that his parents should have arranged a marriage for him to "blunt the thorns" of his sexual feelings. Most of his time in Thagaste was spent with the boys and he joined them in acts of vandalism which, though innocent enough, provided his later guilt-ridden conscience with powerful evidence of original sin.[10]

He was an excellent student. His curriculum included the study of Roman writers, including Vergil, Plautus, Terence, Seneca, Sallust, Apuleius, Horace, Ovid, Juvenal, and Cicero. At sixteen there was no more he could learn from his teachers, and he was advised to move on to Carthage to study rhetoric. Monica objected to the move. The Roman author Salvian had called Africa the cesspool of the Roman Empire, and Carthage the cesspool of Africa. Monica was more worried than ever; her son was rapidly moving beyond her sphere of control.

CARTHAGE

When Patricius succeeded in saving enough money for his son's expenses, Augustine was dispatched to Carthage. The year was AD 371, he was seventeen, and he came alive in the liberating climate of the big city. "I came to Carthage where a cauldron of illicit loves leapt and boiled around me." He plunged joyfully into his academic studies; his intellect exploded into rhetoric, dialectic, geometry, music, mathematics, and law. These were beautiful loves and he wanted never to leave them, so he decided to become a teacher. Carthage offered him a cornucopia of new pleasures: chariot races, gladiatorial combats, the tragedies, comedies, operas, and ballets of the theater which, he said, became "fuel to my raging fire." But it was sex that consumed him. "I was not yet in love, but I was in love with love, and, from the depths of my need, I hated myself for not more keenly feeling the need." (One can hardly decide whether it's Augustine speaking or a recording of his mother's voice playing through his guilty conscience.) "What I needed most was to love and be loved; but most of all when I obtained the enjoyment of the body of the person who loved me . . . I rushed headlong into love, eager to be caught."[11]

Then, in less than a year, everything changed. Augustine fell in love. The girl (we are never told ner name) was from a lower-class Carthaginian family. She became his lover and they set up housekeeping. As Augustine phrased it, not unhappily, he was "washed up on the shores of matrimony." They would be together for fifteen years, and all evidence and intuitions point to their remaining faithful to one another during that time. Formal marriage was out of the question; Romans were rigidly class conscious, and it was forbidden by imperial law for middle-class citizens to marry lower-class women. For Augustine, and probably for the girl as well, this was a beneficial arrangement.[12]

Augustine was eighteen when he and his anonymous mate became parents of a son. They named him Adeodatus, a name common in the Christian community in Carthage. ("Adeo-datus" means "God-given"; but on at least one occasion Augustine refers to him as "the son of my sin.") We know little of this period of Augustine's life, but it was undoubtedly a more stable interlude in a frenetic existence.

At Carthage, Augustine also expected to begin finding answers to his larger questions, and at nineteen he experienced his first "religious" conversion. Working through the syllabus to one of his courses, he came to a book by Cicero titled *The Hortensius* (now lost). "This book, indeed, changed all my way of feeling. It changed my prayers to Thee, O Lord; it gave me entirely different plans and aspirations. Suddenly, all empty hope for my career lost its appeal; and I was left with an unbelievable fire in my heart, desiring the deathless qualities of Wisdom." The key word is "Wisdom," and Cicero now shows Augustine that he can define philosophy as "the soul seeking Wisdom." His search became focused not on some "objective" truth, but on the pursuit of ideas which, when defined as truth, will work pragmatically for him. "I should not chase after this or that philosophical sect, but should love Wisdom, of whatever kind it should be; that I should search for it, follow hard upon it, hold on to it and embrace it with all my strength. That was what stirred me in that discourse,

I am saddened that my tongue cannot live up to my heart.

AUGUSTINE

To Carthage I came, where there sang all around me in my ears a caldron of unholy loves . . . I defiled the spring of friendship with the filth of concupiscence, and I beclouded its brightness with the hell of lustfulness.

AUGUSTINE

The pleasures of this life for which I would weep are in conflict with the sorrows of this life in which I would rejoice, and I know not on which side stands the victory.

AUGUSTINE

Desiderium sinus cordis. It is yearning that makes the heart deep.

AUGUSTINE

set me alight, and left me blazing." But where was he to find such Wisdom? He turned first to the Christian Bible, which was a natural move, but at this stage of his life he was disappointed with what he found. The Old Testament was cluttered with incredulous myths, and the language of the New Testament (which he read in Latin; he didn't know Greek) struck him as crude and uncultured; to an erudite young scholar like Augustine the writings seemed the work of uneducated semiliterates.[13]

The problem of evil had bothered Augustine from at least his adolescence. How could it not bother him? He had been taught that he himself was a shameful mixture of good and evil. His (potentially) good soul was trapped inside an evil body and was locked in a struggle, from birth till death, with the sin-stained physical organism. During every hour of every day, this inner battle was being waged, and any mere mortal man, by himself, was quite incapable of winning the battle.

So Augustine's questions about the nature and origin of evil never left him. "From what cause do we do evil?" What drives it? If God is good, why does he allow it? Why is there so much evil in the world?[14]

Obsessing with this problem, he fell in with the Manichaeans, a highly nonconformist, Christian-Gnostic mystery cult with roots in Persian Zoroastrianism. Augustine expected to find an answer from the Manichaeans since they promised they could answer this and every such question. Whence evil then? The entire cosmos, they taught, is a great battleground between two domains, a Kingdom of Light and a Kingdom of Darkness. The Kingdom of Darkness invades and commits rape on the Kingdom of Light, and a spiritual struggle ensues that will endure to the end of time. Just as the Cosmos is eternally at war with itself, so also the individual soul is at war with itself; both are battlegrounds between good and evil. Man is not free, they said, but the goodness inside us wants to be set free.

For nine years, from the age of twenty, Augustine moved with the Manichees and conducts his search for "Wisdom" within the confines of Mani's Gnostic-Christian worldview. They provided him, for a time, with moderately satisfying solutions. Soul and body "have been enemies since the creation of the worlds," said the *Manichaean Psalmbook*. This made intellectual sense to him; he understood, with their help, why his inner life felt like one long, relentless, painful wrestling match.[15]

Being Augustine, he evangelized for his new faith and made many converts (to his great embarrassment since, later, he must convert them back out of Manichaeism into Christianity). With all his heart he tried to believe. He confesses that he was caught up in Manichaean doctrine partly because it seemed to answer his questions, but more because he was having such fun arguing the issues and always winning. "So it came about that, to a surprising extent, I came to approve of whatever they said— not because I knew any better, but because I wanted it to be true."[16]

But he is still without a remedy for the body's power over, and manipulation of, his will. "The promptings of sensuality are the most strong of all, and so the most hostile to philosophy. . . . What man in the grip of this, the strongest of emotions, can bend his mind to thought, regain his reason, or, indeed, concentrate on anything?" Then, shaking his head sadly, Augustine reminisces and confides (to God): "I, an unfortunate young man, wretched on the threshold of my adult life, used to pray, 'Lord, give me chastity and continence: but not yet!'"[17]

In the fall of AD 373 Augustine returned home to Thagaste to teach literature. He was still a flaming Manichee and was zealous in converting others to his faith; he quickly drew his old friend Alypius and his financial sponsor Romanianus into the cult. But Monica was deeply offended by his (to her) heretical Manichaeism as well as his living with a lowborn girlfriend; she refused to allow her son and his family entrance to her house. Though she soon repented, the scar remained.[18]

O that I had wings like a dove; for then I would fly away and be at rest.

AUGUSTINE

Blessed is he that shall know his soul.

MANICHAEAN PSALMBOOK

On Augustine *Officially, Ambrose converted Augustine to Catholicism; it would be at least a half truth to say instead that Augustine converted the Church to Manichaeism.*

WALLACE I. MATSON

The Devil is not to be blamed for everything: there are times when a man is his own devil.

AUGUSTINE

A year later they returned to Carthage. Augustine continued to ponder Manichaeism and found more and more that its descriptions of the world didn't agree with simple empirical observations. Then the imperial leader of the movement, Faustus of Milevis, came to Carthage. Augustine had been assured that this was the "expert" who would settle his questions, but he listened and was put off by the man's ignorance. "I found at once that the man was not learned in any of the liberal studies save literature, and not especially learned in that either." Just perform the rituals, Faustus counseled. As a result Augustine turned away from Manichaeism. "I could make no progress in it," he said.[19]

So the Manichaean assurances fell apart. He discovered that he had used Manichaean beliefs to avoid having to deal with his guilt, and had therefore failed to resolve it. "For I still held the view that it was not I who was sinning, but some other nature within me."[20]

Once back in Carthage Augustine returned to teaching rhetoric, with not a little success, but he found the students inattentive and hard to handle. He became restless. Through friends he was able to secure the promise of a teaching position in Rome and prepared to set sail from Carthage. This was in the summer of AD 383. Monica was to accompany them. "She, indeed, was in dreadful grief at my going and followed me right to the coast. Then she clung to me, passionately determined that I should either go back home with her or take her to Rome, but I deceived her with the pretence that I had a friend whom I did not want to leave until he had sailed off with a fair wind. Thus I lied to my mother. . . . She would not return home without me, but I managed with some difficulty to persuade her to spend the night in a place near the ship. . . . That night I stole away from her. She remained, praying and weeping. . . . The wind rose and filled our sails, the shore slipped from our sight and on that shore, in the morning light, she stood in a frenzy of grief. She went home, and I to Rome."[21]

MILAN

In Rome Augustine rented some poor quarters and started a search for pupils. His friend Alypius joined them. But the situation in Rome was not congenial. Through the efforts of the Roman senator Symmachus, a former Proconsul in Carthage and now Prefect of Milan, Augustine won an appointment as a professor of rhetoric in Milan. Symmachus was the noblest of the old Romans, and at the time was engaged in a battle over the official disestablishment of the Roman religion; he was urging the Emperor Valentinian to restore the altar to the goddess of Victory in the senate building in Rome, saying that "The heart of so great a mystery can never be reached by following one road only." But he lost the case through the passionate opposition of his cousin Ambrose, the Christian bishop of Milan.

So in the autumn of AD 384 Augustine moved to Milan, and a semblance of a normal working household was finally established. Augustine sent for his wife and son to join them. Monica also joined them, bringing with her Augustine's brother, sister, two of his cousins, and Nebridius, an old friend. Monica became the head and supervisor of this extended-family arrangement.

Bishop Ambrose was one of the most eloquent and powerful Fathers of the Roman Church. (He had brought the Emperor Theodosius to his knees in penance under threat of excommunication.) Augustine attended the cathedral and listened to the bishop's sermons, not, he said, for their content, but rather for their impressive rhetoric; he was also impressed at Ambrose's masterful technique in his debates with heretics; he was always victorious. Augustine, who never bonded with his real father, now found in Ambrose the father he always wanted, and the relationship deepened into one of mutual respect and affection.

I have taken upon me to know.
AUGUSTINE

Uno itinere non potest perveniri ad tam grande secretum. The heart of so great a mystery can never be reached by following one road only.
SYMMACHUS

Wretched, on the threshold of my adult life, I used to pray, "Lord give me chastity and continence: but not yet."

AUGUSTINE

If it was company and good conversation that Adam needed, it would have been much better arranged to have two men together, as friends, not a man and a woman.

AUGUSTINE

What is the difference whether it is in a wife or a mother, it is still Eve that we must beware of in any woman.

AUGUSTINE

Marriage is not good, but it is a good in comparison with fornication.

AUGUSTINE

The understanding flies on ahead, and there follows, oh, so slowly, and sometimes not at all, our weakened human capacity for feeling.

AUGUSTINE

At this juncture Monica persuaded Augustine to send his concubine back to Africa. Augustine later writes: "This was a blow which crushed my heart to bleeding. I loved her dearly." Monica was not unaware of her son's uncontrollable sexual needs and sought to channel them into more acceptable directions, not to make her son happy (she had neither empathy nor sympathy with Augustine's lust for gratification) but to upgrade his social status. "Continual effort was made to have me married." Monica located another young lady, an heiress with a higher social standing, and arranged a betrothal. Though fully sanctioned by Roman law and common practice, Augustine's union had incurred Monica's disapproval from the beginning. She was now in a position to choose what was best for her son, and, moreover, the new fiancée's family would have never agreed to the betrothal if the concubine was allowed to remain. But the new fiancée was "two years under the fit age" (which was the age of twelve; apparently she was only ten at the time of betrothal), and Augustine's "insatiable appetite" rendered a wait of two years out of the question. "Meanwhile," he says, "my sins were being multiplied, and my concubine being torn from my side as a hindrance to my marriage, my heart which clave unto her was torn and wounded and bleeding. And she returned to Africa, vowing unto Thee never to know any other man, leaving with me my son by her. But unhappy I . . . impatient of delay, inasmuch as not till after two years was I to obtain her I sought, not being so much a lover of marriage, as a slave to lust, procured another." So Augustine fell into "a yet deeper gulf of carnal pleasures." The dark night had become reality; he had succumbed, he confessed, to "the disease of my soul."[23]

Augustine's lover undoubtedly returned to Africa reluctantly, but submissively, knowing it had to be, and, according to tradition, she joined a nunnery. It is not surprising that Augustine, at a considerably later time, as a Catholic bishop teaching moral doctrine, should write: If a man's concubine has been "faithful to him, and if, after his marriage to another, she herself gave no thought to marriage, but abstained from all sexual relations, I would not dare to accuse her of adultery—even though she may have been guilty in living with a man who was not her husband."[24]

CONVERSION

Augustine had almost arrived at the point of committing himself to both a life of Wisdom and the life of a Christian. Both paths were taking hold of him, powerfully, but each, in his mind (mirroring the expectations of his Roman society) demanded nonnegotiable sacrifices. Being baptized as a Catholic meant dying to the old way of life to give birth to the new, a complete break with the familiar and the reassuring. And, likewise, becoming a philosopher meant renouncing the world, as Plotinus had done, and letting go of one's dreams of a career, sex, marriage, family and other normal delights of civilized life. No wonder Augustine's soul was being torn apart: Life in this world he had passionately embraced with all his being, or at least with all his physical being if not with his heart, mind, and soul.

In late August of AD 386, Augustine, his mother, and a couple of his friends were together in their house in Milan. Augustine was in great emotional turmoil. In his mind's ear he could hear Ambrose chastising his flock: "How long with your *delights*? How long with your *revelling*? The day of judgement draws ever nearer." Like Buridan's ass, Augustine was paralyzed between choices. "Many years of my life had passed—twelve, unless I was wrong—since I had read Cicero's *Hortensius* at the age of 19, and it had inspired me to study philosophy. But I still postponed my renunciation of this world's joys."[25]

"There was a small garden attached to the house where we lodged. . . . I now found myself driven by the torment in my breast to take refuge in this garden, where no one could interrupt that fierce struggle. . . . I tore my hair and hammered my forehead with my fists; I locked my fingers and hugged my knees." He brooded over the pleasures he would have to give up and was ashamed at the imagery that was projected onto the screen of his mind. But his soul resisted: "Close your ears to the unclean whispers of your body. It tells you of things that delight you, but not of such things as the Law of the Lord your God has to tell.

"In this way I wrangled with myself, in my own heart, about my own self. And all the while Alypius stayed at my side, silently awaiting the outcome of this agitation that was now in me.

"I probed the hidden depths of my soul and wrung its pitiful secrets from it, and when I mustered them all before the eyes of my heart, a great storm broke within me, bringing with it a great deluge of tears. I stood up and left Alypius so that I might weep and cry to my heart's content.

Tolle, lege! Tolle, lege! Take up and read! [voice of a child singing to Augustine]

AUGUSTINE

"Somehow I flung myself down beneath a fig-tree and gave way to the tears which now streamed from my eyes. . . . in my misery I kept crying 'How long shall I go on saying "Tomorrow, tomorrow"?' Why not now? Why not make an end of my ugly sins at this moment?

"I was asking myself these questions, weeping all the while with the most bitter sorrow in my heart, when all at once I heard the sing-song voice of a child in a nearby house. . . . again and again it repeated the refrain *'Tolle, lege! Tolle, lege!'* 'Take up and read, take up and read!' . . . I stemmed my flood of tears and stood up, telling myself that this could only be a divine command to open my book of Scripture and read the first passage on which my eyes should fall. . . . So I hurried back to the place where Alypius was sitting, for when I stood up to move away I had put down the book containing Paul's Epistles. I seized it and opened it, and in silence I read the first passage on which my eyes fell: 'Not in revelling and drunkenness, not in lust and wantonness, not in quarrels and revelries. Rather, arm yourselves with the Lord Jesus Christ, spend no thought on nature and nature's appetites.'"[26]

When you hear a man confessing, you know that he is not yet free.

AUGUSTINE

He had no need to read further. "It was as though the light of confidence flooded into my heart and all the darkness of doubt was dispelled." He marked the place and closed the book.

"Then we went in and told my mother, who was overjoyed. And when we went on to describe how it had all happened, she was jubilant with triumph and glorified You. . . . You converted me to yourself, so that I no longer desired a wife or placed any hope in this world, but stood firmly upon the rule of faith, where you had shown me to her in a dream so many years before. And you *turned her sadness into rejoicing*, into joy far fuller than her dearest wish, far sweeter and more chaste than any she had hoped to find in children begotten of my flesh."[27]

What makes the heart of a Christian heavy? The fact that he is a pilgrim, and longs for his own country.

AUGUSTINE

"Seek and ye shall find" had new meaning. Augustine's search for Wisdom was over, except that it was just beginning. Though he had returned to the simple faith of his mother, it was no longer simple; he had explored, with mind and heart, every facet, every angle, every corner of Christian teaching, and with his uncanny intellect had made it his. "I am just the sort of man," he later wrote, "who is impatient in his longing not only to take what is true on faith, but to come to understand it." Now everything cohered. It made sense. He understood it. After such violent struggles in mind and heart his psyche, at last, could rest. Philosophy and his religious faith had come together as one.[28]

I have loved Thee late, Thou Beauty, so old and so new; I have loved Thee late! And lo! Thou wast within, but I was without, and was seeking Thee there. And into Thy fair creation I plunged myself in my ugliness; for Thou wast with me, and I was not with Thee! Those things kept me away from Thee, which had not been, except they had been in Thee! Thou didst call, and didst cry aloud, and break through my deafness. Thou didst glimmer, Thou didst shine, and didst drive away my blindness. Thou didst breathe, and I drew breath, and breathed in Thee. I tasted Thee, and I hunger and thirst. Thou didst touch me, and I burn for Thy peace. If I, with all that is within me, may once live in Thee, then shall pain and trouble forsake me; entirely filled with Thee, all shall be life to me."[29]

During the previous summer Augustine became ill, possibly from stress and depression. He was plagued by chest pains. Rest was essential. In September of AD 386 he and a few friends retreated to a villa at Cassiciacum, twenty miles north of Milan. It was quiet countryside, near a long blue lake, and from there they could see the Alps. Accompanying Augustine were his son Adeodatus, his brother Navigius, Alypius, some friends, and Monica.

Augustine convalesced and wrote. His strength was gone. He was tired but for the first time felt a healing quietude. He took time to see the beautiful countryside and delighted in the small things in his immediate surroundings. A river of books began to flow from his pen, a stream that continued to the hour of his death forty-four years later.

In March they returned to Milan. Then on the following Easter—on Sunday, April 24, AD 386—Augustine, his son Adeodatus, and his friend Alypius were baptized in the cathedral at Milan. In the baptistry beside the basilica, Bishop Ambrose lowered Augustine into a pool of water for a triune baptism, then before the cathedral's congregation, in a pure white robe, he became for the first time a celebrant in the Christian mystery of the Lord's Supper. He had "put off the old man" and "put on the new man" of a twice-born Christian.[30]

Augustine decided to return to Africa where, near his home, with his mother, his son, and a small group of friends, he would set up a retreat, pursue his studies, and write. In AD 387 they left for Rome, but they found that shipping had been stopped by a naval blockade of the port, so they halted at Ostia. There Monica fell mortally ill. Augustine and Adeodatus wept and promised to carry her body back to Thagaste to be buried beside Patricius, but Monica had a different request: "Bury my body anywhere," she directed, "and trouble not yourselves with it; only this one thing I ask, that you remember me at the altar of my God, wherever you may be."[31]° Nine days later she died in Augustine's arms and was buried at Ostia, at the mouth of the Tiber River. She was fifty-six. Augustine and his small party returned to Rome, waited almost a year till it was safe to sail, then late in AD 388 they took a boat home to north Africa.

LATER YEARS

There is more to the story, forty-two years more, during which time Augustine of Thagaste became the intellectual leader of the Church, not just in north Africa, but throughout the Latin world. The life story, however, from AD 388 on, is entirely different. On the surface it seems to shift from the inner world of contemplation to the outer world of action; but it was really a shift from Augustine's preoccupation with his inner world of emotional conflict to his (still) inner world of intellectual conflict. The emotional hurricanes are no longer even tropical storms. The sea is calm. But Augustine is truly comfortable only with conflict; he seeks it, he thrives on it; he tends to turn any relationship or situation into one of contention where he can make use of his superlative skills for dealing with it. For the rest of his life he is occupied

---

Fides praecedit intellectum.
Faith precedes understanding.

AUGUSTINE

Bury my body anywhere, and trouble not yourselves for it; only this one thing I ask, that you remember me at the altar of my God, wherever you may be.

SAINT MONICA

°*At the close of World War II Monica's admonition was brought back to life when families had to make a decision on whether to bring home the bodies of servicemen killed overseas. See "Let Them Rest in Peace" by Edwin P. Booth in* The Reader's Digest *(May 1947) in which the author urged that the dead be left to rest where buried but "remembered at the altars of God" wherever loved ones happened to be. Prof. Booth had lost a son in the War.*

Through a woman [Eve] we were sent to destruction; through a woman [Mary] salvation was restored to us.

AUGUSTINE

with working out the bugs in his "systematic theology" and, simultaneously, projecting his intellectual system into the public arena for acceptance by all who would seek the truth. This assures a long-running, ever-repeating cycle of dramatic conflict.

Augustine returned to Thagaste hoping to live, for the rest of his life, as a contemplative scholar in a small group of "philosophers." So for three years, from the autumn of AD 388 to early AD 391, he renounced the world and came within a millimeter of achieving his goal. On the estate inherited from his parents he set up a community of recluses that included just a few friends and his son Adeodatus, who was turning out to be a brilliant intellectual, like his father. They thought of themselves as "Servants of God," and their goal was to "to grow god-like in their retirement."

Sometime during the following year Adeodatus died. Augustine wept and whispered Cicero to his lost son: "You are the only man of all men whom I would wish to surpass me in all things." Having lost everything dear, Augustine would live henceforth only to serve his God; for the rest of his life he turned his energies into writing and playing an extremely active role in the development of Christianity in north Africa.[32]

In the spring of AD 391 Augustine journeyed to the maritime town of Hippo to encourage a friend who was toying with the idea of renouncing the world, as Augustine had done. While there he attended services at the cathedral. The elderly bishop of Hippo was no longer able to carry the load of the parish; when the congregation saw Augustine in their midst they shouted and, by acclamation, chose him to be their priest, to assist their bishop. This was a fairly standard procedure for selecting a shepherd of a flock, and Augustine didn't greatly resist. "I was grabbed," he later recalled to his congregation. "I was made a priest . . . and from there, I became your bishop."[33]

From AD 394 till his death in AD 430 Augustine tended his flock in Hippo, a city of some forty thousand people. In the walled-in garden next to the church he established a monastery; this was the beginning of the religious order called Augustinian Hermits. His monastery grew to become an influential theological seminary out of which came many of the leaders of the Western Church. There, in the "Monastery in the Garden," with an ever-growing number of monks, Augustine lived a communal existence. He wore a simple black robe, a cowl, and a leathern girdle, like Eastern monastics. He was a vegetarian. He dined with the other monks, and during meals they read or conversed on spiritual matters. They had a rule never to gossip about someone who was absent. Women were excluded from the monastery; Augustine would never be seen with any woman, including his sister, except when others were present.

From his base in Hippo, Bishop Augustine fought the battles that established theological orthodoxy in the Western Church and wrote the books that were to shape Western thought for the next fifteen hundred years. With Augustine as the center of the hurricane (the metaphor is not inappropriate), north Africa became the intellectual center of the Latin world.

The first round of battle was fought with his former friends the Manichees; he disputed with them on questions of evil and free will. The fight continued with the Donatists on the true nature of the Church and its relationship to society; the Donatists held that the Church was a faithful remnant of God's Chosen People who, in their purity, must recoil from an evil world and protect the truth in their isolation. In contrast to this isolationism, Augustine declared that the Church's mission was not to withdraw from the world but to transform the world; to do this Christians must remain in the arena to take on all enemies who, with God's help, will be van-

Seek not to understand that thou mayest believe, but believe that thou mayest understand.

AUGUSTINE

What is faith save to believe what you do not see?

AUGUSTINE

Give me a man in love: he knows what I mean. Give me one who yearns; give me one who is hungry; give me one far away in this desert, who is thirsty and sighs for the spring of the Eternal country. Give me that sort of man: he knows what I mean. But if I speak to a cold man, he just does not know what I am talking about.

AUGUSTINE

quished. While the Donatist idea of the Church met the us-them need to be morally special in an evil world, it was a counsel of impotence. Augustine, by contrast, saw the Church as a phalanx of divinely empowered warriors preparing for victory in a cosmic battle. Augustine "set the whole African church in motion" against the Donatists. Augustine's greatest battle was with the Pelagians who advocated free will; Augustine passionately opposed them, arguing that man is saved by God's grace, not through his own efforts.

I am the sort of man who writes because he had made progress, and who makes progress by writing.
AUGUSTINE

The library of Augustine's writings is so vast that his biographer Possidius doubted that any one person could ever read all of them. Extant are 113 books, 218 letters, and more than 500 sermons. The most interesting personal works are his *Confessions*, his letters, and the *Retractationes*, a late work, long-planned, in which he did a retrospective on all his writings, with comments and a few revisions. His masterpiece is the massive *City of God*, which took him thirteen years to write. A great bulk of his writings, the "against" books, focused on immediate doctrinal and heretical problems and are invaluable to the historian: *Against the Academics, Against the Pagans, Against Julian, Against the Manichaean Faust, Against the Priscillanists and Origen*, and more. Then there are the theological expositions, the "on" books: *On Genesis, On the Trinity, On Christian Doctrine, On Christian Discipline, On the Immortality of the Soul, On Music, On Order, On Free Will, On the True Religion*, and many more. He wrote a spate of practical books on everyday moral problems: *On Lying, On Fasting, On Virginity, On the Goodness of Marriage*. His "philosophical" subject matter is scattered randomly through his works.

It is written "From much words thou shalt not escape sin." That frightens me considerably.
AUGUSTINE

AUGUSTINE'S THEOLOGY

Augustine was gifted with an incisive logical mind, but he confined the operations of this soaring intellect almost entirely to the circle of faith. *"Fides proecedit intellectum."* "Faith must always precede understanding." *"Nisi credideritis, non intelligetis."* "If one does not believe, then one can't understand." Augustine "never abandoned or depreciated reason, he only subordinated it to faith and made it subservient to the defense of revealed truth. Faith is the pioneer of reason, and discovers the territory which reason explores."[34]

[Legendary child to Augustine] It would be easier for me to pour the sea into this hole than for you to fathom the least part of the mystery of the Trinity.

FAITH AND REASON

Augustine is the supreme harmonizer of the Middle Ages; he resolved the clash of reason and belief in favor of belief. "It is good, then, for me to cleave unto God, for if I remain not in Him, neither shall I in myself."[35] Reason has its place, to be sure, but it is often merely driven by an "impudent curiosity." What this meant, in daily thinking, was that the tenets of Christian doctrine were accepted without question and believed without inspection; the role of the intellect was to explain and defend those doctrines and to make them intellectually respectable to others who might have an inclination toward reasonable doubt.

On Augustine This great mind can make himself so simple that children can understand him.
CASSIODORUS

Augustine's theology is biblical, Pauline, and Neoplatonic. Sounding like a disciple of Plotinus, he taught that God is absolute being and all things derive from him. God is a Trinity of three equal persons, yet one God. The Trinity cannot be rationally understood; it is forever a mystery. Christ is both God and man and is the sole mediator between God and mankind. Humans were designed to be good, but, out of pride, Adam sinned and lost communion with God. So the soul of man, forsaken by God, died; and the human body came under the control of lust. The entire human race existed in the loins of Adam when he sinned; "In him all have sinned,"

Paul wrote. So, as participants in that original sin of Adam, the entire human race is a "mass of perdition," is lost, and merits damnation.[36]

But humans can be saved. The heart of Augustine's theology is the freely given grace of God operating through Christ and the historic Church. God offers redemption to those whom he selects. All human souls are predestined by God both "to punishment and to salvation" (a doctrine called "double predestination"; God himself decides who will be saved and who will be damned). God's election is "irresistible." Baptism erases all sin, original and personal, but even with baptism no one can be absolutely sure that he is saved; for unless God adds perseverance to the will many find it difficult to hold off sinning to the final judgment. God's grace enters the soul at baptism and initiates a transformation of the whole person. There are two final judgments, one upon the death of the individual, another at the end of the world when a general resurrection will take place.

The Church is the instrument of redemption: "the Holy Spirit may be said not to be received except in the Catholic Church." The Church's sacraments are necessary for salvation. Augustine is often thought of as the "father" of the the Catholic sacraments.[37]

ETHICS

Although we usually subsume ethics under philosophy, Augustine's moral reflections, which derive from his theological assumptions about human nature, might be better thought of as theology, for they are biblical, doctrinal, and are sundered from empirical reality. His moral methodology can be summarized in three words: Believing is seeing. He starts from what he thinks to be apriori Christian principles, and these *archai* then determine what he sees and how he sees it.

Moral goodness, he argues, is to be found only within the bounds of Christian faith, apart from which true virtue cannot exist. If a nonbeliever performs some act that would normally be considered virtuous, it is still "prostituted with the influence of obscene and filthy devils." That is, if a certain act of goodwill is performed by both a Christian and a pagan, that action is a virtue for the first, a vice for the second. "Those things which she [the soul] seems to account virtues, and thereby to sway her affections, if they be not all referred unto God, are indeed vices rather than virtues."[38] Augustine's ethical outlook is defined by category: Christians can be good; everyone else can only be bad. But even Christians, depraved by sin, can do no right without divine grace. A recent theologian summarized Augustine's doctrine thus: "If man does something good, God gets the credit; if man does something bad, man gets the blame."[39]

Augustine's view of pleasure—so deeply autobiographical—reflects his inflexible struggle against the body's natural passions—"the diseases of my soul" he calls them. All pleasure is sinful. He spent the first half of a lifetime enjoying the pleasures of the flesh—and hating himself through every minute of it. But even after his baptism, the "peril of pleasure" plagued him constantly; in his soul's ear he never ceased hearing God's warning: "Go not after thy lusts, and from thy pleasure turn away."

Augustine's account of his moral struggle with pleasure is outlined in Book X of the *Confessions*. There he tells us that three great battles rage in his own soul and, by inference (and projection), in the soul of every human being: (1) the battle against the pleasures of sex; (2) the battle with addiction to the senses, especially the eyes (he is not much bothered "with the allurements of smells" and "the delights of the ear," but "the lust of the eyes" is terribly disturbing); and (3) the battle with ambition and pride.

As for "the lust of the flesh," Augustine writes that God had forbidden him to have a concubine (it was really his mother, but Augustine tends to get these things

There is no salvation outside the church.

AUGUSTINE

Every man prefers to grieve in a sane mind, rather than to be glad in madness.

AUGUSTINE

We are ensnared by the wisdom of the serpent; we are set free by the foolishness of God.

AUGUSTINE

It is right that he [Adam] whom that woman [Eve] induced to sin should assume the role of guide lest he fall again through feminine instability.

AMBROSE

I would not believe the gospel, did not the authority of the catholic church compel me.

AUGUSTINE

Parricide is more wicked than homicide, but suicide is most wicked of all.

AUGUSTINE

Augustine's agony of decision in the garden in August, AD 386: "Tolle, lege! Tolle, lege!" the childlike voice repeated. "Take up and read, take up and read."

A man who is afraid of sinning because of Hell-fire is afraid, not of sinning, but of burning.

AUGUSTINE

Far be it from us to think that God would hate in us that which distinguishes us from the beasts. . . . Love understanding wholeheartedly.

AUGUSTINE

mixed up) and then showed him that marriage also is not the high road for a man like him. But whether he is awake or asleep, the images of past sexual encounters replay in his memory (Augustine has a superb memory), and he is haunted by them. When awake he finds he can suppress them, but in night dreams they "are very like reality" and his soul even seems to consent to them. He prays to be drawn closer to his God so that he might be cleansed of "the impure motions of my sleep" and no longer "commit those debasing corruptions, even to pollution of the flesh."

The double bind of pleasure addiction is especially acute in our "eating and drinking," for food holds out to all of us the perpetual promise of pleasure, and the hungrier we are the greater the pleasure when we meet that hunger. Herein lies the "snare of concupiscence." Augustine writes that God has taught him to practice taking in food only as a medicine necessary to sustain the body; eating should never be indulged for pleasure. But this is iffy, for as long as he dwells in a physical body, the necessity of eating, he says, "is sweet unto me." He is determined to fight that sweetness and not be "taken captive"; he will "carry on a daily war by fastings"; but he is still trapped and tricked by this "dangerous pleasure." He can minimize his food intake, slimming it down to just enough to maintain physical health, hoping that "what is enough for health, is too little for pleasure."

But this means walking a very fine line. Too often one cannot be sure whether that felt hunger is the body asking for nourishment or the soul asking for pleasure. Worse yet, "in this uncertainty the unhappy soul rejoiceth" and uses ambiguity as an excuse to sneak in a little pleasure while telling itself its hunger is really for physical maintenance. "Under the cloak of health, it may disguise the matter of gratification." What is the solution to this dilemma? He is not sure. "These temptations I daily endeavour to resist" (though he confesses that "full-feeding sometimes creepeth upon Thy servant"). "I strive daily against concupiscence in eating and drinking," he says, but in the end he must submit the problem to his God: "to Thee do I refer my perplexities; because I have as yet no settled counsel herein."

The pleasure of seeing was particularly unsettling to Augustine, and beauty was a "sweetness" especially enticing and dangerous. "The eyes love fair and varied forms, and bright and soft colours"; but, he prays, "let not these occupy my soul; let God rather occupy it . . . [for] He is my good, not they." "These seductions of the eyes I resist," he writes, "lest my feet wherewith I walk upon Thy way be ensnared; and I lift up mine invisible eyes to Thee, that Thou wouldest pluck my feet out of the snare."

ATTITUDE TOWARD THE SCIENCES

While discussing the temptations of seeing, Augustine digresses to include "another form of temptation more manifoldly dangerous . . . a certain vain and curious desire, veiled under the title of knowledge and learning." Lust for this brand of pleasure, fired by the "disease of curiosity," inspire men "to search out the hidden powers of nature." But this hunger for knowledge "wherein men desire nothing but to know" is a misguided waste of time. Whether it leads us to want to investigate Nature, religious matters, or occult arts, it is "perverted knowledge." He tells us that, in his own life, he has succeeded in removing these "idle interests" so that "nothing of this sort engages my attention. . . . the theatres do not now carry me away, nor care I to know the courses of the stars, nor did my soul ever consult ghosts departed; all sacrilegious mysteries I detest." He is content (as we all should be) to remain "ignorant of the hidden mysteries of heaven and earth."[40]

Should we still harbor questions as to why Augustine exhibits so little interest in things scientific, and why he so deeply despised human curiosity, they are laid to rest by the following passage from the *Enchiridion*, which establishes his priorities:

> When . . . the question is asked what we are to believe in regard to religion, it is not necessary to probe into the nature of things, as was done by those whom the Greeks call *physici*; nor need we be in alarm lest the Christian should be ignorant of the force and number of the elements—the motion, and order, and eclipses of the heavenly bodies; the form of the heavens; the species and the natures of animals, plants, stones, fountains, rivers, mountains; about chronology and distances; the signs of coming storms; and a thousand other things which those philosophers have either found out, or think they have found out. For even these men themselves, endowed though they are with so much genius, burning with zeal, abounding in leisure, tracking some things by the aid of human conjecture, searching into others with the aid of history and experience, have not found out all things; and even their boasted discoveries are oftener mere guesses than certain knowledge. It is enough for the Christian to believe that the only cause of all created things, whether heavenly or earthly, whether visible or invisible, is the goodness of the Creator, the one true God; and that nothing exists but Himself that does not derive its existence from Him; and that He is the Trinity—to wit, the Father, and the Son begotten of the Father, and the Holy Spirit proceeding from the same Father, but one and the same Spirit of Father and Son.[41]

THE SIN OF PRIDE

Lastly, as for pride, Augustine wonders whether it can ever be extinguished in this mortal lifetime. He confesses that he is driven by a need "to be feared and loved of men," but he interprets this *and all self-needs* as residues of original sin that point us away from

Let Thales depart with his water, Anaximenes with the air, the Stoics with their fire, Epicurus with his atoms.

AUGUSTINE

On Augustine *Augustine never mentions the wonderful spring flowers of Africa.*

PETER BROWN

He that is good is free, though he is a slave; he that is evil is a slave, though he be a king.

AUGUSTINE

Saint Augustine leads us to original sin, drops us off, and leaves us there.

JOHN VELASQUEZ

Nisi Credideritis, non intelligetis. If you do not believe, then you will not understand.

ISAIAH 7:9

There is some light in men: but let them walk fast, walk fast, lest the shadows come.

AUGUSTINE

There is nothing evil save that which perverts the mind and shackles the conscience.

AMBROSE

The natural law is in the heart, the written law on tables. All men are under the natural law.

AMBROSE

It is one thing to answer enquiries, another to make sport of them.

AUGUSTINE

It is impossible to meditate on time and the mystery of the creative passage of nature without overwhelming emotion at the limitations of human intelligence.

ALFRED NORTH WHITEHEAD

It is in thee, O my mind, that I measure times.

AUGUSTINE

God and produce in us "a miserable life." We humans should never be praised for what we do, but only for what God does in and through us. Thus Augustine sets the tone for orthodox Christian theology, both Catholic and Protestant, for the next millennium and a half. "We are Thy little flock, O Lord; possess us as Thine, stretch Thy wings over us, and let us fly under them." God's love and grace alone can efface the sin of the prideful self. "Who would be praised of men, when Thou blamest, will not be defended of men, when Thou judgest; nor delivered, when Thou condemnest."

THE PROBLEM OF EVIL

And Augustine finally settled his puzzlement about the nature of evil. "What is called evil is nothing else, surely, than the deprivation of good." When a body is sick, he argues by analogy, it is deprived of health; to heal the body we give it back its health. It is "the will of a good God that good things should be." God created the world out of love, and therefore all things that he created are good. But goodness, like being, comes in degrees; and things are good to the degree that they have being. If something is deprived of being (like a body deprived of its health), then it is also goodness deprived. Its goodness is "diluted." What we call "evil," therefore, is nothing other than the absence of goodness. (This is a drastically revised version of the Neoplatonic idea that all matter is evil because it is distanced from the pure Spirit of God, a notion that Augustine rejected; human evil, he concluded, is found in a depraved will, not in deprived matter.)[42]

All this is noetic theology. It is logical system building, and its internal coherence occupied Augustine's attention for most of his lifetime. A Church historian writes: "It was his need and his delight to wrestle again and again with the hardest problems of thought, and to comprehend to the utmost the divinely revealed matter of the faith."[43] The pragmatic efficacy of his theology is enormous, as evidenced by the millions of individuals who have found it richly meaningful.

AUGUSTINE'S PHILOSOPHY

Sooner or later every curious philosopher will get around to dealing with *time;* with Augustine it is sooner and later: He returned often to probe the mystery of a subject that, early on at least, eluded his understanding; and because it eluded him, he couldn't let go of it. "My soul is on fire to know this most intricate enigma."[44]

It's not an easy problem. "What is time?" he asks. "If no one asks me, I know what it is. But when called on to explain it to someone asking me about it, then I don't know." In his *Confessions* he confessed: "We are forever talking about time and times. . . . They are the most ordinary, common words, and yet they are profoundly obscure and their meaning has yet to be understood."[45]

TIME AND ETERNITY

It is a reader's delight to watch Augustine's mind in action as he works with the problem of time, especially in Book XI of his *Confessions.* "I have taken it upon me to know," he says. By the time he writes this "autobiography" (about AD 397), he has spent years analyzing the problem and had reached his solutions. Still, as he writes it out, he is doing fairly good philosophy; he is searching, honestly and passionately, to *understand* a specific phenomenon; and this is the closest he ever comes to being empirical.[46]

In order to develop ideas, many teacher-writers, sitting at their desks, create a scenario in their minds of an imaginary exchange with students or a mentor or colleague. In like manner, Augustine carries on a running dialogue, in his mind, with

God. Presumably God already knows all about time (he created it, Augustine says), but Augustine talks and thinks like a gifted student attempting to prove to his teacher that he is determined to come to grips with a difficult subject (it's a required assignment!) and to hang onto it till he has solved it. Presumably also, each time he makes a breakthrough in his understanding, Augustine feels a sense of satisfaction, as though his teacher is rewarding him and saying "Well done, thou good and faithful student." He talks with his Teacher as though they are seated together in a classroom. "Please, Lord, let me seek further," he once implores; and again, "I'm just asking, not telling you. Please give me some guidelines." Once, when arguing a point, he reminds God with "But remember, Lord. . . ." (His chatty exchanges with God remind us of the preacher who began his Sunday-morning prayer with, "Dear God, as you saw on television this morning. . . .")

Augustine had special reason to wrestle with time, or at least to wrestle with the mind's concepts of time; but in working with these concepts he comes very close to seeing "the real thing." He is motivated to inquire into the subject because he feels trapped by several logical contradictions, and because these befuddlements are not, to him, merely mind games but have heavy implications for the nature of his God, God's decency and justice, and the intelligibility of the entire scheme of salvation. He feels a mighty pressure to resolve them.

The logical problems are these. (1) His pondering began, he tells us, because he had been asked "What was God doing before He made heaven and earth?" Why, that is, did God just sit around doing nothing for so long a time when he could have been using his time more constructively?! And why did he decide to create the world just at the time he did? If some inner impulse aroused God "to r'ar back and make a world," then clearly God is not the eternal, unchanging Being he is thought to be. As Augustine put the question: "How came it into His mind to make anything, having never before made anything?" (2) Augustine is also logically puzzled by the fact that God revealed future events to the Hebrew Prophets, allowing them to "predict" the future. But how can what doesn't yet exist be known at all? How can even God know (foresee) the future if it hasn't happened yet? "For, what is not, neither can it be taught."[47]

These may be his starting conundrums about time, but they lead on to further questions with weightier implications. (3) If God, being omniscient, foresees all occurrences from the beginning of time to the end of time, then all things must occur as he foresees them (assuming God can't be wrong in what he foresees). How then can we humans have freedom of choice in what we do? Despite the feeling that we are freely exercising our wills, our every move has been foreseen by God and therefore predetermined. This is the hardest of "hard predestination." Consequently (4), if we have no freedom of choice, then how can God hold us responsible for what we do? How can he damn us or reward us for our behavior if we had no choice but to do what we did? (5) Doesn't this reasoning logically imply that God is not good, not just, and not compassionate? He causes us to be bad and then punishes us for it! A decent human father wouldn't treat his child with such callous contempt. (6) One might even be inclined to ask further: If God can foresee everything, then he has always known the personal fate of every soul. Why then does he even bother to create those who will be damned? The obvious (but unacceptable) answer is that God must enjoy damning souls to hell.

Augustine says (to God) that he will give a serious answer to these questions and not be like the man who, when asked what God was doing before he made Heaven and Earth, replied that "He was preparing hell for people who ask such questions." His theory of time and eternity will answer all of them.[48]

To confess that God exists, and at the same time to deny that he has foreknowledge of future things, is the most manifest folly.

AUGUSTINE

On Augustine [Augustinianism] has been the source of as many heresies and deviations as of good fruits.

HENRI I. MARROU

Augustine's solution is ingenious, ingenuous, and logically coherent. He says that there exist two quite different "times"—God's time and our time. Our time is the time of our everyday experience, the time of material objects-in-motion, the time we measure with our notions of "before" and "after." But God's time, called Eternity, is above time and beyond our time. Eternity is "time-less." The notions of "before" and "after" don't apply. "In Eternity nothing happens in sequence, but everything takes place at once in the present." God's today is Eternity; his Eternity is today. "For where the day neither commences with the end of yesterday, nor is ended by the commencement of the morrow, it is forever Today." All our puzzlements come from our confusing these two realms of time.[49]

First, our everyday time. "I heard once from a learned man, that the motions of the sun, moon, and stars, constituted time. But I disagreed. Because, if you want to make such argument, then everything in motion would constitute time." Augustine notes that in the Old Testament, when Joshua commanded the sun to stand still, time continued. "So let no man then tell me that the motions of the heavenly bodies constitute times."[50]

It is in Augustine's nature always to turn inward to find the truth, so in this instance he focuses on our subjective *experience* of time. He begins by analyzing the nature of past, present, and future, and finds that these are only concepts that exist in the mind. "The present time of past things is our memory; the present time of present things is our sight; the present time of future things is our expectation." What about the passing of hours, days, years, and generations? Like "past," "present," and "future" these are categories and measurements employed by the mind to organize and sequence our experience of time, but they are not time itself. "It's perfectly clear and plain that the future and the past don't exist"; or, rather, they exist "in the soul." "It is in thee, O my mind, that I measure times. . . . The impression, which things passing by cause in thee, and which remains [in memory] when the things are gone, is that by which I measure time." So the past is memory, the future is expectation: only the present exists.[51]

But what is the present? If one thinks of the briefest possible instant of time—a duration so short that it can't be subdivided any more—then that unit of time can be called the present. It is this tiny unit of time that flits from the future to the past so fast that "it can't be lengthened out with even the least stay." For if it were lengthened out, it would then be divisible into past and future. The present, he concludes, has no width.[52]

Time is one thing; eternity is something else. Eternity is timeless. It exists, that is, but outside of time. Time involves moving objects; eternity is changeless. Time and the world were created; eternity is uncreated. Time has a beginning and an end; eternity is . . . well . . . eternal. We humans experience events sequentially: One event happens "before" or "after" some other event; but in God's eternity there is no before or after, only an eternal present. To indulge a metaphor, God "looks down" from his Eternal Present and "sees" the entire historical drama, from Eden to the New Jerusalem, at the same "instant." This means that he doesn't foresee or predetermine mundane events; he merely proceeds to ordain what he sees happening ("happening" in the now of his time, "will happen" in the future of our time).

Augustine explores every angle of God's Eternity, and finds biblical support. God said to Moses, "I am Who I Am" (Exodus 3:14–16). This autobiographical "I am" from God means that he is defining himself as Pure Being, and by logical inference everything else "is found not really to be." God's very name means "True Being" or "Pure Being." God alone is pure existence, and the being of all created things diminishes (in good Neoplatonic fashion) as they move farther and farther away from God.

God's Word (the Logos) burst forth from eternity. "There is eternity already then, and the Word already, but not yet time. Why not? Because time too was made." For John 1:3 says "All things were made through him, and without him was made nothing." "All things" must include time. So time was created by the Word/Logos. God calls "creatures of time and makes them eternal." That is, God will collect all generations of men and make them into one generation; and that generation "will share in your eternity." God will not merely make mortal men immortal; he will rather take away time entirely and make them eternal.

If we can "only recognize it properly," Augustine preached to his congregation, we can move out of our time into God's time, and then "God's years will be in us." "God's years are God's eternity; . . . which has nothing changeable about it. There is no past there . . . no future there. . . . There is nothing there except *Is*."[53]

Augustine promised God that he would answer all the questions. "It is one thing to answer enquiries, another to make sport of inquiries," he wrote. So here are his answers. (1) *What was God doing before he created the world?* The question is all wrong. There is no before or after with God. "There was never a time when Thou hadst not made anything, but time itself Thou madest."[54] Besides that, God doesn't "do"; he is unchanging and Eternal in his nature; the act of creation is from his nature, not from his "action." (2) *How could the Hebrew prophets "know" the future?* What is future to us humans is present to God, so from his present he can reveal events that, for us time-trapped humans, will appear as future events. (3) *Doesn't God's "foreseeing" mean predestination?* No, for God doesn't "foresee"; he only sees. Without "foreseeing" there can be no predetermination; therefore his "seeing" does not rob us of our free will. (4) *How can God damn us for doing what we were predestined to do?* God just lets the chips fall: Not being predetermined by God's "foreknowledge," God merely sees what we, on our own, will do; he then determines the punishment or reward that is appropriate. (5) *Doesn't undeserved punishment mean that God is neither good nor just?* No, from his love he wants all souls to be saved, but it is our behavior, not God's willing, that determines our final state. (6) *If God can foresee the damnation of a soul, why does he proceed to create that lost soul?* Everything that God creates is good, but some souls, falling away from their Creator, become deprived of their God-given goodness and are therefore evil; it is us humans, not God, who distance our souls from God's saving grace.

QUOD SI FALLOR, SUM!

Once when Augustine was having a conversation with his friend Evodius, the subject came up whether we can be sure of anything. (Evodius, interestingly, had recently retired from the secret police and would later retire from the world and become a Christian bishop; he was a close friend to Augustine and was with him at Ostia when Monica died.)

"Let's begin with the obvious," Augustine says to Evodius. "I will ask you, first of all, whether you yourself exist. Don't worry about being wrong, because even if you're wrong that would still prove that you exist."

"What's your point?" asks Evodius.

"My point is that, since it is obvious that you exist, and also since it couldn't be obvious to you unless you are alive, it is also obvious that you are alive!"[55]

Presumably he is thinking of applying this argument to God as well. Whether or not God has the capacity to doubt his own existence is arguable, but Augustine thinks that the simple fact that God thinks proves that he exists.

Not everything is about you, Mulder.

"SCULLY"
(*THE X-FILES*)

Quandoquidem etiam si dubitat, vivit. *A man's doubt proves that he exists.*

AUGUSTINE

Who doubts that he lives and thinks? . . . For if he doubts, he lives.

AUGUSTINE

Elsewhere, in his *City of God*, Augustine restates his version of the "Cogito" in replying to the Academic Skeptics who specialized in doubting everything. "I don't need any of the imagination's tricks and fantasies to be sure that I am, and that I know that this is so—and that I love it! . . . There is no need to fear any of the Academics' arguments. They may say, 'What if you're mistaken?' If I'm mistaken, I am! *Quod si fallor, sum!* Someone who doesn't exist can't be mistaken, can he? Therefore I exist if I am mistaken. . . . So, then, even if I were mistaken, there would have to be a self/mind to be mistaken. There can be no doubt whatever that there is one thing I can't doubt: In knowing that I exist I am not mistaken."[56]

This logic leads Augustine to believe that our knowledge of our own soul (or mind or self) is the most surely known of all realities. Descartes will later build an epistemological system on this self-evident datum, but Augustine does not. However, Augustine does insinuate that the "Cogito" may have wider proof value. "If I say I'm not alive, then my saying I'm not alive proves that I am alive." "If I doubt, I am." "If I feel, I am." "If I scream, I am." "If I wheeze, I am." And so on.

A TALE OF TWO CITIES

Augustine is often given credit for "inventing" philosophy of history. By definition, "philosophy of history" is the intellectual discipline that looks at past human events very carefully to find out if there are larger patterns which, when scrutinized, will reveal some sort of hidden meaning. On August 24, AD 410, the Eternal City of Rome ceased to be eternal. It was entered by the Gothic army of Alaric, and for three days, parts of the city were burned, inhabitants raped and tortured, treasures plundered. Citizens were soon starved to the point of cannibalism. The British monk Pelagius was there: "Everyone was mingled together and shaken with fear; every household had its grief and an all-pervading terror gripped us. Slave and noble were one. The same spectre of death stalked before us all." Since Vergil's day it had been taken for granted that the Roman Empire was indestructible and immortal, so for Romans everywhere the shock was unimaginable. The greatness that was Rome; the culture, the achievements in literature, architecture, and the arts; the dignity and pride; the stability—all was lost. "If Rome can perish, what can be safe?" wrote Jerome, the translator of the Vulgate.[57]

The old Romans said the disaster was brought on by the Christians. Because the emperors had chosen Christianity as the official religion, the great gods of ancient Rome had been abandoned: Their temples had fallen into ruin, their festivals prohibited, their priests arrested and burned; they were no longer honored in the senate. Earlier, while Jupiter and the Olympian family had been worshiped, Rome had been powerful; but now, no longer placated by offerings and prayers, they had withdrawn their protection from Rome and its people.

Augustine said that was all wrong. Roman had fallen, he declared, because of the Romans' sins. (All suffering, in Augustine's eyes, is caused by sinning.) The Romans' sins were largely the result of their following immoral gods. "Your stage-plays, those spectacles of uncleanness, those licentious vanities, were not first brought up at Rome by the corruptions of men, but by the direct command of your gods."[58] (Augustine never denied the existence of the "pagan" gods; he considered them to be demons and evil spirits.) Moreover, it was not the case that, in the heyday of the old gods, everything had been all right. For example, when Troy was plundered it certainly wasn't protected by the gods. Furthermore, the reason that the city of Rome wasn't completely razed by Alaric's soldiers was that the Goths were Christian— heretical Arian Christians but still Christian.

Quod si fallor, sum! Because if I'm mistaken, I am.

AUGUSTINE

Scrupulous fear of the gods is the very thing which keeps the Roman Commonwealth together.

POLYBIUS
(GREEK HISTORIAN, C. 208–126 BC)

Thrushes, parrots, ravens, magpies and the like are often taught to say what they do not understand. To know what we are saying—that was granted by God's will to human nature.

AUGUSTINE

But Augustine knew there was far more to a right understanding of what was actually happening. After setting the record straight on the cause of Rome's demise, he proceeded to put into perspective all historical events, large and small, good and evil; he thus developed a monumental theology of history and wrote it out in the *City of God*. The old Romans had believed that the Empire was an instrument of the gods' purpose in history; Christians had bought into this notion, believing that the Empire was indeed an instrument of a divine plan—the Christian God's plan. Augustine, however, was thinking bigger thoughts. For thirteen years he worked to develop an outline of cosmic history that would reveal the Big Picture in its true nature; it would include a complete reappraisal of the Empire's place in God's drama of redemption.

There are two cities, he said, a City of Earth and a City of God. From the beginning of time there have been "two and only two kinds of human beings: those who live according to man, and those who live according to God. These two we call the 'two cities,' one predestined to reign with God eternally, the other predestined to eternal torment with the Devil." All human beings, and all historical events, are to be found in one city or the other, and they are locked forever in a struggle with each other. All of human history, therefore, will be seen by Christian believers as a great struggle between Good and Evil, and they will know themselves to be participants in it.[59] The City of Earth is not coincident with the Roman Empire, though it is the

The law is not made for the just, but for the unjust. The just man is a man unto himself, and he does not need to summon the law from afar, for he carries it enclosed in his heart.

AMBROSE

Ruins of St. Augustine's cathedral and grounds at Hippo as a visitor sees them today.

The purpose of all war is peace.
AUGUSTINE

°*Romans 8:1–39. It is interesting that the four great scriptural doctrines that impacted Augustine's life are from the heart of Paul's letter to the Romans: his dualistic interpretation of history in Chapter 8; the doctrine of original sin and atonement in Chapters 4 and 5; the doctrine of predestination in 8:29ff.; and the famous conversion passage in 13:11–14.*

On Augustine *He is the most authentic, eloquent, and powerful voice of the Age of Faith in Christendom.*
WILL DURANT

On Augustine *[He was] the man who first Christianized the teachings of Plato.*
WILLIAM TURNER

immediate manifestation of it. (Augustine is aware only of Graeco-Roman history; other great civilizations and religious traditions have no existence in his consciousness.) The City of Earth is rather a supratemporal, but very real, abstract entity whose citizenry is composed of all who are dedicated to the pleasures and pursuits of this earthly life. By contrast, the citizens of the City of God are the souls of all times and places who are dedicated to a Godly life. Augustine's "giant book" is an instruction manual for pilgrims yearning for the next life; it shows how to be otherworldly while still trapped in this one. It also explains why the Christian faith is the true religion of the whole human race. The city of Rome fell to the barbarians, therefore, as a part of God's plan. Christians need not fear, for their Heavenly City is not of this world; it is eternally intact, and growing.

While Augustine's vision of history is his own, its raw material came from several preexisting theological systems. The primary source was Saint Paul. In his letter to the Romans,° the Apostle had written that only two kinds of people exist, those who "walk according to the flesh" and those who "walk according to the spirit," and all the latter belong to an eternal "communion of saints." Other ideas that cohered nicely with Saint Paul's dualism derived from the Zoroastrian scenario of a cosmic battle between the Kingdom of Darkness and the Kingdom of Light; from Plato's description of an ideal state existing somewhere in the realm of Real Ideas; and from the closely similar Donatist doctrine that there exists two eternal societies, one of God and one of Satan. (The Donatists, of course, placed themselves in the society of God while relegating Augustine to the society of Satan.) Augustine was well read in all these cosmic speculations and drew them together into his own cosmic vision.

These are noetic, not empirical, concepts. The good-guy/bad-guy theme is subjective and can be placed on any set of persons or events; who or what falls into each category depends on the criteria one uses for separating the "good" from the "bad."

Augustine teaching philosophy and rhetoric, presumably at Carthage.

But Augustine believed that he was dealing with "real" goodness and evil, not merely evaluations; or more accurately, he "knew" that his evaluations corresponded truly to realities. In more concrete situations, he treated individuals as potentially good souls trapped in pushy material bodies; but when thinking in larger abstractions, individuals for him lost their ambiguous complexities and were seen to be either working with God or against God in league with the Devil.

Augustine possessed an extensive repertoire of historical events, mostly derived from Roman history and the Scriptures; but he was not an historian. His "method" did not involve his looking at history "empirically" and then attempting to discern, from his multifarious observations, whether "patterns" really exist, as would an historian or a philosopher of history. His approach was the reverse of this: He began with a belief in the reality of his mental "pattern" and then fitted historical events into that preconceived picture. His interpretation of history, therefore, is highly subjective and was designed to support firmly held theological beliefs. The *City of God* is a theology of history rather than a philosophy of history.[60]

FINAL HOURS

With the completion of the *City of God* in AD 427, he penned a benediction: "With the help of the Lord, I seem to have paid off my debt, in this, a giant of a book." Then he turned his full attention to the other writings on his bookshelves. He had written almost 230 books, volumes of letters and sermons. He wanted to put this literary legacy into chronological order and write brief comments so that readers might get the most from his works. Someone had written, he said, that "From much words thou shalt not escape sin," and he confessed that the thought "frightens me considerably." For three years he gave his retrospective full attention, and completed a review of his major works in his *Retractiones*. He continued to work on his letters and sermons right up to his death.[61]

The Vandal hordes had by this time moved through Spain, crossed the Straits, and began plundering the coastal cities of north Africa; in AD 430 they laid seige to Hippo. During his last years Augustine's health had declined; in August he took down with a fever. Knowing he would die, he "ordered the four psalms of David that deal with penance to be copied out. From his sick-bed he could see these sheets of paper every day, hanging on his walls, and would read them, crying constantly and deeply." Then he asked to be left alone so he could spend his time in prayer. He died on the 28th of August, AD 430. Not long thereafter the Vandals breached the walls, ravaged and burned much of the city. Augustine's library was saved by disciples who escaped by boat into the Mediterranean.'[62]

None save great men have been the authors of great heresies.

AUGUSTINE

Justice being taken away, what are kingdoms but great robberies.

AUGUSTINE

Hear me, you few. I know that many listen to me, few take any notice.

AUGUSTINE

Nothing conquers but truth, and the victory of truth is love.

AUGUSTINE

ENDNOTES

1 Augustine, *Confessions*, IV, i (1).
2 Peter Brown, *Augustine of Hippo* (University of California Press, 1969), p. 160.
3 Augustine, *Confessions*, V, viii (15); IX, ix (22).
4 Augustine, *De cura pro mortuis gerenda*, xiii, 16.
5 Augustine, *Confessions*, I, x (17).
6 Augustine, *Confessions*, III, xii (21); I, x (17).
7 Augustine, *Confessions*, I, xvi (26).
8 Augustine, *Confessions*, II, iv (9).
9 Augustine, *Confessions*, II, iii (7).
10 Augustine, *Confessions*, II, iii (6), ii (3), iii (6), ii (3).
11 Augustine, *Confessions*, III, i (1), ii (2), i (1).

12 Augustine, *Confessions*, II, ii (3).

13 Augustine, *Confessions*, III, iv (7–8).

14 Augustine, *De libero arbitrio*, I, ii, 4.

15 C. R. C. Allberry, *Manichaean Psalmbook*, pt. 2 (Manichaean Manuscripts in the Chester Beatty Collection, 1938), vol. 2, p. 56, in *Augustine of Hippo*, by Brown, p. 49.

16 Augustine, *De ii animae*, 11.

17 Augustine, *Contra Juliano*, IV, xiv, 72; *Confessions*, VIII, vii (17).

18 Augustine, *Confessions*, III, xi (19).

19 Augustine, *Confessions*, V, vi (11), x (18).

20 Augustine, *Confessions*, V, x (18).

21 Augustine, *Confessions*, V, viii (15).

22 Q. Aurelius Symmachus, *Relatio Tertia*.

23 Augustine, *Confessions*, VI, xv (25), xiii (23)–xvii (26).

24 Augustine, *De bono conjugali*, v, 5.

25 Ambrose, *De Helia vel de jejunio*, xxii, 85.

26 Rom. 13:11–14.

27 Augustine, *Confessions*, IX, ii (4).

28 Augustine, *Contra Academicos*, III, xx, 43.

29 Augustine, *Confessions*, X, xxvii (38).

30 Brown, *Augustine of Hippo*, pp. 124f.

31 Augustine, *Confessions*, IX, xi (27). Behind her request is the already common practice of offering prayers for the dead.

32 Cicero, *Op. Imp.*, VI, 22, in Brown, *Augustine of Hippo*, p. 135.

33 Augustine, *Sermons*, 355, 2.

34 Philip Schaff, *History of the Christian Church* (Scribner's, 1910; reprint, Eerdmans, 1950), vol. 3, p. 1004.

35 Augustine, *Confessions*, VII, xi (17).

36 Augustine, *On Original Sin*, 34.

37 Augustine, *On Baptism*, iii, 16, 21.

38 Bertrand Russell, *A History of Western Philosophy* (George Allen and Unwin, Ltd., 1946), p. 381.

39 L. Harold DeWolf, late professor of Systematic Theology, Boston University School of Theology, seminar discussion, 1954.

40 Augustine, *Confessions*, XXXV; the last quote is from the *Enchiridion*, (trans. J. F. Shaw), Chap. 16, in *Greek Science in Antiquity*, by Marshall Clagett (Collier Books, 1955), p. 164..

41 Augustine, *Enchiridion*, Chap. 9.

42 Augustine, *City of God*, xi, 21; *Enchiridion*, 3 (11)–4 (12–13).

43 Schaff, *History*, vol. 3, pp. 997f.

44 Augustine, *Confessions*, XI, xxii (28).

45 Augustine, *Confessions*, XI, xxii (28).

46 Augustine, *Confessions*, XI, xxii (28).

47 Augustine, *Confessions*, XI, x (12), xii (14), xix (25). God's "to r'ar back and make a world" is from *Ol' Man Adam an' His Chillum*, by Roark Bradford (The Military Service Publishing Co., 1944).

48 Augustine, *Confessions*, XI, xii (14).

49 Augustine, *Confessions*, XI, xi (13).

50 Augustine, *Confessions*, XI, xxiii (29–30), xxiv (31).

51 Augustine, *Confessions*, XI, 20, 27.

52 Augustine, *Confessions*, XI, xv (20).

53 Augustine, *Enarrationes in Psalmos*, 101, Sermon II, 10, 11.

54 Augustine, *Confessions*, XI, xiv (17).

55 Augustine, *De libero arbitrio*, II, 3 (7).

56 Augustine, *City of God*, XI, 26; see also *On the Trinity*, X, 10 (16).

57 Pelagius, *Ep. ad Demetriadem*, 30; and Jerome, *Ep. 123*, 16, both in *Augustine of Hippo*, by Brown, p. 289.

58 Augustine, *City of God*, I, 31.

59 Augustine, *City of God*, XV, 1.

60 We know Augustine studied deeply the Book of Judges in the Old Testament; there, the first known theologian of history, the so-called Deuteronomic historian, applied a similar, but very arbitrary, pattern on the events of early Hebrew history. See *Philosophy: An Introduction to the Art of Wondering*, 7th ed., by James L. Christian (Harcourt Brace, 1998), pp. 345, 351f.

61 Augustine, *City of God*, XXII, 30, 149.

62 Possidius, *Sancti Augustini Vita a Possidio episcopo*, XXX, 1–3, in *Augustine of Hippo*, by Brown, p. 432.

CHAPTER 18

PHILOSOPHY DURING THE DARK AGES: THREE

FROM THE CHRISTOLOGICAL BATTLES TO ALCUIN (AD 425–800)

For four hundred years, battles are waged over right and wrong ideas; philosophy continues to be entirely subservient to theology; the problem of harmonizing reason and Scripture occupies fewer minds; then a renewed focus on education begins a brief renewal of intellect and reason.

THE CHRISTOLOGICAL CONTROVERSIES

For over four centuries the task of identifying bad ideas and clarifying good ideas plagued the early Christian church. The series of doctrinal crises called the "Christological controversies" belongs to the history of theology rather than to the history of philosophy; yet a brief survey of the great debates helps to put both theology and philosophy in perspective and begins to answer the question of how such enormous intellectual activity expended over a span of centuries could fail to produce even a modicum of critical philosophizing. The answer is embarrassingly simple: The most creative minds were engaged in all-consuming theological battles. From the opening days of the new faith, Christians had been fighting among themselves over which ideas were right and which were wrong. The "Council of Jerusalem" in AD 50 between Saint Paul and the more conservative Judaizing apostles was a clash over whether Gentiles could also be Christians, and if so, whether they must first be inducted into the Jewish faith by circumcision (females, obviously, were not a party to this debate; Paul had warned women to keep quiet in church and, by implication, in church matters; if they wanted to know something, they were to ask their husbands: see I Cor. 14:34f. and 11:1–16). Paul said yes and no, respectively, on the Gentile question, and won the day; with his victory the Christian religion was ready to open its arms to everyone, whether Jew or Greek, freeman or slave, male or female, Roman, Egyptian, Latin, or whatever.

In the second century bitter disputes arose between the Montanists ("the world is about to end") and mainstream Christian bishops. Theologians fought over the correct wording of creeds and over which books should be included in the scriptural canon. During the next century they fought over the escalating power of the bishop of Rome, over whether one could be saved outside the Catholic church, and over whether God himself had been crucified on the cross. To mention only a few.

If the work of God would be comprehended by reason, it would be no longer wonderful, and faith would have no merit if reason provided proof.
GREGORY I THE GREAT
(540–604)

Fools must be rejected not by arguments, but by facts.
FLAVIUS JOSEPHUS
(AD 37–105)

Then everything changed (and nothing changed) when, in October of AD 312, Constantine defeated his enemies and crossed the Tiber into Rome, believing that the Christian God had given him the victory. As emperor he proceeded to meld the Greek East and Latin West together into one empire; and that empire, he was then convinced, must have just one religion. One empire, one emperor, one law . . . and one religion to act as the glue to bind the diverse peoples of the empire together. But Christians kept squabbling over issues that, to Constantine, were punctilious theological inanities; he watched their bickering spawn dangerous divisions that could destroy his dream of empire. In AD 311 the followers of Donatus split the church in north Africa on the question whether a sinful priest could perform a valid sacrament (they said he couldn't). In AD 314 the diehard Donatists were condemned at a council, and the emperor followed suit in AD 316. But the Donatists held their ground and persecutions ensued, this time Christian against Christian.

In Eastern churches the idea persisted that Christ was really a God, but of a different kind. In Antioch the notion still circulated that God the Father adopted Jesus as his son at his baptism. In Alexandria the belief held on that Father, Son, and Holy Spirit were just different names for the one God. More dangerous in the eyes of the Church Fathers was the Arian heresy that sprang up in Alexandria about AD 320. An honored presbyter named Arius was teaching that Christ had been created by God "out of nothing" just like everything else; at his baptism the Logos entered into Jesus's body and replaced the human soul with a divine spirit. These ideas, at best, made Christ a sort of second-rate God. From Alexandria the dispute spread through the East. It grew bitter, anathemas were hurled, bishops deposed one another. To Constantine it was "an unprofitable question," so he called a council to meet in May, AD 325, to settle the matter.

Out of the billowy smoke of the Nicene Council there finally emerged an acceptable formula regarding the relationship of God and Christ: The Son, like the Father, is uncreated and eternal; he was "begotten, not made." More than that, Father and Son share the same essence (*homo-ousion*, "same nature"). These ideas were shaped into the Nicene Creed.

But soon after this First General Council, a question arose as to where the Holy Spirit fits into all this. That is, what is the Holy Spirit's relationship to the Father and the Son? Bishop Athanasius held that the Holy Spirit shared the divine essence with both Father and Son, and this idea was affirmed by a synod held in Alexandria in AD 362. With the victory of this idea, the doctrine of the Trinity was complete: God is one essence in three hypostases.° In the sixth century one further clarification was added to the Creed. The Eastern Church had long held that the Holy Spirit proceeds from the Father but not from the Son. That was wrong, Augustine had said; the Holy Spirit derives from both the Father and from the Son (*filioque*). This filioque clause, rejected by the Eastern Church, continues today to separate Eastern Christianity from the West.

A Second General Council was summoned to meet in Constantinople in AD 381. The Emperor Theodosius published an edict mandating the existence of only one recognized religion, the Christian—but only the Trinitarian Christian. Heresy was denounced and "heathen" worship forbidden. Deviation from established orthodoxy was treated both as a mortal offense against the Church and a crime against the state.

Theologians were by this time occupied with a new problem. Christ was both God and Man, they knew, but what exactly was the relationship of the divine nature in Christ to the human nature in Christ? If Christ was fully human, how could he be sinless—which they knew him to be? Also, does this double nature mean that he possessed two distinct wills? And if Christ the Man was also fully God, could that mean that God himself was crucified and died on the cross?

In the early fifth century another, quite logical, problem arose. If Christ was both fully divine and fully human, does that make Mary the mother of God? Eastern clerics had traditionally been addressing her as *Theotokos*, "Bearer of God"; others argued against the title, saying it should be "Bearer of Christ."

These disputes spread throughout the empire. A council was needed, so in AD 431 the Emperor Theodosius II called the Third General Council to meet in Ephesus. The delegates who arrived early met and, in a single day, settled the matter before their opponents could arrive. They condemned the critics of Theotokos and concluded that since Christ is fully God then Mary is properly addressed "Mother of God." She is indeed Theotokos. When the opposition party arrived they condemned and deposed the advocates of the Theotokos formula.

But heretics and freethinkers seem to be irrepressible. A minor Eastern cleric with connections continued to preach that Christ possessed two natures before the incarnation but just one nature afterward. The Pope wrote a *Tome* in which he again stated that Christ had "two full and complete natures in one person." The Fourth General Council met at Chalcedon, near Constantinople, in the autumn of AD 451. Called by the emperor Marcian, it finally crystalized the orthodox understanding of the Christological problem. "All with one consent," it said, "we teach men to confess . . .[Christ is] perfect in Godhead and also perfect in manhood, truly God and truly man . . . consubstantial with the Father in his divinity . . . consubstantial with us [humans] in his manhood . . . without sin . . . begotten before all ages . . . born of the Virgin Mary, the Mother of God . . . two natures . . . in one person." This creed formulated at Chalcedon became the official doctrinal standard of the empire.

But countless nonabiders rejected the creed. The most articulate were the Monophysites of Syria and Egypt. Believing still that Christ had but one nature, their creed held that the "Holy God" was "crucified for us." For a century this and related theological issues roiled the empire; bitter condemnations were hurled from every quarter. The Byzantine emperor Justinian summoned the Fifth General Council in AD 553. Held in Constantinople, it condemned all available heresies, but it only attempted to silence Monophysitism without solving the problem. The Egyptian Coptic church still adheres today to the Monophysite doctrine.

More than a century passed before the Sixth General Council was called in AD 680. The Monothelite heresy—teaching that Christ had but one will—had arisen again and had become embroiled in the politics of emperors, popes, and lesser movers and shakers. The emperor attempted to suppress the problem by prohibiting discussion of it, but in vain. The matter was settled by the council: Christ had "two natural wills or willings," human and divine; but in all things his human will subjected itself to and followed (obeyed) his divine will. This formulation assured a complete humanity to Christ and secured universal acceptance.

The Seventh and last General Council was called to assemble in Nicea in AD 787 to deal with major rifts between East and West. Eastern churches had enacted various decrees to which the Western churches strongly objected: Deacons can marry, there was to be no fasting on Saturdays during Lent (it was a "pagan" custom), Christ must not be depicted with the symbol of the lamb, and more. The stormiest issue was the imperial prohibition of the use of pictures in worship. The Council addressed all these problems but resolved only the dispute over the veneration of images. It decreed that religious pictures, along with the cross and the gospels, should receive "honorable reverence" (not worship) since "the honor which is paid to the image passes on to that which the image represents."

These seven General Councils, writes a modern historian, "rise up like lofty peaks or majestic pyramids from the plain of ancient church history, and mark the

True science teaches, above all, to doubt and to be ignorant.
MIGUEL DE UNAMUNO

This is the reason we cannot complain of life: it keeps no one against his will.
SENECA THE YOUNGER (C. 4 BC–AD 65), ROMAN PHILOSOPHER

Philosophy and religion are enemies, and because they are enemies they have need of one another. There is no religion without some philosophic basis, and no philosophy without roots in religion.
MIGUEL DE UNAMUNO

What God has spoken by the council of Nicea abides forever.
ATHANASIUS

Life is a gift of the immortal gods, but living well is the gift of philosophy.
SENECA THE YOUNGER

*Begin at once to live, and count
each separate day as a separate life.*
SENECA THE YOUNGER

ultimate authoritative settlement of the general questions of doctrine and discipline which agitated Christendom in the Graeco-Roman empire."[1] Since AD 842 the Greek and Russian Orthodox Churches have celebrated, on the first Sunday in Lent, the seven ecumenical councils as the triumph of orthodoxy over dangerous heresies. They are esteemed in the Roman and Protestant Churches for the same reason.

PROCLUS OF ATHENS

*Laborare est orare. To labor is
to pray.*
BENEDICT OF NURSIA

In the fifth century AD a philosophic revival of sorts occurred in the Academy at Athens under two scholarchs. The first, Syrianus, attempted to reconcile the apparent disagreement between Plato and Aristotle on exactly what is real, the singular concrete object or the abstract mental univeral idea of the object. That is, which is "more real," this strange-looking diagram of a triangle I just drew on this piece of paper or the mind's abstract concept of triangle which is always perfect? Plato held the abstract concept to be the more real; Aristotle argued that the drawing (in which the ideal concept is applied to a specific instance) is the only reality. Syrianus believed he could solve the problem with numbers. Numbers, he concluded, are real and stand between (link together) the two entities: The drawing of the triangle can be reduced to mathematical quantification; so can the Real Idea of triangle; so the two notions are really the same thing looked at from two different angles.

The Athenian renaissance was more fully developed by a prolific polymath named Proclus. His writings in Neoplatonic metaphysics represent the final flowering of Greek philosophy, and his work was destined to have enormous influence on all speculative thinking during the Dark Ages.

*The toleration of heretics is more
injurious than the devastation of
the provinces by the barbarians.*
POPE GELASIUS I
[D. 496]

Proclus is therefore important in the history of philosophy (1) for fathering the last revival of Greek philosophy; (2) for giving Neoplatonism the final and most complete form that would shape Western theology into a Christian Platonism; (3) for being a major wellspring of Medieval mysticism.

Proclus was born in Constantinople about AD 410 and died in Athens in AD 485. Raised in Lycia (a province in southwestern Asia Minor), he studied Neoplatonic philosophy at Athens and Alexandria under Plutarch and Syrianus. Belonging to an affluent family, he was handsome, self-possessed, and took great pride in his work. Early in life he planned for a career as a lawyer, but he experienced a conversion that turned him to philosophy. He lived as an ascetic, remained single, and poured his creative energies into his teaching, writing, and meditations. Upon Syrianus's death Proclus assumed leadership of the Academy. All his life he was a critic of Christianity and a defender of Greek culture and thought.

By words the mind is winged.
ARISTOPHANES

Proclus's works include *Elements of Theology*, a compendium of Neoplatonic metaphysics; *Platonic Theology*, a prime source of Plato's philosophy for the Middle Ages; *Elements of Physics*, in which he summarized Aristotle's philosophy; commentaries on Plato's dialogues; a few hymns and epigrams; and a large number of treatises on astronomy, mathematics, physics, grammar, and literary criticism.

*The true faith compels us to
believe that there is one holy
Catholic Apostolic Church. . . .
And outside of her there is no
salvation or remission from sins.*
POPE BONIFACE VIII

Proclus's metaphysical theology was thoroughly Neoplatonic, but with its own twists. It includes all the usual structural elements of Plotinus's system—the One, Nous, and Psyche; emanations, a cosmic hierarchy of beings, multiple levels of reality; good spirit versus evil matter; and a universal epistrophic return to the source of being.° Adopting this basic framework, Proclus proceeds to create his own Neoplatonic worldview.

°*Note again the framework of all the
Neoplatonisms, pp. 271ff.*

To Proclus's way of thinking, the only thing that is truly real and truly good is the One; the rest of the cosmos shades off into infinite levels of lower grades of reality and goodness. What is real is consciousness, however, not matter, which is unreal. Consciousness is reality, and reality is consciousness. The substance of consciousness is real, and the substantive contents of that consciousness are comprised of the totality of the mind's ideas and images. If my mind thinks of book or star or pine tree, these items are the substance of consciousness, whether it be my consciousness or the consciousness of the cosmos. All I know of star is the substantive image in my mind; all the cosmos knows of star is the substantive image in the cosmic mind; and they are the same. To think of a star is to give the star reality. Every object that is real is only a thought. Reality and thought are the same.

To return to the metaphor of light, the Cosmic One, the truly real, melts away with distance, and shades down into the unreal. What is it that melts away or shades away? Reality, Oneness, Goodness, Spirit, and Consciousness. The One is beyond knowing, but as its emanating creations distance themselves from the Source (the One), their blinding Unity fades into darker pluralities; and these can be known. This means that each single human being exists at the tail end of the emanating process. He must live and operate with a minimal level of reality, goodness, spirit, and consciousness; and the world of multiplicities he lives in is so far removed from the wholeness of the One that his depraved condition will mean an existence of emptiness and suffering.

The ethic of Proclus therefore calls for a rejection of the sense experiencing of this physical world and an epistrophic return "upward" toward the great nuclear Source of Reality, Goodness, Wholeness, Spirit, and Consciousness. Herein lies Proclus's mysticism; the final achievement will be the absorption of the individual mind (soul) back into the One. This return should be the goal of all our living, and we must do anything we can to effect this movement from the lowest to the highest, that "anything" being whatever works for the individual—meditation, prayer, magic, worshiping the gods or demons, etc.

Proclus is most remembered for having a field day analyzing and complexifying the countless levels of reality, subdividing each of them into functional beings who come and go and influence one another ad infinitum. In one place or another he succeeds in working into his system all the Greek gods, spirits, and heroes.

PSEUDO-DIONYSIUS OF THE AREOPAGUS

About a decade after the death of Proclus an unknown mystic adopted the basic teachings of Neoplatonism and shaped them into Christian doctrine. Derived mostly from Proclus but solidly grounded in Plotinus's mystical theology, the principal Neoplatonic ideas that he used were:

- that God is good and the world is bad;
- that the cosmos is composed of vast emanations of celestial beings;
- that the pure reality of God becomes diluted as it moves farther away from its divine Source;
- that all things long to return to God;
- and that, for humans, this return can be effected only by contemplative ecstasy

After he had transmogrified them, the author considered all these Neoplatonic ideas to be entirely in harmony with Christian orthodoxy.

He (or, God forbid, she?) is called Pseudo-Dionysius through a misidentification. The name "Dionysius" appears once in the treatises, and medieval clerics assumed that the author must be the Dionysius the Areopagite converted by Saint Paul (Acts

An apology to the Devil. It must be remembered that we have heard only one side of the case. God has written all the books.
SAMUEL BUTLER

An honest God's the noblest work of man.
SAMUEL BUTLER

It is part of the cure to wish to be cured.
SENECA THE YOUNGER

All things which are, by the very fact that they are, are good and come from good; but insofar as they are deprived of good, they are neither good nor do they exist.

PSEUDO-DIONYSIUS

Life is not an exact science, it is an art.

SAMUEL BUTLER

°Compare this with St. Paul's angry words in Ephesians 1:20–2:10, 1 Corinthians 12:8, and 1 Timothy 6:20; see also pp. 218f.

Science as a substitute for religion, and reason as a substitute for faith, have always fallen to pieces.

MIGUEL DE UNAMUNO

The most tragic problem of philosophy is to reconcile intellectual necessities with the necessities of the heart and the will.

MIGUEL DE UNAMUNO

17:34). Most probably the anonymous author was a Syrian monk, but his true identity remains known. His aim was to blend together Neoplatonic and Christian ideas and give the result a mystical spin.

The writings of Pseudo-Dionysius, composed about AD 500 and consisting of four treatises and ten letters (all extant), are important in the history of philosophy (1) for their enormous and varied influence on medieval thinkers and mystics; (2) for the notion that the unknowable God can be known, not with concepts and language, but through intuition, feeling, and silence; and therefore (3) for their role in the creation of a mystical Christian Neoplatonism. Pseudo-Dionysius wrote theology but called it philosophy.

The two treatises titled *On the Celestial Hierarchy* and *On the Ecclesiastical Hierarchy* outline the governmental mechanisms through which God and the heavenly host of beings conduct the program of redemption. God is "a unity of three persons, who with his loving providence penetrates to all things, from super-celestial essences to the last things of earth, as being the beginning and cause of all being, beyond all beginning, and enfolding all things transcendentally in his infinite embrace."[2] Emanating from the One are two hierarchies, the celestial and the earthly, each a ninefold arrangement of ranked functionaries by which the work gets done. The celestial hierarchy consists of three triadic levels of beings: (1) seraphim, cherubim, and thrones; (2) dominions, powers, and authorities; (3) principalities, archangels, and angels.° (Dionysius thus continues the Neoplatonic habit of multiplying everything by threes.) All beings are spiritual at the higher levels but become more material and unreal as they descend to lower levels.

Just as God reigns at the head of the celestial hierarchy, Christ stands at the head of the earthly hierarchy, which is a mirror image of the celestial and operates as a preparatory curriculum to lead us to God. It consists of (1) the sacraments of baptism, Eucharist, and holy unction; (2) the ordination of priests, consecration of monks, and anointing of the dead; and (3) the orders of monks, laity, and catechumens. Through these triadic beings God communicates himself to man and carries out the ministrations of the cosmic return.

The long treatise titled *On the Divine Names* describes the beauty and love of God that bathes all his creation with a longing to return to him. All evil in the world is seen to be, not a real thing, but the inability of beings to hold on to God's love. The fourth treatise, *On Mystic Theology*, details the steps in the soul's journey from the world of sense to its mystical absorption into the One. This journey involves the laying to rest of all thought and speech, allowing the soul to penetrate into the unthinkable darkness above knowing where, in silence, it is united with the One.

The Dionysian writings were loved by medieval and Renaissance scholars with a feeling for mysticism. Eriugena translated them, and Maximus the Confessor created out of them a pantheistic interpretation of Christianity. Hugh of Saint Victor, Albertus Magnus and Thomas Aquinas wrote commentaries on them and regarded Dionysius as the prince of theologians. Spanish and Flemish mystics breathed their poetry, and Dante put the author in the company of other great theologians in the fourth heaven of the sun.

BOËTHIUS OF ROME

Two of Rome's greatest statesmen, Boëthius and Cassiodorus, were contemporaries and colleagues. Born about the same time (c. AD 480), the first wrote his most important work while in prison and just before he was executed, the second lived on for another half century, wrote voluminously (including a biography of his old friend), and died peacefully in his own monastery.

In the history of philosophy Boëthius is remembered (1) for his contribution to, and influence on, propositional logic in the cathedral, monastic, and court schools of the Middle Ages; (2) for his use of Aristotelian logic in the analysis and exposition of theological problems; (3) for being an inspiration to all who, during times of misfortune, are determined to maintain their integrity in the face of life's injustices.

Anicius Manlius Severinus Boëthius would doubtless have been the philosopher-king of Plato's dream had conditions been different. Born into the honored and wealthy Roman family of the Anicii, his father had been consul to the senate and twice prefect of Rome. Boëthius too became consul, as did two of his sons. His father died when he was still a boy, and he was raised and educated by the noble patrician Aurelius Symmachus, whose daughter Rusticiana he later married. He studied Neoplatonic philosophy at Athens and developed wide-ranging interests. While still young he entered into a career of public service and, like Plato, felt a calling to help rescue the state from corruption. The king of Italy, Theodoric the Ostrogoth, was an Arian Christian. Though Boëthius persisted in defending his own orthodox Christian ideas, he rose to become Theodoric's prime minister and always faithfully performed his public duties. Though famed in his own time as a statesman, Boëthius's lasting contribution lies in his writings, most of which aimed at providing readable translations of the Greeks. He wrote an astonishing number of works in philosophy, theology, education, and the natural sciences. "The geometry of Euclid, the music of Pythagoras, the arithmetic of Nicomachus, the mechanics of Archimedes, the astronomy of Ptolemy, the theology of Plato, and the logic of Aristotle, with the commentary of Porphyry, were translated and illustrated by the indefatigable pen of the Roman senator."[3] In his scientific writings he described, among other things, the workings of the water clock, sundial, and the motions of the planets which he demonstrated with a globe.

Boëthius was above all a logician and mathematician, and he produced numerous short works on logic. His abundant writings include *Elements of Arithmetic, Elements of Geometry,* and *Elements of Music;* several works reflecting the Christological controversies: *On the Trinity, On the Person and Two Natures in Christ,* and *Against Eutyches and Nestorius.* Among his translations are Porphyry's *Eisagôgê* and Aristotle's *Prior Analytics, Posterior Analytics, Sophistic Arguments,* and the *Categories.* He wrote an influential commentary on the *Categories.* His original plan was to translate all of Plato and Aristotle into Latin, but that was not to be.

Theodoric had invaded Italy in AD 488, rapidly conquered the peninsula, and gained the throne by viciously murdering the royal family at Ravenna with his own sword. He had been educated in Constantinople to be an Arian Christian, and though he accomplished much good during his thirty-three-year reign, he was never secure. He was distrusted by citizens who saw him as a barbarian usurper adhering to a hated religion, and he knew full well that they would rejoice at his downfall. Becoming increasingly paranoid, he came to perceive the senate, composed largely of Romans devoted to the old traditions, as his enemy. After years of defending the senate with his eloquence, Boëthius's signature was found attached to a document (now believed to be a forgery) inviting the Byzantine emperor to liberate Italy from the Goths. Boëthius was charged with treason and imprisoned. To save themselves from Theodoric's wrath, his senatorial colleagues voted to confiscate his property and sentence him to death.

If there is a God, whence proceed so many evils? If there is no God, whence cometh any good?

BOËTHIUS

Then she [Philosophy] said . . . what place can be left for purposelessness when God puts all things in order?

BOËTHIUS

Virginity stands as far above marriage as the heavens stand above the earth.

JOHN CHRYSOSTOM

Boëthius of Rome (470–524)

Nor do I regret that I have lived, since I have so lived that I think I was not born in vain, and I quit life as if it were an inn, not a home.

CICERO

Faith is in its essence simply a matter of will, not of reason, and to believe is to wish to believe, and to believe in God is, before all and above all, to wish that there may be a God.

MIGUEL DE UNAMUNO

While imprisoned in the baptistry in the cathedral tower at Pavia, Boëthius wrote his last work, *On the Consolation of Philosophy*, which assured his immortal fame. It is difficult in imagination to recover the depth of his suffering. If you spend your life teaching and dispensing justice, it is on the edge of impossible to come face-to-face with the final injustice—to lose your life paying for a crime you didn't commit—and, at the same time, to maintain your humanity. Yet Boëthius seems to have accomplished the impossible. Although he was a professing Christian, Boëthius turned to philosophy for help. The book is an allegory, composed partly in poetry, partly in prose, written as a dialogue between Boëthius and a personified Philosophia who comes to him in the guise of a wise and stately woman. Like the later Beatrice of Dante's *Divine Comedy*, she is "the celestial guide whom he had so long invoked at Rome and Athens now condescended to illumine his dungeon, to revive his courage, and to pour into his wounds her salutary balm."[4] In the course of the dialogue Philosophia helps him put his life and death into perspective. He had been fortunate to live a long and prosperous life, she tells him, and by contrast his last misfortune is brief and insignificant. She assures him that the just person who is made to suffer unjustly can find dignity, courage, and even a kind of happiness in the experience of suffering.

When the order for Boëthius's execution finally came, a cord was fastened around his head and tightened, after which he was beaten to death. The year was AD 524. It undoubtedly brought him a modicum of comfort knowing that his wife and sons and his father-in-law Symmachus were safe. He was spared from knowing that the esteemed Symmachus, a few months later, was dragged in chains to the royal palace at Ravenna and executed. (Such events invariably become clothed in myth. The story came to be told that one evening at dinner a large fish was placed before King Theodoric; when he beheld it what he saw was the angry face of Symmachus, with sharklike teeth, about to devour him. He retreated to his chambers where, trembling with fear, he repented his murder of Boëthius and Symmachus. Theodoric died three days later in his palace at Ravenna.[5])

Written while awaiting execution in the cathedral tower at Pavia, Boëthius's Consolation of Philosophy *depicts a personified Philosophia reassuring him that a good person can find dignity and even happiness in suffering.*

Boëthius has sometimes been described as the last of the Romans and the first of the Scholastics. His friend Cassiodorus required his educable monks at Viviers to read his works on the liberal arts, and many of his writings and translations became the basic textbooks for the education of clergy and nobles. His *Consolation* was extremely popular throughout the Middle Ages. It was translated into Greek, Hebrew, French, and old High German; into Anglo-Saxon by King Alfred, into Norman English by Chaucer, into sixteenth-century English by Queen Elizabeth I.

Philosophy is the best medicine for the mind.

CICERO

CASSIODORUS OF VIVIERS

If Cassiodorus could have foreseen the future, he would rest content knowing that his enormous labors had fulfilled his dreams. For a half century he dedicated himself to the task of preserving ancient manuscripts, with laudable success. The picture of Cassiodorus's monks working in the monastery at Viviers is one of the brightest scenes of the Dark Ages; there they collected books, restored them, copied and translated them, and wrote commentaries on what remained of Greek learning and earlier Christian theology.

Cassiodorus is therefore significant in the history of philosophy, not for original ideas, but for his preservation of ancient books and learning. If one compares the vast number of manuscripts available to Islamic scholars with what was available to Latin scholars, one weeps; and what did survive in the Dark Ages owes an incalculable debt to the foresight and labor of Cassiodorus.°

Nothing is so easy as to deceive one's self; for what we wish, we readily believe.

DEMOSTHENES

°*On how this happened, see the story of translations from the Greek, pp. 358ff.*

Like his friend Boëthius, Cassiodorus was a Roman statesman who held important posts under the Gothic kings. Born about AD 480 in Scyllacium (present-day Calabria), his father had been pretorian prefect and senator, then provincial governor, during the reign of Theodoric; and Cassiodorus rose to be a close friend and advisor to the same king and served him as private secretary and then prime minister. Like Boëthius, he worked to reconcile the Gothic rulers with the restive Roman citizens.

When the Byzantine army recaptured Italy from the Goths, Cassiodorus retired from public life to live in the monastery at Viviers, nestled at the foot of Mount Moscius in southwestern Italy. He was about sixty. He had earlier founded the monastery himself, furnished it lavishly with books, and dedicated it to learning and literature; only monks with literate skills and devotion to learning were allowed in residence. While some of the monks translated and copied classical manuscripts, others worked to restore texts, correct errors (Cassiodorus gave them correct spellings of words and lists of errors to avoid), bind and catalogue books. Still others prepared medicines and worked the monastery's gardens. For decades Cassiodorus had collected manuscripts, accumulating a huge library at Rome which he added to the monastery's holdings when he retired.

Poverty is the mother of crime.

CASSIODORUS

His writings reveal great knowledge and erudition. His *Miscellany*, in twelve books, is a collection of 468 documents he issued in the king's name while in office. His *Ecclesiastical History* became the only available history of Christianity during the Middle Ages. Other works include the *Chronicle* (a history of the world from Adam to AD 519), the *Computation of Easter, Origin and History of the Goths* (a history of mankind down to the death of Theodoric, now lost), *Institutions of Sacred and Secular Letters* (his most important work, an encyclopedia of literature for the use of his monks; part two containing an exposition of the seven liberal arts was widely read during the Middle Ages); *The Soul* (which treats the nature of the soul and the afterlife, but goes on to deplore the conflict between Romans and Goths). His treatise titled *Institutiones musicae* con-

[Love] is the sole medicine against death, for it is death's brother.

MIGUEL DE UNAMUNO

tains a summary of medieval musical theory. He also made numerous translations himself and wrote biblical commentaries. Many of his writings are still extant.

Thus Viviers became a sanctuary of learning during the most illiterate of times. Cassiodorus's call for the preservation of books was heard by other monasteries, especially the Benedictine, where the 48th rule of Saint Benedict called for the study and working of manuscripts as a mandatory part of the monk's daily schedule. This is the faint beginning of a revival of education in the Latin West. Monasteries became publishing houses since books were scarce and expensive, and the only way to get new books was to copy old ones. So novices learned to read and write. They also needed to learn how to calculate the dates of Easter and other festival days, so arithmetic was taught. To meet these needs rulers and bishops urged monasteries to establish schools for boys, and these schools, in time, became an accepted feature of the monastic organization. At first monastic schools were open only to young men intending to take vows, but by the ninth century they began to admit *externi*, students not planning to enter the church. Ecclesiastical affairs and ceremonies were conducted in Latin, but the Latin of the Middle Ages had become corrupted, so it became a prime task of the monastic schools to recover the pure Latin of the old Roman authors such as Cicero, Seneca, and Vergil; to accomplish this they copied and preserved the old masters, along with the Vulgate, Patristic writings, Missal and Psalter. As the centuries passed, some of the monasteries became famed for their great libraries, literary activity, and excellence in teaching.

Thus, thanks to Cassiodorus's love of books, much of the Greek and Roman literature and learning that would have been lost was saved from destruction. These became the fertile materials for a gradual revival of intellectual inquiry in the West.

Cassiodorus's last known work, *On Orthography*, was written when he was ninety-three; he died at Viviers sometime between AD 570 and 580.

JOHN PHILOPONUS OF ALEXANDRIA

Strangely, out of the Neoplatonic worldview came a respectable amount of mathematics and physics. In addition to being antiestablishment theologians, two brilliant writers of the late sixth and early seventh centuries AD, John Philoponus and Simplicius, were also able mathematicians.

John Philoponus (often referred to as John the Grammarian) was a Christian Neoplatonist who got into considerable trouble for his stubbornness in maintaining the heretical idea that in Christ there is only one nature, the divine; Christ's human nature, he said, possesses no separate personhood of its own. When condemned for this interpretation, he attempted to "clarify" his thinking on the Trinity, reasoning that each of the three persons of the Trinity really possesses a distinct nature and substance; but this was interpreted by his orthodox opponents as implying the existence of three deities ("tritheism"), and for this he was again condemned as a heretic. (Some days you just can't win.)

In the history of philosophy John Philoponus is important (1) for creating a synthesis of Neoplatonic and Christian ideas that, through Syriac and Arabic translations, had much influence on both Islamic and Latin cultures; (2) for his critical work on Aristotle's mechanics that led to further discoveries in physics, among them the concept of momentum.

Little is known of Philoponus's life. His name derives from a guild of Christian laymen described by the Greek adjective *philoponos*, "labor loving" ("diligent,"

Honi soit qui mal y pense.
Shamed be the one who thinks evil of it.
KING EDWARD III OF
ENGLAND (1312–77)

The facts speak for themselves.
EURIPIDES

Doubt is an angel, not a devil; it assumes an order of truth. Only through the agony of doubt can we have the courage to be.
MARSHALL W.
FISHWICK

Sex and obscenity are not synonymous.
UNITED STATES
SUPREME COURT
(THE ROTH CASE, 1957)

"industrious"). He was a native of Alexandria and studied there with the Aristotelian teacher Ammonius. He was one of the last representatives of Neoplatonism in the East. It was Philoponus who tried, desperately but in vain, to prevent the destruction of the great library at Alexandria by Muslim conquerors.°

°See p. 282.

His works include *On the Eternity of the World*, in which he formulates a creationist cosmogony; *Mediator, or Concerning Union*, his principal theological work, in which he elaborates his views on Christology; several noteworthy commentaries on Aristotle's works (four of his commentaries are extant); two works on grammar that were widely read during the Middle Ages (from which came his title "The Grammarian"); a polemic against Proclus (arguing that the world was created and not eternal); and two treatises on mathematics, one of them the oldest known work on the astrolabe, an instrument used to measure the height of the sun and stars above the horizon.

Among his theological views was the notion that each individual possesses his own distinct intellect and doesn't derive his intellect from a universal mind, as Aristotle had held; this enabled him to turn Aristotle around on the possibility of personal immortality. Philoponus also identified Aristotle's First Cause with the God of Christian belief.

With wisdom grows doubt.
GOETHE

In his treatises on mathematics and physics, Philoponus shows himself to be a good observer. He analyzed Aristotle's views on motion and agreed with him that a falling object's downward motion is the result of its weight, and that in a medium, such as air or water, a heavier object can move through that medium more easily than a lighter object. It "has a greater downward tendency" and "divides the medium better." Obviously, then, the thinner the medium the less resistance the object will encounter and the faster it can fall; if there were no resistance at all (as in a vacuum), the object, set in motion by a (measurable) force, would travel a given distance in a (measurable) amount of time. Less resistance allows the object to move faster; more resistance forces it to move more slowly. Philoponus saw that "Aristotle wrongly assumes that the ratio of the times required for motion through various media is equal to the ratio of the densities of the media." Philoponus apparently ran some sort of experiment and determined motions "by actual observation." What he discovered was that Aristotle's conclusion is "completely erroneous." "For if you let fall from the same height two weights of which one is many times as heavy as the other, you will see that the ratio of the times required for the motion does not depend on the ratio of the weights, but that the difference in time is a very small one . . . an imperceptible difference." (Legend has it that Galileo first performed this experiment by dropping objects from the Tower of Pisa.) Philoponus concludes with a formula stating that the speed of a falling object is proportional to the ratio of force to resistance, that is, velocity is proportional to the amount that force exceeds resistance.[6]

The true God, the all-powerful God, is the God of ideas.
ALFRED VICTOR
(COMTE DE VIGNY,
FRENCH POET,
1797–1863)

In John Philoponus we watch a philosopher attempting to do intelligent and honest physics. His science, however, strikes us as an anomaly when we remember the Neoplatonic worldview in which he moved; but then he wouldn't be the first, or the last, to think empirically with one side of his brain and noetically with the other. Philoponus has been underappreciated in the history of philosophy, either because his theological contributions are negligible or because today the sciences are no longer thought of as "natural philosophy" (even though Aristotle spent considerable time working in precisely these areas of physics).

An unused life is an early death.
GOETHE

Wisdom is found only in truth.
GOETHE

Philoponus's work in mathematics and physics had substantial impact on Islamic thinkers, and through them, on Latin science during the High Scholasticism of the late thirteenth and fourteenth centuries.

I know everything but myself.
FRANÇOIS VILLON
(FRENCH POET,
1431–C. 1465)

SIMPLICIUS OF ATHENS

°See p. 295.

His [the Pope's] judgment may not be revised by anyone, and he alone may revise the judgment of others.
POPE GREGORY VII
(HILDEBRAND)

The Roman Church has never erred, and, according to the scripture, never shall err.
POPE GREGORY VII

Timeo Danaos et dona ferentes. *I fear the Greeks though bearing gifts.*
VIRGIL (ROMAN POET, 70–19 BC)

Simplicius was one of the very last Neoplatonists and is most remembered for being one of a small group of scholars who escaped to Persia when Justinian forcefully closed the Athenian Academy in AD 529 because it was "pagan."° In the history of philsosophy he is appreciated (1) for his commentaries on Aristotle and the Stoics which preserved many fragments from the early Greek philosophers; and (2) for the preservation of a modicum of scientific thinking and performing experiments in physical dynamics.

Simplicius was born in Cilicia in southern Anatolia, studied at Alexandria and Athens, the two great centers of Neoplatonic philosophy. After his return from Persia he wrote commentaries on Aristotle's *Physics, On the Soul, On the Heavens,* and *Categories,* all of which have been preserved. He also wrote a commentary on Epictetus's *Encheiridion* and a work on geometrical constructions. In his commentaries he included much of Theophrastus's material on the presocratic philosophers of nature, extensive passages from Eudoxus, and Strato's observations on mechanics.

Like his contemporary John Philoponus, Simplicius was capable of careful scientific thinking; and like him, when he wants to prove or oppose an idea, he appealed to empirical evidence. He even performed experiments. After attempting to determine whether air or water has "weight in its own place," he wrote, with justfiable pride, "I performed the experiment with the greatest possible care. . . . Now if the result of my experiment is correct, it follows, clearly, that in their respective natural places the elements are without weight, having neither heaviness nor lightness."

Also like Philoponus, Simplicius worked with the physics of falling objects. He was puzzled by the fact that a falling body falls more slowly when first released and then gradually accelerates as it falls. His best hypothesis to explain what he observed was that "objects higher up are supported by a greater quantity of air" while "objects lower down [are supported] by a lesser quantity . . . so it is fair to suppose that . . . the greater the amount of underlying air, the more do lighter objects seem bouyed up."[7]

Simplicius's writings were translated into Latin in the thirteenth century and had considerable impact on scholastic thinking.

GREGORY OF TOURS

Gregory of Tours was a forceful and much-loved monastic leader who personally influenced everyone who knew him. He lived from AD 538 to 594 and became bishop of the bustling city of Tours in AD 573. He entered the priesthood to fulfill a promise he made during an almost fatal illness. His times were violent and Gregory fought vigorously to defend the citizens of Tours against tyrants and stubbornly defended the church's right to provide sanctuary for anyone who was persecuted. He restored and dedicated churches, fought against unfair taxation on behalf of the people of his diocese, and performed numerous other acts of defiance and courage that endeared him to the people of Tours. Gregory wrote continuously in what he himself admitted was poor Latin. His works dealt mostly with the lives of the saints and with miracles. His fame rests on his ten-volume *History of the Franks,* the only surviving dependable source of information for the history of France in the fifth and sixth centuries AD. Written in a lively and dramatic style, his history begins with the creation of the world; events of his own time appear near the end of the first book.

The author of historical narrative inevitably tucks into his account some sort of "philosophy of history," however rudimentary it may be; that is, he assumes ideas (usually unconsciously) about the overall meaning of history and the structures and values that give it shape and by which its "plot" develops. In this sense Gregory's history reveals a very unsophisticated, traditional framework: History is the story of the church fighting to save mankind, of good men versus bad. The good are always rewarded, the evil are always punished, in both this life and the next. It is a narration, he says, of the struggles of "martyrs with the heathen" and of "churches with the heretics." As a trinitarian he could not allow heretics to perform anything good, though he was not hesitant to place adulterous priests and violent bishops on the side of evil even if orthodox in their belief. In the big picture those of orthodox faith (the good guys) will ultimately triumph. The dramatis personae of the historical drama all fit within this simplistic framework.

Gregory's minuscule contribution to the history of philosophy rests on a little book on astronomy (discovered in 1853) titled *The Ecclesiastical Circuit* (but usually called *On the Course of the Stars*). His aim in this work was to provide the clergy with descriptions of stars and constellations and their movements across the sky so ministrants could calculate more precisely the proper times for performing special prayers and ceremonies. Gregory describes the major constellations, tells when they are visible during the year, and often includes diagrams of the stars' relative positions for recognition. In passing he notes that God's universe reveals many natural wonders: the tides, growing plants, volcanoes, hot springs, the course of the Sun, and the phases of the Moon.

In placing his empirical observations wholly in the service of his religious faith, Gregory was a child of the Middle Ages. Virtually all his writings are extant.

ISIDORE OF SEVILLE

Isidore was an esteemed leader of the Spanish Christian Church and the most accomplished scholar of his day. He joins a growing number of medieval writers nicely labeled "encyclopedists," scholars who attempted to collect accumulated information in every area of knowledge, organize it, and make it conveniently accessible. (The word "*encyclopedia*" derives from the Greek *enkyklios paideia*, "general education," and was first used to describe the *Natural History* of the Roman polymath Pliny the Elder about AD 77.)

In the history of philosophy Isidore is remembered for his preservation of Greek and Roman writings in a time of great cultural losses.

Isidore was born about AD 560, became archbishop of Seville c. AD 600, and died there in AD 636. In his own time he was known primarily as a dynamic leader who played important roles in influential church councils, especially the General Council of Toledo in AD 633 which defined the Church's policy on church and state (they were united as one), issued an edict of toleration of Jews, and mandated uniformity in the Spanish mass. He was a staunch defender of orthodoxy and worked tirelessly to convert the Arian Visigoths.

The scope of Isidore's reading was enormous. In his greatest work, the *Etymologies* (or *Origins*, in twenty volumes), he quotes from 154 Greek, Roman, and Patristic writers, and thereby preserves valuable material otherwise lost. In it he summarizes the seven liberal arts (grammar, rhetoric, and dialectic; arithmetic, geometry, music, and astronomy) and in addition writes on biology, botany, mineralogy, geography, architecture, agriculture, chronology, medicine, law, politics, anthropology, angelol-

Omnia vincit Amor. Love conquers all.

VIRGIL

When the mind withdraws into itself and dispenses with facts it makes only chaos.

EDITH HAMILTON

We men have made our gods in our own image.

HESIOD

Sapere aude. Have the courage to be wise.

VIRGIL

What is hateful to thyself do not do to another. This is the whole Law, the rest is Commentary.

RABBI HILLEL
(FL. 30 BC–AD 9)

ogy, and much more. He describes animals (real and mythical), including birds, fish, serpents, worms, and flying insects. His books are mostly compilations; he worked solely from written sources and conducted few if any observations himself. His descriptions are often wrong.

Isidore also wrote a sort of textbook in natural philosophy titled *On the Nature of Things* that became widely used in monastic schools of the Middle Ages. In its forty-eight chapters he analyzes units of time and describes the heavens, the Earth, the waters under the Earth, and meteorology (he tried to work out a theory of climatic zones and apply it to a flat Earth). He often supplies accompanying diagrams.

Numerous other writings were produced from his untiring labors: *History of the Goths, Vandals, and Suevi; The Order of Creation* (dealing with cosmogony, the devil and demons, paradise, purgatory, and the future life); *Books of Differences* (studies of words, synonyms, plus religious and metaphysical ideas); *On the Order of Creatures; Greater Chronicles* (on history); *On the Origin and Death of the Fathers* (brief biographies of eighty-six personages from the Bible); *Catholicism versus the Jews; Three Books of Sentences* (one-liners on morals and religion); *On Church Duties* (on liturgy); and *Synonyms* (a short work on meditation).

Isidore was not in any sense an empiricist, yet his writings are unusually clear of superstition and myth. They were for centuries treated as the final authority in Europe. His *Sentences* became the standard textbook in theology in the West.

JOHN OF DAMASCUS

Legends commonly spring up around the lives of truly great men, and John of Damascus was one of them. Among many apocryphal tales, one story tells of the time the Muslim caliph of Damascus lopped off John's right hand as punishment for treason (the charge was false); but John repositioned the severed hand at the stump of his arm, prayed before an image of the Virgin Mary, and found the amputated limb restored. (That he prayed before an "image" is significant, for John was the outspoken advocate, against the Iconoclasts, of the veneration of "pictures" in Christian worship.)

John Damascene was one of history's great theologians. His contribution to the history of philosophy lies in (1) his application of Aristotle's logic to Christian theology, and in (2) his preservation of Greek learning through his encyclopedic *Fountain of Knowledge* which summarized virtually every minute point in Christian doctrine as well as "all other kinds of knowledge."

Born about AD 675 in Damascus, John was nicknamed Chrysorrhoas ("stream of gold") for his eloquence; his Arabic name was Mansur ("Victor"). He became chief councillor to the Saracen ruler but soon after AD 730 retired from the political arena to a monastery near the Dead Sea where he could study and write. He died about AD 754 and was canonized saint and doctor in both the Greek and Latin churches. He is often called the last of the Greek Fathers and sometimes—for his application of Aristotle's dialectics to Christian theology—the Father of Scholasticism.

John's professional life was spent in zealously defending image worship, for which he was condemned at one council, extolled at another. "The heathens dedicate their images to demons," he wrote, "whom they call gods; we dedicate ours to the incarnate God and his friends, through whom we exorcise demons."[8]

His *Fountain* is a three-volume epitome of Greek theology. The first book expounds Aristotle's *Categories* and Porphyry's *Eisagôgê* and applies Greek logic to

A man's mind stretched by a new idea can never go back to its original dimensions.

OLIVER WENDELL HOLMES

The precepts of the law are these: to live honestly, to injure no one, and to give every man his due.

EMPEROR JUSTINIAN I
(AD 483-565)

Christian doctrine. The second book contains John's compendium of arguments against heresies. The third book (originally organized into one hundred chapters!), titled "*An Accurate Exposition of the Orthodox Faith*," contains a complete synopsis of the doctrines of the Eastern church and treats of angels, demons, paradise, nature, humans, foreknowledge and predestination, the Incarnation, Christological problems, and a multitude of other questions regarding faith and practice. It is in this third book of the trilogy that John reveals his extensive knowledge of the natural sciences.

John Damascene's systematic format and style deeply influenced the theological writings of medieval Schoolmen.

VENERABLE BEDE OF JARROW

In the late seventh and eighth centuries AD, there was an acceleration of intellectual activity in European and English monasteries, and the shining representative of this rebirth of learning was an Anglo-Saxon monk known as the Venerable Bede. (His name, more properly, was Baeda or Beda; and "venerable," an epithet of respect, not age, became permanently associated with his name some two centuries later.)

In the history of philosophy Bede is appreciated (1) for his deep love of learning that rekindled intellectual passions in the West at a time when education seemed to be dying; and (2) for retaining a modicum of empirical connection at a time when sense experience was still considered inappropriate and even dangerous.

Bede's life was outwardly uneventful; except for brief visits to the Holy Island of Lindisfarne and to York, he never left his monastery at Jarrow. However, his inner life was one long, exciting adventure of the mind. Born in AD 673 in the village of Jarrow in Northumbria, he was orphaned before he was seven and placed in the monastery at Wearmouth. One of the largest libraries in England was housed at Wearmouth, and the riches of literature nourished Bede's natural love of learning; he rapidly mastered Latin, Greek, and Hebrew, and began to write. "I always took delight in learning, teaching and writing," he tells us in a short autobiography that he attached to his great work on English history. He became the most knowledgeable man of his age and its greatest author; he once declined election to the office of abbot because, he said, it would interfere with his studies.

Through his inspiration, one of his pupils, Egbert, founded the influential school at York; another, Alcuin, launched the so-called Carolingian renaissance in education on the continent.

Though known during the late Middle Ages primarily for his commentaries on the Scriptures, his enduring fame rests on his *Ecclesiastical History of the English People.* Begun at the suggestion of the English king Ceolwulf, it took him a lifetime to write; he completed it just before his death. His style of writing is simple and clear, he took great care to be accurate, he used the best available sources, he gave credit to those who helped him, and he seems to have made every effort to understand a datum or a statement before he borrowed and made use of it. Material for the first twenty-two chapters he derived from written sources; later chapters were based on his own careful investigation. The work is the only source of English history down to the eighth century. It is a beautiful and valuable piece of writing, and for it Bede is justly called the "Father of English History."

Bede's range of interests was enormous; he wrote treatises on history, theology, chronology, and the natural sciences. During Bede's time there arose an interest in, and need for, materials that could aid clerics in the computation and decipherment of ecclesiastical calendars. Gathered into collections called the "computus," these

Slavery is an institution of the law of nations, against nature, subjecting one man to the dominion of another.

JUSTINIAN I

If a man could kill all his illusions he'd become a god.

COLIN WILSON

Vitam impendere vero. *Stake life upon truth.*

JUVENAL

quasi-scientific creations consisted of tracts, timetables, lists of dates, multiplication tables, diagrams, and mnemonic devices to assist in memorizing dates and times. Extant manuscripts of computi from the eighth to the twelfth centuries number in the hundreds. Bede was a major contributor to this computistical literature with his *On Times* (written in AD 703) and *On the Reckoning of Times* (AD 725). These and others of his works, such as *On the Nature of Things*, did much to stimulate interest in scientific education during the Carolingian period. For example, in Chapter 29 of *On Times* Bede describes the ebb and flow of tides and notes that prevailing or opposing winds can advance or delay the onset of the tides. He also noted that the lag between the Moon's zenith and the arrival of a tide in a specific harbor remains constant, but that the time lag varies from port to port. These statements are supported by Bede with personal observations—a simple but refreshing turn of mind still out of fashion in the medieval worldview.

Bede was known for his learning and his humility. He died at Jarrow in AD 735, probably of pneumonia. He had been working on a translation of the Gospel of John, and it was nearly completed. On Tuesday, May 25, the day before he died, he continued to dictate his translations, saying often to his scribe, "Go quickly and copy. I don't know how long I can hold out before my Maker calls me away." He worked through the night. Early on Wednesday morning he was told that one chapter remained to be translated. Bede told his scribe, "Take your pen, make ready, and write fast." With that he felt his work was complete. He then spoke personally to ·each of his brother monks; they all wept when he told them that they would not see his face again in this world. "The time of my dissolution draws nigh, and I want to die and be with Christ." But in the evening his scribe came to tell him that there was still one sentence that needed to be translated. Bede said, "Then write quickly." With that his translation of the Gospel was indeed finished; Bede sang the *Gloria* and breathed his last. He was buried at Jarrow. In AD 1154 the remains of this simplest of monks was placed in a shrine fashioned of gold and silver and encrusted with jewels; the crypt was destroyed by a violent mob in AD 1541. His burial place is today marked only with a simple inscription.[9]

ALCUIN OF YORK AND THE CAROLINGIAN RENAISSANCE

Two bright suns came together near the end of the eighth century to reignite the lamp of learning in medieval Europe. They were an English monk named Aelwine and the farsighted ruler of the Franks whom we call Charlemagne. With their vision and industry there began a recovery of learning known as the Carolingian Renaissance.

In AD 768 Charlemagne became ruler of the far-flung Frankish empire. His grandfather Charles Martel had stopped the Saracens at Tours and hammered them back over the Pyrenees into Spain; he then began to consolidate the diverse peoples of Europe into one state. Charles's son Pepin continued to quell ethnic and tribal revolts, enlist the support of the papacy, and enforce unity. Pepin's son Charlemagne was determined to bring back civilization to the newly unified kingdom. A genius in executive ability with a powerful urge for taking control, he turned his attention to the problem of educating an illiterate nation. What he needed was a master teacher who could spearhead an innovative program, but qualified literati were few. After several unsuccessful efforts to find the right person, he was introduced to Alcuin, England's greatest teacher, during a trip to Parma. Charlemagne persuaded him to take the post, and in AD 782 Alcuin arrived at the royal court at Aachen (today in northwestern Germany). He was fifty years old.

Aelwine or Ealhwine—better known by his Latin name Alcuin—was a product of the cathedral school at York, in Yorkshire, the first great school in England to attain fame for its teaching. By AD 750 it could boast a large library containing all the Latin works and textbooks then available. Born nearby about AD 735, Alcuin received his education at York under the *scholasticus* Aelbert, who, Alcuin later wrote, "moistened thirsty hearts with diverse streams of teaching and varied dews of learning." When Alcuin succeeded Aelbert as head of the school, his fame as an inspiring teacher spread, and he was able to communicate his love of learning to generations of students.

Behind this vibrant revival in England was an Irish tradition of learning that had escaped the disintegration of culture suffered by England and Europe; scholarship and instruction in the classics had continued there without interruption. Alcuin was the brightest intellectual heir of this tradition, and the knowledge that he carried to the Frankish court was still known as "Irish learning." An Irish monk, Clement of Ireland, accompanied him to the continent as his assistant, and throughout the ninth century educators from Ireland could be found in every monastic and cathedral school.

A school of sorts had long existed at Charlemagne's court, but this "palace school" taught little more than the art of fighting and courtly manners. Alcuin set to work reorganizing the school to include some elementary instruction in "letters." Since those in attendance couldn't read or write, instruction at first was entirely oral. Alcuin prepared questions and answers beforehand, and students were to memorize the answers. Elementary reading and writing skills were taught to all. Subjects

Nor should we listen to those who say "The voice of the people is the voice of God," for the turbulence of the mob is always close to insanity.

ALCUIN OF YORK

Wisdom is not acquired save as the result of investigation.

SHANKARA ACHARYA
(HINDU THEOLOGIAN,
c. 769–820)

*What is beautiful is good,
And who is good will soon be
beautiful.*

SAPPHO OF LESBOS
(GREEK POET, c. 612)

While the Middle Ages were "Dark Ages" with respect to philosophy and the sciences, artistic achievement had its bright moments. This front cover of the Lindau Gospels, set with gold and jewels, dates from c. AD 870.

included poetry, arithmetic, astronomy, the Church Fathers, and theology. Among Alcuin's students were the princes and princesses of the royal family, their relatives, members of the court, visiting dignitaries, invited friends, and the king and queen themselves. Sometimes promising youths from humbler families were allowed to attend. Lively debates and discussions became the order of the day. Charlemagne learned to read Latin but never learned to write it.

After laboring for four years with the palace school, Charlemagne and Alcuin turned their attention to the state of education among the monks and clergy. Curriculum materials and letters were dispatched to bishops and abbots. "We invite those whom we can to master the study of the liberal arts," Charlemagne wrote. In AD 787 he issued a general proclamation on education (composed by Alcuin and signed with Charlemagne's own signature) scolding monks for their illiteracy and urging them to study. The same year he imported a number of monks from Italy and assigned them to the principal monasteries to teach grammar, arithmetic, and music. In AD 789 another decree was issued urging the clergy to live exemplary lives. "Let schools be established in which boys may learn to read. Correct carefully the Psalms, the signs in writing, the songs, the calendar, the grammar, in each monastery and diocese, and the catholic book; because often some desire to pray to God properly, but they pray badly because of incorrect books."[10]

This Carolingian Renaissance checked for a time the decline of literacy and learning and reawakened in susceptible minds a love of knowledge. Together the two leaders initiated a trend that could encourage a substitution of ideas for physical force. They laid the foundations of a new civilized world that could inherit the cultural legacy of the old dying civilization. After Charlemagne's reign there was again a general decline in education, but a number of the centers of learning—Fulda in Germany; Utrecht, Liège, Tournai, St. Laurent in the low countries; Tours, Rheims, Auxerre, and Chartres in France—held on into the ninth and tenth centuries to become celebrated cathedral and monastic schools; a few of these went on to develop into the universities of the twelfth and thirteenth centuries.

In AD 796 Alcuin retired to become abbot of St. Martin of Tours. There he founded another school, wrote, taught, and died in May, AD 804.

Some laws, though unwritten, are more firmly established than all written laws.

SENECA THE ELDER
(SPANISH-BORN
ROMAN RHETORICIAN,
C. 54 BC–AD 39)

ENDNOTES

1 Philip Schaff, *History of the Christian Church* (Scribner's, 1910; reprint, Eerdmans, 1950), vol. 3, p. 331.
2 Schaff, *History*, vol. 4, p. 597.
3 Edward Gibbon, *Decline and Fall of the Roman Empire* (Modern Library edition, n.d.), vol. 2, p. 469.
4 Gibbon, *Decline and Fall*, vol. 2, p. 471.
5 Gibbon, *Decline and Fall*, vol. 2, p. 473.
6 Marshall Clagett, *Greek Science in Antiquity* (Collier Books, 1955), pp. 207ff.
7 Clagett, *Greek Science*, p. 218.
8 Schaff, *History*, vol. 4, p. 630.
9 Schaff, *History*, vol. 4, pp. 671ff.
10 Elwood P. Cubberley, *A Brief History of Education* (Houghton Mifflin, 1922), p. 79.

CHAPTER 19

PHILOSOPHY DURING THE DARK AGES: FOUR

ERIUGENA TO ABÉLARD (AD 870–1142)

The long intellectual night continues into the ninth, tenth, and eleventh centuries; illiteracy and ignorance still prevail; but the lamp of learning is starting to be relit in the inquiring minds of a small number of notable individuals; a few centers of intellectual industry are beginning to flourish.

THE BEGINNINGS OF SCHOLASTICISM

In the decades following the labors of Alcuin and Charlemagne, and largely because of their innovations in education, a major intellectual movement began to arise, slowly, from the shadows of ignorance and superstition. Called Scholasticism, this resurrection of rationality centered in the monastic and cathedral schools; hence its leaders are titled Schoolmen or Scholastics. Scholasticism endured for almost five centuries; it declined during the fourteenth century, partly from exhaustion, partly because the best minds turned to other interests.

The problem that occupied Scholastic minds was not new: It was the unresolved tension between belief and reason—the same problem that provoked such bitter controversy in the first centuries of the Christian era. Whenever and wherever individuals begin to acquire a wider knowledge, to think intelligently, and to "see," then they feel trapped by the world around them that demands uncritical belief and passive acceptance of a body of ideas and the worldview that supports those ideas. Each person is forced to come to grips with the question: How can a bright mind, capable of reasoning about things, engage in simple-minded belief? The answer, of course, is that it can't—not a belief, anyway, that is simple minded. All the medieval thinkers assumed that God creates in us humans the capacities for both faith and reason; therefore, they reasoned, God must also have provided a means of reconciling these two modes of thought. This task of reconciliation was the burden and goal of the early Scholastics. All the Schoolmen sincerely saw themselves as both philosophers and theologians, but they had to work vigilantly to assure themselves that there need be no schizoid antagonisms between the two roles.

So, in the early part of the ninth century, with the new intellectual awakening that resulted from the Carolingian renaissance, the wrestling was renewed. By fits and starts, with setbacks and surges, Scholasticism gained strength through the eleventh century and into the twelfth. Then in the late twelfth century, with the massive

On Scholasticism The philosophy of St. Thomas is Aristotle Christianized.

ANONYMOUS

To question, to doubt, to disbelieve—these were among the deadly sins of the early Middle Ages.
ELLWOOD P. CUBBERLEY

recovery of Greek writings from the Arabs, speculative thinking was again stimulated throughout the Latin West. The result was what is known as the High Scholasticism of the thirteenth century—the "Golden Age of Theology"—the most active intellectual century since the Hellenistic era. Guided by an encyclopedia named Albertus Magnus and a supercomputer named Thomas Aquinas, every question conjurable by the human mind was framed, analyzed, pondered, and supplied with an amazing abundance of answers.

JOHN SCOTUS ERIUGENA OF IRELAND

Let no authority terrify thee.

ERIUGENA

The first clear signs of intellectual challenge to the passive acceptance of ideas are found in the writings of John Scotus Eriugena, an Irish monk who, like Alcuin, journeyed to France and, about AD 843, became principal of the palace school at the court of Charles the Bald. Eriugena was the most knowledgeable scholar of his age; some of his worshipful followers said he knew *everything*. He was comfortable in the use of Latin, perhaps Arabic, and he was one of the very few clerics who could read the New Testament in the original Greek. He had read Plato's *Timaeus* and Aristotle's *Categories*, was deeply immersed in the Neoplatonism of Plotinus, and drew from the Church Fathers, especially from Origen, Basil, Gregory of Nyssa, Augustine, Boëthius, and Pseudo-Dionysius. From his mastery of these works he created the first great philosophic synthesis of the Dark Ages. He wrote critically and unceasingly. A man of great originality and freedom of thought, whose writing is characterized by fresh thinking and bold arguments, he was almost too free to be a Scholastic.

In the history of philosophy Eriugena is remembered (1) for his dangerous championing of reason over orthodoxy; (2) for his fourfold interpretation of nature; and (3) for his translation of Pseudo-Dionysius.

The year 529 thus became a symbol of the way the Christian Church put the lid on Greek philosophy.

JORSTEIN GAARDER

Other than the odd note that he was diminutive in stature, nothing is known of his personal life. Born in Ireland about AD 800 and educated there in a monastic school, he achieved fame and influence in France through his high-profile involvement in doctrinal controversies and his writings. He probably died in France about AD 877. He wrote poetry (some of which is extant), commentaries, theological works, sermons, and translations of Church Fathers. His name, incidentally, was Johannes Scotus, "John the Irishman" (*Scotus* meant both Scotland and Ireland); he seems to have adopted the name Eriugena (or Erigena, Erygena, or Erugena) to indicate his birth in Ireland (the name for Ireland, in its oldest form, was Ériu, which later became Erin).

In the ongoing debate on faith versus reason, Eriugena comes down on the side of reason: Reason, he says, must always be the criterion of truth; and the truth must always be reasonable. Religious truth and philosophical truth are one and the same. Reason is to be given free reign in its interpretation of Scripture and the Church Fathers; the final authority is always the truth, and the ecclesiastical authorities may or may not have it. True religion, that is, does not coincide with Church doctrine; and when there is a conflict, Eriugena takes the side of true religion. In general the authority of the Church Fathers is to be accepted, but when they differ among themselves we must then use reason to decide on the best interpretation.

Divine foresight directs the history of mankind from Adam to the end of time as if it were the story of one man who gradually develops from childhood to old age.

ST. AUGUSTINE

Breaking with the tenor of his times, Eriugena's speculations are grounded not in received doctrine but in a consideration of cosmic realities. All true knowledge, including knowledge of God, nature, the universe, and religious doctrine, are coherent parts of a great harmonious worldview. The cosmos is a rational system, and every part of it must be understood in the light of every other part, and of the whole.

There is the briefest hint of the empirical in his scientific reflections. He wrote a book on astronomy, *Annotations to Martianus Capella*, in which he describes the solar system, saying that all the planets revolve around the Sun, but that this Sun-planet system revolves around the Earth. This places the Earth, still, at the center of the universe. But he found this theory, he says, in Plato; it was not the result of his own observations.

His masterpiece, *On the Division of Nature*, defies classification; it is at once a cosmology, a noetic worldview, and a soteriology. Written in the form of a dialogue between a disciple (a metaphor for the Church) and his teacher (who is reason), it shows that the disciple always, in the end, agrees with his teacher—a very dangerous idea in the ninth century. The work is Eriugena's attempt to show that while theology and philosophy are one, it is philosophy that must take the lead. Its treatment ranges over all the issues of the day in philosophy, theology, cosmology, and anthropology.

By "nature" Eriugena means both everything that exists and everything that doesn't exist. Of the things that "are not" his list includes: (1) whatever can't be known because they are beyond sense and mind; (2) all the things known to higher beings (angels, for example) but not to us humans (or to lower beings in the scale of consciousness, such as animals); (3) whatever is potential but not actual; (4) the fleeting events of the world of material things that have no permanence; (5) all things sinful which signals a loss of divine reality.

On the positive side, cosmic components are divided into four categories that represent four stages in the creative unfolding of God's nature.

(1) *What creates but is not created* (what is unmoved but moves other things). This is the ineffable God as the creative source of everything. This being, so transcendent that he is on the edge of nothingness, contains within his nature all the possibilities of existence, and he proceeds to manifest them.

(2) *What is created but also creates* (what is moved and also moves). This includes the Real Ideas, templates, archetypes, and eternal relations by which all things are formed. As recast into Christian framework, this is the second person of the Trinity.

(3) *What is created but does not create* (what is moved but does not move). This is the world of individual objects (including souls). Nothing that exists possesses a separate being of its own; all existing things are expressions of God's nature and exist in him. God alone has true being. God didn't *make* the world; the world is an expression or manifestation of God's being and therefore embodies his very nature. As God creates the world he is also creating himself. This is the third person of the Trinity who brings about actual creation in space and time.

(4) *What neither creates nor is created* (what doesn't move and is not moved). This is God as the final end of everything. Having exhausted all possible modes of creation, God reabsorbs himself into himself, and rests. Herein lies the goal of everything that exists: to return to God and lose the self in the divine. The entire universe is engaged in—in fact, *is*—a redemption program, and the Christian atonement is just one redemptive moment in the cosmic scheme.

This cosmology is not a repeating cycle (as is the Hindu cosmology, for example, or the Jain); it is a one-shot universe established to create and redeem. But man's misuse of his freedom has interrupted the flow of the redemptive process. It should be the goal of the individual soul, after death, to recover its prefall nature and grow toward reabsorption into God.

Largely because Eriugena's speculations were too bold and smelled of heresy, his influence on subsequent speculation was muted. For a debate held in AD 851 he wrote *On Divine Predestination*, and in it his politically incorrect ideas first became known. He argued that God is all goodness, so if he did predetermine anything, it

He who cannot draw on three thousand years is living from hand to mouth.

GOETHE

Every one is excluded and banned Who does not come clad in Aristotle's armor.

GOTTFRIED OF ST. VICTOR

would always be for grace and happiness, not evil. But in fact, he wrote, God allows us humans to freely exercise our own wills and therefore does not predestine any of our actions. These statements were seen by the authorities to contain wrong-headed ideas, and the work was condemned by two councils. His big book on nature was eagerly devoured by young clerics not yet seduced into rigid orthodoxy, but it too was condemned at a council at Sens. In AD 1225 the pope ordered its destruction saying it was "a book teeming with the worms of heretical depravity." In 1685 Pope Gregory XIII placed it on the *Index Librorum Prohibitorum*. Still, despite all efforts, Eriugena's wide-ranging ideas could not be suppressed; they reappeared persistently in the writings of Schoolmen and mystics of later centuries.

THE PROBLEM OF UNIVERSALS

° See p. 291.

[The Scholastics/Schoolmen] covered their ignorance with a curious and inexplicable web of perplexed words.

JOHN LOCKE

Late in the ninth century the problem of "universals," first introduced by Porphyry,° was rekindled and began to usurp the logical debates of Latin theologians; it grew until, in the thirteenth century, it became the central obsession of the most eminent Schoolmen. The existence and nature of universals had a direct bearing on the validity of many Catholic doctrines, as they were then interpreted; it was also, according to some of the Schoolmen, a key to the reconciliation of faith and reason.

The debate was over whether general concepts are real. At this moment I can count some fifty individual roses in my rose garden; each is a singular, unique, flower in itself. But I also commonly speak of rose in general, as in "The rose is the most fragrant of all flowers." Granted that the single rose exists, does the abstract rose that I know in my mind also have a separate, real existence apart from all the individual flowers? Such abstract general ideas were called by the Schoolmen *universalia*, universals.

Three answers were given to the question, the choice depending on whether the thinker considered empirical objects or ideas to be the most real. ("most real"—this notion alone gives the debate a strange sound to a modern mind: Today we don't think of reality, by any reasonable definition, as something that shades away by degrees, or comes in varying amounts. But the Schoolmen, drawing from Neoplatonism, did think of reality in this way; objects could be "more real" or "less real"; indeed objects can exist without possessing any reality at all!) One answer to the question was pure Platonism: Universals are Real Ideas. They are the archetypes, the mental templates—the blueprints—that exist in the mind of God, and from which God creates everything. They are God's creative ideas. This view was captured in the phrase *universalia ante rem*, universals exist before singular objects. This position, called Realism (but often with qualifying adjectives: Platonic Realism, Extreme Realism, Exaggerated Realism, Ultra Realism), was held by the most orthodox theologians.

A second answer came straight from the epistemology of the Epicureans, Cynics, and Skeptics: Concepts have no real existence at all. They are abstractions created by the mind. After the mind has observed fifty roses, it decides it doesn't want to carry around all fifty separate roses, so it instantly creates the universal concept of "rose" to include all fifty, and the universal concept will then serve me for the rest of my life as a catchall into which I can fit all the roses I ever see, smell, or think about. Universals are nothing more than mental concepts, fictions of the mind said William Ockam, the last great Nominalist (died 1349)—*fictiones, signa mentalia, nomina*. The word "universal," he said, refers to an intellectual act *(actus intelligenda)* and nothing more. (For these and other "heresies" Ockam spent four years in confinement and was excommunicated.) This position was expressed with *universalia post rem*, individual objects exist first, and then the universal concept is created from observing them.

It was called Nominalism (from Latin *nomen*, "name"), Conceptualism, or Terminism (because exponents said words are merely terms that may or may not correspond to any ideas or realities). Nominalism was held by the less orthodox thinkers, and was bitterly opposed by the orthodox. The University of Paris led the fight against it, and in 1339 it was made a crime to teach Nominalism or to listen to its being expounded, either in public or private; in 1473 the French king prohibited the publication and use of any Nominalist writings.

A third answer falls somewhere in between Realism and Nominalism, and was called Aristotelian Realism or Moderate Realism. It held that universals are real, but they exist only as they function to give form to individual concrete objects. The universal concept of rose has a real existence, but it exists only as it acts as a blueprint for giving shape to the single rose. This position, expressed with *universalia in re*, was held by such thinkers as Duns Scotus who finds in the Aristotelian position a sound basis for the classification of genera and species.

What was the relevance of all this? When these varying viewpoints were applied to specific doctrines such as the Trinity, the Atonement, and original sin, their impact becomes intelligible. For example, when Roscellin, a Nominalist, theologized the Trinity, he concluded that Father, Son, and Holy Spirit were three distinct beings, separate but equal. That is, the three persona of the Godhead could not partake of a single universal substance, else the first and third persons would have had to become incarnate and die on the cross along with the second. (That's nonsense, replied Anselm of Canterbury, a Realist; the pond, the brook, and the fountain are three distinct entities, yet they contain the same water.) Similarly, when Otto of Tournai, a Platonic Realist, thought of original sin, the doctrine was easily explained: Adam's sin infected the universal soul of the entire human race and thus all souls, from birth, are contaminated with sin and death.[1]

"With intrepid confidence," writes Philip Schaff, "these busy thinkers ventured upon the loftiest speculations, raised and answered all sorts of doubts and ran every accepted dogma through a fiery ordeal to show its invulnerable nature. They were the knights of theology, its Godfreys and Tancreds. Philosophy with them was their handmaid—*ancilla*—dialectics their sword and lance."[2]

About AD 880 **Eric of Auxerre** worked with universals and took the position that would later be called Nominalism. He wrote that Aristotle and Boëthius were right: Concepts are merely images of objects, and words are only symbols used to express those concepts. Around AD 900, an Irish monk named **Fredegis** wrote a treatise titled *De Nihilo et Tenebris*, in which he attempted to prove that both nothing and darkness are real things; this was a first step toward endorsing Realism. Fredegis's pupil **Remigius of Auxerre** (d. AD 904) tried to reconcile Realism with the Nominalism of his teacher; to this end he studied deeply into Plato's Real Ideas and concluded that they exist somewhere in an invisible sphere, hidden away in the mind of God.

Roscellin of Compiègne (d. c. AD 1100), dubbed Founder of a New Lyceum because he popularized Aristotle's logical ideas, was a radical Nominalist who focused on individual objects. The components of a universal class have no unity of substance, he said; the unity that we think we perceive in such terms as *genus* or *species* is nothing but a fabrication of thought and language. Analyzing a whole into its parts is merely a mental operation and has no objective referent whatever. (Nonsense, Abélard retorted: When Christ ate part of a fish, Roscellinus would be compelled to say that Christ ate part of a word.) Roscellin has been credited with initiating the Age of Dialectical Madness.

William of Champeaux (d. 1121), a logician of sorts and a mystic, opposed the Nominalism of Roscellin with a Moderate Realism, saying that the universal is present as substantial essence in every singular object. (Nonsense, responded Abélard: If the universal essence of humanity is present in Socrates, and present in Plato, then Plato must always be where Socrates is.)

Gilbert de la Porrée (d. AD 1154) was a gifted exponent of Aristotelian logic. He concluded that perceived universality derives from *formae nativae*, the innate or natural forms that inhere in all created things; but it is the human mind that abstracts the (real) universal and makes it into a (mental) universal. Such a position appears safely middle of the road, but it still earned Gilbert the brand of heretic.

One of the most exuberant teachers of Platonic Realism was **William of Conches** (d. c. AD 1152), the first medieval thinker to indicate an acquaintance with Muslim philosophy. Inspired by the Arab physicists, his Realism led him identify the Holy Spirit with the Neoplatonic world-soul. When warned that such a doctrine would bring a charge of heresy, he decided to abandon theology and study psychology instead.

John of Salisbury (d. AD 1182), a humanist and historian (who was with Thomas Becket during his last hours), was wiser than most Scholastics. Recognizing the dangers of a dialectic run riot, he stayed above the fray of rancorous logicians and wrote a history of them instead. The most important of his philosophical works are the *Polycraticus* and the *Metalogicus*. These and other of his writings make John of Salisbury the first medieval historian of philosophy.

GERBERT OF AURILLAC

One of the most colorful personalities of the late tenth century was a monk named Gerbert. A man of extraordinary learning and erudition—"the brightest light in the darkness of the tenth century"—he somehow acquired a reputation as a black-arts magician because of his knowledge of astronomy and his fiddling with mechanical devices.[3]

In the history of philosophy Gerbert is remembered (1) for being one of the first to employ "scholastic method"; (2) for his attempts to give philosophy a wider and more empirical definition; and (3) for importing Arabic learning into Latin Europe.

During persisting dark times Gerbert preserved at Rheims the best of the Scholastic movement. He was a creative teacher of logic, using Aristotle's *Categories*, Porphyry's *Eisagôgê*, and Boëthius's commentaries. Rhetoric he taught using a mechanical apparatus to illustrate various combinations of figures of speech. To teach astronomy he used a set of globes to illustrate the celestial circles, identify constellations, and trace the orbits of the planets. He said they helped to reveal "the horizon and the beauties of the heavens."

Gerbert lived from about AD 950 to 1003. Born near Aurillac in the French province of Auvergne, he was educated there in the Benedictine monastery where he studied grammar, arithmetic, and music. He spent three years in Spain where he encountered Islamic culture, gained (probably) a smattering of Arabic, and learned about Arabic numerals and decimal notations which he introduced into the Latin West. As master of the cathedral school at Rheims he gained renown as scholar and teacher. He was at heart a Socratic dialectician and a man of great wit, intelligence, and charm. He was an avid collector of books, which he kept locked in a half dozen wooden chests. Though he devoured knowledge in every field, his special loves were mathematics, astronomy, physics, and music. Strangely, for a pious monk, most of his writings are in mathematics. His voluminous letters written to kings, queens, bishops, archbishops, popes and other eminent figures are invaluable for the light

Ecce quantum fides proficit, ubi sermo deficit. *Where words give out, there is the more room for faith.*

GERBERT

they shed on events of his time. They also chronicle a life endlessly engaged in power struggles, political intrigues, and bitterly contested innovations, with momentous gains and losses. Always a bold and fearless champion of decency in ecclesiastical politics, he attacked even the papacy for its corruptions. He was also an accomplished musician (he constructed a monochord for studying musical theory) and mechanical genius: He wrote on the uses of the astrolabe, and invented, among other gadgets, a musical organ energized by steam, and a clock.

A delightful encounter occurred between Gerbert, then a cathedral master at Rheims, and Otric, a famed master of a cathedral school in Saxony. The conference, called by the Emperor Otho II, took place in Ravenna in December AD 980. Many distinguished figures, temporal and ecclesiastical, were in attendance. Gerbert opened the discussion with an attempt to define the scope of philosophy: *divinarum et humanarum rerum comprehensio veritatis*, philosophy is the knowledge of all reality, both divine and human. That is, philosophy is knowledge, and knowledge philosophy. Then, following both Plato and Aristotle, he divided the field of philosophy into the theoretical and the practical. Theoretical philosophy, he said, includes physics, mathematics, and theology; practical philosophy includes ethics, economics, and politics.

There followed a discussion on where physiology and philology should place in this scheme. Then the question was asked, "What is the goal of philosophy?" Gerbert reitered that the aim of all philosophy is a comprehensive understanding of everything. Getting back to Aristotle's four *aitia* ("causes")° someone asked "What caused the world?" After a vigorous and vehement exchange (including an analysis of the cause of shadows and a probing into the relationship of abstract concepts of differing generality), the Emperor, toward evening, called for adjournment.

° See pp. 189ff.

Gerbert went home (presumably to his monk's cell) and wrote *Concerning the Rational and the Use of Reason* and addressed it to the Emperor. In it he completes the unfinished analysis and classification of abstractions. Beginning with objections that might be raised to his conclusions, he proceeds, with incisive logic, to annihilate those objections, so that when he comes to state his own position it stands clear and without logical contenders. This treatise is important therefore as the first clear example of "scholastic method" as it will be developed by Abélard in his *Sic et Non* ("Yes and No") and, superlatively, by Thomas Aquinas in his *Summa Theologiae*.[4]°

° See "scholastic method" in lexicon.

On April 9 of the year 999, Gerbert became Sylvester II when he was elevated to the papacy as the first French pope. His influence on his own times was immense: Gerbert was to the tenth century what Eriugena was to the ninth, and what Abélard will be to the eleventh.

ANSELM OF CANTERBURY

Anselm of Canterbury was a brilliant theologian, a fighter for church rights, an advocate of monasticism, a passionate mystic, and a much-loved pastor to his flock. In his theology he was a typical, but exceptionally penetrating, scholastic thinker; he explored Catholic doctrine down to the last detail.

But in the history of philosophy Anselm is remembered for a singular contribution: the famous ontological argument for the existence of God.

THE MAN

Anselm was a Frenchman who gained immortality in England. Born in 1033, he came from a noble family of landowners living in Lombardy, near the border with

Switzerland. His mother was a pious Christian woman, his father a man of the world, rough, harsh and judgmental, who had little time for religion and no sympathy at all for his son's leanings toward the religious life. When only fifteen, he told his father he wanted to become a monk, but his father would have none of it. Sick with disappointment, Anselm's response was one of lassitude and depression, with physical ailments. After a bitter quarrel he left home, crossed the Alps, wandered through Burgundy and Normandy, and finally settled at the Norman abbey of Le Bec to become a devoted Benedictine monk. There he studied under the famed teacher Lanfranc. At 23 he became prior of Le Bec, then abbot in 1078. He developed the monastic school into a renowned center of learning that served all of Europe, and it was at Le Bec that he wrote his most important works.

Only a decade earlier, in 1066, at the Battle of Hastings, William the Norman had conquered England. From him the monastery at Le Bec received considerable land in both Normandy and England, and it fell to Anselm to oversee the properties across the Channel. He made three journeys to Kent during which he endeared himself to the English people. When the archbishop of Canterbury—his old teacher Lanfranc—died in 1089 Anselm was chosen to succeed him.

From 1093 to 1097 Anselm looked after his administrative duties, developed ties with the Roman papacy, and wrote; but his energies were constantly absorbed in a running struggle with the English kings on the rights of the Church in England to control revenues, property, and appointments to office. Anselm's firm stand got him exiled from England on several occasions. The investiture controversy (on who should have the right to appoint church dignitaries, the king or the pope) finally ended with the king's capitulation in 1107.

He who does not believe has not felt, and he who has not felt, does not understand.

ANSELM

Anselm was gifted with an unusual mind and heart. Once, while riding in the countryside, a rabbit chased by hunters tried to hide under his horse; Anselm gave it sanctuary. On another occasion a bird was wounded by a thoughtless child; Anselm prayed for it and tried to ease its suffering. Father and protector, he extended the same solicitous care to his human flock.

Anselm was not by temperament a recluse, but from his earliest days he longed for the monastic life and resented any call that tore him away from it. His attitude toward life in this world was typically that of his Age, only more so. In his *Meditations and Prayers* he employs the metaphor of a soul doomed to walk a narrow bridge spanning a dark abyss filled with horrible writhing things and noxious vapors. The bridge is this present life, and every soul must cross it. Barely a foot wide, the bridge is constructed of steps that fall away behind the soul making the crossing. To complicate the journey great birds swoop down from above to harass the traveler. The falling steps are the days of our lives, the birds are malignant spirits. Sinful souls, blinded by ignorance and unable to stay the path, will fall into the abyss; while pious souls, led by God, will be illuminated safely across the bottomless black ravine of hell.[5]

FAITH AND REASON

[Anselm held it to be] a sin of neglect when he who has faith, does not strive after knowledge.

PHILIP SCHAFF

Anselm could only take a Realist position on universals. He had no problem speaking of ideas as "substances" which exist in the mind of God prior to the existence of individual things. The single object is perceived by sense, the universal is known by intellect.

To Anselm faith and reason—theology and philosophy—go hand in hand, each having its own sphere of operations; they never contradict each other. Reason, by itself, is too feeble to avoid error and can be trusted only when it is illuminated by faith. His *Intelligo ut credam*, "I believe in order to understand," became the standard formula of Scholasticism: Christ must come to the intellect through the door of faith, not faith through the door of intellect.

Anselm's major theological work is *Cur Deus homo?*, "Why Did God Become Man?" In it he intended to show by reason alone why the incarnation necessarily had to occur. In the feudal value system of Anselm's time, if someone committed a crime, then he was judged beholden to the victim of his crime and was bound by law to make "satisfaction" to that person. The weight of the satisfaction was determined by the status of the person offended: Victimizing a woman or a fellow serf was relatively minor, while an offense against a baron or king demanded extreme compensation.

So, when Adam, carrying in his testes the lowly human race, sinned against a perfectly loving God, the satisfaction required became so heavy that no mortal could pay it; finite Man could never give sufficient satisfaction for his crime against an infinite God. Mankind deserves eternal death. How, then, can Man be returned to a right relationship with God? This could happen only when a God-Man who is without sin offers up his perfect life as a "fine" on behalf of depraved Man. This Christ did: the fine was paid, the satisfaction was met. It is the Church's sacrament of baptism, Anselm held, that opens the door to each individual and promises to him this restored relationship. Anselm's satisfaction theory supplanted all other interpretations of the atonement.

THE ONTOLOGICAL ARGUMENT

Anselm's claim to philosophic fame rests on his ontological argument for the existence of God. Anselm wrote a preliminary verson of the argument in his *Monologium*, "Monologue" or "Soliloquy," and then reworked it into a more complete form in the *Proslogium*, "Allocution."

He felt intuitively that he could find a simple argument that could prove God's existence from the nature of ideas alone. (We must remember that Anselm thought of ideas as real entities.) He had been discussing theology with his fellow monks, and at their urging he proceeded to work on his "proof." Day and night he wrestled; at times he could neither eat nor sleep. Then during vigils one night the outlines of the argument came clear in his mind. "I do not seek to understand in order that I may believe," he prayed, "but I believe in order that I may understand, for of this I feel sure, that, if I did not believe, I would not understand."[6]

The argument runs thus: The mind has a concept of a being than which nothing greater can be conceived. This being, than which nothing greater can be conceived, must exist in reality as well as in thought. For if it existed solely in the mind, then it would be possible to think of it as existing also in reality, and this being would then be greater. But this notion is self-contradictory and therefore impossible. This being, therefore, than which nothing greater can be conceived, exists both in the mind and reality. And this being is God.

Anselm was certain of his proof. With heartfelt thanks he exclaims, "So truly dost thou exist, O Lord God, that it is not possible to conceive of thee as not existing. For, if any mind could conceive of anything better than thou art, then the creature would ascend above the Creator and become his judge, which is supremely absurd. Everything else besides thyself can be conceived of as not existing."

The argument drew immediate critical response from fellow Schoolmen who, with piety still but better logic, saw its fallacies. A monk named Gaunilo from the monastery of Marmoutiers replied with a treatise titled *Liber pro Insipiente*, freely translated as "A Book Written on Behalf of the Fool Who Says in His Heart that There Is No God." In it Gaunilo said Anselm had confused thought with reality. Believing that something is real doesn't make it real. He pointed out that, with

Anselm's kind of logic, one could argue for the existence of anything. I can picture in my mind the lost island of Atlantis, he said, but that hardly justifies my concluding that the lost island must exist, just because I can think of it as a real thing.

This exchange between the two thoughtful monastics is one of the gentlest on record. Anselm replied to Gaunilo in his *Liber Apologeticus*, saying, in effect, "That's nice, but you've missed the point. I know the difference between something existing in the mind and something existing out there in reality. But I wasn't talking about lost islands or other created objects, which we can easily imagine as not existing. I was talking about God, a being than whom nothing greater can be conceived. It is not possible to think of this being, God, as not existing. God is the one Being, and the only one, whose non-existence is inconceivable."

For Anselm personally, because of the depth of his belief, this statement was undoubtedly true; but it was not logically true, or true for anyone else of a less tenacious faith. The notion that God's existence is inconceivable is simply false: It can easily be conceived at least six times before breakfast (as Alice, in Wonderland, confides to the Queen). One would have no trouble thinking of Zeus as not existing, or Ishtar, Isis, Thor, Krishna, Kwanyin, or any of the other deities to whom mortal men and woman have raised their suppliant voices. However deep the devotion of their devotees, faith, individually or collectively, does not quite succeed in endowing them with real existence.

The argument is invalid at several other points, though beyond the question of validity it points to serious and important problems in epistemology. For centuries critics have asked questions that effectively demolish the argument's coherence. (1) Is it really true that the human mind has "a concept of a being than which nothing greater can be conceived"? It's very doubtful. The idea of "perfect being" is really so fuzzy with ambiguities that it is useless. (2) What exactly is meant by "reality"? And why is something "more real" if it has concrete existence than if it exists only as idea? Reality, it turns out, is a location, not some sort of qualifying substance that sticks to a noun. (3) Anselm wanted to frame an argument that would, in the end, prove that God exists. So why did he start out, in the first line, with the assumption of what he wanted to prove in the last line? If you assume, up front, what you want your conclusion to prove, then your logical argument leaves a little something to be desired. (4) Immanuel Kant noted another flaw in the argument. "Objective existence," he said, "is not a predicate." For example, I can picture a rose in my mind's eye, and then I can add "red" (in my mind) and say "the rose is red." My predicate red has added a specific quality to my subject the rose—in my mind. But if I picture a rose and then try to add "reality" to my subject rose, well, I can do that too—in my mind. But no matter how strong my faith, I can't add to my rose anything but a *concept* of reality, never true objective existence. So Kant is saying that reality ("real reality," not just my idea of reality) is not a predicate. It's all mind stuff, and I can't jump from the mind to the real thing by thinking it. Even with great faith.

It has been said that the ontological argument is the supreme example of Scholastic logic grounded in faith, and that in Anselm lofty reason and childlike faith were bonded into perfect harmony. That may be so, but it's also an example of childlike belief undercutting the power of reason and shattering its validity. A powerful need to believe often gets in the way of good thinking, and Anselm's argument is a depressing example of this. While the true believer does "know" something—a deep emotional experience—that a mere intellectual observer does not, what he knows is not a true knowledge of the realities of a situation, no matter how strong his conviction that it is. In a purely pragmatic sense, his belief that something is real may indeed be true for him, and for anyone else who believes it deeply enough. But this pragmatic criterion of truth, to the exclusion of other criteria, does not lead to a better knowledge of, or understanding of, the truth of world operations. All in all, Anselm's life was more valid than his famous argument.

Anselm's last two years were spent quietly carrying out the duties of his archdiocese. He died in 1109, at 76, probably at Canterbury where he is buried. In 1163 Thomas Becket submitted Anselm's name to Rome for canonization; in 1720 he was made a Doctor of the Roman Church.

ABÉLARD OF THE PARACLETE

Sometimes the personality and character of an historical figure can be captured by sifting through the literature and gathering the epithets flung at him, both pro and con, in his own day and since. Consider, for example, the man who has inspired the following adjectives: brilliant, gifted, restless, impulsive, undisciplined, innovative, heretical, individualistic, moral, charismatic, magnetic, immoral, intimidating, dignified, pious, tender, callous, daring, creative, combative, forceful, famous, infamous, confident—and much more.

> Nec credi posse aliquid nisi primitus intellectus. *Nothing is to be believed, until it has been understood.*
>
> ABÉLARD

The man who suffered these invectives and accolades is Peter Abélard, a twelfth-century dialectician, teacher, and theologian, but famed, not for his mind but for his heart. He was certainly one of the most colorful and complex figures in Western history, and all these qualitative labels are historically fair, or, at least, contain enough truth to warrant further probing.

IN THE HISTORY OF PHILOSOPHY

Abélard is important for (1) his dogged attempt to break the chains of orthodoxy and recapture the freedom to think critically; (2) for the spirit of philosophic doubt that runs through all his writings: "In the spirit of doubt we approach inquiry, and by inquiry we find out the truth"; (3) for his book *Sic et non*, "Yes and No," that raises scholastic method to its highest level; (4) for his ethical theory of intent that was centuries ahead of its time.

THE MAN

At the age of about 46 he wrote his autobiography, *The Story of My Misfortunes* (even in Latin its title, *Historia calamitatum*, sounds ominous). In it he reveals the story of his love for the beautiful Héloïse and the calamities that befell them both, as well as other details of his stormy life.

> God considered not action, but the spirit of the action. It is the intention, not the deed, wherein the merit or praise of the doer consists.
>
> ABÉLARD

Abélard's original name was Pierre de Pallais, for he was born in the village of Le Pallais in the province of Brittany in western France. The eldest son of a knight, he was destined by his father for a military career, but he soon "abandoned Mars for Minerva" and chose the life of an itinerant scholar serving the goddess of Wisdom. He first studied the quadrivium (geometry, astronomy, music, and arithmetic) with Thierry of Chartres, then dialectics with Roscellin at Besançon. He transferred to Paris where he attended the cathedral school and listened to the lectures of William of Champeaux, one of the ablest teachers of his time. Abélard's incisive mind focused on the fallacies in his teacher's logic; they quarreled, and Abélard left; thus was established a lifelong pattern of dialectical confrontation. After a period of illness he returned to Paris and again challenged his teacher, disagreeing with him openly on the reality of universals. "By the simplest and clearest arguments," he recalls, "I pushed him into changing his mind, in fact, to abandon his position."

On Abélard *His manner more than his matter made him a stormy petrel of theology*

THOMAS GILBY, O.P.

Then adding salt to fresh wounds, Abélard set up a rival school on a vine-covered hill nearby and weaned away William's best students, almost to a man, we are told. He pursued "the art of disputation wherever it was flourishing" and became the foremost dialectician in an age of great logicians and debaters; of course he made enemies at every turn. Later, in 1114 and at the peak of his fame, he sat in on classes in theology taught by Anselm of Laon, a renowned biblical scholar; again the two tangled and Abélard came away saying that Anselm created a wonderful flow of words that contained no thoughts, rather like a barren fig tree that produced leaves but no fruit. "When he lights a fire," Abélard said, "he fills the whole house with smoke."

In about 1115 William of Champeaux retired and Abélard was called to Paris to head St. Geneviève, the cathedral school at Notre Dame; here he began his most brilliant and fruitful years. By this time he was known throughout France; students flocked to hear him lecture on philosophy and theology, and when he visited towns to lecture, crowds lined the streets to catch a glimpse of the celebrated iconoclast. He thought clearly and spoke clearly, refusing to hide behind words. He quoted easily from classical literature and was widely read in the Church Fathers. Entertaining, penetrating, and articulate, giving fashionable ideas an acceptable gloss while just under the surface there lurked the seduction of forbidden thoughts and a daring disregard of authority, he fascinated hearers everywhere. From the fresh sounds they couldn't decide if his was the voice of a new way of thinking or a man digging his own grave. (It turned out to be both, of course.)

His books were widely read not only in cathedral schools, monastic schools, and convents but also at gatherings of nobles and guildworkers. By young clerics they were much appreciated, by orthodox bishops much feared. Doctrinally they were suspect. Charges of heresy were first brought against Abélard at a council at Soissons in 1121. His old teacher Roscellin opened the attack, charging him with giving the

Peter Abélard in the pulpit.

Trinity a Sabellian interpretation (the Godhead is not three separate persons, the third-century Roman theologian Sabellius had held, but just one person wearing three different "masks"). Abélard was convicted by the papal legate, confined to the convent of St. Médard in Soissons, and ordered to burn his book on the Trinity and recite the Athanasian Creed in public.

Then Abélard met Héloïse. The daughter of a canon of the Notre Dame Cathedral, she lived in Paris with her uncle Fulbert, also a canon at Notre Dame. All the records indicate, without exaggeration, that she was the most gifted woman of her time, of incomparable brilliance and beauty. She was seventeen when Abélard was selected to be her private tutor. He moved into the canon's residence, and soon the hours devoted to learning turned into hours dedicated to love. There is little doubt that they fell deeply in love with each other. Abélard later wrote that over their open books they exchanged more love than learning, more kisses than knowledge. When their affair became known, the uncle went into a rage. Abélard transported Héloïse to his home in Brittany and cared for her there. A son was born to them and named Astralabe (Astralabius). To sooth her uncle's raging chemistry, they were secretly married, though for years Héloïse publicly denied the marriage in order to safeguard Abélard's career. (Married men could not become priests in the Catholic Church.) When separated, they wrote one another, and their correspondence has endured in world literature as a moving legacy to their mutual love and tragic fate. In one of her letters Héloïse wrote: "If the name 'wife' seems more proper to you, that's all right. But to me the little word 'friend' has always been more dear. Or if 'friend' is not quite right to you, then I'll happily be to you 'concubine' or even 'harlot'—concubina vel scortum. If Augustus had promised me rule of the whole world in exchange for marriage, I call God as my witness that I would rather be your mistress than his empress—your meretrix than his imperatrix."[7]

But she had set a trap for herself and her husband: Keeping the marriage a secret might save Abelard's career, but it could hardly achieve its purpose of placating her uncle. To protect Héloïse, Abélard moved her to the convent of Argenteuil where she became a nun. There he could visit his wife, if only in secret. Learning of the arrangement Fulbert, still furious and feeling humiliated, and apparently still unaware that a marriage had taken place, plotted revenge. He hired some thugs who, with the aid of one of Abélard's servants, fell upon Abélard at night and castrated him. At one blow his dreams of a life with Héloïse and his plans for a career in the Church were abruptly ended.

Shamed and denied a career in the priesthood, Abélard opted for the monastic life and entered the convent of St. Denis, near Paris. But things only got worse. The monks at St. Denis cherished the belief that their patron saint was the Dionysius converted in Athens by Saint Paul (Acts 17:34). When Abélard pointed out (correctly) that such identification was impossible, the monks made life hell for him. So he sought out a barren plot of land in the province of Champagne, built a small retreat, and called it The Paraclete (named, significantly, after the Holy-Spirit-of-the-future mentioned in John 14:16, where *Paraklêtos* means "Interceder," "Strengthener," "Comforter," or "Advocate"; Latin *advocatus*, "called to one's side"—which Abélard, at this point in his life, desperately needed). Soon flocks of students had again gathered around him. But his enemies still pursued. Abélard said he felt like an ant fighting off lions.

In 1125 he was chosen to become abbot of the Breton monastery of St. Gildas by the sea. It was during the ten years that he was at St. Gildas that Abélard wrote his *Misfortunes*. There the story was repeated: The monks were undisciplined, violent, and twice attempted to murder their new abbot, once by poisoning the wine in the

On Abelard's Ethics *Those who do not know the Gospel obviously commit no fault in not believing in Jesus Christ.*
ÉTIENNE GILSON

The sin, then, consists not in desiring a woman, but in consent to the desire.
ABÉLARD

Travel is fatal to prejudice, bigotry, and narrowmindedness.
MARK TWAIN

holy chalice. In disgust and despair Abélard fled, but in "striving to escape one sword," he said, "I threw myself upon another."

Héloïse and her sister nuns had been driven from the convent at Argenteuil, so Abélard brought her to The Paraclete and placed her in charge. Abélard moved to Paris one more time to teach, and rapidly regained his popularity. Almost immediately the ecclesiastical authorities were notified that "doctrinal novelties" were beginning to resurface, dangerous ideas on the Trinity, Christ, Holy Spirit, and Atonement. A quick scrutiny revealed fourteen dangerous errors.

The first time a woman opened her mouth, she overthrew the world.
BERNARD OF CLAIRVAUX

Bernard of Clairvaux, the most powerful religious leader in Europe, had visited Héloïse at The Paraclete and heard for himself that the Lord's Prayer had been altered to read "Give us this day our supersubstantial bread." Incensed, Bernard visited Abélard in Paris and urged him to correct his errors. To no avail: there's really no problem, Abélard assured him, for at The Paraclete they felt free to experiment with new ideas. Bernard was not assured; the Truth was firmly established and there was no place for experiment. Bernard went away complaining that Abélard knew everything but the word *nescio*, "I don't know." Abélard asked that his case be taken up at a council where he hoped to engage Bernard in direct debate, giving him at least a fighting chance. But by the time the council met at Sens in 1141, Bernard had already lined up the powers of the church, from cardinals and bishops to "all the friends of Christ," against Abélard, whom he called a ravenous lion and a dragon. Finding that the case had already been decided against him, Abélard refused to defend himself and appealed directly to the pope, Innocent II. The prelates at the council recommended that Abélard's ideas be branded as eternally in error—*perpetua damnatione*—and that the thinker be punished. The depth of Bernard's scorn of Abélard was expressed in the hundreds of pages dispatched to the pope and cardinals enumerating the accusations against him. He was a snake come forth from its hole, the monk wrote, and a hydra with seven heads.

The pope descended from his *cathedra* and, with his own hands, burned the fourteen offensive articles in front of St. Peter's Basilica. Abélard was declared a heretic

Abélard reading to Héloïse

and ordered confined and silenced. He received the sentence while he was on his way to Rome, and, in ill health and crushed by the defeat, he stopped at the monastery of Cluny, in Burgundy. There Peter the Venerable befriended and cared for him. Peter dispatched to the pope a request that the wandering scholar be allowed to remain with him. The pope consented and Abélard made Cluny his last home. The spirit broken and the strength gone, he was sent by Peter to nearby Châlons-sur-Saône to convalesce. He died there at the age of 63, on April 21, 1142.

Peter wrote to Héloïse telling her of his death and calling Abélard a philosopher of Christ. "So Master Peter finished his days and he who was known in almost the whole world for his great erudition and ability as a teacher died peacefully in Him who said 'Learn of me, for I am meek and lowly of heart,' and he is, as we must believe, gone to Him."[8]

Abélard's body was taken to the Paraclete and laid to rest in a sarcophagus. Twenty-two years later the body of Héloïse was laid beside him. Over the tomb was placed the inscription:

> The Socrates of the Gauls, the great Plato of the Occidentals, our Aristotle, who was greater or equal to him among the logicians! Abélard was the prince of the world's scholars, varied in talent, subtle and keen, conquering all things by his mental force. And then he became a conqueror indeed, when, entering Cluny, he passed over to the true philosophy of Christ.[9]

In 1816 the sarcophagus holding their remains was removed to the cemetery of Père Lachaise in Paris. There it is today, drawing lovers and other pilgrims from around the Globe who stand silently pondering the ways of the world and wondering, for a moment, why time cannot be turned back to undo the wrongs etched with such bitter tears into the human record.

ABÉLARD'S PHILOSOPHY

Abélard was not a voluminous writer like Augustine or Aquinas, but what he did write sounded strong echoes of the Socratic spirit and challenged entrenched orthodoxies.

The work that has made him immortal, of course, is his autobiography, *The Story of My Misfortunes*, written while he was trying to maintain control of his recalcitrant monks at St. Gildas. But the book that impacted Scholastic thinking was his *Sic et non*, "Yes and No," a scholarly work that assumes an intelligent, critical response on the part of his readers. He also produced several works on theology: *Commentary on the Book of Romans, Introduction to Theology, Christian Theology,* and *Dialogue Between a Philosopher, a Jew, and a Christian.* Most enduring is a collection of love letters between Abélard and Héloïse that they themselves assembled. He also penned a few poems.

SIC ET NON   It was while he was at St. Denis that Abélard began to collect passages from the Church Fathers that seemed to teach varied and contradictory points of view. Church dogma had long held that the Bible never contradicted itself and that the Church Fathers were always in complete agreement with one another. Abélard studied the Fathers and found that this received wisdom was false. He made a collection of 158 disparate passages from the Fathers and arranged the results in his *Sic et non.* Always a teacher, the work was designed as a textbook for his students. It is essentially a workbook, and in the preface he provided guidelines by which students could reconcile the opposing statements.

What is significant in *Sic et non* is that students were not *told* the answers, but had to work out the answers for themselves. This is a sharp break with prevailing practice

God shall never see me a good man; I have suffered too much at his hands.

KING WILLIAM II OF ENGLAND

in education. Most teachers at the time were churchmen or theologians, and they felt constrained to teach the established truth as embodied in Church dogma. When Abélard supplied students with thought problems and asked them to analyze them logically, he was, in effect, giving them freedom to make up their own minds. In the eyes of the authorities this was unconscionable. If the truth is known, they believed, it should be taught. It is the most dangerous of betrayals to set students searching for some illusive "truth" with the clear implication that the truth is not known and must still be discovered. Such heretical pedagogy denies the validity of Church teaching, flaunts the power of the Church, and puts young souls at risk of perdition.

Sic et non appears to us today as the work of a sound critical mind as well as an example of good educational technique. Students were encouraged to assume at least a modicum of freedom and to trust their own abilities to think rationally and intelligently. Abélard suggests that what seem to be contradictions in the writings of the Church Fathers may not be so, because there may be problems in the definitions of words or in our interpretations of ambiguous phrases. The only way to find out for sure is to study and analyze them with reason, and this his students were to do. A critical spirit is the proper spirit in which to approach the Fathers and even the Scriptures. The truth will be found by doubt and hard work, not through blind acceptance of uncriticized dogmas. "In the spirit of doubt we approach inquiry, and by inquiry we find out the truth, as He, who was the Truth said, 'Seek and ye shall find, knock and it shall be opened to you.'"

Orthodox theologians were enraged by this, for it made theology subservient to philosophy, faith subservient to reason. Whereas Anselm defended faith by saying "I believe in order to understand," Abélard preached the opposite: "I understand in order [to know what] to believe." *Nec credi posse aliquid nisi primitus intellectus.* "Nothing is to be believed," he said emphatically, "until it has been understood." Implicit in this stance is the notion that human reason can comprehend the mysteries of faith, an idea not held by a Christian thinker for a thousand years.

Abélard's creative mind, shaped by individualism and humanism, saw everything in a slightly different way.

ON THE ATONEMENT   In his commentary on Paul's letter to the Romans, Abélard wrote that the meaning of Christ's life was to inspire people to love God by example alone. The whole purpose of the Atonement was not to pay a ransom to the Devil, or to appease God's wrath, or to make satisfaction for offenses against divine justice. God's singular purpose was to draw man by love back to himself. He could have done it by other means, but he chose to do it by example: Christ's life is all about love.

ON THE TRINITY   The Father, Son, and Holy Spirit are all one and the same, just different manifestations of the one Being. As the figure of the Father, he is Power. As the son he is Wisdom. As the Holy Spirit he is Love. Abélard supported his theory with passages from Scripture. Nevertheless he was severely attacked because this Trinitarian formula too closely resembled some ancient notions condemned long ago as heresies.

ON UNIVERSALS   Abélard staked out a position in the universals debate that was to be greatly influential, but no one at the time knew what to call it: Realism, Moderate Realism, Conceptualism, and Nominalism were just a few of the names given to it. He reasoned that individuality is real; in fact each single object is real and unique. But when we place objects in a particular class, that abstract class is also real. For example, when we see the similarities that all birds have in common and lump them together and give them a general label called "bird," our placing them in that category is justified because they really belong to that category. The abstraction "bird" is not just a mental artifact created by the mind to organize our bits and pieces of information. The common elements that all birds share really exist.

Abélard would be pleased to have the empirical data we possess in the late twentieth century from genetic research. Today we understand rather precisely why birds are birds. Birds are birds because they share something in common, namely gene codes inherited from common ancestors; but because of the almost infinite possibilities of genetic combination birds are also individually unique. Abélard was asserting, in the twelfth century, what we now have a scientific basis for reasserting. Each individual is a unique single object, but it also truly belongs to a class that we can call "bird."

But Abélard had to resolve the problem without benefit of genetic theory. What *causes* all birds to have these qualities in common? Something must operate to endow common qualities to singular objects. He concluded that universals must in fact exist prior to, and independently of, single objects. He called upon Plato via Neoplatonism for his final answer. He said that universals must exist in God's intellect; they are the abstract idea blueprints by which individual things are created.

While this part of his answer was not new, his conclusion was more insightful: All three positions held by the Schoolmen of his day contain some validity. Universals (1) are real "substances" that exist in the mind of God; (2) they are the source of common qualities shared by individual objects; (3) we know them as abstract concepts created by the mind to describe these real patterns. This threefold position was later adopted by Thomas Aquinas and has since become the official doctrine of the Catholic Church.

On Revelation Abélard seems not to have questioned outright the notion of revelation, but he held that we should accept only from revelation what we can support with reason. It is the business of philosophy to provide this support and to make Christian doctrine intellectually sound. This position established the official definition of theology for the Catholic Church: The business of theology is to render accepted doctrine intelligible to probing minds, to distinguish it from other doctrines, and to defend it from attack.

On Sources of Truth Abélard believed that Christianity is the honored recipient of two streams of revealed tradition, Judaic and Hellenic. The biblical prophets had been inspired in their teachings, but so had the Greek philosophers. The essence of true religion is its ethical teaching; those born outside the Christian tradition—for example, the Old Testament figures who lived before Christ, and the great men and women who belonged to other religions—these individuals could well be Christians, even without the name Christian or the redemptive offices of the Church, if they were moral in conscience and intent. The moral teachings of the Gospel are merely Christian formulations of the natural law discerned by Greek philosophers. (Quite apart from his other "errors," this teaching alone placed Abélard outside the circle of faith and ensured attacks on his thinking.)

On Ethics Abélard's soundest contribution to philosophy lies in his ethical theory. In a little book titled *Scito te ipsum*, "Know Thyself," he said that morality has nothing to do with overt action or one's behavior. It is a matter of the heart—for as a man thinks and feels, so is he. Morality is what one intends, not what one does. One's actions are an expression of character, and it is this character that is morally important, not the actions that proceed from it. If one intends to do right, it is this intention that reveals one's true goodness, not the actions that carry out that intent; for, as we all know, the best of intentions often go awry. If I should intend to harm someone, but through a fluke or bad planning my actions inadvertently help that person instead, there is no way that I can then claim that my actions were moral, even though outwardly they may appear to be so. Of course I can always claim that my original intent was to be helpful, but then I would be lying and that would only compound my immorality.

This definition of moral goodness is also Abélard's definition of sin. Eve's disobedience occurred not when she ate the fruit, but earlier at the moment when she made the decision to disobey God's mandate not to eat. The intent and the will are the only criteria for moral judgment. Whenever one does something "wrong" believing sincerely that it is the right thing to do, then what that person does is not a sin. For example, the act of killing someone is not in itself a sin; its sinfulness depends on the circumstances of the immediate situation and one's intent within the context of that situation. Even those who killed Christ did not sin providing they were convinced in their hearts that they were doing God's will. All our natural feelings—anger, pride, selfishness, even the lust of our sexual passions—are not in themselves evil; sin and guilt arise from our giving in to them in hurtful ways; and it is the "giving in to" that God judges. There is an element of the ridiculous in holding people morally reprehensible for having natural physical responses. God punishes our bad intentions rather than our "bad" actions. In the final analysis, sin is disobedience to conscience; when blinded by ignorance or coerced into performing a forbidden action, so that conscience is not violated, there is no sin. A free conscience must always be our guide.

CODA

Abélard has been likened to a brilliant meteor that streaked through the dark skies of the twelfth century, lighting up the night, and then was too soon gone. In him thoughtful reasoning had a valiant advocate in a time when advocacy was still extremely dangerous, and for it he paid a heavy price. This is Abélard's noblest legacy. He elevated philosophy to a central position as the discipline for distinguishing what is true from what is false, a definition not greatly at variance with those of Plato and Aristotle. Though philosophy will remain for another two centuries the means of harmonizing reason and church doctrine, Abélard's dialectical system will be adopted by later thinkers to become the standard methodology of the Scholastics of the thirteenth century; it will reach the peak of its development in the *Summa Theologiae* of Thomas Aquinas.

ENDNOTES

1 Philip Schaff, *History of the Christian Church* (Scribner's, 1910; reprint, Eerdmans, 1950), vol. 5. pp. 594ff.
2 Schaff, *History*, vol. 5, p. 588f.
3 Schaff, *History*, vol. 4, p. 778ff.
4 The encounter at Ravenna is summarized from *History of Philosophy*, by William Turner (Ginn and Co., 1903), pp. 259f.
5 Schaff, *History*, vol.5, p. 608. This picture of life as a bridge bears haunting resemblance to the Zoroastrian description of souls crossing the Chinvat Bridge. See the *Sardar Bundahishn*, 95.5–20. We have no evidence that Anselm was acquainted with Parsi literature; the similarities are doubtless due to fears, hopes, and attitudes toward life, shared by humans everywhere, giving birth to similar imagery. See also *Philosophy: An Introduction to the Art of Wondering*, by James L. Christian, 6th ed. (Harcourt Brace, 1994), pp. 562f. For comparison also, see Jonathan Edwards's famous sermon "Sinners in the Hand of an Angry God."
6 For a brief but excellent analysis of the ontological argument, see *The Problem of God*, by Peter Angeles (Charles E. Merrill, 1974), pp. 1–16.
7 Schaff, *History*, vol. 5, p. 613.
8 Schaff, *History*, vol. 5, pp. 619f.
9 Schaff, *History*, vol. 5, p. 620.

CHAPTER 20

ARABIAN AND JEWISH PHILOSOPHY DURING THE MIDDLE AGES

The Greek literary heritage is translated into Syriac, Arabic, and Latin and makes its way to European scholars; Arabian philosophy reaches its pinnacle in the writings of ibn-Sīnā and ibn-Rushd; Jewish philosophy peaks in the work of Maimonides; their struggle over reason and belief is a clone of the Latin experience.

SYRIAC BEGINNINGS

Between the Tigris and Euphrates Rivers in northern Mesopotamia, there emerged during the second century AD a kingdom that was destined to play a pivotal role in Western philosophy. The kingdom was Syria, and its language, Syriac, became the prime vehicle by which ancient Greek learning was carried into the Islāmic world whence it was transmitted to the Latin West. Without the labors of the Syrian scholars, almost the entire body of Greek writings might well have perished forever.

Syriac was a Semitic language belonging to the Aramaic family, with a script of consonants only, written from right to left. Aramaic was the native language of Palestine and Western Syria and the tongue spoken by Jesus and his disciples; the daughter dialect, Syriac, is therefore significant for its closeness to early Christian thought and writing. By about AD 200 an extensive Syriac literature was beginning to develop, centered in the city of Edessa, which was by then the intellectual capital of the Christian Orient—the "Athens of Syria." This literature began with the translation of the Bible and Church Fathers into Syriac, then proceeded to include the works of the Greek philosophers, scientists, and medical writers. Fortunately, the earlier renderings into Syriac were very literal, and this fact helped later scholars reconstruct the original Greek texts of works otherwise lost.

In the fifth century a prolonged struggle split the Syrian Church; in AD 489 large numbers of Syrian Christians, including the best scholars, were driven from Edessa. They fled eastward and settled in Persia. Welcomed by Sassanid rulers, Syriac schools soon flourished in Persian cities. One such center, Jundi-Shapur, became a famed center of Greek learning and medical teaching. There Sergius of Reshaina (died c. 536) gained renown as a Christian priest, physician, and translator. He translated into Syriac Aristotle's *Categories* and Porphyry's introduction to the *Categories*; even more famed were his translations of Greek medical writers, including almost all the works of Galen. Then drawing on Greek astronomy he composed two books of

If you have two loaves of bread, sell one and buy a hyacinth.
PERSIAN SAYING

Deliver us, oh Allah, from the sea of names!
IBN AL-'ARABĪ

Cave ab homine unius libri.
Beware the man of one book.
LATIN PROVERB

his own, *On the Influence of the Moon* and *The Movement of the Sun*. Another key figure in the preservation of Greek learning was Severus Sebokt (writing c. 640), who lived at a convent on the Euphrates River where he taught Greek, Greek logic, and astronomy, and translated into Syriac the writings of Aristotle and Ptolemy. By the sixth century Syrian scholars had translated and commented on almost all the Greek philosophers and scientists, and had thus preserved the substance of the Greek intellectual world.

Cucullus non facit monachum.
The cowl does not make a monk.
MEDIEVAL PROVERB

Before the advent of Islāmic religion, Arabians were not well educated. Their heritage was rich in practical wisdom expressed orally in proverbs, anecdotes, wise sayings, and fables, but they possessed no literary tradition. When, as Muslims, they burst out of Arabia in the early seventh century, they came into contact with Greek civilization through the peoples they conquered. They overran Syria in AD 634, Babylonia in 637, Assyria in 640, and Egypt in 642. Wherever the Muslims carried the message of Muhammad they eagerly absorbed the cultural riches of the conquered peoples. In Syria Christian scholars and monks became educators in the Islāmic schools and passed along the Greek learning tradition; the Arabian intellect was soon thoroughly Hellenized. Within a century the Arabs had translated virtually the entire Greek corpus of philosophy and science, some from the original Greek but largely from Syriac. As they moved farther to the east, they came into contact with Hindu scholars and from them learned the use of "Arabic" numerals and algebra. Damascus and Baghdad became cultural hubs from which radiated other learning centers that included schools and universities, libraries, and observatories.

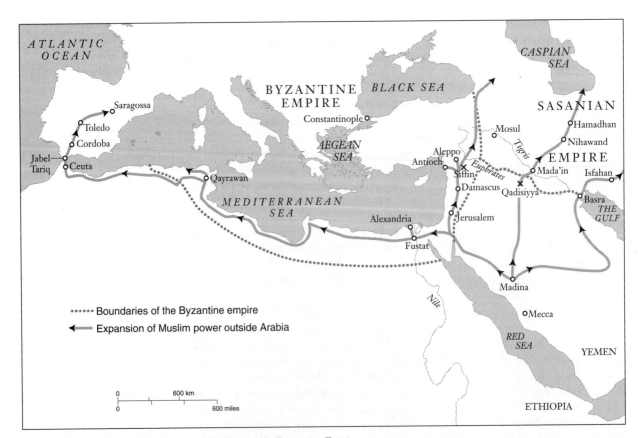

The spread of Muslim hegemony outside Arabia and the Byzantine Empire.

After the Muslims wrested Spain from its Christian roots and established the Moorish kingdom, what survived from the Greek culture was carried westward; a veritable traffic of cultural exchange burgeoned during the ninth to the thirteenth centuries. Muslim pilgrims to Mecca, Medina, and other holy sites returned with new ideas. Muslim students from Spain joined academic circles of Baghdad and Damascus; graduate students from Spanish universities pursued graduate programs at colleges in Syria, Iraq, and the Hijaz. Spanish universities invited eastern professors to give courses. All these carriers of culture brought with them books and knowledge and skills that were eventually to pass into Christian Europe and stimulate the stagnant conditions into a new European Latin Christian civilization.

By AD 900 a substantial intellectual culture had developed at Córdoba, Granada, Toledo, and Seville. Research was conducted in physics, chemistry, astronomy, mathematics, physiology, medicine, surgery, and philosophy. Teachers taught their students geography by the use of globes; hands-on astronomy was taught in observatories; medicine and surgery were taught in classrooms and hospitals; serious research was carried on in well-stocked libraries. Applications of Greek science produced the pendulum clock, compass, and gunpowder. Spanish cities boasted magnificent mosques, public baths, aqueducts, and paved streets lit by lamps.

By AD 1000 Greek philosophy and science in Spain had reached the point where it attracted scholars from Christian Europe. An English monk named Adelhard traveled to Córdoba about AD 1120 and took home the rudiments of arithmetic, geometry, and algebra; he then wrote a textbook on geometry that was widely used in European universities. Gerard of Cremona (died 1187) studied at the university at Toledo and became a sort of translating machine, translating no fewer than eighty books from the Arabic. Those of Gerard's translations that most impacted the West were al-Rāzī's *Comprehensive Book*, four of al-Kindī's scientific treatises, and the giant medical *Canon* of ibn-Sīnā, which was used in the universities of Paris and Louvain till about 1650. Also important were his renderings of Ptolemy's *Almagest*, the Spanish scientist ibn al-Haythan's book on optics, and the Toledan tables of astronomical observations. All these Latin translations Gerard carried back to Italy, whence they were diffused throughout Europe. Monks from other countries studied in Spain all during the twelfth century.

In vino veritas. *In wine is truth.*
QUOTED BY PLATO

BYZANTINE PHILOSOPHY

Early on in the Christian era, philosophy had fallen on hard times. Philo Judaeus had rendered reason essentially impotent by making it submit to theology, and the Church Fathers followed his lead, or ignored philosophy altogether, or—as with Tertullian—fought it tooth and nail. The Byzantine emperor Justinian officially banished "pagan" philosophy from Athens when he forced the Academy to close its doors in AD 529. Also, from about that date, the great Aristotelian school of Alexandria became Christianized and critical intellect was stilled; a century later, in AD 641, when the Muslims took the city, Greek philosophizing came to an end.

But like repressed faculties of the mind, when philosophy is banned in a culture it will invariably go underground and reappear elsewhere to carry on its work. Its first reappearance was at Constantinople. About AD 500 an anonymous Neoplatonic writer whom we call "Pseudo-Dionysius"° had written a series of treatises in which he combined a heady Neoplatonism with Christian doctrine, and this work had a profound effect on the recovery of Byzantine philosophy. Around AD 660 Maximus the Confessor drew upon Pseudo-Dionysius to recast Christian doctrine into a

The whole movement [of Arabian philosophy] is little more than a chapter in the history of Aristotelianism.
WILLIAM WALLACE

"The friends of my youth, where are they?"

The echo answered, "Where are they?"

ARAB SAYING

° See pp. 326ff.

pantheistic and mystical worldview. In the eighth century the theology of John of Damascus reveals his knowledge of, and love of, Aristotle; in the third book of his encyclopedic *Fountain of Knowledge* he was inspired by Aristotle to reflect at length on the stars, planets, comets, oceans, and other subjects in the natural sciences.

In the ninth century Photius, a patriarch of Constantinople and one of the great scholars of the Middle Ages, assembled a massive digest of Greek literature in his *Bibliothêkê* and wrote a series of commentaries on Aristotle. In AD 1045 the University of Constantinople was established, and an interest in philosophy was revitalized. Michael Psellus the Younger, a Neoplatonist, wrote commentaries on Aristotle and Plato. Johannes Italus established a school of Platonism at the imperial court of Constantinople; he wrote ninety-three short treatises in an attempt to syncretize Platonic metaphysics and Aristotelian logic. At a synod in 1082 he was condemned and confined to a monastery for rationalizing the mysteries of faith. Eustratius (c. 1100) wrote commentaries on Aristotle and Plato and was also condemned. In the thirteenth century two great Byzantine scholars Nicephorus Blemmydes and George Pachymeres wrote important treatises derived from Aristotle's philosophy.

The works of these Byzantine thinkers became available to the Latin Schoolmen after the Crusaders took Constantinople in 1204 and returned to Europe laden with treasures; these further stimulated Latin intellectual activity and provided corrections to the texts that had been secured from the Arabs of Spain.

ARABIAN PHILOSOPHY IN THE EAST

There are many paths to the top of the mountain.

THOMAS MERTON

Immediately upon the conquest of new cultures by the Muslims, Islāmic scholars acquired the writings of Aristotle and Plato, and, flushed with the freedom and excitement of critical reflection, began themselves to philosophize and write. So the cultural flow westward included a modicum of Byzantine thought and massive amounts of Arabian speculation.

The greatest Arabian philosophers in the East were al-Kindī, al-Rāzī, al-Fārābī, ibn-Sīnā, al-Ghazālī, and 'Omar Khāyyam. All except 'Omar were devout Aristotelians, and it was they, long before the Latins, who first glorified Aristotle as the supreme thinker of all time, the philosopher in whom human intelligence reached its full potential.

AL-KINDĪ

The full name of this Arab prince was Abū-Yūsuf Ya'Qūb ibn Ishāq al-Kindī; Western Schoolmen knew him as Alkindius. He was the first important Arabian philosopher (that is, of "Arabian blood"; he had Yemeni origins) and therefore became known as "the philosopher of the Arabs." Born about AD 801 (185 AH) in Basra (presently Al-Basrah in Iraq, some forty miles north of the Kuwaiti border), he was educated and lived in Baghdad where he died shortly after 870. Endowed with a gifted intellect, he chose a career in medicine and became court physician and tutor to the royal family in Baghdad. He made translations of Aristotle's writings and wrote commentaries on them. For a century or so he was considered the greatest philosopher of the Aristotelian-Neoplatonic tradition. Al-Kindī was an encyclopedic polymath: At least 361 works are ascribed to him, twenty-seven in philosophy, twenty-two in medicine, twenty-two in psychology, and the rest in various fields—mathematics, music, astronomy, geography, optics, physics, and politics; he even wrote treatises on cooking, sword manufacture, and word-puzzles.

In the history of philosophy al-Kindī is important (1) for preserving Greek philosophy and giving it a home in Arabian thought; (2) for introducing natural theology into Islāmic tradition.

Al-Kindī defined philosophy as "the knowledge of things as they are in reality." It discovers universal knowledge; it is therefore not culture conditioned or limited by time or place or religion. Philosophic reflection can often lead to the same conclusions as theological reflection. By the use of philosophic reasoning tinged with empiricism ("natural theology"), he attempted to prove that the world was created out of nothing at a point in time and that it would dissolve back into nothing at some future date. The content of his philosophy was essentially an Aristotelian framework seen through Neoplatonism and filled in with Islāmic doctrine.

For his philosophic ideas al-Kindī found himself in deep trouble. His view of philosophy as the path to reality was branded by the 'ulamā (orthodox theologians) as dangerous nonsense; at one point they seized his books. So al-Kindī tried to compromise: there can be no contradiction between reason and religion, he decided; the one is for intellectuals who are guided by reason, the other is for the unlettered masses who live by faith. These are really dual expressions of the same truths. This was the first appearance of the "two-truth" doctrine that was to plow a violent path in later Arabic and Christian thinking.

Al-Kindī's influence on Latin philosophy and science was great. In the judgment of the sixteenth-century Italian scholar Geronimo Cardono he was one of the twelve great minds of history. His treatise on optics reopened the science of optics in Europe; his work on musical theory stimulated European musical composition. Of his extant works, most are preserved in Latin.

In silence man can most readily preserve his integrity.
MEISTER ECKHART

AL-RĀZĪ

Known to the Latins as Rhazes, the Arabic name of this celebrated Persian philosopher and physician was Abū Bakr Muhammad ibn Zakarīyā' al-Rāzī. Born near modern Tehran in AD 865, he began his career studying alchemy but ended it as a physician and surgeon. Living an itinerant existence, he received the patronage of various minor rulers before becoming chief physician, first at a hospital in Rayy, then in Baghdad.

In his thinking al-Rāzī was a courageous nonconforming rationalist; he made no attempt to reconcile philosophy and religion because, he said, they were irreconcilable.

In philosophy al-Rāzī thought of himself as an Islāmic Socrates; in medicine he identified himself as an Islāmic Hippocrates. His autobiography is a vigorous defense of the philosophic life. He said that he was a follower of Plato, but his interpretations of the Academic are unique. He studied Democritus (in Arabic) and created his own atomic theory of matter.

Do you not know, my son, with what little understanding the world is ruled?
POPE JULIUS III

Razi's pragmatic thinking was seasoned with more than a pinch of empiricism. When choosing the best location for a hospital in Baghdad, he tested the healthiness of various environments by hanging up strips of meat and then noting the time and amount of spoilage that occurred in each locale. As a radical rationalist he scoffed at the notion of divine prophecy, challenged Qur'ānic doctrine, and said theology must defer to philosophy. All prophets, he said, from Jesus to Muhammad, are frauds, all theologies false.

Al-Rāzī wrote some two hundred works; about half of them survive. His most influential books are in medicine. *The Comprehensive Book (al-Hawi)* was an all-inclusive encyclopedia that summed up all that was known from Greek, Syriac, Persian, Hindu, and early Arabic medicine. Translated into Latin it became a standard textbook in Western medical schools. Numerous other minor medical treatises, including his *Treatise on Smallpox and Measles*, also impacted Western science.

AL-FĀRĀBĪ

Born of Turkish stock in Turkistan about 878, al-Fārābī was taken by his father to Baghdad where he learned Arabic, studied mathematics, medicine, and philosophy, and spent his life in relative quietude. In AD 942 he joined the court of the prince at Aleppo; he died at Damascus about 950.

His full name was Muhammad ibn Muhammad ibn Tarkhān ibn Uzalagh al-Fārābī —Alfarabius to Latin scholars. Known as the greatest teacher since Aristotle, with him Islāmic philosophy came of age. His principal accomplishment was to show how Greek thought could clarify and resolve the bothersome questions that plagued Islāmic thinkers. He judged that, in the Mediterranean world, philosophy had exhausted itself, but that, in Islām, it could acquire new meaning and play a major role in developing Islāmic theology.

Al-Fārābī was essentially a political philosopher, the first in Islāmic tradition. His two major books were *The Political Régime*, inspired by Aristotle's politics, and *An Epistle on the Opinions of the Superior City's People*, a utopian vision modeled on Plato's *Republic* and the *Laws*. He depicted society as a living organism metaphorically similar to the human body. The ruler is the head; he issues directions to the body's organs, which, in turn, transmit instructions to the rest of the system.

Al-Fārābī held the dangerous notion that religious faith could not meet the needs of an intellectual thinker, for whom reason is superior to belief. Religious faith is adequate for the masses; it provides sufficient truth in myths and symbols that can be understood by those not capable of critical thought. But for intellectuals the truth stands clear and unsullied by popular forms of apprehension. Like Plato's philosopher-king—and with a supportive nod to Machiavelli's prince— al-Fārābī envisions the state ruled by philosopher-prophets who understand the function of faith in society and politics; they have the wisdom and the power to transform the truth into mythic form and thereby inspire people to live nobler lives. He believed the world of his time was experiencing chaos because governments were not governed by philosophers.

Al-Fārābī also held the unfashionable conviction that all mankind should have but one religion, though different religions would continue to exist as symbolic expressions of the essential faith. In addressing the problems of daily life, ideas from all religions would be useful. Some ideas are better than others, of course, but every religion can be a rich source of pragmatic ideas for those who believe.

Al-Fārābī's psychology was Aristotelian. The goal of human life is happiness, and this can be achieved only through the development of the intellectual virtues. Those who fail to develop their rational faculties will lose their immortality; for them death will mean the end of the body and soul together.

Al-Fārābī was a major influence on ibn-Sīnā and ibn-Rushd and, through them, on Latin political thought.

IBN-SĪNĀ

His name in Arabic was Abū 'Alī al-Husain ibn 'Abd Allāh ibn Sīnā, but he was known to the West by the Latinized transliteration of ibn-Sīnā—Avicenna. He was one of the great philosopher-scientists of the Arab world, though during his lifetime he was best known as a great physician. In him both philosophy and medicine reached their highest achievement.

In the history of Western philosophy ibn-Sīnā is important (1) for developing further the double-truth doctrine to reconcile reason and faith; (2) for his application of Greek knowledge to the field of medicine; (3) for his impact on Scholastic speculation where traces of his thinking can be found all through thirteenth- and fourteenth-century philosophy.

Born about AD 980 in Bokhara, his entire life was spent in the cities and towns of Khorasan in northeastern Persia. His father was a lay scholar who entertained learned intellectuals in his home; ibn-Sīnā breathed in the rich atmosphere of worthwhile ideas from his earliest days. By the time he was twenty-one he was already famed as a physician. Because of the troubled times, he wandered from place to place healing the sick. At Hamadan he became court physician and vizier. His duties as doctor to the royal family and civil administrator he carried out during the day; his evenings were spent in discussing philosophy with students in sessions that often lasted till the early morning hours; or he would write. The last fourteen years of his life were spent in relative quietude at the court in Isfahan. He fell ill while accompanying the caliph on a military campaign and died at Hamadan in 1037. He was fifty-eight.

Ibn-Sīnā possessed an unusually clear and synoptic mind. He was especially admired for his memory. After reading a page through just a few times he would have it memorized and available for use for the rest of his life. By the time he was ten he had memorized the Qur'ān and vast amounts of Arab classical literature. He studied logic, but quickly learned to outthink his teachers. From ten to eighteen he read, without guidance, everything he could find in philosophy, mathematics, astronomy, and medicine. At the age of seventeen his medical knowledge enabled him to cure the caliph of a serious illness, and as a reward he was allowed access to the volume-rich royal library, which, we are told, he then read and mastered in eighteen months. "By the time I was eighteen I was finished with all of these sciences," he later wrote; "today my knowledge is more mature, otherwise it is the same; nothing has come to me since." By twenty-one he was an accomplished scholar in all known branches of knowledge. For a time he was stymied by Aristotle's *Metaphysics*; even after forty readings he said he still didn't understand it; then he found a copy of al-Fārābī's commentary, and it began to make sense.

The function [of the human soul] is to wait for the revelation of truths.

IBN-SĪNĀ

By virtue of his [Man's] animal soul he shares with the animals; his physical soul links him with the plants; his human soul is a bond between him and the angels.

IBN-SĪNĀ

Ibn Sina surrounded by students

During the political turmoil of his times, ibn-Sīnā wrote continuously; the last period of his life at Isfahan was the most productive. Two of the great books in the history of medicine were his *Book of Healing (Kitab an-najat)*, a veritable encyclopedia of philosophy and the sciences, and the *Canon of Medicine (al-Qanun fi at-tibb)*, often called the most important medical work ever composed. The first, heavily indebted to Aristotle and Neoplatonism and written in Persian, spelled out his philosophy; it has been judged to be the largest work ever written on philosophy by a single author. It opens with logic and then goes on to physics, metaphysics, geology, meteorology, botany and zoology, mathematics and music, and psychology. The *Canon* was a systematic encyclopedia of Greek and Arabic medical knowledge that remained a major textbook in the field till about 1650 in the West and till the nineteenth century in Islām. Its five massive books deal with physiology, pathology, hygiene, methods of treating diseases, and the preparation of medicines.

All together ibn-Sīnā wrote some two hundred treatises, including forty-three medical works, a *Book of Theorems*, works on mysticism, and a poem on the soul. At one point he was told that he didn't understand Arabic philology, so he spent three years studying it and wrote a huge tome on it titled *The Arabic Language (Lisan al-arab)*. His most personal work was the *Book of Directives and Remarks (Kitab al-isharat wa attanbihat)* in which he narrates the soul's mystical journey from its first faithful steps to its final ecstatic illumination in God.

Although he is called the master of the Muslim Aristotelians, his philosophy is more that of Neoplatonism than of Aristotle or Islām. He followed no school of thought slavishly, but studied philosophical systems both East and West and syncretized them into his own worldview. In God essence and existence coincide; what he is and that he is are one and the same; his unchanging attributes are identical with his essence. He is wholly transcendent. He is an uncaused cause. God does not create, he emanates; and the timeless multiplication of beings from the Divine is a result of his self-knowledge. His creation is not ex nihilo, for matter has existed eternally, without beginning or end. Matter (that is, inert, unformed matter—the "primal matter" of Aristotle, the *materia prima* of the Scholastics) is pure potentiality; its timeless existence is wholly independent of God. The physical universe emanates in triadic spheres from him, and the heavenly bodies are given form by the Active Intellect, which also provides motion to the sublunary regions. The Active Intellect is the source of the human soul. All things that exist contingently depend for their existence on a necessary being, which is God. (This may be one source of Anselm's famous Ontological Argument for the existence of God.)

Ibn-Sīnā elaborated the "double-truth" doctrine launched by al-Kindī, applied to politics by al-Fārābī, then revised and given wide recognition by ibn-Rushd. The superior intuitions of men of intellect contrast greatly to the uncritical, literal thinking of the masses. Leaders with clear minds and vivid imaginations can create solutions to society's problems and then persuade the populace to implement those solutions. The ruler, who is an embodiment of the Divine Active Intellect, can translate the truth into the symbolic language of faith of ordinary men, who will then take it literally and act upon it.

Ibn-Sīnā too, in company with the other Arab thinkers, was attacked by defenders of the faith. The idea of physical resurrection is taught explicitly by the Qur'ān, but ibn-Sīnā rejected the notion because a reasoning mind can't make sense of it. His teaching (from Aristotle) that the world is eternal also clashed with the Islāmic tenet that creation took place out of nothing by God's willing at a point in time.

Ibn-Sīnā's influence was enormous. There are hundreds of references to him in Aquinas's works, which became a principal conduit for the entrance of Arab thought into European theology. The universities at Paris, Cologne, and Oxford became centers of Arab studies where students of philosophy and theology knew ibn-Sīnā well. Roger Bacon counted him the greatest scholar since Aristotle.

But in the East, ibn-Sīnā marked the end of speculative thinking among the Arabs; after him intellectual energies were again channeled into theology. "But happily," writes Philip Hitti, "as the sun of philosophy waned in the East it waxed in the West, reaching its meridian in ibn-Rushd, an Arab follower of ibn-Sīnā and native of Spain."[1]

AL-GHAZĀLĪ

It is sad that this Persian theologian must be included in the history of philosophy, for in this context he comes across as a mean-spirited reactionary who spent his life defending the status quo and attacking all who entertained ideas that differed from his. But there is another side to al-Ghazālī: He was, in his time, devoutly loved and admired as a man, a mystic, and a champion of the Islāmic faith; and one senses an authenticity in his spiritual odyssey that drew the devotion of his Sūfī followers, making his story a classic in Sūfī literature. Morever—with not a hint of hypocrisy—he himself espoused mystical doctrines that differed dangerously from mainstream Islāmic orthodoxy and aroused the wrath of the 'ulamā. Known in the West as Algazel, his full name was Abū Hāmid Muhammad al-Ghazālī. He was not a creative philosopher in his own right, but a critic who spent his life explaining mysticism and defending religion against the falāsifa. His writings reveal an obsession with his own inner experience, which he draws upon to schematize the journey of the soul to God. Al-Ghazālī has been called the Augustine of Islām. His influence is still considerable in the Sunni branch of Islām.

Born about 1058 in the northeastern province of Khorasan, he died there in AD 1111. He was educated in the orthodox tradition at Tus and Nīshāpūr and quickly gained recognition as a expert in Islāmic law. But at the age of thirty-six he experienced a personal crisis of faith, a quandary brought on by uncertainty about what he could believe. He found that he didn't believe what he was teaching. He sought something that was deeper and more authentic than the picky legalisms and fine-spun arguments of the theologians. He wanted to know God, not knowledge about God. At the time he was a teacher at a university in Baghdad, but in 1095 he left his job, donned the woolen robe of Sūfī mystics, and wandered for ten years seeking answers to life's problems—answers that would, for him, ring true. "Worldly desires began tugging me with their claims to remain as I was, while the herald of faith was crying out, 'Away! Up and away!'"[2] Searching for this intimate truth, he moved through the Muslim world, visiting Syria, Egypt, and the holy cities of Mecca and Medina. Like Socrates, he sought out members of various religious and theosophical sects and asked them about their criteria for knowing what is true and how they knew it. The Shī'is told him to find an authority and follow him without question, but such unquestioning discipleship seemed fraught with danger; he feared that he might be led, unknowingly, to follow teachings that differed with the Qur'ān. The result, finally, was a recognition that only Muhammad's revelation, the "light that God casts into the hearts of His servants, a gift and present from him," is valid. This result also produced in him a deep revulsion against the inordinate claims of the rational intellect and a lifelong dedication to the tarīqah, the mystical path to knowledge.

Al-Ghazālī can be best understood against the background of Sūfī mysticism, to which he was converted and for which he became the supreme spokesman. Sūfism developed during the eighth and ninth centuries as a way of renouncing the dissolute Islāmic society, and the movement generally maintains a dual stance: love of God vis-à-vis hatred of the world. But renunciation of self—of one's I-hood—was the

The words of Lovers passionate in their intoxication and ecstasy must be hidden away and not spoken of.
AL-GHAZĀLĪ

Allāh knows of the creeping of a black ant upon the rough rock in the dark of night.
AL-GHAZĀLĪ

The highest point a man can attain is not knowledge, or virtue, or goodness, or victory, but something even greater, more heroic and more despairing: sacred awe!
NIKOS KAZANTZAKIS

essential thing if progress is to be achieved in the spiritual life. Early Sūfīs practiced asceticism—fasting, vigils, and meditation on the Scriptures. To symbolize their abandonment of the world and their proverty they wore garments of wool (*sūf*, whence their name). Their goal was to free themselves from every tie except God. "The *zāhid* (ascetic) is one who is controlled by nothing other than God," said the Sūfī Masrūq. "Hands empty of worldly possessions," wrote al-Junayd of Baghdad, "and hearts empty of all attachments"—this is the Sūfī saint.

It is love that moves the sun and other stars.

SŪFĪ MYSTIC

Sūfism soon reached beyond the shadows and began to focus more on the love of God. Al-Ghazālī said that the human quest is complete when the human heart has become fully possessed by God's love. "It is love that moves the sun and the other stars." All love—whatever its object—is a species of God's all-pervasive love and is therefore good. With love, a beauty and a serenity can be detected beneath the surface of even the world's darkest offenses. "Drunken with a drunkenness wherein the sway of intelligence disappears," the self in love is extinguished, and the soul experiences unification with God. Al-Ghazālī and others often used the metaphor of God as divine Lover.

> The beloved knocks at the door of the Lover.
> "Who is there?" asks the Lover.
> "It is I," replies the beloved.
> "This house cannot hold both me and thee," comes the reply. The beloved goes away and, in solitude, weeps and prays. After much time the beloved returns and knocks again.
> The Voice asks, "Who is there?"
> "It is Thou."

Immediately the door opens, and Lover and Beloved are face to face at last.[3] Al-Ghazālī adds, "The words of Lovers lost in the passion of their ecstasy must be honored; they must be respected, and hidden away, and not spoke of."[4]

Out of al-Ghazālī's spiritual crisis came his monumental manifesto of conservatism, *The Revival of the Sciences of Religion (Ihya 'ulum al-din)*. In it he launched his attack on three fronts. (1) He wanted to prove that legalistic theology (*kalām*), as expounded by the orthodox *'ulamā*, was bankrupt. (2) He wanted to expose and destroy every philosophical idea that contradicted the truth of the Qur'ān. (3) He wanted to redirect Sūfī mysticism back to the path from which it had strayed.

Your intuition is excellent, but another viewpoint could be helpful.

CHINESE FORTUNE COOKIE

His *Revival* was an in-depth analysis of what could be called "The Art of Being Islāmic."[5] Not unlike Augustine's *Confessions*, he blazed the trail, in great detail, that the mystic must travel, pointing out temptations and dangers to be faced along the way and describing the milestones that mark the soul's journey. The journey is not the quiescent passage of a Taoist sage or Theravada monk, but an inner *jihād*, a holy wrestling match with the lower nature. It is a touch-and-go struggle between the aspiring soul and the evil within the sinful self. The soul slowly moves from the mundane to the divine, from angst to bliss, from an ego-centered pride to a surrender of self in union with God. Al-Ghazālī avoided the blasphemous sin of *shirk*—placing other beings on a par with God—by making it clear that the soul, in its uniting with the Divine, does not become God. There exists always an awesome gap between God and sinful man. The mystic can experience the ecstasy of a spiritually drunken state, but he would, so to speak, sober up and realize that he was still man, not God.

Al-Ghazālī finally found peace in a mystical certainty that the laws of life are revealed, not by the powers of reason, but by belief in God and the Qur'ān. Only the mystic who is immersed in the love of God is able to see the world as it really is. "Gleams of the truth will shine in his heart" (not in his head, note). The hunger of the heart, which leads to true knowledge, is more important than the acquisitions of the mind, which will deceive.

In his so-called autobiography titled *The Deliverer from Error (al-Munqidh min al-dalal)*, al-Ghazālī speaks of his journey:

> I realized that I was caught in a veritable thicket of attachments. . . . I examined the motives that drove me in my teaching and realized that it was not a pure desire for the things of God. The impulse that moved me was a desire for the prestige of position and public acclaim. I saw clearly that I was standing on a crumbling bank of sand and in certain danger of hell-fire unless I did something about it immediately. . . . So, being driven to Him because I had no other recourse, I abandoned my position and wealth, left behind my children and friends, and sought refuge in the Most High God.[6]

It is understandable that al-Ghazālī came to see philosophy as an insidious force eroding the foundations of Islāmic faith. He therefore concluded that philosophy must begin and end with the truth as revealed in the Qur'ān and the Hadīth. Reason must surrender to faith. God must be removed from analysis and definition. If Muslims did not follow the word of Allāh, they would be abandoned to their own depraved wills and the fallacious speculations of false prophets. To this end he wrote tirelessly, with reason, to destroy the reason of the philosophers. He attacked twenty of their favorite arguments in a famous work (that drew a famous reply from ibn-Rushd) called *The Self-Destruction of the Philosophers (Tahafut al-falisīfa)*. In it he claims to have destroyed the Aristotelian-Neoplatonic doctrines that matter is eternal, that the heavenly bodies have souls, that soul is the cause of motion, and that causality exists in reality. Reason, therefore, as employed by philosophers, cannot be a source of certainty.

The notion of causality was an especially tempting target because it was the foundation stone on which all science rests and, if undermined, could cause the entire empirical structure to collapse. In our experience two events may be observed occurring close together, and we glibly say that one causes the other. But al-Ghazālī argued that a causal connection between the two events is not something we actually see; rather "causality" is a notion that we impose on what we see. The mind associates the two observed events and becomes convinced that they are necessarily connected.° But our assumption of a "principle" of causality is false, he says. The two concurrent events are "caused," not by B necessarily following A, but by the will of God, and it is only in the Divine mind that their connection, if there is one, can be found. He writes: "They are connected as the result of the Decree of God. . . . If one follows the other, it is because He has created them in that fashion, not because the connection in itself is necessary and indissoluble."[7] Therefore, our descriptions of causally connected events do not depict the operations of reality. God is not bound by "laws" or "principles"; he can mandate the occurrence of events at will, and this includes miracles which are deemed impossible under the assumption of real causality. In a word, al-Ghazālī does away with "nature" and "natural causes."

Al-Ghazālī's attack dealt massive blows to critical philosophy in the East. It had less effect in the West. There it was answered by ibn-Rushd in his *Self-destruction of Self-destruction* in which he noted that the spectacle of a thinker using reason to destroy reason seemed like bad logic. The works of al-Ghazālī were well known to the Latin Scholastics.

Al-Ghazālī fails as a critical thinker largely because he does not possess the qualities of critical intellect. Brilliant? Yes. Creative? Yes. Sensitive to fine distinctions? Yes. But suited by aptitude for incisive judgments about words and concepts,

Creativity based on nothing takes place only in theology.
PHILIP HITTI

As the sun of philosophy waned in the East it waxed in the West, reaching its meridian in ibn-Rushd.
PHILIP HITTI

°*To this point his reasoning is pure Hume: "Hume n'a rien dit plus," said Ernst Renan; see Vol. II, pp. 140ff..*

Mystics are always easier neighbors than dogmatists.
KENNETH CRAGG

assumptions and values? No. His natural mode of thought was poetic, metaphorical, emotional, and intuitive. He writes, for example:

> God is above the Throne and the heavens. He is above everything unto the limit of the Pleiades with an aboveness that does not bring Him nearer to the Throne and the heavens, just as it does not make Him farther from the Earth and the Pleiades.[8]

These are not the phrases of a careful thinker, for whom such language would reveal a failure to value clarity; it is the language of the poet who loves words, and for whom such wordplay helps to capture the joyous flights of our wonderful imaginations and deepest emotions. One senses that critical thinking—the objective examination of ideas to establish their acceptability as truth claims—was, for al-Ghazālī, an unnatural mode of thought, as it was for Plotinus, Augustine, and countless other theologians and mystics. In fact, the language of all mysticisms, including Sūfism, is not the language of reason—nor was it ever meant to be. It is designed rather to capture a truth not available to the reasoning mind.

But al-Ghazālī doesn't seem to know this. He seems unaware that his natural mode of thinking is different from the thinking of critical philosophers, and, consequently, he condemns them for the difference. Al-Ghazālī's "spiritual" way of thinking increases the power of religious imagery, contributes to the efficacy of faith, and assists mightily in the solidification of orthodoxy. It is never comfortable with new ideas, new realms of knowledge, and new insights, connections, and understandings; it has no regard whatever for the claims of empirical observation.

'OMAR KHĀYYAM

'Omar's influence on medieval Western thought was minimal—he was not known; and because he is known today for his poetry rather than his philosophy he is not often included in the history of philosophy. Yet, by his contemporaries, 'Omar was considered the greatest thinker of his age, and his poetry reveals an exceptional mind filled with deep thoughts about the confused state of human knowledge, the strange contradictions of our lives, and the predatory sadism of Fate and Fortune. We are enriched by Edward FitzGerald's translation of 'Omar's poignant verse in *The Rubā'iyāt of Omar Khāyyam*, but it is a major loss for both East and West that we don't possess more of his serious philosophic prose.

'Omar Khāyyam was a mathematician, astronomer, philosopher, and poet born about AD 1038 at Nīshāpūr in the extreme northeastern corner of Persia. His full name was Ghiyāthuddīn Abulfath 'Omar ibn Ibrahīm al-Khayyāmī. His talents were evident from his earliest years, and he spent his time (says his translator) "busied in winning knowledge of every kind." He received a good education in science and philosophy at Nīshāpūr and Balkh. He then moved to Samarkand where he wrote a treatise on algebra, a brilliant work that assured his fame as one of the great mathematicians of all time. The work came to the notice of the sultan Malikshah who, in 1074, placed him in charge of an observatory—"House of the Stars"—and assigned him the task of reforming the calendar. He was given a stipend in gold that freed him of material concerns so that he could labor lovingly on his star charts, geometry, mathematics, and poetry. He made a pilgrimage to Mecca following the death of his patron in 1092, then returned to Nīshāpūr where he taught and wrote in philosophy, history, mathematics, medicine, astronomy, and law. Only a few of his writings—mostly on geometry and metaphysics—and scattered epigrams and verses, are extant. Virtually all his prose work is lost.

He was respected by fellow scientists, worshiped by devoted followers, and hated by religious authorities. He spoke his mind fearlessly, criticized bigotry, superstition,

And this was all the Harvest that I reaped—

"I came like Water, and like Wind I go."

'OMAR KHĀYYAM
(STANZA 28)

Illuminated page from Nezāmī Ganjavī's Khamseh (Quintuplet). *Nezāmī (d. 1209), the first great epic poet in Persian literature, was a philosopher in love with language and the sciences. The final poem in the* Khamseh *pentology depicts Alexander the Great seated on a raised throne, meeting with the seven sages of classic antiquity: Aristotle, Apollonius, Socrates, Plato, Thales, Porphyry, and Hermes (the Hermes of Hermetic Literature).*

and mindless adherence to custom. As a result 'Omar was denounced as the "arch-freethinker" of his time and warned "to bridle his tongue." Al-Rāzī derided him as "an unhappy philosopher, atheist, and materialist" who was "confused and in error." Al-Ghazālī hated him. Al-Qifti deplored his rationalism, whose "inward meanings are to the Law stinging serpents." He converted so many to philosophy that the great Sūfī poet Jalāl al-Dīn ar-Rūmī complained "How long [will you study] this philosophy of the Greeks? Study instead the philosophy of the Faithful!" Al-Qazwini tells of a certain theologian who came to 'Omar privately in the early morning for lessons in philosophy but in the evening denounced him from the pulpit as a "freethinker and atheist."

'Omar's intensely personal philosophy is powerfully expressed in his *rubā'īyāt* (quatrains). There one feels the outpourings of a soul undergoing great personal struggle. They express outrage toward Time and Fate and the futility of the human condition. 'Omar's mind clearly sees that religion's preachments about life are all wrong. His Shī'ite tradition supplied him with a full complement of assumptions designed to prepare the believer for death and the afterlife; but these prepackaged ideas didn't satisfy, and he was forced to work out his own realities about life and death, in his own way, with courage and truth. He saw no evidence that there is a God or that we humans are the recipients of providential care. He doubts the possibility of an afterlife. The dogmatic certainty claimed by the *'ulamā* is a sham; there is no certainty. There is nothing in the fashionable corpus of religious ideas that he can put his faith into.

In twelfth-century Persia rubā'īyāt served a special purpose: freedom of expression. Since one might pay a dear price for such subversive activities as thinking, the rubā'īyāt, with veiled allusions, offered some protection from inquisitors. While other verse forms might tell stories or embody religious ideas, the rubā'īyāt

I am the Truth. *Ana-l-Haqq.*
AL-HALLAJ
(THIS STATEMENT LED
TO HIS CRUCIFIXION.)

Your Self is a copy made in the image of God, Seek in yourself all that you desire to know.
JALAL AL-DIN-RUMI

There we all are [in God] before our creation [in time].

JAN VAN RUYSBROECK

contained the more authentic feelings and ideas of its author; the most unorthodox ideas could be given innocuous interpretations so as to offend no one.

Stanzas 82 to 90 (in the fourth edition of *The Rubā'īyāt*) are daring examples of mockery and satire aimed at commonplace religious notions. The poet finds himself alone in a potter's workplace, "surrounded by shapes of Clay" standing along the floor and by the wall. He listens as the pots converse among themselves.

> Said one among them—"Surely not in vain
> My substance of the common Earth was ta'en
> And to this Figure moulded, to be broke,
> Or trampled back to shapeless Earth again."

A second clay pot answers that even the most peevish child would not destroy the bowl from which he had often drunk with much pleasure; and no thoughtful potter, even in angry moments, would shatter the vessels he had lovingly made with his own hand. A third clay pot, crudely deformed, replies that he found it hard to believe that a loving potter could create such misshapen vessels. "What! did the Hand then of the Potter shake?"

To these exchanges a small cooking pot becomes angry with the pointless banter and addresses the larger questions:

> "All this of Pot and Potter—Tell me then,
> Who is the Potter, pray, and who the Pot?"

The "ultimate questions"—who exactly is this Creator we're talking about, and what are these supposed creations?—don't receive convincing answers in the potter's shop any more than in the theological seminary. Another pot makes the observation that some people say that the "luckless Pots" spoiled by the Potter will be tossed into Hell; but that can't be true because, the pondering pot concludes, he's really a "Good Fellow, and 'twill all be well."

Lastly, a long-neglected pot murmurs that the answers make no difference, really, for his clay "is gone dry." Just "fill me with the old familiar Juice," and perhaps, someday, everything will be all right again.

'Omar thus dispenses with the obsessions of the theologians in a few short stanzas, questions that in the devout circles of the serious-minded doctors will fill lifetimes and produce numberless volumes of dialectical argument—in Greek, Arabic, Hebrew, Latin, et al., et al., et al.

People who are on the journey are a lot more interesting than people who, having found answers, are in dry dock.

LORI VILLAMIL

With a rare candor—in great contrast to the all-knowing dogmatisms of the theologians—'Omar says again and again, with a painful but refreshing eloquence, "I don't know!"

> Into this Universe, and Why not knowing
> Nor Whence, like Water willy-nilly flowing;
> And out of it, as Wind along the Waste,
> I know not Whether, willy-nilly blowing.

To be sure, he yearns to know, but . . .

> Not one returns to tell us of the Road,
> Which to discover we must travel too.

Try as he will he can't drive through to a comforting solution of his own. He does decide, in a halfhearted sort of way, that a joyous immersion in the pleasures and beauties of this life is the only alternative left to him.

Ah, make the most of what we yet may spend,
Before we too into the Dust descend; . . .

But halfhearted it remains, for he cannot stop his "seeing"—his awareness of the
Big Picture in which, *sub specie aeternitatis*, his personal strivings are merely an
insignificant and fleeting disturbance. His lines are bitterest when he sees Fate can-
celing all that he has cherished and worked for. All through his poetry one can watch
him rage, ridicule, and try to celebrate; but in the end he despairs.

The Moving Finger writes; and having writ,
Moves on: nor all your Piety nor Wit
Shall lure it back to cancel half a Line,
Nor all your Tears wash out a Word of it.

In this life, therefore, while "the Moving Finger writes," there can be no peace.
Worst of all, perhaps, is the fact that 'Omar's perceptive mind cannot stop "seeing"—at which point he wonders whether a jug of wine might not be the best
answer, even for a philosopher.

YESTERDAY *This* Day's Madness did prepare;
TO-MORROW'S Silence, Triumph, or Despair:
Drink! for you know not whence you came, nor why:
Drink! for you know not why you go, nor where.
Come, fill the Cup, and in the fire of Spring
Your Winter-garment of Repentance fling:
The Bird of Time has but a little way
To flutter—and the Bird is on the Wing.

'Omar died in the town where he was born in 1123. Today his grave is known or visited
by few. It can be found four miles southeast of Neyshābūr, adjacent to a mosque.[9]

ARABIAN PHILOSOPHY IN THE WEST

The best-known Arabian philosophers in the West were ibn-Bājjah (known to Latins
as Avempace), ibn-Tufayl (Abubacer to Schoolmen), ibn-Rushd (the incomparable
Averroës), and the gentle ibn-al-'Arabī, the greatest of the Muslim mystics.

IBN-BĀJJAH

This man was the first Western Arabian thinker in the Aristotelian-Neoplatonic
tradition; indeed what we know of his philosophy has the ring of a faintly Islāmicized

When blindness is universal,
casting stones is not a good idea.
JOAN MORRONE

Faith doesn't need documents.
MARCUS BORG

The Rubá'iyát of 'Omar Khayyam

Neoplatonism—"faintly" because he sounds more like an atheist than a devout Muslim; he rejected the authority of the Qur'ān and held that belief in immortality is wishful thinking. Born around AD 1095 at Saragossa, Spain, little is known of his short life, except that he lived during troubled times when the Christians were recapturing Andalusia. We know his full name: Abū Bakr Muhammad ibn Yahya ibn Assāyigh at-Tujībī al-Andalusī as-Saraqustī; but he was called ibn-Bājjah by Arabs and Avempace by Latins. He was very knowledgeable in medicine, mathematics, and astronomy. He was appointed vizier by the amir of Murcia and was a member of the Almoravid court at Fez, Morocco, when he was poisoned. He died in Morocco in 1138.

Besides his overall impact on the thinking of Latin Scholastics, ibn-Bājjah is important in the history of philosophy primarily for his work *Solitary Man* in which he presents an *itinerarium* for the soul's lonely journey to God.

Ibn-Bājjah wrote philosophical essays, commentaries on Aristotle, songs, poems, and a treatise on botany. The text of the philosophical work that brought him fame, long known only through secondary references, is now available from an original Arabic manuscript. *The Reign of the Solitary Man* (*Tadbīr al-mutawahhid*) is a utopian fantasy modeled on Plato's *Republic*. Designed as an "itinerary" for the journey of the soul upward, it traces the steps that the soul must take to unite itself with the Active Intellect of God. Only the "Solitary Man" can make the journey. Human societies, as we know them now, are dehumanizing collections of very imperfect selves; in them there is little hope for the etherealization of the individual. But in every society there exist spiritualized souls who fix their eyes on the ideal model of what humans can become; these individuals imagine themselves to be members of an ideal state (like Plato's republic or Augustine's city of God) where the noble potential in human life can be achieved. These special people are not really members of degenerate society—they are in it but not of it; and they are therefore "solitaries," men and women who guide themselves by the higher standards of the ideal society. The goal, so ibn-Bājjah implies, is the perfect life not only for the individual, but also for the collective achievement of a perfect society.

The path to be taken by the aspiring soul is both mystical and intellectual and is described by ibn-Bājjah in the language of Neoplatonic soteriology. The human soul, by meditating on forms, must evolve from its trapped state in gross matter to a state of pure spirit where it will become one with the Active Intellect of God. The philosophic mind, that is, rises from a contemplation of forms *with* matter to an experience of forms *without* matter, where it becomes an *intellectus acquisitus*, a mind that has acquired the perfect forms of the mind of God. There it will know the truth, or even become one with the truth. Ibn-Bājjah's *Solitary Man* is a guidebook steering the aspiring soul to its final fulfillment in the Divine.

IBN-TUFAYL

This man's full name was Abū Bakr Muhammad ibn 'Abd al-Malik ibn Muhammad ibn Muhammad ibn Tufayl al-Qaysī. Latins listened to the sound of his first name and called him Abubacer. About a dozen years younger than ibn-Bājjah and fifteen years older than ibn-Rushd, ibn-Tufayl was a celebrated Moorish philosopher and physician, born at Guádix, Spain, in AD 1109. He practiced medicine at Granada where he became secretary to the governor. Late in life he was appointed court physician and vizier to the sultan of Morocco, who was himself an amateur philosopher. The sultan supported scholars and entertained the notion of making Morocco a center of Islāmic learning, modeled on what Baghdad had become in the East. Ibn-Tufayl died in Morocco in 1185.

Ibn-Tufayl's fame rests solely with a charming story that he told of a child stranded on that proverbial desert island. The book was widely known in the Arab

Do not veil the truth with falsehood, nor conceal the truth knowingly.

QUR'ĀN 2:42

God changes not what is in a people, until they change what is in themselves.

QUR'ĀN 13:11

To whomsoever God assigns no light, no light has he.

QUR'ĀN 24:40

world; it became a favorite in Europe and England in its Latin rendering. Titled *The Living—Son of the Awakening One (Risalāt Hayy ibn Yaqdhān)*, the work was a philosophical romance describing the journey of a young truth seeker named Hayy. The boy is born (without parents!) on a desolate island, is raised by a deer, and gradually learns the rudimentary lessons about life and how the world works. He comes to see that he is different from the animals and wonders about his uniqueness. When the deer dies he begins to distinguish between the physical body and the spirit that gave it life. Over a period of fifty years, step by painful step, he comes to realize that there is within him an immortal soul and that above this life there is a God who makes it all happen. On his own, putting the pieces of life's puzzle together with his rational intellect, and using common sense, Hayy raises himself out of the material world to reside in the heavenly forms and become one with the Supreme Intellect. There this hermit-sage from the barren island apprehends the truth about the operations of the universe. He sees the rhythm of emanation and return. He beholds the emanation-beings flowing out of the One, descending from level to level, down to the horizon of the stars where form becomes matter. And he beholds returning spirits moving upward toward the One.

Then Hayy meets another human being, and together they make a visit to human society where Hayy discovers that there is a hierarchy of intelligences, ranging from those who seek the truth through reason to those who are in love with the world and care nothing for the truth. To these latter ones, Hayy advises them to "model themselves after their pious ancestors and leave aside new-fangled ideas"—since this is the only path they are able to follow. Hayy, by contrast, belongs to the few who possess the capacity to ascend to God, and that he has done.

Ibn-Tufayl's vision of a better world is in the tradition of the great utopias, from Plato's Magnesia° to Thomas More's *Utopia*, Voltaire's *Candide*, Rousseau's *Émile*, Defoe's *Robinson Crusoe*, H. G. Wells's *Modern Utopia*, and many others. Something there is in us that yearns deeply to set straight a crazy, broken world, if not in reality then in thought. The cosmic background of the story of Hayy, which gives it its spiritual dimension, is Neoplatonism, and Ibn-Tufayl's tale is a graphic retelling, in the language of philosophic poetry, of ibn-Bājjah's account of the soul's ascent to God.

° See p. 166.

Thou seest the mountains and thou deemest them affixed, but in truth they are as fleeting as the clouds.

QUR'ĀN 27:88

IBN-RUSHD

By far the greatest of the Arabian thinkers to come out of the Islāmicized Spanish culture, this man—Averroës to the Latins—was, like so many of the Muslim intellectuals, a polymath. Renowned especially for his commentaries on Aristotle, for whom he possessed boundless admiration, he was his own thinker; he composed original treatises on law, grammar, astronomy, medicine, theology, and philosophy. He earned his living as a lawyer, physician, and philosopher.

Ibn-Rushd is remembered in the history of philosophy (1) for the doctrine of the unity of intellect; (2) for his refinement of the (misnamed) "double-truth" doctrine designed to reconcile reason and revelation; (3) for his lifelong running battle with orthodox theologians in defense of the intellectual life; (4) for his definition of religion and the religious life; (5) for his considerable influence on the Latin Schoolmen, an impact that endured for over four centuries.

Known as Abū al-Walīd Muhammad ibn Ahmad ibn Muhammad ibn Rushd, he was born in Córdoba in 1126 and died in Morocco in 1198. His family had a long tradition of successful judges and lawyers, and he was himself highly trained in the Islāmic sciences, qualified, that is, to interpret the Qur'ān, Hadīth, and Fiqh—Scripture, Tradition, and Law. In Islām a lawyer was an expert in both civil and divine law; ibn-Rushd was therefore a theologian as well as legal scholar and practitioner.

He who has a thousand friends has not a friend to spare,

And he who has one enemy will meet him everywhere.

ALI IBN-ABI-TALIB

Statue of Ibn Rushd (1126–1198) in Córdoba, Spain

Through ibn-Tufayl he found a patron in the sultan of Marrakesh, abū-Ya'qūb Yusuf, who appointed him to a succession of important positions. In 1169 he was chief justice in Seville where he began his work on Aristotle; in 1171 he was chief justice in Córdoba. He complained that he had to travel so much that little time was left to read and write. Then in 1182 he became court physician and vizier to the sultan in Morocco, the office held earlier by ibn-Tufayl. His first assignment was to prepare a primer on philosophy that could be understood by the layman. Support for critical scholarship continued for a time under Yusuf's successor, al-Mansūr, but pressure from orthodox clerics forced a retreat. In 1194, while a jihād was being waged against the Christians in Spain, ibn-Rushd was branded a traitor to his faith. The sultan imprisoned the sixty-year-old scholar in a village near Córdoba and ordered that his writings be destroyed. Within two years he was back in the sultan's favor, but the fire was gone. Heartbroken over the burning of his books and depressed that his lifelong struggle with the reactionary Mutakallimun had seemingly come to naught, he never recovered. He died on December 10, 1198, in Marrakesh; there he was buried, to be removed later for reinterment in the family tomb at Córdoba. When Sultan al-Mansūr died in AD 1200 the heyday of Arabian philosophy and science came to an end. What writings by ibn-Rushd were lost in the burning is not known.[10]

Ibn-Rushd's first loves were medicine and philosophy, fields in which he produced an enormous literature. He composed a monumental medical encyclopedia titled *General Medicine (al-Kulliyat fi al-Tibb;* the Latins called it *Colliget).* It treats physiology, anatomy, diseases, hygiene, and healing remedies. Among other noteworthy insights, it recognizes the phenomenon of immunity produced by an illness and describes the retina as an organ for the transmission of visual images to the brain.

Ibn-Rushd's lifetime passion was to explain Aristotle, whom he saw as the greatest truth seeker of all time. Of all his [ibn-Rushd's] works, the most esteemed in the West were his Aristotelian commentaries, and for them became known to Latins simply as "The Commentator." Written between AD 1169 and 1195, they were available to European scholars in Latin translations by about 1200. Their immediate effect was (1) to help resurrect the entire Aristotelian corpus and make it available to the Schoolmen; (2) to strengthen the foundations of dialectic (logic) that, due largely to Abélard, was already becoming the universal method of Scholastic thinking; (3) to import Greek ideas (as interpreted in this case by ibn-Rushd) into European thought where they spread like dye to color the thinking of the Latin scholars, and to produce endless and often bitter debate.

Ibn-Rushd's technique was first to master Aristotle's teachings (which he knew only in Arabic translations; he didn't know Greek), survey earlier commentaries on them by Greek and Arabian scholars, then write his own analysis and commentary— which he did, brilliantly, for a total of 38 books, of which 28 survive in Arabic, 36 in Hebrew, and 34 in Latin. Many of the commentaries he wrote in three versions, for beginning, intermediate, and advanced students. For beginners he condensed and simplified the complex philosophic arguments; for more advanced readers he included extended quotations from Aristotle's writings before proceeding with his own comments.

Ibn-Rushd's other principal compositions included three works on theology, faith, and reason. In the *Decisive Treatise on the Agreement Between Religious Law and Philosophy (Fasl al-maqal)*, there is a version of the Cosmological Argument, derived from Aristotle and later redeveloped by Aquinas: Since all motion is caused by prior motion, an infinite regress leads, necessarily, to an uncaused cause, to a Mover that is himself uncaused but who initiates motion; and this is God. In the *Decisive Treatise* he rejects the orthodox doctrines of predestination, physical resurrection, and taught that the world is eternal. He affirmed that God thinks in abstractions or forms; his knowledge of specific events can be likened to what a general manager knows of the detailed execution by hired employees of a company's general policies. Passages in the Qur'ān that depict the rewards of Paradise as sensual (e.g., Sura 56:8–23, 40–43) must be interpreted allegorically, for Heaven's bliss is intellectual and spiritual, not sensual.

In *Examination of the Methods of Proof Concerning the Doctrines of Religion (Manahij)*, an appendix to the *Fasl*, and *The Incoherence of the Incoherence (Tahafut al-tahafut)*, his reply to al-Ghazālī's attack on ibn-Sīnā, and the smaller treatise called *On the Harmony between Religion and Philosophy*, ibn-Rushd worked out in great detail the relationship of the intellectual life to the religious life, including the problem of reason versus revealed truth. There is but one truth, that of the Qur'ān; but that truth is to be structured and interpreted on three levels, corresponding to the different capacities of individuals to understand it. At the lowest level that truth will always be accepted with blind faith and "understood" through pictures, stories, similes, and allegories; and these believers will always be swayable by the popular rhetoric of preachers. There is a middle level composed of hearers who will listen to the logic of the theologians and accept, still uncritically, their limited, dialectical interpretations of the truth. Then there is the highest level of interpretation, the philosophical or metaphysical, that employs the deeper and higher and wider insights of the critical truth seeker. The truth that critical searching can discover will reveal the inner meaning of religion; it will never countermand revealed truth; it will always support it. But it will be interpreted by the unthinking believer and the theologians as heretical and even dangerous because they don't understand it. In *The Incoherence* ibn-Rushd goes farther and says that only the rational metaphysician, who understands these levels of interpretation, has the right to interpret Islāmic doctrine. (Interestingly, ibn-Rushd supports this multilevel theory of truth with passages from the New Testament, e.g., Matt. 13:10–17.°)

° *His disciples asked Jesus, "Why do you speak to them in parables?" Jesus replied: "You are permitted to know the mysteries of the kingdom of Heaven, but they are not. . . . This is why I speak to them in parables, because though they look they do not see, and though they listen they neither hear nor understand."*

Knowledge is the conformity of the object and the intellect.

IBN-RUSHD

Ibn-Rushd's liberal vision was so wide that he advised the true philosopher to choose whatever religion seems best for him. A Muslim thinker will choose Islām, but a Christian thinker may find the religion of Jesus more meaningful, a Jew that of Moses. What this comes down to is a belief that Ultimate Reality can be grasped by different individuals in different ways, each according to his own light. But the essential truth is the same in all religious; the different paths are never incompatible.

Science deals with individual things by the creation of universals abstracted by the mind. Ibn-Rushd accepted Aristotle's analysis of form and matter as the basic principles of being. Matter, he says, is an eternal potency from which the Prime Mover created the world by the use of forms. The physical universe is a dynamic system of eternal motion, and this motion is matter that is striving teleologically toward the perfection of form; but as long as matter is involved in this growth process, perfection can never be reached. Perfection is possible only in pure intellect. The world of nature is struggling to perfect its form; the consummation of all motion will be in the perfect Absolute. The eternal essence of all motion is God, who is its eternal cause.

Just as the sun bathes the objects of the world with light, so also does the Active Intellect communicate with the intellects of individual souls. Indeed each human being is a chosen vessel in which the light of intellect becomes manifest; and as it accepts the light of Divine Intellect, it learns, grows, and becomes ennobled. It grows from a first-stage animal man to the last-stage perfect man, at which point, the soul, while still in this life, can achieve union with the Divine Intellect. When it does this, it becomes one with all other intellects. They are not merely different minds thinking the same thoughts; they are one and the same mind—identical. Thus, intellect is everywhere the same; it differs in individuals only in the degree of illumination it attains. The human race will endure, always, as the honored people in whom the Divine Intellect has chosen to manifest itself. This doctrine—the so-called Unity of Intellect—harmonized nicely with the Neoplatonic assumptions of Latin theologians and, depending on their stance toward standard doctrine, excited or outraged them.

His distinction between rational truth and religious truth led him to clarify the nature of the religious life. Ibn-Rushd was a man of intellect, to be sure; but he was also a man of faith. In defending the rights of reason in matters of this world, he freed faith from the responsibilities of explanation. Religion, for ibn-Rushd, is not a series of empirical observations, or a set of logical syllogisms; nor is it an official list of twenty-five approved dogmas. Faith was for him a personal power, an inward certainty. It is a truth cut especially to meet the spiritual need of each unique individual, a truth that stands apart from, but never contradicts, the rational universals of natural law. If an individual can live with scientific knowledge of the world, so much the better; but if he cannot and finds natural knowledge cold and meaningless, then faith is available—and there need be no contradiction between them.

Ibn-Rushd's thinking became woven into the very fabric of Arabic, Jewish, and Christian philosophy; and, of course, his ideas aroused a storm of protest. The atmosphere in Spain was not conducive to such wild thoughts any more than in Latin Catholicism. More than that, ibn-Rushd joins the burgeoning fellowship of thinkers whose ideas were mischievously misinterpreted and misused. The Latin Averroists of Paris were enamored with his radical thinking, and their adaptation of his ideas served a variety of purposes. The Averroist movement was centered largely in the Latin Quarter of Paris, not far from the University, where large numbers of teachers and students lived. Since both teachers and students came to Paris from all parts of Europe with a Babel of tongues, Latin became the common language used in the classroom, in teaching materials, and in casual conversations. These Latin

Averroists felt autonomous. They thought of themselves as the "philosophers" vis-à-vis the "theologians" in the theological faculty of the University; they concluded that each discipline was self-sufficient and internally coherent within itself. Philosophy had its truth, theology had its truth—and there should be no conflict between them. It was in this context that they transformed ibn-Rushd's multilevel understanding of the one truth into a double-truth doctrine. The Schoolmen, in the eyes of the Averroists, wasted enormous amounts of time trying to reconcile faith and reason. On the hotly debated question of whether the world is eternal or was created, the Averroists said the theologians were right; the world was created by God at a point in time, just as the book of Genesis described. The philosophers were also right when they said the world is eternal and uncreated, just as Aristotle had said. Truth, they argued, is a judgment that has meaning only within a specific frame of reference. It follows that what is true in philosophy may be false in theology, and vice versa.

Such a doctrine was anathema to more orthodox Arabs, Jews, and Christians alike. By contrast ibn-Rushd had clearly said that the truth derived from Scripture (revealed theology) and the truth derived by reason and science (natural theology) are one and the same, though there are many different ways of understanding it. Some of the Latin Averroists went farther and taught that philosophic knowledge is superior to (not the same as) revealed truth and must ultimately supplant it. (This double-truth doctrine also had a purely practical intent at Paris: The Averroists were saying to the intrusive Churchmen on the University faculty "Keep your theological hands off philosophy.")

The Latin Averroists adopted and reworked many of ibn-Rushd's teachings: that God emanates all intelligence; that matter is an eternal potency; that intellect is One; and that there is no free will, moral responsibility, or personal immortality. His notion of the unity of intellect was misunderstood to mean unity of soul—that all humans partook of a universal soul, and, therefore, there was no personal soul to enjoy an afterlife. His multilevel interpretation of truth was given another reductionistic twist: That there is one truth for the masses, another for the intellectual élite, and these may indeed be different truths.

At the University of Paris the reading of ibn-Rushd's works was forbidden in 1210 and 1215; in 1231 they were further banned by papal injunction. The "double-truth" of the Averroists brought official condemnation at Paris in 1270 and 1277. Albertus Magnus fired a broadside with his *Contra Averroistas*, and Thomas Aquinas, about 1269, wrote a *tractatus* against the Averroist movement and its teachings.[11]

IBN-AL-'ARABĪ

To Western minds, he had a name even more formidable than most other Arab thinkers: Muhyi ad-Dīn abū 'Abd Allāh Muhammad ibn 'Alī ibn Muhammad ibn al-'Arabi al-Hātimī at-Tā'ī ibn al'Arabī. Happily, this noble mystic is usually referred to as ibn-al-'Arabī or just ibn-'Arabī. He was also known by the honorific title Ash-Shaykh al-Akbar.

On Ibn-'Arabī When he smiled the flowers blossomed.

The breadth and beauty of ibn-'Arabī's philosophy can be captured in a single paragraph:

> There was a time when I took it amiss in my companion if his religion was not like mine, but now my heart admits every form. It is a pasture of gazelles, a cloister for monks, a temple for idols, a Ka'bah for the pilgrim, the tables of the Torah, and the sacred book of the Qur'ān. Love alone is my religion, and whithersoever man's camels may wonder, then that is my religion and my faith.[12]

This inclusive spirit is unusual in a religion that is largely exclusive, and it begs interpretation. In Islām it could probably happen only in the Sūfī tradition in which an experience of the oneness of all things is the goal of the mystic's journey. Ibn-'Arabī taught that there is but one Reality, and that is God. God is reality; reality is God. God is in everything, in nonmaterial universal forms as well as in material particulars. This "unity of existence" (*wāhdāt āl-wūjūd*) was the central theme of ibn-'Arabī's worldview. Everything preexists in the mind of God as form and imagery before being given expression in the world. This all-pervasive Divine Reality, whose essence is beauty and wisdom, longs to overflow and express its nature, which it does, supremely, in humanity. Any individual, of whatever religion, who discovers the secret of his transcendent unity with God, can move toward fulfillment. In this transcendent unity, every individual can claim to be God. Not *the* God, for that would be *shirk*, but as possessing God within. Islam is merely one "theater of expression" of the One God; so are Christianity and Judaism, and he would undoubtedly add—had he known of them—Hinduism, Buddhism, Taoism, Shinto, and other expressions of the Divine. All revelations are revelations of the same Reality. Humans worship the same God in different ways.

Born in Valencia, Spain, in 1165, ibn-'Arabī died far to the east in Damascus in 1240. He could trace his ancestry back to the Arabian tribe of Tā'ī. After receiving an education in Seville, he remained there for thirty years studying the Islāmic sciences. Early on he was recognized for his unusual qualities. Once in Córdoba he met the great ibn-Rushd, who asked his father to arrange a meeting with the precocious youth, of whom he had heard wonderful things. In this brief encounter ibn-Rushd was overwhelmed and began to tremble in awe at the boy's depth of mind.

In 1198 ibn-'Arabī had a vision in which he was told to leave Spain and begin a pilgrimage. So he set out for the East. As a good Muslim he first visited Mecca, where two events changed his life: He had another vision and he met a young lady. In the vision he learned that the Ka'bah is the place where spiritual Reality touches the world, and he received "a divine commandment" to write a great work on *ishraq*, the systematic formulation of the spiritual essence of the Qur'ān. In a word, his mandate was to produce a worldview that would explain the Sūfī experience within the context of Islāmic faith. This he did in *The Meccan Revelations (al-Futūhāt al-Makkīyya)*, which he completed years later in Baghdad. In 560 chapters the monumental work summarizes, from a mystical point of view, the esoterica of the sciences and includes vital revelations of his own inner journey.

He became acquainted with a young girl in Mecca. Of unusual beauty, ibn-'Arabī saw in her—as he saw in every human being, including himself—the embodiment of Divine beauty and wisdom. Inspired, he penned a collection of love poems titled *The Interpreter of Desires*. She was to him "Sophia" ("Wisdom") and came to play a role in his life not unlike that of the Goddess for Parmenides, Diotima for Socrates, and Beatrice for Dante. Then he wrote a commentary on his book of poems.

His wandering continued. He visited Egypt in 1201, lived briefly in Anatolia, then spent time in Baghdad and Aleppo before settling in Damascus in 1223, where he spent the remaining seventeen years of his life peacefully meditating, teaching, and writing. Some ten years before his death he completed another magnum opus, *The Gems of Wisdom (Fussūs al-hikam)*, which contains his mature philosophy of the mystical experience. He died in Damascus and was buried in a tomb on Qasiyun mountain. It was restored in 1516 and remains today a place of pilgrimage.

Ibn-'Arabī's cosmology is pure Neoplatonism. The cosmos is a spiritual thing. It overflows out of the Divine Being then returns in a cosmic backflow—descent and ascent. As with Plotinus, the outflow was symbolized by light. Why the outflowing?

Because God desires to see his Being reflected back on himself. The Prophet had written "I desired to be known, so I created the creatures in order that I might be known."

The ninety-nine names of God are archetypes for creation, the forms that become manifest in created things. Just as humans begin making things by first conjuring images of what they want to make, so God, the perfect creator, uses perfect forms to create perfect things—including perfect humans. Ibn-'Arabī authored the notion of a "Perfect Man" who fully manifests the nature of God.

It is during the backflow that opportunity presents itself for human aspiration and etherealization. Each human ascends in marked stages in knowledge of himself: "He who knows himself knows his God." On his way he will encounter the living beings who are manifestations of the Names of God, and, ultimately, the veil may be lifted so that the seeker may know God himself. When this happens, the mystic ceases to be aware of separateness and experiences "unity of being." He will know himself to be present in God, and God present in him.

It almost goes without saying that ibn-'Arabī would be attacked by the 'ulamā. He came very close to saying that the great gulf separating God from man had been closed; in the eyes of the literal-minded 'ulamā this would be the final blasphemy, a diabolical demonstration of shirk that obliterated the Almighty. Also his mystical theology of cosmic Oneness struck devout clerics as pantheism, which was forbidden by the Qur'ān. Orthodox theologians prohibited the reading of many of his works. But for most Sūfīs—and for all who identify with his joyous vision of love—he was, and has remained, the saintliest of prophets.

MEDIEVAL JEWISH PHILOSOPHY

The Jews had a long and rich literary tradition, going back at least to 1000 BC/BCE, but that heritage contained almost no material that illustrates critical thinking. It was essentially "existential" literature, a record of the living experience of the Hebrew people and their reflections on that experience, expressed in the language of poetry and myth, allegory, anecdotes and stories, and theological narrative. It possessed intellectual content, but not critical content.

The Judaic understanding of the function of ideas contrasted sharply with the Greek use of ideas. For the Greek thinker ideas were tools to be used to dig with in the course of his excavations; for the Hebrew ideas were containers of a vital truth that must, at all costs, be treasured and held close to one's bosom in order to remain in favor with YHWH/God who is the author of those ideas and even of the words in which they are expressed. The objective study of symbolic thought (semantics) and the careful scrutiny of how and what we know (epistemology) was unthinkable. "Judaism did not speculate much on the nature of the Good," writes Rabbi Abba Hillel Silver, "but it taught man what is good and what the Lord requires of him—'to do justly, to love mercy, and to talk humbly with God.'" A Greek-style dialogue on divine ethics, for the Hebrews, would have smacked of blasphemy, for YHWH/God demanded repentence—not analysis; obedience—not reflection; acceptance—not questions. Even for the great Maimonides, the goal of a human life is to know God, not to study him. "Judaism was not primarily interested in the theoretic elaboration of ethical values but in their realization." The result was that the true nature of human thought and values went unexamined, and the empirical world continued to be seen through the eyes of age-old myths. "On the whole the history of Greek thought is an education of the mind; the history of Hebrew thought is an education of the heart and the spirit."[13]

Anticipate charity by preventing poverty.

MAIMONIDES

Astrology is a disease, not a science.

MAIMONIDES

°*See, for example, 2 Kings 22–3; cf. also Ezra 9–10.*

Generally, it may be stated that what people consider to be good is really bad, and most of the things that are considered bad are really good.

MAIMONIDES

However, from the third century BC/BCE on, there were Jewish intellectuals whose minds were open to the wisdom and knowledge of the cultures in which they lived—at great risk, always, for the Scriptures clearly mandated that a syncretism of divinely revealed truth with foreign ideas was a transgression sure to arouse the wrath of YHWH/God.° Still, there were thinkers who thought of knowledge, wherever found, as God's knowledge. "On seeing the sages of other nations, one should say: Blessed be God Who hath imparted His wisdom to His creatures."[14]

Throughout the reigns of Hellenism and Islām, Jews appropriated the riches of the Greek language. Like the Church Fathers in Christendom, Rabbis feared that Greek ideas would corrupt the young, and during times of persecution their admonitions became extreme. "Cursed be the man who would teach his son Greek Wisdom." But bad times notwithstanding, Judaic literature for a thousand years reveals an in-depth knowledge of Greek philosophic thought, including the sciences, mathematics, and medicine. When the Greek writings were translated into Arabic, Jewish scholars became familiar with the works of Plato and Aristotle and initiated translations into Hebrew. In cultural centers such as Baghdad, Damascus, Cairo, and Córdoba, to be an educated Jew meant to be thoroughly acquainted with Muslim (and therefore Greek) philosophy and science. "Under Moslem impact a veritable Revival of Learning set in among the Jews; poets, scholars, grammarians, philosophers, and scientists shed luster on the most glorious age in medieval Jewish history."[15] Jews under Islām often enjoyed freedom to read and think (even when, as in Spain, Muslim scholars were persecuted and their works burned), a freedom also denied to Latin thinkers. Many of the best minds—ibn-Daud, ibn-Gabirol, and Maimonides, among others—tackled the problem of harmonizing Judaic religion and the results of reason.

MOSES MAIMONIDES

There were many Jewish intellectuals who began to think of their faith in wider and more rational terms, but none could hold a candle to Maimonides. Born at Córdoba in AD/CE 1135, after years of wandering to escape persecution, he died in Cairo in 1204, having become the foremost intellectual figure of medieval Judaism. His name was Moses ben Maimon in Hebrew, ibn-Maymūn in Arabic, and Maimonides to the Latins. He was educated by his scholarly father and Arabic teachers. When he was thirteen years old Córdoba was occupied by an intolerant Islāmic sect, and persecutions began. For ten years Maimonides and his family migrated from place to place, finally settling in Morocco. But the same oppression soon prevailed there, and in 1165 Maimonides moved on to Cairo. His fame in medicine earned him an appointment as personal physician to the sultan Saladin, the Muslim military genius who had recaptured Jerusalem and fought the Crusaders to a standstill. In this more congenial environment Maimonides married, had a family, and became a leader in the Jewish community. He wrote incessantly and once complained that the pressures of his work were undermining his health. He died and was buried at Tiberias in the Holy Land. His tomb is still today visited by pilgrims.

Maimonides' writings profoundly influenced Jewish and Christian philosophy and the sciences of the 13th, 14th, and 15th centuries—despite the fact that much of his work was written in Arabic with Hebrew characters so as to discourage its being read (and misunderstood) by non-Jewish readers. His strategy largely failed. Within a few years of his death his works were translated into Arabic and Latin and reactions begin to appear in the writings of European scholars. His ideas were at once praised and scorned. To most Jews he seemed the consummate interpreter of the Jewish faith; to Latins he appeared like an Aristotle *redivivus*, a master analyst who had

Moses Maimonides
(CE 1135–1204)

A sixteenth century Persian illumination depicting a group of turbaned Muslim astronomers at work in their observatory using a variety of instruments derived from Greek models preserved through Syriac and Arabian traditions: compasses, a world globe, astrolabes, and a mechanical clock.

deeply, and successfully, wrestled with the problems of faith and reason. But he was also denounced as an enemy of religion. An anti-Maimonidist movement arose in France and his works were banned. In 1233 there was a bonfire of his books in the public square in Paris. A prominent Rabbi in Barcelona prohibited the study of all philosophy and science (except medicine) by anyone under the age of 25 (or 30, by another account), but then only if the reader had already been safely grounded in the Talmud and rabbinical literature.

Maimonides is remembered in the history of philosophy (1) for his harmonizing synthesis of reason and belief; (2) for the doctrine of "acquired immortality"; (3) for his "negative theology"; (4) for his idea that we can know God by studying nature; (5) for his powerful influence on Arabian, Jewish, and Christian religious thought.

Maimonides wrote his first work, a treatise on logical and metaphysical terms, at sixteen. Other minor works followed on Jewish law, medicine and health, and the sciences. Current issues were addressed in *Treatise on Resurrection, Letter on Apostasy*, and *Letter on Astrology*. In a medical work, *Moses' Chapters*, he attacked the Greek physician Galen for his unfair criticism of the Torah. *The Torah Reconsidered* is a "revised standard version" of the Torah and Talmud, written in a flowing Hebrew style, his intent was to make the Torah more accessible to the lay reader. Two other works on Jewish law were his *Book of Precepts*, designed also to be read by less-literate layman, and *Laws of Jerusalem*, a compendium of the laws found in the Palestinian Talmud. He wrote *Epistle to Yemen* to refute the claims of a would-be messiah who had appeared on the scene in Yemen.

Maimonides' enduring fame rests on two massive works.

(1) His *Commentary on the Mishnah (Kitab al-Siraj)*, commenced when he was twenty-three and completed at thirty-three, is a summary and clarification of Jewish law as embodied in the Mishnah (a digest of legal cases compiled by Rabbi Judah the Patriarch in the late second century AD/CE). Maimonides' aim was to make the ancient work relevant to Jews of his own time; to this end he wrote in Arabic so all

Any man born is free to become as righteous as Moses, as wicked as Jeroboam, a student or an ignoramus, kind or cruel, generous or niggardly.

MAIMONIDES

The law as a whole aims at two things: the welfare of the soul and the welfare of the body.

MAIMONIDES

Jews living under Muslim rule could read it. After his introductory essays dealing with philosophic questions raised in the Mishnah, he anthologizes the corpus of rabbinical decisions in historic Judaism. He analyzes words and phrases, many of which would be unfamiliar to contemporary Jewry; and he illuminates their meaning by supplying pertinent data from theology and the sciences. He includes a chapter on ethics and a list of the thirteen basic precepts of the Jewish faith. Maimonides is still quoted today as the supreme authority on Jewish religious law, and his thirteen cardinal principles are printed in the *Daily Prayer Book* for use in the morning service.

(2) Maimonides' greatest work is *A Guide for the Perplexed* (*Dalālat al-Hāa'irīn*). Written in Arabic it is a critical reexamination of the entire Jewish faith. Rephrasing the book's title, with a little latitude, its purpose stands clear: *A Guidebook for the Confused*, or *A Guidebook for Those Who Hesitate between Two Contradictory Points of View*, or *Guidebook for Those Who Feel Trapped between Belief and Reason*. A fair but still accurate paraphrase of the author's intent might read: "This book is a tour guide and road map for winding one's way through the thicket of seemingly contradictory concepts that arise inevitably in the rational mind of an intelligent and knowledgeable devout Jew as he reads through the revealed Word of God."

The book makes the case for a more rational approach to religion, and especially the Jewish religion. In doing this, his principal task is to work out a harmony between belief and reason. Such men as Maimonides—and al-Kindī, al-Rāzī, ibn-Sīnā, ibn-Bājjah, ibn-Tufayl, and ibn-Rushd—were scientists as well as devout believers; all were tied to the empirical world with tight bonds through their roles as specialists in medical theory and technology, an eminently practical field in which causality and observational data are essential items of knowledge. But all were also committed to their faith. Maimonides, a universal genius, wrote authoritative works in both religion and medicine. So the dilemma between the demands of religion and the demands of empirical reality became personal for each of them, even more personal than with the Latin Schoolmen who, with few exceptions, had meager or no roots in science or medicine (Albertus Magnus was a notable exception).

Maimonides assumes that all intelligent believers will share his dilemma. He is sure that most Jews see and feel a deep contradiction between Greek science and the doctrines of Judaism. So his aim is to help them accept philosophy and science without giving up their religious observances.

His arguments follow many paths. First of all, God cannot be known by either faith or science. All our mundane statements *about* God are anthropomorphisms; we attach a host of finite attributes to an infinite Being and convince ourselves that we know God. But God is beyond knowing. He exists, but he is beyond being. All we can say is what God is not. These are the most extreme statements of "negative theology" since Philo Judaeus and Plotinus.

But if we can't know God then how can we be sure that he exists? Because he is the Prime Mover. Maimonides adopts Aristotle's "proof" of God as the Unmoved Mover. A careful look at physical motions reveals that every moving thing was set in motion by a prior moving thing, and so on, but maybe not ad infinitum; for reason demands that there was a point in time when motion had to begin, and only a Prime Mover who is himself unmoved could have initiated the causal sequence of moving things. Therefore, although we can't know *about* God, we can be assured that he exists. Maimonides also attempted to prove God's existence with other "classical" arguments, such as the distinction between necessary being and possible being, and between necessity and contingency.

There is something more that we can know. We can learn a considerable amount about God by observing his "behavior"—that is, by observing nature. Nature's physical dynamics are God's active manifestations. Therefore, to study nature is to study God. Science is the study of God's governance of the world. God is, in his essence, pure intellect, and that divine intellect is manifest in the coherence of the natural world. The cosmos is an ordered cosmos, as the Greeks well knew and described with the word *nous*° ("mind"). Similarly, Maimonides reasons that the Divine Intellect is the source of that order.

° *See lexicon.*

Maimonides' notion of God as cause leads him to make an important epistemic judgment. Nature causes all kinds of disasters, from floods and fires to disease and death. Does that mean that God is the *cause* of evil? Not at all, judges Maimonides.

Scholastic theologians spent much time showing that the Jews are in error. These statues at Strasbourg Cathedral contrast the divine vision of the Church (left) with the blindness of the Synagogue (right).

Natural events are, in themselves, neutral; it is we humans who evaluate nature's doings as good or bad, helpful or destructive. This insight is a rare recognition during medieval times that the real (the event) must be carefully distinguished from the experiential (our human judgments and feelings about that event).

What do we do with the traditional statements that attribute qualities to God? Many biblical passages reveal that, like human beings, God "plans" future events, gets angry, makes self-centered demands, punishes good intentions, and punishes for no apparent reason. Such images, Maimonides reasons, are formulations intended for ordinary people who can identify with them. They have practical value in assisting an irrational populace to curb the natural instincts. Widely held religious beliefs that may not be true are still necessary for the maintenance of a just and ordered society. A simple religious faith seems to be an unavoidable fact of man's social existence. In contrast, there is a loftier morality accessible to those who understand and live by rational principles.

Nature, in Maimonides' view, is a manifestation of the organizing principle of the Divine Intellect. It follows from this that God "thinks" in abstractions (as in nature's "laws"), and is remotely connected, if at all, to singular objects. Just as nature is not concerned with individuals, so also statesmen and lawgivers must be concerned primarily with the common Good of society. The welfare of individuals must be secondary to the health of the community.

What is important in humans—intellect—is not a given thing. We are born with a soul, but the intellect is developed through time and experience. This intellect is the immortal part of us; it survives our death. But this immortality is impersonal, for intellect is cosmic, devoid of personal qualities. "My" mind is not "mine" but a local manifestation of a universal process. This doctrine of "acquired immortality" became a distinctive doctrine of the medieval Jewish philosophers.

When thinkers went to work on accepted ideas, they saw problems that faithful laymen didn't see. For their seeing they were both praised and villified. Just believe, they were warned, or you'll disturb the sleeping faith. It was safer to believe than to think. Safety, however, was not a priority concern. The problem of predestination and free will, which occupied much of Maimonides time, is a good example. The given doctrines are, on their face, clear but contradictory. Is God all-knowing? Does his knowing constitute predestination? (That is, if God foresees that something is going to happen, must it then happen as he sees it?) If we are predestined, how can we be held accountable for our actions? If we are not accountable, how can we justly be punished or rewarded?°

° Compare Augustine's time-related solution to this problem, pp. 313ff.

Maimonides answered that God wills that humans should have free will, though some have a greater capacity for freedom than others.

> God does not decree that a man should be good or evil. It is only fools and ignoramuses among Gentiles and Jews who maintain that God decrees at a man's birth whether he shall be righteous or wicked. Any man born is free to become as righteous as Moses, as wicked as Jeroboam, a student or an ignoramus, kind or cruel, generous or niggardly. The subject of man's freedom and God's fore-knowledge is profoundly difficult for man to grasp, as difficult as it is for man to understand God. We believe that the actions of man are in God's hands, and yet God does not coerce man or direct him to act one way or another.[16]

One of Maimonides' critics, Abraham ben David of Posquières, responded that that was not much of an answer, and if he didn't really have an answer he should have kept quiet. The result of opening the matter, he said, was to raise doubts in the simpleminded and disturb the innocence of their faith.

ENDNOTES

1 Philip K. Hitti, *Islām: A Way of Life*, Gateway ed. (Henry Regnery Co., 1971), p. 131.
2 Albert Hourani, *A History of the Arab Peoples* (Harvard University Press, 1991), p. 168.
3 Rewritten from *Mysticism: A Study and an Anthology*, by F. C. Happold (Penguin Books, 1963), p. 98.
4 Rewritten from *Mysticism*, by Happold, p. 229.
5 Kenneth Cragg, *The House of Islām* (Dickenson Publishing Co., 1969), p. 64.
6 *Al-Munqudh min al-Dalāl*, in *House of Islām*, by Cragg, p. 66.
7 Paul McLean, Chap. 46 on Islām, in *Religions of the World* (St. Martin's Press, 1983), p. 634.
8 Cragg, *House of Islam*, p. 14.
9 Much of this account of 'Omar and his philosophy is plagiarized from James L. Christian, *Philosophy: An Introduction to the Art of Wondering* (Harcourt Brace, 6th ed., 1994), pp. 604-607. The author didn't object and the publisher gave his permission. The quatrains are from *The Rubaiyat of Omar Khāyyam*, by Edward FitzGerald, 4th ed., Stanzas 82–90 (the clay pots), 29, 64, 24, 71, 74, 7.
10 Hitti, *Islām*, pp. 133ff.
11 Wallace I. Matson, *A New History of Philosophy* (Harcourt Brace, 1987), vol. 1, pp. 231f.
12 Rewritten from *The History of Religions*, by G. F. Moore (Scribner's, 1919), p. 450. Found in many translations.
13 Abba Hillel Silver, *Where Judaism Differed* (Macmillan, 1956), p. 28; and Isaac Husik, *Philosophical Essays* (1952), pp. 11–12.
14 *Berachot*, 58A, in *Where Judaism Differed*, by Silver, p. 27. Silver gives a helpful but brief history of Jewish "receptivity," pp. 22–37.
15 Silver, *Where Judaism Differed*, p. 32.
16 Hilch. Teshubah, Chaps. 5, 6, in *Where Judaism Differed*, by Silver, p. 303.

CHAPTER 21

HIGH SCHOLASTICISM

THE GOLDEN AGE OF THEOLOGY

Stimulated by the recovery of Aristotle's physical and metaphysical writings, the thirteenth century witnesses a great outburst of intellectual activity known as Scholasticism; this Golden Age of Theology peaks with the work of Thomas Aquinas; then Scholasticism dies as the best minds turn to more worldly concerns.

RECOVERY OF INTELLECT

The student of the history of philosophy can be startled, again and again, when he watches what happens each time the Greek writings are rediscovered. What he sees is an awesome example of the power of ideas as well as a puzzling phenomenon that begs for explanation. And now, in the thirteenth-century, there is just cause to be startled in a big way.

This century is called the Golden Age of Scholastic Theology and is represented by the best minds of the late Middle Ages—Albertus Magnus, Thomas Aquinas, Bonaventura, and Roger Bacon, among others; and it was these men, building on the work of Latin thinkers of the 11th and 12th centuries,° who carried theological speculation to both its height and its depth. Their nuclear goal did not differ from that of centuries of Greek, Latin, Arabian, and Jewish theologians: to reconcile philosophic reasoning with official doctrine. What distinguished the work of the thirteenth-century Latin thinkers were two things: system and exhaustiveness. In their attempt to explain Christian doctrine they asked every imaginable question and gave definitive answers to all of them. In their more balanced moments they gave noble treatment to the great themes of historic Christianity such as the existence of God, the meaning of the Atonement, and the efficacy of the sacraments. But in their attempt at completeness, they went further, asked a million questions and gave a billion answers that, to a modern mind, appear piddling, picky, and irrelevant—"silly stuff" a recent theologian has called it.

Because their creative minds produced such a mass of material, system was required to give it order and usability. These orderly structures, called *summae theologiae*, were encyclopedias of theological knowledge, indexed to answer every possible question that a Christian could ask about the World, God, and Christ; about Man, sin, and salvation; the Church, priesthood, and sacraments; marriage, morals, and manners; the soul, final Judgment, and the Hereafter.

That critical third quarter of the thirteenth century . . . marked the first decisive philosophical encounter between Hellenism and Christianity.

ANTON PEGIS

°*For Scholastic beginnings, see pp. 340ff.*

Contemplata aliis tradere. *To give to others the fruits of contemplation.*

MOTTO OF SAINT
DOMINIC

The immediate cause of the intellectual explosion that occurred during the first decades of the 1200s was the recovery of the complete corpus of Aristotle's writings. Before the thirteenth century only scattered texts containing Greek learning were available to Latin scholars. Aristotle's *Interpretation* was known in the ninth century; Boëthius's translation of Aristotle's *Categories* was used in the tenth. In the twelfth century three more treatises in his *Organon* (the *Prior Analytics*, *Topics*, and *Sophistic Reasonings*) became known. The works of Plato were also largely unknown, though his *Timaeus* was apparently used in the original Greek by Irish monks and in a Latin translation in Europe as early as the fifth century. From the fourth century on, Plato's ideas had been filtered through Neoplatonism to become leaven in the thoughts of virtually all Western Christians; but the originals of Plato's texts remained lost to the West.

Then in the late twelfth and early thirteenth centuries, a spate of new Greek writings began to become available to Latin Schoolmen, and through their influence theology flowered into High Scholasticism. Transmitted through Syriac, Arabic, and Hebrew, a large body of Greek philosophical literature was rendered into Latin and introduced into the cathedral schools and universities. These included Aristotle's *Posterior Analytics*, *Ethics*, *Metaphysics*, *Physics*, *Psychology*, and several of his shorter works. Because of the Carolingian Renaissance and the creative thinking of men like Eriugena and Abélard, educated Latin minds had advanced to the point of being open to Greek learning, even if channeled through "heretical" Muslims and Jews. Foundations had been laid in the cathedral schools through expanded teaching of the trivium and quadrivium (which included, among other subjects, logic, arithmetic, geometry, and astronomy), so that Greek thinking was rapidly assimilated. For almost four centuries Aristotle was to dominate all theological and philosophical thought, largely replacing the Platonism of Augustine. Deductive logic, sprinkled with a seasoning of naive empiricism, became the preferred machinery for the creation of this new Christian worldview. The ecclesiastical establishment went with the flow, adopting the new philosophy and ushering it as best it could through the thorny thickets of dangerous reason.

Aristotle was to the High Scholastics the master thinker; Aquinas habitually referred to him simply as "the Philosopher." He was in their minds a forerunner of the Christian faith—*precursor Christi in naturalibus*. Dante praised him, but because he was, after all, a pagan, he could not allow him access to Paradise or Purgatory; so he placed him in the anteroom of Hell where he would not have to suffer. During the first half of the thirteenth century Aristotle's teachings were suspect in the eyes of popes and councils, but from about AD 1250 on, his authority was unquestioned. The saying of Gottfried of St. Victor circulated in Paris: "Every one is excluded and banned / Who does not come clad in Aristotle's armor."

Before the thirteenth century, therefore, Western Europe presented a dreary contrast to the brilliant Islāmic culture of the Arab world and Spain. Among the Christian masses simple faith still prevailed; among Christian intellectuals simple faith was still defended. Clerics and monks generally regarded philosophy as heretical, and what little they knew of the sciences was, to them, "black art."

With the renewal of intellectual activity in the thirteenth century, European civilization was well on its way to a rebirth. The long night of the Dark Ages was poised for a new dawning, though for two more centuries reason and faith will continue to be locked in a love-hate embrace. Then the Renaissance and Reformation will bring about even more drastic changes in our assumptions, values, thinking habits, and the way we look at ourselves and the world.

It is not easy to account for the repeated impact of Greek ideas. What is startling is the way Greek critical thinking creates a vigor and excitement each time Greek

Foundations must be laid in heaven.
WILLIAM WORDSWORTH

writings are brought to light. They have a liberating affect on minds that are prepared to think, giving them permission to break the restraining bonds of blind belief and stimulating a metanoia in our thinking that launches productive questions of a new kind—questions better designed to discover the truth about how the world works and what our human place is in it.

FIRST STIRRINGS

As the High Scholastics saw it, their task was to reorganize the entire body of Christian doctrine and to present it in systematic form so that everyone—theologians and laymen, believers and skeptics, Christians and non-Christians—could understand its logic and find it persuasive. This they did, brilliantly. What they achieved was almost entirely noetic theology rather than philosophy; it did nothing to extend knowledge into new fields, and it added nothing to what was already known about nature or human beings. With only one or two exceptions, the "puzzled wonderment" about the natural world that had driven Aristotle's research was at an all-time low; the "moon, sun, and stars" had receded from the Scholastics' mental horizons. What the Schoolmen succeeded in doing was to examine every detail of traditional religious thought no matter how obscure, to raise every conceivable question, and to provide ready-made arguments and answers for use by all who might ever find it necessary to defend the faith.

Although they attempted to show that some Christian doctrines could be proven by logic, the Scholastics all subordinated reason to faith. They all accepted, without question, the truth of the Scriptures and Church Fathers, whose teachings remained to them uncriticized *archai*. Nor did they search the Scriptures for new truths. Their job was to employ reason and knowledge to confirm what they had inherited. From their time to ours "scholastic method" has come to mean just this: *Using reason and knowledge to explain and defend already established truth.* The results of the Scholastics' labors were so elegantly and thoroughly executed that they have remained to this day, with only minor revisions, the foundational theology of the Roman Catholic Church, still binding on all Catholics. On August 4, 1879, Pope Leo XIII reaffirmed the theology of Thomas Aquinas to be the standard of Catholic orthodoxy.

ALEXANDER OF HALES

Alexander of Hales' *Summa* was not the first great compendium of theology; Robert of Melun and Stephen Langton had composed *Summae* in the twelfth century. But Alexander was the first Scholastic theologian to attempt such an encyclopedia after all of Aristotle's writings were available, and in it scholastic method is fully developed. Building on the systematic theology of Abélard and Peter Lombard, Alexander listed arguments on both sides of a question, then proceeded to give the correct answer. This is the method that Aquinas will follow in his *Summae*, and Alexander's significance in the history of philosophy lies in his development of scholastic method.

Born in Gloucestershire, England, about AD 1180, he spent most of his life in Paris, where he joined the Franciscan order in 1222, became a celebrated teacher at the University of Paris, and died in 1245. He became known as the *Doctor Irrefragabilis*, the Irrefragable Doctor who is "impossible to refute."

Alexander's lasting contribution was to the theology of Catholic doctrine and sacraments. He taught that in the bread of the Eucharist Christ's divine and human elements are both always present. It was he who first spelled out the four stages of penance: contrition, confession, satisfaction, and absolution, and declared that the priest has the power to absolve a sinner from both guilt and punishment in this world and in purgatory. The theology of indulgences (reducing one's time in purgatory with good works performed now) was largely authored by Alexander, as was the *thesaurus meritorum*, the "treasury of merit" which could be drawn upon to forgive sins or to shorten one's normal stay in purgatory. He defined original sin as a "deficiency of original righteousness" and helped to clarify the five "locations" where souls may proceed after death—heaven, hell, purgatory, limbo for the Fathers *(limbus patrum)*, and limbo for unbaptized babies *(limbus infantum)*.

Known in his time as "the king of theologians," Alexander's most important writing was his *System of Universal Theology* (a work so massive that Roger Bacon said it weighed "more than a horse"). He accepts the validity of Anselm's ontological argument and concluded that man has a natural faculty for knowing God. Our knowledge of *rationes aeternae*, the spiritual first principles, depends on a special, prevenient divine illumination. As for reason and belief, knowledge of the world derives from reason while knowledge of spiritual things derives from faith. The knowledge that nourishes the spirit is distilled from experience, he said, not from study.

Alexander's work was a comprehensive attempt to correlate the new material from Aristotle and the Arabians with established Neoplatonic Augustinian theology. He exercised a powerful influence on the thinking of all subsequent Schoolmen, and especially on Albertus Magnus, Thomas Aquinas, and Bonaventura. Bonaventura and Roger Bacon were among his outstanding pupils.

ALBERTUS MAGNUS

Albertus Magnus—called "the Great" even during his lifetime—was by far the most learned scholar of his age, and the most prolific, officially titled Doctor Universalis by the Church for his encyclopedic knowledge. In physical stature he was diminutive, but he cast a lengthy shadow over the intellectual world of the thirteenth century. He was supreme as naturalist, philosopher, and theologian.

IN THE HISTORY OF PHILOSOPHY

Albert is important (1) for accomplishing fully what he set out to do—"to give Aristotle to the Latins"; (2) for his *System of Nature*, a massive compilation of the entire body of knowledge that existed in his time; (3) for creating a new synthesis of Christian doctrine on which Thomas Aquinas would soon build his great theological system; (4) his emphasis on "experience" and observation as the proper channels for acquiring scientific knowledge (an Aristotelian idea that, ironically, will soon undermine the very foundations of medieval Aristotelianism); (5) for creating, in all his writings, a sourcebook of Greek and Arabian thought that helped preserve these intellectual treasures for Western civilization.

THE MAN

Albert was born in Bavaria about 1200, the eldest son of a wealthy family of nobles. His family planned for him to be a soldier, but after he was sent away to Padua for his schooling he turned instead to the religious life. The master general of the Dominican Order arrived at the university in Padua in the summer of 1223 to recruit new members, and Albert was persuaded; over the strenuous objections of his family, he

On Albert *The honor of first mastering all the works of Aristotle and putting them into the service of Christian philosophy belongs to Albertus.*

DAVID SCHAFF

became a Dominican friar. He immersed himself in the liberal arts curriculum at Padua, then continued his studies at Bologna and in Germany. He was assigned to teach theology in various Dominican convents in Germany and finally settled at Cologne, which became a sort of home base. Though he preferred the quietude of the monastic life, he traveled much; and legend has it that he walked barefoot on his journeys.

In 1240 he received his degree from the University of Paris, and in 1245, as a Doctor of Theology, began to teach at the Dominican convent of Saint-Jacques at the University. It was at this time that he discovered the newly translated works of Aristotle, as well as commentaries on Aristotle by the Arabian philosophers. In 1245 he received his baccalaureate degree from the theological faculty and stayed on to occupy the Dominican chair "for foreigners." He lectured for two years on the Bible, then another two years on the *Sentences* of Peter Lombard, the standard textbook on theology of the late Middle Ages. He rose rapidly to fame for his brilliance and mastery of his subject; Thomas Aquinas, then twenty years old, joined him at the University in 1245 and remained with him for about three years; as teacher and student, and as friends, they profoundly influenced one another till Thomas's early death in 1274.

In 1248 his order transferred Albert back to Cologne to set up an educational center for the study of the liberal arts *(studium generale)*, over which he presided for six years. Aquinas was with him at Cologne but returned to Paris in 1252. In 1254, quite against his wishes, he was appointed head of a German province of Dominicans. In 1259, still reluctant, he accepted the pope's appointment as bishop of the See of Regensburg where a corrupt prelate had squandered the wealth of the church. When he arrived Albert found "not a coin of gold in the Treasury, not a drop of wine in the cellars, and in the barns not a grain of corn"—says his chronicler. These jobs were not to his liking because they took him away from his studies. When the pope

> *We pass over what the ancients have written on this topic because their statements do not agree with experience.*
>
> ALBERTUS MAGNUS

The rebirth of Greek philosophy as Renaissance humanism is graphically expressed in Raphael's painting The School of Athens *(1501–1511). Raphael embodies the fashionable attempt to harmonize Plato (center, on the left) and Aristotle (on the right), believing the two philosophers "agree in substance while they disagree in words." Plato holds the* Timaeus *and points upward (he's the idealist); Aristotle holds a copy of the* Ethics *and points downward (as a good empiricist must). High above, two niches contain statues of Apollo (on Plato's side) and Athena (on Aristotle's side), the gods, respectively, of poetry and reason.*

died, Albert resigned (1262) and returned to Cologne to teach. But his ecclesiastical responsibilities continued to call him away. In 1263 and 1264 he traveled through Germany and Bohemia at the pope's behest preaching a crusade in a time when crusades, with two centuries of failure behind them, were not in fashion. In 1270 he was back in Cologne. In 1274 he went to France to urge the election of Rudolf as the German king. In 1277 he had the sad task of going to Paris to fight off attacks on the doctrines and the memory of his student Thomas. Shortly after that, back at Cologne, Albert descended into senility and died at the age of about eighty. He is buried in St. Andreas church in Cologne. Not long before his death Albert was visited in his cloistered cell by his archbishop, who knocked and asked "Albert, are you there?" "No," the great man replied, "Albert is not here. He used to be here, but he is not here anymore."

HIS WORK

Albertus Magnus left a reputation for almost superhuman knowledge and an uncanny wealth of written material. In his forty years of writing he produced more than twenty-seven thousand pages (in the 1890 Borgnet edition, two columns per page) in thirty-eight volumes. He wrote on philosophy and the natural sciences (twelve volumes), commentaries on the Bible (ten volumes), and theology (fourteen volumes).

His great work was his *System of Nature (Summa de Creaturis)*, in which he shines as the supreme naturalist of his time. In it he attempts to explain the world. He treats astronomy (motions of stars, the Milky Way, comets; he is especially concerned to vindicate man's free will in a cosmos that seems ordered by causal sequences); physics (atmosphere, the propagation of light), meteorology (winds, lightning, thunder, cyclones, rainbows), geography (rivers, "spongy" regions under the Earth's surface), mineralogy and alchemy ("lab work" with sulphur, arsenic, mercury, and other chemicals; he used the term "affinity" to describe the tendency for elements to combine), biology, botany, physiology, medicine, et al. He wrote voluminously on logic, rhetoric, mathematics, ethics, economics, politics, and metaphysics. His metaphysics includes treatment of the Devil, demons, and angels; Man, body and soul; intellect and reason; sleep and digestion.

But it is not sufficient to know something as included in a universal; but we strive to know each thing as it is in its own individual kind of being, for this is the best and perfect kind of knowing.

ALBERTUS MAGNUS

No one since Aristotle had attempted to understand so much. Albert had remarkable powers of observation, an unusual memory for details, and a gift for seeing connections and creating syntheses. His most striking intellectual quality was his trust in experience as the correct means of gathering dependable information about the world. "We pass over what the ancients have written on this topic because their statements do not agree with experience."[1] In an age in which almost no one gave even a nod to personal experience as a means of apprehending what is real, this is an astonishing exception. Albert makes a clear distinction between percepts (of individual things) and mind-generated abstract concepts that place those things into a class. Knowledge of the physical world, he said, is best known through what he called "experiment," the investigation of single objects through precise observation, exact description, and careful classification. Albert listened attentively to Aristotle's "scientific method" and by its lead went far to return Western thinkers to an appreciation of empirical reality. In 1941 Albertus Magnus became, by papal decree, the patron saint of the natural sciences.

Albert's answers are, for many, of less interest than his questions. His cosmic framework is largely Neoplatonic. The cosmos is a multilevel hierarchy of emanations from God. Being was the first created thing (an idea derived from Aristotle's *Categories*); this being connects with God as cause and with single objects as creator.

There are ignorant men who would fight by every means the employment of philosophy; and particularly the Franciscans— brutish beasts who blaspheme that which they do not know.

ALBERTUS MAGNUS

Reality is a divine order structured by the Divine Intellect; the human intellect, as another manifestation of the Divine Intellect, runs parallel to the order of nature and allows us to understand it. Each human intellect is separate and unique in itself. The soul is created directly by God, and is immortal.

On the subject of universals, Albert held (1) that abstract concepts preexist as divine ideas; (2) that they exist as forming agents for individual objects (as Aristotle had said); and (3) they are created by the mind as abstractions designed to apply to the many.

Reason and religion are friends, not enemies. Philosophy and science draw upon competent past authorities then create new knowledge through observation. These data are then employed by the mind to develop abstract categories to the highest level. Some facts can be known only by revelation, while others can be known by both revelation and reason (another notion to be developed by Aquinas). Truth is one; all parts are in harmony; faith and reason never contradict. Albert vigorously opposed the Averroists' two-truth doctrine.

SCHOLASTIC SPECULATIONS

There were Schoolmen before Albertus Magnus who outdid themselves in their attempts to be exhaustive, but Albert's imaginative intellect seems to have been especially equipped to go beyond the bounds of good sense. The topics that received most attention from the Scholastic theologians were the angels, the Virgin Mary, the Devil, creation, and bodily resurrection, though no subject was exempt from scrutiny. Here is a representative sampling of the probing questions asked by a century of perseverating Schoolmen.

Can several angels stand in the same place at the same time? (No, they would get confused.)

Can an angel be in two places at the same time? (No.)

If angels are immaterial spirits, what do they use for vocal cords? (After all, they do sing.)

Do evil souls who have gone to Hell continue to sin?

How do demons in Hell cope with the smokey atmosphere?

What age will souls be when they rise from the dead?

Resurrected souls will be given a spiritual body according to St. Paul, so how tall will they be?

As saved souls watch damned souls writhe in agony, does that vision increase or diminish their bliss? (Their joy will increase, said Albert and Thomas, as they realize that they themselves have been redeemed.)

When the Devil fell from Heaven, what did he fall into?

What happens to a mouse that eats the consecrated bread of the Eucharist? (Nothing, wrote Thomas, because the mouse is not capable of "sacramental" eating; Bonaventura said the actual body of Christ would be "withdrawn"; Peter the Lombard said God only knows.)

If an ass drinks holy water intended for baptism, what will happen to him? (Nothing, answered Duns Scotus; the question is *subtilitas asinina*, for the ass can inbibe only the water, not the water's virtue.)

Why did God create man? (To serve God, to praise Him, to enjoy Him; also to fill up the empty spaces left by the fallen angels.)

Could God have made a better world?

What, if anything, did Adam and Eve eat before they ate the apple?

Could Eve conceive before she ate the apple? (That is, could the first couple have sex before they were punished by being made aware of their nakedness?)

On the night of the Last Supper, did Judas partake of the true body and blood of Christ?

When the disciples celebrated the Eucharist after Christ's death and before the resurrection, what exactly did they eat? (Hugo of St. Victor refused to discuss the problem, saying it was better to worship than to analyze.)

Was Peter's denial of Christ a mortal sin?

Who suffers the better death, a crusader going to the Holy Land or one returning from it?

Where do evil spirits live? (In the midzone of the superterrestrial atmosphere where it is cold and dark; from there they create tempests and thunders to frighten human beings.)

Can demons foretell the future? (Yes.)

Can evil spirits perform miracles? (Yes.)

Can demons have sex with mortal women? (Yes, as the *incubus*; and with men as the *succubus*, though demons could change sex, change form, or do about anything they damn well pleased.)

When the angels fell, did they lose their intellects? (No.)

Was it more difficult for God to create the universe than for him to create man?

Are angels brighter in the morning or in the evening?

If Eve alone had eaten the apple, would original sin be passed to one's offspring? (No, the active generative principle is in the male, said Aquinas; so that, if only Adam had sinned, original sin would still have been passed on through the male line.)

At what hour of the day did Adam sin? (Alexander of Hales decided it was the ninth hour, the hour at which Christ died.)

Did God love the human race more than he loved Christ?

Could God have chosen to become incarnate as a woman? (Peter the Lombard posed the question, to which Walter of St. Victor replied that the better question would have been why Peter didn't appear on Earth as an ass.)

At the Last Judgment, will a resurrected man receive back his lost rib?

Whose sin was greatest, Adam's or Eve's? (Eve's was greater, said Peter Lombard; Adam ate the apple only to avoid offending Eve. Albert said Adam was the worse offender since it was he who carried, in his testicles, the future of the entire human race; hence his responsibility was the weightiest. Bonaventura argued that Adam's was the greater since he sinned against God's goodness, but Eve's was greater when judged by the degree of lust that drove her to disobey God's mandate.)

Until the advent of Roger Bacon—the apostle of common sense (see Chapter 22, pp. 427ff.)—all the Latin theologians took part in this kind of pursuit. The peak of this specious speculation was reached in the queries of Duns Scotus (died AD 1308) who, more than any other theologian of the age, was responsible for giving Scholasticism its reputation for empty irrelevance.

In fairness, the above questions are extracted from context, and must be balanced by the enormous positive labors carried on by these theologians in their better moments. Still, they are important as indicators of the kind of sophistry that brought the Scholastic movement into disrepute, exhausted it, and rerouted the best minds to other interests.[2]

There is something terrible in the laughing of a God.
MALACHY CARROLL

Without Albert Thomas would have been impossible.
WILL DURANT

"The Apotheosis of St. Thomas Aquinas" by Francisco de Zurbarán, now in the Museo de Bellas Artes, Seville, Spain.

SAINT THOMAS AQUINAS OF PARIS: THE ANGELIC DOCTOR

THEOLOGIAN

The literature on Thomas Aquinas is filled with superlatives. He was canonized saint in 1323 and made Doctor Angelicus of the Roman Church in 1567. In 1879 a papal encyclical pronounced Thomas's teachings to be the safest guide for all who are still engaged in the struggle between philosophy and religion, for it was he who "set to rest once and for all the discord between faith and reason, exalting the dignity of each and yet keeping them in friendly alliance."[3] The following year he was made the patron of Catholic Schools.

Aquinas is considered to be one of the three greatest theological minds of all time, joining Augustine and John Calvin; and he was one of the most prolific, writing some sixty books during the twenty-year period from 1252 to 1273. The twenty-one volumes of the *Summa theologiae* supply ample evidence of his organizing genius, clarity of thought, and simple honesty. Reading through the questions in the *Summa* one feels himself in the presence of a mind and heart that are wholly trustworthy in intent, without guile, driven by a divine impulse to seek out the compelling logic of the Christian message. Though he does attempt to persuade, he never intends to manipulate unfairly or to deceive. Never does his work suffer from failure of intellect or loss of vision. Or lack of courage: There is nothing fainthearted in his attempt to grasp and reshape the whole of Western "sacred doctrine." Thomas's philosophic labors do indeed suffer, but their deepest flaws are largely the result of his being trapped in the noetic worldview of the thirteenth century, and from the limited state of knowledge that prevailed in the natural sciences, psychology and physiology, epistemology and semantics. They are further vitiated by the unempirical (i.e. unrealistic) assumptions and values of his age. Writes Anton Pegis, the editor of the Modern Library abridgment of the *Summae*, "his age influenced him much more than it listened to him. It gave him the problems with which he was to be concerned; in many cases it even set for him directions that he was to follow, explore and complete. It is impossible to understand the works of St. Thomas without seeing them in the context of his world; . . ."[4] In a word, like all the greater philosophers, Thomas Aquinas strove to rise above the Zeitgeist of time and place, but in the end he failed to achieve the impossible and succumbed to the frustrating limitations that keep us all earthbound.

On Aquinas Delicate and not exclusive, he will yet be of our day: his heart, for all its contemplation, will yet know the works of men.
JACQUES MARITAIN

IN THE HISTORY OF PHILOSOPHY (AS DISTINCT FROM THEOLOGY)

Thomas is important (1) for supplying the Latin Church with its final resolution to the long-running battle between faith and reason and defining clearly the legitimate sphere of each; (2) for grounding scientific knowledge in sense perception and thereby opening the door (in theory) for the Church to support the natural sciences; (3) for his five "classical" arguments for God's existence; (4) for replacing Platonism/Neoplatonism with Aristotelianism and making Aristotle the ultimate authority in the structure of all human knowledge.

To the credo ut intelligam and the intelligo ut credam of the scholastics, the mystics added Amo ut intelligam—"I love so that I may understand."
WILLIAM TURNER

THE MAN

Thomas was born in the family castle at Roccasecca, four miles north of the little town of Aquino situated on the Via Latina between Rome and Naples. Early in the thirteenth century devastating feudal wars had begun in southern Italy between the

Nihil est in intellectu quod prius non fuerit in sensu. *All knowledge begins with sense knowledge.*

THOMAS AQUINAS

Each man is the weaver of his own dreams.

MALACHY CARROLL

pope and emperor—between the spiritual and the temporal; the Roccasecca castle, a stronghold atop a barren rock rising from the plain of Terra di Lavora, had been captured by the Aquino family and was held as a small feudal enclave. They had earned distinction fighting on the side of the emperor in his war with the papacy.

Thomas's father Landolfo, a descendent of the princely house of Lombardy, was the count of Aquino, Belcastro, and Roccasecca. His mother, Teodora, the Countess of Teano, was descended from the French Normans who had only recently captured southern Italy. She was the granddaughter of Tancred, the noblest of the Crusaders, "the parfite gentil knyght" described by Chaucer, and the conscience of the First Crusade. Thomas Aquinas was therefore an imperial prince with the royalty of Aragon, Castille, Sicily, and France in his veins. Thomas had two brothers and two sisters. Both brothers were older and chose careers as soldiers in the Ghibelline army of the emperor Frederick II.

Born about AD 1225 in what was then the Saracen Kingdom of Sicily, the first five years of Thomas's life were spent in the isolation of a privileged family who believed that wealth, status, display, and power were the true criteria of nobility. These were values entirely uncongenial to the spiritual temperament of the young Thomas. At the age of five he was sent to the Benedictine monastery at Monte Cassino, a dozen miles away, where his uncle Sinnebald was abbot. He was enrolled as an *oblatus* (one intending to take monastic vows)—his family hoped, with an eye to power and prestige, that he too might eventually become abbot of the monastery, thus attaining a feudal lordship of great dignity and princely power over a vast territory and episcopal head of multiple dioceses. At Monte Cassino he began his elementary studies—grammar, rhetoric, logic, poetry, and perhaps the first elements of philosophy—and, tradition says, his mind began to ponder *Quid est Deus?*, "What is God?" His quiet demeanor and introspection (his "introversion") was apparent during these early years. He spent nine years in the majestic fortress-monastery; then Sinnebald died and the monks were expelled by the emperor who feared their close ties to the pope.

Thomas returned to Roccasecca, but the busyness of the Castle was not to his liking. The abbot of Monte Cassino had advised his parents to be aware of Thomas's special gifts and not let them go undeveloped; so, at fourteen, he proceeded south to enter the liberal arts program at the University of Naples. The University had recently been founded by the Emperor Frederick to assist struggling students. Himself an undisciplined, restless man of action and a voluptuary, Frederick was also a talented scholar whose head of tousled red hair (his enemies called him "a raving red beast") could often be seen during late-night hours poring over manuscripts in six languages. Frederick (who was a distant relative of Aquinas) was hostile to all things religious, and especially to the papacy and mendicant orders; and Naples had become a hotbed of student rebellion and antireligious sentiments. Thomas's teacher in grammar was Pietro Martini, in logic and the sciences Petrus Hibernus. The story is recorded that a teacher once asked Thomas to summarize the lecture just presented, a common procedure in medieval classrooms. Thomas, we are told, was accustomed to sitting motionless among the other students, seemingly vacuous and inattentive, for which behavior he had earned from his classmates the epithet *bovem mutum*, "the dumb ox."° When he rose to recite, Thomas summarized the entire lecture with scholarly precision and impressive clarity. From that moment, according to his chronicler, his reputation for genius spread. *Fama ejus per Neapolim volitabat.* "His fame circulated throughout Naples."

For five years Thomas studied in the noisy university atmosphere, then decided that he belonged in the cloistered quietness of the monastic life. Ignoring the plans of his family, and having come under the oratory of John of St. Julian of the Dominican

°*The Latin* mutus *means "mute," "still," "quiet," "silent," and "inarticulate"; it does not mean "dense" or "stupid."*

convent in Naples, he donned the white garb of the Order of Saint Dominic and became a mendicant friar.

Thus at the age of nineteen, his life path was chosen and he could proceed with the career of his choice. Or so it seemed. But the wishes of his parents were not to be so easily ignored. The Countess Teodora came to Naples to reason with Thomas; but the Dominicans, realizing that she might try to take him away, dispatched him to Rome. But near the town of Aquapendente Thomas was waylaid by his brothers at his mother's instigation, taken by force back to Roccasecca and held captive in the fortress of San Giovanni, to be sequestered till he came to his senses and agreed to uphold the honor of the Aquinos. He was incarcerated for almost two years. With the help of a sister he obtained some books and devoted himself to diligent study of the Scriptures, Aristotle, and Peter Lombard.

But Thomas stubbornly resisted every persuasion. At one point, in a last-ditch attempt to seduce Thomas back to the real world, his brothers sought out a prostitute and introduced her into Thomas's room. Thomas grasped a burning stick from the fire, drove the young woman from the room, and burned a charcoal-black cross of Christ into the white-washed wall. Then he knelt in prayer, asking God to help him preserve his steadfast devotion to the spiritual life. (The legend records that he fell into a deep sleep, during which two angels appeared to him saying, "We gird thee with the girdle of perpetual virginity.") Sometime after this failure to persuade, the family began to back off and Thomas escaped from the fortress, being lowered in a basket to waiting Dominicans. He had used his time wisely, they noted, and "had made such progress that it was as though he had been attending a *studium generale*." The young friar proceeded to Rome where he stayed in the Dominican Convent of Santa Sabina, not far from the papal palace of Sevelli. The pope questioned him and satisfied himself regarding Thomas's true intent. But his mother pursued him even to Rome and threatened to raise havoc with the Dominican monks. "*La Comtesse d'Aquin faisait retenir toute la ville de Rome de ses plaintes*," writes the chronicler Touron; "the Countess threatens to hold up the whole city of Rome with her complaints." The pope ordered that there should be no further interference with Thomas's vocation, and he was taken directly to Paris by the Master General of the Dominican order.

PARIS

The year was AD 1244 or 1245. *Fourmillante cité, cité pleine de rêves*, Baudelaire described the metropolis: "A city swarming like an ant hill, a city filled with dreams." There Thomas found sanctuary in the University where he studied under the tutelage of Albertus Magnus, also a man of noble lineage, already famed for an insatiable thirst for knowledge that matched that of Thomas, a man so learned, his followers said, that nature revealed all her secrets to him. Albert recognized Aquinas's greatness: "We call this man a dumb ox," he said; "Well, the deep lowings of this dumb ox will become so thunderous that the centuries will resound with their echo."[5] Albert and Thomas formed a lifelong friendship.

When Albert was sent to Cologne in the summer of 1248 Thomas accompanied him and remained with him till 1252. While at Cologne, probably in 1250, he was ordained to the priesthood. In 1252 Thomas was sent back to Paris to teach theology in the Dominican *studium* at the University. During this time, from 1252 to 1256, while working on his degrees, he began to write commentaries on the Gospels and Peter Lombard's *Sentences*. In 1256 he was awarded the *licentia docendi* permitting him to teach, and shortly thereafter received the master's degree and was made *regens primarius* in one of the two Dominican schools that were incorporated into the

It is only after a long process of training that the mind, by reflecting on its own acts, comes to know itself.

WILLIAM TURNER

Evil has no formal cause, but is rather a privation of form.

THOMAS AQUINAS

University of Paris. For three years he fulfilled his dream of being a teacher of "divine wisdom," and his excellence as both teacher and writer began to be known. During this time he was preparing to take the degree of Doctor of Theology, which he received in October of 1257. In his teaching and writing, Thomas had a twofold purpose: to defend the truth against the attacks of antagonists, and to create a systematic theology that will include every detail of Christian doctrine.

In 1259 Thomas returned to Italy in the service of the Pontifical Curia in Rome. Papal courts existed in many Italian cities, and for nine years Thomas taught and served the papacy in Anagni, Orvieto, Rome, and Viterbo. At Orvieto he met a fellow Dominican, William Moerbake, who began translating Aristotle's writings from Greek into a literal Latin that Thomas found especially helpful.

In 1268 he returned to Paris to teach theology. During the next four years he was engaged in a series of bitter struggles, though in fact his entire teaching career was never free from contention. His first battle was with the Latin Averroists in the faculty of arts of the University. Under the leadership of Siger of Brabant, several of ibn-Rushd's doctrines, including the misinterpreted doctrine of "double-truth," were becoming popular in theological circles, and Thomas countered Siger directly, debated with him, and about 1269 wrote a strong treatise against the Averroist movement, *De unitate intellectus contra Averroistas*.

The second struggle was over the rights of the mendicant orders to teach at the University of Paris. The Dominicans, like the Franciscans, had been founded as "begging monks" whose apostolic poverty, self-sacrifice, asceticism, devotion, and great learning could outpace all others in Christlikeness and missionary zeal. They established monasteries and carried on their work quite separate from the ordained clergy who were assigned to parishes; they could preach and absolve anywhere they liked. Reading like a series of events from a black comedy, a great conflagration began in 1229 in a tavern brawl with a bunch of unruly students who "find by chance wine very good and sweet to drink" and are soon *clerici potantes*, quite drunk, busting the tavern to pieces and "setting the wine-taps aflowing." The chronicler of the account, Matthew of Paris, tells us the matter reached the attention of the queen, who ordered the students punished. But, it appears, the punishers punished the wrong students. The University authorities came to the students' aid and protested by shutting down the University. This left a teaching vacuum, so the Dominicans of Saint-Jacques were invited to fill in, being offered two teaching positions in theology. When the regular faculty returned in 1231, the Dominicans were firmly in control of the University; so the Secular faculty passed a law limiting the mendicant orders to just a single teaching position. By the time Aquinas took up residence in Paris all parties were firmly entrenched and battle lines drawn. He entered into the fray and spent his first years defending the right of the mendicant orders to teach in a "secular" University. William of Saint Amour wrote a treatise attacking the whole concept of mendicancy as unchristian, saying that lazy beggars inevitably become flatterers, liars, and robbers. The dispute could be settled only by the pope, so representatives of all sides were sent to the papal court at Anagni. Though much preferring to stay at home with his scrolls, Aquinas obeyed a summons to the Dominican convent at Anagni to defend the case for the mendicants. The Dominicans were aware that he could be invincible when roused by a dangerous idea. Pope Alexander had his best theologians examine the arguments in William's book. Aquinas presented an eloquent case that was much admired by the pope. Even before William arrived the book was condemned and ordered to be burned.

On another occasion an invitation from King Louis IX arrived at the Dominican monastery at Saint-Jacques, requesting the monks' attendance at a royal banquet; the

On Thomas Aquinas *How little the beauty of nature really meant to Thomas. His landscapes were the landscapes of the mind, and the interplay of ideas made the colors of his sunsets.*

MALACHY CARROLL

famed theologian, Br. Thomas Aquinas, was specifically invited. His chronicler remarks that Thomas really didn't belong in the courtly atmosphere; he was like a rhinoceros ordered to savor a dish of strawberries and cream. As the dishes came and went, Thomas's mind withdrew from the social trivia and returned to the congenial domain of thought. He had recently been brooding over the Manichaean answer as to the origins of evil, ° and suddenly, with an intuitive flash, the solution to the problem came to him. His fist came down triumphantly on the table as he exclaimed, quite aloud, "That's the decisive argument against the Manichaeans!" Greatly embarrassed, his Prior attempted to apologize for Thomas's outburst, but the King reacted with poise and appreciation: "Bring writing materials to Brother Thomas immediately lest these treasures be lost."

°See pp. 303, 313 for Augustine's reaction to the same problem.

In stature Thomas towered above others; he was a large man, tall and dark, with a heavy build, later in life almost rotund (a configuration that gave rise to a legend about a "half-moon cut in the refectory table" where Thomas sat), with a large head that was slightly balding. His walk was easy and graceful, almost majesterial. By common judgment he was handsome, well proportioned. His complexion was "the color of new wheat." His eyes, noted by all who knew him, possessed an all-seeing quietness. By nature he was calm, pensive, meditative, and unflappable; he was an observer, not one eager to participate or get involved in any social occasion. And he was an ecstatic: that is, he was given to withdrawing deeply into his own thoughts. There are many reports, derived from observers and from Thomas himself, that he experienced angelic visions and divine visitations, including epiphanies from the Virgin Mary, Peter, and Paul, who gave him guidance and reassurance.

The great wheels of Heaven can often be set in motion by a mere rose petal falling on them.
MALACHY CARROLL

WRITINGS

Throughout his adult life Aquinas actively preached, taught, and debated, but despite these burdens he never ceased writing, often dictating to as many as four amanuenses at once (his own penmanship was almost unreadable, as shown by the original manuscript of the *Summa contra gentiles* which is in the Vatican Library). Though he often preached in his native Italian, he wrote only in Latin. From about 1254 to 1256 he worked on a commentary on Peter Lombard's theological textbook titled *Commentaria in Libros Sententiarum*; from 1257 to 1261 he wrote commentaries on Boëthius and Pseudo-Dionysius, and began writing commentaries on the Scriptures. A series of treatises collectively titled *Disputed Questions* was inspired by his classroom teaching; when his students encountered tough problems that required their teacher's intellectual power, he wrote an analysis of the issue. Among these *Quaestiones disputatae* are *On Truth* (1256–1259), *On the Power of God* (1259 to 1263), *On Evil* (1263–1268), *On Spiritual Creatures* (1269), and *On the Soul* (1269–1270). His *Quodlibeta (Various Discussions)* contains answers to questions his students had asked him. In the *Contra Averroists* he attacked the doctrines that all men share a single soul and the two-truth perversion of ibn-Rushd's teaching about multilevel understandings of true ideas. His *Summa de veritate catholicae fidei contra gentiles* (usually abbreviated to *Summa contra gentiles*), the supreme medieval work on natural theology, was written for the purpose of defending Catholic doctrine against the Jews and Arabian pantheists in Spain; it was written in Rome from 1261 to 1264.

The masterwork which makes Thomas immortal and which has done so much to shape Western religious thought is his great *Summa theologiae*, intended to be a summary of all knowledge; it was begun at Bologna about 1271. His *Compendium of Theology* dates from 1273. The commentaries on Aristotle's works, which he worked on as a labor of love all his adult life, covered almost the entire Aristotelian corpus. Thomas penned various shorter treatises called *Opuscula* and composed some of the loveliest eucharistic hymns in the Catholic liturgy, including "Sacris Solemniis," "Pange Lingua," and the "Lauda Sion" of the Mass.

LAST YEARS

In 1261 Thomas left his teacher's post at the University of Paris and taught for brief periods at Bologna, Rome, and other Italian cities. In 1265 the pope moved to appoint Thomas archbishop of Naples, but Thomas asked to be excused because it would mean abandoning his writing. The years 1272 and 1273 were spent living in the Dominican convent in Naples and teaching at his alma mater the University of Naples. He was working on the third part of his *Summa theologiae* and had reached the ninetieth question when, on the 6th of December, 1273, he grew weak and could no longer teach or write. When his assistant, Father Reginald, begged him to continue writing, Thomas answered, "I can do no more. Such secrets have been revealed to me that everything that I have written appears to me as worthless straw."

It is good for a man to return home when his work is done and when the lights are dimming on the stage of his life.

MALACHY CARROLL

Still, in January of 1274, Thomas was summoned by the pope to a council in Lyons, to be convened May 1. Two hundred years earlier, in AD 1054, the pope had excommunicated the patriarch of Constantinople over political and sacramental disputes, causing a formal schism between the Greek and the Latin Churches. This Second Council of Lyons was called by Pope Gregory X to address that rift and to take steps toward healing it. Thomas was asked to bring along his treatise *Against the Errors of the Greeks* that he had composed at the request of the former pope. Obedient as always, Thomas began the journey on foot but fell ill on the way and collapsed near Terracina. He was taken to the Castle of Maienza, the home of his niece Francesca. When the Cistercian monks at the abbey of Santa Maria at nearby Fossanuova heard of his plight they invited him into their cloister. Fra Reginald urged him to remain at the Castle, but Thomas replied "If the Lord wishes to summon me, then it is better that I be found in a religious house than in that of a layman." Arriving at the monastery he whispered, "This is my rest forever and ever." He died there on March 7, 1274, having spent his last days dictating a commentary on the Song of Songs. The abbey was just a few miles west of his birthplace at Roccasecca. He was forty-nine.

FAITH AND PHILOSOPHY

Aquinas's settlement of the controversy between faith and reason has the appearance of utter simplicity, so that one may wonder why such a solution didn't occur centuries earlier. We use philosophy, he said, to understand the world; we use theology to understand sacred doctrine. Philosophic thinking begins with sense perceptions and from them, using reason, infers general principles; theological thinking begins with revealed doctrines and proceeds, using reason, to illuminate them. Philosophy reasons from an empirical database to discover new knowledge; theology reasons from a revealed database in order to better understand God's truths. The goal of theology is to clarify revealed truth, work out apparent inconsistencies, and to find ways of applying it. Theology does not employ reason to prove revealed doctrine, for faith entails acceptance of true doctrine without proof. Theology is a higher discipline than philosophy because its content is certain and can therefore be used to explain everything else; it is also the nobler science because, as Thomas sees it, the capacity for faith is a prevenient gift from God.

It ill becomes a preacher to turn aside from the solid highways of truth to the byways of fruitless speculation.

AQUINAS

Thus, Aquinas did his best to separate philosophy from theology and to reserve for each a legitimate sphere of operations. In the study of the visible world, philosophy takes precedence over faith; in the study of the unseen world, faith takes precedence over philosophy. Rightly interpreted there can never be any contradiction between the two, for both are wellsprings of knowledge from the one God.

(Aquinas's metaphysical framework is the standard, almost universal, division of existence into two orders of reality, the supernatural and the natural. This two-order universe is accepted by him "on faith" and remains entirely unexamined; it is after all the bedrock of virtually all humankind's great religions, including the Judeo-Christian. His vision of the roles of theology and philosophy is thus easily simplified: Philosophy studies the natural order of reality, theology the supernatural order of reality. Thus philosophy and theology nicely complement one another as coworkers.)

But, in Thomas's mind, knowledge of the world was not important in itself. Its value was entirely instrumental: to know God and to understand the Christian message of salvation.

Thus the goal of empirical knowledge is the same as the goal of divine knowledge attained through faith. Since the operations of nature as known through the sciences are God's "behavioral patterns," we study nature to find out about God. Presumably, if one wished to study nature just to know about nature, then Thomas would shrug and say "Well (in Latin), that's okay too, but you're missing the true purpose of our being in the world—to be saved for all eternity."

THE SPHERE OF PHILOSOPHY

There are three categories of knowledge in Aquinas's system. (1) Some things can be known only (or primarily) through philosophic reasoning (for instance, that there is but one universe and not many). (2) Some things can be known only through revelation (that the Incarnation and Atonement have occurred in history, that God is a Trinity, that he created the world at a point in time, that angels exist). (3) Then there is a third category of truths that can be known through both revelation and reason (such as the existence of God). These latter are special items of knowledge called "natural theology." Through almost all of Aquinas's writings the subject under investigation is indicated as belonging to one or the other of these categories.

Thomas's masterpiece is the *Summa theologiae*, though his *Summa contra gentiles* must be ranked close behind. His procedure in both works is a model of organization and clarity. He tells us, in the prologue to the great *Summa*, that his purpose in style is to avoid the useless questions, confused order, and repetitions common to such Scholastic works, problems "that begat disgust and confusion in the minds of learners." The twenty-one volumes of the *Summa theologiae* are divided simply into three books dealing with God, Man, and Christ, which are divided into 518 questions, which are divided into 2,652 articles. (Thomas left the *Summa* unfinished; his original plan, it seems, was to complete 3,000 articles; it was completed posthumously with additions from his commentary on the Lombard's *Sentences*.) Each article deals with a single topic or question which he states at the outset: "Is theology a science?" "Does God exist?" "Do other worlds exist?" "Is God the cause of evil?" "Does man have free will?"—and so on, through 2,652 carefully worded analyses. Each article has five parts. First, he states the question: "Here is the problem," he says. Second, he lists all the wrong arguments that he has read, heard, or discerned through his own reasoning: "Here are the wrong answers." Third, he states the correct answer: "On the contrary," he writes, almost always quoting a line or two from Scripture, Aristotle, Augustine, or some other ancient authority. Fourth, he supplies, in greater detail, the correct answer to the original question: "I answer that . . ." Fifth, he answers, one by one, the wrong arguments summarized at the beginning of the article: "Replies to objections."

His questions are sincere; they are not meant as displays of erudition, though they are erudite. Each is an honest attempt to find the true answers that he himself longed to know about his God, the world, and the contents of experience; he supplies the

I have spread my dreams.
WILLIAM BUTLER
YEATS

The Light of Light looks on the motive, not the deed.
WILLIAM BUTLET
YEATS

most curious Christian—as well as the least curious—with everything he needs to know about his salvation.

Almost any article could be selected as typical and would illustrate both Aquinas's strengths and weaknesses. His treatment of the possible existence of other worlds belongs to the first category—things that can be known by reason. Book I, Question 47, Article 3, asks the question "Are there other worlds?" He begins with the "wrong answers." The first is: Yes, there must be many worlds, for God's power is not limited to the creation of just one world; he could create as many as he wanted; therefore he must have created many worlds. (This is a common form of Scholastic argument: Is something possible? Since God can do everything, that something is possible; if it's possible God would have done it; therefore it is.)

The second "wrong answer" is: If one world is good, then two must be better, and many would be better still. God always does what is best, and "best" implies that he would create many worlds. Therefore, many worlds exist.

The third "wrong answer": Drawing on Aristotle's doctrine of form and matter, the form of "world" is a universal abstraction given concreteness by the existence of "this world." (To Aristotle, remember, form is found only in connection with singular objects.) Since the form "world" is available as a blueprint, God might as well have used it to make other worlds.

Then Thomas says "On the contrary" and quotes a passage from the Gospel of John (1:10): "the world came into existence through him." Since the verse refers to "the world" (singular) there is therefore only one world.

The correct answer is then spelled out: This world is an ordered cosmos, given oneness by God. God himself is perfect order, and the world, as a manifestation of his ordering intellect, is one order, not many. (Being careful not to backread from modern astrophysics, this argument is somewhat analogous to saying that the "laws of physics" prevail everywhere in the universe; in which case Thomas's "world" means the entire universe.) He adds, with perhaps a hint of disdain, that the only thinkers who could honestly argue for the existence of other worlds would be nontheists like Democritus who believe that the world is just a collection of atoms brought together by chance.

Lastly, Aquinas replies to the initial objections. His first reply (which is a restatement of his "on the contrary" argument and fails entirely to address the first objection) is that the world is one because there exists but one order and one end toward which it moves. The second reply points out that the phrase "many worlds" refers to lumps of physical substance, while the proper criterion for judging what is "best" is God's intention, not merely multiple copies of matter. That is, "good," "better," and "best" have to do with quality, not quantity. His third reply is that "the world" by definition includes everything, and, moreover, other worlds would naturally gravitate toward the Earth as the center of this (geocentric) cosmos; but since they don't, then they must not exist.

Today we would go about answering this question in an entirely different way. First, we would ask for definition. What is meant by "other worlds"? Do we mean other planets? other solar systems? other habitable planets? other galaxies? other big-bang universes? After defining the subject we would proceed to set up our telescopes and spectrographs and *look*—because (1) we think that the best way to describe a tree is to look at a tree; and (2) we now possess the knowledge, tools, and skills that will give us enough trustworthy data to make inroads into the question.

Aquinas possessed no such tools, of course, and he was limited to using the best information and reasoning at his command. The Achilles' heel of the problem is the fact that the question *is* an empirical question. Thomas knew this; he had made it

[In Aquinas's view] theology views truth in the light of divine revelation, while philosophy views truth in the light of human reason. . . . Thomas taught that where science ends faith begins.

WILLIAM TURNER

Abstraction tends to grow on the saint, so that he may eventually need a man of affairs at his elbow to remind him of such details of life as eating and sleeping.

MALACHY CARROLL

clear that knowledge of the world must be acquired through sense observation. Still, he possessed no empirical data that could lead him to a satisfying answer.

We might observe, looking back, that there did exist in his time an accumulation of scientific facts that would at least have steered him in a more fruitful direction. But although Aquinas had read in the scientific literature, he didn't trust this kind of information, partly because much of it didn't cohere with revealed truth, partly because he possessed firm archai from which he had to work, partly because he just wasn't interested in "seeing" the world. (He was concerned with "knowing" but not "seeing.")

So Aquinas found himself forced to deal with an empirical question with unempirical procedures. This problem was a thorn to Plato (though, ironically, not to Aristotle): How does one describe a tree without ever looking at a tree? One can gather answers from other people who have looked at trees, and if their answers happen to be embedded in canonized records, then, no matter how outlandish those answers might seem when judged by immediate sense experience, we suspend our critical faculties and accept them as the truth.

THE SPHERE OF THEOLOGY

In Book I, Question 46, Article 2, Aquinas poses the question, "Is the creation of the world something we know by faith?" or can we know this by philosophic reasoning? In his objections he faithfully records the arguments for the eternity of the world. There are eight "wrong answers," most of them gleaned from philosophic literature. Alexander of Hales had argued that since God is the cause of the world, and all "causes" produce their "effects" at a point in time, then reasoning can prove that the world was created and is not an item of faith. Further, if God created the world, then he made it of either something or nothing; but it can't have been made from something because, if it were, then matter predated the world, and Aristotle said that couldn't be the case. Therefore, it was made from nothing "and thus it has being after non-being, and therefore it must have begun to be." So, again, reasoning has proved that the world was created in time and is not a matter of faith. Through six more arguments Aquinas sets them up, so that, after his statement of the correct answer, he can show wherein they are fallacious.

That correct answer is: "That the world did not always exist we hold by faith alone: it cannot be proved demonstratively. . . . that the world began to exist is an object of faith, but not of demonstration or science." All attempts to prove by reasoning that the world was created are weak arguments that might "give unbelievers the occasion to ridicule, thinking that on such [shaky] grounds we believe the things that are properly matters of faith."

THE SPHERE OF NATURAL THEOLOGY

The third category includes doctrines that can be known by both faith and reason. In Book I, Question 2, Article 3 of the *Summa theologiae*, Aquinas submits the question "Does God exist?" For Christians with the capacity for faith, of course, God's existence is not in question. But for anyone with a tendency to doubt, Thomas's five proofs for God's existence are supplied as compelling evidence to back up faith.

Then Aquinas says, "The existence of God can be proved in five ways." The first four proofs are called, somewhat arbitrarily, "cosmological arguments"; the fifth is called, with better reason, a "teleological argument."

(1) The first proof is a recycling of Aristotle's argument from motion.° Aquinas thinks of it as an empirical argument and begins with what is "evident to our senses," that motion exists and that "whatever is moved must be moved by another. If that by

°*See pp. 191f.*

which it is moved be itself moved, then this also must needs be moved by another, and that by another again. But this cannot go on to infinity, because then there would be no first mover.... Therefore it is necessary to arrive at a first mover, moved by no other; and this everyone understands to be God." (Aquinas ties this Prime Mover argument to Aristotle's definition of motion: Motion, Aquinas says, "is nothing else than the reduction of something from potentiality to actuality. But nothing can be reduced from potentiality to actuality except by something in a state of actuality"; and the only thing that is entirely actual and without potential is God. Therefore God exists.)

(2) Drawing from Aristotle's notion of "efficient cause," Aquinas argues that it is impossible to conceive of an infinite series of causes, so that, like the problem of motion, there must have existed a First Cause. "There is no case known (neither is it, indeed, possible) in which a thing is found to be the efficient cause of itself." So, if we envision a chain of causal connections, the mind is led back inevitably to "a first efficient cause, to which everyone gives the name of God."

(3) Our common experience in nature is to find that things exist, and then, suddenly, they don't exist anymore, having died or disintegrated. They are, and then they aren't. Anything that is has the potential not to be. Nothing can last forever. But "if everything can not-be, then at one time there was nothing in existence"; since nothing comes from nothing, nothing would exist now. But that's false. Therefore, while most things are "merely possible," something must exist which possesses "necessary existence" as a part of its being. "This all men speak of as God."

(4) Aquinas's fourth proof is an argument from perfection, and this too purports to be derived from observation. What we find in the world, he tells us, is a hierarchy of graduated levels of reality. We find that things are good, true, noble, and so on; but then we discover that some things are better or worse than others, truer or less true than others, nobler or less noble than others. (Note that Aquinas is operating on the belief that "good" and "bad," etc., are not just evaluations, but real qualities that inhere in real objects/events; "good" is an actual substance that infects objects in themselves quite apart from our experience of them.) Thomas argues that when we speak of "more" or "less" we are tacitly assuming the existence of a maximum as a standard against which we are measuring "more" or "less." For instance there is a maximal hot (he says it's fire) which gives meaning to our judgments of more hot and less hot; that is, "a thing is said to be hotter according as it more nearly resembles that which is hottest." If there were no maximal standards then our judgments of gradations would be meaningless. Moreover, it is from these maximal states that all the things in a class derive their qualities: The hotness of a cup of coffee, for example, gets its hotness from the maximal state, fire. Now these "maximal standards" exist for truth and being just as much as for goodness and hotness. Therefore there exists in reality, necessarily, an absolute standard of truth and an absolute standard of being—perfect truth and perfect being; "and this we call God."

(5) The fifth proof is the argument from the teleological nature of all existence, again a repetition of Aristotle's doctrine of "final cause." Everything, Aquinas says, behaves as though it is working toward some goal, even mindless things that "lack knowledge" such as seeds and flowers. But "whatever lacks knowledge cannot move towards an end unless it be directed by some being endowed with knowledge and intelligence." Obviously, therefore, this goal-oriented design implies a designer, an intelligent being "by whom all natural things are directed to their end; and this being we call God."

According to Aquinas, therefore, we know that God exists by both revelation and philosophic reasoning; so the level of "perhaps" is raised above doubt to absolute

---

Infinite series without a beginning and an end have been successfully treated in mathematics; there is nothing paradoxical in them. To object that there must have been a first event, a beginning of time, is the attitude of an untrained mind.

Hans Reichenbach

If we ever did find a First Cause we could intelligibly ask "What caused it?" And if that is found: "What caused it?"—ad infinitum in a sequence into the past.

Peter Angeles

certainty. Those with a capacity for faith, of course, don't need logical proof: "there is nothing to prevent a man, who cannot grasp a proof, from accepting, as a matter of faith, something which in itself is capable of being scientifically known and demonstrated."[6]

THOMAS'S THEOLOGY

Thomas's theology (he referred to it as "sacred doctrine" and rarely used the word "theology") consists of all the doctrines known by faith. We have them on God's authority and can therefore be absolutely certain of them. Theology is partly divine, partly human; for it begins with principles from divine revelation and is then developed, from premise to conclusion, by natural reason. The following are just a few of the highlights of his systematic theology.

The *creation* of the world was an expression of God's love, not an act brought about by causal necessity. God is not bound by necessity, but operates freely; he chooses not to break into the natural order of things, but rather operates outside that order, using the mechanics of nature to bring about "accidents" and "coincidences" which, if we see them rightly, are God's ways of controlling events in our lives.

The *cosmos* is characterized by levels of being, a hierarchy of God's creation. At the top of the ladder are God and the angels; at the bottom are material things, the elements, plants, and animals. Man occupies a special rung in the middle of the ladder because he has a material body and a spiritual soul.

Truth is the equation of thought and thing.
THOMAS AQUINAS

St. Thomas Aquinas lecturing in the schoolyard of Albertus Magnus.

All *knowledge of God* is indirect and only approximate. We can be sure that God is, but not what he is. Knowledge of God can be attained in two ways: by analogy and by negation. In everyday language we say that things are good, beautiful, wise, and powerful; we can employ these same adjectives for God in their superlative form: God is perfect goodness, perfect beauty, perfect in wisdom and power. By negation, Aquinas argues that we can be sure that God is *not* matter, *not* limited, *not* evil, *not* complex, and so on through this "darkness of unknowing" until we develop a residual notion of what God might be.

It was most appropriate that Thomas was honored with the title of *doctor angelicus*, for he devotes 358 articles of his *Summa* to *angels*. He follows the ninefold ordering of celestial beings suggested by Pseudo-Dionysius and groups the angels into three triadic levels: seraphim, cherubim, and thrones; dominions, powers, and authorities; principalities, archangels, and just angels (the garden variety, presumably). Angels are immaterial beings, each angel belonging to its own species. Angels move themselves by thinking, and can therefore move very fast, but how fast depends on angelic will: A strong-willed angel can move really fast. They can move in a continuous vector, or (like a quantum particle) they can move from one place to another without crossing the space in between. Angels are normally not visible to us humans, but on occasion they can assume a quasi-material form and be seen.

The more one knows, the greater one's desire to know.

THOMAS AQUINAS

Predestination is a problem for Thomas as it was for Augustine, and he can be quoted on several sides of the issue. "It is fitting that God should predestine men, for all things are subject to his Providence." Some men "are ordained to eternal life" while God permits others "to fall away from that end." That is, God does not predestine souls to hell, for he loves everyone; but he does leave all humans to their own free-will devices and many therefore damn themselves. "Man has free choice, or otherwise counsels, exhortations, commands, prohibitions, rewards and punishments would be in vain." By a fiat of prevenience, Aquinas tries to salvage both God's providence and Man's freedom. "Man's turning to God is by free choice . . . but free choice can be turned to God only when God turns it. . . . Man's preparation for grace is from God, as mover, and from free choice, as moved."[7] God has predestined certain individual souls to salvation to replace the angels who fell from grace.

Adam, Eve, and the Fall endlessly occupy Thomas's curiosity; after all, the sinful condition of the entire human race was initiated in the Garden of Eden. Like other Scholastics Thomas asked trivial questions about the first sinless state but is balanced somewhat by better common sense. Through Adam and Eve's disobedience of God's mandate not to eat, original sin effected a moral disorder in the universal human soul. Adam carried in his testes the seed of the entire human race and thus bequeathed the blot of that first sin to all his descendents. Just as a disease can infect the body, original sin infects the soul with a corrupt disposition, *habitus corruptus*. It shows itself most obviously in the sexual passions. Original sin was brought about through an inordinate love of self and prevents man from doing anything good of his own natural will.

By faith we know certain things about God which are so sublime that reason cannot reach them by means of demonstration.

THOMAS AQUINAS

Atonement through Christ is God's providential antidote to the guilt condition of the whole human race, which is so massive that only the Son of God himself can make atonement. As a result of the working of God's love in each soul, faith opens the heart to God's grace and salvation through the Atonement.

Sacraments are the Church's means of imparting God's grace to redeemed sinners. Just as there are seven mortal sins and seven cardinal virtues, there must be seven sacraments. The efficacy of the sacrament is inherent in the sacrament itself and is not conditioned by the moral nature of the priest or the faith of the recipient. Three of the sacraments—baptism, confirmation, and ordination—effect permanent, ineradicable changes in the soul. Baptism cleanses the soul of its original sin. In the Eucharist the bread and wine are both transubstantiated into the very substance of the body and blood of Christ, though outward appearance ("accidents") such as texture and taste of the bread and wine may remain the same. Penance is for erasing sin incurred after baptism.

Children who are unbaptized have no hope for salvation. Baptism washes away original sin, so if a baby dies in the unwashed state and therefore has no connection with Christ's redeeming power, then it is forever lost and will be detained in hell.

Last days are elaborated by Thomas in detail. The resurrected body, as described by Paul (1 Thess. 4:13–5:11) will be physically identical to the one we have now, and therefore the fires of hell, which are very real, will be felt just as fire is felt on Earth. (This gives meaning to the agony of souls in Dante's *Inferno*, which is a pictorial version of Aquinas's theological vision.)

On the question of *evil* Aquinas follows Augustine: Evil is not a thing, but a lack of something, namely goodness. God, therefore, being perfect Goodness, did not, and cannot, create evil. It exists because God permits all possible grades of being in this world. Out of evil God produces good. Evil is experienced in three forms: Natural evils are from nature, as in earthquakes and floods. Moral evils are committed by humans as a result of the misuse of their freedom. Punitive evils are God's way of rendering justice for man's sins and are, in the divine economy, really good.

THOMAS'S PHILOSOPHY

Although Aquinas supplies criteria for distinguishing theology from philosophy, the two disciplines are often difficult to separate. His treatment of evil for example: We would normally consider the "problem of evil" to be an empirical problem—we sense pain, we feel bereavement, we empathize with the sufferings of others—but Thomas's answers regarding the origin and nature of evil are theological and very *un*empirical.

Aquinas's notion of the *sciences* is heavily indebted to Aristotle's *Posterior Analytics*, on which he wrote a commentary. There is little doubt that Thomas knew of, and fully understood, the world of the natural sciences that his mentor Albertus Magnus loved and mastered; but Thomas is not interested in specifics (his mind, it seems, is not comfortable with induction) but is concerned only to go beyond specifics to the creation of abstract principles that give him knowledge, as he defines it. Science is a knowledge of the causes of objects/events, "causes" meaning universal causal principles or "causal laws" that can be trusted again and again to describe natural events. Science is the study of the necessary and the universal that lie behind and under the eternally changing face of natural phenomena; it is the search for being in the becoming. But whatever concepts the mind develops from sense, they must harmonize with concepts already established through revelation. The scientific principles derived from nature, especially from the study of physics, were valued by Aquinas because they represent another way of knowing God: One can come to know something of the Creator by studying his creations—and his creatings. Aquinas treats the natural sciences most directly in Book II of the *Summa contra gentiles*, in *De principiis naturae*, and in his treatise *De aeternitate mundi*.

(Repeatedly, in his science, Aquinas shows an uncanny resemblance to Aristotle: They both wanted to understand the world; they both had a passion for ordered knowledge; both sought abstract principles underlying phenomena; and both created vast, synoptic syntheses. The difference is that, for their initial database, Aristotle looked at the world he wanted to describe while Thomas looked at Aristotle. And yet, paradoxically, in scientific matters Thomas held that the appeal to authority is the

The knowledge of faith does not set the desire at rest, but inflames it; for everyone desires to see what he believes.

THOMAS AQUINAS

°*See pp. 179ff.*.

weakest kind of argument and chastises those who quote Aristotle as the final word. In any case, the similarity between Aristotle and Thomas goes beyond the fact that the Schoolman practically memorized the Philosopher; they also shared many personal qualities of character and feeling.°)

So Aquinas's science, to no one's surprise, is Aristotelian, though in content it is prosaic: The world is geocentric; the Earth is enclosed within some half hundred concentric spheres; and so on. More important than his content is the fact that his dogmatism in doctrine contrasts with his open-mindedness in the sciences where he admonishes a student to consider all the different theories, to remain open to further information, and to hold answers provisionally.

The *universals* problem, for Thomas, was largely solved by Aristotle. Although the Real Ideas of Plato don't exist, the universal concepts and judgments created by our minds do have a real basis; that is, the attributes that all objects in a class have in common are real. The abstraction "bird" is not a figment. Only individual birds really exist, but the fact that all birds share similar characteristics points to a real basis for our generalized abstractions. Therefore, the universal existed in the mind of God as a template; it exists in our human minds as a mentally created abstraction; *and* it exists as the essence of things; and because that essence is real, there is a justifiable foundation for scientific knowledge: Both induction and deduction are absolutely valid procedures. This is "Aristotelian realism" or "moderate realism."°

°*See pp. 343ff.*

Space and *Time* intrigue Aquinas, but he follows Aristotle closely and invests less thought in the problem. Space is real, in his judgment, but it exists only as a matrix for physical bodies; where there are no lumps of matter there is no space. Space, therefore, is coterminous with the physical universe; beyond that there exists only potential space. Regarding time, the now of consciousness is the result of the mind's "alternation" of the present instant, thus creating a succession of instants that we experience as a continuum. We use the experience of time, and measure time, only in regard to the before and after of things in motion. His final position sounds Augustinian: "*Si non esset anima, non esset tempus.*" "If it's not in the soul, then it's not in time."[8] Eternity is another matter altogether. It too is real and possesses duration, but is without beginning or end, before and after, or any sequence of instants; eternity is not "stretched out" but exists all at once.

Aquinas's *metaphysics* is almost entirely Aristotelian. Physical objects are created from primal matter (the *materia prima* of Aristotle) and form; neither exists by itself. The existence of everything is accounted for with Aristotle's four "causes" (*aitia*).°

°*See pp. 189ff.*

Every being is composed of potentiality and actuality. Matter is potentiality; primal matter is pure potentially and nothing more. Form confers actuality on objects. In living things form is the source of life and motion. Angels are pure form without matter. Matter is composed of the four classical elements, fire, earth, air, and water; the heavenly bodies are composed of some other kind of matter entirely.

"Being" is the most universal of all the mind's ideas; it is both real and mental, but it can't be defined; it simply is, and it is one. It applies to the highest actuality as well as the lowest. Being is the first object of cognition. Between God (who is pure actuality, *Actus Purus*) and primal matter (which is pure potentiality) is a graded hierarchy of all other existing things, all of which are combinations of potentiality and actuality in varying amounts. Everything, therefore, is a blend of essence and existence—except God, whose essence is also his existence. "God exists" is an analytical proposition, argues Aquinas; for if our minds were up to comprehending the nature of existence, we would find that "God" includes the predicate "existence." But because of our mental limitations, we must think of the proposition as a posteriori and seek proof of God's existence.

Aquinas's *epistemology* also follows Aristotle. The mind is a blank tablet, and the senses activate the mind's potential. All knowledge begins with the senses: *"Nihil est in intellectu quod prius non fuerit in sensu."* "Nothing is in the intellect that is not first in the senses." The intellect goes to work only after the senses have submitted their input. As an object acts, the senses react. Thomas makes a distinction between what will later be termed primary qualities (motion, shape, size, etc.; *sensibilia communia*) that inhere in real objects and secondary qualities (color, sound, taste, etc.; *sensibilia propria*) that are in objects only potentially; that is, they exist only when an object is perceived. What we perceive is a physiological counterpart of the physical process that takes place in the real world; and between the object and the senses there exists some sort of connecting media *(species sensibiles)* that facilitate a correspondence between image and object. The intellect captures this sense knowledge, screens out the material elements of the sense images, and creates an imageless universal idea or concept; and this concept is the proper object of knowledge which we employ in subsequent reasoning tasks and to make comparative judgments. This process of creating knowledge Thomas likens to the impression of a seal on wax: What is impressed on the wax is the form of the seal, but not the seal. The mind, therefore, knows the form of the object, not the object. So while a full knowledge of the object may escape us, the form is known with clarity and certainty. Of course our sensing can give us faulty information when the sense is not working properly, when it is plagued with fatigue, and when we confuse the secondary with the primary qualities.

The central fact of Thomas's *psychology* is that the human being is a union of matter and form, that is, body and soul. Man is a compound, not a mixture. The soul is created by God and infused into the body at the moment of conception. The body requires the soul for life and action; the soul requires the body for its sustenance and mobility. The soul is the self-originating principle that is the basis of—or is—the vital functions and motion of an organism. (This is Aquinas's definition of "life"— self-motion.) The soul does nothing in which the body does not participate, and the body does nothing in which the soul doesn't participate (if the body drinks, the soul gets drunk, quipped Mark Twain). However, the intellect, while dependent on the functioning body, is yet independent of it; for in the act of pure thought it transcends all material conditions and proves that the soul is immaterial. And being immaterial the soul at death survives the body but finds itself in an unnatural, restless state until it is reunited with its new body at the resurrection. The soul is a form and is therefore incorruptible. All life is a victory of form over matter. Perfection of the soul is achieved through knowledge and virtue, which are attained by transcending the material conditions of life, that is, by distancing ourselves from physical matter. Since death is the final separation of the soul from matter, death brings a perfecting of the soul.

Ethics occupies almost a third of Thomas's system of theology and receives detailed treatment. The final goal of a human life is "blessedness" which rests on a vision of God, who alone can still the restlessness of the human heart. Complete happiness can be realized only in the next life, but a happiness of sorts can be achieved in this life providing we possess health, a modicum of necessary things, and good friends. As for moral action, if circumstances and intention are good, then the action is good. *"Bonum ex integra causa; malum ex quocumque defectu."* "Moral decency arises from good intent, moral evil from a defective intent."[9]

Politics in Aquinas's system is essentially a baptized Aristotelianism. The state exists only to enable each individual to grow in faith and to redeem his soul; to this end it must provide its citizens with education and meet their existence needs. The state is subservient to the Church which holds temporal leaders in check to prevent

An astronomer, a scribe, and a mathematician are hard at work using newly resurrected sciences. A painting from a Psalter (Book of Psalms) used by St. Louis and Blanche of Castille.

tyranny. Just as a man's spirit is master of his body, the Church is master of the state. Kings are subject to the pope; civil authorities are subject to ecclesiastical authorities. Rome is the supreme head of all Christendom; to obey Rome is to obey God. Obedience to the pope is necessary to salvation, and it follows that the pope is infallible in faith and morals. Thomas is the first theologian to discuss papal infallibility. Civil authority must concern itself with the welfare, not of individuals, but of the body social. Laws in a society must be founded on moral principles and must be reasonable. Aquinas sees three kinds of laws: divine law, natural law, and positive law. Natural law derives from divine law and is inscribed on "the tables of the heart."

Heresy is a crime subject to punishment, just as murder and theft. No one can be forced to enter the Church, but once a member he can be compelled, by violent means if necessary, to adhere to the truth—*haeretici sunt compellendi ut fidem teneant.* To save their souls, persecution of heretics is permitted even to death.

SYNTHESIZER

Thomas Aquinas was not a great creator; he was a synthesizer. More than any other thinker, he is responsible for the creation of the new medieval Christian worldview that brought coherence to countless fragments of myth, knowledge, and speculation and which was to cause enormous problems during the next few centuries as philosophic intellects attempted desperately to move out of and beyond this medieval world; his anointing of Aristotle with final authority in so many realms of philosophy was especially troublesome. In his attempt to be complete he was the greatest of the Schoolmen; and he was by far the greatest in his conviction that all knowledge, whatever its source, could be fitted together into one coherent, harmonious whole.

THE MEDIEVAL MIND

Such things have been revealed to me, wordless things, that everything I have written seems to me to be straw, worthless straw.
THOMAS AQUINAS

For the medieval mind, religion supplied complete answers to the two universal questions addressed by all humans in all cultures in every century: How does the world work? What is the meaning of a human life? After a thousand years of accumulated doctrine, and after the logical minds of the thirteenth century had completed their work, these and all related questions had been given final answers.

According to medieval man each individual human person is a union of a body and a soul. His soul, unfortunately, is diseased; it became infected by the original sin of Adam and Eve's disobedience in the Garden of Eden. Because it is diseased, the soul lost its power for good and is subject to the maulings of the body with its prideful cravings and insidious urges.

Life's purpose, therefore, lies entirely in the struggle to achieve a cleansing of the soul of this lethal disease. The Church exists solely to effect this cleansing through the sacrament of baptism that washes away the infection and restores the soul to health, so that the purified soul may enter into the sacred body of Christ; and the other sacraments and ministrations of the Church exist to support and sustain the soul through the rest of its precarious earthly sojourn, so it can attain eternal life with God. Therefore, the meaning of human life—and its only meaning—lies in discovering God's plan and saving one's soul by being baptized, believing in Christ, and doing his will.

From these revealed archai or first principles, the rest of the medieval worldview follows logically.

(1) The world is a stage on which the drama of salvation takes place, and history is the unfolding of that dramatic plot from its beginning (in the Garden) to its climactic ending (with the return of Christ).

On Aquinas *He laboured as if all depended on his own efforts and prayed as if all depended on God.*
                                        D. J. KENNEDY

(2) Humans, therefore, are not part of a natural historical process, but of a suprahistorical drama. Indeed, there is no such thing as "a natural historical process," for all events happen as effects of God's will and therefore have meaning only in terms of his intent and plan. If a child does poorly in school, the "cause" cannot be traced to influences in the home. If he joins a gang, finishes college, becomes a priest or fisherman, or dies in a rockfall, such "effects" have complex supernatural antecedents and are not to be "explained" as "natural historical causal processes." Man is a player in a supranatural story, the other determinative players being God, the Devil, angels, demons, saints, et al.

(3) What we call nature (physical nature, the cosmos, the world, the universe) has no meaning in itself apart from this salvation drama. It is merely a background staging area. It is, however, the carefully designed backdrop which, when studied carefully, can reveal valuable information about God and his great drama.

(4) Everything is teleological; nothing happens without a purpose, since, after all, it is a small part of the great purposive drama. The spiritually wise person will interpret every object/event in the light of its (divinely intended) purpose. If a feather falls to earth, it has a purpose, and one should ask, What is that purpose? If a flood or drought destroys a crop, it has a purpose: What is that purpose? If a loved one dies, or a volcano erupts, or a comet passes over the Earth, each is driven by an intended purpose: What might that purpose be? (With this interpretation, one must be very careful, of course: The cosmos is filled with evil spirits as well as good spirits, and nature's phenomena just might be signals from the demons or the Devil that would lead one away from God; one can't always be sure.)

(5) This present life is relatively unimportant. It is but a fleeting "overture" (*allegro vivace*—it passes very fast!) that, if lived properly, will lead to continued existence in Eternity. Whether one's life is long or short means nothing; its value lies solely in its being lived virtuously so as to merit eternal life. All material things, all

A panel by Pedro Berruguete depicting St. Dominic presiding over an Auto-da-fé; now in the Museo del Prado, Madrid. Berruguete's style is usually described in such terms as "eclectic, a mixture of the Flemish, Spanish Gothic, and Italian Renaissance, but never imitative; he combines luxurious ornament and gold decoration with simplicity and ease." (The burning flesh is never mentioned.)

enjoyments, all pleasures are essentially evil since they can seduce us away from the spiritual life, which is our true purpose in being here. The individual, as an individual, with unique personal experiences, is of little or no significance; it is the drama that is significant, not the dramatis personae.

(6) Like it or not, we humans must adjust to and learn to live in a universe of preestablished values. Values are not ideas that we humans create in our minds when we value things. Goodness, truth, and beauty—and purity, nobleness, sanctity, meaning, and so on—are actual qualities that inhere in real objects/events. Also real are evil, ugliness, corruption, and sin. No qualities are merely "in the eye of the beholder." God is a valuer, just like us humans, and he has created a cosmic order that embodies these (his) values. These values, which are guarded, interpreted, and taught by the Church, can meet all of one's needs, material and spiritual. The individual's task is not to fabricate new and different values, but to accept God's eternal, unchanging judgments and live by them.

ENDNOTES

1 Francis J. Catania, "Albert the Great," in Paul Edwards' *The Encyclopedia of Philosophy* (Macmillan, 1967), vol. 1, p. 65. Also quoted from Catania are the marginal quotations on pp. 390 and 391.

2 Philip Schaff [David S. Schaff], *History of the Christian Church* (Eerdmans, 1949), vol. 5, pp. 593f., 657ff., 719ff., 884ff.

3 *Encyclical*, August 4, 1879. The encomium reads: [Thomas is] *"inter scholasticos doctores omnium princeps et magister . . . ingenio docilis et acer, memoriae facilis et tenax, vitae integerrimus, veritatis, unice amator, devina humanaque scientia praedives."*

4 Anton C. Pegis, *Introduction to Saint Thomas Aquinas* (The Modern Library, 1948), p. xi.

5 Tocco, *Vita*, Cap. 3. The Latin reads, *"Nos vocamus istum bovem mutum, sed ipse adhuc talem dabit in doctrina mugitum quod in toto mundo sonabit."*

6 Thomas Aquinas, *Summa theologiae*, book I, ques. 2, art. 2. For a logical analysis of Aquinas's five proofs, see *The Problem of God*, by Peter Angeles (Charles E. Merrill, 1974).

7 See *Summa theologiae*, by Thomas Aquinas, I, 23, I, 3; I, 83, 1; I, 23, 3; I–II, 109, 6; I-II, 112, 2, 3. Thomas Aquinas, *Summa contra gentiles*, III, 163; III, 73.

8 Thomas Aquinas, *Summa theologiae*, Ia, X, 4: *"Fluxus ipsius nunc, secundum quod alternatur ratione, est tempus"*; *Commentary on the Books of Sentences*, I, Dist. XIX, II, 1.

9 Thomas Aquinas, *Summa theologiae*, Ia IIae, XVIII, 1.

CHAPTER 22

PHILOSOPHY DURING THE RENAISSANCE

The Renaissance represents a transition from the Middle Ages to the modern era, from the Greek *thanatos* of medieval theology to the Greek *eros* with its love of life, feeling for nature, sense of history, and respect for reason; the battle is waged by semihumanists such as Roger Bacon, Dante, and Copernicus, and by full-fledged humanists like Petrarca, da Vinci, and Erasmus.

THE RESURRECTION OF EROS

The Renaissance era is a nightmare to the student of the history of philosophy because it seems as though everything was happening *but* philosophy. Momentous revolutions were occurring in every field, but there were no major figures in philosophy that loom like the giants of the past. There were great painters such as Fra Angelico, da Vinci, Botticelli, and Raphael; and superlative sculptors such as Donatello and Michelangelo; and great architects—Alberti, Brunelleschi, Palladio; and many great writers, among them Dante, Erasmus, and Montaigne. There were also outstanding innovators in politics, business and trade, exploration, education, and religion. But great thinkers whose lives were specifically dedicated to the critical evaluation of thinking and knowing are notably absent.

The thousand-year-old philosophic tradition can be likened to a great river that vanishes underground. When we last see the river around AD 1300 it is still basking in the glory of Scholasticism; when it reemerges into view around 1600, Scholasticism is history and represents to scholars an awkward, primitive stage of human thinking. In 1300 humans lived in a teleological universe, filled with spiritual beings good and bad, and run by God for the benefit of man; in 1600 the universe was turning out to be more like a great autonomous machine ordered by mathematical principles, and man is, in some sense, a part of that machinery. In 1300 philosophy was still passionately in love with the next world; in 1600 it had found that it could largely ignore that other world, with impunity, and live a joyous existence in this one.

The primary cause of this transformation was the revitalization of the Greek *eros*. In Greek mythology Eros was the god of love, the first god who, at the beginning of time, emerged from chaos and brought order to the world. In time the word *eros* came to mean the love of beauty and goodness. Freud adopted the terms *eros* ("love") and *thanatos* ("death") to symbolize opposing psychic orientations: "life-force" and

It is not love towards God of which we are in search . . . but love towards things with life, that is, where there can be a return of affection.

ARISTOTLE

Immortal God! What a world I see dawning! Why can I not grow young again?

DESIDERIUS ERASMUS
(1517)

"death-wish." In the human organism, he said, there is an irreconcilable struggle between eros that seeks to preserve and enrich life, and thanatos, the death instinct that yearns to return life energy to the quietude of nothingness. When an individual or society is driven by thanatos he/it is fearful of life and seeks escape. When an individual or society is infused with eros, then he/it loves life and aggressively seeks the adventure, beauty, pleasure, and attainments that body and soul, working together, can achieve. In a word, eros is the love of life. The Greeks of the Golden Age possessed this love of life and reveled in the creation of the arts, sciences, and philosophies. Life is good, they said, not bad. No one has understood the depths of human tragedy better than the Greeks, but they still believed that a life well lived is worth living. Even in life's bitter reversals, the freedom to rise, Phoenixlike, to greater heights of character and nobility is always there. By contrast the Dark Ages and the Scholastic era were dominated by thanatos: Men strove to escape life, to nullify the needs of the body (the "prison of the soul"), to minimize pleasure, to negate the self, and to insist that happiness is to be found only in meditating on the things of the spirit. "To the monk beauty was a snare, woman a temptation, pleasure a sin, the world vanity of vanities."[1] The individual dominated by eros wants to live, while one dominated by thanatos wants to have done with this life and move on to an existence elsewhere.

Renaissance men brought eros back to life by resurrecting the high culture of Greece and Rome. The word *"renaissance"* means "rebirth" and to fifteenth- and sixteenth-century scholars it referred to a reawakening to the Greek creative genius after the long night of the Dark Ages. For a thousand years eros had been lost in the dismal imagery of Heaven, Hell, and Purgatory so vividly depicted in Dante's *Divine Comedy*. The Church had succeeded in persuading the Western world that *the* purpose of this life is to allow the soul time to make preparations for its existence in eternity. Now this doctrine is called into question as millions of souls discover that the experiences of this life can be fulfilling ends in themselves.

This revival had begun about AD 1200 with the recovery of Aristotle's works, but at that time the excitement was largely limited to scholastics who saw in Greek writings new ways of examining and defending Church doctrine.° With few exceptions, the Schoolmen of the thirteenth century performed their work within rigid parameters established by the Church. Occasionally, of course, a few scholars threatened to push their interests beyond the boundaries of orthodoxy: Abélard loved Virgil's *Aenead*, and Schoolmen commonly quoted from Cicero, Livy, Tacitus, Suetonius, Ovid and other Latin authors. But popes saw in such a trend a grave threat to the faith and banned reading of the classics. Under papal threat, the University of Paris removed all Latin literature from its courses.

With the coming of the Renaissance—because of "all the other things that happened" during the fourteenth and fifteenth centuries—excitement over the classics came from a different source. It was the nonclerical scholars who read the classics and became inspired when they found ideas and values that the Churchmen had ignored. They read the "pagan" literature with different eyes and felt they had been given new life.

Herein lies the significance of the Renaissance. By AD 1600 virtually every ingredient in the medieval worldview had been challenged, analyzed, criticized, and found to be very low in nutritional value, or even toxic to the human system. It was this critical awareness that gave birth to modern civilization.

Bernard of Clairvaux represents the mind and heart of the medieval world. On a trip from Rome back to his Cistercian monastery, he traveled all day along the shores of Lake Geneva, with snowy Mont Blanc in the distance shining down on

Eros, son of Aphrodite, was a favorite deity of the Athenians and shared in the love goddess's cultic festivities. Here the infant Eros adorns a gold earring.

It is a joy to live!
ULRICH VON HUTTEN
(THE SPIRIT OF THE
RENAISSANCE)

Wisdom confers on man powers which perfect his nature.
NICOLA ABBAGNANO

° See pp. 340ff. and 386ff.

Out of the astronomy of the Arabs the Christians got only astrology; out of their chemistry they got only alchemy.
ELWOOD CUBBERLEY

That a Renaissance should have been needed is a startling fact in the history of human development and demands explanation.
DAVID SCHAFF

velvet-green pine forests and the blue waters of Lac Léman. With his cowl over his head, Bernard was meditating on the sins of mankind, and in the evening, when the party stopped at Lausanne, he asked his companions what scenery they had passed on the journey, for he had beheld none of it. But had Bernard raised his eyes to see, he would have seen, not the pale rose of a sunset illuminating the Alps, but God sending a message to a depraved humanity. "The trees and rocks will teach thee what thou canst not hear from human teachers."[2]

Francesco Petrarca was the literary genius of the early Renaissance humanists. "Today," he wrote one day about AD 1336, "I ascended the highest mountain in this region, which, not without cause, they call the Windy Peak." And why did Petrarch climb Windy Peak? "Nothing but the desire to see its conspicuous height was the reason for this undertaking. . . . At first I stood there almost benumbed, over-whelmed by a gale such as I had never felt before and by the unusually open and wide view. I looked around me: clouds were gathering below my feet, and Athos and Olympus grew less incredible . . . The Alps were frozen stiff and covered with snow. . . . They looked as if they were quite near me, though they are far, far away. . . . I admired every detail, now relishing earthly enjoyment." But then, from some strange feeling of guilt (Freud would undoubtedly label it "pleasure anxiety"), Petrarch opened a copy of Augustine's *Confessions* which he says he always carried with him. There he read "And men go to admire the high mountains, the vast floods of the sea, the huge streams of the rivers, the circumference of the ocean, and the revolutions of the stars—and desert themselves." Petrarch says he was stunned and sat meditating, till he realized that it was not really the mountain or sea or ocean that is great, but the human mind which, "compared to *its* greatness nothing is great."[3]

RENAISSANCE TRENDS:
THE OTHER THINGS THAT HAPPENED

When Duns Scotus died in AD 1308, scholasticism was finished. For various reasons it had lost the respect of both thinkers and laymen and rapidly passed into history; the average believer had become bored by it all, and most Schoolmen came to realize only very late how trivial their obsessions had become. Men's minds, sated on metaphysics and put off by an unimaginative rehash of the same old questions, were beginning to turn back to a real world that had for a thousand years been neglected. Movements started up, it seems, in every human endeavor, all working together to close out the medieval era.

THE CRUSADES
Charlemagne died in AD 814, and the empire he had created rapidly began to fall apart, and the sundry enclaves of western Europe were forced to reorganize as best they could. Small landowners, freemen, and serfs turned to noblemen for protection in exchange for work, and the feudal system was born. From about 900 to about 1250 feudalism was the prevailing form of political arrangement. But this lord-and-vassal system could not be a permanent solution, for the history of feudalism is largely the story of nobles quarreling and fighting among themselves.

The Crusades went far to undermine the feudal system. The first wave of Christian soldiers was blessed and sent on their way by Pope Urban II in July, 1095; great armies of devout "soldiers of Christ" left their homes and began the long trek to the Holy Land where they hoped to liberate Jerusalem from the Saracens (Muslims) who of late had been harrassing Christian pilgrims. Of the millions of men, women, and children (there was even a "Children's Crusade" in AD 1212) who started the journey, a few thousand reached the Holy City, and in one of the bloodiest scenes in all of history the Saracens were slaughtered and Jerusalem once again flew the Christian flag. All told, seven Crusades occupied Europeans from 1095 to 1270.

Europe was transformed by the Crusades. The pope had urged nobles to stop fighting among themselves and fight the Infidels instead; so the Crusades created a goal that gave Christians a common purpose against a common foe. The knights and nobles with red crosses emblazoned on white tunics, priests and monks, and soldiers from all the European nations (except Spain) marched toward the Holy Land.

Those who returned from the impossible dream had been introduced to a larger world. They had seen a civilization far superior to theirs that could boast of wealthy cities and well-run governments. They saw wonders of art and architecture. They heard new languages and watched devotees practicing alien religions. They were baffled by strange customs, outlandish dress, new flora and fauna, and exotic foods. They had fought side by side with brother Crusaders from every nation, and the traditional boundaries that separated them began to seem less important. When they returned home they brought back an enriched experience of *this* world that made the medieval depictions of the *next* world seem irrelevant and far away. They had all faced danger and survived. Countless numbers of ordinary men returned with a new sense of worth that emboldened them to raise their voices for the first time ever and make themselves heard.

These thoughts and feelings resulted in a surge of new activities: exploration and discovery of new worlds and peoples; a revival of trade and industry; burgeoning cities with new classes of craftsmen, merchants, and bankers; a new middle class of freemen and burghers; new educational systems; and the first seeds of what would germinate into modern nations. Driving these pursuits was a revitalized sense of human dignity and self-confidence, a brand-new individualism of the kind not known since the best days of Athens, and a Zeitgeist permitting human beings to be themselves, to value mind and body, and to make the most of the days we have on Earth, not as a prelude to a far-off, iffy Paradise, but as a sure existence filled with experiences that are their own reward.

Not until the world could shake off this medieval attitude toward scientific inquiry and make possible honest doubt was any real intellectual progress possible.

ELWOOD CUBBERLEY

EXPLORATION AND DISCOVERY

A direct outgrowth of the Crusades was a new era of geographic exploration and discovery. In 1295 Marco Polo returned from the East and told outlandish tales of new lands and peoples. About 1400, with the perfection of the campass, longer sea voyages were undertaken. Portuguese sailors discovered the Canary Islands in 1402, the Madeiras in 1419, the Cape Verdes in 1460. Then the Portuguese, fired by the notion of driving the Muslims out of north Africa, sailed down the west African coast. What they discovered was that the Muslims were entrenched but that black Africans could be taken back to Europe and sold for a handsome profit.

When the Turks closed down the Venetian trade route through the Mediterranean, European traders began a search for new ways to the Orient. Believing that the world is round, Columbus, sailing west to go east, serendipitously came across a new continent in 1492. In 1496 John Cabot sailed into the north Atlantic and claimed everything he found for England. In 1497 Vasco da Gama rounded the tip of Africa and opened a passage to India where he established a trading post on the Malabar coast. In 1499 South America was discovered by Europeans (or the native Indians, already there, discovered the Europeans). In 1518 Spanish conquistadors explored the Gulf of Mexico; in 1519 Cortés destroyed the Aztec nation; by 1525 the

Society . . . really consists only of people.

J. W. N. WATKINS

Spaniards had crossed Panamá to the Pacific coast; and in 1533 Pizarro and 180 soldiers ascended into the Peruvian Andes and, with the help of 37 horses, weapons of steel, and smallpox, against which the natives had no immunity, made short work of the Inca nation. Magellan sailed around the globe from 1519 through 1521 and finally proved that the world is round (actually Magellan died in the Philippines; his surviving crew proved that the world is round).

After a century of discovery, the European consciousness had been turned outward, or at least westward, and its major preoccupations were with silver and gold, not universals and essences. The Franciscan missionaries who accompanied these expeditions were motivated by faith, of course, but the men whose names we read in our history books were mostly driven by the promise of wealth and immortality, preferably in this life.

GROWTH OF CITIES

The importance that the modern world attaches to human personality is the consequence of an attitude made possible by Renaissance humanism.

NICOLA ABBAGNANO

The growth of cities was a major factor in shaping a new worldview. In the 11th century Italian cities began to overthrow their rulers, the prince-bishops, and to transmutate into city-states much like those of ancient Greece; in them a coherent city life emerged in northern and central Italy. Elsewhere in Europe, by about 1200, cities were becoming numerous and important. Inevitably, these urban centers organized, passed laws, and began to demand greater autonomy. Revolts against overlords became common, and by means of power struggles and/or negotiations, rights were secured and charters drawn and sealed. By such means hundreds of self-governing "free towns" arose throughout Europe, demanding a franchise to elect their own magistrates and levy taxes. In these city-states emerged new classes of citizens and new associations of merchants, artisans, and businessmen who, also, began to demand rights and privileges. These "freemen," "burghers," and "bourgeoisie" were the beginning of a middle class, and they were always restive under the Church's restraints. They developed new educational systems independent of ecclesiastical control. Autonomous guilds were established by likeminded men in their respective vocations: craft guilds organized by bakers, tanners, carpenters, fishers, butchers, and leather workers; merchant guilds of shippers, businessmen, and shopkeepers; guilds of scholars, teachers, and copyists—and these associations, too, increasingly demanded their freedoms.

NATIONALISM

Parallel to the growth of cities, beginning in the latter half of the thirteenth century, was the emergence of a new nationalism, the feeling that one's common interests as a Frenchman, say, or an Englishman, constitute one's identity and have first claim on one's loyalties; all other named associations and individuals are deemed to be foreign, even the pope. This growing sense of a local and national belonging worked to erode the Augustinian claim that all men everywhere belong to a world sovereignty—the City of God—under the world rulership of the papacy.

EDUCATION

In education new philosophies and systems replaced those created and run by the Church during the Middle Ages. From about the middle of the fourth century AD, all education was designed, directly or indirectly, to prepare the soul for the next life. Salvation rested on one's faith in true doctrine, so that education aimed at conditioning the mind and heart to submit to the truth, with tenacity but without intelligence or critical thought. The goals of Greek and Roman education—to develop character and to prepare men to be wise leaders and intelligent citizens—were abandoned.

In 1416 a complete copy of Quintilian's *Institutes of Oratory* had been discovered at Saint Gall giving a detailed summary of Roman education, and this helped to inspire a reappraisal of teaching. It inspired a return to classic ideals, and humanist schools were everywhere started by scholars and teachers and supported enthusiastically by merchants, officials, and the upper classes. Italian education emphasized the growth and fulfillment of the individual and resulted in only minor religious and moral reforms, while northern European and English systems concentrated on moral and religious living and practical usefulness. As a result students were given a thorough grounding in Greek and Latin history and literature, supported by training in manners and morals using the writings of Livy and Plutarch as guides to conduct. To develop the whole person, as did the Greeks and Romans, the curriculum included fencing, wrestling, track, dancing, and competitive games. Humanist education prepared the student for a useful and enjoyable life here and now. It encouraged him to appreciate the accomplishments of the past and to know them as his heritage. This program was vastly superior to anything the cathedral schools could offer. These innovations flowed from Italy to France and Germany and permanently changed the purpose of Western education.

UNIVERSITIES

One of the most significant events of the thirteenth century was the evolution of the universities. The Church had already established specialized schools: monastic schools by the tenth century, convent schools by the eleventh; and in the larger cities cathedral schools, song schools, parish schools, and chantry schools (the last endowed by bequests). For more than six hundred years these institutions constituted the educational system of western Europe.

But as time passed the cathedral schools gradually concentrated more on advanced studies, leaving the other schools to take over the elementary subjects of reading, writing, and grammar (because of their emphasis on grammar they were called "grammar schools"). The curriculum of the cathedral schools included some or all of the seven liberal arts of the Middle Ages: the *trivium*—grammar, rhetoric, and logic; and the *quadrivium*—geometry, arithmetic, music, and astronomy. When a student became well versed in the liberal arts, he could then proceed to ethics, metaphysics, and—if he was planning a career in the Church—theology.

By a natural process, some of the cathedral schools rose above others by offering superior instruction and/or boasting a staff of famous teachers and scholars. These schools attracted the brightest and best of European youth, many traveling great distances to pursue their education. Stimulated by the new interest in Greek studies, certain cathedral schools grew rapidly: York and Canterbury in England; Paris, Chartres, and St. Gaul in France (the latter famed for its music, Paris for its theological studies); Bologna and Padua in Italy (acclaimed for teaching civil and canon law). These places came to be known as *studia generalia*, recognized centers of education where lectures were open to students of all countries and all social and economic backgrounds.

By AD 1200, to protect against intrusion from outside interference, students and teachers began to organize themselves into associations and to seek recognition of the rights and privileges essential to their craft—freedom to discuss ideas and to teach different points of view; freedom to read and copy manuscripts without censorship; the right to conduct examinations of their students and to issue licenses to those they judged qualified to teach; the right to discipline (or not to discipline) students for infractions. In time, charters guaranteeing these rights were given to the burgeoning cathedral schools by kings and popes.

Despite Aquinas' deep study of every aspect of the Aristotelian corpus, he utterly failed to understand the true spirit and methods of natural science.

A. R. HALL

There is . . . no qualitative similarity between the thermodynamic properties of a gas and the mechanical properties of its elements.

W. H. DRAY

From these teacher-student associations arose the universities of western Europe. Their chartered teaching organizations were part of a much wider movement of autonomous associations sweeping Europe during the eleventh, twelfth, and thirteenth centuries, resulting in the creation of arts-and-crafts guilds, merchant guilds, and other groups of men with common interests, the purpose for all being to withstand outside oppression and control. Soon there were four distinct faculties in many of the great universities—Arts, Law, Medicine, and Theology. These divisions were well established by the fourteenth century, and each faculty gradually became more autonomous and more militant in defining and defending its rights and freedoms.

Two of the rights obtained early on by the universities were the privileges of *cessatio* and the issuing of teachers' licenses. The cessatio was the right to go on strike—to stop lectures, close libraries, even to shut down the university (which the University of Paris did repeatedly when it needed to excercise political clout) to redress grievances against outside authorities, both civil and ecclesiastical. The right to license students gave the universities control of academic standards without the intrusion of dogmatic churchmen or ignorant civil officials. These all-important early victories paved the way for even greater academic freedoms: freedom to seek the truth and to allow reason to lead where it will; freedom to harbor unpopular opinions and argue unpopular causes; freedom to follow the dictates of conscience. The universities of the fourteenth century were virtually the only centers of free thought. They were the most democratic institutions of the time, and they became role models—not always appreciated—for a more democratic way of thinking. Both the institutions and individual members of the faculties began to express their opinions on public matters and to offer counsel to kings and popes, who often found it expedient to heed their advice.

The universities were the first organizations to challenge the monopoly of the Catholic Church in its control of thinking, teaching, and learning; and, in the long run, that challenge succeeded. During the Dark Ages manuscripts and learning were preserved in monasteries, but with the growth of the universities all knowledge, research, and the copying and cataloguing of ancient texts, came to rest in the hands of trained scholars and teachers of the arts and sciences; and these men increasingly asserted their independence from the dictates of both Church and State and became critics of Western culture. It was from the faculties of Medicine that graduates went on to battle against superstition and bigotry and lay foundations for the future growth of the medical sciences. Graduates from the faculties of Law took the lead in writing charters and working for political and economic rights to benefit the common man. It was from the faculties of Theology that graduates emerged to criticize corruption in the Church and mount attacks on the ignorance, superstition, insensitivity, and immorality of priests and monks, and even the malfeasance of popes; and when all else failed, they launched a Reformation.

THE PROTESTANT REFORMATION

On the 31st of October, AD 1517, at twelve o'clock noon, a disgruntled monk walked to the castle-church at Wittenberg, Saxony, and nailed some papers to the big wooden doors. Written on them in Latin were ninety-five brief statements of Church doctrine that he wanted to debate. He was especially distraught by the Church's teaching on penitence and its flagrant marketing of indulgences. The opening inscription on the papers read: "In the desire and with the purpose of elucidating the truth, a disputation will be held on the underwritten propositions at Wittenberg, under the presidency of the Reverend Father Martin Luther, Monk of the Order of St. Augustin, Master of Arts and of Sacred Theology." If one couldn't attend the debate, he added, then write a letter. "In the name of our Lord Jesus Christ. Amen."

[During the Renaissance] the mind of God was transferred to the mind of Man.

ROBERT HUGHES

Man alone knows what suffering is, hence in inflicting it he becomes a monster.

GEORGIO DE SANTILLANA

This was the opening shot in the Protestant Reformation that was to dis-integrate and then renew European civilization. The Ninety-five Theses were immediately translated into German and within two weeks had been published all over Germany. Luther, at this time, intended no revolt against the Church, but his protest touched a nerve and the rebellion spread. He was excommunicated in 1520, but he publicly burned the letter of excommunication along with a volume of canon law.

Luther's revolt was merely one of the powerful forces working to erode papal authority. The best men of the Latin Church, sick at the dissolute morals of church-men at all levels, had been pushing for reform for more than two centuries, but the lack of change left them discouraged. One of Boccaccio's stories in the *Decameron* tells of a Jew named Abraham who resisted all attempts to get him to convert to Christianity. He decided to go to Rome to study the religion for himself. What he found was a Church rotten to the core, corrupt at every level, including cardinals openly living with concubines in sensuous luxury. He concluded that Christianity is clearly the religion of God, else it could not possibly have survived. So he joined the faith.

The German culture critic and philosopher Friedrich Nietzsche later judged that the Renaissance provided Western civilization a glorious opportunity to free itself of the life-denying Christian morality; but that the opportunity was lost because of Martin Luther. "Luther, this calamity of a monk, restored the church and, what is a thousand times worse, Christianity, at the very moment *when it was vanquished*."

In light of the Church's refusal to heed the signs of discontent, reformation was inevitable. With minor variations the Protestant Reformation engulfed and split all of Europe: northern and western Germany went with Luther, as did Denmark, Norway, Sweden, and Finland. The other reformers, Zwingli and Calvin, carried part of Switzerland, northern France, the Netherlands, Scotland, and parts of England. The English parliament in 1534 severed all ties with the papacy and established the Anglican Church. Most of France, Switzerland, and eastern and southern Europe remained with Rome. In general, those parts of western Europe that had once been a part of the old Roman Empire stayed loyal to the Roman Church, while the regions of the old Germanic tribes joined the Protestants.

Luther declared his freedom from Rome, but he was unable to grant it to others who held beliefs that differed from his; this was true also of the other reformers, and notably John Calvin. So for two centuries the various religious factions warred on one another until the peace of Westphalia in 1648 which stopped the bloody Thirty Years' War. Though this treaty embodied the viable seeds of religious freedom, they were not to germinate for another century, during which, haltingly, words began to replace the sword and schools the torch as the arena of battle.

The effect of the Reformation was

- to replace the authority of the Church with the authority of the Bible;
- to replace the Church's responsibility to dispense salvation with personal responsibility for one's own salvation;
- to replace the Church's claim that only it can interpret Scripture with the freedom of each individual to interpret it for himself;
- to replace the Church's interposition of itself between God and the believer by giving each believer his own intimate access to his God;
- to replace the Church's moral formalism with the individual's informed conscience.

This shift in focus from the priestly collective to the individual supported the forces of humanism and helped establish a trust in human nature and natural reason. It also required that education be made available to everyone so that each person could

[I regret the time spent] on philosophy and all that devil's muck, when I could have been busy with poetry and legend and so many good things.
MARTIN LUTHER

Erasmus is an enemy of all religion, he is the true adversary of Christ, a perfect replica of Epicurus and Lucian. Whenever I pray, I pray for a curse on him.
MARTIN LUTHER

participate knowledgeably in religious affairs. Hence, the Protestant nations took education very seriously and created schools in which these values could be taught; out of these schools came new leaders in all spheres of life. The rights and freedoms given to individuals in religious matters led directly to a spate of struggles for more democratic arrangements. The great struggles of the sixteenth and seventeenth centuries were for religious freedom and tolerance; the struggles of the eighteenth and nineteenth centuries were for political rights and freedoms; the prevailing struggles of the twentieth century have been for universal human rights and equality.

ART, LITERATURE, AND PHILOSOPHY

With Freud, man lost his Godlike mind; with Darwin his exalted place among the creatures on earth; with Copernicus man had lost his privileged position in the universe.

NORWOOD RUSSELL
HANSON

The Renaissance has always been most visible in the arts, literature, and philosophy—the humanities. If the thirteenth century was the Golden Age of Theology, the fourteenth century was the Golden Age of the Humanities. Native literatures were springing up all over Europe, and Dante wrote his *Divina Comedia*, not in Latin, but in Italian. National epics—the Arthurian legends, Chansons, Nibelungen Lied, and El Cid—were being reduced to writing. The process of making paper became known in Europe near the end of the thirteenth century, and books became more available in Italian, French, Provençal, Tuscan, Spanish, Catalan, English, and German, with a corresponding neglect of Latin. Troubadours and minnesingers carried a new poetry of love and nature to courts, hamlets, and festivals. All these were momentous changes that awakened Renaissance Man's consciousness of his power, gave him confidence in himself and his creations, showed him the beauty of the world and the joy of life, restored his connections to the historic past and inspired a vision of a future that, with imagination and courage, he might create. The Renaissance began in Italy where much of the old Roman culture still lingered, and where Italians felt themselves the heirs of Imperial Rome. Petrarch is honored with the title the "Morning Star of the Renaissance," and his life and writings embody the full complement of humanist qualities. His friend Boccaccio shared that spirit. Both men spent their lives combing the libraries of monasteries and castles searching for ancient manuscripts. Petrarch made his first important find at Liège—two unknown orations of Cicero; then at Verona he discovered half of one of Cicero's lost letters. Others took up the quest for ancient writings, and by the end of the fourteenth century vast treasures of Latin literature had been recovered and made available to scholars everywhere.

Greek literature was not far behind. Manuel Chrysoloras, a Byzantine Greek scholar, began teaching Greek literature at Florence in 1396 and, from that time, a passion for Greek began spreading through the universities. In 1408 Guarino Veronese brought some fifty Greek manuscripts home from a visit to Constantinople; he later established a chair in the Greek and Latin classics at Florence. After the Turks conquered Constantinople in 1453 Italy became a refuge for scholars and educated laymen who escaped and brought with them the riches of Greek culture. A new wave of learning swept Italy, firing the keenest young minds with a love of classic literature, and inspiring the more important cities to found academies (modeled on Plato's Academy) to promote literary studies. Wealthy merchants, nobles, and sometimes churchmen gave the movement financial support, especially for collecting and copying manuscripts and establishing libraries. Lorenzo de' Medici sent two expeditions to Greece to search for manuscripts for his library in Florence. Two of the world's great extant libraries, at Urbino and the Vatican, were founded at this time.

These enthusiastic Italian youth—who often adopted Latin names and celebrated Greek festivals—are credited with opening the Western mind to the classic humanities.

PAPERMAKING AND PRINTING

The Greeks had rediscovered the art of making paper about 1250, and the first paper mill was founded in Italy in 1276; by 1450 paper had replaced parchment everywhere in Europe and was ready for the printing press. The invention of printing from movable type by Johannes Gutenberg in 1453 allowed books to be published rapidly and inexpensively. Ideas and information became available to everyone, textbooks could be bought by students, and all forms of education were accelerated. This dissemination of classic ideas—which means revolutionary ideas—spelled the death of the Middle Ages and the beginning of the Modern Era.

PHILOSOPHY DURING THE RENAISSANCE

HUMANISM, NATURALISM, AND INDIVIDUALISM

The Renaissance era shattered the Middle Ages with three major shifts in the way men thought. These were humanism, naturalism, and individualism. The word "humanism" derives from the Latin *humanitas*, "human nature," "human feeling," "kindness," "education," "culture." In Roman times the word was used to translate the Greek *paideia*, which meant "education" in general but implied education in the liberal arts that enable one to develop his human potential. With the recovery of Greek and Latin literature, the Renaissance humanists defined themselves as students of the *literae humanae*, the "humane studies" necessary for a human being to recover his lost humanity.

The essential idea of *humanism* is that being human is good, not bad. Human nature is trustworthy; it is promising; it is the source of creation, delight, wisdom, and progress. Man himself is the criterion for judging good and evil, sin and virtue, the beautiful and the ugly. Being fully human is the only source of personal fulfillment, and the capacity to be fully human is made possible through a resurrection of the eros and culture of the classical era. The humanists believed that the Greeks and Romans were the first human beings to achieve the golden ideal of being human. That humanness is to be found in their poetry, dramas, histories, art, architecture, and sculpture; in their ethics, politics, and lifestyles; and in their freedom, critical spirit, and creativity. The humanist scholars, therefore, saw their life work to be that of searching for ancient manuscripts, restoring and understanding them, teaching their secrets, and thereby resurrecting the life of Greece and Rome.

"*Naturalism*" refers to a sensitivity to nature. It meant the attempt to understand and feel a kinship with nature, and to understand human beings as creations of natural processes. Renaissance artists made great strides in representing nature accurately in art, sculpture, and literature. The striking illusion of depth in Mantegna's *Pietà* reveals a new perception of spatial relationships. The visible foreshortening in Tintoretto's *Last Supper* demonstrates an awareness of perspective that the human eye actually sees. Fra Angelico's *Annunciation* depicts garden plants as a scientist might describe them. Men felt free to observe what is taking place in physical nature, biology, psychology, history, and politics. The result was a new empiricism. Leonardo's notebooks reveal a deep involvement in all the arts and sciences and abound with insights into nature. Medieval art had been largely symbolic because it focused on the nonmaterial and supernatural; it made little difference if an artist captured the details of visible reality. By contrast, Renaissance artists returned to representational art and found that, in order to be precise and honest in their creations, they must learn to be observant.

The word *"individualism"* also needs definition. It refers to the capacity to see and appreciate differences in things without obliterating their distinctiveness. It means letting things be themselves. After all, each single object *is* unique, and philosophic individualism allows that object to retain its uniqueness. Differences are the facts of our hourly experience, providing our conceptualizing minds will allow us to see them. Our human faces all look different. Our ideas are different (that's why we have arguments, write editorials, fund PACs, get divorces, and have summit talks, wars, and philosophers' conventions). We have different religious beliefs and moral convictions. Artists have different styles. In contrast to the Dark Ages when different ideas and beliefs were branded "heresy" and their thinkers were hastened to the stake, the humanist considers differences to be good. He values differences and stresses uniqueness. Objects in a landscape painting are separated by space and have their own place in the foreground or background. Sculptors depict the facial lines and contours of real individuals rather than an abstract ideal as exemplified in Greek statues. The humanist encourages each person to be himself/herself. "The importance that the modern world attaches to human personality is the consequence of an attitude made possible by Renaissance humanism."[4]

Individualism implied the possibility of tolerance and peaceful coexistence. Humanists felt they understood the human impulses that create differences in religious belief and found those needs to be the same everywhere. The religious wars of past centuries resulted from our blindness to this shared humanness. If we humans were allowed to be ourselves, to have our own ideas and values, there is no reason why we cannot live together in peace.

This humanism/naturalism/individualism came nearer than any other to being the true philosophy of the Renaissance. (Hereafter the word "humanism" will be understood to include naturalism and individualism.) Humanism began in Italy about 1350, then spread rapidly to the other European countries.

There were many threads in the warp and woof of this old/new humanism, most of which had not been seen for a thousand years. One thread was the conviction that *humans are a part of nature.* "My home is the world," exclaimed Dante (implying, interestingly, that the three-storied afterworld of his *Divine Comedy* was not his home after all). The humanists, for the most part, accepted the notion of a soul, but they were convinced that the body is also rather important for living in this world, and its needs are to be taken seriously. Medieval asceticism annoyed them. Man's task is to become what he is, not what some theologian says he should (but cannot possibly, in this life) be. What he is, of course, can be left to drift in the animal state or be worked over, polished, and made wise. The important point, to the humanist, is that man has the power to improve himself, and he bears a moral responsibility to do so.

THE EMPIRICAL SPIRIT

The gradual recovery of the empirical spirit allowed the humanists to see the natural world through different eyes. They started with the conviction that a human being possesses the two tools necessary to understand nature: the senses and a rational mind. But there were two major obstacles to progress in the sciences: the attitude of the Church toward empirical observation, and the authority of Aristotle's answers (as opposed to his method). The power of both had to be broken, and the humanists, with a little help, did so successfully.

It was the humanist decision to live in the world that provoked a love of empiricism. The empirical psyche, however, was not easy to come by. Men had to learn to see again. When one is conditioned not to see, the recovery of seeing will be accompanied by confusion and guilt. It requires letting go of authority, giving in to a forbidden curiosity, indulging one's native puzzlement, learning to observe causal processes and patterns, developing viable hypotheses, and continually monitoring one's objectivity for the unwanted intrusion of ignorance and biases. The empirical mind cherishes verifiable facts, is excited by connections, goes ecstatic over insights, and is put off by fact claims filtered through emotional needs.

Empirical honesty often begins with a realization that the old ideas don't work, that is, they don't accurately describe the world; and this insight becomes clear only as one musters the courage to trust the senses—when one decides that the facts of experience, not authorities, must dictate one's beliefs. A confidence in the self, in the power of the rational mind to perceive reality, and a willingness to allow the truth of careful observation to lead where it must—these are the requisites that medieval man did not possess and that the humanists came to prize. The sciences were the happy result of this return to good sense.

MAN AND HISTORY

Another thread, precious to the humanists, was a recovered understanding of man as part and parcel of the historical process. History is an account of linear, historic causal effects and their consequences, and this is the only proper context for studying man. Therefore the accurate reconstruction of the past became very important during the Renaissance, for it was upon the truth of historic events that lessons can be learned and insights from past minds given new life. So the humanists strove to recover the Graeco-Roman culture as it actually existed in ancient times, and then to develop what they discovered from inside out; that is, to let Plato remain Plato without transmogrifying him into various revised versions—neo-Plato, Gnostic Plato, Christian Plato, and so on. Should Plato the man be resurrected and invited to their banquets, the humanists wanted Plato to be able to recognize his own thoughts. Having restored the historic figures and their ideas, the humanists then proceeded to apply the ancients' lessons to their own life and times. Though they didn't always succeed, the touchstone of historic integrity endured.

It was this sense of history that allowed the humanists to recognize the existence of "two Aristotles" and begin to correct a mistake that had prevailed during the Dark Ages and High Scholasticism. There was the logical Aristotle of the *Prior Analytics* who had been used to underwrite the great doctrinal systems of the Scholastics. And there was the empirical Aristotle of the *Posterior Analytics* who outlined the most sublime science of the classical world. To Aristotle, of course, these were one: observation and logic must work together; unless one's archai (starting points) are empirically sound, then the best logic will still lead to false conclusions. But theologians had used Aristotle's logic in such an insidious way, not to seek truth, but to defend noetic doctrine, that the humanists almost threw the baby out with the bathwater. That is, they were tempted to dismiss Aristotle altogether, as Francis Bacon would, as the source of all intellectual mischief. But Aristotle's sensible foundations remained rock solid, and humanists, seeing through the paradox, appropriated the Greek building blocks and allowed the natural sciences to blossom. The nature of the Great Perversion was perceived by only some of the Renaissance thinkers, of course. Others continued to use Aristotle to refute Aristotle.

RECOVERY OF THE SENSES

The phrase "recovery of the senses" may sound strange to a modern mind. But consider: If an individual has been told that the senses lie and can't be trusted, that pleasure is evil, that happiness is to be found only in denying one's normal feelings, that to be saved (approved of) one must "walk according to the spirit," not "according to the flesh"—if one has been conditioned from birth to know and feel these things, then the necessity of a resurrection of the body becomes understandable. The recovery of the senses meant recovering the capacity for experiencing pleasure and delight. In his *De voluptate* Lorenzo Valla (d. 1457) went farther and argued that pleasure is the sole goal of a human life, and is, in fact, what all human activity is designed to achieve. The raison d'être of government, economics, education, medicine, and art is to create and enhance human pleasure. Human endeavor is not to be judged by such puerile criteria as power, status, or wealth, but solely by its capacity to allow one to experience pleasure and give it to others. The recovery of Lucretius's *De rerum natura* led to a new appreciation of Epicurus, who the humanists felt to be, of all past philosophers, the closest to a correct assessment of human nature.°

°Compare to Epicurus's estimate of the role of pleasure in our lives, pp. 238ff.

CRITICAL SPIRIT

The development of a critical spirit was basic to humanists. Criticism, to humanists, was a positive frame of mind that meant honoring man's capacity to judge, with intelligence, what is true or false, right or wrong, good or bad, beneficial or detrimental. The critical psyche contrasts with the believing psyche, and makes a clean break with Scholastic method. This rebirth of criticism allowed scholars to collect, examine, question, correct, and edit the ancient texts and to reconstruct the daily life and thought of the Greeks and Romans. Driving it was a craving for truth, an awakening of an historical sense, and an appreciation of beauty in literature, nature and art. When this critical spirit was directed at Church doctrine and practice it resulted in the Reformation; when directed at nature it resulted in the sciences; when directed at politics it brought down kings and led to democracy.

FROM BACON TO BACON:
THE RETURN OF EMPIRICISM

EMPIRICISM

The three centuries that separate Roger Bacon from Francis Bacon—from 1300 to 1600—is, from a philosophical perspective, one continuous struggle, with numerous advances and setbacks, for the freedom to look carefully at the world and to discover what is actually going on. After a delay of almost two millennia, the dream of the presocratic philosopher/scientists and of Aristotle was called forth from near death and set afoot on a quickened pace toward the modern world.

Thus the Greek empirical psyche was resurrected. The essence of empiricism is what has been called "the authority of facts." The data/ideas employed by medieval thinkers derived from the Scriptures, from Aristotle or some other ancient writer, or from "the Church." But it was becoming clear to the new breed of critical intellects that these fact claims could not be trusted without first having their validity judged; and the only way they could be judged was to subject them to the truth of immediate experience. This meant the development of careful methods of observation and the precise application of inductive and deductive rules of reasoning. It was these double-checked data/ideas—critically established "facts"—that were replacing the outdated (and invalid) appeals to authority.

The adjective "empirical" comes from the Greek *empeiros*, "experienced" or "acquainted with" (the substantive plural *hoi empeiroi* means "things that are experienced"); and this gave birth to the Latin noun *experia*, "experience." In the history of

Roger Bacon dispatching the manuscript of his Opus majus to Pope Clement IV from his Franciscan prison cell in Paris.

philosophy, the word has generally been used to refer to knowledge derived from sense experience, and, by derivation, to the mood and movement in the Western philosophical tradition that has argued that all dependable knowledge must ultimately be gleaned from the senses; that is, only knowledge that is supported by sense data is sure and true. The shibboleth employed by empiricists has long been the phrase "There is nothing in the intellect which was not previously in the senses."

ROGER BACON

There were numerous precursors of the Renaissance spirit in whose life and work one can watch the wrestling between the noetic and the empirical. One especially deserves notice—Roger Bacon. Bacon was a star in the thirteenth-century galaxy of great thinkers and shines with the same magnitude as Albert and Thomas. But a combination of factors robbed him of his place in history.

In the literature Bacon is usually described as the first reformer of science, the first advocate of science education, a pioneer of scientific method, a prophet of the modern scientific age, the father of invention, the founder of chemistry, the founder of experimental method—"the greatest scientific light of the 13th century." There is truth in all these interpretations. Firm facts known to us include: Bacon experimented with black powder, constructed an android, worked with lenses and mirrors, described (or actually constructed) an eyeglass, magnifying glass, and camera (a box with a pinhole in it, the so-called *camera obscura*, through which he viewed a solar eclipse); he wrote of seeing distant stars up close, implying that he knew something of the telescope; he predicted flying machines, hot-air balloons, motorboats, and cars; he theorized about light, heat, forces, the cause of tides and melting snows. And much more. Therefore, though he died in 1294, Roger Bacon is clearly one of the first Renaissance men. Right?

Now consider the following descriptions found in Baconian literature: Bacon belonged to the Middle Ages; he was a thoroughgoing scholastic, one of the greatest theological minds of the era; to him theology was the Queen of the Sciences; all his life he adhered devoutly to orthodox doctrine. The purpose of science, he said, is to clarify God's word and support the authority of the Church, which alone has the right to interpret all knowledge, including scientific data. He pushed textual criticism so the Bible could be read more accurately. Philosophy, he believed, comes only through divine illumination. His dream was to establish a world system of believers under the rulership of the pope.

Clearly, Bacon lived somewhere on the boundary line between the medieval and modern worldviews, and kept one foot in each. But—since such appellations are usually meant as true descriptions of the man, and since we all must guard against our love of neat labels and simple categories—the question still persists: Was Bacon really a Schoolman or a Renaissance scientist? The answer, of course, is that there

When the flame of powder touches the soul of man, it burneth exceeding deep.
ROGER BACON

One science is the mistress of the others, namely, theology.
ROGER BACON

are inherent problems in the way we classify things. We classify ideas, objects, and events to organize our knowledge, that is, to meet a subjective need for order and system; but classifying doesn't alter the object. Bacon was Bacon—who else? It would seem epistemically wise to abandon efforts to fit Bacon into our categories and attempt to create categories that will fit Bacon. Ideas should be custom-made so they will describe realities, though too often we try to fit realities into our prefabricated ideas. (Quite often our classifications tell us more about ourselves as classifiers than about the objects classified.)

The history of Christianity throughout all the Dark Ages is a history of the distrust of inquiry and reason, and the emphasis of blind emotional faith.

ELWOOD CUBBERLEY

If you could ask Bacon in person about when or where he really belonged, he would doubtless complain that he was born in the wrong time and place. Philosophically, he lived on the cusp between the medieval and modern worlds. The medieval world demanded rigid adherence to religious doctrine and frowned on empirical observation; Bacon stubbornly resisted blind adherence to dogma and found great joy in looking at the world. So he led a vigorous, creative life in both worlds. How then did he avoid becoming schizoid? How did he avoid becoming a casualty in the grind and crush of opposing claims? We can give an interpretive answer to the first question; the answer to the second question—He didn't!—is a matter of historical record.

THE MAN   Bacon was an Englishman, born at Ilchester in Gloucestershire about AD 1214. Our knowledge of his early life is a blank, and the most probable chronology of his life finds him at Oxford University about 1230, at age sixteen, working on his master's degree, and coming under the influence of several Oxonian scholars. In 1237, at twenty-two, he was in Paris studying for a second master's, lecturing at the university, and writing. While in Paris he was privileged to listen to two great minds in action, Alexander of Hales and Albertus Magnus; but Bacon was critical of both for their nitpicking. He also watched the impressive William of Auvergne in public debate.

Reasoning does not suffice, but experience does.

ROGER BACON

In 1247 he returned to Oxford to study under two renowned scholar-scientists, Robert Grosseteste and Adam Marsh. These teachers changed Bacon's life. Sometime between 1247 and 1257 he joined the Franciscan Order, for we know that in 1257 he was forcibly taken to Paris by his Franciscan brothers and put under house arrest in a cell belonging to the Friars. For a decade—from 1257 to 1267—he was restricted. In ill health much of this time, he channeled his energy into writing. In 1266 his life was reinvigorated by a letter from the pope; this happier period lasted for two years, till 1268 when those hopes were dashed. Then in 1277 his troubles began in earnest with another confinement that lasted fourteen years. Finally freed in 1292, he found that his voice had been silenced; he was forgotten and unknown. He had only a few months of writing—still vigorous and clear—before his death, the exact date of which is not recorded. This is a bare outline of the life of a genius-out-of-time. Bacon's life is the classic account of a thinker who tries to live in two incompatible worlds and finds that his creative strength is largely sapped and drained by that attempt. Till the age of about thirty-three Bacon was devoted to the Catholic faith and conformed to orthodox doctrine and practice, though he does confess to a minor indifference to "what the crowd thinks." While studying at the University of Paris he mastered Aristotle's writings and the Arabian commentators on Aristotle; then he lectured on Aristotle, one of the first to do so after the papal ban on Aristotle's writings had been lifted. He proceeded to write commentaries on several of Aristotle's treatises, including the *Quaestiones* on the *Physics, Metaphysics,* and *De sensu et sensibili.* Bacon thought of himself as a pure Aristotelian.

To this point Roger Bacon received the typical education of a cleric or theologian. But then he underwent a *metanoia,* a reversal, an about-face; he transitioned from his red period to his blue period. In 1247, with his return to Oxford, the empirical Aristotle took hold, probably under the guidance of Grosseteste and Marsh, and Bacon fell in love with science. He began to dream of creating a universal science that would decipher all the secrets of nature. Though his roots were deep in doctrine, he became possessed by a passion for empirical knowledge. Working with boundless energy, he immersed himself in the sciences. He analyzed the processes of sense experience, developed the idea of experiment, and became enthralled with gadgets. Bacon would call this his awakening.

THE EMPIRICIST   From this time on Bacon never stopped "doing" science. He studied mathematics, astronomy, optics, chemistry, mechanics, geography, chronology, and agriculture. He always loved languages, so he studied Greek, Hebrew, and Arabic to enable him to conduct textual criticism. He tells us that he spent much time and energy and enormous sums of money (£2,000, he says) on research, books, instruments, and training assistants.

He cleared the way by noting the four mistakes we commonly make that short-circuit our finding the truth. (1) We put our faith in "authorities" who are really incompetent and have nothing to tell us; (2) we buy into the customs and values of society without realizing how much false information they convey to us; (3) we also buy into the myths and prejudices that are in fashion among an uninformed public; and (4) we commonly make the mistake of trying to conceal our ignorance by pretending that we know something when we don't.

Inspired by Arab scientists, Bacon had a special interest in optics—in using parabolic mirrors and lenses, and studying the reflection and refraction of light. One of his sentences reads "thus from an incredible distance we may read the smallest letters"—implying that he discovered the magnifying glass or the eyeglass. Another line tells us that "the Sun, Moon, and stars may be made to descend hither in appearance"—implying that he knew how to put together a telescope; he probably used it, for elsewhere he describes the Milky Way as composed of a multitude of stars (*habens multas stellas congregatas*) and concludes that the smallest star is larger than the Earth. He adds that people just wouldn't believe what he had seen.

Another claim to fame was his "invention" of black powder. About 1242 he wrote down, in his *Epistola*, the formula for making it from saltpetre, sulfur, and charcoal. Black powder had apparently been discovered in the ninth century by the Chinese, carried westward by the Arabs, and found its way to Latin Europe through Muslim Spain; Bacon (who could read Arabic) "reinvented" black powder for the West, improved its explosive power with finer blends, and ignited the fuse of a new era in European warfare. He knew that the compound could be used to propel rockets, and he may have been aware of its explosive potential. Fearing what might happen if his formula became known, he encoded his recipe in the form of a Latin anagram. The final words of his encryption are, "And so thou wilt call up thunder and destruction if thou know the art." (Only seventy years later black powder was used to propel projectiles, and was thereafter known as "gunpowder.") This is just one example of Bacon's work in chemistry (then called "alchemy" because no good word existed for what we know as chemistry). He seems to have had a laboratory in which he studied the behavior of liquids, solids, and gases. These and other hands-on investigations earned Bacon the titles "father of experimental method" and "father of European invention."

Like a delighted child, and with great imagination, Bacon toyed with mechanical contraptions. For underwater exploration he envisioned "machines that can be made for walking in the sea and rivers." Large ships can be navigated by machines; aircraft (*instrumenta volandi*) can be built with flapping wings and operated by just one man

Sine experientia nihil sufficienter sciri potest. *Without experience nothing, not even mathematical proof, is sufficient.*

ROGER BACON

sitting in the middle. "Likewise cars may be made so that, without an animal to pull them, they will move at inestimable speed." He also envisioned locomotives (*currus etiam possunt fieri*), suspension bridges, and balloons made of thin copper sheeting and energized by "liquid fire" so they will float on the air.

Bacon shows himself to be a faithful Aristotelian, for from observed facts he moved to theory. Many of the Franciscans were mathematicians, and Bacon never stoped praising the virtues of mathematics as the only way to understand nature. And he understood something of scientific method as it involves observation, hypothesis, mathematical description, and verification. Above everything, Bacon was an empiricist in the study of the world. All knowledge must be verified by experience; nothing persuades but experience; no man can be trusted who has not trusted his senses to inform him about nature. A man may be told that fire is hot, Bacon observes, but until he has put his hand in the flame, he is not quite convinced. "Therefore," he writes in his *Opus majus*, "reasoning doesn't suffice, but experience does."

His insistence that all knowledge must be checked against experience is Bacon's most significant contribution to the sciences. He wrote repeatedly of the importance of "experiment" (*scientia experimentalis*), but what he had in mind was merely careful, steady, and intelligent observation—"informed seeing." His famous analysis of rainbows is a good example. While observing a rainbow, move a few steps to the left and then to the right; you find that the rainbow moves with you so that the center of the rainbow will always be at the center of your vision. "We learn by experiment that there are as many rainbows as there are observers. . . . Therefore it's impossible for two people to see the same rainbow (though it's hard to convince an ignorant person that this is so)."[5]

THE ICONOCLAST   Is there any wonder that, in the eyes of monks and public, Bacon was seen as a wonder-worker, and, for his attempts to control nature, was judged by the Church to be a dabbler in the black arts serving the Devil? Combine his revolutionary ideas with Bacon's lack of respect for authority; his bold criticisms of everyone (Albert and Thomas were "boys who became teachers before they had learned anything"); his easy dismissal of anyone who disagreed with him; his attacks on the ignorance of mendicants, the avarice of bishops, and the arrogance of the papal court ("their vices are a scandal to laymen"); his caustic broadsides against the immorality of university faculties; his belief that his interpretations were better than anyone else's (they often were!); his attack on the universities for ignoring the sciences; his insistence that the teachings of the Church Fathers be judged by intelligence and reason; his recommendation that other religions be studied; his condemnation of deductive reasoning (so misused by the Schoolmen); his dismissal of the whole of Scholasticism as nothing but word fights, frivolous metaphysics, and a waste of time (a "universal," he said, is nothing other than what two men share that is not shared by a pig or jackass); his pronouncements that all translations of the Vulgate are corrupt; his threat to burn all of Aristotle's books (if he could get them) because they too are corrupt; his grandiose vision of the unification of all the sciences which *he* would accomplish—given all this, it was inevitable that Bacon would eventually be silenced, despite the fact that he professed to be a faithful son of the Church.

The first blow came while he was teaching at Oxford in 1257. He was hustled to Paris by his fellow Franciscans and placed in confinement (the exact charges are unknown to us). Initially he was not allowed to write, only to teach languages to young students. Though dejected and feeling abandoned, he returned to Oxford to continue writing.

A year or so earlier Bacon had become friends with a bishop named Guy de Foulques and had written to him about his scientific interests. Bacon believed that a better science would only confirm the doctrines of the Bible and support the Church. Now de Foulques had become Pope Clement IV, and on June 22, 1266 he asked Bacon to send him a copy of his work. Bacon was aghast, for the project—a gigantic encyclopedia of all knowledge—was only in the planning stage. Bacon's response reveals much about his genius and industry. He was hopeful again and alive with energy. The Vicar of Christ, he said, "has deigned to petition me. I have been given superhuman powers . . . ." Elated, he began work on the big work, to be titled *Communia naturalium*, but it soon became apparent that his proposal was too grandiose, and in January 1267 he revised his plan and started work on a more modest "summary of everything." With prodigious strength, and within a period of eighteen months, he completed the *Opus majus*, *Opus minus*, and *Opus tertium*— "Great Work," "Lesser Work," and "Third Work." Bacon put a pragmatic spin on his science, urging the pope to consider the enormous practical advantages that will accrue from a true knowledge of chemistry, astronomy, and mechanics. A subtitle given to his *Opus majus* was "On the Utility of Knowledge."

Bacon sent his new books to Pope Clement IV, along with a treatise on chemistry, a concave lens, and a map of the world. For reasons not clear, the request from the pope had been sent with a command for secrecy, and the project was not known even to his Franciscan superiors. When they noticed Bacon's changed routines they became alarmed, and, he says, subjected him to "unspeakable violence." But within months his plans abruptly ended; in November 1268 the pope died. Bacon, discouraged and alone, began work again on the big *Communia*.

Then in 1277 the minister-general of the Franciscan order became suspicious of certain "novelties" in his thinking and again demanded that Bacon give an account of his theories. Almost immediately his writings were condemned as "heretical," and he was imprisoned on a charge of insubordination, this time for fourteen years. He was returned to freedom shortly before his death.

BACON'S THEOLOGY   Any account of Roger Bacon would not be complete without a note on his theology, although none of it is unfamiliar, and his ideas were soon to belong to a bygone era. (Knowing that his religious ideas were unacceptable, he most likely reserved his creative energies for writing in the sciences.) His cosmology is Neoplatonism colored by the Arabian commentators. He believed in the existence of the *rationes seminales*.° In a most unorthodox manner, he recommended the study of non-Christian religions since there is really only one God and one revelation. Greek philosophy was God's gift, and its development was guided providentially; the Church should make use of all sources of revelation; all Christians should study philosophy. Laymen should be allowed to read the Scriptures (a right soon to be a keystone of Protestantism). Theology is still the ruler and judge over the sciences. He believed that theology could organize the sciences into an all-inclusive wisdom, and that this wisdom could unite the world into a single Christian republic ruled by the pope. Revelation and reason are in agreement since both result from a divine "inner illumination" (an idea adopted from Augustine). God gives us the capacity for reason, though actual thoughts are ours and we must be responsible for them.

°*See* logos spermatikos *in lexicon.*

Given the stresses of his long life, it is astounding that Bacon was able to write so productively (or perhaps it was *because* of his prolonged confinements). In addition to the three opera completed at Paris, he produced a *Greek Grammar*, parts of a *Hebrew Grammar*, commentaries on Aristotle's treatises, a *Compendium of Philosophical Studies*, a *General Principles of Mathematics*, and numerous scientific reports and treatises. He was working on a *Compendium of Theology* at the time of his death. Bacon lies buried in the Franciscan church in Oxford, England. Officially, he still bears the title of *doctor mirabilis*, the "Wonderful Teacher" of the Church.

Leonardo da Vinci (1452–1519), self-portrait in red chalk.

Roger Bacon's personal struggles can serve as a metaphor for the philosophical struggles of the Renaissance era. His love of "experience" and the demand to be free to follow that experience parallels the striving of all the Renaissance thinkers who were attempting to return to this world and make sense of it. To some extent, all of them (with the possible exception of Machiavelli) moved in two worlds; nevertheless critical thinking and scientific thinking continued to evolve in the creative work of men such as da Vinci, Machiavelli, Copernicus, Kepler, and Francis Bacon.

LEONARDO DA VINCI

Leonardo is best known as artist, scientist, and inventor, all of which he was, in superlative measure. Less known is the fact that he merits attention as a relentless advocate of empiricism and a fair epistemologist. His writings contain not only sketches of mechanical gadgets and anatomical drawings, but numerous philosophic notations about what the human mind can and cannot know, and how it can know it.

When da Vinci died in France in 1519 his legacy included a vast collection of notebooks containing thousands of pages of random jottings, drawings, and studies for future work. Despite the fact that his fame rests on a few paintings—notably *Mona Lisa* and *The Last Supper*—it is his notebooks that contain the heart and soul of his creative genius. Of some forty notebooks left to his friend and executor Francesco Melzi, thirty-one (or about 3500 pages) have survived intact; scores of others have been lost or broken up and their pages scattered around the world. He had a driving passion to draw and kept pieces of paper near at hand or small sketch pads tucked in his belt; he would later put the notes in order and enter them into his notebooks. When he began keeping notebooks in Milan at the age of thirty, he noted "This will be a collection without order." He planned to rework the entire assemblage at some later date to produce formal treatises. From about 1490 on, his life plan called for the writing of four great books on painting, architecture, mechanics, and human anatomy. Only the *Treatise on Painting* was completed, being assembled posthumously by his friend Melzi from notebook material.

Where there is great feeling, there is great suffering.

LEONARDO DA VINCI

What the notebooks reveal is a man of enormous energy, irrepressible curiosity, tireless intellect, and stubborn determination to tackle and subdue a problem. His drawings include designs for contraptions of all kinds, among them a flying machine, parachute, and helicopter; heavy engines of war, a rapid-fire machine gun, hydraulic machines (the hydrometer for measuring the specific gravity of liquids was his invention). They include engineering studies for canals, bridges, and fortifications; architectural plans of all sorts; mathematical and geometrical notations; trial drawings of details for his paintings and sculptures; studies of light and shade and perspective. Not least, they include his famous anatomical drawings, with diagrams of skeletal structure, musculature, organs, and the circulatory system.

Where there is shouting there is no true science.
LEONARDO DA VINCI

The textual material in his notebooks was generally intended to illustrate the drawings, rather than the drawings the texts. Leonardo was apparently left-handed and found it natural to write from right to left in mirror-writing (his texts are easily read with a mirror); but he was also at ease with "normal" writing. The neatly written texts cover everything from studies of the growth of trees, the dynamics of birds' wings, geological formations, air currents, and whirlpools to theories of perception, scientific method, and philosophic comments on nature.

No one should read me who is not a mathematician.
LEONARDO DA VINCI

His notebooks, however, tell us little about Leonardo the man. He was not a gossip and was never involved in the petty occupations of ordinary life. He never reveals his personal feelings about anyone or anything; he speaks nowhere of love interests or tells us of his family. When his father died, Leonardo gave the occasion only passing notice. He was not seriously religious, had a superficial, pragmatic interest in the Church, and suffered no patriotic feelings. "He lacked the sensual worldliness of a Boccaccio or a Chaucer, the recklessness of a Rabelais, the piety of a Dante, or the religious passion of a Michelangelo."[6] His human qualities must be inferred, gingerly, from the mass of "objective" materials that contain his art, science, and philosophy.

There is no certainty in sciences where one of the mathematical sciences cannot be applied.
LEONARDO DA VINCI

The testimony of friends paints a picture of a man who was generous and thoughtful, charming in social gatherings, and completely at home as pageant master in the festive courts where he wrote and recited humorous skits, fables, satires, and allegories. He was loved for his sense of humor and his music, and during his early years, with his golden hair, he presented a striking figure as he stood before audiences in a rose-colored cloak expounding on such topics as the dynamics of bird flight or rerouting a canal past the city. He especially enjoyed the company of men of talent and intellect. He inspired loyalty in friends and disciples, and, not surprisingly, was known for his gentleness toward animals. But paradoxically, he was a loner who watched the parade of life with detached amusement and sadness. Loneliness was a cross he bore all his life. As a youth he spent considerable time by himself, and seclusion was always precious time for creative concentration. In his notebooks is found the comment, "The painter must be solitary, especially when he is intent on those speculations and considerations, which if they are kept continually before the eyes give the memory the opportunity of mastering them. For if you are alone you are completely yourself, but if you are accompanied by a single companion you are only half yourself."[7]

Mechanics is the paradise of mathematical sciences, because it is there that one plucks the mathematical fruit.
LEONARDO DA VINCI

Marvelous is Thy justice, O Primo Motore! Thou hast seen to it that no power lacks the order and value of your necessary governance.
LEONARDO DA VINCI

THE MAN   Leonardo's youth was spent in the Tuscan village of Vinci where he was born and whence the family name. His father Ser Piero da Vinci was a notary at the Palazzo in the city of Florence, some fifteen miles to the east of Vinci. His mother Caterina was a peasant girl who married an artisan shortly after Leonardo's birth and had no influence on her son. He was raised by his father almost as an only child, for though he had eleven siblings, the oldest was twenty-four years younger than he, all borne by Ser Piero's third and fourth wives. In contrast to an Augustine who tells us so much about his youth, da Vinci avoids the subject. We do know that on one occasion a neighbor asked him if he would paint a dragon on a shield. Leonardo made a small collection of lizards, crickets, snakes, butterflies, grasshoppers, and bats, used them as models, and painted "a great ugly creature" near enough to satisfy the need for a dragon. On another occasion he is said to have bought captive birds in the marketplace so he could take them home and set them free. His intellectual absorption was evident from his earliest years; he often secluded himself in thought and would forget to rest or eat.

His early education was conventional; he learned the usual skills in arithmetic and reading and writing in his native Italian; after that, through diligent study, he taught himself the basics of Latin, science, mathematics, history, and philosophy. The upside to being self-educated was that, having no ties to the universities, he managed to maintain the autonomy of his genius untrammeled by the constraints of academic tradition. The downside is that his thinking suffers from lack of rigor, and because he was not deeply informed in the history of philosophic inquiry, he tends to plow the old fields unaware that they are fallow. He was annoyed by sophistic arguments "through which men are always disputing with noise and much moving of hands." He distrusted those who profess only book learning.

His father was aware of his son's unusual abilities and at about seventeen apprenticed him to the Florentine workshop of Andrea del Verrocchio. There exists a legend (but based on fact) that, at the time of Leonardo's first visit, Verrocchio was working on a baptismal scene for the monastery at Vallombrosa, and Leonardo was invited to finish the figure of an angel in the left-hand corner of the painting. When Verrocchio returned and saw the bright little angel he was breathless with admiration and muttered that it wasn't right "that a boy should know more of the art than his teacher." (The painting is now in the Uffizi Gallery in Florence.) By the age of twenty-five Leonardo had his own studio in Florence and was supporting himself with commissions.

Da Vinci's adult life was spent moving from city to city searching for patrons, receiving assignments, and leaving before completing his work. From the age of thirty to forty-eight he worked in Milan as "painter and engineer of the Duke," Ludovico Sforza; there he painted, sculpted, designed pageants for the festive court, and served as consultant in architectural and military matters. He established his own expansive workshop and gathered about him apprentices and students. He was obsessive about his work and often labored furiously from sunrise to dark; after that he would back off for a few days to gain perspective, and then go back to work. While in Milan he painted *The Last Supper* on the refectory wall of the monastery of Santa Maria delle Grazie, and planned a gigantic bronze equestrian statue in honor of Francesco Sforza. But times changed, and the metal for the statue was melted down for cannonballs. His scientific interests took more and more of his time at Milan, and he began to experiment with the possibility of applying mathematical analysis to his painting.

When forty-eight he moved back to Florence where he was treated as a celebrity. He left his home city for ten months to serve at the itinerant court of Cesare Borgia where he was engrossed in military engineering, cartography, and scientific studies; there he met Machiavelli and received a commission from him. At fifty-four he moved back to Milan and continued to develop his knowledge of the sciences and to create a unified theory of art and science. He also gave much time to the study of human anatomy, for which, he tells us, he dissected some thirty cadavers.

In 1513 he proceeded to Rome, but younger artists were garnering attention and Leonardo felt left out. He was sixty-one, without work, and becoming bitter. For three years he worked on mathematical studies, drew maps, and strolled the city, alone. When in 1516 he was invited to come to France by the young king, Francis I—who was awed by da Vinci's work and reputation—he accepted and spent the last two and a half years of his life in a palatial residence near the king's summer retreat at Amboise on the Loire. Though his official title was *"Premier peintre, architecte et méchanicien du Roi,"* he was called on for little but conversation and occasional advice. Greatly admired at court, he spent much of his time designing scenes for pageants and festivals and editing his scientific studies, striving to give some order to his papers. But he was exhausted; he suffered a mild paralysis that made painting difficult, and he grew weak. On the eve of Easter, 1519, he made out his will, leaving his manuscripts to Melzi and four hundred ducats to his half brothers. He died on the 2nd of May. His burial place in the palace church was destroyed during the French Revolution and the location of his grave is now unknown.

WINDOW OF THE SOUL   If the Renaissance can be interpreted as Western man's return to the world, then da Vinci represents a return in a specific and unique way. His entire life was influenced and shaped by the sense of sight—by seeing. The eye, he wrote, is "lord of the senses"; it is the "window of the soul"; it is "the principal means by which the central sense can most completely and abundantly appreciate the infinite works of nature." "He who loses his sight loses his view of the universe, and is like one interred alive who can still move about and breathe in his grave. Do you not see that the eye encompasses the beauty of the whole world?"[8]

But Leonardo looked at reality through different eyes. As a representational artist aiming at realistic portrayal, he was compelled to be a keen observer; but he developed his capacity for seeing far beyond the ordinary and then embedded that gift in a philosophy that drove it to astounding heights. At one point he reminds himself to draw "the three chief positions of the wings of birds in descent" and to be aware of "the formation of clouds, and the cause of snow and hail, and of the new shapes that snow forms in the air, and of the trees in cold countries with the new shape of the leaves." The lifelong theme of both his art and his science was *saper vedere,* "knowing how to see"—seeing objects in great detail and with unprecedented precision. Much of Leonardo's epistemology is a recycling of Greek thinking, but with his own personal twist. "You who speculate on the nature of things, don't be too sure that you understand exactly how nature operates as she follows her own rules and maneuvers toward her own ends; just be glad that you can experience and understand the creations of your own mind."

Reality, he is saying, just may be off-limits to human investigation. "The ability to define the whatness of the elements is not in man's power, but many of their effects can be known by man." While the mind can't know the reality of concrete events, it can apprehend with mathematics the laws that govern physical motion. Ordinary language is useless in this business of apprehending reality; it is too static, too fuzzy. But mathematics can capture the structure of physical reality. Leonardo studied mathematics all his life and believed that he had found the key to nature's secrets. ("No one should read me," he warned, "who is not a mathematician.")

Through vision and mathematics, therefore, da Vinci believed he had glimpsed the essence of nature's operations. Of the senses, sight is the most trustworthy, for it can furnish immediate and precise data. The artist, carefully trained in saper vedere, is doubly endowed with good seeing and a steady hand; his is the high calling to reproduce accurately what he sees and lay the foundations for a "science of reality." Thus Leonardo's empiricism makes a clean break with the ruling Platonic tradition that scorned those "who turn their eye intently on things in the hope of grasping them through the senses." In the final analysis, all knowledge is empirical. Da Vinci argued that any contents of the mind that have not been derived from the senses is useless for it "brings forth no truth."

Mental things which have not gone in through the senses are vain and bring forth no truth except detrimental.
LEONARDO DA VINCI

As a day well spent gives joyful sleep, so does a life well spent gives joyful death.
LEONARDO DA VINCI

If you are alone you are completely yourself, but if you are accompanied by a single companion you are only half yourself.
LEONARDO DA VINCI

Anyone who in discussion relies upon authority uses, not his understanding, but rather his memory.
LEONARDO DA VINCI

The definition of the whatness of the elements is not in the power of man, but many of their effects are known.
LEONARDO DA VINCI

Wisdom is the daughter of experience.
LEONARDO DA VINCI

Experience never errs; it is only your judgments that err.
LEONARDO DA VINCI

Since experience has been the mistress of whoever has written well, I take her as my mistress, and to her on all points make my appeal.
LEONARDO DA VINCI

My intention is to consult experience first and then with reasoning show why such experience is bound to operate in such a way.
LEONARDO DA VINCI

Without experience nothing can be sufficiently known.
LEONARDO DA VINCI

Leonardo developed the grand plan of observing all objects in the world in this way so as to reveal their form and structure. What he called "the science of painting" would aim at gradually knowing all objects as they really are. For Leonardo science and art work toward the same goal—the comprehension of the real world. From about 1495 on he planned to devote the rest of his life to this "visible cosmology," and his copious notebook drawings all serve this end. His plan called for rendering the animal world first, then the plant world, and lastly the world of nonliving natural forces.

Thus da Vinci rejects the medieval notion that we live in a universe that is scaled up and down with qualities and values; he looked carefully at the world, and what he found was that all of its components appear to be reducible to quantitative measurement. Leonardo was deeply moved when he pondered the mathematical order of the cosmos—a true miracle of nature: "O wondrous and awesome necessity! With your law you constrain all effects to result from their causes by the shortest path, and according to the highest and irrevocable law every natural action obeys you with the briefest operation." Building on the assumption of universal causality, he studied statics and dynamics and made significant contributions to the concept of force, including inertia and the principle of action and reaction. He noted that a physical universe that follows causal principles could not permit miracles or magic. This does not mean that Leonardo was a secular humanist, for he attributes this cosmic order to a Prime Mover *(Primo Motore)*, which he defines as "a force divine or otherwise."

RECAPITULATION Since da Vinci's epistemology is uniquely his, and since he nowhere wrote down a systematic statement of his philosophy, a recap of what he was envisioning seems in order.

At his point in time there existed no massive accumulation of scientific information about the world, and what noetic speculators had come up with, after two thousand years of headwork, was . . . nothing. No one since Aristotle had *looked at the world* with sustained gazing, with careful method, and with empirical intelligence. There were, of course, bits and pieces of insights that *might be true* and might arbitrarily be made to fit together by creative minds; but these bits and pieces lay around like rags in a monkey cage, without meaning or coherence. Da Vinci shared with many great thinkers a passion to see the world, that is, to understand it as it actually is. He was aware of his special gifts of sight and intellect, and, since he lived in an era when looking at the world was again in fashion, he believed he could utilize his unusual abilities to make inroads, at last, on the big questions about "reality": How does the world work? What is our human place in it?

So, insofar as humanly possible, he wanted to *look* at everything with his special eyes, to observe precisely what is going on; and then, by using his rational intellect, organize what he had seen into a coherent picture of reality. Since this is the job of a "scientist," da Vinci assumes the role; but since success also depends on the artist who has the eyes and hands to transcribe what the scientist finds, then he must be both scientist and artist.

This dual role gave his life a sustained teleological purpose. He will focus the floodlight of his analytical intellect on three problems, work them through to clarity, and create a new science of reality. They are (1) to define exactly how science and art can be brought together as working partners; (2) to lay out the mathematical basis of painting, that is, to apply mathematics to its component elements such as geometrical design, balance, perspective, proportion, and the interplay of light and shadow; and (3) to apprehend and reduce to theoretical system the forms and patterns that are to be found in dynamic nature.

Carrying out this philosophic goal requires saper vedere, which in turn involves a mastery of the techniques of painting, the physics of engineering, an understanding of mechanics and model construction, a firm grasp of optics, light, and perspective . . . and, it seems, *everything else!* Add to this the fact that he had a philosophic mind that insisted on fitting all these puzzle pieces together into a coherent picture—the enormity of Leonardo's vision is staggering. No wonder that his dream of developing a "perceptual cosmology" played a significant role in the rise of Renaissance humanism and inspired generations of artists. One can't but stand in amazement at the power of his intellect and the range of his seeing. His creations shine brilliantly as expressions of human creativity at its peak.

Leonardo's philosophic humanism revolved around one momentous idea: that a human being, in order to save himself, must work toward the fulfillment of his true nature. In this notion da Vinci can be seen as the incarnation of all we mean by the word "Renaissance."

All our knowledge has its origins in our perceptions.
LEONARDO DA VINCI

NICCOLÒ MACHIAVELLI

Machiavelli's philosophy treats humans harshly, and history has returned the favor. One can discern in the literature a noticeable absence of appreciation of the man and his ideas and a strong tendency to misinterpret him. He joins the company of innovative thinkers—Aristotle, Epicurus, Nietzsche, and Marx come to mind—whose very names have come to stand for principles they themselves angrily disowned. Just as the word "Epicureanism" has been perverted to mean gluttony, and "Nietzschean" is widely used to imply fascism, the word "Machiavellian" is thought to refer to the sinister doctrine that evil succeeds where goodness fails. "Machiavellianism," according to *The American Heritage Dictionary*, stands for the doctrine that "denies the relevance of morality in political affairs and holds that craft and deceit are justified in pursuing and maintaining political power." While this use of "Machiavellian" is not entirely off the wall, such a definition, if taken from context, makes Machiavelli appear more diabolical than he really was and encourages readers to miss the point of his writing.

Niccolò Machiavelli was an erudite Italian humanist who pursued the truth in a field of activity that had always been rife with myth and lies; this was a dangerous thing to do, and for this he has been much maligned. His public career was a seesaw opportunism. After an early rise to power, he fell out of favor and never again achieved the heights he sought and never fully actualized the talents he knew he possessed. We find in his writing outbursts of bitterness that make him seem remote and ill-humored. It is not easy to see the humanness in Machiavelli, partly because he cloaked the real self in a robe of formalism, partly because his jarring pronouncements offend us, and partly because he has been the victim of so much malinterpretation. Still, on occasion, we have glimpses of the man that reveal the person behind the persona. After the Medicis seized power in Florence in 1512, he sought refuge on his small farm outside the city. There he lived with his family, wrote, and tried to adjust to his humiliating exile. In a letter written to Francesco Vettori he described a typical day in his frustrated existence:

We Italians are irreligious and corrupt above others.
NICCOLÒ MACHIAVELLI

Though a prince need not possess all the virtues, to seem *to have them is useful; as, for example, to seem* merciful, loyal, humane, religious, *and* sincere; *it is also useful to* be *so, but with a mind so flexible that if the need arise he can be the contrary.*
NICCOLÒ MACHIAVELLI

When neither their property nor their honor is touched, the majority of men live content.
NICCOLÒ MACHIAVELLI

> I seat myself along the road, by the tavern, I talk to those passing by, I ask news of their own parts. I hear many things, and take note of sundry ways and diverse fancies of men. Thus comes time for dinner, and with my family I eat of such fare as this my poor farm and minute patrimony consent. Then back to the tavern, where I find per usual the owner, a butcher, a miller, a couple of brickmakers. With these I go their loutish way, playing

The world has always been inhabited by human beings who have always had the same passions.
NICCOLÒ MACHIAVELLI

checkers all afternoon, whence spring up a thousand quarrels and number-less insulting spites, and as we argue about a farthing you might hear us shout as far as San Casciano. Thus involved among these lice I keep my mind from going sour, and I yield myself to the malice of this beastly fate of mine, not minding that it should tread me in the mire in this fashion, so haply it might be driven to shame.

When evening comes, I go home and enter my study; at the door I dis-card these daily clothes full of dirt and dust, and put on regal and curial robes, and thus condignly clad I enter the ancient courts of ancient men, where I am received by them lovingly, and partake of that nourishment which alone is mine, and for it was I born. Then I am bold to converse with them, and question them as to the reasons of their actions, and they out of their courtesy willingly answer me; and during those four hours I am above any trouble, I fear not poverty, nor does death appall me; I utterly become one with them. [9]

> *It is necessary for a prince who wishes to maintain himself to learn how* not *to be good, and to use this knowledge and not use it according to the necessities of the case.*
> NICCOLÒ MACHIAVELLI

> *Whoever desires to found a state and give it laws, must start with assuming that all men are bad and ever ready to display their vicious nature, whenever they may find occasion for it.*
> NICCOLÒ MACHIAVELLI

> *The fact is that a man who wants to act virtuously in every way necessarily comes to grief among so many who are not virtuous.*
> NICCOLÒ MACHIAVELLI

> *For the great majority of mankind are satisfied with appearances, as though they were realities and are often more influenced by the things that* seem *than by those that* are.
> NICCOLÒ MACHIAVELLI

The wife who put up with this temperamental misanthrope and shared his penu-rious lifestyle was Marietta Corsini, who, since their marriage twelve years earlier (1501) had borne five children. As a husband and father Niccolò receives passing marks, barely, but—as the above passage implies—his basic needs were nourished elsewhere. He yearned for the company of people, and without them he became restive and bored. He lived for the times when he could share the prestige of the famous and powerful who could validate his existence, and the motivating drive behind all his writing was the hope that he could so impress the Florentine movers and shakers that he would be returned to positions in which his considerable talents could be put to use. In the introduction to *The Discourses* he notes that although his writing "may prove difficult and troublesome," he hopes that it "may also bring me some reward in the approbation of those who will kindly appreciate my efforts." To this end his writing contains revolutionary (read "politically incorrect") ideas, irritat-ing sentences, and sensational exaggerations that make him appear dour and sar-donic. It has been noted that in his private living, however, he followed the old-fashioned virtues, remained faithful to his friends (though not his wife), and worked responsibly in the positions he held.

Machiavelli was born in the city-state of Florence in 1449, the son of a lawyer who belonged to a prominent, but poor, Florentine family. Early in life, he says, he "learned to do without." He received only a fair formal education; he said he got more from reading books at home than from his schooling; from this we infer that he lacked training in disciplined scholarship but, at the same time, escaped the cus-tomary conditioning that academia demanded of its students, leaving him free from the constraints of orthodox thinking habits. At 29 he secured a responsible post in the city government and was sent on diplomatic missions to other cities in Italy, and to France and Germany. His abilities were acknowledged, and at 49 he became an assistant to the secretary of state. But when the Medicis overthrew the republican government in 1512 Machiavelli found himself without a place in the new regime.

So the exiled Machiavelli began to write. His immortal fame rests on *The Prince* (written 1513) and *The Discourses*, commentaries on the ten books of the Roman his-torian Livy (written about 1516); it is largely from this latter work that he learned to read "the lessons of history." He also wrote a play, *La Mandragola* (1518), a bold satire on corruption in high places; and a *History of Florence*, which he presented to the pope in 1525. He also wrote a book of fiction and some poetry. Thus Machia-velli's literary career was a sidetrip, a detour, unplanned and unforeseen, resulting from the accident of unemployment; and because his writing was never a passionate first love, his pages reveal the ulterior motives that drove his labors. In the 1520s, when the pope appointed him to some lesser offices, he put off his writing, and never returned. He became ill and died in 1527. In writing *The Prince* and *The Discourses* Machiavelli was attempting to break new ground: "animated by that desire which impels me to do what may prove for the common benefit of all, I have resolved to open a new route which has not yet been followed by anyone." He applied empirical method to politics in an attempt to understand man's political machinations and find out, not what men *should* be doing, but what they actually do. Machiavelli had a scientific mind, and *The Prince* is a scientific analysis of how rulers gain and keep power. He doesn't ask whether the prince's power is a good thing, whether it benefits people, or whether it is moral or decent or life affirming—such judgments are inapplicable. To be sure, he is a moralist, for he deals with "shoulds" and "oughts"; but he is an amoral moralist whose only interest is the nourishment of "the state." His literary style, elegant in its simplicity, embodies the "street smarts" that is a far cry from the speculations of the Greek thinkers whose classic prose spelled out their dreams of a better world. Machiavelli's intent is to state the truth, to make objective statement; and for this he is credited with founding the discipline of Political Science.

The ruler, he says, will adhere to the ideas and principles that will lead him to success. These are:

- politics is an "autonomous discipline" governed by its own unique set of rules;
- these rules derive from nature, not man, and are immutable and irrevocable;
- therefore the usual notions about right and wrong don't apply to politics, for it is an amoral discipline;
- the sole objective of a good ruler is to preserve and strengthen the state;
- the ruler's end success in accomplishing this goal provides the only criterion for judging the "rightness" or "wrongness" of his means ("the end justifies the means");
- the ruler will not be bound by constraining principles and stands ready to perform *any act* that will work to secure the state;
- the ruler cares not about being liked, respected, or honored, for these tender needs are irrelevant to success ("it is much safer to be feared than to be loved");
- expedient ideas and actions will be chosen by a ruler within the context of each unique situation, for only in concrete circumstances can one's actions achieve pragmatic efficiency (for this Machiavelli is sometimes called a "contextualist").[10]

Machiavelli argues that a careful reading of history will show that these are the rules that have worked for successful leaders, and they will continue to work because they are founded on the "laws of nature." Whereas Plato wrote *The Republic* and *The Laws* to show how to set up a government by using reason, Machiavelli is convinced that political states are neither caused nor governed by human reason, but are the creations of nature's inexorable laws as they operate in human societies. All human relationships, that is, are nonrational, and Aristotle's dream of a society of individuals enjoying the fruits of reason is only a utopian wish-fulfillment. Human nature is a natural system, and humans will always behave in the same way in a given situation. "The world has always been inhabited by human beings who have always had the same passions." While the masses of humankind will slavishly follow the dictates of this natural law, enlightened leaders can by force of will lead a citizenry toward

He who usurps the government of any state should execute all the cruelties which he thinks material all at once, that he may have no occasion to renew them often.
NICCOLÒ MACHIAVELLI

For when men are well governed, they neither seek nor desire any other liberty.
NICCOLÒ MACHIAVELLI

War should be the only study of a prince. He should consider peace only as a breathing-time which gives him leisure to contrive, and furnishes ability to execute.
NICCOLÒ MACHIAVELLI

collective action and move the political body toward survival, growth, and well-being. Masses are entropic, but leaders can establish antientropy in the body politic.

How perilous it is to free a people who prefer slavery.
NICCOLÒ MACHIAVELLI
(ATTRIBUTED)

Any political or ethical system that ignores this natural basis of human relationships must necessarily fail. Machiavelli excoriates Christianity for supplying an instruction manual for living counter to nature's rules, thereby creating a way of life that is "unnatural." "Thus the world has fallen prey to scoundrels who can rule it in all impunity, because people, in order to go to heaven, prefer to bear and bewail their abuses rather than punish them."

If you have to choose between the two, it is much safer to be feared than to be loved.
NICCOLÒ MACHIAVELLI

Machiavelli possessed an unusually dismal view of human nature, and his political philosophy is a logical projection of his thoughts and feelings about people: The masses ("the herd" Nietzsche would call them) are "naturally bad" and must be controlled. "The people resemble a wild beast," he wrote. "It may be said of men in general that they are ungrateful and fickle, dissemblers, avoiders of danger, and greedy of gain." "Whoever desires to found a state and give it laws, must start with assuming that all men are bad and ever ready to display their vicious nature, whenever they may find occasion for it." In the introduction to *The Discourses* he laments that men are "so prompt to blame and so slow to praise." The individual who seeks nobility will have a rough time, for "the fact is that a man who wants to act virtuously in every way necessarily comes to grief among so many who are not virtuous." "You do not know the unfathomable cowardice of humanity," he said or wrote somewhere (at least the words are attributed to him); they are "servile in the face of force, pitiless in the face of weakness, implacable before blunders, indulgent before crimes." Little wonder that Machiavelli would become the voice for all the misanthropes who need comfort and support in their misery.[11]

For our country, wrong is right.
NICCOLÒ MACHIAVELLI
(ATTRIBUTED)

People care little for the truth, "for the great majority of mankind are satisfied with appearances, as though they were realities and are often more influenced by the things that *seem* than by those that *are*." "There are three classes of intellects," he writes, "one which comprehends by itself; another which appreciates what others comprehend; and a third which neither comprehends by itself nor by the showing of others; the first is the most excellent, the second is good, the third is useless."[12]

War is, and will always be, the order of the day. The ruler "should consider peace only as a breathing-time that gives him leisure to contrive" his next wartime strategies.[13]

No good man will ever reproach another who endeavors to defend his country, whatever be his mode of doing so.
NICCOLÒ MACHIAVELLI

Machiavelli might well be considered the author of the simple-minded patriotism on which nationalism feeds so ravenously. "No good man will ever reproach another who endeavors to defend his country, whatever be his mode of doing so." "For *our* country, wrong is right." "Whenever the survival of one's country depends wholly on a decision that one has to make, then no consideration should be given to questions of justice and injustice, kindness or cruelty, or to its being praiseworthy or ignominious. All these considerations must be set aside, so that the only alternative that exists is that of saving the existence of the country and preserving its freedom." These comments reveal the parameters of Machiavelli's investment. When one is reminded that he is advocating an unthinking loyalty to a rather small Italian city-state, the narrowness of his identification becomes frightening. His principles, of course, can be applied to all states of whatever size; but in any case his lack of empathy with other perspectives invites attack from those with larger vision and expanded loyalties.

Politics has no relations to morals.
NICCOLÒ MACHIAVELLI

Savage is he who saves himself.
NICCOLÒ MACHIAVELLI

Perception is everything, authentic being is meaningless. "Though a prince need not possess all the virtues, to *seem* to have them is useful; as, for example, to *seem* merciful, loyal, humane, religious, and sincere; it is also useful to *be* so, but with a mind so flexible that if the need arise he can be the contrary."

Machiavelli's writing has been a wellspring of ideas which men, through the ages, have turned to to find support for their own beliefs and behavior, especially for unpopular actions they feel a need to defend. He exposed to the light what all successful rulers know but keep in the dark. For almost five centuries this "political realism" has been shared by leaders and admirers of similar temperament; by gentler idealists he has always been deemed too cynical, too callous, too bitter to be a worthy guide—even when he speaks the truth.

NICHOLAS COPERNICUS

May 24 in the year AD 1543 was the saddest and most joyous of days. Eighteen months earlier Nicholas Copernicus had placed the manuscript of a great book—his life's work—into the hands of his faithful friend Tiedemann Giese to be carried to the publisher. Then late in 1542 Copernicus suffered a brain hemorrhage that left him half paralyzed and bedridden. He clung to life, barely holding on, till the first copy of his *Revolutions* was brought to him on his deathbed. "He had lost his memory and mental vigor many days before," Giese recounts, "and he saw his completed work only at his last breath upon the day that he died."[14]

Nor did Copernicus ever know that his book had suffered a monstrous humiliation. Sick and unable to guide his book through the press, his friends shouldered the burden. Giese sent the manuscript on to Georg Rhäticus, a young German scholar and disciple of Copernicus, to find a publisher in Nuremberg, which he did. But then Rhäticus was transferred to Leipzig University, so he turned the precious pages over to a local Lutheran pastor named Andreas Osiander. Osiander wrote a brief, unsigned preface and inserted it into the manuscript. The preface stated that the purpose of the book was to facilitate the reckoning of dates for the ecclesiastical calendar; it was purely hypothetical and was never intended as a description of the actual motion of the celestial bodies. Osiander's preface perverted the book's intent and robbed it of its scientific integrity; it also postponed for a half century the sting of heresy. To compound the humiliation the original manuscript was lost, and various "improvements" were made to the text by scholars who felt they knew the subject better than Copernicus, or wanted to correct him. The corrupt Nuremberg edition became the standard text until the original manuscript was rediscovered in the nineteenth century. Corrections have since been made in printed editions, and the results reveal the brilliant quality of Copernicus's science and the slow, painstaking process by which he constructed his theory. In 1843, on the four hundredth anniversary of his death, Copernicus's book was finally published as he wrote it.

Fortune [chance, accident] is the arbiter of one half our actions, but she still leaves us to direct the other half.
NICCOLÒ MACHIAVELLI

Gold alone will not procure good soliders, but good soldiers will always procure gold.
NICCOLÒ MACHIAVELLI

Copernicus (1473–1543)

For his elegantly simple but earthshaking notion that the Earth orbits the Sun, Nicholas Copernicus ranks among the greats of world exploration. His one book nailed the coffin lid tight on all other cosmologies and prepared the ground for more precise views of the world.

THE MAN   His first glimpse of the larger universe came on February 19, 1473, at Toruń (or Thorn), a small trading town on the banks of the Vistula in eastern Poland. His mother, Barbara, came from the affluent family of Waczenrodes; his father, Nicholas, was a respected merchant and magistrate in Toruń. He was the youngest of four children. Whether his lineage was Polish or German is unknown (nor would he have cared, except that it might have made a difference in how he spelled his name: Mikolaj Kopernik in Polish, Niklas Koppernick in the German-Prussian dialect; the Latinized Nicholas Copernicus—which he adopted—is a fair rendering now anointed by time).

No contemporary biography of Copernicus exists (his friend Georg Rhäticus wrote one, but it was lost), and the details of his life are sketchy. His father died when he was only ten, and the children were raised by their maternal uncle, Lucas Waczenrode, a priest and distinguished scholar. At eighteen he matriculated at the University of Kraków where he was introduced to Italian humanism, learned Latin, studied geometry, geography, and philosophy, fell in love with astronomy, and began collecting books on mathematics and astronomy. In the autumn of 1496, at twenty-two, he was sent to the University of Bologna in Italy where he delved into mathematics, Greek, and Plato; he updated himself on the latest in astronomical studies. He was twenty-four when he began serious sky watching by recording (on March 9, 1497) the eclipse of the red star Aldebaran by the Moon. His notes show that, from 1497 to 1529, he made twenty-seven observations from which he calculated the paths of the Sun, Moon, and planets as they supposedly orbit the Earth.

At twenty-eight he began a four-year program in medicine at the university medical school at Padua, with time out in 1503 to finish a doctorate in canon law at the University of Ferrara. His formal education completed, Copernicus returned to Frauenburg as a churchman (not a priest), a physician, and a doctor in church law. He was nicely prepared with special language skills (he knew German, Polish, Latin, Greek, probably Italian, and possibly Hebrew), financial theory, economics, administration, and some politics.

By the age of thirty he was permanently settled in Poland working as general assistant and personal physician to his uncle (and second father) Lucas Waczenrode, bishop of Ermland. His residence until his uncle's death in 1512 was at the episcopal palace at Heilsberg, and it was there that he settled to the task of refashioning mankind's flawed picture of the world. He had come to believe that explanations of nature should be quite simple, and when they seem complicated it is because we don't understand. It was at Heilsberg that Copernicus wrote the first account of the new system in his *Little Commentary* and circulated a few copies among his friends.

After 1512 Copernicus retired to the cathedral at Frauenburg where he remained for the rest of his life. Within a few years he had completed the first draft of his big book on the new system. He lived in one of the turret-towers attached to the wall of the Frauenburg cathedral; from its roof he could spend long nights watching and measuring the paths of planets and stars.

Copernicus's scientifically trained mind became increasingly intolerant of prevailing astronomical explanations. They weren't working. As early as the third century BC, Greek thinkers had suggested alternative Sun-centered theories, but they were never taken seriously because (1) they were not supported by precise observations; (2) they slammed hard against the commonsense experience we all have of watching the Sun blaze across the sky each day and the stars each night; (3) this commonsense experience had made its way into Scripture as revealed truth and was therefore set in stone. The result, as Thomas Digges would later say it, is that "the world hath so longe a time bin carried with an opinion of the earths stabilitye, as the contrary cannot but be nowe very imperswasible."[15]

So as the centuries passed, one cosmological model—the Ptolemaic—became the accepted dogma that displaced all others. The Alexandrian astronomer Claudius Ptolemaeus (fl. AD 127–45) had devised an elaborate geocentric model using large circles to represent planetary orbits around the Earth and small circles to represent "epicycles." Each planet was located on the circumference of a small circle, whose center was located on the path of the large circle. Thus each planet traces a small circle while it is orbiting the Sun on the big circle. All the orbits, on the authority of Aristotle, had to be perfect circles.

This Ptolemaic model was able to explain the three observed data that had always baffled observers: (1) the planets' changes in brightness as they move along their orbital paths; (2) the erratic changes in the planets' velocities; and (3) their retrograde motions. This last was especially puzzling. If you're tracking Mars, for instance, what you actually see as you observe it over a period of months is the Red Planet moving from west to east, then slowing down, stopping motionless for a time, then moving backwards toward the west, stopping again, then resuming its original journey across the night sky from west to east. Without a coherent theory this behavior makes no sense at all, and for two thousand years the best minds had not come up with a satisfactory explanation. Ptolemy's theory had been widely accepted, but as observations became more precise, it was increasingly unable to predict the position of the planets, and a spate of minor modifications was required to keep it viable. Copernicus concluded that a model that required so much fixing needed overhauling. He was convinced that there must be a simpler explanation. Having read the early Greek scientists, he was aware of the heliocentric hypothesis; so his task, as he saw it, was to check the validity of the age-old idea against observed facts. To do this he had to make his own careful observations.

Copernicus started with a simple question: What if the platform we observers stand on is a moving platform? This was a counterintuitive assumption, for, after all, it's obvious to everyone with common sense that the Earth stands still while the heavens move. That is, the platform is stationary, and the perceived motion of the celestial bodies is real. But what if? When Copernicus figured out what *motion* this moving platform must have to account for the peculiar movements of the planets, what he discovered was that this platform would have to orbit around the Sun. In other words, if he *assumed* that the Earth orbits the Sun, then the actual motions of the planets begin to make sense.

Copernicus's plan was to work out the details of this model and give it mathematical support. It was a gargantuan undertaking requiring precise observation and detailed analysis of the motions of all the heavenly bodies. For thirty years he labored, all the while resisting publication. He knew the theory was not perfect, and this troubled him. (He had made the mistake of assuming that orbits are circular—a notion soon to be shattered by Kepler; and this assumption forced him to bring back epicycles into his model—but only seventeen epicycles as compared to Ptolemy's eighty-three!) He was also keenly aware of the furor his ideas would create. So he continued to buy time by working with his system, bolstering it with more mathematics and better explanations.

His *Little Commentary* circulated well beyond his circle of friends and made his ideas generally known among scholars, churchmen, and learned men everywhere. In

On Copernicus *The fool will turn the whole science of Astronomy upside down. But, as Holy Writ declares, it was the Sun and not the Earth which Joshua commanded to stand still.*
MARTIN LUTHER

1514 Pope Leo X asked him to assist in reforming the calendar, but he declined. His system was presented before Pope Clement VII; he liked it. Rhäticus and others continued to urge him to publish his big book. He even received a formal request from Cardinal Schönberg in Rome begging him to publish his system. Already he was being praised for his science and vilified for his heresy. Rarely do Protestants and Catholics agree on much, but they were one in condemning Copernicus. "The fool will turn the whole science of Astronomy upside down!" steamed Martin Luther. "But, as Holy Writ declares, it was the Sun and not the Earth which Joshua commanded to stand still."[16] In 1540 he finally consented to publication and gave the manuscript to Giese.

After the spring of 1543 Copernicus was beyond praise and vilification. He had succeeded in dethroning the Earth from its hallowed position at the center of Everything. What is called "the Copernican Revolution" was slow in coming because of the massive opposition, but it gradually won acceptance among educated minds everywhere. The name "Copernicus" became a battle cry against entrenched ideas, whether in religion, science, or philosophy.

Copernicus's work led to at least three major developments in the physical sciences. (1) Sky watchers began to understand that all cosmic motion is relative to the position of the observer. That is, what we see the planets doing is not what the planets are doing, but is the result of our own motion. (2) Copernicus took the first giant step that enabled cosmologists to envision an open and infinite universe. The logic was compelling: If the Earth revolves around the Sun, inscribing an orbit with a diameter of some two hundred million miles, then observers on this moving platform should be able to see the stars shift their positions. But they don't. The explanation must be that the fixed stars are so far away that the shifts are not discernible. This realization led to the concept of an infinitely large universe with stars scattered throughout in three-dimensional space. (3) Greek natural philosophers had described the action of falling bodies as a natural inclination to fall toward the center of the universe; but if the Earth is not that center, then why do they fall *down* in such a manner? This line of questioning led inexorably to the idea of universal gravity.

Copernicus loved his solitude, always, but his rush onto sacred ground had scared away even angels. By fashionable standards his ideas were explosively incorrect, which distanced many; but worse, he had been tolerant toward Protestants, and most of his colleagues in his immediate establishment were conservative Catholics. So friends grew scarce, and, though Rhäticus and Giese stood by him, his last months were times of loneliness. In December, 1542, Giese had written to a canon of the Frauenburg Cathedral asking him to stand by Copernicus and "take care of the man whom you, with me, have ever loved, so that he may not lack brotherly help in his distress, and that we may not appear ungrateful to a friend who has richly deserved our love and gratitude."[17]

Copernicus was buried in Frauenburg Cathedral, though the exact location of the crypt is now uncertain. His books and papers were kept in the Cathedral library, but during the Thirty Years War they were taken to Sweden and are now in the Swedish University library at Upsala.

Copernicus was the first modern scientific man to make an impression on the thinking of mankind.

ELWOOD CUBBERLEY

THE CENTURY OF EMPIRICAL FOUNDATIONS

The era from roughly 1550 to 1650 witnessed the firm recovery of the empirical spirit and the laying of empirical foundations in many of the sciences. The basic principles of mathematics and mechanics had been discovered. Whereas in 1450 about all that was taught in schools were Arabic numerals and elementary Euclidian geometry, by 1650 the West had developed the decimal system, symbolic algebra, plane and spherical trigonometry, mechanics, logarithms, conic sections, and would soon (1667–87) add calculus. In 1569 Mercator had printed a map of the world; in 1572 the calendar had at last been revised with the introduction of the Gregorian calendar. Various practical gadgets had come into common use during this time, including the barometer, thermometer, air pump, pendulum clock, and telescope. Alchemy was well on the way to becoming chemistry; astrology was being nosed out by astronomy. Anatomy had made strides, and all scientific research, especially medicine, had been reinforced with the microscope. Theories were rapidly developing about the nature and behavior of light, gases, and gravity.

These advances had all been made during the century following the work of Nicholas Copernicus. The seekers of a new and better truth had proven that the human mind can know the ways of nature, and rapid advances were made in the sciences.

Aristotle had looked carefully at the world—as carefully as humanly possible in 350 BC—and created the reigning model of how the heavens behave, or ought to behave; and his theory had prevailed until the work of Copernicus. But when better observations could be made, Aristotle's model turned out to be wrong in all its details, and its hold on men's mind had to be broken. This could be accomplished only through a series of courageous intellectual steps that became possible with the gradual accumulation of new knowledge, all of which had been won in the face of enormous religious and scientific resistance.

Before Copernicus, Roger Bacon fought, with delayed success, a running battle for a careful examination of nature, and he initiated a method for doing so.

Bacon was followed by a church reformer and cardinal, *Nicholas of Cusa*, who wrote a book with the delightful title of *Learned Ignorance* (1440); in it he declared the universe to be *interminatum*, "interminate," that is, *not* enclosed in a series of Aristotelian shells.

Then in 1543 Copernicus gave the world the first broad outlines of the universe that we know today: a Sun-centered system with the Earth, other planets, and stars orbiting along predictable paths.

A few years after Copernicus, in 1576, an Englishman named *Thomas Digges* began replacing the closed universe with an open one. "The orbe of the starres fixed infinitely up extendeth hit self in altitude sphericallye. . . ."[18] Thus in Digges's diagram, the stars spread out in every direction from the central Sun and solar system.

Then a quarter of a century later an Italian ex-Dominican named *Giordano Bruno* became impressed by Copernicus's views and in his book *On the Infinite Universe and Worlds* (1584) drew out their implications. His conclusion: there exists an infinite number of worlds, with many solar systems, some of which are inhabited by human beings not unlike us. Each will think that his world is the center of the universe, but "the Earth no more than any other is at the center."[19] With this vision from Bruno, mankind's uniquely privileged position at the center of the world began to fade. For it Bruno was imprisoned by the Inquisition for eight years and then torched at the stake on February 17, AD 1600.

Contemporary with Bruno was *Tycho Brahe*, a Danish instrument maker and the most meticulous of all the sky watchers. Brahe had his own observatory and night after night recorded the precise positions of the planets. He rejected Copernicus's heliocentric model because of the absence of observable seasonable shifts in stellar positions, but his observation of a brightening supernova in the constellation Cassiopeia in 1572 destroyed Aristotle's notion that the heavens are perfect and

> *Our intellect . . . never grasps the truth with such precision that it could not be comprehended with infinitely greater precision.*
> NICHOLAS OF CUSA

> *The Earth is not in the center of the universe; it is central only to our surrounding space.*
> GIORDANO BRUNO

Giordano Bruno (c. 1548–1600)

unchangeable. Five years later Brahe tracked a comet across the sky and, using trigonometry, found that it was moving between the planets without visibly crashing through Aristotle's spherical shells. Step by step Aristotle's model was eroding.

The next giant step was taken by *Johannes Kepler* in his *New Astronomy* published in 1609. Kepler was the son of a swashbuckling German soldier and an innkeeper's daughter (later tried as a witch). He learned his craft as an assistant to Brahe. A scholar of infinite patience and respect for facts, Kepler's curious mind sought the meaning behind Brahe's collection of observations. Why, he asked, do the distant planets move slower than the closer ones. Why does Jupiter take twelve times, and Saturn thirty times, as long as the Earth to complete a journey back to where it started? Kepler concluded that, somehow, the planet's distance from the Sun held the key. Some physical force *coming from the Sun* must be influencing, and perhaps even determining, the movement of the planets. He focused primarily on Mars, whose orbital motion had always been puzzling. What he found was that Mars' speed varies in inverse proportion to its distance from the Sun, and that a straight line drawn from a moving Mars to the Sun will sweep out equal distances in equal times. This is known as Kepler's "Second Law of Motion." Careful observation had also revealed that Mars' orbit is not circular, so when Kepler tried out the possibility that it is an ellipse, the theory worked. But why did it work? "Is it not unbelievable that the celestial bodies should be like huge magnets?" So he tested the magnet hypothesis. The result was conclusive: "Gravity is the mutual bodily tendency between cognate bodies towards unity or contact (of which kind the magnetic force also is)."[20] He went on to develop the first and third laws of motion. First Law: A planet follows an elliptical orbit around the Sun which is positioned at one of the two elliptical foci. Third Law: The planetary year of each planet will be proportional to the cube of its semimajor axis. Kepler had determined once and for all that the solar system has a mathematical structure.

During the seventeenth century three major figures carried the joyous burden—Francis Bacon, Galileo, and Newton. Each made monumental contributions to the growth of Western thought.

Francis Bacon is often called the father of scientific method. "I was fitted for nothing so well as for the study of Truth," he wrote. Bacon spent his life doing battle against the wrongheaded use of Aristotle's logic that he believed had blighted human progress for a thousand years. Bacon's *The Advancement of Learning* (1605) contained his bold reclassification of all the sciences; his *Novum Organum* (1620) was a critical search to find where deductive thinking had gone wrong and a detailed description of induction and scientific method.

Galileo Galilei is generally accorded the honor of being the founder of modern physics. It was he who, in the shivering cold of the Paduan winter in January 1610, turned his homemade telescope on the heavens and watched the big/little moons of Jupiter circle their father planet. From such observations, and especially from his decipherment of the phases of Venus, he demolished for all time the geocentric worldview. But even in his day—almost a hundred years after Copernicus—this still meant trouble. His small Latin pamphlet called *The Starry Messenger* (1610) invited the charge of heresy. In 1616 the Pope's special commission told Galileo: "The view that the Sun stands motionless at the center of the universe is foolish, philosophically false, and utterly heretical, because contrary to Holy Scripture"; also the view that the Earth "has a daily rotation is philosophically false, and at least an erroneous belief." Finally, on June 21, 1633, Galileo was forced to kneel before the judges of the Inquisition and recant his errors.

Then there was Isaac Newton, for whom Alexander Pope wrote a memorable epitaph:

> Nature and Nature's laws lay hid in night:
> God said, "Let Newton be!" and all was light.

Newton took the tangled threads of this new cosmology and wove them together into a single fabric. He published the great *Principia Mathematica* in 1687. Having surveyed Kepler's laws, and using Kepler's discovery that orbits are elliptical, Newton concluded that the simplest explanation for planetary motion is that some kind of force exists to hold the planets to the Sun, providing a centripetal force that keeps each planet moving in its own orbit. Newton also found that that force is proportional to the mass of the planet and inversely proportional to the square of the distance from the planet to the Sun. By unlocking the secret of planetary motion, Newton was able to infer the Universal Law of Gravitation, a formula that describes the mutual interaction between all objects anywhere in the universe.

ENDNOTES

1 David S. Schaff, in *History of the Christian Church*, by Philip Schaff (Eerdmans, 1949), vol. 6, p. 565.

2 Bernard of Clairvaux, *Vita prima*, III. 2, in Schaff, *History*, vol.5, p. 346. This account emphasizes but one side of the complex Bernard, for on other occasions he expressed an unusual appreciation of nature.

3 Petrarch, *The Ascent of Mount Ventoux*, trans. H. Nachod, in *The Renaissance Philosophy of Man*, ed. Ernst Cassirer, P. O. Kristeller, and George Herman Randall Jr. (University of Chicago Press, 1948), pp. 36–46.

4 Nicola Abaggnano, "Humanism," in *The Encyclopedia of Philosophy*, ed. Paul Edwards (Macmillan and Free Press, 1967), vol. 4, p. 71.

5 Roger Bacon, *Opus majus*, pt. 6, Chap. 7.

6 Daniel J. Boorstin, *The Creators* (Random House, 1992), p. 401.

7 Boorstin, *The Creators*, p. 402.

8 Boorstin, *The Creators*, p. 399.

9 Giorgio de Santillana, ed., *The Age of Adventure* (Mentor, 1956), pp. 107f.

10 Niccolo Machiavelli, *The Prince*, Chaps. 8 and 17.

11 Niccolo Machiavelli, *Discourses upon the First Ten Books of Livy*, book 2, Chap. 2.

12 Machiavelli, *The Prince*, Chap. 18; *Discourses*, book 1, Chaps. 16, 3; *The Prince*, Chap. 5; attributed.

13 Machiavelli, *Discourses*, book 1, Chap. 25; *The Prince*, Chap. 22.

14 Machiavelli, *The Prince*, Chap. 14.

15 Angus Armitage, *The World of Copernicus* (Mentor, 1956), p. 102.

16 Martin Luther, *A Perfit Discription*, in *From the Closed World to the Infinite Universe*, by Alexandre Koyré (Harper Torchbooks, 1958), p. 38. If you care to examine Joshua's command, which in Hebrew is poetry, not descriptive prose, see Josh. 10:12–14.

17 Armitage, *The World of Copernicus*, p. 94.

18 Armitage, *The World of Copernicus*, p. 102.

19 Koyré, *From the Closed World to the Infinite Universe*, p. 36.

20 Koyré, *From the Closed World to the Infinite Universe*, p. 41f.

21 Stephen Toulmin and June Goodfield, *The Fabric of the Heavens* (Harper Torchbooks, 1961), pp. 206, 208.

A woodcut depicting humankind's restless curiosity to know how the universe works. Here an adventurer travels to the edge of the world, pokes his head through the firmament, and beholds the cosmic machinery that drives the heavenly bodies. Renaissance philosophers went far to liberate the long-suppressed curiosity that, after five more centuries, would allow scientific inquiry to make great strides toward the fulfillment of this dream.

LEXICON

Included in many of the following entries is the name of the philosopher most closely associated with the word or idea, but of course the word may have been used by others. I am especially indebted to Peter Angeles's *Dictionary of Philosophy* (Barnes & Noble Books, 1981) for assistance in the development of this lexicon.

absurd (from Latin *absurdus*, "harsh," "unmelodious," "foolish"); an adjective describing a fact, statement, or situation that is so unreasonable that it defies all human understanding.

acquired immortality Doctrine taught by Medieval Jewish philosophers: the immortal part of a human is not soul but intellect that can develop and grow through time and experience.

actuality That which exists (in experience or in reality) (as opposed to the potential which does not yet exist); see **potential**.

aêr Greek for "atmosphere"; the atmosphere that surrounds the Earth was thought by the Greeks to have two levels: *aither* ("ether") was the bright blue "ethereal" sky at the upper level; while *aêr* was the lower, heavier atmosphere in which humans and animals live; compare with *pneuma*.

agora Greek for marketplace or place of assembly (from *agoreuein*, "to address," "to speak in an assembly," "to harangue").

aither "Ether." In Greek thought, the pure upper air, the sparkling blue ethereal sky. See *aêr* and *pneuma*.

aitia Greek for "cause"; the reason why something is what it is. Aristotle identified four *aitiai* that fully account for something's becoming what it is.

akrasia Greek for "immoderate" or "intemperate," lacking self-control; the opposite of *sôphrosynê* (one of the cardinal Greek virtues).

anangkê Greek for "mechanical necessity"; whatever is inevitable that human intent must bow to and accept. To Plato it meant the recalcitrance that makes matter resist shaping by the rational or by the **Demiurge**.

anamnêsis Greek for "recollection" or "remembrance." Socrates believed that universal abstract ideas are recalled from a previous lifetime; this is the source of Plato's famous doctrine of Real Ideas (Forms).

andreios Greek for "manly" and "masculine"; "bold" and "courageous"; also "macho" and "stubborn." The subject of Socrates's discussions in the *Lachês*.

anthropomorphic (from Greek *anthropos*, "man," and *morphê*, "shape" or "form"); the projection of human qualities onto any non-human object of thought. Xenophanes was one of the first to be aware of this fallacy.

antinomian (from Greek *anti-nomos*, literally "against the law"); one who wants to live outside the prevailing rules and customs established by some group (church, society, legal system).

apatheia (from the Greek alpha privative that negates or expresses the absence of something, and *pathos*, "suffering"); the Stoic doctrine and practice of cultivating "indifference to pain" in order to achieve peace of mind.

apeiron "Boundless," "unlimited," "infinite"; from the Greek *a*, "not," and *peras*, "end," "limit," or "boundary"; term used by several early Greek philosophers, but Anaximander was the first to use *apeiron* to refer to an open universe that has no boundaries and from which all things come into being.

aposteriori (*a posteriori*) Literally "coming after" or "that which follows"; refers to any of the mind's contents that result from experiencing. See **apriori**.

apriori (*a priori*) Literally "coming before," "that which precedes"; ideas, experiences, or structures that exist in the mind prior to the arrival of sensory input; (Kant) the "forms of perception" that enable the mind to experience objects in space and time. See **aposteriori**. A proper Latinist would insist that apriori be written *a priori*, but to avoid having to pause and reread the phrase each time one comes across it in the text, it will here be Anglicized (not italicized as a "foreign" word) and rendered apriori.

archê Greek for "beginning," "origin," "first cause"; the original stuff of which anything is made; (Anaximander) the primal substance or "first principle" out of which all things emerge or come to be; (Aristotle) an axiomatic starting point in a developing line of thought or argument.

aretê Greek for "virtue" or the "functioning excellence" of a thing; the virtue of anything is determined by its nature and function. "When something performs the function it is designed to perform and it does this excellently then it has *aretê*. . . . A human's *aretê* consists of the development and use of his reason to the utmost level of functioning excellence." (Peter Angeles) See Socrates's search for definition.

aristocentric (from Greek *aristos*, the superlative of *agathos*, "good," and *kentron*, "center"; hence "the best of its kind" or "the most to be valued"); refers to an inordinate claim to a position of superiority for oneself or one's group. Aristocentric claims are most often made on behalf of one's ethnic group or race, one's tribe or nation, or one's religion. Aristocentric claims are ubiquitous.

aristocracy (from Greek *aristos*, "best," and *kratos*, "sovereignty," "power," "strength," "might"); a state ruled by those most qualified to rule (in terms of intellect, training, moral virtue, nobility, or wealth).

ataraxia (from Greek *a*, "not," and *tarazein*, "to agitate," "to bother," "to disturb"); hence "tranquility," "peace of soul," "unflappable"; the goal of life for Epicureans.

Atê As a common noun *atê* refers to a foolhardy or reckless impulse resulting from clouded judgment caused by unchecked passions or stubbornness; but *Atê* (personified) is a mischievous goddess who leads men to destroy themselves.

atomos (from Greek alpha privative and *tomos*, "cuttable," "divisible," hence "uncuttable," "indivisible"—whence our word "atom"); (Democritus) the indivisible particles of matter that are ultimate constituents of all physical reality; atoms are without qualities in themselves but produce perceptions of color, smell, and taste as they interact with the senses.

atomism The view that everything in the universe is composed of invisible material particles that clump together to create the objects of perception.

autarkeia (Greek for "autonomy," "sufficiency in oneself," "self-reliance," "self-starting," "individualism"). A central tenet of Socrates's teachings that resulted in his being charged with "corrupting the young"; (Aristotle) an essential ingredient of *eudaimonia*, "happiness"; (Zeno) a Stoic ethical doctrine counselling independence so that one doesn't have to rely on others.

axiom (from Greek *axioma*, "a worthwhile idea"); a "self-evident" idea that can serve as a secure starting point in geometry and on which a logical system can be built deductively.

being In Greek thought being is best understood when made to contrast with **becoming**. Being (existing, actual existence, the truly real) refers to what is eternal and unchanging, while becoming refers to the physical world that we perceive with our senses which, because it is ever-changing, is not really real. To Plato being and becoming were fundamental categories for apprehending reality: being (what actually exists, the "most real") exists only in the realm of Real Ideas (Forms), while becoming is the illusory realm of sense where everything is forever in process of becoming something else.

being, scale of The Thomastic doctrine that there are grades or levels of being, a sort of hierarchy of the real shading from something that is one hundred percent real (usually God) to that which is barely real at all (usually thought to be physical matter); the doctrine rests on the assumption that "reality" is a quality of things (that reality is real!). Plotinus used the metaphor of light to illustrate a similar doctrine. See **emanation**.

becoming The process of changing from being one thing to being something else (not just a change of position while remaining otherwise the same). Plato: the ever-changing processes of physical nature given to us by our senses; contrasts with the realm of Real Ideas that are eternal and unchanging. Aristotle's definition of motion, a kind of change by which the potential becomes actual and thereby realizes its end-goal or purpose in existing (its *entelecheia*).

belief (Pragmatism) personal commitment to an idea in order to make that idea work in the pragmatic sense; this commitment involves acceptance that the idea is in some sense true, valid, and worthwhile.

bios Greek for "life" as in "lifetime" and "she lived a good life" (not as in "the patient clings to life"); the "life" that is the subject of biography.

catharsis (Aristotle) See *katharsis*.

cause (Aristotle) See *aitia*.

causality The theory that every event must be preceded by a cause and that this causal pattern is a universal fact of physical nature. Hume argued that such a "principle" is not observed in nature and is only a concept that the mind finds convenient. Kant interpreted causality to be one of the categories used by the mind to give meaning to perceptual experience.

change See *kinêsis*.

coherence Truth test developed by Spinoza holding that only or primarily by means of logial consistency can the truth of an idea be assured.

cosmogony (From Greek *kosmos*, "universe" and *gignesthai*, "to be born"); study and theory of the origins of the universe. Compare with **cosmology**.

cosmological argument Any argument for God's existence based on the order, patterns, consistencies, and designs observed in nature.

cosmology (From Greek *kosmos*, "world," and *logos*, "the study of"); the attempt to discern the structure of the world; (Plotinus) a rational attempt to explain the coherent structure of the spiritual universe; (Einstein) speculation about the origin and structure of the physical universe based on observations from modern astronomy and physics.

cosmos See *kosmos*.

critic, critical, criticism See *krino*.

daimôn (commonly transliterated as *daemôn* or *daimonion*). To the Greeks a *daimôn* was a spiritual being superior to man but inferior to the gods. Socrates individualized the notion into an experience: his *daimôn* was a private inner voice (not unlike a guardian angel of a later age) that acted as guide and conscience. At his trial Socrates tells the jury that "in the past the prophetic voice to which I have become accustomed has always been my constant companion, opposing me even in quite trivial things if I was going to take the wrong course" (*Apology* 40A). The word came to mean demon or devil in New Testament usage.

definition Defining a thing or idea establishes its most important characteristics, the ultimate goal being clarity regarding the objects of thought; both Socrates and Plato sought universal and essential definitions, believing that meanings are not subjective and arbitrary but real existents that derive from the realm of Real Ideas.

Demiurge In the *Timaeus* Plato refers to *demiourgos* as the creative principle or force in the universe; it ("It" or "He" when personified) uses Real Ideas to shape recalcitrant matter into rational objects; the Demiurge is the creator and architect of the universe.

demythologizing Replacing the need for mythical explanations (1) by appealing to rational and empirical explanation and (2) by understanding the function of myth as meaningful expressions of the human psyche.

determinism Doctrine that all events (in both physical nature and human action) result from antecedent causes; in its theological form ("predestination") the doctrine holds that all events are willed by God (or the Fates) and human effort is helpless to alter them. Aquinas taught a paradoxical doctrine that God determines everything, including man's free will. Spinoza taught that human thoughts, decisions, and emotions are exactly what they must be since nothing (not even God) can be other than what it is.

dialectic (from Greek *dialectikê*, "the art of conversation" or "the art of reasoning"). Plato made a sharp distinction between dialectic employed in the pursuit of truth and dialectic used just to win an argument. Socrates used dialectic as a means of seeking knowledge through question and answer. See *eristic*.

dikaiosynê Commonly translated as "justice," *dikaiosynê* had for the Greeks many of the same rich connotations that it has for us in English. A man who was *dikaios* was law-abiding, decent, good, moral, well-ordered, and civilized; he had a passion to do what is right, being driven by an inner sense of rightness. To Plato, the individual who has achieved integration of the three conflicting psychic faculties (reason, will, desire), is said to be *dikaios*. The citizen of a polis with *dikaiosynê* works to achieve a functioning harmony of all parts of the community.

docetic (from Greek *dokêsis*, "fancy"; "apparition," "not truly seen"). Docetism was taught by the Gnostics who held that Jesus could not have been crucified because his body was merely an apparition and not real matter.

doxa (Greek, "belief," "mere speculation," "conjecture," "popular opinion," "what others think"). To

Parmenides *doxa* is inferior to true knowledge obtained through reason. Plato contrasts *doxa*, "belief" (probably mistaken), with *epistêmê*, true knowledge. *Doxa* was the mental process by which information from the senses produces "belief" or "judgment." To Aristotle *doxa* is frequently a synonym for *hypolêpsis* ("hasty judgment"). See *epistêmê*.

double-truth doctrine A distinctive doctrine of medieval Islamic philosophers holding that there are two levels of truth, one for the mind and one for the heart. There were two versions of the doctrine: one held that there is one truth for individuals who live by faith, another for individuals guided by reason; the other version sought to reconcile the life of reason with the life of faith in each individual .

ego (Greek *egô*, the personal pronoun, first person singular, that is declined as "I," "we" "us" etc.). A synonym for "self," the underlying cause of mental functions. In Freudian theory the *ego* is the psychic system that mediates between the id and the super-ego to get our needs met.

egocentric predicament Phrase coined by Ralph Barton Perry to describe the logical (epistemological) predicament of not being able to know if human observation changes the existence or the nature of real objects.

eidos (Greek for "form," "shape," "figure," "idea.") Plato used *eidos* to refer to universal abstract ideas he believed to be real; such ideas were to him the perfect, unchanging blueprints used by the Demiurge to organize matter into existing objects. This is Plato's famous doctrine of Real Ideas (or "Forms"). See **universals**.

elenctic dialectic (From Greek *elenchos* [also transliterated *elengchos*], "cross-examination" and "confutation"), an adversarial style of debate developed by Protagoras designed to demolish an opponent's argument. Socrates was a formidable opponent in this form of debate but in adult life seems to have abandoned elenctic as harsh and unfair.

emanation Neoplatonist metaphor to explain the universe: the universe is a spiritual emanation from God (the Sun) flowing outward and radiating away its heat and light until darkness overwhelms all. The Gnostic Valentinus and Ibn-Sīnā taught similar doctrines. See *epistrophe*.

empathy (Greek *empathês*, an emotional state during which one can be especially vulnerable to another). To empathize is to recognize and identify the feelings, sufferings, and torments of another person, to understand them intellectually without experiencing those feelings oneself. Empathy is intellectual identification in contrast to sympathy, which is affective identification.

empyrean (Greek *empyreuein*, "to light a fire"); in ancient cosmology, the highest heaven; the outer spherical shell in Aristotle's heavenly schematic thought of as a sphere of fire or light; by implication, the sphere of lofty ideas.

empirical (Greek *empeiros*, to be acquainted with something, to know a thing by experience). The view that all knowledge derives ultimately from sense experience.

empiricism The view that all knowledge is ultimately derived from sense experience, and all claims to knowledge are to be questioned until they reveal their empirical sources.

empiricism, loose An empiricism that accepts information not only from sense but from the full spectrum of human experience, including dreams, emotions, esthetic experiences, values, etc. See **narrow empiricism**.

empiricism, narrow An empiricism that insists that true knowledge must rest only on the immediate perception of the senses and what can be validly inferred from them and must not include other kinds of human experience. See **loose empiricism**.

entelechy See *entelecheia*.

entelecheia ("being complete") Entelechy. Aristotle's word for the impulse in every living thing to grow toward the fulfillment or completion of whatever it is supposed to be. The definition of a thing must include not only what it is, but what it "intends" to become; e.g. the definition of a peach seed must include its *entelecheia* that strives to become a peach tree. In other words, the potential is an aspect of the actual (a strange notion until resurrected by quantum physics).

epigonos (pl. *epigonoi*) (from Greek *epigignomai*, "to be born after"); as a substantive adjective it refers to someone "born too late" to be a participant in some momentous event; hence, an imitative follower of a creative thinker, writer, musician, or artist. According to Webster's *Third New International Dictionary* "epigonism" is "artistic, literary, or intellectual imitation esp. by a later generation than the artist, writer, or thinker imitated." The Latin is *epigonus* and (pl.) *epigoni*.

epistêmê (whence "epistemology" and "epistemological"); "knowledge," but with the connotation of its being true knowledge (in contrast to *doxa*, false knowledge which one may believe but which in fact is not true); systematic knowledge, scientific knowledge, science. Epistemology, then, is the science of true knowledge.

epistemological nihilism The view that all knowledge is illusory, relative, and meaningless, that there is no basis for knowing reality. Nietzsche was convinced that the world is meaningless, reality is meaningless, history is meaningless—and that truth is an illusion.

epistrophe (Literally, a "wheeling about," "a return motion"). In the Neoplatonic and Gnostic myths the emanating spiritual light is drawn to return to its source, the God/Sun; and human souls (in which the spiritual light dwells) yearn to return to the source of their being. In Plotinus's system, emanation is the outflowing of the spiritual light while epistrophe is the "backflowing."

epochê (in Greek a "halting," the point where something suddenly comes to a standstill); doctrine taught by the Skeptics advocating deliberate suspension of judgment about all things that can't be known. Husserl developed *epochê* into a technique for systematically removing all particulars from consciousness in order to discover the pure experiencing ego.

eristic (From Greek *eris*, "quarrel," "contention," "to meet in battle"; as a proper name **Eris** was the Greek goddess who incites men to war); used by Homer to suggest intense rivalry in contests for prizes, it later suggests domestic or political strife, discord, or wrangling. Eristic was an adversarial debating technique taught by the Sophists.

eros (Greek for "love," "desire"; as a proper name **Eros** was the god of love). One of the two forces in Empedocles' Love-Strife cosmology that represent attraction and repulsion. The subject of Socrates's speech in the *Symposium* in which he searches for "who and what sort of being is Eros," the inspirer of man's quest for beauty and goodness. The resurrection of *eros* was a key factor in the revitalization of Greek learning during the Renaissance.

Eros Greek god of love, son of Aphrodite. See *eros*.

esoteric Intended for a small, select group only, something that would be difficult for outsiders to understand. Pythagoras's community was divided into those who could hear, the *esoterica*, and those who had not yet been initiated, the *exoterica*.

essence (Latin *essentia*, from *esse*, "to be," "to exist") The idea (belief) that everything in a category or class possesses defining characteristics without which it would not be what it is but something else. Virtually all philosophers from Socrates on were convinced that essences exist, and that they are real, even though their existence can be known only through mental abstraction. See **universal**. To Aristotle the essence of something is not what it is now but what it will be when its **entelechy** has been fully achieved. Sartre insisted that "essence" refers to nothing whatever.

ether See *aither*.

eudaimonia ("happiness,"; Greek prefix *eu*, "well," "good"; and *daimon*, "inner spirit"); the deepest sense of well-being that comes through self-realization of the human soul. To Aristotle *eudaimonia* is the principal ingredient in the human entelechy. To the Stoics *eudaimonia* can be achieved by "going with the flow," cultivating *apatheia*, and learning to live with nature.

evil An adjective used to describe one's feelings regarding a thing, process, person or deed about which one feels intensely negative and desires to make an evaluation. The word is entirely reflexive; it refers not to objects or to qualities in objects but only to the values (ideas and feelings) of the individual making the evaluation. Evil is not real. Epicurus, the Skeptics and many others worked on the problem.

existence, existential The Latin *existere* merely means "to appear," "to exist," and refers to what concretely exists in contrast to creations of thought. In philosophy the word has often been used to refer to a *quality of existence*, a special existence that includes a heightened awareness that one *is*, a vivid sense of the real, living in the present, being intensely involved in experiencing (as over against being merely an observer).

exoteric See esoteric.

geocentric Ptolemy's theory that the Earth is the center of the solar system, an idea overthrown by empirical observation by Copernicus.

gnosis (Greek for "knowledge," "knowing someone," "recognizing someone"); knowledge in general, but often with the connotation of a special knowledge of some sort. To the Gnostics *gnosis* meant a saving knowledge vouchsafed to only a chosen few.

Gnosticism A pre-Christian mystical movement extremely popular in Roman times. It taught a great cosmic myth and offered a plan of salvation based on an esoteric revealed *gnosis*. Earthly men were of three kinds: hylics, psychics, and pneumatics, with the psychics redeemed by faith and the pneumatics by *gnosis*. Saint Paul confronted the Gnostics at Ephesus and Colossae.

Hadês In Greek myth the underworld realm of the dead. Socrates said he hoped to continue asking questions even in Hadês.

Hadîth The body of traditions collected from the time of Muhammad that together constitute the basis of Islamic theological orthodoxy.

happiness See *eudaimonia*

harmonia Pythagoras believed that all the vibrations of the cosmos are (or could be) in harmony. "They [the Pythagoreans] supposed the whole heaven to be a *harmonia* and a number," wrote Aristotle. The ideal human life should be in harmony with the cosmos.

hedonism (Greek *hedone*, "pleasure") The ethical view that the proper aim of a human life should be the pursuit of pleasure in all its forms, and all human actions should be judged on whether, and to what degree, they produce pleasure. This was the teaching of the Cyrenaic hedonists.

humanism One of the three major philosophic developments of the Renaissance. The main idea of humanism is that being human is good, not bad, as the church had always taught. The other major developments were **naturalism** and **individualism**.

hubris (sometimes spelled *hybris* since the Greek "u" was transliterated by Latins into a "y"); (Greek, "pride," "arrogance"); going beyond one's abilities and making a fool of oneself; an overbearing insolence that ultimately brings retribution from the gods (*nemesis*, divine indignation) causing one to bring about his own destruction.

hylozoism (from Greek *hylê*, "matter," "the physical stuff from which a thing is made"; and *zoê*, "life"); the notion that all matter is alive, a doctrine held by all three Milesian philosophers.

hypostasis (Greek for "derived essence," "that which is subsumed under"). In Neoplatonism the Godhead (the One) is the ineffable source that manifests itself in two hypostases, Mind/*Nous* and Soul/*Psyche*. In Christian theology Athanasius taught that God is one essence in three hypostases; this became the accepted doctrine of the Trinity at the Synod of Alexandria in AD 362.

idea See *eidos*.

idealism The view that the primary reality of the universe is not physical matter but something else,

usually thought to be mind (*nous*), soul (*psyche*) or spirit. This notion is the essence of Platonism: that the only ultimate reality is Idea. See **Real Ideas**. Hegel also considered the *Geist*/Spirit to be the only ultimate reality.

individualism One of the three major new views that arose during the Renaissance: it meant the capacity to see and appreciate differences in things without obliterating their distinctiveness. See **naturalism** and **humanism**.

intuition A human faculty that enables one to know something immediately and directly without (or prior to) the use of reason or reflection. One of the two ways of knowing, said Bergson; see **intellect**. Kant's term for the mind's faculty that allows empirical information to be assimilated so real objects can be experienced in space and time.

jihâd Arabic "holy war," any battle waged by the Faithful on behalf of Islâm; a description of the life journey of the soul in its unending wrestling-match with its lower nature.

justice See *dikaiosynê*.

kairos (Greek, "the proper time or season for action," "the right moment for something to happen," "the opportune moment.") Human time is marked by moments of greater or lesser significance. *Kairos* is seizing the right moment.

katharsis (Greek for "cleansing," "purification"). According to Aristotle the principal function of tragic drama is to purge the emotional system of excess "humors" such as fear and pity, leading us to cry and thereby effect a return to emotional stability and health. See *mimêsis*.

kinêsis (Greek for "movement" or "motion"; from *kinein*, "to set in motion," "to set agoing," "to arouse," "to cause"); any kind of change. Heraclitus was the earliest philosopher to argue that *kinêsis* is the fundamental nature of the world for everything is in a condition of perpetual change. See *panta rhei*. Aristotle defined *kinêsis* as the process by which potential becomes actual. Note that the Eleatic logicians Parmenides and Zeno denied the existence of motion and change.

kosmos (from Greek *kosmeo*, "I order," "I arrange," "I systematize"); "the world" or "the universe," but always with the implication that the universe is an ordered whole.

logic (Greek *logikê*, "logic"); the study of the rules of right reasoning. To Aristotle logic was the intellectual tool by which the sciences can carry on their work; it included both deduction and induction.

logion (Greek *logion*, "a saying"; pl. *logia*). Literally, announcements, oracles, sayings; commonly refers to groups of Jesus's sayings found outside the gospel tradition.

logos A richly meaningful Greek noun for "word," "proposition," "meaning," "language," "speech," "story," "narrative," "definition," "thought," "reason," sometimes "soul"; any channel by which inward thought becomes expressed. Heraclitus was the first to use *logos* as an interpretative category: to him *logos* was the source of order; whatever in the universe remains the same when everything else changes is an expression of the *logos*'s ordering power. The Stoics saw *logos* as the cosmic principle of intelligence; it is manifest in nature as natural law but is available to human intellect for use in its rational function to understand the world and life. Philo Judaeus reasoned that God governs the world by laws of nature planted into physical matter by the *Logos* during the original creation.

I. F. Stone (*The Trial of Socrates*, Little, Brown, 1988, p. xi) makes a comment worth repeating on the word *logos* (and by extension on all words from ancient languages). He writes: "How can one understand the word *logos*, for example, from any one English translation, when the definition of this famous term—in all its rich complexity and creative evolution—requires more than five full columns of small type in the massive unabridged Liddell-Scott-Jones *Greek-English Lexicon*? A thousand years of philosophic thought are embodied in a term that begins by meaning 'talk' in Homer, developed into 'reason'—with a capital R, as the divine ruler of the universe—in the Stoics, and ends up in the Gospel of St. John—by a subtle borrowing from biblical sources—as the creative Word of God, His instrument in the Creation." For New Testament usage, read the famous "logos prologue" in the Gospel of John 1:1-18.

Logos orthos (In Greek "right reason," "correct thinking," "sound argument"). Sophist phrase for the logical principles that establish proper reasoning and make for the strongest case when one is defending a position.

Logos Spermatikos (Greek, "life-giving word") One of the Stoics' favorite phrases for God/Nature as the generative principle (literally "sperm" or "seed") that effects the continual and everlasting creation of everything in the cosmos, which itself is a living organism.

maiutic (from Greek **maia**, "midwife"). Socrates's chosen vocation, his calling. Socrates said he specialized in helping others give birth to ideas, not to birthing ideas himself. This is one element of **Socratic method**.

metanoia (Greek, "about-face," "repentence"); literally, to change one's mind and go in the opposite direction; it is usually a deliberate act not forced by external conditions. See for example Augustine's multidirectional search for moral goodness.

metaphysics (Greek *meta ta physica*, "after the physics"); the rational attempt to discover the ultimate reality (or realities) of the universe as a whole. Metaphysics attempts to "get under" the palpable visible components and to concentrate on structures and universal essences that are assumed to be elements of the real, e.g. existence, cause-and-effect, motion, time, space, substance, unity, and variety. As a self-critical discipline metaphysics attempts to fathom the mind's operations in its search to understand what is real.

metaphysics Bergson radically redefined metaphysics by insisting that a true empiricism will not settle with scratching surfaces but will move into objects empathetically "by a kind of spiritual *auscultation*." A metaphysics that fails to perceive the inner (experiential) realities of people and things is no true metaphysics.

midwifery (Socrates) See **maiutic**.

mimêsis (Greek "imitation," "representation"). Aristotle's theory that art imitates life, and those of us who watch a staged tragedy find that, "through pity and fear," this *mimêsis* brings about a purging (*katharsis*) of our emotions.

monism The philosophical view that all is One, meaning that everything in the universe is a form of just one thing and can be explained in terms of that one thing, whether it be spirit, mind, matter, form, God, or energy.

naturalism One of the three major shifts in thinking that occurred during the Renaissance. The central theme of naturalism was a new sensitivity to nature that resulted in a new empiricism. See **humanism** and **individualism**.

natural moral law Diogenes the Cynic declared that his "natural rights" commanded more authority than social conventions. The Stoics dreamed of and worked for a "cosmopolis," a single city-state in which all human beings would live and be judged by a single standard.

natural selection Theories associated with Empedocles and Darwin describing how better adapted animal species have survived.

negative theology The doctrine that a positive knowledge of God is impossible, being off-limits to the human intellect; therefore only negative statements can be made about God: that he is not evil, that he is not infinite, that he is not limited in time, etc.

neikos (Greek, "strife," "quarrel"). Along with Love, one of two forces in Empedocles' cosmology that provide the attraction and repulsion causing the elements to mix.

nihilism See **epistemological nihilism.**

noetic (from Greek *noêtikos*, "intelligent" and *noêtos*, "perceptible to the mind," "thinkable"). Knowledge that is arrived at through pure thought without input from the senses; non-empirical knowledge.

nominalism (from Latin *nōmen*, "name"). One of three basic theories of universals; objects exist first and then the mind creates universals from them; essences refer to nothing in reality. See **realism**; see **universals.**

nous (Greek, "mind," "reason," "intellect"; often a close synonym for *noêsis*, "intelligence," "thought"). *Nous*, to Anaxagoras, is the force that binds everything together, initiates motion, and makes for order in the cosmos.

Olympiad The interval of four years between Olympic games used by the Greeks to reckon dates.

ontological argument Anselm's famous argument for the existence of God; in it he attempted to prove God's existence by a sort of "internal logic" within the nature of ideas alone. Descartes devised at least three ideas along the same line.

ontology (from Greek *onta*, "existing things," "reality," "the truth of what is"; and *logos*, "the study of"). The study of being, abstract being in itself, apart from existing things; the branch of philosophy that attempts to describe the order and structure of reality; what Aristotle referred to as "first philosophy."

opinion See *doxa.*

original sin The doctrine (*peccatum originis*) in Christian theology holding that the sin of Adam that brought about the Fall and his expulsion from Paradise was transmitted down through time and history, from generation to generation, so that every descendant of Adam must be regarded as being originally in a state of perversion and depravity; only the washing away of original sin through baptism and grace can redeem the sinner.

pagan (from Latin *pagani* which meant "peasantry"). Word first used in a law passed under the emperor Valentinian in AD 368; at the time it merely meant "non-Christian."

panta rhei (Greek, "everything flows"). "Everything flows and nothing abides; everything gives way and nothing stays fixed." Thus Heraclitus expressed his most fundamental conviction about the world: everything is in a state of change, everything is in motion, nothing endures.

pantheism (from Greek *pan*, "all," and *theos*, "God"). The belief that God and Nature are to be identified as one; that is, God and universe are one and the same, or in some way God is the soul of Nature.

pathei mathos Greek adage meaning "taught by suffering." Doctrine enunciated by Aeschylus (*Agamemnon* lines 177f.) that "wisdom is achieved only through suffering." Toynbee makes *pathei mathos* a major theme of his philosophy.

perceptions In philosophy perception means sense perception, the awareness of basic input from sight, taste, touch, sound, etc. Perceptions are entirely subjective, but in ordinary experience we would not long survive if we couldn't depend upon them to inform us about our environment. The problem of exactly how the mind organizes perceptions into concepts, and whether and to what extent perceptions tell us about reality, are major preoccupations of philosophers from the presocratics to the present day.

philosophy (from Greek *philos*, "love," and *sophia*, "wisdom," "knowledge," "intelligence"). The love of wisdom. The word was first used by Pythagoras, the first man also to claim to be a philosopher.

physis (Greek, "nature," "the law of nature," "the universe"). In general *physis* meant Nature or physical matter. When applied to the physical world it often meant the source of a thing, or its structure, or the stuff out of which it is made; applied to humans it meant man's fundamental nature. Plato used the word to refer to the essential natures of things and to Real Ideas. Aristotle used *physis* to refer to a thing's natural *entelecheia* that drives it to become what it is.

pistis (Greek, "faith," "belief"). When discussing branches of knowledge, Plato (*Republic*, Book VII, 534) uses *pistis* for the third division. Shorey (the Loeb translator) translates it as "belief" and warns (vol. II, p. 205 n⁸) "always avoid "faith" in translating Plato. *Pistis* was the ubiquitous New Testament term for "faith," "faithfulness," "trust," and "confidence."

Platonism A general term not for Plato's philosophy but for the philosophic system that developed during the centuries after Plato. It is a fallacious concept, for there never existed in Plato's lifetime, a Platonism.

plenum (from Latin *plēnus*, "full," "filled," "satisfied," "complete"; derived from the Greek *plêrês*, "full," "complete"). Parmenides' notion that empty space can't exist because it is a *plenum*, absolutely and completely filled. Reality is one, he said, eternal, indivisible, immovable and unchanging.

plêroma (Greek "fullness," "full measure"). In the great Gnostic myth, Pleroma is the halo of brilliant light formed by the Aeons around the Deep.

pluralism (from Latin *pluralis*, "more"). The view that there exists more than one fundamental reality in the world and that they are independent and irreducible. The universe, therefore, is not a coherent unity, not a harmonious thing, but a disparate pile of separate entities.

pneuma (whence "pneumatic" and "pneumonia"). Greek for "air" but with connotations of "moving air," "a blast of air," "a blowing," "a wind"; also the air that is breathed, "breath": and by extension "the breath of life," "spirit." Compare with *aêr*.

polis (Greek, "city," "state"). The autonomous Greek city-state. Aristotle contended that "the city-state is a natural creation and man is by nature a political animal." By definition the state must be "a community of well-being."

potential See **actuality**.

pragmatic paradox A paradox of belief: an idea must be believed to be a true description of reality (on the correspondence test) in order for the mind to accept the idea on faith (and make it work on the pragmatic test). If one does not believe an idea to be true to reality, then it has no faith value.

pragmatic truth test Truth test holding that only by practical application to real situations can the truth of an idea be determined. See **coherence** and **correspondence**.

primary and secondary qualities See **qualities, primary and secondary**.

Prime Mover Aristotle reasoned that an infinite regress in causality is illogical; therefore at the beginning (of time?) there must have existed an "unmoved mover," and this Aristotle called the "Prime Mover" or "Uncaused Cause"; only with

reluctance did he think of it as divine. Aquinas developed the idea as one of his five ways of proving the existence of God. His "cosmological argument" is a repeat of Aristotle's argument from motion. To Aquinas of course it referred to the Judeo/Christian Creator God.

psychê (Greek "breath," "soul," "spirit," "breath of life"; Latin *anima*). The principle of life and in higher organisms the source of consciousness. There are three grades of soul, Aristotle contended, the nutritive, sensitive, and rational; the soul is the locus of an organism's *entelecheia*.

psychology In the broadest sense psychology is the attempt to make sense of the human person, especially the experiencing self. Precritical psychology is endemic to every culture; critical psychology began with the Greeks; scientific or empirical psychology arose in the late nineteenth and early twentieth centuries.

pyr (Greek, "fire"). Heraclitus's chosen symbol for the perpetual change that is the essential nature of the world. "This universe always has been, is, and always will be an ever-living fire."

quadrivium The higher four of the seven liberal arts studied in the cathedral schools of the late Middle Ages; it included geometry, arithmetic, music, and astronomy. See *trivium*.

qualities, primary and secondary Primary qualities refers to qualities that inhere in real objects (solidity, extension, figure, motion, etc.); while secondary qualities are located entirely in our experience (color, taste, smells, etc.)

quod si fallor, sum! "If I fail, I am!" Augustine's version of the **cogito**; see *je pense, donc je suis*.

rational (from Latin *ratio*, "reason"). The capacity to be reasonable, the ability to function rationally. Also to be rational implies the ability to understand and to be understood. Intelligible. Sensible.

rationes seminales (Latin for "causal reasons"; Latin equivalent of *logos spermatikos*). Roger Bacon accepted the doctrine of *rationes seminales*, a divine illumination of the mind that allows certainty and permits an understanding and appreciation of the wonders of nature.

real Existing apart from perception, having objective existence. The word, in philosophy, has the function of establishing the *location* of an object/event as taking place either in the human experiential system or in the real world "out there."

reality That which exists. The sum total of everything that exists apart from, and outside of, the realm of human perception. The opposite of reality is appearance.

realism One of the three basic medieval theories of universals. Realism (following Plato) held that universals are not mental abstractions but are real ideas, archetypal templates that exist in the mind of God. See **conceptualism** and **nominalism**; see also **universals**.

Real Ideas, doctrine of (usually referred to as Plato's "theory of forms"). Plato's powerful notion that there exists a realm of abstract ideas or "forms" that in themselves are unchanging and eternal. These "ideal forms" are the sources, the templates, the origins, for the entire world of changing things. See *eidos*.

reductio ad absurdum (Latin "reduction to absurdity"). Method of arguing in which a statement is deemed true because its opposite would lead to an absurd conclusion. Argument used effectively by the Eleatics.

reification The fallacy of treating ideas as though they were real, for example, treating "evil" as a real thing and not just an idea. When applied to imaginary persons (e.g. angels), then the fallacy is a "personification." See also **anthropomorphic**.

reincarnation The doctrine that we humans (and perhaps animals as well) live our lives repeatedly more or less as the same person. Pythagoras just assumed such repeated existences. The notion is frequently treated as a reward system: good people will return as upgraded souls of some sort, bad people will return as lower animals and even demons.

relativism Doctrine taught by Protagoras and the Sophists that whatever is held to be true by a community is in fact true for that community. "Man is the measure of all things; of things that are that they are, and of things that are not that they are not." The doctrine also applies to individuals: if I believe something is true, then it *is* true *for me*—and that's an end to the matter.

rhetoric (from Greek *rhêtorikê*, "rhetoric," "the art of public oratory"). The art of persuading through public speaking. In Plato's *Gorgias* Socrates and three well-known Sophists examine the relationship between rhetoric and living the good life. Gorgias argues that rhetoric is the supreme art form because it enables one to make everyone else do what he wants.

roots Empedocles' term for the four elements (fire, earth, air, and water) of which everything is made, and which are driven by Love and Strife.

shirk In Islamic theology, the most serious sin of placing other beings on a par with Allah.

skeptic (from Greek *skeptikos*, "thoughtful," "curious"; from *skeptisthai*, "to examine," "to look about carefully"). One who suspends judgment about something awaiting further evidence, or one who is constitutionally habituated to doubting until proven otherwise.

Skeptics Movement in late Greek philosophy founded by Pyrrhon of Êlis about 300 BC that had a pervasive influence on philosophic thinking for the next four centuries.

Socratic ignorance Ever since Socrates professed that he knew nothing (at least he knew what he didn't know), this brand of "Socratic ignorance" has been a precious tenet of our Western intellectual tradition. "I myself know nothing, except just a little, enough to extract an argument from another man who is wise and to receive it with an open mind."

Socratic method Four words or concepts lie at the heart of Socrates's "method" and go far toward explaining why he was so popular (with young lions) and unpopular (with the citizens of Athens). See **dialectic, maiutic, elenctic, eristic.**

sophia (Greek, "wisdom"). The highest intellectual attainment, according to Aristotle, and therefore the highest of all the virtues. He distinguished *sophia*, "theoretical wisdom," from *phronêsis*, "practical wisdom."

Sophia (Gnostics) one of the two Aeons that play special roles in the great cosmic drama (the other being "Primal Man"). Also a Meccan girl who became the embodiment of Wisdom to Ibn-'Arabī, inspiring him to write a book of poems.

Sophists Movement in Greek education during the late fifth century BC. The sophists were itinerant teachers who traveled from city to city offering courses in a wide range of practical arts and skills. They were constant antagonists of Socrates and his followers.

sophistry The attitude and teachings that the sophist movement developed late in its career; the word had come to mean shallow, quarrelsome, and dishonest.

sôphrosynê (from Greek *sôphrôn*, "sensible," "discreet," "of sound mind"). "Moderation" or "temperance"; but the word possessed numerous overtones, such as "sobriety," "discretion," "self-control," "chastity," "sanity"; it usually referred to a person who had full control over his passions and was chaste and sober.

telos (Greek, "fulfillment," the "completion" of anything; "proposed end," "consummation," "achieved result"). Aristotle believed there is a *telos* in the soul of every living thing that guides in the direction of its fulfillment. See *entelecheia*.

theism (from Greek *theos*, "divine," "God"). Belief in a God or gods.

trivium The first level of courses in the cathedral schools of the Middle Ages. The *trivium* included grammar, rhetoric, and logic. See **quadrivium**.

truth Quality of ideas and statements that makes them true. Truth of an idea can be known only after having been judged on one or more of the truth-tests that provide criteria for establishing what quality of truth is in the idea. See **coherence, pragmatic**.

two-truth doctrine See **double-truth doctrine**.

unity of existence Central doctrine of Ibn-'Arabī's worldview: that God is in everything and everything is One, including other religions.

universals "Universals" are the mind's general abstractions; the debate raged for a thousand years among theologians over whether such abstractions are real or only mental. There were three basic theories of universals. See **realism**, and **nominalism**.

Unmoved Mover See **Prime Mover**.

virtue See *aretê*.

Weltanschauung (German "world view"). A comprehensive view of the whole of reality.

wisdom Human knowledge and understanding of what is true, right, good—a right-mindedness that permits one to lead a fulfilling life. Socrates and Plato both believed that if one knows what is right, he will do what is right. Knowledge, therefore, is the path to wisdom.

Zeitgeist (German, "the spirit of the time"). The total fabric of thought and value, taste, and outlook characterizing a certain epoch, era, century, or other block of time. In general it is the *Zeitgeist* that thinkers of all ages are trying to escape from.

CREDITS

INDEX

F